Network Algorithmics

The Morgan Kaufmann Series in Networking

Series Editor, David Clark, M.I.T.

Network Algorithmics: An Interdisciplinary Approach to Designing Fast Networked Devices
George Varghese

Network Recovery: Protection and Restoration of Optical, SONET-SDH, IP, and MPLS
Jean Philippe Vasseur, Mario Pickavet, and Piet Demeester

Routing, Flow, and Capacity Design in Communication and Computer Networks
Michal Pióro and Deepankar Medhi

Wireless Sensor Networks: An Information Processing Approach
Feng Zhao and Leonidas Guibas

Communication Networking: An Analytical Approach
Anurag Kumar, D. Manjunath, and Joy Kuri

The Internet and Its Protocols: A Comparative Approach
Adrian Farrel

Modern Cable Television Technology: Video, Voice, and Data Communications, 2e
Walter Ciciora, James Farmer, David Large, and Michael Adams

Bluetooth Application Programming with the Java APIs
C. Bala Kumar, Paul J. Kline, and Timothy J. Thompson

Policy-Based Network Management: Solutions for the Next Generation
John Strassner

Computer Networks: A Systems Approach, 3e
Larry L. Peterson and Bruce S. Davie

Network Architecture, Analysis, and Design, 2e
James D. McCabe

MPLS Network Management: MIBs, Tools, and Techniques
Thomas D. Nadeau

Developing IP-Based Services: Solutions for Service Providers and Vendors
Monique Morrow and Kateel Vijayananda

Telecommunications Law in the Internet Age
Sharon K. Black

Optical Networks: A Practical Perspective, 2e
Rajiv Ramaswami and Kumar N. Sivarajan

Internet QoS: Architectures and Mechanisms
Zheng Wang

TCP/IP Sockets in Java: Practical Guide for Programmers
Michael J. Donahoo and Kenneth L. Calvert

TCP/IP Sockets in C: Practical Guide for Programmers
Kenneth L. Calvert and Michael J. Donahoo

Multicast Communication: Protocols, Programming, and Applications
Ralph Wittmann and Martina Zitterbart

MPLS: Technology and Applications
Bruce Davie and Yakov Rekhter

High-Performance Communication Networks, 2e
Jean Walrand and Pravin Varaiya

Internetworking Multimedia
Jon Crowcroft, Mark Handley, and Ian Wakeman

Understanding Networked Applications: A First Course
David G. Messerschmitt

Integrated Management of Networked Systems: Concepts, Architectures, and Their Operational Applications
Heinz-Gerd Hegering, Sebastian Abeck, and Bernhard Neumair

Virtual Private Networks: Making the Right Connection
Dennis Fowler

Networked Applications: A Guide to the New Computing Infrastructure
David G. Messerschmitt

Wide Area Network Design: Concepts and Tools for Optimization
Robert S. Cahn

For further information on these books and for a list of forthcoming titles, please visit our website at http://www.mkp.com.

Network Algorithmics

An Interdisciplinary Approach to Designing
Fast Networked Devices

George Varghese
University of California, San Diego

AMSTERDAM • BOSTON • HEIDELBERG • LONDON
NEW YORK • OXFORD • PARIS • SAN DIEGO
SAN FRANCISCO • SINGAPORE • SYDNEY • TOKYO

ELSEVIER
MORGAN KAUFMANN PUBLISHERS IS AN IMPRINT OF ELSEVIER

MORGAN KAUFMANN PUBLISHERS

Elsevier/Morgan Kaufmann
Publishing Director: Diane D. Cerra
Senior Acquisitions Editor: Rick Adams
Associate Editor: Karyn Johnson
Editorial Coordinator: Mona Buehler
Publishing Services Manager: Simon Crump
Senior Project Manager: Angela Dooley
Cover Design Manager: Cate Rickard Barr
Cover Design: Yvo Riezebos Design

Cover Image: Getty Images
Text Design: Michael Remener
Composition: CEPHA
Technical Illustration: Dartmouth Publishing, Inc.
Copyeditor: Elliot Simon
Proofreader: Phyllis Coyne et al.
Indexer: Northwind Editorial
Interior Printer: The Maple-Vail Book Manufacturing Group
Cover Printer: Phoenix Color

Morgan Kaufmann is an imprint of Elsevier.
500 Sansome Street, Suite 400, San Francisco, CA 94111

This book is printed on acid-free paper.

Library of Congress Cataloging-in-Publication Data
Application submitted

ISBN-13: 978-0-12-088477-3
ISBN-10: 0-12-088477-1

For information on all Morgan Kaufmann publications,
visit our website at www.mkp.com.

Printed in the United States of America
08 07 06   5 4 3 2

For Aju and Tim and Andrew, who made all this possible . . .

CONTENTS

PART II   Playing with Endnodes   *105*

CHAPTER 5   Copying Data   *107*

PREFACE

Computer networks have become an integral part of society. We take for granted the ability to transact commerce over the Internet and that users can avail themselves of a burgeoning set of communication methods, which range from file sharing to Web logs. However, for networks to take their place as part of the fundamental infrastructure of society, they must provide performance guarantees.

We take for granted that electricity will flow when a switch is flicked and that telephone calls will be routed on Mother's Day. But the performance of computer networks such as the Internet is still notoriously unreliable. While there are many factors that go into performance, one major issue is that of network bottlenecks. There are two types of network bottlenecks: *resource bottlenecks* and *implementation bottlenecks*.

Resource bottlenecks occur when network performance is limited by the speed of the underlying hardware; examples include slow processors in server platforms and slow communication links. Resource bottlenecks can be worked around, at some cost, by buying faster hardware. However, it is quite often the case that the underlying hardware is perfectly adequate but that the real bottleneck is a design issue in the implementation. For example, a Web server running on the fastest processors may run slowly because of redundant data copying. Similarly, a router with a simple packet classification algorithm may start dropping packets when the number of ACL rules grows beyond a limit, though it keeps up with link speeds when classification is turned off. This book concentrates on such network implementation bottlenecks, especially at servers and routers.

Beyond servers and routers, new breeds of networking devices that introduce new performance bottlenecks are becoming popular. As networks become more integrated, devices such as storage area networks (SANs) and multimedia switches are becoming common. Further, as networks get more complex, various special-purpose network appliances for file systems and security are proliferating. While the first generation of such devices justified themselves by the new functions they provided, it is becoming critical that future network appliances keep up with link speeds.

Thus the objective of this book is to provide a set of techniques to overcome implementation bottlenecks at *all* networking devices and to provide a set of principles and models to help overcome current and *future* networking bottlenecks.

AUDIENCE

This book was written to answer a need for a text on efficient protocol implementations. The vast majority of networking books are on network protocols; even the implementation books are, for the most part, detailed explanations of the protocol. While protocols form the foundation of the field, there are just a handful of fundamental network infrastucture protocols left, such as TCP and IP. On the other hand, there are many implementations as most companies and start-ups customize their products to gain competitive advantage. This is exacerbated by the tendency to place TCP and IP everywhere, from bridges to SAN switches to toasters.

Thus there are many more people implementing protocols than designing them. *This is a textbook for implementors, networking students, and networking researchers, covering ground from the art of building a fast Web server to building a fast router and beyond.*

To do so, this book describes a collection of efficient implementation techniques; in fact, an initial section of each chapter concludes with a Quick Reference Guide for implementors that points to the most useful techniques for each topic. However, the book goes further and distills a fundamental method of crafting solutions to new network bottlenecks that we call *network algorithmics*. This provides the reader tools to design different implementations for specific contexts and to deal with new bottlenecks that will undoubtedly arise in a changing world.

Here is a detailed profile of our intended audience.

- *Network Protocol Implementors:* This group includes implementors of endnode networking stacks for large servers, PCs, and workstations and for network appliances. It also includes implementors of classic network interconnection devices, such as routers, bridges, switches, and gateways, as well as devices that monitor networks for measurement and security purposes. It also includes implementors of storage area networks, distributed computing infrastructures, multimedia switches and gateways, and other new networking devices. This book can be especially useful for implementors in start-ups as well as in established companies, for whom improved performance can provide an edge.

- *Networking Students:* Undergraduate and graduate students who have mastered the basics of network protocols can use this book as a text that describes how protocols should be implemented to improve performance, potentially an important aspect of their future jobs.

- *Instructors:* Instructors can use this book as a textbook for a one-semester course on network algorithmics.

- *Systems Researchers:* Networking and other systems researchers can use this text as a reference and as a stimulus for further research in improving system performance. Given that disributed operating systems and distributed computing infrastructures (e.g., the Grid) rely on an underlying networking core whose performance can be critical, this book can be useful to general systems researchers.

WHAT THIS BOOK IS ABOUT

Chapter 1 provides a more detailed introduction to network algorithmics. For now, we informally define network algorithmics as an interdisciplinary systems approach to streamlining network implementations. Network algorithmics is *interdisciplinary*, because it requires techniques from diverse fields such as architecture, operating systems, hardware design, and algorithms. Network algorithmics is also a *systems* approach, because routers and servers are systems in which efficiencies can be gained by moving functions in time and space between subsystems.

In essence, this book is about three things: fundamental networking implementation bottlenecks, general principles to address new bottlenecks, and techniques for specific bottlenecks that can be derived from the general principles.

Fundamental bottlenecks for an endnode such as a PC or workstation include data copying, control transfer, demultiplexing, timers, buffer allocation, checksums, and protocol processing. Similarly, fundamental bottlenecks for interconnect devices such as routers and SAN switches include exact and prefix lookups, packet classification, switching, and the implementation of measurement and security primitives. Chapter 1 goes into more detail about the inherent causes of these bottlenecks.

The fundamental methods that encompass network algorithmics include implementation models (Chapter 2) and 15 implementation principles (Chapter 3). The implementation models include models of operating systems, protocols, hardware, and architecture. They are included because the world of network protocol implementation requires the skills of several different communities, including operating system experts, protocol pundits, hardware designers, and computer architects. The implementation models are an attempt to bridge the gaps between these traditionally separate communities.

On the other hand, the implementation principles are an attempt to abstract the main ideas behind many specific implementation techniques. They include such well-known principles as "Optimize the expected case." They also include somewhat less well-known principles, such as "Combine DRAM with SRAM," which is a surprisingly powerful principle for producing fast hardware designs for network devices.

While Part I of the book lays out the methodology of network algorithmics, Part II *applies* the methodology to specific network bottlenecks in endnodes and servers. For example, Part II discusses copy avoidance techniques (such as passing virtual memory pointers and RDMA) and efficient control transfer methods (such as bypassing the kernel, as in the VIA proposal, and techniques for building event-driven servers).

Similarly, Part III of the book applies the methodology of Part I to interconnect devices, such as network routers. For example, Part III discusses effficient prefix-lookup schemes (such as multibit or compressed tries) and efficient switching schemes (such as those based on virtual output queues and bipartite matching).

Finally, Part IV of the book applies the methodology of Part I to new functions for security and measurement that could be housed in either servers or interconnect devices. For example, Part IV discusses efficient methods to compress large traffic reports and efficient methods to detect attacks.

ORGANIZATION OF THE BOOK

This book is organized into four overall parts. Each part is made as self-contained as possible to allow detailed study. Readers that are pressed for time can consult the index or Table of Contents for a particular topic (e.g., IP lookups). More importantly, the opening section of each chapter concludes with a Quick Reference Guide that points to the most important topics for implementors. The Quick Reference Guide may be the fastest guide for usefully skimming a chapter.

Part I of the book aims to familiarize the reader with the rules and philosophy of network algorithmics. It starts with Chapter 2, which describes simple models of protocols, operating systems, hardware design, and endnode and router architectures. Chapter 3 describes in detail the 15 principles used as a cornerstone for the book. Chapter 4 rounds out the first part by providing 15 examples, drawn for the most part from real implementation problems, to allow the reader a first opportunity to see the principles in action on real problems.

Part II of the book, called "Playing with Endnodes," shows how to build fast endnode implementations, such as Web servers, that run on general-purpose operating systems and standard computer architectures. It starts with Chapter 5, which shows how to reduce or avoid extra data copying. (Copying often occurs when network data is passed between implementation modules) and how to increase cache efficiency. Chapter 6 shows how to reduce or avoid the overhead of transferring control between implementation modules, such as the device driver, the kernel, and the application. Chapter 7 describes how to efficiently manage thousands of outstanding timers, a critical issue for large servers. Chapter 8 describes how to efficiently demultiplex data to receiving applications in a single step, allowing innovations such as user-level networking. Chapter 9 describes how to implement specific functions that often recur in specific protocol implementations, such as buffer allocation, checksums, sequence number bookkeeping, and reassembly. An overview of Part II can be found in Figure 1.1.

Part III of the book, called "Playing with Routers," shows how to build fast routers, bridges, and gateways. It begins with three chapters that describe state lookups of increasing complexity. Chapter 10 describes exact-match lookups, which are essential for the design of bridges and ARP caches. Chapter 11 describes prefix-match lookups, which are used by Internet routers to forward packets. Chapter 12 describes packet classification, a more sophisticated form of lookup required for security and quality of service. Chapter 13 describes how to build crossbar switches, which interconnect input and output links of devices such as routers. Finally, Chapter 14 describes packet-scheduling algorithms, which are used to provide quality-of-service, and Chapter 15 discusses routers as distributed systems, with examples focusing on performance and the use of design and reasoning techniques from distributed algorithms. While this list of functions seems short, one can build a fast router by designing a fast lookup algorithm, a fast switch, and fast packet-scheduling algorithms. Part IV, called "Endgame," starts by speculating on the potential need for implementing more complex tasks in the future. For example, Chapter 16 describes efficient implementation techniques for measurement primitives, while Chapter 17 describes efficient implementation techniques for security primitives. The book ends with a short chapter, Chapter 18, which reaches closure by distilling the unities that underly the many different topics in this book. This chapter also briefly presents examples of the use of algorithmics in a canonical router (the Cisco GSR) and a canonical server (the Flash Web server). A more detailed overview of Parts III and IV of the book can be found in Figure 1.2.

FEATURES

The book has the following features that readers, implementors, students, and instructors can take advantage of.

Intuitive introduction: The introductory paragraph of each chapter in Parts II, III, and IV uses an intuitive, real-world analogy to motivate each bottleneck. For example, we use the analogy of making multiple photocopies of a document for data copying and the analogy of a flight database for prefix lookups.

Quick Reference Guide: For readers familiar with a topic and pressed for time, the opening section of each chapter concludes with a Quick Reference Guide that points to the most important implementation ideas and the corresponding section numbers.

Chapter organization: To help orient the reader, immediately after the Quick Reference Guide in each chapter is a map of the entire chapter.

Summary of techniques: To emphasize the correlation between principles and techniques, at the start of each chapter is a table that summarizes the techniques described, together with the corresponding principles.

Consistent use of principles: After a detailed description in Chapter 3 of 15 principles, the rest of the book consistently uses these principles in describing specific techniques. For reference, the principles are summarized inside the front cover. Principles are referred to consistently by number — for example, **P9** for Principle 9. Since principle numbers are hard to remember, three aids are provided. Besides the inside front cover summary and the summary at the start of each chapter, the first use of a principle in any chapter is accompanied by an explicit statement of the principle.

Exercises: Chapter 4 of the book provides a set of real-life examples of applying the principles that have been enjoyed by past attendees of tutorials on network algorithmics. Every subsequent chapter through Chapter 17 is followed by a set of exercises. Brief solutions to these exercises can be found in an instructor's manual obtainable from Morgan Kaufmann.

Slides: Lecture slides in pdf for most chapters are available at Morgan Kaufmann's Web site www.mkp.com.

USAGE

This book can be used in many ways.

Textbook: Students and instructors can use this book as the basis of a one-semester class. A semester class on network algorithmics can include most of Part I and can sample chapters from Part II (e.g., Chapter 5 on copying, Chapter 6 on control overhead) and from Part III (e.g., Chapter 11 on prefix lookups, Chapter 13 on switching).

Implementation guide: Implementors who care about performance may wish to read all of Part I and then sample Parts II and III according to their needs.

Reference book: Implementors and students can also use this book as a reference book in addition to other books on network protocols.

WHY THIS BOOK WAS WRITTEN

The impetus for this book came from my academic research into efficient protocol implementation. It also came from three networking products I worked on with colleagues: the first bridge, the Gigaswitch, and the Procket 40 Gbps router. To prove itself against detractors, the first bridge was designed to operate at wire speed, an idea that spread to routers and the entire industry. My experience watching the work of Mark Kempf on the first bridge (see Chapter 10) led to a lasting interest in speeding up networking devices.

Next, the DEC Gigaswitch introduced me to the world of switching. Finally, the Procket router was designed by an interdisciplinary team that included digital designers who had designed processors, experts who had written vast amounts of the software in core routers, and some people like myself who were interested in algorithms. Despite the varied backgrounds, the team produced innovative new ideas, which convinced me of the importance of interdisciplinary thinking for performance breakthroughs. This motivated the writing of Chapter 2 on implementation models, an attempt to bridge the gaps between the different communities involved in high-performance designs.

For several years, I taught a class that collected together these techniques. The 15 principles emerged as a way to break up the techniques more finely and systematically. In retrospect, some principles seem redundant and glib. However, they serve as part of a first attempt to organize a vast amount of material.

I have taught five classes and three tutorials based on the material in this book, and so this book has been greatly influenced by student responses and ideas.

ACKNOWLEDGMENTS

A special thanks to my editors: Karen Gettman and Rick Adams and Karyn Johnson; to all my advisors, who taught me so much: Wushow Chou, Arne Nillson, Baruch Awerbuch, Nancy Lynch; to all my mentors: Alan Kirby, Radia Perlman, Tony Lauck, Bob Thomas, Bob Simcoe, Jon Turner; to numerous colleages at DEC and other companies, especially to Sharad Merhotra, Bill Lynch, and Tony Li of Procket Networks, who taught me about real routers; to students who adventured in the field of network algorithmics with me; to numerous reviewers of this book and especially to Jon Snader, Tony Lauck, Brian Kernighan, Craig Partridge, and Radia Perlman for detailed comments; to Kevin D'Souza, Stefano Previdi, Anees Shaikh, and Darryl Veitch for their reviews and ideas; to my family, my mother, my wife's father and mother, and my sister; and, of course, to my wife, Aju, and my sons, Tim and Andrew.

I'd like to end by acknowledging my heroes: four teachers who have influenced me. The first is Leonard Bernstein, who taught me in his lectures on music that a teacher's enthusiasm for the material can be infectious. The second is George Polya, who taught me in his books on problem solving that the process of discovery is as important as the final discoveries themselves. The third is Socrates, who taught me through Plato that it is worth always questioning assumptions. The fourth is Jesus, who has taught me that life, and indeed this book, is not a matter of merit but of grace and gift.

PART I

The Rules of the Game

"Come, Watson, come!" he cried. *"The game is afoot!"*

—ARTHUR CONAN DOYLE IN *The Abbey Grange*

The first part of this book deals with specifying the rules of the network algorithmics game. We start with a quick introduction where we define network algorithmics and contrast it to algorithm design. Next, we present models of protocols, operating systems, processor architecture, and hardware design; these are the key disciplines used in the rest of the book. Then we present a set of 15 principles abstracted from the specific techniques presented later in the book. Part I ends with a set of sample problems together with solutions obtained using the principles. Implementors pressed for time should skim the Quick Reference Guides directly following the introduction to each chapter.

CHAPTER 1

Introducing Network Algorithmics

*What really makes it an invention is that someone decides not to change the solution
to a known problem, but to change the question.*

—DEAN KAMEN

Just as the objective of chess is to checkmate the opponent and the objective of tennis is to win matches, the objective of the network algorithmics game is to battle networking implementation bottlenecks.

Beyond specific techniques, this book distills a fundamental way of crafting solutions to internet bottlenecks that we call *network algorithmics*. This provides the reader tools to design different implementations for specific contexts and to deal with new bottlenecks that will undoubtedly arise in the changing world of networks.

So what is network algorithmics? Network algorithmics goes beyond the design of efficient algorithms for networking tasks, though this has an important place. In particular, network algorithmics recognizes the primary importance of taking an interdisciplinary systems approach to streamlining network implementations.

Network algorithmics is an *interdisciplinary* approach because it encompasses such fields as architecture and operating systems (for speeding up servers), hardware design (for speeding up network devices such as routers), and algorithm design (for designing scalable algorithms). Network algorithmics is also a *systems* approach, because it is described in this book using a set of 15 principles that exploit the fact that routers and servers are systems, in which efficiencies can be gained by moving functions in time and space between subsystems.

The problems addressed by network algorithmics are fundamental networking performance *bottlenecks*. The solutions advocated by network algorithmics are a set of fundamental *techniques* to address these bottlenecks. Next, we provide a quick preview of both the bottlenecks and the methods.

1.1 THE PROBLEM: NETWORK BOTTLENECKS

The main problem considered in this book is how to make networks *easy to use* while at the same time realizing the *performance* of the raw hardware. Ease of use comes from the use of powerful network abstractions, such as socket interfaces and prefix-based forwarding. Unfortunately, without care such abstractions exact a large performance penalty when compared to the capacity of raw transmission links such as optical fiber. To study this performance gap in more detail we examine two fundamental categories of networking devices, *endnodes* and *routers*.

1.1.1 Endnode Bottlenecks

Endnodes are the endpoints of the network. They include personal computers and workstations as well as large servers that provide services. Endnodes are specialized toward computation, as opposed to networking, and are typically designed to support *general-purpose* computation. Thus endnode bottlenecks are typically the result of two forces: structure and scale.

- *Structure:* To be able to run arbitrary code, personal computers and large servers typically have an operating system that mediates between applications and the hardware. To ease software development, most large operating systems are carefully structured as *layered software*; to protect the operating system from other applications, operating systems implement a set of *protection mechanisms*; finally, core operating systems routines, such as schedulers and allocators, are written using *general mechanisms* that target as wide a class of applications as possible. Unfortunately, the combination of layered software, protection mechanisms, and excessive generality can slow down networking software greatly, even with the fastest processors.

- *Scale:* The emergence of large servers providing Web and other services causes further performance problems. In particular, a large server such as a Web server will typically have thousands of concurrent clients. Many operating systems use inefficient data structures and algorithms that were designed for an era when the number of connections was small.

Figure 1.1 previews the main endnode bottlenecks covered in this book, together with causes and solutions. The first bottleneck occurs because conventional operating system structures cause packet data *copying* across protection domains; the situation is further complicated

Bottleneck	Chapter	Cause	Sample Solution
Copying	5	Protection, structure	Copying many data blocks without OS intervention (e.g., RDMA)
Context switching	6	Complex scheduling	User-level protocol implementations Event-driven Web servers
System calls	6	Protection, structure	Direct channels from applications to drivers (e.g., VIA)
Timers	7	Scaling with number of timers	Timing wheels
Demultiplexing	8	Scaling with number of endpoints	BPF and Pathfinder
Checksums/ CRCs	9	Generality Scaling with link speeds	Multibit computation
Protocol code	9	Generality	Header prediction

FIGURE 1.1   Preview of endnode bottlenecks, solutions to which are described in Part II of the book.

in Web servers by similar copying with respect to the file system and by other manipulations, such as checksums, that examine all the packet data. Chapter 5 describes a number of techniques to reduce these overheads while preserving the goals of system abstractions, such as protection and structure. The second major overhead is the *control overhead* caused by switching between threads of control (or protection domains) while processing a packet; this is addressed in Chapter 6.

Networking applications use timers to deal with failure. With a large number of connections the timer overhead at a server can become large; this overhead is addressed in Chapter 7. Similarly, network messages must be demultiplexed (i.e., steered) on receipt to the right end application; techniques to address this bottleneck are addressed in Chapter 8. Finally, there are several other common protocol processing tasks, such as buffer allocation and checksums, which are addressed in Chapter 9.

1.1.2 Router Bottlenecks

Though we concentrate on Internet routers, almost all the techniques described in this book apply equally well to any other network devices, such as bridges, switches, gateways, monitors, and security appliances, and to protocols other than IP, such as FiberChannel.

Thus throughout the rest of the book, it is often useful to think of a *router* as a "generic network interconnection device." Unlike endnodes, these are special-purpose devices devoted to networking. Thus there is very little structural overhead within a router, with only the use of a very lightweight operating system and a clearly separated forwarding path that often is completely implemented in hardware. Instead of structure, the fundamental problems faced by routers are caused by *scale* and *services*.

- *Scale:* Network devices face two areas of scaling: *bandwidth scaling* and *population scaling*. Bandwidth scaling occurs because optical links keep getting faster, as the progress from 1-Gbps to 40-Gbps links shows, and because Internet traffic keeps growing due to a diverse set of new applications. Population scaling occurs because more endpoints get added to the Internet as more enterprises go online.

- *Services:* The need for speed and scale drove much of the networking industry in the 1980s and 1990s as more businesses went online (e.g., Amazon.com) and whole new online services were created (e.g., Ebay). But the very success of the Internet requires careful attention in the next decade to make it more effective by providing guarantees in terms of performance, security, and reliability. After all, if manufacturers (e.g., Dell) sell more online than by other channels, it is important to provide *network guarantees* — delay in times of congestion, protection during attacks, and availability when failures occur. Finding ways to implement these new services at high speeds will be a major challenge for router vendors in the next decade.

Figure 1.2 previews the main router (bridge/gateway) bottlenecks covered in this book, together with causes and solutions.

First, all networking devices forward packets to their destination by looking up a forwarding table. The simplest forwarding table lookup does an exact match with a destination address, as exemplified by bridges. Chapter 10 describes fast and scalable exact-match lookup schemes. Unfortunately, population scaling has made lookups far more complex for routers.

Bottleneck	Chapter	Cause	Sample Solution
Exact lookups	10	Link speed scaling	Parallel hashing
Prefix lookups	11	Link speed scaling Prefix database size scaling	Compressed multibit tries
Packet classification	12	Service differentiation Link speed and size scaling	Decision tree algorithms Hardware parallelism (CAMs)
Switching	13	Optical-electronic speed gap Head-of-line blocking	Crossbar switches Virtual output queues
Fair queueing	14	Service differentiation Link speed scaling Memory scaling	Weighted fair queueing Deficit round robin DiffServ, Core Stateless
Internal bandwidth	15	Scaling of internal bus speeds	Reliable striping
Measurement	16	Link speed scaling	Juniper's DCU
Security	17	Scaling in number and intensity of attacks	Traceback with bloom filters Extracting worm signatures

FIGURE 1.2 Preview of router bottlenecks, solutions to which are described in Parts III and IV of the book.

To deal with large Internet populations, routers keep a single entry called a *prefix* (analogous to a telephone area code) for a large group of stations. Thus routers must do a more complex *longest-prefix-match* lookup. Chapter 11 describes solutions to this problem that scale to increasing speeds and table sizes.

Many routers today offer what is sometimes called *service differentiation*, where different packets can be treated differently in order to provide service and security guarantees. Unfortunately, this requires an even more complex form of lookup called *packet classification*, in which the lookup is based on the destination, source, and even the services that a packet is providing. This challenging issue is tackled in Chapter 12.

Next, all networking devices can be abstractly considered as switches that shunt packets coming in from a set of input links to a set of output links. Thus a fundamental issue is that of building a high-speed switch. This is hard, especially in the face of the growing gap between optical and electronic speeds. The standard solution is to use parallelism via a *crossbar switch*. Unfortunately, it is nontrivial to schedule a crossbar at high speeds, and parallelism is limited by a phenomenon known as *head-of-line blocking*. Worse, population scaling and optical multiplexing are forcing switch vendors to build switches with a large number of ports (e.g., 256), which exacerbates these other problems. Solutions to these problems are described in Chapter 13.

While the previous bottlenecks are caused by scaling, the next bottleneck is caused by the need for new services. The issue of providing performance guarantees at high speeds is treated in Chapter 14, where the issue of implementing so-called QoS (quality of service) mechanisms is studied. Chapter 15 briefly surveys another bottleneck that is becoming an increasing problem: the issue of bandwidth within a router. It describes sample techniques, such as striping across internal buses and chip-to-chip links.

The final sections of the book take a brief look at emerging services that must, we believe, be part of a well-engineered Internet of the future. First, routers of the future must build in support for measurement, because measurement is key to engineering networks to provide guarantees. While routers today provide some support for measurement in terms of counters and NetFlow records, Chapter 16 also considers more innovative measurement mechanisms that may be implemented in the future.

Chapter 17 describes security support, some of which is already being built into routers. Given the increased sophistication, virulence, and rate of network attacks, we believe that implementing security features in networking devices (whether routers or dedicated intrusion prevention/detection devices) will be essential. Further, unless the security device can keep up with high-speed links, the device may miss vital information required to spot an attack.

1.2 THE TECHNIQUES: NETWORK ALGORITHMICS

Throughout this book, we will talk of many specific techniques: of interrupts, copies, and timing wheels; of Pathfinder and Sting; of why some routers are very slow; and whether Web servers can scale. But what underlies the assorted techniques in this book and makes it more than a recipe book is the notion of *network algorithmics*. As said earlier, network algorithmics recognizes the primary importance of taking a *systems* approach to streamlining network implementations.

While everyone recognizes that the Internet is a system consisting of routers and links, it is perhaps less obvious that every networking device, from the Cisco GSR to an Apache Web server, is also a system. A system is built out of interconnected subsystems that are instantiated at various points in time. For example, a core router consists of line cards with forwarding engines and packet memories connected by a crossbar switch. The router behavior is affected by decisions at various time scales, which range from manufacturing time (when default parameters are stored in NVRAM) to route computation time (when routers conspire to compute routes) to packet-forwarding time (when packets are sent to adjoining routers).

Thus one key observation in the systems approach is that one can often design an efficient subsystem by moving some of its functions in *space* (i.e., to other subsystems) or in *time* (i.e., to points in time before or after the function is apparently required). In some sense, the practitioner of network algorithmics is an unscrupulous opportunist willing to change the rules at any time to make the game easier. The only constraint is that the functions provided by the overall system continue to satisfy users.

In one of Mark Twain's books, a Connecticut Yankee is transported back in time to King Arthur's court. The Yankee then uses a gun to fight against dueling knights accustomed to jousting with lances. This is an example of changing system assumptions (replacing lances by guns) to solve a problem (winning a duel).

Considering the constraints faced by the network implementor at high speeds — increasingly complex tasks, larger systems to support, small amounts of high-speed memory, and a small number of memory accesses — it may require every trick, every gun in one's arsenal, to keep pace with the increasing speed and scale of the Internet. The designer can throw hardware at the problem, change the system assumptions, design a new algorithm — whatever it takes to get the job done.

This book is divided into four parts. The first part, of which this is the first chapter, lays a foundation for applying network algorithmics to packet processing. The second chapter of the first part outlines models, and the third chapter presents general principles used in the remainder of the book.

One of the best ways to get a quick idea about what network algorithmics is about is to plunge right away into a warm-up example. While the warm-up example that follows is in the context of a device within the network where new hardware can be designed, note that Part 2 is about building efficient servers using only software design techniques.

1.2.1 Warm-up Example: Scenting an Evil Packet

Imagine a front-end network monitor (or intrusion detection system) on the periphery of a corporate network that wishes to flag suspicious incoming packets — packets that could contain attacks on internal computers. A common such attack is a *buffer overflow* attack, where the attacker places machine code C in a network header field F.

If the receiving computer allocates a buffer too small for header field F and is careless about checking for overflow, the code C can spill onto the receiving machine's stack. With a little more effort, the intruder can make the receiving machine actually execute evil code C. C then takes over the receiver machine. Figure 1.3 shows such an attack embodied in a familiar field, a destination Web URL (uniform resource locator). How might the monitor detect the presence of such a suspicious URL? A possible way is to observe that URLs containing evil code are often too long (an easy check) and often have a large fraction of unusual (at least in URLs) characters, such as #. Thus the monitor could mark such packets (containing URLs that are too long and have too many occurrences of such unusual characters) for more thorough examination.

It is worth stating at the outset that the security implications of this strategy need to be carefully thought out. For example, there may be several innocuous programs, such as CGI scripts, in URLs that lead to false positives. Without getting too hung up in overall architectural implications, let us assume that this was a specification handed down to a chip architect by a security architect. We now use this sample problem, suggested by Mike Fisk, to illustrate algorithmics in action.

Faced with such a specification, a chip designer may use the following design process, which illustrates some of the principles of network algorithmics. The process starts with a strawman design and refines the design using techniques such as designing a better algorithm, relaxing the specification, and exploiting hardware.

FIGURE 1.3   Getting wind of an evil packet by noticing the frequency of unprintable characters.

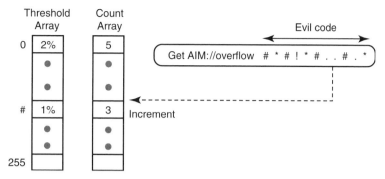

FIGURE 1.4 Strawman solution for detecting an evil packet by counting occurrences of each character via a count array (middle) and then comparing in a final pass with an array of acceptable thresholds (left).

1.2.2 Strawman Solution

The check of overall length is straightforward to implement, so we concentrate on checking for a prevalence of suspicious characters. The first strawman solution is illustrated in Figure 1.4. The chip maintains two arrays, T and C, with 256 elements each, one for each possible value of an 8-bit character. The threshold array, T, contains the acceptable percentage (as a fraction of the entire URL length) for each character. If the occurrences of a character in an actual URL fall above this fraction, the packet should be flagged. Each character can have a different threshold.

The count array, C, in the middle, contains the current count $C[i]$ for each possible character i. When the chip reads a new character $"i"$ in the URL, it increments $C[i]$ by 1. $C[i]$ is initialized to 0 for all values of i when a new packet is encountered. The incrementing process starts only after the chip parses the HTTP header and recognizes the start of a URL.

In HTTP, the end of a URL is signified by two newline characters; thus one can tell the length of the URL only after parsing the entire URL string. Thus, after the end of the URL is encountered, the chip makes a final pass over the array C. If $C[j] \geq L \cdot T[j]$ for any j, where L is the length of the URL, the packet is flagged.

Assume that packets are coming into the monitor at high speed and that we wish to finish processing a packet before the next one arrives. This requirement, called *wire speed processing*, is very common in networking; it prevents processing backlogs even in the worst case. To meet wire speed requirements, ideally the chip should do a small constant number of operations for every URL byte. Assume the main step of incrementing a counter can be done in the time to receive a byte.

Unfortunately, the two passes over the array, first to initialize it and then to check for threshold violations, make this design slow. Minimum packet sizes are often as small as 40 bytes and include only network headers. Adding 768 more operations (1 write and 1 read to each element of C, and 1 read of T for each of 256 indices) can make this design infeasible.

1.2.3 Thinking Algorithmically

Intuitively, the second pass through the arrays C and T at the end seems like a waste. For example, it suffices to alarm if *any* character is over the threshold. So why check all characters?

FIGURE 1.5   Avoiding the final loop through the threshold array by keeping track only of *Max*, the highest counter encountered so far relative to its threshold value.

This suggests keeping track only of the largest character count c; at the end perhaps the algorithm needs to check only whether c is over threshold with respect to the total URL length L.

This does not quite work. A nonsuspicious character such as "e" may well have a very high occurrence count. However, "e" is also likely to be specified with a high threshold. Thus if we keep track only of "e" with, say, a count of 20, we may not keep track of "#" with, say, a count of 10. If the threshold of "#" is much smaller, the algorithm may cause a *false negative*: The chip may fail to alarm on a packet that should be flagged.

The counterexample suggests the following fix. The chip keeps track in a register of the highest counter relativized to the threshold value. More precisely, the chip keeps track of the highest relativized counter *Max* corresponding to some character k, such that $C[k]/T[k] = Max$ is the highest among all characters encountered so far. If a new character i is read, the chip increments $C[i]$. If $C[i]/T[i] > Max$, then the chip replaces the current stored value of *Max* with $C[i]/T[i]$. At the end of URL processing, the chip alarms if $Max \geq L$.

Here's why this works. If $Max = C[k]/T[k] \geq L$, clearly the packet must be flagged, because character k is over threshold. On the other hand, if $C[k]/T[k] < L$, then for any character i, it follows that $C[i]/T[i] \leq C[k]/T[k] < L$. Thus if *Max* falls below threshold, then no character is above threshold. Thus there can be no false negatives. This solution is shown in Figure 1.5.

1.2.4 *Refining the Algorithm: Exploiting Hardware*

The new algorithm has eliminated the loop at the end but still has to deal with a divide operation while processing each byte. Divide logic is somewhat complicated and worth avoiding if possible — but how?

Returning to the specification and its intended use, it seems likely that thresholds are not meant to be exact floating point numbers. It is unlikely that the architect providing thresholds can estimate the values precisely; one is likely to approximate 2.78% as 3% without causing much difference to the security goals. So why not go further and approximate the threshold by some power of 2 less than the exact intended threshold? Thus if the threshold is 1/29, why not approximate it as 1/32?

FIGURE 1.6 Using a wide word and a coalesced array to combine 2 reads into one.

Changing the specification in this way requires negotiation with the system architect. Assume that the architect agrees to this new proposal. Then a threshold such as 1/32 can be encoded compactly as the corresponding power of 2 — i.e., 5. This threshold *shift* value can be stored in the threshold array instead of a fraction.

Thus when a character j is encountered, the chip increments $C[j]$ as usual and then shifts $C[j]$ to the left — dividing by $1/x$ is the same as multiplying by x — by the specified threshold. If the shifted value is higher than the last stored value for *Max*, the chip replaces the old value with the new value and marches on.

Thus the logic required to implement the processing of a byte is a simple shift-and-compare. The stored state is only a single register to store *Max*. As it stands, however, the design requires a Read to the Threshold array (to read the shift value), a Read to the Count array (to read the old count), and a Write to the Count array (to write back the incremented value).

Now reads to memory — 1–2 nsec even for the fastest on-chip memories but possibly even as slow as 10 nsec for slower memories — are slower than logic. Single gate delays are only in the order of picoseconds, and shift logic does not require too many gate delays. Thus the processing bottleneck is the number of memory accesses.

The chip implementation can combine the 2 Reads to memory into 1 Read by coalescing the Count and Threshold arrays into a single array, as shown in Figure 1.6. The idea is to make the memory words wide enough to hold the counter (say, 15 bits to handle packets of length 32K) and the threshold (depending on the precision necessary, no more than 14 bits). Thus the two fields can easily be combined into a larger word of size 29 bits. In practice, hardware can handle much larger words sizes of up to 1000 bits. Also, note that extracting the two fields packed into a single word, quite a chore in software, is trivial in hardware by routing wires appropriately between registers or by using multiplexers.

1.2.5 Cleaning Up

We have postponed one thorny issue to this point. The terminal loop has been eliminated while leaving the initial initialization loop. To handle this, note that the chip has spare time for initialization after parsing the URL of the current packet and before encountering the URL of the next packet.

Unfortunately, packets can be as small as 50 bytes, even with an HTTP header. Thus even assuming a slack of 40 non-URL bytes other than the 10 bytes of the URL, this still does not suffice to initialize a 256-byte array without paying $256/40 = 6$ more operations per byte than during the processing of a URL. As in the URL processing loop, each initialization step requires a Read and Write of some element of the coalesced array.

A trick among lazy people is to postpone work until it is absolutely needed, in the hope that it may never be needed. Note that, strictly speaking, the chip need not initialize a $C[i]$ until character i is accessed for the first time in a subsequent packet. But how can the chip tell that it is seeing character i for the first time?

To implement lazy evaluation, each memory word representing an entry in the coalesced array must be expanded to include, say, a 3-bit generation number $G[i]$. The generation number can be thought of as a value of clock time measured in terms of packets encountered so far, except that it is limited to 3 bits. Thus, the chip keeps an additional register g, besides the extra $G[i]$ for each i, that is 3 bits long; g is incremented mod 8 for every packet encountered. In addition, every time $C[i]$ is updated, the chip updates $G[i]$ as well to reflect the current value of g.

Given the generation numbers, the chip need not initialize the count array after the current packet has been processed. However, consider the case of a packet whose generation number is h, which contains a character i in its URL. When the chip encounters i while processing the packet the chip reads $C[i]$ and $G[i]$ from the Count array. If $G[i] \neq h$, this clearly indicates that entry i was last accessed by an earlier packet and has not subsequently been initialized. Thus the logic will write back the value of $C[i]$ as 1 (initialization plus increment) and set $G[i]$ to h. This is shown in Figure 1.7.

The careful reader will immediately object. Since the generation number is only 3 bits, once the value of g wraps around, there can be aliasing. Thus if $G[i]$ is 5 and entry i is not accessed until eight more packets have gone by, g will have wrapped around to 5. If the next packet contains i, $C[i]$ will not be initialized and the count will (wrongly) accumulate the count of i in the current packet together with the count that occurred eight packets in the past.

The chip can avoid such aliasing by doing a separate "scrubbing" loop that reads the array and initializes all counters with outdated generation numbers. For correctness, the chip must guarantee one complete scan through the array for every eight packets processed. Given that one has a slack of (say) 40 non-URL bytes per packet, this guarantees a slack of 320 non-URL

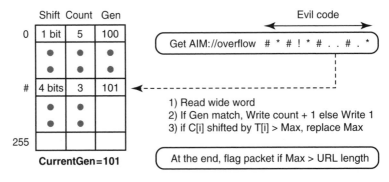

FIGURE 1.7   The final solution with generation numbers to finesse an initialization loop.

bytes after eight packets, which suffices to initialize a 256-element array using one Read and one Write per byte, whether the byte is a URL or a non-URL byte. Clearly, the designer can gain more slack, if needed, by increasing the bits in the generation number, at the cost of slightly increased storage in the array.

The chip, then, must have two states: one for processing URL bytes and one for processing non-URL bytes. When the URL is completely processed, the chip switches to the "Scrub" state. The chip maintains another register, which points to the next array entry s to be scrubbed. In the scrub state, when a non-URL character is received, the chip reads entry s in the coalesced array. If $G[s] \neq g$, $G[s]$ is reset to g and $C[s]$ is initialized to 0.

Thus the use of 3 extra bits of generation number per array entry has reduced initialization processing cycles, trading processing for storage. Altogether a coalesced array entry is now only 32 bits, 15 bits for a counter, 14 bits for a threshold shift value, and 3 bits for a generation number. Note that the added initialization check needed during URL byte processing does not increase memory references (the bottleneck) but adds slightly to the processing logic. In addition, it requires two more chip registers to hold g and s, a small additional expense.

1.2.6 Characteristics of Network Algorithmics

The example of scenting an evil packet illustrates three important aspects of network algorithmics.

a. Network algorithmics is interdisciplinary: Given the high rates at which network processing must be done, a router designer would be hard pressed not to use hardware. The example exploited several features of hardware: It assumed that wide words of arbitrary size were easily possible; it assumed that shifts were easier than divides; it assumed that memory references were the bottleneck; it assumed that a 256-element array contained in fast on-chip memory was feasible; it assumed that adding a few extra registers was feasible; and finally it assumed that small changes to the logic to combine URL processing and initialization were trivial to implement.

For the reader unfamiliar with hardware design, this is a little like jumping into a game of cards without knowing the rules and then finding oneself finessed and trumped in unexpected ways. A contention of this book is that mastery of a few relevant aspects of hardware design can help even a software designer understand at least the feasibility of different hardware designs. A further contention of this book is that such interdisciplinary thinking can help produce the best designs.

Thus Chapter 2 presents the rules of the game. It presents simple models of hardware that point out opportunities for finessing and trumping troublesome implementation issues. It also presents simple models of operating systems. This is done because end systems such as clients and Web servers require tinkering with and understanding operating system issues to improve performance, just as routers and network devices require tinkering with hardware.

b. Network algorithmics recognizes the primacy of systems thinking: The specification was relaxed to allow approximate thresholds in powers of 2, which simplified the hardware. Relaxing specifications and moving work from one subsystem to another is an extremely common systems technique, but it is not encouraged by current educational practice in universities, in which each area is taught in isolation.

Thus today one has separate courses in algorithms, in operating systems, and in networking. This tends to encourage "black box" thinking instead of holistic or systems thinking.

The example alluded to other systems techniques, such as the use of *lazy evaluation* and *trading memory for processing* in order to scrub the Count array.

Thus a feature of this book is an attempt to distill the systems principles used in algorithmics into a set of 15 principles, which are catalogued inside the front cover of the book and are explored in detail in Chapter 3. This book attempts to explain and dissect all the network implementations described in this book in terms of these principles. The principles are also given numbers for easy reference, though for the most part we will use both the number and the name. For instance, take a quick peek at the inside front cover and you will find that relaxing specifications is principle **P4** and lazy evaluation is **P2a**.

c. Network algorithmics can benefit from algorithmic thinking: While this book stresses the primacy of systems thinking to finesse problems wherever possible, there are many situations where systems constraints prevent any elimination of problems. In our example, after attempting to finesse the need for algorithmic thinking by relaxing the specification, the problem of false positives led to considering keeping track of the highest counter relative to its threshold value. As a second example, Chapter 11 shows that despite attempts to finesse Internet lookups using what is called *tag switching*, many routers resort to efficient algorithms for lookup.

It is worth emphasizing, however, that because the models are somewhat different from standard theoretical models, it is often insufficient to blindly reuse existing algorithms. For example, Chapter 13 discusses how the need to schedule a crossbar switch in 8 nsec leads to considering simpler maximal matching heuristics, as opposed to more complicated algorithms that produce optimal matchings in a bipartite graph.

As a second example, Chapter 11 describes how the BSD implementation of lookups blindly reused a data structure called a Patricia trie, which uses a skip count, to do IP lookups. The resulting algorithm requires complex backtracking.[1] A simple modification that keeps the actual bits that were skipped (instead of the count) avoids the need for backtracking. But this requires some insight into the black box (i.e., the algorithm) and its application.

In summary, the uncritical use of standard algorithms can miss implementation breakthroughs because of inappropriate *measures* (e.g., for packet filters such as BPF, the insertion of a new classifier can afford to take more time than search), inappropriate *models* (e.g., ignoring the effects of cache lines in software or parallelism in hardware), and inappropriate *analysis* (e.g., order-of-complexity results that hide constant factors crucial in ensuring wire speed forwarding).

Thus another purpose of this book is to persuade implementors that insight into algorithms and the use of fundamental algorithmic techniques such as divide-and-conquer and randomization is important to master. This leads us to the following.

Definition: Network algorithmics is the use of an interdisciplinary systems approach, seasoned with algorithmic thinking, to design fast implementations of network processing tasks at servers, routers, and other networking devices.

---

[1]The algorithm was considered to be the state of the art for many years and was even implemented in hardware in several router designs. In fact, a patent for lookups issued to a major router company appears to be a hardware implementation of BSD Patricia tries with backtracking. Any deficiencies of the algorithm can, of course, be mitigated by fast hardware. However, it is worth considering that a simple change to the algorithm could have simplified the hardware design.

Focus	Chapter	Motivation	Sample Topic
Models	2	Understand simple models for OS, hardware, networks	Memory technology techniques (interleaving, mixing SRAM/DRAM)
Strategies	3	Learn systems principles for overcoming bottlenecks	Pass hints, evaluate lazily Add state, exploit locality
Problems	4	Practice applying principles on simple problems	Designing a lookup engine for a network monitor

FIGURE 1.8 Preview of network algorithmics. Network algorithmics is introduced using a set of models, strategies, and sample problems, which are described in Part I of the book.

Part I of the book is devoted to describing the network algorithmics approach in more detail. An overview of Part I is given in Figure 1.8.

While this book concentrates on networking, the general algorithmics approach holds for the implementation of any computer system, whether a database, a processor architecture, or a software application. This general philosophy is alluded to in Chapter 3 by providing illustrative examples from the field of computer system implementation. The reader interested only in networking should rest assured that the remainder of the book, other than Chapter 3, avoids further digressions beyond networking.

While Parts II and III provide specific techniques for important specific problems, the main goal of this book is to allow the reader to be able to tackle *arbitrary* packet-processing tasks at high speeds in software or hardware. Thus the implementor of the future may be given the task of speeding up XML processing in a Web server (likely, given current trends) or even the task of computing the chi-square statistic in a router (possible because chi-square provides a test for detecting abnormal observed frequencies for tasks such as intrusion detection). Despite being assigned a completely unfamiliar task, the hope is that the implementor would be able to craft a new solution to such tasks using the models, principles, and techniques described in this book.

1.3 EXERCISE

1. **Implementing Chi-Square:** The chi-square statistic can be used to find if the overall set of observed character frequencies are unusually different (as compared to normal random variation) from the expected character frequencies. This is a more sophisticated test, statistically speaking, than the simple threshold detector used in the warm-up example. Assume that the thresholds represent the expected frequencies. The statistic is computed by finding the sum of

$$(ExpectedFrequency[i] - ObservedFrequency[i])^2 / ExpectedFrequency[i]$$

for all values of character i. The chip should alarm if the final statistic is above a specified threshold. (For example, a value of 14.2 implies that there is only a 1.4% chance that the difference is due to chance variation.) Find a way to efficiently implement this statistic, assuming once again that the length is known only at the end.

CHAPTER 2

Network Implementation Models

A rather small set of key concepts is enough. Only by learning the essence of each topic, and by carrying along the least amount of mental baggage at each step, will the student emerge with a good overall understanding of the subject.

— CARVER MEAD AND LYNN CONWAY

To improve the performance of endnodes and routers, an implementor must know the rules of the game. A central difficulty is that network algorithmics encompasses four separate areas: protocols, hardware architectures, operating systems, and algorithms. Networking innovations occur when area experts work together to produce synergistic solutions. But can a logic designer understand protocol issues, and can a clever algorithm designer understand hardware trade-offs, at least without deep study?

Useful dialog can begin with *simple models* that have explanatory and predictive power but without unnecessary detail. At the least, such models should define terms used in the book; at the best, such models should enable a creative person *outside* an area to play with and create designs that can be checked by an expert *within* the area. For example, a hardware chip implementor should be able to suggest software changes to the chip driver, and a theoretical computer scientist should be able to dream up hardware matching algorithms for switch arbitration. This is the goal of this chapter.

The chapter is organized as follows. Starting with a model for protocols in Section 2.1, the implementation environment is described in bottom-up order. Section 2.2 describes relevant aspects of hardware protocol implementation, surveying logic, memories, and components. Section 2.3 describes a model for endnodes and network devices such as routers. Section 2.4 describes a model for the relevant aspects of operating systems that affect performance, especially in endnodes. To motivate the reader and to retain the interest of the area expert, the chapter contains a large number of networking examples to illustrate the application of each model.

Quick Reference Guide

Hardware designers should skip most of Section 2.2, except for Example 3 (design of a switch arbitrator), Example 4 (design of a flow ID lookup chip), Example 5 (pin count limitations and their implications), and Section 2.2.5 (which summarizes three hardware design principles useful in networking). Processor and architecture experts should skip Section 2.3 except for Example 7 (network processors).

Implementors familiar with operating systems should skip Section 2.4, except for Example 8 (receiver livelock as an example of how operating system structure influences protocol implementations). Even those unfamiliar with an area such as operating systems may wish to consult these sections if needed after reading the specific chapters that follow.

2.1 PROTOCOLS

Section 2.1.1 describes the transport protocol TCP and the IP routing protocol. These two examples are used to provide an abstract model of a protocol and its functions in Section 2.1.2. Section 2.1.3 ends with common network performance assumptions. Readers familiar with TCP/IP may wish to skip to Section 2.1.2.

2.1.1 Transport and Routing Protocols

Applications subcontract the job of reliable delivery to a transport protocol such as the Transmission Control Protocol (TCP). TCP's job is to provide the sending and receiving applications with the illusion of two shared data queues in each direction — despite the fact that the sender and receiver machines are separated by a lossy network. Thus whatever the sender application writes to its local TCP send queue should magically appear in the same order at the local TCP receive queue at the receiver, and vice versa. TCP implements this mechanism by breaking the queued application data into segments and retransmitting each segment until an acknowledgment (ack) has been received. A more detailed description of TCP operation can be found in Section A.1.1.

If the application is (say) a videoconferencing application that does not want reliability guarantees, it can choose to use a protocol called UDP (User Datagram Protocol) instead of TCP. Unlike TCP, UDP does not need acks or retransmissions because it does not guarantee reliability.

Transport protocols such as TCP and UDP work by sending segments from a sender node to a receiver node across the Internet. The actual job of sending a segment is subcontracted to the Internet routing protocol IP.

Internet routing is broken into two conceptual parts, called *forwarding* and *routing*. Forwarding is the process by which packets move from source to destination through intermediate routers. A *packet* is a TCP segment together with a routing header that contains the destination Internet address.

While forwarding must be done at extremely high speeds, the forwarding tables at each router must be built by a routing protocol, especially in the face of topology changes, such as link failures. There are several commonly used routing protocols, such as distance vector (e.g., RIP), link state (e.g., OSPF), and policy routing (e.g., BGP). More details and references to other texts can be found in Section A.1.2 in the Appendix.

2.1.2 Abstract Protocol Model

A protocol is a state machine for all nodes participating in the protocol, together with interfaces and message formats. A model for a protocol state machine is shown in Figure 2.1.

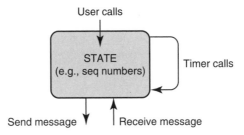

FIGURE 2.1   Abstract model of the state machine implementing a protocol at a node participating in a protocol.

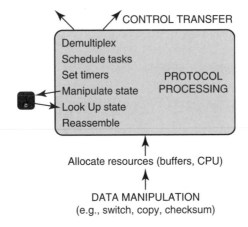

FIGURE 2.2   Common protocol functions. The small shaded black box to the lower left represents the state table used by the protocol.

The specification must describe how the state machine changes state and responds (e.g., by sending messages, setting timers) to interface calls, received messages, and timer events.

For instance, when an application makes a connect request, the TCP sender state machine initializes by picking an unused initial sequence number, goes to the so-called SYN-SENT state, and sends a SYN message. As a second example, a link state routing protocol like OSPF has a state machine at each router; when a link state packet (LSP) arrives at a router with a higher sequence number than the last LSP from the source, the new LSP should be stored and sent to all neighbors. While the link state protocol is very different from TCP, both protocols can be abstracted by the state machine model shown in Figure 2.1.

This book is devoted to protocol implementations. Besides TCP and IP, this book will consider other protocols, such as HTTP. Thus, it is worth abstracting out the *generic and time-consuming functions* that a protocol state machine performs based on our TCP and routing examples. Such a model, shown in Figure 2.2, will guide us through this book.

First, at the bottom of Figure 2.2, a protocol state machine must receive and send data packets. This involves *data manipulations*, or operations that must read or write every byte in a packet. For instance, a TCP must copy received data to application buffers, while a router has to switch packets from input links to output links. The TCP header also specifies a checksum that must be computed over all the data bytes. Data copying also requires allocation of resources such as buffers.

Second, at the top of Figure 2.2, the state machine must *demultiplex* data to one of many clients. In some cases, the client programs must be activated, requiring potentially expensive control transfer. For instance, when a receiving TCP receives a Web page, it has to demultiplex the data to the Web browser application using the port number fields and may have to wake up the process running the browser.

Figure 2.2 also depicts several generic functions shared by many protocols. First, protocols have crucial state that must be looked up at high speeds and sometimes manipulated. For instance, a received TCP packet causes TCP to *look up* a table of connection state, while a received IP packet causes IP to look up a forwarding table. Second, protocols need to efficiently set *timers*, for example, to control retransmission in TCP. Third, if a protocol module is handling several different clients, it needs to efficiently *schedule* these clients. For instance, TCP must schedule the processing of different connections, while a router must make sure that unruly conversations between some pair of computers do not lock out other conversations. Many protocols also allow large pieces of data to be fragmented into smaller pieces that need *reassembly*.

One of the major theses of this book is that though such generic functions are often expensive, their cost can be mitigated with the right techniques. Thus each generic protocol function is worth studying in isolation. Therefore after Part I of this book, the remaining chapters address specific protocol functions for endnodes and routers.

2.1.3 Performance Environment and Measures

This section describes some important measures and performance assumptions. Consider a system (such as a network or even a single router) where jobs (such as messages) arrive and, after completion, leave. The two most important metrics in networks are throughput and latency. *Throughput* roughly measures the number of jobs completed per second. *Latency* measures the time (typically worst case) to complete a job. System owners (e.g., ISPs, routers) seek to maximize throughput to maximize revenues, while users of a system want end-to-end latencies lower than a few hundred milliseconds. Latency also affects the speed of computation across the network, as, for example, in the performance of a remote procedure call.

The following performance-related observations about the Internet milieu are helpful when considering implementation trade-offs.

- *Link Speeds:* Backbone links are upgrading to 10 Gbps and 40 Gbps, and local links are upgrading to gigabit speeds. However, wireless and home links are currently orders of magnitude slower.

- *TCP and Web Dominance:* Web traffic accounts for over 70% of traffic in bytes or packets. Similarly, TCP accounts for 90% of traffic in a a recent study [Bra98].

- *Small Transfers:* Most accessed Web documents accessed are small; for example, a SPEC [Car96] study shows that 50% of accessed files are 50 kilobytes (KB) or less.

- *Poor Latencies:* Real round-trip delays exceed speed-of-light limitations; measurements in Crovella and Carter [CC95] report a mean of 241 msec across the United States compared to speed-of-light delays of less than 30 msec. Increased latency can be caused by efforts to improve throughput, such as batch compression at modems and pipelining in routers.

- *Poor Locality:* Backbone traffic studies [TMW97] show 250,000 different source–destination pairs (sometimes called *flows*) passing through a router in a very short duration. More recent estimates show around a million concurrent flows. Aggregating groups of headers with the same destination address or other means does not reduce the number of header classes significantly. Thus locality, or the likelihood of computation invested in a packet being reused on a future packet, is small.

- *Small Packets:* Thompson et al. [TMW97] also show that roughly half the packets received by a router are minimum-size 40-byte TCP acknowledgments. To avoid losing important packets in a stream of minimum-size packets, most router- and network-adaptor vendors aim for "wire speed forwarding" — this is the ability to process minimum-size (40-byte) packets at the speed of the input link.[1]

- *Critical Measures:* It is worth distinguishing between *global* performance measures, such as end-to-end delay and bandwidth, and *local* performance measures, such as router lookup speeds. While global performance measures are crucial to overall network performance, this book focuses only on local performance measures, which are a key piece of the puzzle. In particular, this book focuses on forwarding performance and resource (e.g., memory, logic) measures.

- *Tools:* Most network management tools, such as HP's OpenView, deal with global measures. The tools needed for local measures are tools to measure performance within computers, such as profiling software. Examples include Rational's Quantify (http://www.rational.com) for application software, Intel's VTune (www.intel.com/software/products/vtune/), and even hardware oscilloscopes. Network monitors such as tcpdump (www.tcpdump.org) are also useful.

Case Study 1: SANs and iSCSI

This case study shows that protocol features can greatly affect application performance. Many large data centers connect their disk drives and computers together using a *storage area network (SAN)*. This allows computers to share disks. Currently, storage area networks are based on FiberChannel [Ben95] components, which are more expensive than say Gigabit Ethernet. The proponents of iSCSI (Internet storage) [SSMe01] protocols seek to replace FiberChannel protocols with (hopefully cheaper) TCP/IP protocols and components.

SCSI is the protocol used by computers to communicate with local disks. It can also be used to communicate with disks across a network. A single SCSI command could ask to read 10 megabytes (MB) of data from a remote disk. Currently, such remote SCSI commands run over a FiberChannel transport protocol implemented in the network adaptors. Thus a 10-MB transfer is broken up into multiple FiberChannel packets,

---

[1]The preoccupation with wire speed forwarding in networking is extremely different from the mentality in computer architecture, which is content with optimizing typical (and not worst-case) performance as measured on benchmarks.

sent, delivered, and acknowledged (acked) without any per-packet processing by the requesting computer or responding disk.

The obvious approach to reduce costs is to replace the proprietary FiberChannel transport layer with TCP and the FiberChannel network layer with IP. This would allow us to replace expensive FiberChannel switches in SANs with commodity Ethernet switches. However, this has three implications. First, to compete with FiberChannel performance, TCP will probably have to be implemented in hardware. Second, TCP sends and delivers a byte stream (see Figure A.1 in the Appendix if needed). Thus multiple sent SCSI messages can be merged at the receiver. Message boundaries must be recovered by adding another iSCSI header containing the length of the next SCSI message.

The third implication is trickier. Storage vendors [SSMe01] wish to process SCSI commands out of order. If two independent SCSI messages C1 and C2 are sent in order but the C2 data arrives before C1, TCP will buffer C2 until C1 arrives. But the storage enthusiast wishes to steer C2 directly to a preallocated SCSI buffer and process C2 out of order, a prospect that makes the TCP purist cringe. The length field method described earlier fails for this purpose because a missing TCP segment (containing the SCSI message length) makes it impossible to find later message boundaries. An alternate proposal suggests having the iSCSI layer insert headers at periodic intervals in the TCP byte stream, but the jury is still out.

2.2 HARDWARE

As links approach 40-gigabit/sec OC-768 speeds, a 40-byte packet must be forwarded in 8 nsec. At such speeds, packet forwarding is typically directly implemented in hardware instead of on a programmable processor. You cannot participate in the design process of such hardware-intensive designs without understanding the tools and constraints of hardware designers. And yet a few simple models can allow you to understand and even play with hardware designs. Even if you have no familiarity with and have a positive distaste for hardware, you are invited to take a quick tour of hardware design, full of networking examples to keep you awake.

Internet lookups are often implemented using combinational logic, Internet packets are stored in router memories, and an Internet router is put together with components such as switches, and lookup chips. Thus our tour begins with logic implementation, continues with memory internals, and ends with component-based design. For more details, we refer the reader to the classic VLSI text [MC80], which still wears well despite its age, and the classic computer architecture text [HP96].

2.2.1 Combinatorial Logic

Section A.2.1 in the Appendix describes very simple models of basic hardware gates, such as NOT, NAND, and NOR, that can be understood by even a software designer who is willing to read a few pages. However, even knowing how basic gates are implemented is not required to have some insight into hardware design.

The first key to understanding logic design is the following observation. Given NOT, NAND, and NOR gates, Boolean algebra shows that any Boolean function $f(I_1, \ldots, I_n)$ of n inputs can be implemented. Each bit of a multibit output can be considered a function of the input bits. Logic minimization is often used to eliminate redundant gates and sometimes to increase speed. For example, if $+$ denotes OR and $\cdot$ denotes AND, then the function $O = I_1 \cdot I_2 + I_1 \cdot \overline{I_2}$ can be simplified to $O = I_1$.

◆ **Example 1.** Quality of Service and Priority Encoders: Suppose we have a network router that maintains n output packet queues for a link, where queue i has higher priority than queue j if $i < j$. This problem comes under the category of providing quality of service (QOS), which is covered in Chapter 14. The transmit scheduler in the router must pick a packet from the first nonempty packet queue in priority order. Assume the scheduler maintains an N-bit vector (bitmap) I such that $I[j] = 1$ if and only if queue j is nonempty. Then the scheduler can find the highest-priority nonempty queue by finding the smallest position in I in which a bit is set. Hardware designers know this function intimately as a *priority encoder*. However, even a software designer should realize that this function is feasible for hardware implementation for reasonable n. This function is examined more closely in Example 2.

2.2.2 Timing and Power

To forward a 40-byte packet at OC-768 speeds, any networking function on the packet must complete in 8 nsec. Thus the maximum signal transmission delay from inputs to outputs on any logic path must not exceed 8 nsec.[2] To ensure this constraint, a model of signal transmission delay in a transistor is needed.

Roughly speaking, each logic gate, such as a NAND or NOT gate, can be thought of as a set of capacitors and resistors that must be charged (when input values change) in order to compute output values. Worse, charging one input gate can cause the outputs of later gates to charge further inputs, and so on. Thus for a combinatorial function, the delay to compute the function is the sum of the charging and discharging delays over the worst-case path of transistors. Such path delays must fit within a minimum packet arrival time. Besides the time to charge capacitors, another source of delay is wire delay. More details can be found in Section A.2.2.

It also takes energy to charge capacitors, where the energy per unit time (power) scales with the square of the voltage, the capacitance, and the clock frequency at which inputs can change; $P = CV^2 f$. While new processes shrink voltage levels and capacitance, higher-speed circuits must increase clock frequency. Similarly, parallelism implies more capacitors being charged at a time. Thus many high-speed chips dissipate a lot of heat, requiring nontrivial cooling techniques such as heat sinks. ISPs and colocation facilities are large consumers of power. While our level of abstraction precludes understanding power trade-offs, it is good to be aware that chips and routers are sometimes power limited. Some practical limits today are 30 watts per square centimeter on a single die and 10,000 watts per square foot in a data center.

◆ **Example 2.** Priority Encoder Design: Consider the problem of estimating timing for the priority encoder of Example 1 for an OC-768 link using 40-byte packets. Thus the circuit has 8 nsec to produce the output. Assume the input I and outputs O are N-bit vectors such that $O[j] = 1$ if and only if $I[j] = 1$ and $I[k] = 0$ for all $k < j$. Notice that the output is represented in unary (often called 1-hot representation) rather than binary. The specification leads directly to the combinational logic equation $O[j] = \overline{I[1]} \ldots \overline{I[j-1]} I[j]$ for $j > 0$.

---

[2]Alternatively, parts of the function can be parallelized/pipelined, but then each part must complete in 8 nsec.

This design can be implemented directly using N AND gates, one for each output bit, where the N gates take a number of inputs that range from 1 to N. Intuitively, since N input AND gates take $O(N)$ transistors, we have a design, Design 1, with $O(N^2)$ transistors that appears to take $O(1)$ time.[3] Even this level of design is helpful, though one can do better.

A more area-economical design is based on the observation that every output bit $O[j]$ requires the AND of the complement of the first $j - 1$ input bits. Thus we define the partial results $P[j] = \overline{I[1]} \ldots \overline{I[j-1]}$ for $j = 2 \ldots N$. Clearly, $O[j] = I[j]P[j]$. But $P[j]$ can be constructed recursively using the equation $P[j] = P[j-1]\overline{I[j]}$, which can be implemented using N two-input AND gates, connected in series. This produces a design, Design 2, that takes $O(N)$ transistors but takes $O(N)$ time.

Design 1 is fast and fat, and Design 2 is slow and lean. This is a familiar time–space trade-off and suggests we can get something in between. The computation of $P[j]$ in Design 2 resembles an unbalanced binary tree of height N. However, it is obvious that $P[N]$ can be computed using a fully balanced binary of 2-input AND gates of height $\log N$. A little thought then shows that the partial results of the binary tree can be combined in simple ways to get $P[j]$ for all $j < N$ using the same binary tree [WH00].

For example, if $N = 8$, to compute $P[8]$ we compute $X = \overline{I[0]} \ldots \overline{I[3]}$ and $Y = \overline{I[4]} \ldots \overline{I[7]}$ and compute the AND of X and Y at the root. Thus, it is easy to calculate $P[5]$, for instance, using one more AND gate by computing $X \cdot \overline{I[4]}$. Such a method is very commonly used by hardware designers to replace apparently long $O(N)$ computation chains with chains of length $2 \log N$. Since it was first used to speed up carry chains in addition, it is known as *carry look-ahead* or simply *look-ahead*. While look-ahead techniques appear complex, even software designers can master them because at their core they use divide-and-conquer.

2.2.3 Raising the Abstraction Level of Hardware Design

Hand designing each transistor in a network chip design consisting of 1 million transistors would be time consuming. The design process can be reduced to a few months using building blocks. A quick description of building block technologies, such as PLAs, PALs, and standard cells, can be found in Section A.2.5.

The high-order bit, however, is that just as software designers reuse code, so also hardware designers reuse a repertoire of commonly occurring functions. Besides common computational blocks, such as adders, multipliers, comparators, and priority encoders, designs also use decoders, barrel shifters, multiplexers, and demultiplexers. It is helpful to be familiar with these "arrows" in the hardware designer's quiver.

A decoder coverts a $\log N$–bit binary value to an N-bit unary encoding of the same value; while binary representations are more compact, unary representations are more convenient for computation. A barrel shifter shifts an input I by s positions to the left or right, with the bits shifted off from an end coming around to the other end.

A *multiplexer* (mux) connects one of several inputs to a common output, while its dual, the *demultiplexer*, routes one input to one of several possible outputs. More precisely, a multiplexer (mux) connects one of n input bits I_j to the output O if a $\log n$–bit select signal S encodes the value j in binary. Its dual, the demultiplexer, connects input I to output O_j if the signal S encodes the value j in binary.

---

[3]A more precise argument, due to David Harris, using the method of Sutherland et al. [SSH99] shows the delay scales as $\log(N \log N)$ because of the effort required to charge a tree of N transistors in each AND gate.

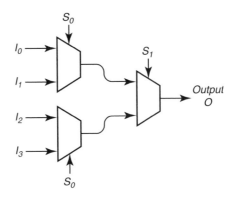

FIGURE 2.3 Building a 4-input mux with select bits S_0 and S_1 from three 2-input muxes. The figure uses the standard trapezoidal icon for a mux.

Thus the game becomes one of decomposing a complex logic function into instances of the standard functions, even using recursion when needed. This is exactly akin to reduction and divide-and-conquer and is easily picked up by software designers. For example, Figure 2.3 shows the typical Lego puzzle faced by hardware designers: Build a 4-input multiplexer from 2-input multiplexers. Start by choosing one of I_0 and I_1 using a 2-input mux and then choosing one of I_2 and I_3 by another 2-input mux. Clearly, the outputs of the 2-input muxes in the first stage must be combined using a third 2-input mux; the only cleverness required is to realize that the select signal for the first two muxes is the least significant bit S_0 of the 2-bit select signal, while the third mux chooses between the upper and lower halves and so uses S_1 as the select bit.

The following networking example shows that reduction is a powerful design tool for designing critical networking functions.

◆ **Example 3.** Crossbar Scheduling and Programmable Priority Encoders: Examples 1 and 2 motivated and designed a fast priority encoder (PE). A commonly used router arbitration mechanism uses an enhanced form of priority encoder called a programmable priority encoder (PPE). There is an N-bit input I as before, together with an additional $\log N$-bit input P. The PPE circuit must compute an output O such that $O[j] = 1$, where j is the first position beyond P (treated as a binary value) that has a nonzero bit in I. If $P = 0$, this reduces to a simple priority encoder.

PPEs arise naturally in switch arbitration (see Chapter 13 for details). For now, suppose a router connects N communication links. Suppose several input links wish to transmit a packet at the same time to output link L. To avoid contention at L, each of the inputs sends a request to L in the first time slot; L chooses which input link to grant a request to in the second slot; the granted input sends a packet in the third time slot.

To make its grant decision, L can store the requests received at the end of Slot 1 in an N-bit request vector R, where $R[i] = 1$ if input link i wishes to transmit to L. For fairness, L should remember the last input link P it granted a request to. Then, L should confer the grant to the first input link beyond P that has a request. This is exactly a PPE problem with R and P as inputs. Since a router must do arbitration for each time slot and each output link, a fast and area-efficient PPE design is needed. Even a software designer can understand and possibly repeat the process [GM99a] used to design the PPE found in the Tiny Tera, a switch built at Stanford and later commercialized. The basic idea is reduction: reducing the design of a PPE to the design of a PE (Example 2).

The first idea is simple. A PPE is essentially a PE whose highest-priority value starts at position P instead of at 0. A barrel shifter can be used to shift I first to the left by P bits. After this a simple PE can be used. Of course, the output-bit vector is now shifted; we recover the original order by shifting the output of the PE to the right by P bits. A barrel shifter for N-bit inputs can be implemented using a tree of 2-input multiplexers in around $\log N$ time. Thus two barrel shifters and a PE take around $3 \log N$ gate delays.

A faster design used in Gupta and McKeown [GM99a], which requires only $2 \log N$ gate delays is as follows. Split the problem into two parts. If the input has some bit set at position P or greater, then the result can be found by using a PE operating on the original input after setting to zero all input bits with positions less than P.[4] On the other hand, if the input has no bit set at a position P or greater, then the result can be found by using a PE on the original input with no masking at all. This results in the design of Figure 2.4, which, when tested on a Texas Instrument Cell Library, was nearly twice as fast and took three times less area than the barrel shifter design for a 32-port router.

The message here is that the logic design used for a time-critical component of a very influential switch design can be achieved using simple reductions and simple models. Such models are not beyond the reach of those of us who do not live and breathe digital design.

2.2.4 Memories

In endnodes and routers, packet forwarding is performed using combinational logic, but packets and forwarding state are stored in *memories*. Since memory access times are significantly slower than logic delays, memories form major bottlenecks in routers and endnodes.

Further, different subsystems require different memory characteristics. For example, router vendors feel it is important to buffer 200 msec — an upper bound on a round-trip delay — worth of packets to avoid dropping packets during periods of congestion. At, say, 40 Gbit/sec per link, such packet buffering requires an enormous amount of memory. On the other hand, router lookups require a smaller amount of memory, which is accessed randomly. Thus it helps to have simple models for different memory technologies. Next, we describe registers, SRAMs, DRAMs, and interleaved memory technology. Simple implementation models of these memory components can be found in Section A.2.4 in the Appendix.

REGISTERS

A *flip-flop* is a way of connecting two or more transistors in a feedback loop so that (in the absence of Writes and power failures) the bit stays indefinitely without "leaking" away. A *register* is an ordered collection of flip-flops. For example, most modern processors have a collection of 32- or 64-bit on-chip registers. A 32-bit register contains 32 flip-flops, each storing a bit. Access from logic to a register on the same chip is extremely fast, around 0.5–1 nsec.

---

[4]This can be done by ANDing the input with P encoded as a mask; such a mask is commonly known in the hardware community as a *thermometer* encoding of P.

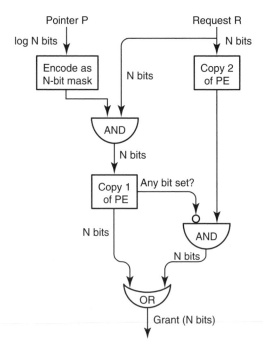

FIGURE 2.4 The Tiny Tera PPE design uses copy 1 of a priority encoder to find the highest bit set, if any, of all bits greater than *P* using a mask encoding of *P*. If such a bit is not found, the output of a second copy of a priority encoder is enabled using the bottom AND gate. The results of the two copies are then combined using an *N*-input OR gate.

SRAM

A static random access memory (SRAM) contains *N* registers addressed by log *N* address bits *A*. SRAM is so named because the underlying flip-flops refresh themselves and so are "static." Besides flip-flops, an SRAM also needs a decoder that decodes *A* into a unary value used to select the right register. Accessing an SRAM on-chip is only slightly slower than accessing a register, because of the added decode delay. At the time of writing, it was possible to obtain on-chip SRAMs with 0.5-nsec access times. Access times of of 1–2 nsec for on-chip SRAM and 5–10 nsec for off-chip SRAM are common.

Dynamic RAM

An SRAM bit cell requires at least five transistors. Thus SRAM is always less dense or more expensive than memory technology based on dynamic RAM (DRAM). The key idea is to replace the feedback loop (and extra transistors) used to store a bit in a flip-flop with an output capacitance that can store the bit; thus the charge leaks, but it leaks slowly. Loss due to leakage is fixed by refreshing the DRAM cell externally within a few milliseconds. Of course, the complexity comes in manufacturing a high capacitance using a tiny amount of silicon.

DRAM chips appear to quadruple in capacity every 3 years [FPCe97] and are heading towards 1 gigabit on a single chip. Addressing these bits, even if they are packed together as 4- or even 32-bit "registers," is tricky. Recall that the address must be decoded from (say) 20 bits

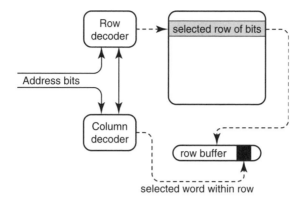

FIGURE 2.5 Most large memories are organized two-dimensionally in terms of rows and columns. Selecting a word consists of selecting first the row and then the column within the row.

to (say) one of 2^{20} values. The complexity of such decode logic suggests divide-and-conquer. Why not decode in two stages?

Figure 2.5 shows that most memories are internally organized two-dimensionally into rows and columns. The upper address bits are decoded to select the row, and then the lower address bits are used to decode the column. More precisely, the user first supplies the row address bits and enables a signal called RAS (row address strobe); later, the user supplies the column address bits,[5] and enables a signal called CAS (column address strobe). After a specified time, the desired memory word can be read out. Assuming equal-size rows and columns, this reduces decode gate complexity from $O(N)$ to $O(\sqrt{(N)})$ at the expense of one extra decode delay. Besides the required delay between RAS and CAS, there is also a *precharge* delay between successive RAS and CAS invocations to allow time for capacitors to charge.

The fastest off-chip DRAMs take around 40–60 nsec to access (latency), with longer times, such as 100 nsec, between successive reads (throughput) because of precharge restrictions. Some of this latency includes the time to drive the address using external lines onto the DRAM interface pins; recent innovations allow on-chip DRAM with lower access times of around 30 nsec. It seems clear that DRAM will always be denser but slower than SRAM.

Page-Mode DRAMs

One reason to understand DRAM structure is to understand how function can follow form. A classic example is a trick to speed up access times called *page mode*. Page mode is beneficial for access patterns that exhibit spatial locality, in which adjacent memory words are successively accessed. But having made a row access in Figure 2.5, one can access words within the row without incurring additional RAS and precharge delays. Video RAMs exploit the same structure by having a row read into an SRAM, which can be read out serially to refresh a display at high speed. Besides page mode and video RAMS, perhaps there are other ideas that exploit DRAM structure that could be useful in networking.

---

[5]Many DRAM chips take advantage of the fact that row and column addresses are not required at the same time to multiplex row and column addresses on the same set of pins, reducing the pin count of the chip.

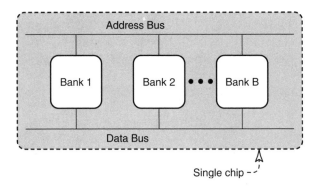

FIGURE 2.6   The idea behind RAMBUS, SDRAM, and numerous variants is to create a single chip containing multiple DRAM parallel memories to gain memory bandwidth while using only one set of address and data lines.

INTERLEAVED DRAMS

While memory latency is critical for computation speed, memory throughput (often called *bandwidth*) is also important for many network applications. Suppose a DRAM has a word size of 32 bits and a cycle time of 100 nsec. Then the throughput using a single copy of the DRAM is limited to 32 bits every 100 nsec. Clearly, throughput can be improved using accesses to multiple DRAMs. As in Figure 2.6, multiple DRAMs (called *banks*) can be strung together on a single bus. The user can start a Read to Bank 1 by placing the address on the address bus. Assume each DRAM bank takes 100 nsec to return the selected data.

Instead of idling during this 100-nsec delay, the user can place a second address for Bank 2, a third for Bank 3, and so on. If the placing of each address takes 10 nsec, the user can "feed" 10 DRAM banks before the answer to the first DRAM bank query arrives, followed 10 nsec later by the answer to the second DRAM bank query, and so on. Thus the net memory bandwidth in this example is 10 times the memory bandwidth of a single DRAM, as long as the user can arrange to have consecutive accesses touch different banks.

While using multiple memory banks is a very old idea, it is only in the last 5 years that memory designers have integrated several banks into a single memory chip (Figure 2.6), where the address and data lines for all banks are multiplexed using a common high-speed network called a *bus*. In addition, page-mode accesses are often allowed on each bank. Memory technologies based on this core idea abound, with different values for the DRAM sizes, the protocol to read and write, and the number of banks. Prominent examples include SDRAM with two banks and RDRAM with 16 banks.

◆ **Example 4.** Pipelined Flow ID Lookups: A flow is characterized by source and destination IP addresses and TCP ports. Some customers would like routers to keep track of the number of packets sent by each network flow, for accounting purposes. This requires a data structure that stores a counter for each flow ID and supports the two operations of *Insert (FlowId)* to insert a new flow ID, and *Lookup (FlowId)* to find the location of a counter for a flow ID. Lookup requires an exact match on the flow ID – which is around 96 bits – in the time to receive a packet. This can be done by any exact-matching algorithm, such as hashing.

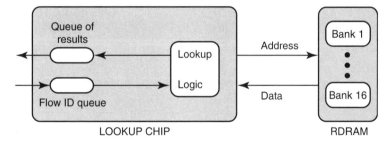

FIGURE 2.7 Solving the flow ID lookup problem by using a pipelined lookup chip that works on up to 16 concurrent flow ID lookups, each of which accesses an independent bank of the RDRAM. The lookup chip returns an index to, say, a network processor that updates the flow ID counter.

However, if, as many router vendors wish to do, the worst-case lookup time must be small and bounded, binary search [CLR90] is a better idea. Assume that flow ID lookups must be done at wire speeds for worst-case 40-byte packets at 2.5 Gbits/sec or OC-48 speeds. Thus the chip has 128 nsec to look up a flow ID.

To bound lookup delays, consider using a balanced binary tree, such as a B-tree. The logic for tree traversal is fairly easy. For speed, ideally the flow IDs and counters should be stored in SRAM. However, current estimates in core routers [TMW97] show around a million concurrent flows. Keeping state for a million flows in SRAM is expensive. However, plain DRAM using a binary tree with a branching factor of 2 would require $\log_2 1,000,000 = 20$ memory accesses. Even assuming an optimistic DRAM cycle time of 50 nsec, the overall lookup time is 1 usec, which is too slow.

A solution is to use pipelining, as shown in Figure 2.7, where the pipelined logic accesses flow IDs stored in an RDRAM with 16 banks of memory as shown in Figure 2.6. All the nodes at height i in the binary tree are stored in Bank i of the RDRAM. The lookup chip works on 16 flow ID lookups (for 16 packets) concurrently. For example, after looking at the root node for Packet 1 in Bank 1, the chip can look up the second-level tree node for Packet 1 in Bank 2 and (very slightly after that) look up the root for Packet 2 in Bank 1. When Packet 1's lookup "thread" is accessing Bank 16, Packet 16's lookup thread is accessing Bank 1. Since direct RDRAM runs at 800 MHz, the time between address requests to the RAMBUS is small compared with the read access time of around 60 nsec. Thus while a single packet takes around $16 * 60$ nsec to complete, processing 16 packets concurrently allows a throughput of one flow ID lookup every 60 nsec.

Unfortunately, a binary tree with 16 levels allows only $2^{16} = 64K$ flow IDs, which is too small. Fortunately, RAMBUS allows a variation of page mode where 8 data words of 32 bits can be accessed in almost the same time as 1 word. This allows us to retrieve two 96-bit keys and three 20-bit pointers in one 256-bit memory access. Thus a tree with 3-way branching can be used, which allows potentially 3^{16}, or potentially 43 million, flow IDs.

2.2.5 *Memory Subsystem Design Techniques*

The flow ID lookup problem illustrates three major design techniques commonly used in memory subsystem designs for networking chips.

- **Memory Interleaving and Pipelining:** Similar techniques are used in IP lookup, classification, and in scheduling algorithms that implement QoS. The multiple banks can be implemented using several external memories, a single external memory like a RAMBUS, or on-chip SRAM within a chip that also contains processing logic.

- **Wide Word Parallelism:** A common theme in many networking designs, such as the Lucent bit vector scheme (Chapter 12), is to use wide memory words that can be processed in parallel. This can be implemented using DRAM and exploiting page mode or by using SRAM and making each memory word wider.

- **Combining DRAM and SRAM:** Given that SRAM is expensive and fast and that DRAM is cheap and slow, it makes sense to combine the two technologies to attempt to obtain the best of both worlds. While the use of SRAM as a cache for DRAM databases is classical, there are many more creative applications of the idea of a memory hierarchy. For instance, the exercises explore the effect of a small amount of SRAM on the design of the flow ID lookup chip. Chapter 16 describes a more unusual application of this technique to implement a large number of counters, where the low-order bits of each counter are stored in SRAM.

It is more important for a novice designer to understand these design techniques (than to know memory implementation details) in order to produce creative hardware implementations of networking functions.

2.2.6 Component-Level Design

The methods of the last two subsections can be used to implement a *state machine* that implements arbitrary computation. A state machine has a current state stored in memory; the machine processes inputs using combinatorial logic that reads the current state and possibly writes the state. An example of a complex state machine is a Pentium processor, whose state is the combination of registers, caches, and main memory. An example of a simpler state machine is the flow ID lookup chip of Figure 2.7, whose state is the registers used to track each of 16 concurrent lookups and the RDRAM storing the B-tree.

While a few key chips may have to be designed to build a router or a network interface card, the remainder of the design can be called component-level design: organizing and interconnecting chips on a board and placing the board in a box while paying attention to form factor, power, and cooling. A key aspect of component-level design is understanding pin-count limitations, which often provide a quick "parity check" on feasible designs.

◆ *Example 5.* Pin-Count Implications for Router Buffers: Consider a router than has five 10 Gb/sec links. The overall buffering required is 200 msec * 50 Gb/sec, which is 10 gigabits. For cost and power, we use DRAM for packet buffers. Since each packet must go in and out of the buffer, the overall memory bandwidth needs to be twice the bandwidth into the box — i.e., 100 Gb/sec. Assuming 100% overhead for internal packet headers, links between packets in queues, and wasted memory bandwidth, it is reasonable to aim for 200-Gb/sec memory bandwidth.

Using a single direct RDRAM with 16 banks, specifications show peak memory bandwidth of 1.6 GB/sec, or 13 Gb/sec. Accessing each RDRAM requires 64 interface pins for data and 25 other pins for address and control, for a total of 90 pins. A 200-Gbps memory bandwidth requires 16 RDRAMs, which require 1440 pins in total. A conservative upper bound on the number of pins on a chip is around 1000. This implies that even if the router vendor were to build an extremely fast custom-designed packet-forwarding chip that could handle all packets at the maximum box rate, one would still need at least one more chip to drive data in and out of the RAMBUS packet buffers. Our message is that pin limitations are a key constraint in partitioning a design between chips.

2.2.7 Final Hardware Lessons

If all else is forgotten in this hardware design section, it is helpful to remember the design techniques of Section 2.2.5. A knowledge of the following parameter values is also useful to help system designers quickly weed out infeasible designs without a detailed knowledge of hardware design. Unfortunately, these parameters are a moving target, and the following numbers were written based on technology available in 2004.

- **Chip Complexity Scaling:** The number of components per chip appears to double every 2 years. While 0.13-micron processes are common, 90-nm technology is ramping up, and 65-nm technology is expected after that. As a result, current ASICs can pack several million gate equivalents (that's a lot of combinatorial logic) plus up to 50 Mbits (at the time of writing, using half a 12-mm/side die) of on-chip SRAM on an ASIC.[6] Embedded DRAM is also a common option to get more space on-chip at the cost of larger latency.

- **Chip Speeds:** As feature sizes go down, on-chip clock speeds of 1 GHz are becoming common, with some chips even pushing close to 3 GHz. To put this in perspective, the clock cycle to do a piece of computation on a 1-GHz chip is 1 nsec. By using parallelism via pipelining and wide memory words, multiple operations can be performed per clock cycle.

- **Chip I/O:** The number of pins per chip grows, but rather slowly. While there are some promising technologies, it is best to assume that designs are pin limited to around 1000 pins.

- **Serial I/O:** Chip-to-chip I/O has also come a long way, with 10-Gbit serial links available to connect chips.

- **Memory Scaling:** On-chip SRAM with access times of 1 nsec are available, with even smaller access times being worked on. Off-chip SRAM with access times of 2.5 nsec are commonly available. On-chip DRAM access times are around 30 nsec, while off-chip DRAM of around 60 nsec is common. Of course, the use of interleaved DRAM, as discussed in the memory subsection, is a good way to increase memory subsystem throughput for certain applications. DRAM costs roughly 4–10 times less than SRAM per bit.

- **Power and Packaging:** The large power consumption of high-speed routers requires careful design of the cooling system. Finally, most ISPs have severe rack space limitations, and so there is considerable pressure to build routers that have small form factors.

These parameter values have clear implications for high-speed networking designs. For instance, at OC-768 speeds, a 40-byte packet arrives in 3.2 nsec. Thus it seems clear that all

---

[6]FPGAs are more programmable chips that can only offer smaller amounts of on-chip SRAM.

state required to process the packet must be in on-chip SRAM. While the amount of on-chip SRAM is growing, this memory is not growing as fast as the number of flows seen by a router. Similarly, with 1-nsec SRAMs, at most three memory accesses can be made to a *single* memory bank in a packet arrival time.

Thus the design techniques of Section 2.2.5 must be used within a chip to gain parallelism using multiple memory banks and wide words and to increase the usable memory by creative combinations that involve off- and on-chip memory. However, given that chip densities and power constraints limit parallelism to, say, a factor of at most 60, the bottom line is that all packet-processing functions at high speeds must complete using at most 200 memory accesses and limited on-chip memory.[7] Despite these limitations, a rich variety of packet-processing functions have been implemented at high speeds.

2.3 NETWORK DEVICE ARCHITECTURES

Optimizing network performance requires optimizing the path of data through the internals of the source node, the sink node, and every router. Thus it is important to understand the internal architecture of endnodes and routers. The earlier part of this chapter argued that logic and memory can be combined to form state machines. In essence, both routers and endnodes are state machines. However, their architectures are optimized for different purposes: endnode architectures (Section 2.3.1) for general *computation* and router architectures (Section 2.3.2) for Internet *communication*.

2.3.1 Endnode Architecture

A processor such as a Pentium is a state machine that takes a sequence of instructions and data as input and writes output to I/O devices, such as printers and terminals. To allow programs that have a large state space, the bulk of processor state is stored externally in cheap DRAM. In PCs, this is referred to as *main memory* and is often implemented using 1 GB or more of interleaved DRAM, such as SDRAM. However, recall that DRAM access times are large, say, 60 nsec. If processor state were stored only in DRAM, an instruction would take 60 nsec to read or write to memory.

Processors gain speed using *caches*, which are comparitively small chunks of SRAM that can store commonly used pieces of state for faster access. Some SRAM (i.e., the L1 cache) is placed on the processor chip, and some more SRAM (i.e., the L2 cache) is placed external to the processor. A cache is a hash table that maps between memory address locations and contents. CPU caches use a simple hash function: They extract some bits from the address to index into an array and then search in parallel for all the addresses that map into the array element.[8] When a memory location has to be read from DRAM, it is placed in the cache, and an existing cache element may be evicted. Commonly used data is stored in a *data cache*, and commonly used instructions in an *instruction cache*.

---

[7]Of course, there are ways to work around these limits, for instance, by using multiple chips, but such implementations often do badly in terms of cost, complexity, and power consumption.

[8]The number of elements that can be searched in parallel in a hash bucket is called the *associativity* of the cache. While router designers rightly consider bit extraction to be a poor hash function, the addition of associativity improves overall hashing performance, especially on computing workloads.

Caching works well if the instructions and data exhibit temporal locality (i.e., the corresponding location is reused frequently in a small time period) or spatial locality (i.e., accessing a location is followed by access to a nearby location). Spatial locality is taken advantage of as follows. Recall that accessing a DRAM location involves accessing a row R and then a column within the row. Thus reading words within row R is cheaper after R is accessed. A Pentium takes advantage of this observation by prefetching 128 (*cache line size*) contiguous bits into the cache whenever 32 bits of data are accessed. Accesses to the adjoining 96 bits will not incur a cache miss penalty.

Many computing benchmarks exhibit temporal and spatial locality; however, a stream of packets probably exhibits only spatial locality. Thus improving endnode protocol implementations often requires paying attention to cache effects.

The foregoing discussion should set the stage for the endnode architecture model shown in Figure 2.8. The processor, or CPU — e.g., a Pentium or an Alpha — sits on a bus. A bus can be thought of as a network like an Ethernet, but optimized for the fact that the devices on the bus are close to each other. The processor interacts with other components by sending messages across the bus.

The input–output (I/O) devices are typically *memory mapped*. In other words, even I/O devices like the network adaptor and the disk look like pieces of memory. For example, the adaptor memory may be locations 100–200 on the bus. This allows uniform communication between the CPU and any device by using the same conventions used to interact with memory. In terms of networking, a Read (or Write) can be thought of as a message sent on the bus addressed to the memory location. Thus a Read 100 is sent on the bus, and the device that owns memory location 100 (e.g., the adaptor) will receive the message and reply with the contents of location 100.

Modern machines allow direct memory access (DMA), where devices such as the disk or the network adaptor send Reads and Writes directly to the memory via the bus without processor intervention. However, only one entity can use the bus at a time. Thus the adaptor has to contend for the bus; any device that gets hold of the bus "steals cycles" from the processor. This is because the processor is forced to wait to access memory while a device is sending messages across the bus.

In Figure 2.8 notice also that the adaptor actually sits on a different bus (system bus or memory bus) from the bus on which the network adaptor and other peripherals (I/O bus) sit.

FIGURE 2.8 Model of a workstation.

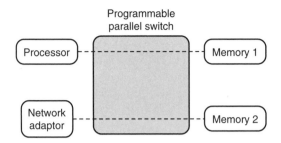

FIGURE 2.9 Using parallel connections within an endnode architecture to allow concurrent processing and network traffic via a parallel switch.

The memory bus is designed for speed and is redesigned for every new processor; the I/O bus is a standard bus (e.g., a PCI bus) chosen to stay compatible with older I/O devices. Thus the I/O bus is typically slower than the memory bus.

A big lesson for networking in Figure 2.8 is that the throughput of a networking application is crucially limited by the speed of the slowest bus, typically the I/O bus. Worse, the need for extra copies to preserve operating system structure causes every packet received or sent by a workstation to traverse the bus multiple times. Techniques to avoid redundant bus traversals are described in Chapter 5.

Modern processors are heavily pipelined with instruction fetch, instruction decode, data reads, and data writes split into separate stages. *Superscalar* and *multithreaded* machines go beyond pipelining by issuing multiple instructions concurrently. While these innovations (see, for example, the classic reference on endnode architecture [HP96]) remove computation bottlenecks, they do little for data-movement bottlenecks. Consider instead the following speculative architecture.

◆ **Example 6.** Endnode Architecture Using a Crossbar Switch: Figure 2.9 shows the endnode bus being replaced by a programmable hardware switch, as is commonly used by routers. The switch internally contains a number of parallel buses so that any set of disjoint endpoint pairs can be connected in parallel by the switch. Thus in the figure the processor is connected to Memory 1, while the network adaptor is connected to Memory 2. Thus packets from the network can be placed in Memory 2 without interfering with the processor's reading from Memory 1. If the processor now wishes to read the incoming packet, the switch can be reprogrammed to connect the processor to Memory 2 and the adaptor to Memory 1. This can work well if the queue of empty packet buffers used by the adaptor alternates between the two memories.

There are recent proposals for Infiniband switch technology to replace the I/O bus in processors (Chapter 5). The ultimate message of this example is not that architectures such as Figure 2.9 are necessarily good but that simple architectural ideas to improve network performance, such as Figure 2.9, are not hard for even protocol designers to conceive, given simple models of hardware and architecture.

2.3.2 Router Architecture

A router model that covers both high-end routers (such as Juniper's M-series routers) and low-end routers (such as the Cisco Catalyst) is shown in Figure 2.10. Basically, a router is a

FIGURE 2.10 A model of a router labeled with the three main bottlenecks in the forwarding path: address lookup (**B1**), switching (**B2**), and output scheduling (**B3**).

box with a set of input links, shown on the left, and a set of output links, shown on the right; the task of the router is to switch a packet from an input link to the appropriate output link based on the destination address in the packet. While the input and output links are shown separately, the two links in each direction between two routers are often packaged together. We review three main bottlenecks in a router: lookup, switching, and output queuing.

LOOKUP

A packet arrives on, say, the left link, input link *i*. Every packet carries a 32-bit Internet (IP) address.[9] Assume that the first six bits of the destination address of a sample packet are 100100. A processor in the router inspects the destination address to determine where to forward the packet.

The processor consults a forwarding table to determine the output link for the packet. The forwarding table is sometimes called a *FIB*, for *forwarding information base*. The FIB contains a set of *prefixes* with corresponding output links. The reason for prefixes will be explained in Chapter 11; for now think of prefixes as variable-length "area codes" that greatly reduce the FIB size. A prefix like 01*, where the * denotes the usual "don't care" symbol, matches IP addresses that start with 01. Assume that prefix 100* has associated output link 6, while prefix 1* has output link 2. Thus our sample packet, whose destination address starts with 100100, matches *both* prefix 100* and 1*. The disambiguating rule that IP routers use is to match an address to the *longest matching prefix*. Assuming no longer matching prefixes, our sample packet should be forwarded to output link 6.

The processor that does the lookup and basic packet processing can be either shared or dedicated and can be either a general processor or a special-purpose chip. Early router designs used a shared processor (or processors), but this proved to be a bottleneck. Later designs, including Cisco's GSR family, use a dedicated processor per input link interface. The earliest designs used a standard CPU processor, but many of the fastest routers today, such as Juniper's M-160, use a dedicated chip (ASIC) with some degree of programmability. There has been a

---

[9]Recall that while most users deal with domain names, these names are translated to an IP address by a directory service, called DNS, before packets are sent.

backlash to this trend toward ASICs, however, with customers asking routers to perform new functions, such as Web load balancing. Thus some new routers use *network processors* (see Example 7), which are general-purpose processors optimized for networking.

Algorithms for prefix lookups are described in Chapter 11. Many routers today also offer a more complex lookup called *packet classification* (Chapter 12), where the lookup takes as input the destination address *as well as* source address and TCP ports.

SWITCHING

After address lookup in the example of Figure 2.10, the processor instructs an internal switching system to transfer the packet from link *i* to output link 6. In older processors, the switch was a simple bus, such as shown in Figure 2.8. This proved to be a major bottleneck because, if the switch has N input links running at B bits per second, the bus would have to have a bandwidth of $B \cdot N$. Unfortunately, as N increases, electrical effects (such as the capacitive load of a bus) predominate, limiting the bus speed.

Thus the fastest routers today internally use a parallel switch of the sort shown in Figure 2.9. The throughput of the switch is increased by using N *parallel* buses, one for each input and one for each output. An input and an output are connected by turning on transistors connecting the corresponding input bus and output bus. While it is easy to build the data path, it is harder to schedule the switch, because multiple inputs may wish to send to the same output link at the same time. The switch-scheduling problem boils down to matching available inputs and outputs every packet arrival time. Algorithms for this purpose are described in Chapter 13.

QUEUING

Once the packet in Figure 2.10 has been looked up and switched to output link 6, output link 6 may be congested, and thus the packet may have to be placed in a queue for output link 6. Many older routers simply place the packet in a first-in first-out (FIFO) transmission queue. However, some routers employ more sophisticated output scheduling to provide fair bandwidth allocation and delay guarantees. Output scheduling is described in Chapter 14.

Besides the major tasks of lookups, switching, and queuing, there are a number of other tasks that are less time critical.

HEADER VALIDATION AND CHECKSUMS

The version number of a packet is checked, and the header-length field is checked for options. Options are additional processing directives that are rarely used; such packets are often shunted to a separate route processor. The header also has a simple checksum that must be verified. Finally, a time-to-live (TTL) field must be decremented and the header checksum recalculated. Chapter 9 shows how to incrementally update the checksum. Header validation and checksum computation are often done in hardware.

ROUTE PROCESSING

Section A.1.2 describes briefly how routers build forwarding tables using routing protocols. Routers within domains implement RIP and OSPF, while routers that link domains also must implement BGP.[10] These protocols are implemented in one or more route processors.

---

[10]It is possible to buy versions of these protocols, but the software must be customized for each new hardware platform. A more insidious problem, especially with BGP and OSPF, is that many of the first implementations of these

For example, when a link state packet is sent to the router in Figure 2.10, lookup will recognize that this is a packet destined for the router itself and will cause the packet to be switched to the route processor. The route processor maintains the link state database and computes shortest paths; after computation, the route processor loads the new forwarding databases in each of the forwarding processors through either the switch or a separate out-of-band path.

In the early days, Cisco won its spurs by processing not just Internet packets but also other routing protocols, such as DECNET, SNA, and Appletalk. The need for such multiprotocol processing is less clear now. A much more important trend is multi-protocol-label switching (MPLS), which appears to be de rigeur for core routers. In MPLS, the IP header is augmented with a header containing simple integer indices that can be looked up directly without a prefix lookup; Chapter 11 provides more details about MPLS.

PROTOCOL PROCESSING

All routers today have to implement the simple network management protocol (SNMP) and provide a set of counters that can be inspected remotely. To allow remote communication with the router, most routers also implement TCP and UDP. In addition, routers have to implement the Internet control message protocol (ICMP), which is basically a protocol for sending error messages, such as "time-to-live exceeded."

FRAGMENTATION, REDIRECTS, AND ARPs

While it is clear that route and protocol processing is best relegated to a route processor on a so-called "slow path," there are a few router functions that are more ambiguous. For example, if a packet of 4000 bytes is to be sent over a link with a maximum packet size (MTU) of 1500 bytes, the packet has to be fragmented into two pieces.[11] While the prevailing trend is for sources, instead of routers, to do fragmentation, some routers do fragmentation in the fast path. Another such function is the sending of Redirects. If an endnode sends a message to the wrong router, the router is supposed to send a Redirect back to the endnode. A third such function is the sending of address resolution protocol (ARP) requests, whose operation is explored in the exercises.

Finally, routers today have a number of other tasks they may be called on to perform. Many routers within enterprises do content-based handling of packets, where the packet processing depends on strings found in the packet data. For example, a router that fronts a Web farm of many servers may wish to forward packets with the same Web URL to the same Web server. There are also the issues of accounting and traffic measurement. Some of these new services are described in Chapter 16.

◆ *Example 7.* Network Processors: Network processors are general-purpose programmable processors optimized for network traffic. Their proponents say that they are needed because the unpredictable nature of router tasks (such as content-based delivery) makes committing router forwarding to silicon a risky proposition. For example, the Intel IXP1200 network processor evaluated in Spalink et al. [SKP00] internally contains six processors, each running at

---

protocols vary in subtle ways from the actual specifications. Thus a new implementation that meets the specification may not interoperate with existing routers. Thus ISPs are reluctant to buy new routers unless they can trust the "quality" of the BGP code, in terms of its ability to interoperate with existing routers.

[11] Strictly speaking, since each fragment adds headers, there will be *three* pieces.

177 MHz with a 5.6-nsec clock cycle. Each processor receives packets from an input queue; packets are stored in a large DRAM; after the processor has looked up the packet destination, the packet is placed on the output queue with a tag describing the output link it should be forwarded to.

The biggest problem is that the processors are responsible for moving packets in and out of DRAM. In the IXP1200, moving 32 bytes from the queue to the DRAM takes 45 clock cycles, and moving from the DRAM to the queue takes 55 cycles. Since a minimum-size packet is at least 40 bytes, this requires a total of 200 cycles = 1.12 usec, which translates to a forwarding rate of only around 900K packets/second. The IXP1200 gets around this limit by using six parallel processors and an old architectural idea called *multithreading*. The main idea is that each processor works on multiple packets, each packet being a thread; when the processing for one packet stalls because of a memory reference, processing for the next thread is resumed. Using fast context switching between threads, and four contexts per processor, the IXP1200 can theoretically obtain 6 * 4 * 900 = 21.4M packets/second.

Network processors also offer special-purpose instructions for address lookup and other common forwarding functions. Some network processors also streamline the movement of data packets by having hardware engines that present only the header of each data packet to the processor. The remainder of the data packet flows directly to the output queue. The processor(s) read the header, do the lookup, and write the updated header to the output queue. The hardware magically glues together the updated header with the original packet and keeps all packets in order. While this approach avoids the movement of the remainder of the packet through the processor, it does nothing for the case of minimum-size packets.

Case Study 2: Buffering and Optical Switching

As fiber-optic links scale to higher speeds, electronics implementing combinational logic and memories in core routers becomes a bottleneck. Currently, packets arrive over fiber-optic links with each bit encoded as a light pulse. Optics at the receiver convert light to electrical pulses; the packet is then presented to forwarding logic implemented electronically. The packet is then queued to an outbound link for transmission, upon which the transmitting link optics convert electrical bits back to light. The electronic bottleneck can be circumvented by creating an all-optical router without any electro-optical conversions.

Unfortunately, doing IP lookups optically, and especially building dense optical packet memories, seems hard today. But switching light between several endpoints is feasible. Thus the numerous startups in the buzzing optical space tend to build optical *circuit switches* that use electronics to set up the circuit switch. A circuit switch connects input X to output Y for a large duration, as opposed to the duration of a single packet as in a packet switch. Such circuit switches have found use as a flexible "core" of an ISP's network to connect conventional routers. If traffic between, say, routers $R1$ and $R2$ increases, an ISP operator can (at a large time scale of, say, minutes) change the circuit switches to increase the bandwidth of the $R1$-to-$R2$ path. However, the wastefulness of reserving switch paths for small flow durations makes it likely that packet-switched routers will continue to be popular in the near future.

2.4 OPERATING SYSTEMS

An operating system is software that sits above hardware in order to make life easier for application programmers. For most Internet routers, time-critical packet forwarding runs directly on the hardware (Figure 2.10) and is *not* mediated by an operating system. Less time-critical code runs on a router operating system that is stripped down such as Cisco's IOS. However, to improve end-to-end performance for, say, Web browsing, an implementor needs to understand the costs and benefits of operating systems.

Abstractions are idealizations or illusions we invent to deal with the perversity and irregularity of the real world. To finesse the difficulties of programming on a bare machine, operating systems offer abstractions to application programmers. Three central difficulties of dealing with raw hardware are dealing with interrupts, managing memory, and controlling I/O devices. To deal with these difficulties, operating systems offer the abstractions of *uninterrupted computation*, *infinite memory*, and *simple I/O*.

A good abstraction increases programmer productivity but has two costs. First, the mechanism implementing the abstraction has a price. For example, scheduling processes can cause overhead for a Web server. A second, less obvious cost is that the abstraction can hide power, preventing the programmer from making optimal use of resources. For example, operating system memory management may prevent the programmer of an Internet lookup algorithm from keeping the lookup data structure in memory in order to maximize performance. We now provide a model of the costs and underlying mechanisms of the process (Section 2.4.1), virtual memory (Section 2.4.2), and I/O (Section 2.4.3) abstractions. More details can be found in Tanenbaum [Tan92].

2.4.1 Uninterrupted Computation via Processes

A program may not run very long on the processor before being interrupted by the network adaptor. If application programmers had to deal with interrupts, a working 100-line program would be a miracle. Thus operating systems provide programmers with the abstraction of uninterrupted, sequential computation under the name of a *process*.

The process *abstraction* is realized by three *mechanisms*: context switching, scheduling, and protection, the first two of which are depicted in Figure 2.11. In Figure 2.11, Process P1 has the illusion that it runs on the processor by itself. In reality, as shown on the timeline below, Process P1 may be interrupted by a timer interrupt, which causes the OS scheduler program to run on the processor. Displacing P1 requires the operating system to save the state of P1 in memory. The scheduler may run briefly and decide to give Process P2 a turn. Restoring P2 to

FIGURE 2.11 The programmer sees the illusion of an uninterrupted timeline shown above, while the real processor timeline may switch back and forth between several processes.

FIGURE 2.12   The processing of a received Internet packet in BSD is divided between the network adaptor, the kernel, and the destined process.

run on the processor requires restoring the state of P2 from memory. Thus the actual time line of a processor may involve frequent context switches between processes, as orchestrated by the scheduler. Finally, *protection* ensures that incorrect or malicious behavior of one process cannot affect other processes.

As agents of computation, "processes" come in three flavors — interrupt handlers, threads, and user processes — ranked in order of increasing generality and cost. *Interrupt handlers* are small pieces of computation used to service urgent requests, such as the arrival of a message to the network adaptor; interrupt handlers use only a small amount of state, typically a few registers. *User processes* use the complete state of the machine, such as memory as well as registers; thus it is expensive to switch between user processes as directed by the scheduler. Within the context of a single process, threads offer a cheaper alternative to processes. A *thread* is a lightweight process that requires less state, because threads within the same process share the same memory (i.e., same variables). Thus context switching between two threads in the same process is cheaper than switching processes, because memory does not have to be remapped. The following example shows the relevance of these concepts to endnode networking.

◆ **Example 8.** Receiver Livelock in BSD Unix: In BSD UNIX, as shown in Figure 2.12, the arrival of a packet generates an interrupt. The interrupt is a hardware signal that causes the processor to save the state of the currently running process, say, a Java program. The processor then jumps to the interrupt handler code, bypassing the scheduler for speed. The interrupt handler copies the packet to a kernel queue of IP packets waiting to be consumed, makes a request for an operating system thread (called a *software interrupt*), and exits. Assuming no further interrupts, the interrupt exit passes control to the scheduler, which is likely to cede the processor to the software interrupt, which has higher priority than user processes.

The kernel thread does TCP and IP processing and queues the packet to the appropriate application queue, called a *socket* queue (Figure 2.12). Assume that the application is a browser such as Netscape. Netscape runs as a process that may have been asleep waiting for data and is now considered for being run on the processor by the scheduler. After the software interrupt exits and control passes back to the scheduler, the scheduler may decide to run Netscape in place of the original Java program.

Under high network load, the computer can enter what is called *receiver livelock* [MR97], in which the computer spends all its time processing incoming packets, only to discard them later because the applications never run. In our example, if there is a series of back-to-back packet arrivals, only the highest-priority interrupt handler will run, possibly leaving no time for the software interrupt and certainly leaving none for the browser process. Thus either the IP or socket queues will fill up, causing packets to be dropped after resources have been invested in their processing. Methods to mitigate this effect are described in Chapter 6.

Notice also that the latency and throughput of network code in an endnode depend on "process" activation times. For example, current figures for Pentium IV machines show around 2 μsec of interrupt latency for a null interrupt call, around 10 μsec for a Process Context switch on a Linux machine with two processes, and much more time for Windows and Solaris on the same machine. These times may seem small, but recall that 30 minimum-size (40-byte) packets can arrive in 10 μsec on a Gigabit Ethernet link.

2.4.2 Infinite Memory via Virtual Memory

In virtual memory (Figure 2.13), the programmer works with an abstraction of memory that is a linear array into which a compiler assigns variable locations. Variable *X* could be stored

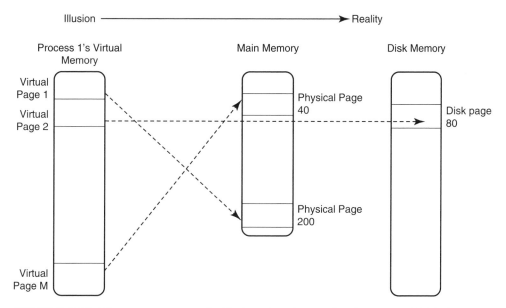

FIGURE 2.13 The programmer sees the illusion of contiguous virtual memory, which is, in reality, mapped to a collection of main memory and disk memory pages via page tables.

in location 1010 in this imaginary (or virtual) array. The virtual memory abstraction is implemented using the twin mechanisms of page table mapping and demand paging. Both these mechanisms are crucial to understand in order to optimize data transfer costs in an endnode.

Any virtual address must be mapped to a physical memory address. The easiest mapping is to use an offset into physical memory. For example, a virtual array of 15,000 locations could be mapped into physical memory from, say, 12,000 to 27,000. This has two disadvantages. First, when the program runs, a block of 15,000 contiguous locations has to be found. Second, the programmer is limited to using a total memory equal to the size of physical memory.

Both problems can be avoided by a mapping based on table lookup. Since it takes too much memory to implement a mapping from any virtual location to *any* physical location, a more restricted mapping based on *pages* is used. Thus for any virtual address, let us say that the high-order bits (e.g., 20 bits) form the page number and that the low-order bits (e.g., 12 bits) form the location within a page. All locations within a virtual page are mapped to the same relative location, but individual virtual pages can be mapped to arbitrary locations. Main memory is also divided into physical pages, such that every group of 2^{12} memory words is a physical page.

To map a virtual into a physical address, the corresponding virtual page (i.e., high-order 20 bits) is mapped to a physical page number while retaining the same location within the page. The mapping is done by looking up a page table indexed by the virtual page number. A virtual page can be located in any physical memory page. More generally, some pages (e.g., Virtual Page 2 in Figure 2.13) may not be memory resident and can be marked as being on disk. When such a page is accessed, the hardware will generate an exception and cause the operating system to read the page from the disk page into a main memory page. This second mechanism is called *demand paging*.

Together, page mapping and demand paging solve the two problems of storage allocation and bounded memory allocations. Instead of solving the harder variable size storage allocation problem, the OS needs only to keep a list of fixed size free pages and to assign some free pages to a new program. Also, the programmer can work with an abstraction of memory whose size is bounded only by the size of disk and the number of instruction address bits.

The extra mapping can slow down each instruction considerably. A Read to virtual location X may require two main memory accesses: a page table access to translate X to physical address P, followed by a Read to address P. Modern processors get around this overhead by caching the most recently used mappings between virtual and physical addresses in a *translation lookaside buffer* (TLB), which is a processor-resident cache. The actual translation is done by a piece of hardware called the *memory management unit* (MMU), as shown in Figure 2.8.

The page table mapping also provides a mechanism for protection between processes. When a process makes a Read to virtual location X, unless there is a corresponding entry in the page table, the hardware will generate a page fault exception. By ensuring that only the operating system can change page table entries, the operating system can ensure that one process cannot read from or write to the memory of another process in unauthorized fashion.

While router forwarding works directly on physical memory, all endnode and server networking code works on virtual memory. While virtual memory is a potential *cost* (e.g., for TLB misses), it also reflects a possible *opportunity*. For example, it offers the potential that packet copying between the operating system and the application (see Example 8) can be done more efficiently by manipulating page tables. This idea is explored further in Chapter 5.

2.4.3 Simple I/O via System Calls

Having an application programmer be aware of the variety and complexity of each I/O device would be intolerable. Thus operating systems provide the programmer with the abstraction of the devices as a piece of memory (Figure 2.14) that can be read and written.

The code that maps from a simple I/O interface call to the actual physical Read (with all parameters filled in) to the device is called a *device driver*. If abstraction were the only concern, the device driver code could be installed in a library of commonly available code that can be "checked out" by each application. However, since devices such as disks must be shared by all applications, if applications directly control the disk, an erroneous process could crash the disk. Instead, secure operating system design requires that only the buggy application fail.

Thus it makes sense for the I/O calls to be handled by device drivers that are in a secure portion of the operating system that cannot be affected by buggy processes. This secure portion, called the *kernel*, provides a core of essential services, including I/O and page table updates, that applications cannot be trusted to perform directly.

Thus when a browser such as Netscape wants to make a disk access to read a Web page, it must make a so-called *system call* across the application–kernel boundary. System calls are a protected form of a function call. The hardware instruction is said to "trap" to a more privileged level (kernel mode), which allows access to operating system internals. When the function call returns after the I/O completes, the application code runs at normal privilege levels. A system call is more expensive than a function call because of the hardware privilege escalation and the extra sanitizing checks for incorrect parameter values. A simple system call may take a few microseconds on modern machines.

The relevance to networking is that when a browser wishes to send a message over the network (e.g., Process 2 in Figure 2.14), it must do a system call to activate TCP processing. A few microseconds for a system call may seem small, but it is really very high overhead on a fast Pentium. Can applications speed up networking by bypassing the system call? If so,

FIGURE 2.14 The programmer sees devices as disparate as a disk and a network adaptor as pieces of memory that can be read and written using system calls, but in reality the kernel manages a host of device-specific details.

does OS protection get tossed out of the window? Answers to these tantalizing questions are postponed to Chapter 6.

2.5 SUMMARY

This chapter is best sampled based on the reader's needs. Structurally, the chapter works its way through four abstraction levels that affect performance: hardware, architecture, operating systems, and protocols. Viewing across abstraction levels is helpful because packet-processing speeds can be limited by transistor paths implementing packet processing, by architectural limits such as bus speeds, by OS abstraction overheads such as system calls, and finally even by protocol mechanisms. Several examples, which look ahead to the rest of the book, were described to show that performance can be improved by understanding each abstraction level.

Designers that consider all four abstraction levels for each problem will soon be lost in detail. However, there are a *few* important performance issues and major architectural decisions for which simultaneous understanding of all abstraction levels is essential. For example, the simple models given in this chapter can allow circuit designers, logic designers, architects, microcoders, and software protocol implementors to work together to craft the architecture of a world-class router. They can also allow operating system designers, algorithm experts, and application writers to work together to design a world-class Web server. As link speeds cross 40 Gbps, such interdisciplinary teams will become even more important. This need is alluded to by Raymond Kurzweil in a different context [Kur]:

> *There's another aspect of creativity. We've been talking about great individual contributors, but when you're creating technology it's necessarily a group process, because technology today is so complex that it has to be interdisciplinary. . . . And they're all essentially speaking their own languages, even about the same concepts. So we will spend months establishing our common language. . . . I have a technique to get people to think outside the box: I'll give a signal-processing problem to the linguists, and vice versa, and let them apply the disciplines in which they've grown up to a completely different problem. The result is often an approach that the experts in the original field would never have thought of. Group process gives creativity a new dimension.*

With fields like hardware implementation and protocol design replacing signal processing and linguistics, Kurzweil's manifesto reflects the goal of this chapter.

2.6 EXERCISES

1. **TCP Protocols and Denial-of-Service Attacks:** A common exploit for a hacker is to attempt to bring down a popular service, such as Yahoo, by doing a denial-of-service (DOS) attack. A simple DOS attack that can be understood using the simple TCP model of Figure A.1 is TCP *Syn-Flooding*. In this attack, the hacker sends a number of SYN packets to the chosen destination D (e.g., Yahoo) using randomly chosen source addresses. D sends back a SYN-ACK to the supposed source S and waits for a response. If S is not an active IP address, then there will be no response from S. Unfortunately, state for S is kept in a pending connection queue at D until D finally times out S. By periodically sending bogus connection attempts pretending to be from different sources,

the attacker can ensure that the finite pending connection queue is always full. Thereafter, legitimate connection requests to D will be denied.

- Assume there is a monitor that is watching all traffic. What algorithm can be used to detect denial-of-service attacks? Try to make your algorithm as fast and memory efficient as possible so that it can potentially be used in real time, even in a router. This is a hard problem, but even starting to think about the problem is instructive.

- Suppose the monitor realizes a TCP flood attack is under way. Why might it be hard to distinguish between legitimate traffic and flood traffic?

2. **Digital Design:** Multiplexers and barrel shifters are very useful in networking hardware, so working this problem can help even a software person to build up hardware intuition.

- First, design a 2-input multiplexer from basic gates (AND, OR, NOT).

- Next, generalize the idea shown in the chapter to design an N-input multiplexer from $N/2$ input multiplexers. Use this to describe a design that takes $\log N$ gate delays and $O(N)$ transistors.

- Show how to design a barrel shifter using a reduction to multiplexers (i.e, use as many muxes as you need in your solution). Based on your earlier solutions, what are the gate and time complexities of your solution?

- Try to design a barrel shifter directly at the transistor level. What are its time and transistor complexities? You can do better using direct design than the simple reduction earlier.

3. **Memory Design:** For the design of the pipelined flow ID lookup scheme described earlier, draw the timing diagrams for the pipelined lookups. Use the numbers described in the chapter, and clearly sketch a sample binary tree with 15 leaves and show how it can be looked up after four lookups on four different banks. Assume a binary tree, not a ternary tree. Also, calculate the number of keys that can be supported using 16 banks of RAMBUS if the first k levels of the tree are cached in on-chip SRAM.

4. **Memories and Pipelining Trees:** This problem studies how to pipeline a heap. A heap is important for applications like QoS, where a router wishes to transmit the packet with the earliest timestamp first. Thus it makes sense to have a heap ordered on timestamps. To make it efficient, the heap needs to be pipelined in the same fashion as the binary search tree example in the chapter, though doing so for a heap is somewhat harder. Figure 2.15 shows an example of a P-heap capable of storing 15 keys. A P-heap [BL00] is a full binary tree, such as a standard heap, except that nodes anywhere in the heap can be empty as long as all children of the node are also empty (e.g., nodes 6, 12, 13).

For the following explanations consult Figures 2.15 and Figure 2.16. Consider adding key 9 to the heap. Assume every node N has a count of the number of empty nodes in the subtree rooted at N. Since 9 is less than the root value of 16, 9 must move below. Since both the left and right children have empty nodes in their subtrees, we arbitrarily choose to add 9 to the left subtree (node 2). The index, value, and position values shown on the left of each tree are registers used to show the state of the current operation. Thus in Figure 2.15, part (b), when 9 is added to the left subtree, the index represents the depth

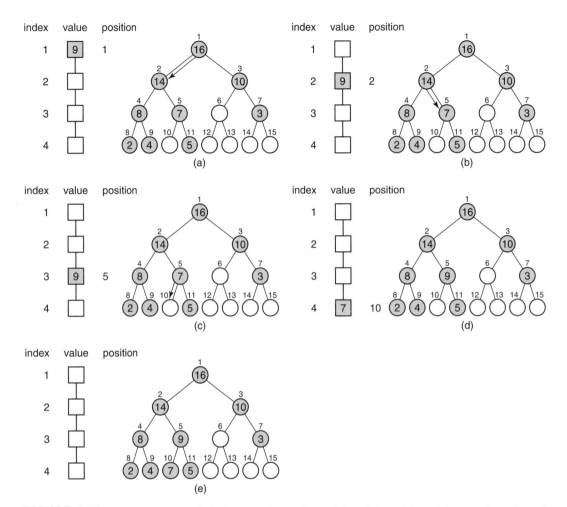

FIGURE 2.15 An enqueue example in five snapshots to be read from left to right and then top down. In each snapshot, the index represents the depth of the subtree, and the position is the number of the node that the value is being added to.

of the subtree (depth 2) and the position is the number of the node (i.e., node 2) that the value 9 is being added to.

Next, since 9 is less than 14 and since only the right child has space in its subtree, 9 is added to the subtree rooted at node 5. This time 9 is greater than 7, so 7 is replaced with 9 (in node 5) and 7 is pushed down to the empty node, 10. Thus in Figure 2.15, part (d), the index value is 4 (i.e., operation is at depth 4) and the position is 10. Although in Figure 2.15 only one of the registers at any index/depth has nonempty information, keeping separate registers for each index will allow pipelining.

Consider next what is involved in removing the largest element (dequeue). Remove 16 and try to push down the hole created until an empty subtree is created. Thus in Step 3,

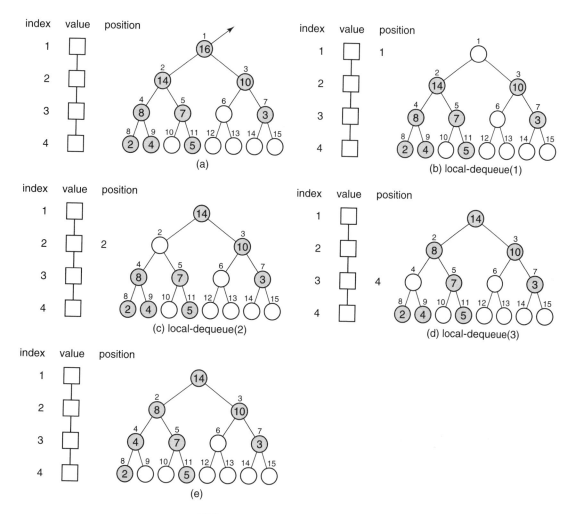

FIGURE 2.16   Dequeue example.

the hole is moved to node 2 (because its value, 14, is larger than its sibling, with value 10), then to node 4, and finally to node 9. Each time a hole is moved down, the corresponding nonempty value from below replaces the old hole.

- In order to make the enqueue operation work correctly, the count of empty subtree nodes must be maintained. Explain briefly how the count should be maintained for each enqueue and dequeue operation (the structure will be pipelined in a moment, so make sure the count values respect this goal).

- A logical thing to do is to pipeline by level, as we did for the binary tree in the chapter. However, here we have a problem. At each level (say, inserting 9 at the root) the operation has to consult the two children at the next level as well. Thus when the first operation moves down to level 2, one cannot bring in a second operation to level 1 or there will be memory contention. Clearly waiting till one operation finishes completely will work, but this reduces to sequential processing of operations. What is the fastest rate you can pipeline the heap?

- Consider the operations "Enqueue 9; Enqueue 4.5; Dequeue" pipelined as you have answered earlier. Show six consecutive snapshots of the tree supporting these three operations.

- Assume that each level memory is an on-chip SRAM that takes 5 nsec for a memory access. Assume that you can read and write the value and count fields together in one access. Remember that some of the memories can be queried in parallel. What is the steady-state throughput of the heap, in operations per second?

- Could one improve the number of memory references by using a wider memory access and laying out the tree appropriately?

- Before this design, previous designs used a memory element for each heap element as well as logic for each element. Thus the amount of logic required scaled directly with heap size, which scales poorly in terms of density and power. In this design, the memory scales with the number of heap elements and thus scales with SRAM densities and power, but the logic required scales much better. Explain.

5. **Architecture, Caches, and Fast Hash Functions:** The L1 cache in a CPU provides essentially a fast hash function that maps from a physical memory address to its contents via the L1 cache. Suppose that one wants to teach an old dog (the L1 cache) a new trick (to do IP lookups) using a method suggested in Chieuh and Pradhan [CP98]. The goal is to use the L1 cache as a hash table to map 32-bit IP addresses to 7-bit port numbers. Assume a 16-KB L1 cache, of which the first 4 KB are reserved for the hash table, and a 32-byte cache block size. Assume a byte-addressable machine, a 32-bit virtual address, and a page size of 4 KB. Thus there are 512 32-byte blocks in the cache. Assume the L1 cache is directly indexed (called *direct mapped*). Thus bits 5 through 13 of a virtual address are used to index into one of 512 blocks, with bits 0 through 4 identifying the byte within each block.

- Given pages of size 4 KB and that the machine is byte addressable, how many bits in a virtual address identify the virtual page? How many bits of the virtual page number intersect with bits 5 through 13 used to index into the L1 cache?

- The only way to ensure that the hash table is not thrown out of the L1 cache when some other virtual pages arrive is to mark any pages that could map into the same portion of the L1 cache as uncacheable at start-up (this can be done). Based on your previous answer and the fact that the hash table uses the first 4 KB of L1 cache, precisely identify which pages must be marked as uncacheable.

- To do a lookup of a 32-byte IP address, first convert the address to a virtual address by setting to 0 all bits except bits 5 through 11 (bits 12 and 13 are zero because only the top quarter of the L1 cache is being used). Assume this is translated to the exact same physical address. When a Read is done to this address, the L1 cache hardware will return the contents of the first 32-bit word of the corresponding cache block. Each 32-bit word will contain a 25-bit tag and a 7-bit port number. Next, compare all bits in the IP address, other than bits 5 through 11, with the tag, and keep doing so for each 32-bit entry in the block. How many L1 cache accesses are required in the worst case for a hash lookup? Why might this be faster than a standard hash lookup in software?

6. **Operating Systems and Lazy Receiver Processing:** Example 8 described how BSD protocol processing can lead to receiver livelock. Lazy receiver processing [DB96] combats this problem via two mechanisms.

   • The first mechanism is to replace the single shared IP processing queue by a separate queue per destination socket. Why does this help? Why might this not be easy to implement?

   • The second mechanism is to implement the protocol processing at the priority of the receiving process and as part of the context of the received process (and not a separate software interrupt). Why does this help? Why might this not be easy to implement?

CHAPTER 3

Fifteen Implementation Principles

Instead of computing, I had to think about the problem, a formula for success that I recommend highly.

— IVAN SUTHERLAND

After understanding how queens and knights move in a game of chess, it helps to understand basic strategies, such as castling and the promotion of pawns in the endgame. Similarly, having studied some of the rules of the protocol implementation game in the last chapter, you will be presented in this chapter with implementation strategies in the form of 15 principles. The principles are abstracted from protocol implementations that have worked well. Many good implementors *unconsciously* use such principles. The point, however, is to articulate such principles so that they can be *deliberately* applied to craft efficient implementations.

This chapter is organized as follows. Section 3.1 motivates the use of the principles using a ternary CAM problem. Section 3.2 clarifies the distinction between algorithms and algorithmics using a network security forensics problem. Section 3.3 introduces 15 implementation principles; Section 3.4 explains the differences between *implementation* and *design* principles. Finally, Section 3.5 describes some cautionary questions that should be asked before applying the principles.

Quick Reference Guide

The reader pressed for time should consult the summaries of the 15 principles found in Figures 3.1, 3.2, and 3.3. Two networking applications of these principles can be found in a ternary CAM update problem (Section 3.1) and a network security forensics problem (Section 3.2).

3.1 MOTIVATING THE USE OF PRINCIPLES — UPDATING TERNARY CONTENT-ADDRESSABLE MEMORIES

Call a string *ternary* if it contains characters that are either 0, 1, or *, where * denotes a wildcard that can match both a 0 and a 1. Examples of ternary strings of length 3 include $S1 = 01*$ and $S2 = *1*$; the actual binary string 011 matches both S1 and S2, while 111 matches only S2.

Number	Principle	Used In
P1	Avoid obvious waste	Zero-copy interfaces
P2 P2a P2b P2c	Shift computation in time Precompute Evaluate lazily Share expenses, batch	Application device channels Copy-on-write Integrated layer processing
P3 P3a P3b P3c	Relax system requirements Trade certainty for time Trade accuracy for time Shift computation in space	Stochastic fair queueing Switch load balancing IPv6 fragmentation
P4 P4a P4b P4c	Leverage off system components Exploit locality Trade memory for speed Exploit existing hardware	Locality-driven receiver Processing; Lulea IP lookups Fast TCP checksum
P5 P5a P5b P5c	Add hardware Use memory interleaving and pipelining Use wide word parallelism Combine DRAM and SRAM effectively	Pipelined IP lookups Shared memory switches Maintaining counters

FIGURE 3.1   Summary of Principles 1–5 — systems thinking.

Number	Principle	Networking Example
P6	Create efficient specialized routines	UDP checksums
P7	Avoid unnecessary generality	Fbufs
P8	Don't be tied to reference implementation	Upcalls
P9	Pass hints in layer interfaces	Packet filters
P10	Pass hints in protocol headers	Tag switching

FIGURE 3.2   Summary of Principles 6–10 — recovering efficiency while retaining modularity.

Number	Principle	Networking Example
P11 P11a	Optimize the expected case Use caches	Header prediction Fbufs
P12 P12a	Add state for speed Compute incrementally	Active VC list Recomputing CRCs
P13	Optimize degrees of freedom	IP trie lookups
P14	Use bucket sorting, bitmaps	Timing wheels
P15	Create efficient data structures	Level-4 switching

FIGURE 3.3   Summary of Principles 11–15 — speeding up key routines.

FIGURE 3.4   Example of using a ternary CAM for prefix lookups.

A ternary content-addressable memory (CAM) is a memory containing ternary strings of a specified length together with associated information; when presented with an input string, the CAM will search all its memory locations in parallel to output (in one cycle) the lowest memory location whose ternary string matches the specified input key.

Figure 3.4 shows an application of ternary CAMs to the longest-matching-prefix problem for Internet routers. For every incoming packet, each Internet router must extract a 32-bit destination IP address from the incoming packet and match it against a forwarding database of IP prefixes with their corresponding next hops. An IP prefix is a ternary string of length 32 where all the wildcards are at the end. We will change notation slightly and let * denote any number of wildcard characters, so 101* matches 10100 and not just 1010.

Thus in Figure 3.4 a packet sent to a destination address that starts with 010001 matches the prefixes 010001* and 01* but should be sent to Port P5 because Internet forwarding requires that packets be forwarded using the longest match. We will have more to say about this problem in Chapter 11. For now, note that if the prefixes are arranged in a ternary CAM such that all longer prefixes occur before any shorter prefixes (as in Figure 3.4), the ternary CAM provides the matching next hop in one memory cycle.

While ternary CAMs are extremely fast for message forwarding, they require that longer prefixes occur before shorter prefixes. But routing protocols often add or delete prefixes. Suppose in Figure 3.4 that a new prefix, 11*, with next hop Port 1 must be added to the router database. The naive way to do insertion would make space in the group of length-2 prefixes (i.e., create a hole before 0*) by pushing up by one position all prefixes of length 2 or higher.

Unfortunately, for a large database of around 100,000 prefixes kept by a typical core router, this would take 100,000 memory cycles, which would make it very slow to add a prefix. We can obtain a better solution systematically by applying the following two principles (described later in this chapter as principles **P13** and **P15**).

UNDERSTAND AND EXPLOIT DEGREES OF FREEDOM

In looking at the forwarding table on the left of Figure 3.4 we see that all prefixes of the same length are arranged together and all prefixes of length i occur after all prefixes of length $j > i$.

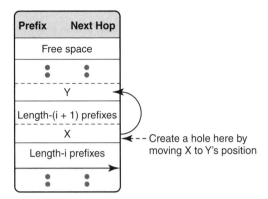

FIGURE 3.5 Finding a spot for the new prefix by moving X to Y's position recursively requires us to find a spot to move Y.

However, in the figure all prefixes of the same length are also sorted by value. Thus 00* occurs before 01*, which occurs before 10*. But this is unnecessary for the CAM to correctly return longest matching prefixes: We only require ordering between prefixes of *different* lengths; we do not require ordering between prefixes of the *same* length.

In looking at the more abstract view of Figure 3.4 shown in Figure 3.5, we see that if we are to add an entry to the start of the set of length-i prefixes, we have to create a hole at the end of the length-$(i + 1)$ set of prefixes. Thus we have to move the entry X, already at this position, to another position. If we move X one step up, we will be forced into our prior inefficient solution.

However, our observation about degrees of freedom says that we can place X *anywhere* adjacent to the other length-$(i + 1)$ prefixes. Thus, an alternative idea is to move X to the position held by Y, the last length-$(i + 2)$ prefix. But this forces us to find a new position for Y. How does this help? We need a second principle.

USE ALGORITHMIC TECHNIQUES

Again, recursion suggests itself: We solve a problem by reducing the problem to a "smaller" instance of the same problem. In this case, the new problem of assigning Y a new position is "smaller" because the set of length-$(i + 2)$ prefixes are closer to the free space at the top of the CAM than the set of length-$(i + 1)$ prefixes. Thus we move Y to the end of the length-$(i + 3)$ set of prefixes, etc.

While recursion is a natural way to think, a better implementation is to unwind the recursion by starting from the top of the CAM and working downward by creating a hole at the end of the length-1 prefixes,[1] creating a hole at the end of the length-2 prefixes, etc., until we create a hole at the end of the length-i prefixes. Thus the worst-case time is $32 - i$ memory accesses, which is around 32 for small i.

---

[1] For simplicity, this description has assumed that the CAM contains prefixes of all lengths; it is easy to modify the algorithm to avoid this assumption.

Are we done? No, we can do better by further exploiting degrees of freedom. First, in Figure 3.5 we *assumed* that the free space was at the *top* of the CAM. But the free space could be placed anywhere. In particular, it can be placed after the length-16 prefixes. This reduces the worst-case number of memory accesses by a factor of 2 [SG01].

A more sophisticated degree of freedom is as follows. So far the specification of the CAM insertion algorithm required that "a prefix of length i must occur before a prefix of length j if $i > j$." Such a specification is *sufficient* for correctness but is not *necessary*. For example, 010* can occur before 111001* because there is no address that can match both prefixes!

Thus a less exacting specification is "if two prefixes P and Q can match the same address, then P must come before Q in the CAM if P is longer than Q." This is used in Shah and Gupta [SG01] to further reduce the worst-case number of memory accesses for insertion for some practical databases.

While the last improvement is not worth its complexity, it points to another important principle. We often divide a large problem into subproblems and hand over the subproblem for a solution based on a specification. For example, the CAM hardware designer may have handed over the update problem to a microcoder, specifying that longer prefixes be placed before shorter ones.

But, as before, such a specification may not be the only way to solve the original problem. Thus changes to the specification (principle **P3**) can yield a more efficient solution. Of course, this requires curious and confident individuals who understand the big picture or who are brave enough to ask dangerous questions.

3.2 ALGORITHMS VERSUS ALGORITHMICS

It may be possible to argue that the previous example is still essentially algorithmic and does not require system thinking. One more quick example will help clarify the difference between algorithms and algorithmics.

SECURITY FORENSICS PROBLEM

In many intrusion detection systems, a manager often finds that a flow (defined by some packet header, for example, a source IP address) is likely to be misbehaving based on some probabilistic check. For example, a source doing a port scan may be identified after it has sent 100,000 packets to different machines in the attacked subnet.

While there are methods to identify such sources, one problem is that the evidence (the 100,000 packets sent by the source) has typically disappeared (i.e., been forwarded from the router) by the time the guilty source is identified. The problem is that the probabilistic check requires accumulating some state (in, say, a suspicion table) for every packet received *over some period of time* before a source can be deemed suspicious. Thus if a source is judged to be suspicious after 10 seconds, how can one go back in time and retrieve the packets sent by the source during those 10 seconds?

To accomplish this, in Figure 3.6 we keep a queue of the last 100,000 packets that were sent by the router. When a packet is forwarded we also add a copy of the packet (or just keep a pointer to the packet) to the head of the queue. To keep the queue bounded, when the queue is full we delete from the tail as well.

The main difficulty with this scheme is that when a guilty flow is detected there may be lots of the flow's packets in the queue (Figure 3.6). All of these packets must be placed in

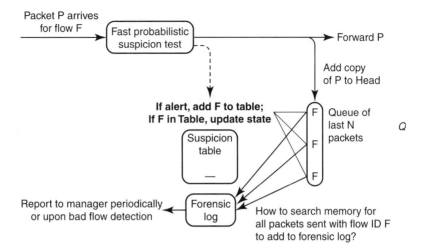

FIGURE 3.6 Keeping a queue of the last 100,000 packets that contains forensic information about what suspicious flows have been sent in the past.

the forensic log for transmission to a manager. The naive method of searching through a large DRAM buffer is very slow.

The textbook algorithms approach would be to add some index structure to search quickly for flow IDs. For example, one might maintain a hash table of flow IDs that maps every flow to a list of pointers to all packets with that flow ID in the queue. When a new packet is placed in the queue, the flow ID is looked up in the hash table and the address of the new packet in the queue is placed at the end of the flow's list. Of course, when packets leave the queue, their entries must be removed from the list, and the list can be long. Fortunately, the entry to be deleted is guaranteed to be at the head of the queue for that flow ID.

Despite this, the textbook scheme has some difficulties. It adds more space to maintain these extra queues per flow ID, and space can be at a premium for a high-speed implementation. It also adds some extra complexity to packet processing to maintain the hash table, and requires reading out all of a flow's packets to the forensic log before the packet is overwritten by a packet that arrives 100,000 packets later. Instead the following "systems" solution may be more elegant.

SOLUTION

Do not attempt to immediately identify all of a flow F's packets when F is identified, but *lazily* identify them as they reach the end of the packet queue. This is shown in Figure 3.7. When we add a packet to the head of the queue, we must remove a packet from the end of the queue (at least when the queue is full).

If that packet (say, Q, see Figure 3.6) belongs to flow F that is in the Suspicion Table and flow F has reached some threshold of suspicion, we then add packet Q to the forensic log. The log can be sent to a manager. The overhead of this scheme is significant but manageable; we have to do two packet-processing steps, one for the packet being forwarded and one for the packet being removed from the queue. But these two packet-processing steps are also required in the textbook scheme; on the other hand, the elegant scheme requires no hashing and uses much less storage (no pointers between the 100,000 packets).

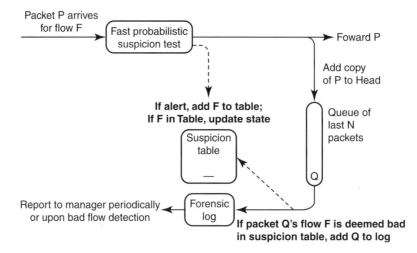

FIGURE 3.7 Keeping a queue of the last 100,000 packets that contains forensic information about what suspicious flows have been sent in the past.

3.3 FIFTEEN IMPLEMENTATION PRINCIPLES — CATEGORIZATION AND DESCRIPTION

The two earlier examples and the warm-up exercise in Chapter 1 motivate the following 15 principles, which are used in the rest of the book. They are summarized inside the front cover. To add more structure they are categorized as follows:

- **Systems Principles:** Principles 1–5 take advantage of the fact that a system is constructed from subsystems. By taking a systemwide rather than a black-box approach, one can often improve performance.

- **Improving Efficiency While Retaining Modularity:** Principles 6–10 suggest methods for improving performance while allowing complex systems to be built modularly.

- **Speeding It Up:** Principles 11–15 suggest techniques for speeding up a key routine considered by itself.

Amazingly, many of these principles have been used for years by Chef Charlie at his Greasy Spoon restaurant. This chapter sometimes uses illustrations drawn from Chef Charlie's experience, in addition to computer systems examples. One networking example is also described for each principle, though details are deferred to later chapters.

3.3.1 Systems Principles

The first five principles exploit the fact that we are building systems.

P1: AVOID OBVIOUS WASTE IN COMMON SITUATIONS

In a system, there may be wasted resources in special sequences of operations. If these patterns occur commonly, it may be worth eliminating the waste. This reflects an attitude of thriftiness toward system costs.

For example, Chef Charlie has to make a trip to the pantry to get the ice cream maker to make ice cream and to the pantry for a pie plate when he makes pies. But when he makes pie à la mode, he has learned to eliminate the obvious waste of two separate trips to the pantry.

Similarly, optimizing compilers look for obvious waste in terms of repeated subexpressions. For example, if a statement calculates $i = 5.1 * n + 2$ and a later statement calculates $j := (5.1 * n + 2) * 4$, the calculation of the common subexpression $5.1 * n + 2$ is wasteful and can be avoided by computing the subexpression once, assigning it to a temporary variable t, and then calculating $i := t$ and $j := t * 4$. A classic networking example, described in Chapter 5, is avoiding making multiple copies of a packet between operating system and user buffers.

Notice that each operation (e.g., walk to pantry, line of code, single packet copy) considered by itself has no obvious waste. It is the sequence of operations (two trips to the pantry, two statements that recompute a subexpression, two copies) that have obvious waste. Clearly, the larger the exposed context, the greater the scope for optimization. While the identification of certain operation patterns as being worth optimizing is often a matter of designer intuition, optimizations can be tested in practice using benchmarks.

P2: SHIFT COMPUTATION IN TIME

Systems have an aspect in space and time. The space aspect is represented by the subsystems, possibly geographically distributed, into which the system is decomposed. The time aspect is represented by the fact that a system is instantiated at various time scales, from fabrication time, to compile time, to parameter-setting times, to run time. Many efficiencies can be gained by shifting computation in time. Here are three generic methods that fall under time-shifting.

- *P2a: Precompute.* This refers to computing quantities before they are actually used, to save time at the point of use. For example, Chef Charlie prepares crushed garlic in advance to save time during the dinner rush. A common systems example is table-lookup methods, where the computation of an expensive function f in run time is replaced by the lookup of a table that contains the value of f for every element in the domain of f. A networking example is the precomputation of IP and TCP headers for packets in a connection; because only a few header fields change for each packet, this reduces the work to write packet headers (Chapter 9).

- *P2b: Evaluate Lazily.* This refers to postponing expensive operations at critical times, hoping that either the operation will not be needed later or a less busy time will be found to perform the operation. For example, Chef Charlie postpones dishwashing to the end of the day. While precomputation is computing before the need, lazy evaluation is computing only when needed.

    A famous example of lazy evaluation in systems is *copy-on-write* in the Mach operating system. Suppose we have to copy a virtual address space A to another space, B, for process migration. A general solution is to copy all pages in A to B to allow for pages in B to be written independently. Instead, copy-on-write makes page table entries in B's virtual address space point to the corresponding page in A. When a process using B writes to a location, then a separate copy of the corresponding page in A is made for B, and the write is performed. Since we expect the number of pages that are written in B to be small compared to the total number of pages, this avoids unnecessary copying.

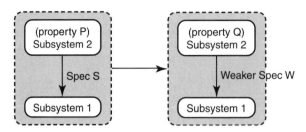

FIGURE 3.8 Easing the implementation of Subsystem 1 by weakening its specification from S to, say, W, at the cost of making Subsystem 2 do more work.

A simple networking example occurs when a network packet arrives to an endnode X in a different byte order than X's native byte order. Rather than swap all bytes immediately, it can be more efficient to wait to swap the bytes that are actually read.

- *P2c: Share Expenses.* This refers to taking advantage of expensive operations done by other parts of the system. An important example of expense sharing is *batching*, where several expensive operations can be done together more cheaply than doing each separately. For example, Charlie bakes several pies in one batch. Computer systems have used batch processing for years, especially in the early days of mainframes, before time sharing. Batching trades latency for throughput. A simple networking example of expense sharing is timing wheels (Chapter 7), where the timer data structure shares expensive per-clock-tick processing with the routine that updates the time-of-day clock.

P3: RELAX SYSTEM REQUIREMENTS

When a system is first designed top-down, functions are partitioned among subsystems. After fixing subsystem requirements and interfaces, individual subsystems are designed. When implementation difficulties arise, the basic system structure may have to be redone, as shown in Figure 3.8.

As shown in Chapter 1, implementation difficulties (e.g., implementing a Divide) can sometimes be solved by relaxing the specification requirements for, say, Subsystem 1. This is shown in the figure by weakening the specification of Subsystem 1 from, say, S to W, but at the cost of making Subsystem 2 obey a stronger property, Q, compared to the previous property, P.

Three techniques that arise from this principle are distinguished by how they relax the original subsystem specification.

- *P3a: Trade Certainty for Time.* Systems designers can fool themselves into believing that their systems offer deterministic guarantees, when in fact we all depend on probabilities. For example, quantum mechanics tells us there is some probability that the atoms in your body will rearrange themselves to form a hockey puck, but this is clearly improbable.[2] This opens the door to consider randomized strategies when deterministic algorithms are too slow.

  In systems, randomization is used by millions of Ethernets worldwide to sort out packet-sending instants after collisions occur. A simple networking example of

---

[2]Quote due to Tony Lauck.

randomization is Cisco's NetFlow traffic measurement software: If a router does not have enough processing power to count all arriving packets, it can count random samples and still be able to statistically identify large flows. A second networking example is stochastic fair queuing (Chapter 14), where, rather than keep track exactly of the networking conversations going through a router, conversations are tracked probabilistically using hashing.

- *P3b: Trade Accuracy for Time.* Similarly, numerical analysis cures us of the illusion that computers are perfectly accurate. Thus it can pay to relax accuracy requirements for speed. In systems, many image compression techniques, such as MPEG, rely on lossy compression using interpolation. Chapter 1 used approximate thresholds to replace divides by shifts. In networking, some packet-scheduling algorithms at routers (Chapter 14) require sorting packets by their departure deadlines; some proposals to reduce sorting overhead at high speeds suggest approximate sorting, which can slightly reduce quality-of-service bounds but reduce processing.

- *P3c: Shift Computation in Space.* Notice that all the examples given for this principle relaxed requirements: Sampling may miss some packets, and the transferred image may not be identical to the original image. However, other parts of the system (e.g., Subsystem 2 in Figure 3.8) have to adapt to these looser requirements. Thus we prefer to call the general idea of moving computation from one subsystem to another ("robbing Peter to pay Paul") *shifting computation in space*. In networking, for example, the need for routers to fragment packets has recently been avoided by having end systems calculate a packet size that will pass all routers.

P4: LEVERAGE OFF SYSTEM COMPONENTS

A black-box view of system design is to decompose the system into subsystems and then to design each subsystem in isolation. While this top-down approach has a pleasing modularity, in practice performance-critical components are often constructed partially bottom-up. For example, algorithms are designed to fit the features offered by the hardware. Here are some techniques that fall under this principle.

- *P4a: Exploit Locality.* Chapter 2 showed that memory hardware offers efficiencies if related data is laid out contiguously — e.g., same sector for disks, or same DRAM page for DRAMs. Disk-search algorithms exploit this fact by using search trees of high radix, such as B-trees. IP-lookup algorithms (Chapter 11) use the same trick to reduce lookup times by placing several keys in a wide word, as did the example in Chapter 1.

- *P4b: Trade Memory for Speed.* The obvious technique is to use more memory, such as lookup tables, to save processing time. A less obvious technique is to *compress* a data structure to make it more likely to fit into cache, because cache accesses are cheaper than memory accesses. The Lulea IP-lookup algorithm described in Chapter 11 uses this idea by using sparse arrays that can still be looked up efficiently using space-efficient bitmaps.

- *P4c: Exploit Hardware Features.* Compilers use *strength reduction* to optimize away multiplications in loops; for example, in a loop where addresses are 4 bytes and the index i increases by 1 each time, instead of computing $4 * i$, the compiler calculates the new array index as being 4 higher than its previous value. This exploits the fact that multiplies are more expensive than additions on many modern processors. Similarly, it pays to

manipulate data in multiples of the machine word size, as we will see in the fast
IP-checksum algorithms described in Chapter 9.

If this principle is carried too far, the modularity of the system will be in jeopardy. Two
techniques alleviate this problem. First, if we exploit other system features only to improve
performance, then changes to those system features can only affect performance and not
correctness. Second, we use this technique only for system components that profiling has
shown to be a bottleneck.

P5: Add Hardware to Improve Performance

When all else fails, goes the aphorism, use brute force. Adding new hardware,[3] such as buying
a faster processor, can be simpler and more cost effective than using clever techniques. Besides
the brute-force approach of using faster infrastructure (e.g., faster processors, memory, buses,
links), there are cleverer hardware–software trade-offs. Since hardware is less flexible and has
higher design costs, it pays to add the minimum amount of hardware needed.

Thus, baking at the Greasy Spoon was sped up using microwave ovens. In computer
systems, dramatic improvements each year in processor speeds and memory densities suggest
doing key algorithms in software and upgrading to faster processors for speed increases. But
computer systems abound with cleverer hardware–software trade-offs.

For example, in a multiprocessor system, if a processor wishes to write data, it must inform
any "owners" of cached versions of the data. This interaction can be avoided if each processor
has a piece of hardware that watches the bus for write transactions by other processors and
automatically invalidates the cached location when necessary. This simple hardware snoopy
cache controller allows the remainder of the cache-consistency algorithm to be efficiently
performed in software.

Decomposing functions between hardware and software is an art in itself. Hardware offers
several benefits. First, there is no time required to fetch instructions: Instructions are effectively hardcoded. Second, common computational sequences (which would require several
instructions in software) can be done in a single hardware clock cycle. For example, finding
the first bit set in, say, a 32-bit word may take several instructions on a RISC machine but can
be computed by a simple priority encoder, as shown in the previous chapter.

Third, hardware allows you to explicitly take advantage of parallelism inherent in the
problem. Finally, hardware manufactured in volume may be cheaper than a general-purpose
processor. For example, a Pentium may cost $100 while an ASIC in volume with similar speeds
may cost $10.

On the other hand, a software design is easily transported to the next generation of faster
chips. Hardware, despite the use of programmable chips, is still less flexible. Despite this,
with the advent of design tools such as VHDL synthesis packages, hardware design times have
decreased considerably. Thus in the last few years chips performing fairly complex functions,
such as image compression and IP lookups, have been designed.

Besides specific performance improvements, new technology can result in a complete
paradigm shift. A visionary designer may completely redesign a system in anticipation of

---

[3]By contrast, Principle **P4** talks about exploiting existing system features, such as the existing hardware. Of
course, the distinction between principles tends to blur and must be taken with a grain of salt.

such trends. For example, the invention of the transistor and fast digital memories certainly enabled the use of digitized voice in the telephone network.

Increases in chip density have led computer architects to ponder what computational features to add to memories to alleviate the processor-memory bottleneck. In networks, the availability of high-speed links in the 1980s led to use of large addresses and large headers. Ironically, the emergence of laptops in the 1990s led to the use of low-bandwidth wireless links and to a renewed concern for header compression. Technology trends can seesaw!

The following specific hardware techniques are often used in networking ASICs and are worth mentioning. They were first described in Chapter 2 and are repeated here for convenience.

- **P5a: Use Memory Interleaving and Pipelining.** Similar techniques are used in IP lookup, in classification, and in scheduling algorithms that implement QoS. The multiple banks can be implemented using several external memories, a single external memory such as a RAMBUS, or on-chip SRAM within a chip that also contains processing logic.

- **P5b: Use Wide Word Parallelism.** A common theme in many networking designs, such as the Lucent bit vector scheme (Chapter 12), is to use wide memory words that can be processed in parallel. This can be implemented using DRAM and exploiting page mode or by using SRAM and making each memory word wider.

- **P5c: Combine DRAM and SRAM.** Given that SRAM is expensive and fast and that DRAM is cheap and slow, it makes sense to combine the two technologies to attempt to obtain the best of both worlds. While the use of SRAM as a cache for DRAM databases is classical, there are many more creative applications of the idea of a memory hierarchy. For instance, the exercises explore the effect of a small amount of SRAM on the design of the flow ID lookup chip. Chapter 16 describes a more unusual application of this technique to implement a large number of counters, where the low-order bits of each counter are stored in SRAM.

3.3.2 Principles for Modularity with Efficiency

An engineer who had read Dave Clark's classic papers (e.g., Ref. Cla85) on the inefficiences of layered implementations once complained to a researcher about modularity. The researcher (Radia Perlman) replied, "But that's how we got to the stage where we could complain about something." Her point, of course, was that complex systems like network protocols could only have been engineered using layering and modularity. The following principles, culled from work by Clark and others, show how to regain efficiencies while retaining modularity.

P6: CREATE EFFICIENT SPECIALIZED ROUTINES BY REPLACING INEFFICIENT GENERAL-PURPOSE ROUTINES

As in mathematics, the use of abstraction in computer system design can make systems compact, orthogonal, and modular. However, at times the one-size-fits-all aspect of a general-purpose routine leads to inefficiencies. In important cases, it can pay to design an optimized and specialized routine.

A systems example can be found in database caches. Most general-purpose caching strategies would replace the least recently used record to disk. However, consider a query-processing routine processing a sequence of database tuples in a loop. In such a case, it is the most recently used record that will be used furthest in the future so it is the ideal candidate for replacement.

Thus many database applications replace the operating system caching routines with more specialized routines. It is best to do such specialization only for key routines, to avoid code bloat. A networking example is the fast UDP processing routines that we describe in Chapter 9.

P7: AVOID UNNECESSARY GENERALITY

The tendency to design abstract and general subsystems can also lead to unnecessary or rarely used features. Thus, rather than building several specialized routines (e.g., **P6**) to replace the general-purpose routine, we might remove features to gain performance.[4]

Of course, as in the case of **P3**, removing features requires users of the routine to live with restrictions. For example, in RISC processors, the elimination of complex instructions such as multiplies required multiplication to be emulated by firmware. A networking example is provided by *Fbufs* (Chapter 5), which provide a specialized virtual memory service that allows efficient copying between virtual address spaces.

P8: DON'T BE TIED TO REFERENCE IMPLEMENTATIONS

Specifications are written for clarity, not to suggest efficient implementations. Because abstract specification languages are unpopular, many specifications use imperative languages such as C. Rather than precisely describe *what* function is to be computed, one gets code that prescribes *how* to compute the function. This has two side effects.

First, there is a strong tendency to overspecify. Second, many implementors copy the reference implementation in the specification, which is a problem when the reference implementation was chosen for conceptual clarity and not efficiency. As Clark [Cla85] points out, implementors are free to change the reference implementation as long as the two implementations have the same external effects. In fact, there may be other structured implementations that are efficient as well as modular.

For example, Charlie knows that when a recipe tells him to cut beans and then to cut carrots, he can interchange the two steps. In the systems world, Clark originally suggested the use of upcalls [Cla85] for operating systems. In an upcall, a lower layer can call an upper layer for data or advice, seemingly violating the rules of hierarchical decomposition introduced in the design of operating systems. Upcalls are commonly used today in network protocol implementations.

P9: PASS HINTS IN MODULE INTERFACES

A hint is information passed from a client to a service that, if correct, can avoid expensive computation by the service. The two key phrases are *passed* and *if correct*. By *passing* the hint in its request, a service can avoid the need for the associative lookup needed to access a cache. For example, a hint can be used to supply a direct index into the processing state at the receiver. Also, unlike caches, the hint is not guaranteed to be correct and hence must be checked against other certifiably correct information. Hints improve performance if the hint is correct most of the time.

This definition of a hint suggests a variant in which information is passed that is guaranteed to be correct and hence requires no checking. For want of an established term, we will call such information a *tip*. Tips are harder to use because of the need to ensure correctness of the tip.

---

[4]Butler Lampson, a computer scientist and Turing Award winner, provides two quotes: *When in doubt, get rid of it* (anonymous) and *Exterminate Features* (Thacker).

As a systems example, the Alto File system [Lam89] has every file block on disk carry a pointer to the next file block. This pointer is treated as only a hint and is checked against the file name and block number stored in the block itself. If the hint is incorrect, the information can be reconstructed from disk. Incorrect hints must not jeopardize system correctness but result only in performance degradation.

P10: PASS HINTS IN PROTOCOL HEADERS

For distributed systems, the logical extension to Principle **P9** is to pass information such as hints in message headers. Since this book deals with distributed systems, we will make this a separate principle. For example, computer architects have applied this principle to circumvent inefficiencies in message-passing parallel systems such as the Connection Machine.

One of the ideas in active messages (Chapter 5) is to have a message carry the address of the interrupt handler for fast dispatching. Another example is tag switching (Chapter 11), where packets carry additional indices besides the destination address to help the destination address to be looked up quickly. Tags are used as hints because tag consistency is not guaranteed; packets can be routed to the wrong destination, where they must be checked.

3.3.3 Principles for Speeding Up Routines

While the previous principles exploited system structure, we now consider principles for speeding up system routines considered in isolation.

P11: OPTIMIZE THE EXPECTED CASE

While systems *can* exhibit a range of behaviors, the behaviors often fall into a smaller set called the "expected case" [HP96]. For example, well-designed systems should mostly operate in a fault- and exception-free regime. A second example is a program that exhibits *spatial locality* by mostly accessing a small set of memory locations. Thus it pays to make common behaviors efficient, even at the cost of making uncommon behaviors more expensive.

Heuristics such as optimizing the expected case are often unsatisfying for theoreticians, who (naturally) prefer mechanisms whose benefit can be precisely quantified in an average or worst-case sense. In defense of this heuristic, note that every computer in existence optimizes the expected case (see Chapter 2) at least a million times a second.

For example, with the use of paging, the worst-case number of memory references to resolve a PC instruction that accesses memory can be as bad as four (read instruction from memory, read first-level page table, read second-level page table, fetch operand from memory). However, the number of memory accesses can be reduced to 0 using caches. In general, caches allow designers to use modular structures and indirection, with gains in flexibility, and yet regain performance in the expected case. Thus it is worth highlighting caching.

P11a: USE CACHES

Besides caching, there are subtler uses of the expected-case principle. For example, when you wish to change buffers in the EMACS editor, the editor offers you a default buffer name, which is the last buffer you examined. This saves typing time in the expected case when you keep moving between two buffers. The use of header prediction (Chapter 9) in networks is another example of optimizing the expected case: The cost of processing a packet can be greatly reduced by assuming that the next packet received is closely related to the last packet processed (for example, by being the next packet in sequence) and requires no exception processing.

Note that determining the common case is best done by measurements and by schemes that automatically learn the common case. However, it is often based on the designer's intuition. Note that the expected case may be incorrect in special situations or may change with time.

P12: ADD OR EXPLOIT STATE TO GAIN SPEED

If an operation is expensive, consider maintaining additional but redundant state to speed up the operation. For example, Charlie keeps track of the tables that are busy so that he can optimize waiter assignments. This is not absolutely necessary, for he can always compute this information when needed by walking around the restaurant.

In database systems, a classic example is the use of secondary indices. Bank records may be stored and searched using a primary key, say, the customer Social Security number. However, if there are several queries that reference the customer name (e.g., "Find the balance of all Cleopatra's accounts in the Thebes branch"), it may pay to maintain an additional index (e.g., a hash table or B-tree) on the customer name. Note that maintaining additional state implies the need to potentially modify this state whenever changes occur.

However, sometimes this principle can be used without adding state by exploiting existing state. We call this out as Principle **P12a**.

P12a: COMPUTE INCREMENTALLY

When a new customer comes in or leaves, Charlie increments the board on which he notes waiter assignments. As a second example, strength reduction in compilers (see example in **P4c**) incrementally computes the new loop index from the old using additions instead of computing the absolute index using multiplication. An example of incremental computation in networking is the incremental computation of IP checksums (Chapter 9) when only a few fields in the packet change.

P13: OPTIMIZE DEGREES OF FREEDOM

It helps to be aware of the variables that are under one's control and the evaluation criteria used to determine good performance. Then the game becomes one of optimizing these variables to maximize performance. For example, Charlie first used to assign waiters to tables as they became free, but he realized he could improve waiter efficiency by assigning each waiter to a set of contiguous tables.

Similarly, compilers use coloring algorithms to do register assignment while minimizing register spills. A networking example of optimizing degrees of freedom is multibit trie IP lookup algorithms (Chapter 11). In this example, a degree of freedom that can be overlooked is that the number of bits used to index into a trie node can vary, depending on the path through the trie, as opposed to being fixed at each level. The number of bits used can also be optimized via dynamic programming (Chapter 11) to demand the smallest amount of memory for a given speed requirement.

P14: USE SPECIAL TECHNIQUES FOR FINITE UNIVERSES SUCH AS INTEGERS

When dealing with small universes, such as moderately sized integers, techniques like bucket sorting, array lookup, and bitmaps are often more efficient than general-purpose sorting and searching algorithms.

To translate a virtual address into a physical address, a processor first tries a cache called the TLB. If this fails, the processor must look up the page table. A prefix of the address bits is used to index into the page table directly. The use of table lookup avoids the use of hash tables or binary search, but it requires large page table sizes. A networking example of this technique is timing wheels (Chapter 7), where an efficient algorithm for a fixed timer range is constructed using a circular array.

P15: USE ALGORITHMIC TECHNIQUES TO CREATE EFFICIENT DATA STRUCTURES

Even where there are major bottlenecks, such as virtual address translation, systems designers finesse the need for clever algorithms by passing hints, using caches, and performing table lookup. Thus a major system designer is reported to have told an eager theoretician: "I don't use algorithms, son."

This book *does not* take this somewhat anti-intellectual position. Instead it contends that, in context, efficient algorithms can greatly improve system performance. In fact, a fair portion of the book will be spent describing such examples. However, there is a solid kernel of truth to the "I don't use algorithms" putdown. In many cases, Principles **P1** through **P14** need to be applied before any algorithmic issues become bottlenecks.

Algorithmic approaches include the use of standard data structures as well as generic algorithmic *techniques*, such as divide-and-conquer and randomization. The algorithm designer must, however, be prepared to see his clever algorithm become obsolete because of changes in system structure and technology. As described in the introduction, the real breakthroughs may arise from applying algorithmic *thinking* as opposed to merely reusing existing algorithms.

Examples of the successful use of algorithms in computer systems are the Lempel–Ziv compression algorithm employed in the UNIX utility *gzip*, the Rabin–Miller primality test algorithm found in public key systems, and the common use of B-trees (due to Bayer–McCreight) in databases [CLR90]. Networking examples studied in this text include the Lulea IP-lookup algorithm (Chapter 11) and the RFC scheme for packet classification (Chapter 12).

3.4 DESIGN VERSUS IMPLEMENTATION PRINCIPLES

Now that we have listed the principles used in this book, three clarifications are needed. First, conscious use of general principles does not eliminate creativity and effort but instead channels them more efficiently. Second, the list of principles is necessarily incomplete and can probably be categorized in a different way; however, it is a good place to start.

Third, it is important to clarify the difference between system *design* and *implementation* principles. Systems designers have articulated principles for system *design*. Design principles include, for example, the use of hierarchies and aggregation for scaling (e.g., IP prefixes), adding a level of indirection for increased flexibility (e.g., mapping from domain names to IP addresses allows DNS servers to balance load between instances of a server), and virtualization of resources for increased user productivity (e.g., virtual memory).[5]

A nice compilation of design principles can be found in Lampson's article [Lam89] and Keshav's book [Kes97]. Besides design principles, both Lampson and Keshav include a few

---

[5]The previous chapter briefly explains these terms (IP prefixes, DNS, and virtual memory).

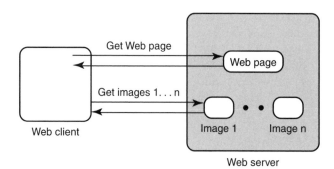

FIGURE 3.9   Retrieval of a Web page with images typically requires one request to get the page that specifies the needed images and more requests to retrieve each specified image. Why not have the Web server download the images directly?

implementation principles (e.g., "use hints" and "optimize the expected case"). This book, by contrast, assumes that much of the network design is already given, and so we focus on principles for efficient protocol *implementation*. This book also adds several principles for efficient implementation not found in Keshav [Kes91] or Lampson [Lam89].

On the other hand, Bentley's book on "efficient program design" [Ben82] is more about optimizing small code segments than the large systems that are our focus; thus many of Bentley's principles (e.g., fuse loops, unroll loops, reorder tests) are meant to speed up critical loops rather than speed up systems as a whole.

3.5 CAVEATS

Performance problems cannot be solved only through the use of Zen meditation.

— Paraphrased from Jeff Mogul, a computer scientist at HP Labs

The best of principles must be balanced with wisdom to understand the important metrics, with profiling to determine bottlenecks, and with experimental measurements to confirm that the changes are really improvements. We start with two case studies to illustrate the need for caution.

Case Study 1: Reducing Page Download Times

Figure 3.9 shows that in order for a Web client to retrieve a Web page containing images, it must typically send a GET request for the page. If the page specifies inline images, then the client must send separate requests to retrieve the images before it can display the page. A natural application of principle **P1** is to ask why separate requests are needed. Why can't the Web server automatically download the images when the page is requested instead of waiting for a separate request? This should reduce page download latency by at least half a round-trip delay.

To test our hypothesis, we modified the server software to do so and measured the resulting performance. To our surprise, we found only minimal latency improvement.

Using a network analyzer based on tcpdump, we found two reasons why this seeming improvement was a bad idea.

- **Interaction with TCP:** Web transfer is orchestrated by TCP as described in Chapter 2. To avoid network congestion, TCP increases its rate slowly, starting with one packet per round-trip, then to two packets per round-trip delay, increasing its rate when it gets acks. Since TCP had to wait for acks anyway to increase its rate, waiting for additional requests for images did not add latency.

- **Interaction with Client Caching:** Many clients already cache common images, such as .gif files. It is a waste of bandwidth to have the Web server unilaterally download images that the client already has in its cache. Note that having the client request the images avoids this problem because the client will only request images it does not already have.

A useful lesson from this case study is the difficulty of improving part of a system (e.g., image downloading) because of interactions with other parts of the system (e.g., TCP congestion control.)

Case Study 2: Speeding Up Signature-Based Intrusion Detection

As a second example, many network sites field an intrusion detection system, such as Snort [Sno], that looks for suspicious strings in packet payloads that are characteristic of hacker attacks. An example is the string "perl.exe", which may signify an attempt to execute perl and then to execute arbitrary commands on a Web server. For every potentially matching rule that contains a string, Snort searches for each such string separately using the Boyer–Moore algorithm [CLR90]. The worst case happens to be a Web packet that matches 310 rules. Simple profiling using gprof reveals [FV01] that 30% of the overhead in Snort arises from string searching.

An obvious application of **P1** seemed to be the following: Instead of separate searches for each string, use an integrated search algorithm that searches for all possible strings in a single pass over the packet. We modified Boyer–Moore to a set Boyer–Moore algorithm that could search for all specified strings in one pass. Implemented in a library, the new algorithm performed better than the Snort algorithm by a factor of 50 for the full Snort database. Unfortunately, when we integrated it into Snort, we found almost no improvement on packet traces [FV01]. We found two reasons for this.

- **Multiple string matching is not a bottleneck for the trace:** For the given trace, very few packets matched multiple rules, each of which contained separate strings. When we used a trace containing only Web traffic (i.e., traffic with destination port 80), a substantial improvement was found.

- **Cache Effects:** Integrated string searching requires a data structure, such as a trie, whose size grows with the number of strings being searched. The simplest way to do integrated set searching is to place the strings contained in all rules in a single trie. However, when the number of strings went over 100, the trie did not fit in cache, and performance suffered. Thus the system had to be reimplemented to use collections of smaller sets that took into account the hardware (**P4**).

A useful lesson from this case study is that purported improvements may not really target the bottleneck (which in the trace appears to be single-string matching) and can also interact with other parts of the system (the data cache).

3.5.1 Eight Cautionary Questions

In the spirit of the two case studies, here are eight cautionary questions that warn against injudicious use of the principles.

Q1: IS IT WORTH IMPROVING PERFORMANCE?

If one were to sell the system as a product, is performance a major selling strength? People interested in performance improvement would like to think so, but other aspects of a system, such as ease of use, functionality, and robustness, may be more important. For example, a user of a network management product cares more about features than performance. Thus, given limited resources and implementation complexity, we may choose to defer optimizations until needed. Even if performance is important, which performance metric (e.g., latency throughput, memory) is important?

Other things being equal, simplicity is best. Simple systems are easier to understand, debug, and maintain. On the other hand, the definition of simplicity changes with technology and time. Some amount of complexity is worthwhile for large performance gains. For example, years ago image compression algorithms such as MPEG were considered too complex to implement in software or hardware. However, with increasing chip densities, many MPEG chips have come to market.

Q2: IS THIS REALLY A BOTTLENECK?

The 80–20 rule suggests that a large percentage of the performance improvements comes from optimizing a small fraction of the system. A simple way to start is to identify key bottlenecks for the performance metrics we wish to optimize. One way to do so is to use profiling tools, as we did in Case Study 2.

Q3: WHAT IMPACT DOES THE CHANGE HAVE ON THE REST OF THE SYSTEM?

A simple change may speed up a portion of the system but may have complex and unforeseen effects on the rest of the system. This is illustrated by Case Study 1. A change that improves performance but has too many interactions should be reconsidered.

Q4: DOES THE INITIAL ANALYSIS INDICATE SIGNIFICANT IMPROVEMENT?

Before doing a complete implementation, a quick analysis can indicate how much gain is possible. Standard complexity analysis is useful. However, when nanoseconds are at stake, constant factors are important. For software and hardware, because memory accesses are a bottleneck, a reasonable first-pass estimate is the number of memory accesses.

For example, suppose analysis indicates that address lookup in a router is a bottleneck (e.g., because there are fast switches to make data transfer not a bottleneck). Suppose the standard algorithm takes an average of 15 memory accesses while a new algorithm indicates a worst case of 3 memory accesses. This suggests a factor of 5 improvement, which makes it interesting to proceed further.

Q5: IS IT WORTH ADDING CUSTOM HARDWARE?

With the continued improvement in the price–performance of general-purpose processors, it is tempting to implement algorithms in software and ride the price–performance curve. Thus if we are considering a piece of custom hardware that takes a year to design, and the resulting price–performance improvement is only a factor of 2, it may not be worth the effort. On the other hand, hardware design times are shrinking with the advent of effective synthesis tools. Volume manufacturing can also result in extremely small costs (compared to general-purpose processors) for a custom-designed chip. Having an edge for even a small period such as a year in a competitive market is attractive. This has led companies to increasingly place networking functions in silicon.

Q6: CAN PROTOCOL CHANGES BE AVOIDED?

Through the years there have been several proposals denouncing particular protocols as being inefficient and proposing alternative protocols designed for performance. For example, in the 1980s, the transport protocol TCP was considered "slow" and a protocol called XTP [Che89] was explicitly designed to be implemented in hardware. This stimulated research into making TCP fast, which culminated in Van Jacobson's fast implementation of TCP [CJRS89] in the standard BSD release. More recently, proposals for protocol changes (e.g., tag and flow switching) to finesse the need for IP lookups have stimulated research into fast IP lookups.

Q7: DO PROTOTYPES CONFIRM THE INITIAL PROMISE?

Once we have successfully answered all the preceding questions, it is still a good idea to build a prototype or simulation and actually test to see if the improvement is real. This is because we are dealing with complex systems; the initial analysis rarely captures all effects encountered in practice. For example, understanding that the Web-image-dumping idea does not improve latency (see Case Study 1) might come only after a real implementation and tests with a network analyzer.

A major problem is finding a standard set of benchmarks to compare the standard and new implementations. For example, in the general systems world, despite some disagreement, there are standard benchmarks for floating point performance (e.g., Whetstone) or database performance (e.g., debit–credit). If one claims to reduce Web transfer latencies using differential encoding, what set of Web pages provides a reasonable benchmark to prove this contention? If one claims to have an IP lookup scheme with small storage, which benchmark databases can be used to support this assertion?

Q8: WILL PERFORMANCE GAINS BE LOST IF THE ENVIRONMENT CHANGES?

Sadly, the job is not quite over even if a prototype implementation is built and a benchmark shows that performance improvements are close to initial projections. The difficulty is that the improvement may be specific to the particular platform used (which can change) and may take advantage of properties of a certain benchmark (which may not reflect all environments in which the system will be used). The improvements may still be worthwhile, but some form of sensitivity analysis is still useful for the future.

For example, Van Jacobson performed a major optimization of the BSD networking code that allowed ordinary workstations to saturate 100-Mbps FDDI rings. The optimization, which we will study in detail in Chapter 9, assumes that in the normal case the next packet is from the same connection as the previous packet, P, and has sequence number one higher than P. Will this assumption hold for servers that have thousands of simultaneous connections to clients? Will it hold if packets get sent over parallel links in the network, resulting in packet reordering? Fortunately, the code has worked well in practice for a number of years. Despite this, such questions alert us to possible future dangers.

3.6 SUMMARY

This chapter introduced a set of principles for efficient system implementation. A summary can be found in Figures 3.1, 3.2, and 3.3. The principles were illustrated with examples drawn from compilers, architecture, databases, algorithms, and networks to show broad applicability to computer systems. Chef Charlie's examples, while somewhat tongue in cheek, show that these principles also extend to general systems, from restaurants to state governments. While the broad focus is on performance, cost is an equally important metric. One can cast problems in the form of finding the fastest solution for a given cost. Optimization of other metrics, such as bandwidth, storage, and computation, can be subsumed under the cost metric.

A preview of well-known networking applications of the 15 principles can be found in Figures 3.1, 3.2, and 3.3. These applications will be explained in detail in later chapters. The first five principles encourage systems thinking. The next five principles encourage a fresh look at system modularity. The last five principles point to useful ways to speed up individual subsystems.

Just as chess strategies are boring until one plays a game of chess, implementation principles are lifeless without concrete examples. The reader is encouraged to try the following exercises, which provide more examples drawn from computer systems. The principles will be applied to networks in the rest of the book. In particular, the next chapter seeks to engage the reader by providing a set of 15 self-contained networking problems to play with.

3.7 EXERCISES

1. **Batching, Disk Locality, and Logs:** Most serious databases use log files for performance. Because writes to disk are expensive, it is cheaper to update only a memory image of a record. However, because a crash can occur any time, the update must also be recorded on disk. This can be done by directly updating the record location on disk, but random writes to disk are expensive (see **P4a**). Instead, information on the update is written to a sequential log file. The log entry contains the record location, the old value (undo information), and the new value (redo information).

   • Suppose a disk page of 4000 bytes can be written using one disk I/0 and that a log record is 50 bytes. If we apply batching (**2c**), what is a reasonable strategy for updating the log? What fraction of a disk I/O should be charged to a log update?

- Before a transaction that does the update can commit (i.e., tell the user it is done), it must be sure the log is written. Why? Explain why this leads to another form of batching, *group commit*, where multiple transactions are committed together.

- If the database represented by the log gets too far ahead of the database represented on disk, crash recovery can take too long. Describe a strategy to bound crash recovery times.

2. **Relaxing Consistency Requirements in a Name Service:** The Grapevine system [Be82] offers a combination of a name service (to translate user names to inboxes) and a mail service. To improve availability, Grapevine name servers are replicated. Thus any update to a registration record (e.g., Joe $\rightarrow$ MailSlot3) must be performed on all servers implementing replicas of that record. Standard database techniques for distributed databases require that each update be atomic; that is, the effect should be as if updates were done simultaneously on all replicas. Because atomic updates require that all servers be available, and registration information is not as important as, say, bank accounts, Grapevine provides only the following loose semantics (**P3**): All replicas will *eventually* agree if updates stop. Each update is timestamped and passed from one replica to the other in arbitrary order. The highest timestamped update wins.

   - Give an example of how a user could detect inconsistency in Joe's registration during the convergence process.

   - If Joe's record is deleted, it should eventually be purged from the database to save storage. Suppose a server purges Joe's record immediately after receiving a Delete update. Why might Add updates possibly cause a problem? Suggest a solution.

   - The rule that the latest timestamp wins does not work well when two administrators try to create an entry with the same name. Because a later creation could be trapped in a crashed server, the administrator of the earlier creation can never know for sure that his creation has won. The Grapevine designers did not introduce mechanisms to solve this problem but relied on "some human-level centralization of name creation." Explain their assumption clearly.

3. **Replacing General-Purpose Routines with Special-Purpose Routines and Efficient Storage Allocators:** Consider the design of a general storage allocator that is given control of a large contiguous piece of memory and may be asked by applications for smaller, variable-size chunks. A general allocator is quite complex: As time goes by, the available memory fragments and time must be spent finding a piece of the requested size and coalescing adjacent released pieces into larger free blocks.

   - Briefly sketch the design of a general-purpose allocator. Consult a textbook such as Horwitz and Sahni [HS78] for example allocators.

   - Suppose a profile has shown that a large fraction of the applications ask for 64 bytes of storage. Describe a more efficient allocator that works for the special case (**P6**) of allocating just 64-byte quantities.

   - How would you optimize the expected case (**P11**) and yet handle requests for storage other than 64 bytes?

4. **Passing Information in Interfaces**: Consider a file system that is reading or writing files from disk. Each random disk Read/Write involves positioning the disk over the correct track (seeking). If we have a sequence of say three Reads to Tracks 1, 15, and 7, it may pay to reorder the second and third Reads to reduce waste in terms of seek times. Clearly, as in **P1**, the larger the context of the optimization (e.g., the number of Reads or Writes considered for reordering), the greater the potential benefits of such *seek optimization*.

   A normal file system only has an interface to open, read, and write a single file. However, suppose an application is reading multiple files and can pass that information (**P9**) in the file system call.

   • What information about the pattern of file accesses would be useful for the file system to perform seek optimization? What should the interface look like?

   • Give examples of applications that process multiple files and could benefit from this optimization. For more details, see the paper by H. Patterson et al. [Pe95]. They call this form of tip a *disclosure*.

5. **Optimizing the Expected Case, Using Algorithmic Ideas, and Scavenging Files:** The Alto computer used a scavenging system [Lam89] that scans the disk after a crash to reconstruct file system indexes that map from file names and blocks to disk sectors. This can be done because each disk sector that contains a file block also contains the corresponding file identifier. What complicates matters is that main memory is not large enough to hold information for every disk sector. Thus a single scan that builds a list in memory for each file will not work. Assume that the information for a single file will fit into memory. Thus a way that will work is to make a single scan of the disk for each file; but that would be obvious waste (**P1**) and too slow.

   Instead, observe that in the expected case, most files are allocated contiguously. Thus suppose File X has pages 1–1000 located on disk sectors 301–1301. Thus the information about 1000 sectors can be compactly represented by three integers and a file name. Call this a run node.

   • Assume the expected case holds and that all run nodes can fit in memory. Assume also that the file index for each file is an array (stored on disk) that maps from file block number to disk sector number. Show how to rebuild all the file indexes.

   • Now suppose the expected case does not hold and that the run nodes *do not* all fit into memory. Describe a technique, based on the algorithmic idea of divide-and-conquer (**P15**), that is guaranteed to work (without reverting to the naive idea of building the index for one file at a time unless strictly necessary).

CHAPTER 4

Principles in Action

System architecture and design, like any art, can only be learned by doing. ...The space of possibilities unfolds only as the medium is worked.

— CARVER MEAD AND LYNN CONWAY

Having rounded up my horses, I now set myself to put them through their paces.

— ARNOLD TOYNBEE

The previous chapter outlined 15 principles for efficient network protocol implementation. Part II of the book begins a detailed look at specific network bottlenecks such as data copying and control transfer. While the principles are used in these later chapters, the focus of these later chapters is on the specific bottleneck being examined. Given that network algorithmics is as much a way of thinking as it is a set of techniques, it seems useful to round out Part I by seeing the principles in action on small, self-contained, but nontrivial network problems.

Thus this chapter provides examples of applying the principles in solving specific networking problems. The examples are drawn from real problems, and some of the solutions are used in real products. Unlike subsequent chapters, this chapter is not a collection of new material followed by a set of exercises. Instead, this chapter can be thought of as an extended set of exercises.

In Section 4.1 to Section 4.15, 15 problems are motivated and described. Each problem is followed by a hint that suggests specific principles, which is then followed by a solution sketch. There are also a few exercises after each solution. In classes and seminars on the topic of this chapter, the audience enjoyed inventing solutions by themselves (after a few hints were provided), rather than directly seeing the final solutions.

Quick Reference Guide

In an ideal world, each problem should have something interesting for every reader. For those readers pressed for time, however, here is some guidance. Hardware designers looking to sample a few problems may wish to try their hand at designing an Ethernet monitor (Section 4.4) or doing a binary search on long identifiers (Section 4.14). Systems people looking for examples of how systems thinking can finesse algorithmic expertise may wish to tackle a problem on application device channels (Section 4.1) or a problem on compressing the connection table (Section 4.11). Algorithm designers may be interested in the problem of identifying a resource hog (Section 4.10) and a problem on the use of protocol design changes to simplify an implementation problem in link state routing (Section 4.8).

4.1 BUFFER VALIDATION OF APPLICATION DEVICE CHANNELS

Usually, application programs can only send network data through the operating system kernel, and only the kernel is allowed to talk to the network adaptor. This restriction prevents different applications from (maliciously or accidentally) writing or reading each other's data. However, communication through the kernel adds overhead in the form of system calls (see Chapter 2). In application device channels (ADCs), the idea is to allow an application to send data to and from the network by *directly* writing to the memory of the network adaptor. Refer to Chapter 5 for more details. One mechanism to ensure protection, in lieu of kernel mediation, is to have the kernel set up the adaptor with a set of valid memory pages for each application. The network adaptor must then ensure that the application's data can only be sent and received from memory in the valid set.

In Figure 4.1, for example, application P is allowed to send and receive data from a set of valid pages $X, Y, \ldots, L, A$. Suppose application P queues a request to the adaptor to receive the next packet for P into a buffer in page A. Since this request is sent directly to the adaptor, the kernel cannot check that this is a valid buffer for P. Instead, the adaptor must validate this request by ensuring that A is in the set of valid pages. If the adaptor does not perform this check, application P could supply an invalid page belonging to some other application, and the adaptor would write P's data into the wrong page. The need for a check leads to the following problem.

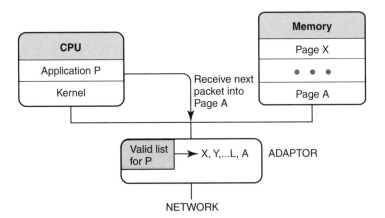

FIGURE 4.1 In application device channels, the network adaptor is given a set of valid pages (X, Y, L, A, etc.) for a given application P. When application P makes a request to receive data into page A, the adaptor must check if A is in the valid list before allowing the receive.

When application *P* does a Receive, the adaptor must validate whether the page belongs to the valid page set for *P*. If the set of pages is organized as a linear list [DDP94], then validation can cost $O(n)$, where *n* is the number of pages in the set. For instance, in Figure 4.1, since *A* is at the end of the list of valid pages, the adaptor must traverse the entire list before it finds *A*. If *n* is large, this can be expensive and can slow down the rate at which the adaptor can send and receive packets. How can the validation process be sped up? Try thinking through the solution before reading the hint and solutions that follow.

Hint: A good approach to reduce the complexity of validation is to use a better data structure than a list (**P15**). Which data structure would you choose? However, one can improve worst-case behavior even further and get smaller constant factors by using system thinking and by passing hints in interfaces (**P9**).

An algorithmic thinker will immediately consider implementing the set of valid pages as a *hash table* instead of a *list*. This provides an $O(1)$ average search time. Hashing has two disadvantages: (1) good hash functions that have small collision probabilities are expensive computationally; (2) hashing does not provide a good worst-case bound. Binary search does provide logarithmic worst-case search times, but this is expensive (it also requires keeping the set sorted) if the set of pages is large and packet transmission rates are high. Instead, we replace the hash table lookup by an indexed array lookup, as follows (try using **P9** before you read on).

The adaptor stores the set of valid pages for each application in an array, as shown in Figure 4.2. This array is updated only when the kernel updates the set of valid pages for the application. When the application does a Receive into page *A*, it also passes to the adaptor a handle (**P9**). The handle is the index of the array position where *A* is stored. The adaptor can use this to quickly confirm whether the page in the Receive request matches the page stored in the handle. The cost of validation is a bounds check (to see if the handle is a valid index), one array lookup, and one compare.

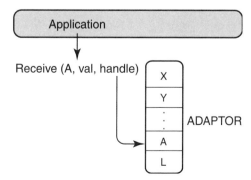

FIGURE 4.2 Finessing the need for a hash table lookup by passing a handle across the interface between the application and adaptor.

- Is the handle a hint or a tip? Let's invoke principle **P1**: If this is a handle, why pass the page number (e.g., *A*) in the interface? Why does removing the page number speed up the confirmation task slightly?

- To find the array corresponding to application *P* normally requires a hash table search using *P* as the key. This weakens the argument for getting rid of the hash table search to check if the page is valid — unless, of course, the hash search of *P* can be finessed as well. How can this be done?

4.2 SCHEDULER FOR ASYNCHRONOUS TRANSFER MODE FLOW CONTROL

In asynchronous transfer mode (ATM), an ATM adaptor may have hundreds of simultaneous virtual circuits (VCs) that can send data (called cells). Each VC is often flow controlled in some way to limit the rate at which it can send. For example, in rate-based flow control, a VC may receive credits to send cells at fixed time intervals. On the other hand, in credit-based flow control [KCB94, OSV94], credits may be sent by the next node in the path when buffers free up.

Thus, in Figure 4.3 the adaptor has a table that holds the VC state. There are four VCs that have been set up (1, 3, 5, 7). Of these, only VCs 1, 5, and 7 have any cells to send. Finally, only VCs 1 and 7 have credits to send cells. Thus the next cell to be sent by the adaptor should be from either one of the eligible VCs: 1 or 7. The selection from the eligible VCs should be done fairly, for example, in round-robin fashion. If the adaptor chooses to send a cell from VC 7, the adaptor would decrement the credits of VC 7 to 1. Since there are no more cells to be sent, VC 7 now becomes ineligible. Choosing the next eligible VC leads to the following problem.

PROBLEM

A naive scheduler may cycle through the VC array looking for a VC that is eligible. If many of the VCs are ineligible, this can be quite inefficient, for the scheduler may have to

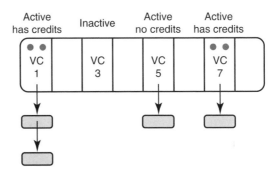

FIGURE 4.3   An ATM virtual circuit is eligible to send data if it is active (has some outstanding cells to send in the queue shown below the VC) and has credits (shown by black dots above the VC). The problem is to select the next eligible VC in some fair manner without stepping through VCs that are ineligible.

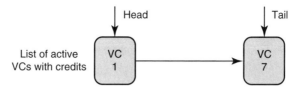

FIGURE 4.4 Maintaining a list of eligible VCs to speed up the scheduler main loop.

step through several VCs that are ineligible to send one cell from an eligible VC. How can this inefficiency be avoided?

Hint: Consider invoking **P12** to add some extra state to speed up the scheduler main loop. What state can you add to avoid stepping through ineligible VCs? How would you maintain this state efficiently?

SOLUTION

Maintain a list (Figure 4.4) of eligible VCs in addition to the VC table of Figure 4.3. The only problem is to efficiently *maintain* this state. This is the major difficulty in using **P12**. If the state is too expensive to maintain, the added state is a liability and not an asset. Recall that a VC is eligible if it has both cells to send and has credits. Thus a VC is removed from the list after service if VC becomes inactive or has no more credits; if not, the VC is added to the tail of the list to ensure fairness. A VC is added to the tail of the list either when a cell arrives to an empty VC cell queue or when the VC has no credits and receives a credit update.

EXERCISES ─────────────────────────────

• How can you be sure that a VC is not added multiple times to the eligible list?

• Can this scheme be generalized to allow some VCs to get more opportunities to send than other VCs based on a weight assigned by a manager?

4.3 ROUTE COMPUTATION USING DIJKSTRA'S ALGORITHM

How does a router S decide how to route a packet to a given destination D? Every link in a network is labeled with a cost, and routers like S often compute the shortest (i.e., lowest-cost) paths to destinations within a local domain. Assume the cost is a small integer. Recall from Chapter 2 that the most commonly used routing protocol within a domain is OSPF based on link state routing.

In link state routing, every router in a subnet sends a link state packet (LSP) that lists its links to all of its neighbors. Each LSP is sent to every other router in the subnet. Each router sends its LSP to other routers using a primitive flooding protocol [Per92]. Once every router receives an LSP from every router, then every router has a complete map of the network. Assuming the topology remains stable, each router can now calculate its shortest path to every other node in the network using a standard shortest-path algorithm, such as Dijkstra's algorithm [CLR90].

In Figure 4.5, source S wishes to calculate a shortest-path tree to all other nodes (A, B, C, D) in the network. The network is shown on the left frame in Figure 4.5 with links numbered with their cost. In Dijkstra's algorithm, S begins by placing only itself in the shortest-cost tree.

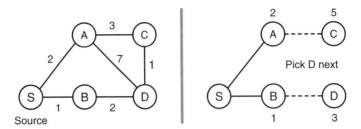

FIGURE 4.5   In Dijkstra's algorithm, the source *S* builds a shortest-path tree rooted at *S*. At each stage, the closest node not in the tree is added to the tree.

S also updates the cost to reach all its direct neighbors (e.g., *B*, *A*). At each iteration, Dijkstra's algorithm adds to the current tree the node that is closest to the current tree. The costs of the neighbors of this newly added node are updated. The process repeats until all nodes in the network belong to the tree.

For instance, in Figure 4.5, after adding *S*, the algorithm picks *B* and then picks *A*. At this iteration, the tree is as shown on the right in Figure 4.5. The solid lines show the existing tree, and the dotted lines show the best current connections to nodes that are not already in the tree. Thus since *A* has a cost of 2 and there is a link of cost 3 from *A* to *C*, *C* is labeled with 5. Similarly, *D* is labeled with a cost of 2 for the path through *B*. At the next iteration, the algorithm picks *D* as the least-cost node not already in the tree. The cost to *C* is then updated using the route through *D*. Finally, *C* is added to the tree in the last iteration.

This textbook solution requires determining the node with the shortest cost that is not already in the tree at each iteration. The standard data structure to keep track of the minimum-value element in a dynamically changing set is a priority queue. This leads to the following problem.

PROBLEM

Dijkstra's algorithm requires a priority queue at each of *N* iterations, where *N* is the number of network nodes. The best general-purpose priority queues, such as heaps [CLR90], take $O(\log N)$ cost to find the minimum element. This implies a total running time of $O(N \log N)$ time. For a large network, this can result in slow response to failures and other network topology changes. How can route computation be speeded up?

Hint: Consider exploiting the fact that the link costs are small integers **(P14)** by using an array to represent the current costs of nodes. How can you efficiently, at least in an amortized sense, find the next minimum-cost node to include in the shortest-path tree?

SOLUTION

The fact that the link costs are small integers can be exploited to construct a priority queue based on bucket sorting **(P14)**. Assume that the largest link cost is *MaxLinkCost*. Thus the maximum cost of a path can be no more than *Diam* ∗ *MaxLinkCost*, where *Diam* is the diameter of the network. Assume *Diam* is also a small integer. Thus one could imagine using an array with a location for every possible cost *c* in the range $1 \ldots Diam * MaxLinkCost$. If during the course of Dijkstra's algorithm the current cost of a node *X* is *c*, then node *X* can be placed in a list pointed to by element *c* of the array (Figure 4.6). This leads to the following algorithm.

FIGURE 4.6 Using a priority queue based on bucket sorting to speed up Dijkstra's algorithm.

Whenever a node X changes its cost from c to c', node X is removed from the list for c and added to the list for c'. But how is the minimum element to be found? This can be done by initializing a pointer called *CurrentMin* to 0 (which corresponds to the cost of S). Each time the algorithm wishes to find the minimum-cost node not in the tree, *CurrentMin* is incremented by 1 until an array location is reached that contains a nonempty list. Any node in this list can then be added to the tree. The algorithm costs $O(N + Diam * MaxLinkCost)$ because the work done in advancing *CurrentMin* can at most be the size of the array. This can be significantly better than $N \log N$ for large N and small values of *Diam* and *MaxLinkCost*.

A crucial factor in being able to efficiently use a bucket sort priority queue of the kind described earlier is that the node costs are always ahead of the value of *CurrentMin*. This is a monotonicity condition. If it were not true, the algorithm would start checking for the minimum from 1 at each iteration, instead of starting from the last value of *CurrentMin* and never backing up. The monotonicity condition is fairly obvious for Dijktra's algorithm because the costs of nodes not already in the tree have to be larger than the costs of nodes that are already in the tree.

Figure 4.6 shows the state of the bucket sort priority queue after A has been added to the tree. This corresponds to the right frame of Figure 4.5. At this stage, *CurrentMin* = 2, which is the cost of A. At the next iteration, *CurrentMin* will advance to 3, and D will be added to the tree. This will result in the C's cost being reduced to 4. We thus remove C from the list in position 5 and add it to the empty list in position 4. *CurrentMin* is then advanced to 4, and C is added to the tree.

Exercises

- The algorithm requires a node to be removed from a list and added to another, earlier list. How can this be done efficiently?

- In Figure 4.6, how can the algorithm know that it can terminate after adding C to the tree instead of advancing to the end of the long array?

- In networks that have failures, the concept of diameter is a highly suspect one because the diameter could change considerably after a failure. Consider a wheel topology where all N nodes have diameter 2 through a central spoke node; if the central spoke node fails, the diameter goes up to $N/2$. In actual practice the diameter is often small. Can this cause problems in sizing the array?

• Can you circumvent the problem of the diameter completely by replacing the linear array of Figure 4.6 with a circular array of size *MaxLinkCost*? Explain. The resulting solution is known as Dial's algorithm [AMO93].

4.4 ETHERNET MONITOR USING BRIDGE HARDWARE

Alyssa P. Hacker is working for Acme Networks and knows of the Ethernet bridge invented at Acme. A bridge (see Chapter 10) is a device that can connect together Ethernets. To forward packets from one Ethernet to another, the bridge must look up the 48-bit destination address in an Ethernet packet at high speeds.

Alyssa decides to convert the bridge into an Ethernet traffic monitor that will passively listen to an Ethernet and produce statistics about traffic patterns. The marketing person tells her that she needs to monitor traffic between arbitrary source–destination pairs. Thus for every active source–destination pair, such as A, B, Alyssa must keep a variable $P_{A,B}$ that measures the number of packets sent from A to B since the monitor was started. When a packet is sent from A to B, the monitor (which is listening to all packets sent on the cable) will pick up a copy of the packet. If the source is A and the destination is B, the monitor should increment $P_{A,B}$. The problem is to do this in 64 μsec, the minimum interpacket time on the Ethernet. The bottleneck is the lookup of the state $P_{A,B}$ associated with a pair of 48-bit addresses A, B.

Fortunately, the bridge hardware has a spiffy lookup hardware engine that can look up the state associated with a *single* 48-bit address in 1.4 μsec. A call to the hardware can be expressed as *Lookup*(X, D), where X is the 48-bit key and D is the database to be searched. The call returns the state associated with X in 1.4 μsec for databases of less than 64,000 keys. What Alyssa must solve is the following problem.

PROBLEM

The monitor needs to update state for AB when a packet from A to B arrives. The monitor has a lookup engine that can look up only *single* addresses and not address *pairs*. How can Alyssa use the existing engine to look up address pairs? The problem is illustrated in Figure 4.7.

Hint: The problem requires using **P4c** to exploit the existing bridge hardware. Since 1.4 μsec is much smaller than 64 μsec, the design can afford to use more than one hardware lookup. How can a 96-bit lookup be reduced to a 48-bit lookup using three lookups?

A naive solution is to use two lookups to convert source A and destination B into smaller ($<$24-bit) indices I_A and I_B. The indices I_A and I_B can then be used to look up a two-dimensional array that

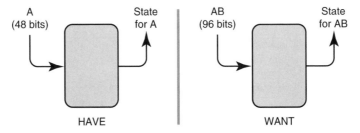

FIGURE 4.7 Adapting an engine that does destination lookup to doing destination-source lookups.

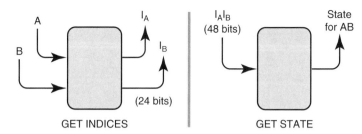

FIGURE 4.8 Converting a 96-bit lookup into a 48-bit lookup by first converting each 48-bit address into a 24-bit index and concatenating the indices.

stores the state for AB. This requires only two hardware lookups plus one more memory access, but it can require large amounts of memory. If there are 1000 possible sources and 1000 possible destinations, the array must contain a million entries. In practice, there may be only 20,000 active source–destination pairs. How could you make the required amount of memory proportional to the number of actual source–destination pairs?

SOLUTION

As before, first use one lookup each to convert source A and destination B into smaller ($<$24-bit) indices I_A and I_B. Then use a third lookup to map from $I_A I_B$ to AB state. The solution is illustrated in Figure 4.8. The third lookup effectively compresses the two-dimensional array of the naive solution. This solution is due to Mark Kempf and Mike Soha.

EXERCISES _____

- Can this problem be solved using only two bridge hardware lookups without requiring extra memory?

- The set of active source–destination pairs may change with time, because some pairs of addresses stop communicating for long periods. How can this be handled without keeping the state for every possible address pair that has communicated since the monitor was powered on?

4.5 DEMULTIPLEXING IN THE X-KERNEL

The x-kernel [HP91] provides a software infrastructure for protocol implementation in hosts. The x-kernel system provides support for a number of required protocol functions. One commonly required function is protocol *demultiplexing*. For example, when the Internet routing layer IP receives a packet, it must use the protocol field to determine whether the packet should be subsequently sent to TCP or UDP.

Most protocols do demultiplexing based on some identifier in the protocol header. These identifiers can vary in length in different protocols. For example, Ethernet-type fields can be 5 bytes while TCP port numbers are 2 bytes long. Thus the x-kernel allows demultiplexing based on variable-length protocol identifiers. When the system is initialized, the protocol routine can register the mapping between the identifier and the destination protocol with the x-kernel.

FIGURE 4.9 Demultiplexing in the x-kernel is done by hashing the protocol identifier K and (potentially) using a byte-by-byte comparison with the key L stored at the hash table entry.

At run time, when a packet arrives the protocol routine can extract the protocol identifier from the packet and query the x-kernel demultiplexing routine for the destination protocol. Since packets can arrive at high speeds, the demultiplexing routine should be fast. This leads to the following problem.

PROBLEM

On average, the fastest way to do a lookup is to use a hash table. As shown in Figure 4.9, this requires computing some hash function on the identifier K to generate a hash index, using this index to access the hash table, and comparing the key L stored in the hash table entry with K. If there is a match, the demultiplexing routine can retrieve the destination protocol associated with key L. Assume that the hash function has been chosen to make collisions infrequent.

However, since the identifier length is an arbitrary number of bytes, the comparison routine that compares the two keys must, in general, do byte-by-byte comparisons. However, suppose the most common case is 4-byte identifiers, which is the machine word size. In this case, it is much more efficient to do a word comparison. Thus the goal is to exploit efficient word comparisons (**P4c**) to optimize the expected case (**P11**). How can this be done while still handling arbitrary protocols?

Hint: Notice that if the x-kernel has to demultiplex a 3-byte identifier, it has to use a byte-by-byte comparison routine; if the x-kernel has to demultiplex a 4-byte identifier and 4 bytes is the machine word size, it can use a word compare. The first degree of freedom that can be exploited is to have different comparison routines for the most common cases (e.g., word compares, long-word compares) and a default comparison routine that uses byte comparisons. Doing so trades some extra space for time (**P4b**). For correctness, however, it is important to know which comparison routine to use for each protocol. Consider invoking principles **P9** to pass hints in interfaces and **P2a** to do some precomputation.

SOLUTION

Each protocol has to declare its identifier and destination protocol to the x-kernel when the system initializes. When this happens, each protocol can predeclare its identifier length, so the x-kernel can use a specialized comparison routines for each protocol. Effectively, information is being passed between the client protocol and the x-kernel (**P9**) at an earlier time (**P2a**). Assume that the x-kernel has a separate hash table for each client protocol and that the x-kernel knows the context for each client in order to use code specialized for that client.

- Code up byte-by-byte and word comparisons on your machine and do a large number of both types of comparisons and compare the overall time taken for each.

- In the earlier ADC solution, the hash table lookup was finessed by passing an index (instead of the identifier length as earlier). Why might that solution be difficult in this case?

4.6 TRIES WITH NODE COMPRESSION

A *trie* is a data structure that is a tree of nodes, where each node is an array of M elements. Figure 4.10 shows a simple example with $M = 8$. Each array can hold either a key (e.g., KEY 1, KEY 2, or KEY 3 in Figure 4.11) or a pointer to another trie node (e.g., the first element in the topmost trie node of Figure 4.10, which is the root). The trie is used to search for exact matches (and longest-prefix matches) with an input string. Tries are useful in networking for such varied tasks as IP address lookup (Chapter 11), bridge lookups (Chapter 10), and demultiplexing filters (Chapter 8).

The exact trie algorithms do not concern us here. All one needs to know is how a trie is searched. Let $c = \log_2 M$ be the chunk size of a trie. To search the trie, search first breaks the input string into chunks of size c. Search uses successive chunks, starting from the most significant, to index into nodes of the trie, starting with the root node. When search uses chunk j to index into position i of the current trie node, position i could contain either a pointer or a key. If position i contains a nonnull pointer to node N, the search continues at node N with chunk $j + 1$; otherwise, the search terminates.

To summarize, each node is an array of pointers or keys, and the search process needs to index into these arrays. However, if many trie nodes are sparse, there is considerable wasted space (**P1**). For example, in Figure 4.10, only 4 out of 16 locations contain useful information. In the worst case, each trie node could contain 1 pointer or key and there could be a factor of M in wasted memory. Assume $M \leq 32$ in what follows. Even if M is this small, a 32-fold increase in memory can greatly increase the cost of the design.

An obvious approach is to replace each trie node by a linear list of pairs of the form (i, val), where *val* is the nonempty value (either pointer or key) in position i of the node. For example,

Trie Node (space not used by pointers is wasted)

Key 1

Key 2   Key 3

FIGURE 4.10 Trie storing three keys. Notice the wasted space in the trie nodes.

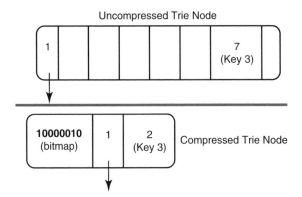

FIGURE 4.11 Compressing a trie node using a bitmap and bit counting to efficiently translate from an uncompressed index to a compressed index.

the root trie node in Figure 4.10 could be replaced by the list $(1, ptr); (7, KEY1)$, where $ptr1$ is the pointer to the bottom trie node. Unfortunately, this can slow down trie search by a factor of M, because the search of each trie node may now have to search through a list of M locations, instead of a single indexing operation. This leads to the following problem.

PROBLEM

How can trie nodes be compressed to remove null pointers without slowing down search by more than a small factor?

Hint: Despite compressing the nodes, array indexing needs to be efficient. If the nodes are compressed, how might information about which array elements are removed be represented? Consider leveraging off the fact that M is small by following **P14** (exploit the small integer size) and **P4a** (exploit locality).

SOLUTION

Since $M < 32$, a bitmap of size 32 can easily fit into a computer word (**P14** and **P4a**). Thus null pointers are removed after adding a bitmap with zero bits indicating the original positions of null pointers. This is shown in Figure 4.11. The trie node can now be replaced with a bitmap and a compressed trie node. A compressed trie node is an array that consists only of the nonnull values in the original node. Thus in Figure 4.11, the original root trie node (on the top) has been replaced with the compressed trie node (on the bottom). The bitmap contains a 1 in the first and seventh positions, where the root node contains nonnull values. The compressed array now contains only two elements, the first pointer and KEY 3. This still begs the question: How should a trie node be searched?

Since both uncompressed and compressed nodes are arrays and the search process starts with an index I into the uncompressed node, the search process must consult the bitmap to convert the uncompressed index I into a compressed index C into the compressed node. For example, if I is 1 in Figure 4.11, C should be 1; if I is 7, C should be 2. If I is any other value, C should be 0, indicating that there is only a null pointer.

Fortunately, the conversion from I to C can be accomplished easily by noting the following. If position I in the bitmap contains a 0, then $C = 0$. Otherwise, C is the number of 1's in the first I bits of the bitmap. Thus if $I = 7$, then $C = 2$, since there are two bits set in the first seven bits of the bitmap.

This computation requires at most two memory references: one to access the bitmap (because the bitmap is small (**P4a**)) and one to access the compressed array. The calculation of the number of bits set in a bitmap can be done using internal registers (in software) or combinatorial logic (in hardware). Thus the effective slowdown is slightly more than a factor of 2 in software and exactly 2 in hardware.

EXERCISES

- How could you use table lookup (**P14, P2a**) to speed up counting the number of bits set in software? Would this necessarily require a third memory reference?

- Suppose the bitmap is large (say, $M = 64$ K). It would appear that counting the number of bits set in such a large bitmap is impossibly slow in hardware or software. Can you find a way to speed up counting bits in a large bitmap (principles **P12** and **P2a**) using only one extra memory access? This will be extremely useful in Chapter 11.

4.7 PACKET FILTERING IN ROUTERS

Chapter 12 describes protocols that set up resources at routers for traffic, such as video, that needs performance guarantees. Such protocols use the concept of packet filters, sometimes called *classifiers*. Thus, in Figure 4.12 each receiver attached to a router may specify a packet filter describing the packets it wishes to receive. For example, in Figure 4.12 Receiver 1 may be interested in receiving NBC, which is specified by Filter 4. Each filter is some specification of the fields that describe the video packets that NBC sends. For example, NBC may be specified by packets that use the source address of the NBC transmitter in Germany and use a specified TCP destination and source port number.

Similarly, in Figure 4.12 Receiver m may be interested in receiving ABC Sports and CNN, which are described by Filters 1 and 7, respectively. Packets arrive at the router at high speeds and must be sent to all receivers that request the packet. For example, Receivers 1 and 2 may both wish to receive NBC. This leads to the following problem.

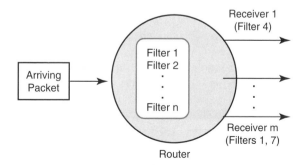

FIGURE 4.12 Packet filtering in a router may require a slow linear scan of all filters followed by making a copy of the packet for all filters that match.

PROBLEM

Each receiving packet must be matched against all filters and sent to all receivers that match. A simple linear scan of all filters is expensive if the number of filters is large. Assume the number of filters is over a thousand. How can this expensive process be sped up?

Hint: One might think of optimizing the expected case by caching (**P11a**). However, why is caching difficult in this case? Consider adding a field (**P10**) to the packet header to make caching easier. Ideally, which protocol layer should this be added to? Adding a fixed well-known field for each possible video type is not a panacea because it requires global standardization, and filters can be based on other fields, such as the source address. Assume the field you add does not require globally standardized identifiers. What properties of this field must the source ensure?

SOLUTION

Caching (**P11a**), the old workhorse of system designers, is not very straightforward in this problem. In general, a cache stores a mapping between an input a and some output $f(a)$. The cache then consists of a set of pairs of the form $(a, f(a))$. This set of pairs is stored as a database keyed by values of a. The database can be implemented as a hash table (in software) or a content-addressable memory (in hardware). Given input a and the need to calculate $f(a)$, the database is first checked to see if a is already in the database. If so, the fast path exits with the existing value of $f(a)$. If not, $f(a)$ is computed using some other (possibly expensive) computation and the pair $(a, f(a))$ is then inserted into the cache database. Subsequent inputs with value a can then be calculated very fast.

In the packet filtering problem, the goal is to calculate the set of receivers associated with a packet P. The problem is that the output is a function of a (potentially) large number of packet header fields of P. Thus to use caching, one has to store a large portion of the headers of P associated with the set of receivers for P. Storing a mapping between 64 bytes of packet header and an output set of receivers is an expensive proposition. It is expensive in time, since searching the cache can take longer because the keys are wide. It is also clearly expensive in storage. The large storage needs in turn imply that fewer mappings can be cached for a given cache size, which leads to a poorer cache hit rate.

The ideal is to cache a mapping between one or two packet fields and the output receiver set. This would speed up cache search time and improve the cache hit rate. These fields should also preferably be in the routing header, which routers examine anyway. The problem is that there may be no such field that uniquely fingerprints packet P.

However, suppose we are system designers designing the routing protocol. We can add a field to the routing header. The problem might seem trivial if we could assign each possible stream of packets a unique global identifier. For example, if we could assign NBC identifier 1, ABC identifier 2, and CNN identifier 3, then we could cache using the identifier as the key. Such a solution would require some form of global standards committee responsible for naming every application stream. Even if that could be done, the receiver filter might ask for all NBC packets from a given source, and the filter could depend on other packet fields. This leads to the following final idea.

Change the routing header to add a flow identifier F (Figure 4.13), whose meaning depends on the source. In other words, different sources can use the same flow identifier because it is the combination of the source and the flow identifier that is unique. Thus there is no need for global standardization (or other global coordination) of flow identifiers. A flow identifier is only a local counter maintained by the source. The idea is that a sending application at the

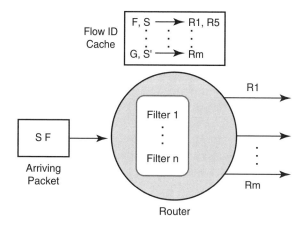

FIGURE 4.13 Adding a flow identifier (which is unique only with respect to a source) can speed up packet filtering.

sender can ask the routing layer for a flow identifier. This identifier is added to the routing header of all the packets for this application.

As usual, when the application packet first arrives, the router does a (slow) linear search to determine the set of receivers associated with the packet header. Because identifiers are not unique across sources, the router caches the mapping using the concatenation of the packet source address *and* the flow identifier as the key. Clearly, correctness depends on the sender application's not changing fields that could affect a filter without also changing the flow identifier in the packet.

EXERCISES

- What can go wrong if the source crashes and comes up again without remembering which identifiers it has assigned to different applications? What can go wrong when a receiver adds a new filter? How can these problems be solved?

- In the current solution, the flow identifier is used as a tip (Chapter 3) and not as a hint. What additional costs would be incurred if the flow identifier-source address pair is treated as a hint and not as a tip?

4.8 AVOIDING FRAGMENTATION OF LINK STATE PACKETS

The following problem actually arose during the design of the OSI and OSPF [Per92] link state routing protocols. This problem is about protocol design, as opposed to protocol implementation once the design is fixed. Despite this, it illustrates how design choices can greatly affect implementation performance.

Chapter 2 and Section 4.3 described link state routing. Recall that in link state routing, a router must send a link state packet (LSP) listing all its neighbors. The link state protocol consists of two separate processes. The first is the update process that sends link state packets reliably from router to router using a flooding protocol that relies on a unique sequence number

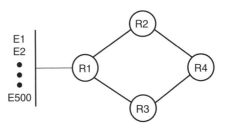

FIGURE 4.14 The link state packet of router $R1$ (with even 500 endnode neighbors) may be too large to fit into a data link frame. Without a clever idea, this would require inefficient fragmentation and reassembly of the router at every hop.

per link state packet. The sequence number is used to reject duplicate copies of an LSP. Whenever a router receives a new LSP numbered x from source S, the router will remember number x and will reject any subsequent LSPs received from S with sequence number x. After the update process does its work, the decision process at every router applies Dijkstra's algorithm to the network map formed by the link state packets.

While a router may have a small number of router neighbors, a router may have a large number of host computers (endnodes) that are connected directly to the router on the same LAN. For example, in Figure 4.14, router $R1$ has 500 endnode neighbors $E1 \ldots E500$. Large LANs may even have a larger number of endnodes. This leads to the following problem.

PROBLEM

At 8 bytes per endnode (6 bytes to identify the endnode and 2 bytes of cost information), the LSP can be very large (40,000 bytes for 5000 endnodes). This is much too huge for the link state packet to fit into a maximum-size frame on many commonly used data links. For example, Ethernet has a maximum size of 1500 bytes and FDDI specifies a maximum of 4500 bytes. This implies that the large LSP must be fragmented into many data link frames on each hop and reassembled at each router before it can be sent onward. This requires an expensive reassembly process at each hop to determine whether all the pieces of a LSP have been received.

It also increases the latency of link state propagation. Suppose that each LSP can fit in M data link frames, that the diameter of the network is D, and that the time to send a data link frame over a link is 1 time unit. Then with hop-by-hop reassembly, the propagation time of an LSP can be $D \cdot M$. If a router did not have to wait to reassemble each LSP at each hop, the propagation delay would be only $M + D$. When the link state protocol was being designed, these problems were discovered by implementors reviewing the initial specification.

On the other hand, it seems impossible to propagate the fragments independently because the LSP carries a single sequence number that is crucial to the update process. Simply copying the sequence number into each fragment will not help, because that will cause the later fragments to be rejected, since they have the same sequence number as the first fragment. The problem is to make the impossible possible by shifting computation around in space to avoid the need for hop-by-hop fragmentation. Changes to the LSP routing protocol are allowed.

Hint: Does the information about all 5000 endnodes have to be in the same LSP? Consider invoking **P3c** to shift computation in space.

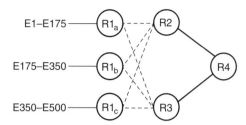

FIGURE 4.15 Avoiding hop-by-hop fragmentation by dividing a large router into pseudo-routers.

SOLUTION

If the individual fragments of the original LSP of $R1$ are to be propagated independently without hop-by-hop reassembly, then each fragment must be a separate LSP by itself, with a separate sequence number. This crucial observation leads to the following elegant idea.

Modify the link state routing protocol to allow any router $R1$ to be multiple pseudo-routers $R1_a, R1_b, R1_c$ (see Figure 4.15). The original set of endnodes are divided among these pseudo-routers, so the LSP of each pseudo-router can fit into most data link frames *without* the need for fragmentation. For example, if most data link sizes are at least 576 bytes, roughly 72 endnodes can fit within a data link frame.

How is this concept of a pseudo-router actually realized? In the original LSP propagation, each router had a 6-byte ID that is placed in all LSPs sent by the router. To allow for pseudo-routers, we change the protocol to have LSPs carry a 7-byte ID (6-byte router ID + 1-byte pseudo-router ID). The pseudo-router ID can be assigned by the actual router that houses all the pseudo-routers. By allowing 256 pseudo-routers per router, roughly 18,000 endnodes can be supported per router.

While the LSP propagation treats pseudo-routers separately, it is crucial that route computation treat the separate pseudo-routers as one router. After all, the endnodes are all directly connected to $R1$ in our example. But this is easily done, because all the LSPs with the same first 6 bytes can be recognized as being from the same router.

In summary, the main idea is to shift computation in space (**P3c**) by having the source fragment the original LSP into independent LSPs instead of having each data link do the fragmentation. This is a good example of systems thinking. Needless to say, the implementors liked this solution (invented by Radia Perlman) much better than the original approach.

EXERCISES

- How can a router assign endnodes to pseudo-routers? What happens if a router initially has a lot of endnodes (and hence a lot of pseudo-routers) and then most of the endnodes die? This can leave a lot of pseudo-routers, each of which has only a few endnodes. Why is this bad, and how can it be fixed?

- As in the relaxed-consistency examples described in Chapter 3, this solution can lead to some unexpected (but not very serious) temporary inconsistencies. Assuming a solution to the previous exercise, describe a scenario in which a given router, say, $R2$, can find (at some instant) that its LSP database shows the same endnode (say, E1) belonging to two pseudo-routers, $R1_a$ and $R1_c$. Why is this no worse than ordinary LSP routing?

4.9 POLICING TRAFFIC PATTERNS

Some network protocols require that sources never send data faster than a certain rate. Instead of merely specifying the average rate over long periods of time, the protocol may also specify the maximum amount of traffic, B, in bits a source can send in any period of T seconds. This does limit the source to an average rate of B/T bits per second. However, it also limits the "burstiness" of the users' traffic to at most one burst of size B every T units of time. For example, choosing a small value of the parameter T limits the traffic burstiness considerably. Burstiness causes problems for networks because periods of high traffic and packet loss are followed by idle periods.

If every source meets its contract (i.e., sends no more than the specified amount in the specified period), the network can often guarantee performance and ensure that no traffic is dropped and that all traffic is delivered in timely fashion. Unfortunately, this is like saying that if everyone follows the rules of the road, traffic will flow smoothly. Most people do follow the rules: some because they feel it is the right thing to do, and many because they are aware of penalties that they have to pay when caught by traffic police. Thus policing is an important part of an ordered society.

For the same reason, many designers advocate that the network should periodically police traffic to look for offenders that do not meet their contracts. Without policing, the offenders can get an unfair share of network bandwidth.

Assume that a traffic flow is identified by the source and destination address and the traffic type. Thus each router needs to ensure that a particular traffic flow sends no more than B bits in any period of T seconds. The simplest solution is for the router to use a single timer that ticks every T seconds and to count the number of bits sent in each period using a counter per flow. At the end of each period, if the counter exceeds B, the router has detected a violation.

Unfortunately, the single timer can police only some periods. For example, assume without loss of generality that the timer starts at time 0. Then the only periods checked are the periods $[0, T], [T, 2T], [2T, 3T], \ldots$. This *does not* ensure that the source flow does not violate its contract in a period like $[T/2, 3T/2]$, which overlaps the periods that are policed. For example, in the left side of Figure 4.16, the flow sends a burst of size B just before the timer ticks at time T and sends a second burst of size B just after the timer ticks at time T.

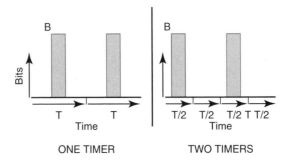

FIGURE 4.16 The naive use of a single or multiple timers (to check whether a flow sends no more than B every T seconds) does not catch all violations.

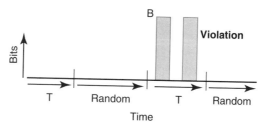

FIGURE 4.17 Picking a random gap of T seconds between policing intervals allows the router to catch a violating flow with high probability.

One attempt to fix this problem is for the router to use multiple timers and counters. For example, as shown on the right of Figure 4.16, the router could use one timer that starts at 0 and a second timer that starts at time $T/2$. Unfortunately, the flow can still violate its contract by sending no more than B in each policed period but sending more than B in some overlapping period.

For instance, in the right frame of Figure 4.16 an offending flow sends a first burst of B at the end of the first period and a second burst of B at the start of the third period, sending $2B$ within a period slightly greater than $T/2$. Unfortunately, neither of the timers will detect the flow as being a violator. This leads to the following problem.

PROBLEM

Multiple timers are expensive and do not guarantee that the flow will not violate its traffic contract. It is easy to see that with even a single timer, the flow can send no more than $2B$ in any period of T seconds. One approach is simply to assume that a factor-of-2 violation is not worth the effort to police. However, suppose that bandwidth is precious on a transcontinental link and that a factor-of-2 violation is serious. How could a violating flow still be caught using only a single timer?

Hint: Consider exploiting a degree of freedom (**P13**) that has been assumed to be fixed in the naive solution. Do the policing intervals have to start at fixed intervals? Also consider using **P3a**.

SOLUTION

As suggested in the hints, the policing intervals need not be fixed. Thus, there can be an arbitrary gap between policing intervals. How should the gap be picked? Since a violating flow can pick its violating period of T to start at any instant, a simple idea is to invoke **P3a** to yield the following idea (Figure 4.17).

The router uses a single timer of T units and a single counter, as before. A policing interval ends with a timer tick; if the counter is greater than B, a violation is detected. Then a flag is set indicating that the timer is now used only for inserting a random gap. Then the timer is restarted for a random time interval between 0 and T. When the timer ticks, the flag is cleared and the counter is initialized, and the timer is reset for a period of T to start policing again.

EXERCISES _____

• Suppose the counter is initialized and maintained during the gap period as well as during policing periods. Can the router make any valid inference during such a period, even if the gap period is less than T units?

FIGURE 4.18   Finding the source that is a resource hog.

- (Open Problem): Suppose the flow is adversarial. What is a good strategy for the flow to consistently violate the contract by as high a margin as possible and still elude the randomized detector described earlier? The flow strategy can be randomized as well. A good answer should be supported by a probabilistic analysis.

4.10 IDENTIFYING A RESOURCE HOG

Suppose a device wishes to keep track of resources, like the packet memory allocated to various sources in a router. The device wants a cheap way to find the source consuming the most memory so that the device can grab memory back from such a resource hog. Figure 4.18 shows five sources with their present resource consumption of 1, 9, 30, 24, and 7 units, respectively. The resource hog is S3.

A simple solution to identify the resource hog is to use a heap. However, if the number of sources is a thousand or more, this may be too expensive at high speeds. Assume that the numbers that describe resource usage are integers in the range from 1 to 8000. Thus bucket sort techniques won't work well because we may have to search 8000 entries to find the resource hog.

Suppose, instead, that the device does not care about the exact maximum as long as the result comes within a factor of 2 (perfect fairness is unimportant as in **P3b**). For example, in the figure, assume it is fine to get an answer of 24 instead of 30. This leads to the following problem.

PROBLEM

A software or hardware module needs to keep track of resources required by various users. The module needs a cheap way to find the user consuming the most resources. Since ordinary heaps are too slow, the device designers are willing to relax the system requirements (**P3b**) to be off by a factor of 2. Can this relaxation in accuracy requirements be translated into a more efficient algorithm?

Hint: Consider using three principles: trading accuracy for computation (**P3b**), using bucket sorting (**P14**), and using table lookups (**P4b, P2a**).

SOLUTION

Since the answer can be off by a factor of 2, it makes sense to aggregate users whose resources are within a factor of 2 into the same "resource usage group." This can be a win if the resulting number of groups is much smaller than the original number of users; finding the largest group then will be faster than finding the largest user. This is roughly the same idea behind aggregation in hierarchical routing, where a number of destinations are aggregated

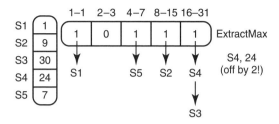

FIGURE 4.19 Aggregating users with resource consumption within a factor of 2 leads to a small number of aggregates whose membership can be represented using a bitmap.

behind a common prefix; this can make routing less accurate but reduces the number of routing entries. This leads to the following idea (try to work out the details before you read further).

Binomial bucketing can be used, as shown in Figure 4.19, where all users are grouped into buckets according to resource consumption, where bucket i contains all users whose resource consumption lies between 2^i and $2^{i+1} - 1$. In Figure 4.19, for instance, users S3 and S4 are both in the range $[16, 31]$ and hence are in the same bucket.

Each bucket contains an unsorted list of the resource records of all the users that fall within that bucket range. Thus in Figure 4.19, S3 and S4 are in the same list. The data structure also contains a bitmap, with one bit for every bucket, that is set if the corresponding bucket list is nonempty (Figure 4.19). Thus in Figure 4.19, the bits corresponding to buckets [1,1], [4,7], [8,15], and [16,31] are set, while the bit corresponding to [2,3] is clear.

Thus to find the resource hog, the algorithm simply looks for the bit position i corresponding to the rightmost bit set in the bitmap. The algorithm then returns the user at the head of the bucket list corresponding to position i. Thus in Figure 4.19, the algorithm would return S4 instead of the more accurate S3.

EXERCISES _____

- How is this data structure maintained? What happens if the resources in a user (e.g., S3) are reduced from 30 to 16? What kind of lists are needed for efficient maintenance?

- How large is each bitmap? How can finding the rightmost bit set be done efficiently?

4.11 GETTING RID OF THE TCP OPEN CONNECTION LIST

A transport protocol such as TCP [Ste94] in computer X keeps state for every concurrent conversation that X has with other computers. Recall from Chapter 2 that the technical name for the shared state between the two endpoints of a conversation is a *connection*. Thus if a user wishes to send mail from X to another workstation, Y, the mail program in X must first establish a connection (shared state) to the mail program in Y. A busy server like a Web server may have lots of concurrent connections.

The state in a connection consists of things like the numbers of packets sent by X that have not been acknowledged by Y. Any packets that have not been acknowledged for a long time must be retransmitted by X. To do retransmission, transport protocols typically have a

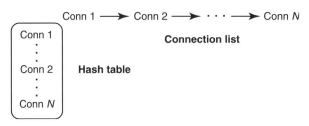

FIGURE 4.20 The x-kernel implementation uses a hash table mapping connections to state (for packet dispatching) as well as a linked list of connections (for timer processing). The redundant state causes dilution of the data cache.

periodic timer that triggers the retransmission of any packets whose acknowledgments have been outstanding for a while.

The freely available Berkeley (BSD) TCP code [Ste94] keeps a list of open connections (Figure 4.20) to examine on timer ticks in order to perform any needed retransmissions. However, when a packet arrives at X, TCP at X must also quickly determine which connection the packet belongs to in order to update the state for the connection. Each connection is identified by a connection identifier that is carried in every packet.

Relying on the list to determine the connection for a packet would require searching the entire list, in the worst case; this could be slow for servers with large numbers of connections. Thus the x-kernel implementation [HP91] added a hash table to the BSD implementation (**P15**) to efficiently map from connection identifiers in packets to the corresponding state for the connection. The hash table is an array of pointers indexed by hash value that points to lists of connections that hash to the same value. In addition, the original linked list of connections was retained for timer processing, while the hash table was supposed to speed up packet processing.

Oddly enough, measurements of the new implementation actually showed a slowdown! Careful measurements traced the problem to the fact that information about connections was stored redundantly, and this reduced the efficiency of the data cache when implemented on modern processors (see Chapter 2 for a model of a modern processor). This illustrates question **Q3** in Chapter 3, where an obvious improvement to one part of the system can affect other parts of the system. Note that while main memory may be cheap, fast memory such as the data cache is often limited. Commonly used structures such as the connection list should float into the data cache as long as they are small enough to fit.

The obvious solution is to avoid redundancy. The hash table is needed for fast lookups. The timer routine must also periodically and efficiently scan through all connections. This leads to the following problem.

PROBLEM

Can you get rid of the waste caused by the explicit connection list while retaining the hash table? It is reasonable to add a small amount of extra information to the hash table. When doing so, observe that the original connection list was made doubly linked to allow easy deletion when connections terminate. But this adds storage and dilutes the data cache. How can a singly linked list be used *without slowing down deletion*?

Hint: The first part is easy to fix by linking the valid hash table entries in a list. The second part (avoiding the doubly linked list, which would require two pointers per hash table entry) is a bit harder.

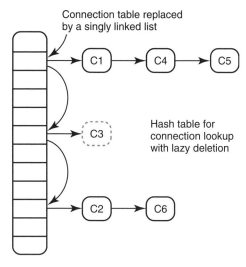

FIGURE 4.21 Linking the valid hash table entries using forward pointers and lazy deletion. The dashed lines imply connection records that have been marked as deleted but that will be processed only in the next iteration.

A connection list consists of nodes, each of which contains a connection ID (96 bits for IP) plus two pointers (say, 32 bits each) for easy deletion. Since the hash table is needed for fast demultiplexing, the connection list can be removed if the valid hash table entries are linked together as shown in Figure 4.21 and a pointer is kept to the head of the list. On a timer tick, the retransmit routine will periodically scan this list. Scanning the complete hash table is less efficient because the hash table may have many empty locations.

The naive solution would add two pointers to each valid hash table entry to implement a doubly linked list. Since these pointers can be hash table indexes instead of arbitrary pointers to memory, the indexes need not be larger than the size of the hash table: Even the largest hash table storing connections should require no more than 16 bits, often much less. The naive solution does well, adding at most 32 bits per entry instead of 160 bits per entry, a savings of 128 bits. However, it is possible to do better and to add only 16 bits per entry. Consider using lazy evaluation (**P2b**) and relaxing the specification (**P3**).

SOLUTION

A doubly linked list is useful only for efficient deletions. When a connection (say, Connection *C*3 in Figure 4.21) is terminated, the delete routine would ideally like to find the previous valid entry (i.e., the list containing Connection *C*1 in Figure 4.20) in order to link the previous list to the next list (i.e., the list containing *C*2). This would require each hash table entry to store a pointer to the previous valid entry in the list.

Instead, consider principle **P3**, which asks whether the system requirements can be relaxed. Normally, one assumes that when a connection terminates, its storage must be reclaimed immediately. To reclaim storage, the hash table entry should be placed in a free list, where it can be used by another connection. However, if the hash table is a little larger than strictly necessary, it is not essential that the storage used by a terminated connection be reused immediately.

Given this relaxation of requirements, the implementation can *lazily* delete the connection state. When a connection is terminated, the entry must be marked as unused. This requires an extra bit of state, as in **P12**, but is cheap. The actual deletion of unused hash table entry E involves linking the entry before E to the entry after E and also requires returning E to a free list. However, this deletion can be done on the next list traversal when the traversal encounters an unused entry.

EXERCISES ———————————————————————————————

- Write pseudocode for the addition of a new connection, the termination of a connection, and the timer-based traversal.

- How can we get away with singly linked lists for the lists of connections in each hash table list?

- Hugh Hopeful is always interested in clever tricks that he never thinks through completely. He suggests a way to avoid back pointers in any doubly linked list. Suppose a node X needs to be deleted. Normally, the deletion routine is passed a handle to retrieve X, which is typically a pointer to node X. Instead, Hugh suggests that the handle be a pointer to the node *before* X in the linked list (except when X is the head of the list when the handle is a null pointer). Hugh claims that this allows his implementation to efficiently locate both the node prior to X and the node after X using only forward pointers. Present a counter-example to stop Hugh before he writes some buggy code.

4.12 ACKNOWLEDGMENT WITHHOLDING

Transport protocols such as TCP ensure that data is delivered to the destination by requiring that the destination send an acknowledgment (ack) for every piece of received data. This is analogous to certified mail. Packets and acks are numbered. Acks are often cumulative; an ack for a packet numbered N implicitly acknowledges all packets with numbers less than or equal to N.

Cumulative acks allow the receiver the flexibility of not sending an ack for every received packet. Instead, acks can be batched (**P2c**). For example, in Figure 4.22 a file transfer program is sending file blocks, one in every packet. Blocks 1 and 2 are individually acknowledged, but blocks 3 and 4 are acknowledged with a single ack for block 4.

Reducing acks is a good thing for the sender and receiver. Although acks are small, they contain headers that must be processed by every router and the source and the destination. Further, each received packet, however small, can cause an interrupt at the destination computer, and interrupts are expensive. Thus ideally, a receiver should batch as many acks as possible. But what should the receiver batching policy be? This leads to the following problem.

PROBLEM

Ack withholding is difficult at a receiver that is not clairvoyant. In Figure 4.22, for example, if block 3 arrives first and is processed quickly, how long should the receiver wait for block 4 before sending the ack for block 3? If block 4 never arrives (because the sender has no more data to send), then withholding the ack for block 3 would cause incorrect behavior. The classical solution is to set an ack-withholding timer; when the timer expires, a cumulative ack is sent. This limits the time that an ack can be withheld.

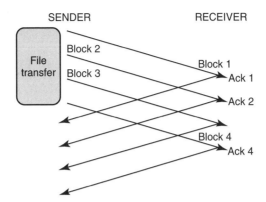

FIGURE 4.22 The use of cumulative acks allows the receiver to acknowledge several packets with one ack (e.g., Blocks 3 and 4) but introduces the problem of determining a good receiver ack policy.

However, the withholding timer also causes problems. Some applications are sensitive to latency. Adding an ack-withholding timer can increase latency in cases where the sender has no more data to send. If the transport protocol could be modified, what information could be added to avoid unnecessary latency and yet allow acks to be effectively batched?

Hint: In an application such as FTP, which software module "knows" that there is more data to be sent? For ack withholding, which software module would ideally like to know that there is more data to be sent? Now consider using **P9** and **P10**.

SOLUTION

In an application such as file transfer, the sender *application* knows that there is more data to be sent (e.g., there will be a block 4 after block 3). The sending application may also be willing to tolerate the latency due to batching of acks. However, it is the transport module at the receiver that needs to know this information. This observation leads to a simple proposal.

The sender application passes a bit to the sender transport (in the application–transport interface) that is set when the application has more data to send. Assume that the transport protocol can be modified to carry a withhold bit. The sending transport can use the information passed by the application to set a withhold bit w in every packet that it sends; w is cleared when the sender wants an immediate ack. The moral, of course, is that it is better for the sender to telegraph his intentions than for the receiver to make guesses about the future!

For example, in Figure 4.23 the sender transport is informed by the sending file transfer application that there are four blocks to be sent. Thus the sender transport sets the withhold bit on the first three packets and clears the bit in the fourth packet. The receiver acts on this information to send one ack instead of four. On the other hand, an application that is latency sensitive can choose not to pass any information about data to be sent. Note also that the withhold bit is a hint; the receiver can choose to ignore this information and send an ack anyway. Despite its apparent cleverness, this solution is a bad idea in today's TCP. See the exercises for details.

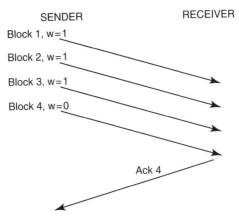

FIGURE 4.23 Telegraphing the sender's intentions using a withhold bit *w*.

EXERCISES

- Another technique for reducing acks is to piggyback acks on data flowing from the receiver to the sender. To support this, most transport protocols, such as TCP, have extra fields in data packets to convey reverse ack information. However, piggybacking has the same classical trade-off between latency and piggybacking efficiency. How long should the receiver transport wait for reverse data? On the other hand, there are common applications where the sender application knows this information. How could the solution outlined earlier be extended to support piggybacking as well as ack batching?

- Recall that Chapter 3 outlined a set of cautionary questions for evaluating purported improvements. For example, **Q3** asks whether a change can affect the rest of the system. Why might aggressive ack withholding interact with other aspects of the transport protocol, such as flow and congestion control [Ste94]?

4.13 INCREMENTALLY READING A LARGE DATABASE

Suppose a user continuously reads a large database stored on a Web site. The Web page can change and the reader only wants the incremental (**P12a**) updates since the last read of the database. Thus, in Figure 4.24 there is a database of highly popular food items that is being read constantly by readers around the world who wish to keep up with culinary fashion. Fortunately, food fashions change slowly.

Thus a reader that last read at 2 pm and reads again at 6 pm only wants the differences: Coke to Pepsi, and Wheaties to Cheerios. If, on the other hand, a different user reads at 3 pm and then at 6 pm, she, too, only wants the difference: Wheaties to Cheerios. This leads to the following problem.

PROBLEM

Find a way for the database to efficiently perform such incremental queries. One solution is to have the database remember what each user has previously read. However, it is unreasonable

FIGURE 4.24 A slowly changing database of food items shown at three different times: 2 pm, 3 pm, and 6 pm. Notice that only the soft drink has changed from 2 to 3 pm and that only the cereal has changed from 3 to 6 pm. Thus a reader who is constantly monitoring the database wishes to find only the differences from the last time the database was read.

for the database to remember what each user has previously read, since there may be millions of users. Find another solution that is less burdensome for the database program.

Hint: If the database does not store any information about the last Read performed by a user, then it follows that user Read requests must pass some information (**P10**) about the last Read request made by the same user. Passing the entire details of the last Read would be overkill and inefficient. What simple piece of information can succinctly characterize the user's last request? Now consider adding redundant state (**P12**) at the database that can easily be indexed using the information passed by the user to facilitate efficient incremental query processing.

Solution

As said earlier, user Read requests must pass some information (**P10**) about the last Read request made by the same user. The most succinct and relevant piece of information about the last user request is the *time* at which it was made. If user requests pass the time of the last Read, then the database needs to be organized to efficiently compute all updates after any given time. This can be done by storing copies of the database at all possible earlier times. This is clearly inefficient and can be avoided by storing only the incremental changes (**P12a**). This leads to the following algorithm.

Add an update history list to the database, with most recent updates closer to the head of the list. Read requests carry the time T of the last Read, so a Read request can be processed by scanning the update list from the head to find all updates after T.

For example, in Figure 4.25 the head of the update history list has the latest change (compare with Figure 4.24) at 6 pm from Wheaties to Cheerios and the next earliest change at 3 pm from Coke to Pepsi. Consider a Read request that has a last Read time of 5 pm. In this case, when scanning the list from the head, the request processing will find the 6 pm update and stop when it reaches the 3 pm update because $3 < 5$. Thus the Read request will return only the first update.

Exercises

- If a single entry changes multiple times, a single entry change can be stored redundantly in the list, which costs space and time. What principle can you use to avoid this redundancy?

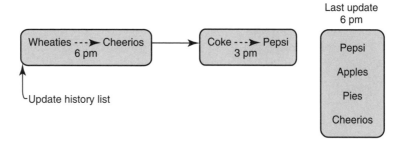

FIGURE 4.25   Solving the incremental-update problem using an update history list.

Assume the database is just a collection of records and that you want each record to appear at most once in the incremental list.

- If the number of records is large or the foregoing trick is not adopted, the incremental list size will grow very big. Suggest a sensible policy for periodically reducing the size of the incremental list.

4.14 BINARY SEARCH OF LONG IDENTIFIERS

The next-generation Internet (IPv6) plans to use larger, 128-bit addresses to accommodate more Internet endpoints. Suppose the goal is to look up 128-bit addresses. Assume the algorithm works on a machine whose natural word size is 32 bits. Then each comparison of two 128-bit numbers will take $128/32 = 4$ operations to compare each word individually. In general, suppose each identifier in the table is W words long. In our example, $W = 4$. Naive binary search will take $W \cdot \log N$ comparisons, which is expensive. Yet this seems obviously wasteful. If all the identifiers have the same first $W - 1$ words, then clearly $\log N$ comparisons are sufficient. The problem is to modify binary search to take $\log N + W$ comparisons. The strategy is to work in columns, starting with the most significant word and doing binary search in that column until equality is obtained in that column. At that point, the algorithm moves to the next word to the right and continues the binary search where it left off.

Thus in Figure 4.26, which has $W = 3$, consider a search for the three-word identifier *BMW*. Pretend each character is a word. Start by comparing in the leftmost column in the middle element, as shown by the arrow labeled 1.[1] Since the *B* in the search string matches the *B* at the arrow labeled 1, the search moves to the right (not shown) to compare the *M* in *BMW* with the *N* in the middle location of the second column. Since $N < M$, the search performs the second probe at the quarter position of the second column. This time the two *M*'s match and the search moves rightward and finds *W*, but (oops!) the search has found *AMW*, not *BMW* as desired. This leads to the following problem.

---

[1] Many implementors implement binary search to pick the 4th element from the top (i.e., the first *B*) as the middle and not the 5th element as we have done. Keep this somewhat unusual convention in mind while following the example.

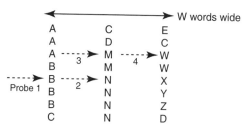

FIGURE 4.26 Binary search of long identifiers can result in a multiplicative factor of W, the number of words in an identifier. The naive method of reducing this to an additive factor by moving to the right on equality fails.

PROBLEM

Find some state that can be added to each element in each column that can fix this algorithm to work correctly in $\log N + W$ comparisons.

Hint: The problem is caused by the fact that when the search moved to the quarter position in column 2, it assumed that all elements in the quarter of the second column begin with B. This assumption is false in general. What state can be added to avoid making this false assumption, and how can the search be modified to use this state?

SOLUTION

The trick is to add state to each element in each column, which can constrain the binary search to stay within a guard range. This is shown in Figure 4.27. In the figure, for each word like B in the leftmost (most significant) column, add a pointer to the range of all other words that also contain B in this position. Thus the first probe of the binary search for BMW starts with the B in BNX. On equality, the search moves to the second column, as before. However, search also keeps track of the guard range corresponding to the B's in the first column. The figure shows that the guard range includes only rows 4 through 7. This guard range is stored with the first B compared (see arrows in Figure 4.27).

Thus when the search moves to column 2 and finds that M in BMW is less than the N in BNX, it attempts to halve the range as before and to try a second probe at the third entry (the M in AMT). However, the third entry is lower than the high point of the current guard range (4 through 6, assuming the first element is numbered 1). So without doing a compare, the search

FIGURE 4.27 Adding a guard range to every element in a column to allow binary search to work correctly when switching columns.

tries to halve the binary search range again. This time the search tries entry 4, which is in the guard range. The search finds equality, moves to the right, and finds *BMW*, as desired.

In general, every multiword entry $W_1, W_2, \ldots, W_n$ will store a precomputed guard range. The range for W_i points to the range of entries that have $W_1, W_2, \ldots, W_i$ in the first i words. This ensures that on a match with W_i in the ith column, the binary search in column $i + 1$ will search only in this guard range. For example, the N entry in *BNY* (second column) has a guard range of 5–7, because these entries all have *BN* in the first two words.

The resulting search strategy takes $\log_2 N + W$ probes if there are N identifiers. The cost is the addition of two 16-bit pointers to each word. Since most word sizes are at least 32 bits, this results in adding 32 bits of pointer space for each word, which can at most double memory usage. Besides adding state, a second dominant idea is to use precomputation (**P2a**) to trade a slower insertion time for a faster search. The idea is due to Butler Lampson.

EXERCISE _____

- (This is harder than the usual exercises.) The naive method of updating the binary search data structure requires rebuilding the entire structure (especially because of the precomputed ranges) when a new entry is added or deleted. However, the whole scheme can be elegantly represented by a binary search tree, with each node having the usual > and < pointers but also an = pointer, which corresponds to moving to the next column to the right, as shown earlier. The subtree corresponding to the = pointer naturally represents the guard range. The structure now looks like a trie of binary search trees. Use this observation and standard update techniques for balanced binary trees and tries to obtain logarithmic update times.

4.15 VIDEO CONFERENCING VIA ASYNCHRONOUS TRANSFER MODE

In asynchronous transfer mode (ATM), the network first sets up a virtual circuit through a series of switches before data can be sent. Standard ATM allows one-to-many virtual circuits, where a virtual circuit (VC) can connect a single source to multiple receivers. Any data sent by the source is replicated and sent to every receiver in the one-to-many virtual circuit.

Although it is not standardized, it is also easy to have many-to-many VCs, where every endpoint can be both a source and a receiver. The idea is that when any source sends data, the switches replicate the data to every receiver. Of course, the main problem in many-to-many VCs is that if two sources talk at the same time, then the data from the two sources can be arbitrarily interleaved at the receivers and cause confusion. This is possibly why many-to-many VCs are not supported by standards, though it is often easy for switch hardware to support many-to-many VCs.

Figure 4.28 shows a simple topology consisting of an ATM switch that connects N workstations. To showcase the bandwidth of the switch, the system designers have designed a videoconferencing application. The conferencing application can allow users at any of the N workstations to have a videoconference with each other. The application should bring up a screen (on every workstation in the conference) that displays at least the current speaker and also plays the speech of the current speaker. In addition, in the event of a conversation, it is desirable to see the expressions of the participants. The designers soon run into the following problem.

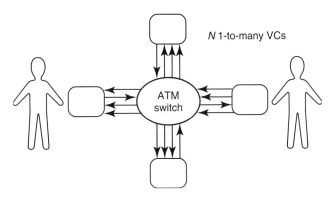

FIGURE 4.28 A videoconferencing system that uses an ATM switch with the ability to support many-to-many virtual circuits.

PROBLEM

The naivest solution would use up to N^2 point-to-point connections between every pair of participating workstations. A better solution is shown in Figure 4.28. It uses up to N many-to-many VCs between each participating workstation and the other workstations. The video and speech of each workstation is connected by a one-to-many virtual circuit to every other participating workstation. Thus every participating workstation gets the video output of all participants and the application can choose which one (or ones) to display. Unfortunately, the ATM switch requires that bandwidth on the switch be statically divided among the N one-to-many VCs. Given a minimum bandwidth for video quality of B_{min} and a total switch bandwidth of B, this limits the number of participating workstations to be less than B/B_{min}. Is there a more scalable solution?

Hint: Consider exploiting the switch hardware's ability to support many-to-many VCs (**P4c**). However, to prevent confusion, only one source should transmit at a time in any many-to-many VC. Instead of developing a complex protocol to ensure such a constraint, what hardware can be added (**P5**) to ensure this constraint?

SOLUTION

As suggested in the hint, the designers chose to exploit the many-to-many VC capability of the switch to replace N one-to-many VCs with a constant number of many-to-many VCs. This allowed the fixed switch bandwidth to scale to a large number of participants. However, this generic idea requires elaboration. How many many-to-many VCs should be used? How is the potential confusion caused by many-to-many VCs resolved? Here are the details of a solution worked out by Jon Turner at Washington University.

First, consider the use of a *single* many-to-many VC named C. A naive solution to the confusion problem entails a protocol (say, a round-robin protocol) that ensures that only one workstation at a time connects its video output to C. Such protocols require coordination, and the coordination adds latency and expense. Instead, as systems thinkers, the designers observed that, at a minimum, only the current speaker needs to be displayed.

Thus the designers added extra hardware (**P5**) in the form of a speech detector to the input at each workstation. If the detector detects significant speech activity at a workstation X, then

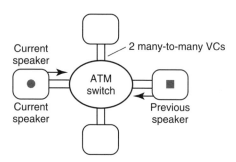

FIGURE 4.29 Replacing *N* one-to-many VCs with two many-to-many VCs through the use of a speech detector and a simple hardware state machine at each input.

the detector connects the video input of *X* to *C*; otherwise, the video input of *X* is not connected to *C*. Since this hardware was quite cheap, the extra scalability came at a reasonable price.

Next, the designers observed that keeping a video image of the last speaker provides visual continuity in the expected case when there is a dialog between two participants. Thus instead of one many-to-many VC, they used *two* many-to-many VCs, *C* and *L*, one for the current speaker and one for the last speaker, as shown in Figure 4.29.

EXERCISES

- Write pseudocode (using some state variables) for the hardware at each workstation to update its connections to *C* and *L*. Assume the speech detector output is a function.

- What happens if more than one user speaks at one time? What could you add to the hardware state machine so that the application displays something reasonable? For instance, it would be unreasonable for the images of the two speakers to be morphed together in this case.

PART II

Playing with Endnodes

The supreme accomplishment is to blur the line between work and play.

— ARNOLD TOYNBEE

The second part of the book deals with *endnode algorithmics*. This is the application of network algorithmics to building fast protocol implementations at endnodes, especially at servers. If you like, you can think of it as a systematic collection of techniques for building fast servers. The techniques are applied mostly in a software setting. Much of it has to do with getting around operating system structure to enable high-speed data transfers. We study how to reduce the overhead incurred by copying, control transfer, demultiplexing, timers, and other generic protocol-processing tasks.

CHAPTER 5

Copying Data

Copy from one, it's plagiarism; copy from two, it's research.

— WILSON MIZNER

Imagine an office where every letter received is first sent to shipping and receiving. Shipping and receiving opens the letter, figures out which department it's meant for, and makes a photocopy for their records. They then hand it to the security department, which pores over every line of the letter, looking for signs of industrial esponiage. To maintain an audit trail for possible later use, the security department also makes a photocopy of the letter, for good measure. Finally, the letter, somewhat the worse for wear, reaches the intended recipient in personnel.

You would probably think this a pretty ludicrous state of affairs, worthy to be featured in a Charlie Chaplin movie. But then you might be surprised to learn that most Web servers, and computers in general, routinely make a number of extra copies of received and sent messages. Unlike photocopies, which take up only a small amount of paper, power, and time, extra copying in a computer consumes two precious resources: memory bandwidth and memory itself. Ultimately, if there are k copies involved in processing a message in a Web server, the throughput of the Web server can be k times slower.

Thus this chapter will focus on removing the obvious waste (**P1**) involved in such unnecessary copies. A copy is unnecessary if it is not imposed by the hardware. For example, the hardware does require copying bits received by an adaptor to the computer memory. However, as we shall see, there is no essential reason (other than those imposed by conventional operating system structuring) for copying between application and operating system buffers. Eliminating redundant copies allows the software to come closer to realizing the potential of the hardware, one of the goals of network algorithmics.

This chapter will also briefly talk about other operations (such as checksumming and encryption) that touch all the data in the packet and other techniques to more closely align protocol software to hardware constraints, such as bus bandwidths and caches. While we will briefly repeat some of the relevant operating systems and architectural facts, it will help the reader to be familiar with endnode architecture and operating system models of Chapter 2. In summary, this chapter surveys techniques for reducing the costs of data manipulation without sacrificing modularity and without major changes to operating system design.

This chapter is organized as follows. Section 5.1 describes why and how extra data copies occur. Section 5.2 describes a series of techniques to avoid copies by local restructuring of the operating system and network code at an endnode. Section 5.3 shows how to avoid both copy and control overhead for large transfers, using remote DMA techniques that involve protocol changes.

Section 5.4 broadens the discussion to consider the file system in, say, a Web server, and it shows how to avoid wasteful copies between the file cache and the application. Section 5.5 broadens the discussion to consider other operations that touch all the data, such as check-summing and encryption, and introduces a well-known technique called *integrated layer processing.* Section 5.6 broadens the discussion beyond copying to show that without careful consideration of cache effects, instruction cache effects can swamp the effects of copying for small messages.

Although this is the first chapter of the book that is devoted to techniques for overcoming a specific bottleneck, the techniques are based on the principles described in Part I of the book. The techniques and the corresponding principles are summarized in Figure 5.1.

Quick Reference Guide

The most useful sections for an implementor today are as follows. Section 5.3.1 on remote direct memory access (RDMA) describes techniques to avoid memory copying overheads in computing and storage clusters. Section 5.4.2 describes a fairly radical way, called IO-lite (involving some operating system surgery), to improve the performance of a server by consistently passing buffers by reference, even between the file and networking systems. IO-lite builds on an idea called *fbufs* that is introduced in Section 5.2.3. Section 5.4.3 describes a less radical but effective method called *I/O splicing* to directly connect I/O subsystems. Finally, Section 5.6.1 describes techniques to improve I-cache performance.

Number	Principle	Used In
P13	Memory location (on adaptor) as degree of freedom	Afterburner
P2b	Lazy copying using copy-on-write	Mach
P11a P7	Cache VM mappings per path Uniform fbuf space across processes	Solaris fbufs
P10	Pass buffer name and offset in packet	RDMA systems
P4	VM mapping to avoid copies in cache and application	Flash
P11a	Cache VM mappings per path Buffer sequence numbers enable checksum caching	Flash-lite
P6	New system call that splices I/O	Sendfile()
P1	Avoid repeated memory access across manipulations	ILP
P13	Layout code to minimize i-cache misses	x-kernel
P13	Layer processing order as degree of freedom	LDRP

FIGURE 5.1   Techniques for copy avoidance and cache efficiency that are discussed in this chapter, together with the corresponding principles.

FIGURE 5.2 Redundant copies involved in handling a GET request at a server.

5.1 WHY DATA COPIES

In Figure A.1 in the Appendix, we describe how TCP works in the context of a Web server. Figure A.1 only shows the sending of the GET request for a file, followed by the file data itself in two TCP segments. What Figure A.1 does not show is how the Web server processes the GET request. In this chapter, we ignore the control transfer required to transfer the request to some application server process. Instead, Figure 5.2 shows the sequence of data transfers involved in reading file data from the disk (in the worst case) to the sending of the corresponding segments via the network adaptor.

The main hardware players in Figure 5.2 are the CPU, the memory bus, the I/O bus, the disk, and the network adaptor. The main software players are the Web server application and the kernel. There are two main kernel subsystems involved, the file system and the networking system. For simplicity, the picture shows only one CPU in the server (many servers are multiprocessors) and focuses only on requests for static content (many requests are for dynamic content that is served by a computer-generated imagery (CGI) process).[1]

Intuitively, the story is simple. The file is read from disk into the application buffer via, say, a *read()* system call. The combination of the HTTP response and the application buffer is then sent to the network over the TCP connection to the client by, say, a *write()* system call. The TCP code in the network subsystem of the kernel breaks up the response data into

---

[1] The picture makes it appear that the code for the file system and the TCP/IP code is on the processor. In reality, the code is also stored in memory and is fetched by the processor. However, the portion of the code that fits into the processor instruction cache indeed can be considered to be in the processor.

bite-size segments and transmits them to the network adaptor after adding a TCP checksum to each segment.

In practice, the story is often more messy in the details. First, the file is typically read into a piece of kernel memory, called the *file cache*, in what we call Copy 1. This is a good idea because subsequent requests to a popular file can be served from main memory without slow disk I/O. The file is then copied from the file cache into the Web server application buffer in Copy 2 shown in Figure 5.2. Since the application buffer and the file cache buffer are in different parts of main memory, this copy can only be done by the CPU's reading the data from the first memory location and writing into the second location across the memory bus.

The Web server then does a *write()* to the corresponding socket. Since the application can freely reuse its buffer (or even deallocate it) at any time after the *write()*, the network subsystem in the kernel cannot simply transmit out of the application buffer. In particular, the TCP software may need to retransmit part of the file after an unpredictable amount of time, by which time the application may wish to use the buffer for other purposes.

Thus UNIX (and many other operating systems) provides what is known as *copy* semantics. The application buffer specified in the *write()* call is copied to a socket buffer (another buffer within the kernel, at a different address in memory than either the file cache or the application buffer). This is called Copy 3 in Figure 5.2. Finally, each segment is sent out to the network (after IP and link headers have been pasted) by copying the data from the socket buffer to memory within the network adaptor. This is called Copy 4.

In between, before transmission to the network, the TCP software in the kernel must make a pass over the data to compute the TCP checksum. Techniques for efficiently implementing the TCP checksum are described in Chapter 9, but for now it suffices to think of the TCP checksum as essentially computing the sum of 16-bit words in each TCP segment's data.

Each of the four copies and the checksum consume resources. All four copies and the checksum calculation consume bandwidth on the memory bus. The copies between memory locations (Copies 2 and 3) are actually worse than the others because they require one Read and one Write across the bus for every word of memory transferred. The TCP checksum requires only one Read for every word and a single Write to append the final checksum. Finally, Copies 1 and 4 can be as expensive as Copies 2 and 3 if the CPU does the heavy lifting for the copy (so-called programmed I/O); however, if the devices themselves do the copy (so-called DMA), the cost is only a single Read or Write per word across the bus.

The copies also consume I/O bus bandwidth and ultimately memory bandwidth itself. A memory that supplies a word of size W bits every x nanoseconds has a fundamental limit on throughput of W/x bits per nanosecond. For example, even assuming DMA, these copies ensure that the memory bus is used seven times for each word in the file sent out by the server. Thus the Web server throughput cannot exceed $T/7$, where T is the smaller of the speed of the memory and the memory bus.

Second, and more basically, the extra copies consume *memory*. The same file (Figure 5.2) could be stored in the file cache, the application buffer, and the socket buffer. While memory seems to be cheap and plentiful (especially when buying a PC!), it does have some limits, and Web servers would like to use as much as possible for the file cache to avoid slow disk I/O. Thus triply replicating a file can reduce the file cache by a factor of 3, which in turn can dramatically reduce the cache hit rate and, hence, overall server performance.

In summary, redundant copies hurt performance in two fundamental and orthogonal ways. First, by using more bus and memory bandwidth than strictly necessary, the Web server runs slower than bus speeds, even when serving documents that are in memory. Second, by using more memory than it should, the Web server will have to read an unduly large fraction of files from disk instead of from the file cache.

Note also that we have only described the scenario in which static content is served. In reality the SPECweb benchmarks assume that 30% of the requests are for dynamic content. Dynamic content is often served by a separate CGI process (other than the server application) that communicates this content to the server via some interprocess communication mechanism, such as a UNIX pipe, which often involves another copy.

Ideally, all these pesky extra bus traversals should be removed. Clearly, Copy 1 is not required if the data is in cache and so we can ignore it (if it's not in cache, the server runs at disk speed, which is too slow anyway). Copy 2 seems unnecessary. Why can't the data be sent directly from the file cache memory location to the network? Similarly, Copy 3 seems unnecessary. Copy 4 is unavoidable.

5.2 REDUCING COPYING VIA LOCAL RESTRUCTURING

Before tackling the full complexity of eliminating all redundant copies in Figure 5.2, this section starts by concentrating on Copy 3, the fundamental copy made from the application to kernel buffers (or vice versa) when a network message is sent (received). This is a fundamental issue for networking, independent of file system issues. It also turns out that general solutions that eliminate all redundant I/O copies (Section 5.4) build on the techniques developed in this section.

This section assumes that the protocol is fixed but the local implementation (at least the kernel) can be restructured. The goal, of course, is to perform minimal restructuring in order to continue to leverage the vast amount of investment in existing kernel and application software. Section 5.2.1 describes techniques based on exploiting adaptor memory. Section 5.2.2 describes the core idea behind copy avoidance (by remapping shared physical pages) and its pitfalls. Section 5.2.3 shows how to optimize page remapping using precomputation and caching based on I/O streams; however, this technique involves changing the application programming interface (API). Finally, Section 5.2.4 describes another technique, one that uses virtual memory but does not change the API.

5.2.1 Exploiting Adaptor Memory

The simple idea here is to exploit a degree of freedom (**P13**) by realizing that memory can be located *anywhere* on the bus in a memory-mapped architecture. Recall from Chapter 2 that memory mapping means that the CPU talks to all devices, such as the adaptor and the disk, by reading and writing to a portion of the physical memory space that is located on the device.

Thus while kernel memory is often resident on the memory subsystem, there is no reason why part of the kernel memory cannot be on the adaptor itself, which typically contains some memory. By leveraging off the existing adaptor memory (**P4**) and utilizing this degree of freedom in terms of placement of kernel memory, we can place kernel memory on the adaptor. The net result is that once the data is copied from application to kernel memory it is already in the adaptor and so does not need to be copied again for transmission to the network. This is shown in Figure 5.3.

FIGURE 5.3   The Witless (afterburner) approach eliminates the need for the kernel-to-adaptor copy by placing kernel buffers in the adaptor.

Compare Figure 5.3 to Figure 5.2. Notice that Figure 5.3 ignores any disk-to-memory transfer. Essentially, the useless Copy 3 in Figure 5.2 is now combined with the essential Copy 4 in Figure 5.2 to form a single copy in Figure 5.3.

What about the checksum? We will see this in more general form in Section 5.5, but the main idea is to use principle **P2c**, expense sharing. When data is being moved from the application buffer to the adaptor resident kernel memory by the processor (using so-called programmed I/O, or PIO, which is I/O under processor control), the CPU is reading every word of the packet anyway. Since such bus reads are expensive, the CPU might as well piggyback the checksum computation with the copy process by keeping a register that accumulates the running sum of words that are transferred.

This idea, first espoused by Van Jacobson and called the Witless (or simple-minded) approach, was never built. Later this approach was used by Banks and Prudence [BP93] at Hewlett-Packard labs and called the Afterburner adaptor. In the Afterburner approach, the CPU did not transfer data from memory to the adaptor. Instead, the adaptor did so, using so-called direct memory access, or DMA. Thus since the CPU is no longer involved in the copy process, the adaptor should do the checksum. The Afterburner adaptor had special (but simple) checksum hardware that checksummed words as the DMA transfer takes place.

While the idea is a good one, it has three basic flaws. First, it implies that the network adaptor needs lots of memory to provide support for many high-throughput TCP connections (which require large window sizes); the memory required may make the adaptor more expensive than one wishes. Second, in the Witless approach, where the checksum is calculated by the CPU, doing the checksum while copying a received packet to the application buffer can imply that corrupted data can be written to application buffers. Though this can be discovered at the end, when the checksum does not compute, it does cause some awkwardness to prevent applications from reading incorrect data. A third problem with delayed acknowledgments is explored in the exercises.

5.2.2 Using Copy-on-Write

While the basic idea in the Witless approach can be considered to be eliminating the kernel-to-adaptor copy, the alternate idea pursued in the next three subsections is to eliminate the application-to-kernel copy (in most cases) using virtual memory remappings. Recall that one reason for the separate copy was the possibility that the application would modify the buffer and hence violate TCP semantics. A second reason is that the application and kernel use different virtual address spaces.

Some operating systems (notably Mach) offer a facility called copy-on-write (COW) that allows a process to replicate a virtual page in memory at low cost. The idea is to make the copy point to the original physical page P from which it was copied. This only involves updating a few descriptors (a few words of memory) instead of copying a whole packet (say, 1500 bytes of data). However, the nice thing about copy-on-write is that if the original owner of the data modifies the data, the OS will detect this condition automatically and generate two separate physical copies, P and P'. The original owner now points to P and can make modifications on P; the owner of the copied page points to the old copy, P'. This works fine if the vast majority of times pages are not modified (or only a few pages are modified) by the original owner.

Thus in a copy-on-write system, the application could make a copy-on-write copy for the kernel. In the hopefully rare event that the application modifies its buffer, the kernel makes an (expensive) physical copy. However, that should be uncommon. Clearly, we are using lazy evaluation (**P2b**) to minimize overhead in the expected case (**P11**). Finally, in Figure 5.4 the checksum can be piggybacked either with the copy to or from adaptor memory or by using CRC hardware on the adaptor.

Unfortunately, many operating systems, such as UNIX[2] and Windows, do not offer copy-on-write. However, much of the same effect can be obtained by understanding the basis behind the copy-on-write service, which is the use of virtual memory.

IMPLEMENTING COPY-ON-WRITE

Recall from Chapter 2 that most modern computers use virtual memory. Recall that the programmer works with an abstraction of infinite memory that is a linear array into which she (or more accurately her compiler) assigns variable locations, so, say, location X would be location 1010 in this imaginary (or virtual) array. These virtual addresses are then mapped into physical memory (which can reside on disk or in main memory) using a page table (Chapter 2).

For any virtual address, the high-order bits (e.g., 20 bits) form the page number, and the low-order bits (e.g., 12 bits) form the location within a page. Main memory is also divided into physical pages such that (say) every group of 2^{12} memory words is a physical page. Recall that a virtual address is mapped to a physical address by mapping the corresponding virtual page to a physical page number by looking up a page table indexed by the virtual page number. If the desired page is not memory resident, the hardware generates an exception that causes the

---

[2]System V UNIX does implement copy-on-write when a process is forked. The pages shared between the child and the parent process are shared with the copy-on-write bit set.

FIGURE 5.4 Using copy-on-write.

operating system to read the page from disk into main memory. Recall also that the overhead of reading page tables from memory can be avoided in the common case using a TLB (translation look-aside buffer), which is a processor resident cache.

Looking under the hood, virtual memory is the basis for the copy-on-write scheme. Suppose virtual page X is pointing to a physical memory–resident page P. Suppose that the operating system wishes to replicate the contents of X onto a new virtual page, Y. The hard way to do this would be to allocate a new physical page, P', to copy the contents of P to P', and then to point Y to P' in the page table. The simpler way, embodied in copy-on-write, is to *map* the new virtual page, Y, back to the old physical page, P, by changing a page table entry. Since most modern operating systems use large page sizes, changing a page table entry is more efficient than copying from one physical page to another.

In addition, the kernel also sets a COW protection bit as part of the page table entry for the original virtual page, X. If the application tries to write to page X, the hardware will access the page table for X, notice the bit set, and generate an exception that calls the operating system. At this point the operating system will copy the physical page, P, to another location, P', and then make X point to P', after clearing the COW bit. Y continues to point to the old physical page, P. While this is every bit as expensive as physical page copying, the point is that this expense is incurred only in the (hopefully) rare case when an application writes to a COW page.

The explanation of how COW works should present the following opportunity. While operating systems such as UNIX and Windows do not offer COW, they still offer virtual memory. Virtual memory (VM) presents a level of indirection that can be exploited by changing page table entries to finesse physical copying. Thus much of the core idea behind Figure 5.4 can be reused in most operating systems. All that remains is to find an alternate way to protect against application Writes in place of COW protection.

FIGURE 5.5 Basic operations involved in making a copy of a page using virtual memory.

5.2.3 Fbufs: Optimizing Page Remapping

Even ignoring the aspect of protecting against application writes, Figure 5.5 implies that a large buffer can be transferred from application to kernel (or vice versa) with a Write to the page table. This simplistic view of page remapping is somewhat naive and misleading.

Figure 5.5 shows a concrete example of page remapping. Suppose the operating system wishes to make a fast copy of data of Process 1 (say, the application) in Virtual Page (VP) 10 to some virtual page (e.g., VP 8) in the page table of Process 23's (say, the kernel). Naively, this seems to require only changing the page table entry corresponding to Virtual Page 8 in Process 2 to point to the packet data to which that Virtual Page table entry 10 in Process 1 already points. However, there are several additional pieces of overhead that are glossed over by this simple description.

- *Multiple-level page tables:* Most modern systems use multiple levels of page table mappings because it takes too much page table memory to map from, say, 20 bits of a virtual page. Thus the real mapping may require changing mappings in at least a first- and a second-level page table. For portability, there are also both machine-independent and machine-dependent tables. Thus there are several Writes involved, not just one.

- *Acquiring locks and modifying page table entries:* Page tables are shared resources and thus must be protected using locks that must be acquired and released.

- *Flushing translation look-aside buffers (TLBs):* As we said earlier, to save translation time, commonly used page table mappings are cached in the TLB. When a new virtual page location for VP 8 is written, any TLB entries for VP 8 must be found and flushed (i.e., removed) or corrected.

- *Allocating VM in destination domain:* While we have assumed that virtual memory location 8 was the location for the destination page, some computation must be done to find a free page table entry in the destination process before the copy can take place.

- *Locking the corresponding pages:* Physical pages can be swapped out to disk to make room for other virtual pages currently on disk. To prevent pages from being swapped out, pages have to be locked, which is additional overhead.

All these overheads are exacerbated in multiprocessor systems. The net result is that while the page table mapping can seem very good (the mapping seems to take a constant time, independent of the size of the packet data), the constant factors (see **Q4** in the discussion of caveats) are actually a big overhead. This was experimentally demonstrated by experiments performed by Druschel and Peterson [DP93] in the early 1990s. In the decade that followed, if anything, page mapping overheads have only increased.

Druschel and Peterson, however, did not stop with the experiments but invented an operating system facility called *fbufs* (short for "fast buffers"), which actually removes most or all of the four sources of page remapping overhead. Their idea can be described as follows in terms of the principles used in this book.

FBUFS

The main idea in fbufs is to realize that if an application is sending a lot of data packets to the network through the kernel, then a buffer will probably be reused multiple times, and thus the operating system can precompute (**P2a**) all the page mapping information for the buffer ahead of time and then avoid much of the page mapping overhead during the actual data transfer. Alternatively, the mappings can be computed lazily (**P2b**) when the data transfer is first started (causing high overhead for the first few received packets) but can be cached (**P11a**) for the subsequent packets. In this version, page remapping overheads are eliminated in the common case.

The simplest way to do this would be to use what is called *shared memory*. Map a number of pages $P_1, \ldots, P_n$ into the virtual memory tables of the kernel as well as all sending applications $A_1, \ldots, A_k$. However, this is a bad idea, because we now can have (say) application A_1 reading the packets sent by application A_2.[3] This would violate security and fault-isolation goals.

A more secure notion would be to reserve (or lazily establish) mapped shared pages for each application-to-kernel transfer, and vice versa. For example, there could be one set of buffers (pages) for FTP, one set for HTTP, and so on. More generally, some operating systems define multiple security subsystems besides kernel and application. Thus the fbuf designers call a path a sequence of security domains. For our simple examples described earlier, it suffices to think of a path as either kernel, application or application, kernel (e.g., FTP, kernel or kernel, HTTP). We will see why paths are unidirectional — that is, why each application needs two paths in both directions — in a minute.

Figure 5.6 shows a more complex example of paths, where the Ethernet software is implemented as a kernel-level driver, the TCP/IP stack is implemented as a user-level security domain, and, finally, the Web application is implemented at the application layer. Each security domain has its own set of page tables. The receiving paths are Ethernet, TCP/IP, Web and Ethernet, OSI, FTP.

To implement the fbuf idea the operating system could take some number of physical pages $P_1, \ldots, P_k$ and premap them onto the page tables of the Ethernet driver, the TCP/IP code, and the Web application. The same operation could be performed with a different set of physical pages for Ethernet, OSI, and FTP. Thus we are using Principle **2a** to precompute mappings. Reserving physical pages for each path could be wasteful, because traffic is bursty; instead, a better idea is to lazily establish (**P2b**) such mappings when a path becomes busy.

Lazy establishment avoids the overheads of updating multiple levels of page tables, acquiring locks, flushing TLBs, and allocating destination virtual memory after the first few data packets arrive and are sent. Instead, all this work is done once, when the transfer first starts. To make fbufs work, it is crucial that when a packet arrives, the lowest-level driver (or even the

---

[3]It is worth knowing that the virtual memory hardware normally enforces this security constraint by making sure that any accesses by A_2 can access only physical pages mapped into the page tables of A_2.

FIGURE 5.6 Premapping or lazily establishing buffer pages into the page tables of each domain in a path avoids the expense of page remapping in the real-time path, after the initial setup.

adaptor itself) be able to quickly figure out what the complete path the packet will be mapped to when receiving a packet from the network. This function, called *early demultiplexing*, is described in detail in Chapter 8. Intuitively, in Figure 5.6 this is done by examining all the packet headers to determine (for instance) that a packet with an Ethernet, IP, and HTTP header belongs to Path 1.

The driver (or the adaptor) will then have a list of free buffers for that path, which will be used by the adaptor to write the packet to; when the adaptor is done it will pass the buffer descriptor to the next application in the path. Note that a buffer descriptor is only a pointer to a shared page, not the page itself. When the last application in the path finishes with the page, it passes it back to the first application in the path, where it again becomes a free buffer, and so on.

At this point, the reader may wonder why paths are unidirectional. Paths are made unidirectional because the first process on each path is assumed to be a writer and the remaining processes are assumed to be readers. This can be enforced during the premapping by setting a write-allowed bit for the first application in its page table entry, and a read-only bit in the page table entries of all the other applications. Clearly, this is asymmetric in both directions and requires unidirectional paths. But this does ensure some level of protection.

This is shown in Figure 5.7 with just two domains in a path. Note that the writer writes packets into buffers described by a queue of free fbufs and then puts the written descriptor on to a queue of written fbufs that are read by the next application (only one is shown in Figure 5.7).

So far, it is possible that premapped page 8 in the first application on a path is mapped to page 10 in the second application. This is painful because when the second application reads a descriptor for page 8, it must somehow know that it corresponds to its own virtual page 10. Instead, the designers used the principle of avoiding unnecessary generality (**P7**) and insisted that the fbuf get mapped to the *same* virtual page in all applications on the path. This can be done by reserving some number of initial pages in the virtual memory of all processes to be fbuf pages.

At this point, we may feel that we are finished, but there are still a few thorny problems. To achieve protection, we allowed only a single writer and had multiple readers. However, that means that pages are *immutable*; only the writer can touch them. But what about adding headers when one goes down the stack. The solution to this problem is shown in Figure 5.8, where a packet is really an aggregate data structure with pointers to individual fbufs so that headers can be added by adding an ordinary buffer or an fbuf to the aggregate.

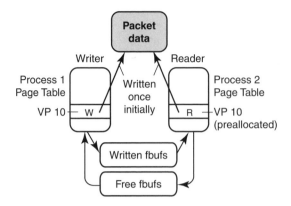

FIGURE 5.7   The single writer optimization.

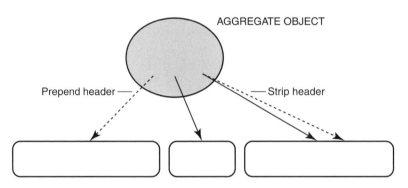

FIGURE 5.8   Using aggregate objects to allow adding layers to add headers while allowing only a single writer.

This is not as big a deal as it sounds because the commonly used UNIX mbufs (see Chapter 9) are also composites of buffers strung together.[4]

So far, the fbuf scheme has used the underlying VM mapping ideas in Figure 5.4 except that it has made them more efficient by amortizing the mapping costs over (hopefully) a large number of packet transfers. Page table updates are removed in the common case. This can be done in ordinary operating systems. In fact, after the fbufs paper, Thadani and Khalidi [TK95] extended the idea and implemented it in Sun's Solaris operating system. But this begs the question: How are standard copy semantics preserved? What if the application does a Write? A standard operating system such as UNIX cannot depend on copy-on-write as in Figure 5.4.

The ultimate answer in fbufs is that *standard copy semantics are not preserved*. The API is changed. Application writers must be careful not to write to an fbuf when it has been handed to the kernel until the fbuf is returned by the kernel in a free list. To protect against buggy or malicious code, the kernel can briefly toggle the write-enable bit when an fbuf is transferred

---

[4]To be precise, UNIX mbufs are strung together in a linear topology, while buffer aggregates form a more general tree topology, but the performance costs due to chaining and indexing are similar.

from the application to the kernel; the bit is set again when the fbuf is given back. If the application does a Write when it does not have write permission, an exception is generated and the application crashes, leaving other processes unaffected.

Since the toggling of the write-enable bits requires some of the overhead that fbufs worked hard to avoid, the fbuf facility also allows another form of fbufs, called *volatile*. Observe that if the writer is a trusted entity (such as the kernel), then there is no point enforcing write protection. If the kernel has a bug that causes it to make unexpected writes, the whole system will crash anyway.

Changing the API in this way sounds dramatic. Does this mean that the huge amount of existing UNIX application software (which uses the networking stack) must be rewritten? Since this is infeasible, there are several ways out. First, the existing API can be augmented with new system calls. For example, the Solaris extensions in Thadani and Khalidi [TK95] add a *uf_write( )* call in addition to the standard *write( )* call. Applications interested in performance can be rewritten using these new calls.

Second, the extensions can be used in implementing common I/O substrates (such as the UNIX *stdio* library) that are a part of several applications. Applications that are linked to this library do not need to be changed and yet can potentially benefit in performance.

Eventually, the pragmatic consideration is not whether the API changes but how hard it is to modify applications to benefit from the API changes. The experiences described in Thadani and Khalidi [TK95] and Pai et al. [PDZ99b] for a number of applications indicate that the changes required in an application to migrate to an fbuf-like API are small and localized.

5.2.4 Transparently Emulating Copy Semantics

One reaction to the new fbuf API is simply to modify applications to gain performance. It is worth pointing out that while the changes may be simple and localized, the mental model that a programmer has of a buffer changes in a fairly drastic way. In the standard UNIX API, the application assigns buffer addresses; in fbufs, the buffers are assigned by the kernel from the fbuf address space. In the standard UNIX API, the programmer can design the buffer layout anyway he pleases, including the use of contiguous buffers. In fbufs, data received from the network can be arbitrarily scattered into pieces linked together by a buffer aggregate, and the application programmer must deal with this new buffer model chosen by the kernel.

Thus a reasonable question is whether many of the benefits of fbufs can be realized *without modifying the UNIX API*. Theoretically, application software will continue to run, and one might get performance without recoding applications.

In a series of papers, Brustoloni and Steenkiste (e.g., Ref. BS96) showed that there is a clever mechanism, which they call *TCOW* (for transient copy-on-write), that makes this possible. While preserving the API theoretically allows unmodified applications to enjoy better performance, there is no experimental confirmation of this possibility. Thus in practice, it is likely that applications have to be modified (perhaps in more intuitive ways) to take advantage of the underlying kernel implementation changes. Nevertheless, the idea is simple and clever and worth pointing out.

Recall that the standard API requires allowing an application to write or deallocate a buffer passed to the kernel at any time. The fbuf design changes the API by making it illegal for an application to do this. Instead, to preserve the API while doing only virtual memory mappings, the operating system must deal with these two potential threats, application writes and application deallocates, during the period the buffer is being used by the kernel to send or retransmit a packet. In the Genie system [BS96], VM mapping is used, as in fbufs, but these two threats are dealt with as follows.

Countering Write Threats by Modifying the VM Fault Manager: First, when an application does a Write, the buffer is marked specially, as Read Only. Thus if the application does a Write, the VM fault manager is invoked. Normally, this should cause an exception. But, of course, if the OS is preserving copy semantics, this should not be an error. Thus Genie modifies the exception handler as follows. First, for each such page/buffer, Genie keeps track of whether there are outstanding sends (sends to the network) using a simple counter that is incremented when the Send starts and decremented when the Send completes. Second, the fault handler is modified to make a separate copy of the page for the application (which incorporates the new Write) if there is an outstanding Send. Of course, this makes performance suffer, but it does preserve the standard copy semantics of APIs such as UNIX. This technique, called transient copy-on-write protection, is invoked only when needed — when the buffer is also being read out by the network subsystem.

Countering Deallocate Threats by Modifying the Pageout Daemon: In a standard virtual memory system, there is a process that is responsible for putting deallocated pages into a free list from which pages may be written to disk. This pageout daemon can be modified not to deallocate a page when the page is being used to send or receive packets.

Interestingly these two ideas are both instances of Principle **P3c**, shifting computation in space. The work of checking for unexpected writes is moved to the VM fault handler, and the work of dealing with deallocates is moved to the page deallocation routine.

These two ideas are sufficient for *sending* a packet but not for receiving. On receiving, Genie needs to depend, like fbufs, on hardware support[5] in the adaptor to split a packet's headers into one buffer and the remaining data into a page-size buffer that can be swapped to the application's buffer.

To do so without a physical copy, the kernel's data buffer must start at the same offset within the page as the application's receive buffer. For a large buffer, the first and last pages (which can be partially filled) are probably most efficiently handled by a physical copy; however, the intermediate pages that are full can simply be swapped from the kernel to the application by the right page table mappings. There is a cute optimization called *reverse copyout* that is explored in the exercises.

Given the complexity that underlies page table remapping, it is unclear how page remapping is done efficiently in Genie. One possibility is that Genie uses the same fbuf idea of caching VM mappings on a path basis[6] to avoid the overhead of TLB flushing, dealing with multiple page tables, and so on.

When all is said and done, can the TCOW idea benefit legacy applications? There is no experimental confirmation of this in Brustaloni and Steenkiste [BS96] and Brustoloni [Bru99] because the experiments use a simple copy benchmark and not an existing application such as

---

[5]Hardware support for parsing in the adaptor is the simplest alternative proposed by the Genie system; there are a number of more baroque mechanisms proposed as part of the Genie system to get around this hardware requirement, but they seem too complicated and full of side effects to be useful in practice.

[6]The Genie experiments were done on an ATM network, where the virtual circuit identifier can provide a quick mapping to the path.

a Web server. Fundamentally, it seems hard for an existing legacy application to benefit from the new kernel implementation of the existing API.

Consider an application running over TCP that supplies a buffer to TCP. Since there is no feedback to the application (unlike fbufs), the application does not know when it can safely reuse the buffer. If the application overwrites the buffer too early while TCP is holding the buffer for retransmission, then safety is not compromised, but performance is compromised because of the physical copy involved in copy-on-write. It appears improbable that an unmodified application could choose the times to modify buffers in accordance with TCP sending times and would have aligned its buffers well enough to allow page swapping to work well.

Thus applications do need to be modified to take full advantage of the Genie system. Even if they do, there is still the hard problem of knowing when to reuse a buffer, because of the lack of feedback. The application could monitor TCOW faults and accordingly modify its reuse pattern. But if applications need to be modified in subtle ways to take full advantage of the new kernel, it is unclear what benefit was gained from preserving the API. Nevertheless, the ideas in Genie are fun to study, and they fall nicely within the general area of network algorithmics.

5.3 AVOIDING COPYING USING REMOTE DMA

While fbufs provide a reasonable solution to the problem of avoiding redundant application-to-kernel copies, there is a more direct solution that also removes an enormous amount of control overhead. Normally, if a 1-MB file is transferred between two workstations on an Ethernet, the file is chopped up into 1500-byte pieces. The CPU is involved in processing each of these 1500-byte pieces to do TCP processing and copying each packet (possibly via a zero-copy interface such as fbufs) to application memory.

On the other hand, recall from Chapter 2 how a CPU orchestrates a direct memory access (DMA) operation between, say, disk and memory for, say, a 1-MB transfer. The CPU sets up the DMA, tells the disk the range of addresses into which the data must be written, and goes about its business. One megabyte of data later, the disk interrupts the CPU to essentially say, "Master, your job is done." Note that the CPU does not micromanage every piece of this transfer, unlike in the earlier case of the corresponding network transfer.

This analogy suggests the vision of doing DMA across the network, or RDMA as it is sometimes called. In fact, it is hardly surprising that this networking feature was first proposed in VAX Clusters by a group of computer architects [KLS86]. It is said that breakthroughs often come via outsiders to an area. There is an apocryphal story about how one of the inventors of VAX Clusters came to the networking people at DEC and asked to learn about networking. They laughed at him and gave him a copy of the standard undergraduate text at that time. He came back 6 months later with the RDMA design.

The intent is that data should be transferred between two memories in two computers across the network without per-packet mediation by the two CPUs. Instead, the two adaptors conspire to read from one memory and to write to the other: DMA across the network. To realize this vision two problems must be solved: (1) how the receiving adaptor knows where to place the data — it cannot ask the host for help without defeating the intent; (2) how security is maintained. The possibility of rogue packets coming over the network and overwriting key pieces of memory should make one pause.

This section starts by describing this very early idea and then moves on to describe modern incarnations of this idea in the Fiber Channel and RDMA [Cona] proposals.

5.3.1 Avoiding Copying in a Cluster

In the last few years, clusters of workstations have become accepted as a cheaper and more effective substitute for large computers. Thus many Web servers are really server farms. While this appears to be recent technology, 20 years ago Digital Equipment Corporation (DEC) introduced a successful commercial product called VAX Clusters to provide a platform for scalable computing for, say, database applications. The heart of the system was a 140-Mbit network called the computer interconnect, or CI, which used an Ethernet-style protocol. To this interconnect, customers could connect a number of VAX computers and network-attached disks. The issue of efficient copying was motivated by the need to transfer large amounts of data between the remote disk and the memory of a VAX. RDMA was born from this need.

RDMA requires that packet data containing part of a large file go into its final destination when it gets to the destination adaptor. This is trickier than it sounds. In traditional networking, when the packet arrives the processor is involved in at least examining the packet and deciding where the packet is to go. Even if the CPU looks at headers, it can only tell based on the destination application which queue of receive buffers to use.

Suppose the receiving application queues Pages 1, 2, and 3 to the receiving adaptor for Application 1. Suppose the first packet arrives and is sent to Page 1, the third packet arrives out of order and is put in Page 2 instead of Page 3. Assume that Pages 1, 2, and 3 should store the receiving file. The CPU can always remap pages at the end, but remapping all the pages at the end of the transfer for a large file can be painful. Out-of-order arrival can always happen, even on a FIFO link, because of packet loss.

Instead, the idea in VAX Clusters is first to have the destination application lock a number of physical pages (such as Pages 11 and 16 in Figure 5.9) that comprise the destination memory for the file transfer. The logical view presented, however, is a buffer of consecutive logical pages (e.g., Pages 1 and 2 in Figure 5.9) called, say, *B*. This buffer name *B* is passed to the sending application.

The source now passes (**P10**, pass information in protocol headers) the buffer name and offset with each packet it sends. Thus when sending Packet 3 out of order in our last example,

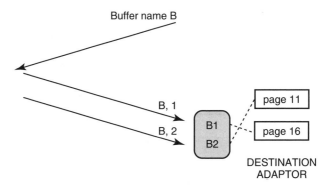

FIGURE 5.9 Doing DMA across the network.

Packet 3 will contain *B* and Page 3 and so can get stored in Page 3 of the buffer even though it arrives before Packet 2. Thus after all packets arrive there is no need for any further page remapping. This is an example of **P10**: passing information, such as a buffer name, in message headers.

To realize the ideal of not bothering the processor on every packet arrival, there are several additional requirements. First, the adaptor must implement the transport protocol (and do all the checking for duplicates, etc.), as in TCP processing. Second, the adaptor must be able to determine where the data begins and where the headers stop so as only to copy the data into the destination buffer.

Finally, it is somewhat cavalier to allow any packet carrying a buffer ID from the network to be written directly into memory. This could be a security hole. To mitigate against this, the buffer IDs contain a random string that is hard to guess. More importantly, VAX Clusters are used only between trusted hosts in a cluster. It is more difficult to imagine scaling this approach to Internet data transfers.

5.3.2 Modern-Day Incarnations of RDMA

VAX Clusters introduced a very early *storage area network*. Storage area networks (SANs) are back-end networks that connect many computers to shared storage, in terms of network-attached disks. There are several recent successors to VAX Clusters that provide SAN technology. These range from the venerable Fiber Channel [Ben95] technology to modern upstarts such as InfiniBand [Assa] and iSCSI [SSMe01].

FIBER CHANNEL

In 1988, the American National Standards Institute (ANSI) Task Group X3T11 began work on a standard called Fiber Channel [Ben95]. One of the goals of Fiber Channel was to take the standard SCSI (small computer system interface) between a workstation and a local disk and extend it over larger distances. Thus in many Fiber Channel installations, SCSI is still used as the protocol that runs over Fiber Channel.

Fiber Channel goes further than VAX Clusters in the underlying network, using modern network technology such as point-to-point fiber links connected with switches. This allows speeds of up to 1 Gbps and allows a larger distance span than in the Vax Cluster network. Switches can even be remotely connected, allowing a trading firm to have backup storage of all trades at a remote site. The use of switches requires attention to such issues as flow control, which is done very carefully to avoid dropping packets where possible.

Finally, Fiber Channel makes slightly more concession to security than VAX Clusters. In VAX Clusters, any device with the right name can overwrite the memory of any other device. Fiber Channel allows the network to be virtualized into zones. Nodes in a zone cannot access the memory of nodes in other zones. Some recent products go even further and propose techniques based on authentication.

However, other than these differences in the underlying technology, the underlying ideas are the same. RDMA via named buffers is still a key enabling idea.

INFINIBAND

Infiniband starts with the observation that the internal I/O bus used within many workstations and PCs, the PCI bus, is showing its age and needs replacement. With a maximum bandwidth of 533 MB/sec, the PCI bus is being overwhelmed by modern high-speed peripherals, such as Gigabit Ethernet interface cards. While there are some temporary alternatives, such as the PCI-X bus, the internal computer interconnect needs to scale in the same way as the external Internet has scaled from, say, 10-Mbit Ethernet to Gigabit Ethernet.

Also, observe that there are three separate networking technologies within a computer: the network interface (e.g., Ethernet), the disk interface (e.g., SCSI over Fiber Channel), and the PCI bus. Occam's razor suggests substituting these three with one network technology. Accordingly, Compaq, Dell, HP, IBM, and Sun banded together to form the Infiniband Trade Association.

The Infiniband specifications use many of the ideas in Fiber Channel's underlying network technology. The interconnect is also based on switches and point-to-point links. Infiniband has a few additional twists. It uses the proposal for 128-bit IP addresses in the next-generation Internet as a basis for addressing. It allows individual physical links to be virtualized into separate virtual links called *lanes*. It has features for quality of service and even multicast. Once again, RDMA is the key technology to avoid copies.

iSCSI

At the time of writing, Fiber Channel parts appear to be priced higher than equivalent-speed Gigabit Ethernet parts. Given that IP has invaded various other networking spaces, such as voice, TV, and radio, a natural consequence is to invade the storage space. This, the argument goes, should drive down prices (while also opening up new markets for network vendors). Further, Fiber Channel and Infiniband are being extended to connect remote data centers over the Internet. This involves using transport protocols that are not necessarily compatible with TCP in terms of reacting to congestion. Why not just adapt TCP for this purpose instead of trying to modify these other protocols to be TCP-friendly?

For the purposes of this chapter, the most interesting thing about iSCSI is the way it must emulate RDMA over standard IP protocols. In particular, recall that in all RDMA implementations, the host adaptor implements the transport protocol in hardware. In the Internet world, the transport protocol is TCP. Thus adaptors must implement TCP in hardware. This is not too hard, and chips that perform TCP offload are becoming widely available.

The harder parts are as follows. First, as we saw in Case Study 1 of Chapter 2, TCP is a streaming protocol. The application writes bytes to a queue, and these bytes are arbitrarily segmented into packets. The RDMA idea, on the other hand, is based on messages, each of which has a named buffer field. Second, RDMA over TCP requires a header to hold named buffers.

The RDMA [Cona] proposal solves both these problems by logically layering three protocols over TCP. The first protocol, MPA, adds a header that defines message boundaries in the byte stream. The second and third protocols implement the RDMA header fields but are separated as follows. Notice that when a packet carries data, all that is needed is a buffer name and offset. Thus this header is abstracted out into a so-called DDA (for direct data access) header together with a command verb (such as READ or WRITE).

The RDMA protocol that is layered over DDA adds a header with a few more fields. For example, for an RDMA remote READ, the initial request must specify the remote buffer name (to be read) and the local name (to be written to). One of these two buffer names can be placed in the DDA header, but the other must be placed in the RDMA header. Thus, except for control messages such as initiating a READ, all data carries only a DDA header and not an RDMA header.

During the evolution from VAX Clusters to the RDMA proposal, one interesting general-ization was to replace a *named* buffer with an *anonymous* buffer. In this case, the DDA header contains a queue name, and the packet is placed in a buffer corresponding to the buffer at the head of the free queue at the receiver.

5.4 BROADENING TO FILE SYSTEMS

So far this chapter has concentrated only on avoiding redundant copies that occur while sending data between an application (such as a Web server) and the network. However, Figure 5.2 shows that even after removing all redundant overhead due to network copying, there are still redundant copies involving the file system. Thus in this section, we will cast our net more widely. We leverage our intellectual investment by extending the copy-avoidance techniques discussed so far to the file system.

Recall from Figure 5.2 that to process a request for File *X*, the server may have to read *X* from disk (Copy 1) into a kernel buffer (representing the file cache) and then make a copy from the file cache to the application buffer (Copy 2). Copy 1 goes out of the picture if the file is already in cache, a reasonable assumption for popular files in a server with sufficient memory. The main goal is to remove Copy 2. Note that in a Web server, unnecessarily doubling the number of copies not only halves the effective bus bandwidth but potentially halves the size of the server cache. This in turn reduces server performance by causing a larger miss rate, which implies that a larger fraction of documents is served at disk speeds and not bus speeds.

This section surveys three techniques for removing the redundant file system copy (Copy 2). Section 5.4.1 describes a technique called *shared memory mapping* that can reduce Copy 2 but is not well integrated with the network subsystem. Section 5.4.2 describes IO-Lite, essentially a generalization of fbufs to include the file system. Finally, Section 5.4.3 describes a technique called *I/O splicing* that is used by many commercial Web servers.

5.4.1 Shared Memory

Modern UNIX variants [Ste98] provide a convenient system call known as *mmap()* to allow an application such as a server to map a file into its virtual memory address space. Other operating systems provide equivalent functions. Conceptually, when a file is mapped into an application's address space, it is as if the application has cached a copy of the file in its memory. This seems redundant because the file system also maintains cached files. However, using the magic of virtual memory (**P4**, leverage off system components), the cached file is really only a set of mappings, so other applications and the file server cache can gain common access to one set of physical pages for the file.

The Flash Web server [PDZ99a] avoids Copy 1 and Copy 2 in Figure 5.2 by having the server application map frequently used files into memory. Given that there are limits on the number of physical pages that can be allocated to file pages and limits on page table mappings, the Flash Web server has to treat these mapped files as a cache. Instead of caching whole files, it caches segments of files and uses an LRU (least recently used) policy to unmap files that have not been used for a while.

Note that such cache maintenance functions are duplicated by the file system cache (which has a more precise view of resources such as free pages because it is kernel resident). However, this can be looked on as a necessary evil to avoid Copies 1 and 2 in Figure 5.2. While Flash uses *mmap( )* to avoid file system copying, it runs over the UNIX API. Hence, Flash is constrained to make an extra copy in the network subsystem (Copy 3 in Figure 5.2). Just when progress is being made to eliminate Copy 2, pesky Copy 3 reappears again!

Copy 3 can be avoided by combining emulated copying using TCOW [BS96] with *mmap( )*. However, this has some of the disadvantages of TCOW mentioned earlier. It is also not a complete solution that generalizes to avoid copying for interaction with a CGI process via a UNIX pipe.

5.4.2 IO-Lite: A Unified View of Buffering

While combining emulated copy with *mmap( )* does away with all redundant copying, it still has some missing optimizations. First, it does nothing to avoid the copying between any CGI application generating dynamic content and the Web server. Such an application is typically implemented as a separate process[7] that sends dynamic content to the server process via a UNIX pipe. But pipes and other similar interprocess communication typically involve copying the content between two address spaces.

Second, notice that none of our schemes so far has done anything about the TCP checksum, an expensive operation. But if the same file keeps hitting in the cache, other than the first response containing the HTTP header, all subsequent packets that return the file contents stay the same for every request. Why can't the TCP checksums be cached? However, that requires a cache that can somehow map from packet contents to checksums. This is inefficient in a conventional buffering scheme.

This section describes a buffering scheme called IO-Lite that generalizes the fbuf ideas to include the file system. IO-Lite not only eliminates all redundant copies in Figure 5.2, but also eliminates redundant copying between the CGI process and the server. It also has a specialized buffer-numbering scheme that lets a subsystem (such as TCP) efficiently realize that it is resending an earlier packet.

IO-Lite is the intellectual descendant of fbufs, though integration with the file system adds significantly more complexity. It is first worth noting that fbufs cannot be combined with *mmap*, unlike TCOW, which is combined with *mmap* in Brustoloni [Bru99]. This is because in *mmap* the application picks the address and format of an application buffer, while in fbufs the kernel picks the address and format of a fast buffer. Thus if the application has mapped a file using a buffer in the application virtual address space, the buffer cannot be sent using an fbuf (kernel address space) without a physical copy.

Since fbufs cannot be combined with *mmap*, IO-Lite generalizes fbufs to include the file system, making *mmap* unnecessary. Also, IO-Lite is implemented in a a general-purpose operating system (UNIX), as opposed to fbufs. But setting aside these two differences, IO-Lite borrows all the main ideas from fbufs: the notion of read-only sharing via immutable buffers (called *slices* in IO lite), the use of composite buffers (called *buffer aggregates*), and the notion of a lazily created cache of buffers for a path (called an *I/O stream* in IO-Lite).

---

[7]Because of the overhead of copying data between a CGI process generating dynamic content and the server process, some vendors have proposed merging the CGI code within the server process. However, that makes the system more brittle because faulty third-party content-generation software can crash the server. Better solutions, such as Windows ASP, propose incorporating safe languages into Web pages such that the server executes the code and puts the result in the page it serves. Thus, despite the references to CGI processes in this chapter, CGI may well be obsolete.

FIGURE 5.10 IO-Lite removes all the redundant copying in Figure 5.2 by effectively passing around pointers (via VM mappings) to a single IO-Lite buffer. Assuming the file, the TCP checksum, and the HTTP response are all cached, the Web server only has to transmit these cached values in a single copy to the network interface.

Despite the core similarities, IO-Lite requires solving difficult problems to integrate with the file system. First, IO-Lite must deal with complex sharing patterns, where several applications may have buffers pointing to the IO-Lite buffer together with the TCP code and the file server. Second, an IO-Lite page can be both a virtual memory page (backed up by the paging backup file on disk) and at the same time a file page (backed up by the actual disk copy of the file). Thus IO-Lite has to implement a complex replacement policy that integrates both the standard page replacement rules together with file cache replacement policies [PDZ99b]. Third, the goal of running over UNIX requires careful thought to find a clean way to integrate IO-Lite without major surgery throughout UNIX.

Figure 5.10 shows the steps in responding to the same GET request pictured in Figure 5.2. When the file is first read from disk into the file system cache, the file pages are stored as IO-Lite buffers. When the application makes a call to read the file, no physical copy is made, but a buffer aggregate is created with a pointer to the IO-Lite buffer. Next, when the application sends the file to TCP for transmission, the network system gets a pointer to the same IO-Lite pages. To prevent errors, the IO-Lite system keeps a reference count for each buffer and reallocates a buffer only when all users are done.

Figure 5.10 also shows two more optimizations. The application keeps a cache of HTTP responses for common files and can often simply append the standard response with minimal modifications. Second, every buffer is given a unique number (**P12**, add redundant state) by IO-Lite, and the TCP module keeps a cache of checksums indexed by buffer number. Thus when a file is transmitted multiple times, the TCP module can avoid calculating the checksum after the first time. Notice that these changes eliminate all the redundancy in Figure 5.2, which speeds up the processing of a response.

IO-Lite can also be used to implement a modified pipe program that eliminates copying. When this IPC mechanism is used between the CGI process and the server process, all copying is eliminated without compromising the safety and fault isolation provided by implementing the two programs as separate processes. IO-Lite can also allow applications to customize their buffer-caching strategy, allowing fancier caching strategies for Web servers based on both size and access frequency.

It is important to note that IO-Lite manages these performance feats without completely eliminating the UNIX kernel and without closely tying the application with the kernel. The Cheetah Web server [EKO95] built over the Exokernel operating system takes a more extreme position, allowing each application (including the Web server) to completely customize its network and file system. The Exokernel mechanisms allow such extreme customization from each application without compromising safety. By dint of these customizations, the Cheetah Web server can eliminate all the copies in Figure 5.2 and also eliminate the TCP checksum calculation using a cache.

While Cheetah does allow some further tricks (see the Exercises), the enormous software engineering challenge of designing and maintaining custom kernels for each application makes approaches such as IO-Lite more attractive. IO-Lite comes close to the performance of customized kernels like Cheetah with a much smaller set of software engineering challenges.

5.4.3 *Avoiding File System Copies via I/O Splicing*

In the commercial world, Web servers are measured by commercial tests such as the SPECweb tests [Conb] for Web servers and the Web polygraph tests [Assb] for Web proxies. In the proxy space, there is an annual cache-off, in which all devices are measured together to calculate the highest cache hit rate, normalized to the price of the device. The SPECweb benchmarks use a different system, in which manufacturers submit their own experimental results to the benchmark system, though these results are audited. In the Web polygraph tests at the time of writing, a Web server technology based on I/O-Lite ideas was among the leaders.

However, in the SPECweb benchmarks, a number of other Web servers also show impressive performance. Part of the reason for this is just faster (and more expensive) hardware. However, there are two simple ideas that can avoid the need for complete model shifts as is the case in IO-Lite.

The first idea is to push the Web server application completely into the kernel. Thus in Figure 5.2, all copies can be eliminated because the application and the kernel are part of the same entity. The major problem with this approach is that such in-kernel Web servers have to deal with the idiosyncrasies of operating system implementation changes. For example, for a popular high-performance server that runs over Linux, every internal change to Linux can invalidate assumptions made by the server software and cause a crash. Note that a conventional user-space server does not have this problem because all changes to the UNIX implementation still preserve the API.

The second idea keeps the server application in user space but relies on a simple idea called *I/O splicing* to eliminate all the copying in Figure 5.2. I/O splicing, shown in Figure 5.11, was first introduced in Fall and Pasquale [FP93]. The idea is to introduce a new system call that *combines* the old call to read a file with the old call (**P6**, efficient specialized routines) to send

FIGURE 5.11 In I/O splicing, all the indirection caused by copying to and from user-space buffers is removed by a single system call that "splices" together the I/O stream from the disk with the I/O stream to the network. As always, Copy 1 can be removed for files in the cache.

a message to the network. By allowing the kernel to splice together these two hitherto-separate system calls, we can avoid all redundant copies. Many systems have system calls such as *sendfile()*, which are now used by several commercial vendors. Despite the success of this mechanism, mechanisms based on *sendfile* do not generalize well to communication with CGI processes.

5.5 BROADENING BEYOND COPIES

Clark and Tennehouse, in a landmark paper, suggested generalizing Van Jacobson's idea (described earlier) of integrating checksums and copying. In more detail, the Jacobson idea is based on the following observation. When copying a packet word from a location (say, $W10$ in adaptor memory in Figure 5.12) to a location in memory (say, $M9$ in memory in Figure 5.12), the processor has to load $W10$ into a register and then store that register to $M9$. Typically, most RISC processors require that, between a load and a store, the compiler insert a so-called *delay slot*, or empty cycle, to keep the pipeline working correctly (never mind why!). That empty cycle can be used for other computation. For example, it can be used to add the word just read to a register that holds the current checksum. Thus with no extra cost the copy loop can often be augmented to be the checksum loop as well.

But there are other data-intensive manipulations, such as encrypting data and doing format conversions. Why not, Clark and Tennehouse [CT90] argued, integrate all such manipulations into the copy loop? For example, in Figure 5.12 the CPU could read $W10$ and then decrypt

FIGURE 5.12   Integrating checksumming and copying.

*W*10 and write the decrypted word to *M*9 rather than have that done in another loop. They called this idea *integrated layer processing*, or ILP. The essential idea is to avoid obvious waste (**P1**), in terms of reading (and possibly) writing the bytes of a packet several times for multiple data-manipulation operations on the same packet.

Thus ILP is a generalization of copy-checksum integration to other manipulations (e.g., encryption, presentation formatting). However, it has several challenges.

- **Challenge 1:** Information needed for manipulations is typically at different layers (e.g., encryption is at the application layer, and checksumming is done at the TCP layer). Integrating the code from different layers without sacrificing modularity is hard.

- **Challenge 2:** Each manipulation may operate on different-size chunks and different portions of the packet. For example, TCP works in 16-bit quantities for a 16-bit checksum, while the popular DES encryption works in 64-bit quantities. Thus while working with one 32-bit word, the ILP loop has to deal with two TCP checksum words and half a DES word.

- **Challenge 3:** Some manipulations may be dependent on each other. For example, one should probably not decrypt a packet if the TCP checksum fails.

- **Challenge 4:** ILP can increase cache miss rate because it can reduce locality within a single manipulation. If we did TCP separately and DES separately instead of in a single loop, the code we'd use at each instant is smaller for the two single loops as opposed to the single loop. This makes it more likely that the code will be found in the instruction cache in the more naive implementation. Increasing integration beyond a certain point can destroy code locality so much that it may even have adverse effects. Some studies have shown this to be a major issue.

The first three challenges show that ILP is hard to do. The fourth challenge suggests that integrating more than a few operations can possibly even reduce performance. Finally, if the packet data is used multiple times, it could well reside in the data cache (even in a naive implementation), making all the bother about integrating loops unnecessary. Possibly for these reasons, ILP has remained a tantalizing idea. Beyond the copy–checksum combination, there has been little follow-up work in integrating other manipulations in academic or commercial systems.

5.6 BROADENING BEYOND DATA MANIPULATIONS

So far this chapter has concentrated on reducing the memory (and bus) bandwidth caused by data-manipulation operations. First, we concentrated on removing redundant data copying between the network and the application. Second, we addressed redundant copying between the file system, the application, and the network. Third, we looked at removing redundant memory reads and writes using integrated layer processing when several data-manipulation operations operate over the same packet. What is common to all these techniques is an attempt to reduce pressure on the memory and the I/O bus by avoiding redundant reads and writes.

But once this is done, there are still other sources of pressure that appear within an endnode architecture as shown in Figure 5.2. This is alluded to in the following excerpt from e-mail sent after the alpha release of a fast user-level Linux Web server [Ric01]:

> *With zero-copy sendfile, data movement is not an issue anymore, asynchronous network IO allows for really inexpensive thread scheduling, and system call invocation adds a very negligible overhead in Linux. What we are left with now is purely wait cycles, the CPUs and the NICs are contending for memory and bus bandwidth.*

In essence, once the first-order effects (such as eliminating copies) are taken care of, performance can be improved only by paying attention to what might be thought of as second-order effects. The next two subsections discuss two such architectural effects that greatly impact the use of bus and memory bandwidth: the effective use of caches and the choice of DMA versus PIO.

5.6.1 Using Caches Effectively

The architectural model of Figure 5.2 avoids two important details that were described in Chapter 2. Recall that the processor keeps one or more data caches (d-caches), and one or more instruction caches (I-caches). The data cache is a table that maps from memory addresses to data contents; if there are repeated reads and writes to the same location L in memory and L is cached, then these reads and writes can be served directly out of the data cache without incurring bus or memory bandwidth. Similarly, recall that programs are stored in memory; every line of code executed by the CPU has to be fetched from main memory unless it is cached in the instruction cache.

Now, packet data benefits little from a data cache, for there is little reuse of the data and copying involves writing to a *new* memory address, as opposed to repeated reads and writes from the *same* memory address. Thus the techniques already discussed to reduce copies are useful, despite the presence of a large processor data cache. However, there are two other items stored in memory that can benefit from caches. First, the program executing the protocol code to process a packet must be fetched from memory, unless it is stored in the I-cache. Second, the state required to process a packet (e.g., TCP connection state tables) must be fetched from memory, unless it is stored in the d-cache.

Of these two other possible contenders for memory bandwidth, the code to be executed is potentially a more serious threat. This is because the state, in bytes, required to process a packet (say, one connection table entry, one routing table entry) is generally small. However, for a small, 40-byte packet, even this can be significant. Thus avoiding the use of redundant state (which tends to pollute the d-cache) wherever possible can improve performance, as was described in Problem 11 of Chapter 4.

However, the code required to execute all of the networking stack (Data Link, TCP, IP, socket layer, and kernel entry and exit) can be much larger. For example, measurements in Blackwell [Bla96] show a total code size of 34 KB using a 1995 NetBSD TCP implementation. Given that even large packets on an Ethernet are at most 1.5 KB, the effort to load the code from memory can easily dwarf the effort to copy the packet multiple times.

In particular, if the I-cache is 8 KB (typical for older machines, such as the early Alpha machines used in Blackwell [Bla96]), this means that at most a quarter of the networking stack can fit in the cache. This in turn could imply that all or most of the code has to be fetched from memory every time a packet needs to be processed. Modern machines have not improved their I-cache sizes significantly. The Pentium III uses 16 KB. Thus effective use of the I-cache could be a key to improved performance, especially for small packets.

We now describe two techniques that can be used to improve I-cache effectiveness: code arrangement and locality-driven-layer processing.

CODE ARRANGEMENT

It is hard to realize when one is writing networking code that the actual layout of code in memory (and hence in the I-cache) is a degree of freedom that can be exploited (**P13**) with some effort. The key idea in code arrangement [MPBM96] is to lay out code in memory to optimize the common case (**P11**) such that commonly used code fits in the I-cache and the effort of loading the I-cache is not wasted.

At first glance, this seems to require no extra work. Since a cache should favor frequently used code over infrequently used code, this should happen automatically. Unfortunately, this is incorrect because of the following two aspects of the way I-caches are implemented.

- *Direct mapping:* An I-cache is a mapping of memory addresses to contents; the mapping is usually implemented by a simple hash function that optimizes for the case of sequential access. Thus most processors use direct-mapped I-caches, where the low-order bits of a memory address are used to index the I-cache array. If the high-order bits match, the contents are returned directly from cache; otherwise, a Read to memory is done across the bus, and the new data value and high-order bits are stored in the same location.

  Figure 5.13 shows the effect of this implementation artifact. The figure on the left shows the memory layout of code for two networking functions, with black code denoting infrequently used code. Since the I-cache size is only half the total size of the code, it is possible for two frequently accessed lines of code (such as X and Y, with addresses that are the same modulo the I-cache size) to map to the same location in the I-cache. Thus if both X and Y are used to process every packet, they will keep evicting each other from the cache even though they are both frequently used.

- *Multiple instructions per block:* Many I-caches can be thought of as an array of blocks, where multiple instructions (say, eight) are stored in a block. Thus when an instruction is fetched, all eight instructions in the same block are also fetched on the assumption of spatial locality: With sequential access, it seems probable that the other seven instructions will also be fetched, and it is cheaper to read multiple instructions from memory at the same time.

  Unfortunately, much of networking code contains error checks such as "If error E do X, else do Z." Z is hardly ever executed, but a compiler will often arrange the code for Z immediately after X. For example, in Figure 5.13 imagine that code for Z immediately

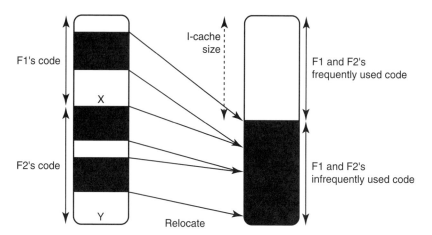

FIGURE 5.13 The figure on the left shows networking code that is laid out in memory so that frequently used (white) and infrequently used (black) code are arbitrarily intermixed. Using a direct-mapped cache of half the size of the total code can lead two frequently used instructions, such as X and Y, to collide. This problem can be avoided by relocating all frequently used code to be contiguous, as shown on the right.

follows X. If X and Z fall in the same block of eight instructions, then fetching frequently accessed X also results in fetching infrequently used Z. This makes loading the cache less efficient (more useless work) and makes the cache less useful after loading (less useful code in cache).

Note that both of these effects are caused by the fact that real caches imperfectly reflect temporal locality. The first is caused by an imperfect hash function that can cause collisions between two frequently used addresses. The second is caused by the fact that the cache also optimizes for spatial locality.

Both effects can be mitigated by reorganizing networking code [MPBM96] so that all frequently used code is contiguous (see right of Figure 5.13). For example, in the case "If error E do X, else do Z," the code for Z can be moved far away from X. This does require an extra jump instruction to be added to the code for Z so that it can jump back to the code that followed Z in the unoptimized version. However, this extra jump is taken only in the error case, and so it is not much of a cost.

This is an example of realizing that the memory location of code is a degree of freedom that can be optimized (**P13**) and an example of optimizing the expected case (**P11**) despite increasing the code path for infrequently used code.

LOCALITY-DRIVEN LAYER PROCESSING

Code reorganization can help up to a point but fails if the working set (i.e., the set of instructions actually accessed for almost every packet) exceeds the I-cache size. For example, in Figure 5.13, if the size of the white, frequently used instructions is larger than the I-cache, code reorganization will still help (fewer loads from memory are required because each load

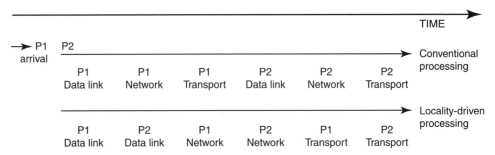

FIGURE 5.14   In a conventional processing timeline (shown from left to right), all the networking layers of packet *P*1 are processed before those of packet *P*2. In locality-driven receiver processing, each layer code is executed multiple times for multiple received packets (two in the picture) before moving on to the next layer.

loads only useful instructions). However, every instruction will still have to be fetched from memory.

While the working set of the networking stack may fit into a modern I-cache (which is getting bigger), it is possible that more complicated protocols (that run over TCP/IP) may not. The idea behind locality-driven layer processing [Bla96] is to be able to use the I-cache effectively as long as the code for each layer of the networking stack fits into the I-cache. By repeatedly processing the code for the same layer across multiple packets, the expense of loading the I-cache is shared (**P2c**) over multiple packets.

Consider the top timeline in Figure 5.14. In a conventional processing timeline (shown from left to right in the figure), all the networking layers of packet *P*1 are processed before those of packet *P*2. Imagine that two packets *P*1 and *P*2 arrive at a server. In a conventional implementation, all the processing of *P*1 is finished, starting with the data link layer (e.g., Ethernet driver) and ending with the transport (e.g., TCP) layer. Only then is the processing of packet *P*2 started.

The main idea in locality-driven processing is to exploit another degree of freedom (**P13**) and to process all the layer code for as many received packets as possible before moving on to the next layer. Thus in the bottom timeline, after the data link layer code for *P*1 is finished, the CPU moves on to execute the data link layer code for *P*2, *not* the network layer code for *P*1. This should not affect correctness because code for a layer should not depend on the state of lower layers. By contrast, integrated layer processing has more subtle dependencies and failure cases.

Thus if the code for each layer (e.g., the data link layer) fits into the I-cache while the code for all layers does not, then this optimization amortizes the cost of loading the I-cache over multiple packets. This is effectively using batch processing (**P2c**, expense sharing). The larger the size of the batch, the more effective the use of the I-cache.

The implementation can be made to tune the size of the batch dynamically [Bla96]. The code can batch-process up to, say, *k* packets from the queue of arrived packets, where *k* is a parameter that limits the latency. If the system is lightly loaded, then only one message at a time will be processed. On the other hand, if the system is heavily loaded, the batch size increases to make more effective use of memory bandwidth when it is most needed.

SOFTWARE ENGINEERING CONSIDERATIONS

Optimizations such as code restructuring (Figure 5.13) and locality-driven processing (Figure 5.14) also need to be evaluated by their effects on code modularity and maintenance. After all, one could rewrite the kernel and all applications using assembly language to more perfectly optimize for memory bandwidth. But it would be difficult to get the code to work or be maintainable.

Code restructuring is best done by a compiler. For example, error-handling code can be annotated with hints [MPBM96] suggesting which branches are more frequently taken (generally obvious to the programmer), and a specially augmented compiler can restructure the code for I-cache locality. Algorithms for this purpose are described in Mosberger et al. [MPBM96].

On the other hand, locality-driven processing preserves modularity within layers. Communication between layers must be changed as follows. If each layer code passes a packet to the code for a higher layer with a procedure call, this code must be modified to add packets to a *queue* for the higher layer. Similarly, when a layer is called, it removes packets from its read queue until the queue is exhausted; after processing each packet, it places it on the queue for its next-higher layer. This strategy works well when each layer can reuse buffers from other layers, as is the case for UNIX mbufs. Overall, the code changes may not be severe.

5.6.2 Direct Memory Access versus Programmed I/O

Earlier sections stated that the Witless scheme uses programmed I/O, or PIO (i.e., the processor or CPU is involved on every word transferred between memory and adaptor), while other schemes, such as VAX Clusters, use DMA (where the adaptor copies data directly to memory). It may seem that DMA is always better than PIO. However, comparisons between DMA and PIO are tricky because each method has subtle implications for the overall memory bandwidth used.

For instance, PIO has one advantage in that the data flows through the processor and thus ends up in the processor cache. This can be useful to prevent loss of memory bandwidth for subsequent access. Also, with PIO it is easy to integrate other functions, such as checksums, without requiring adaptor hardware to do the same function.

However, some studies have shown that if data arrives and is used much later (e.g., one scheduling quantum later) by the application, then placing data in the d-cache too early is wasteful of the d-cache and lowers rather than raises d-cache hit rate. On the other hand, DMA can steal cycles from the CPU and also requires some careful cache invalidation when data is written into a memory location (that could also be cached). So the jury is still out. The choice between the two is best decided on a case-by-case basis, taking into account architectural considerations and the application at hand. A more detailed study of the issues involved can be found in Mogul and Ramakrishnan [MR97].

5.7 CONCLUSIONS

As networks get faster, links today, such as Gigabit Ethernet, are often faster than the buses and memories within desktop computers and servers. Thus memory and bus bandwidth are crucial resources. This chapter describes techniques to optimize the use of memory and bus bandwidth for processing IP and Web packets, the dominant traffic streams found today in the Internet.

To this end, the chapter started by showing how to remove redundant copies involved in processing an IP packet using adaptor memory or virtual memory remapping. We then showed how to remove redundant copies involved in processing Web requests at a server by generalizing virtual memory remapping to include the file system or by combining file system and network I/O in a single system call. We then showed how to combine various data manipulations in one fell swoop. All of these techniques require changes to the application and kernel, but the changes are fairly localized and mostly preserve modularity.

We finally showed that, without care, protocol processing can dwarf copy overhead, and we described techniques to optimize the instruction cache. Comments such as Riccardi's [Ric01] indicate that modern Web servers may already be optimized for zero-copy implementations using *sendfile()*-style system calls. However, Riccardi [Ric01] indicates that such servers still burn processor cycles waiting for memory. Thus, techniques to improve I-cache efficiency may provide the next round of optimizations for Web servers. Figure 5.1 presents a summary of the techniques used in this chapter, together with the major principles involved.

It is important to state that all the performance problems involved in building a modern Web server have not been eliminated. Complex Web sites, such as amazon.com, often use several tiers of processing to respond to Web requests, including an application server, a Web server, and a database server. Such database-driven Web servers introduce new bottlenecks that may require new techniques beyond those described in this chapter. However, the underlying principles should hopefully remain the same.

In terms of principles, this chapter is about the repeated use of **P1**, avoiding obvious waste, where the waste is unnecessary reads and writes that consume precious memory and bus bandwidth. At first glance, principle **P1** seems vacuous or at best a cliché. What makes this principle deeper is that the waste is not apparent unless one broadens one's vision to see as much of the system as possible.

Within each local subsystem (e.g., application to kernel, kernel to network, disk to file system) there is no wasted memory bandwidth. It is only when one follows the adventures of a received packet that one discovers the redundancy between application-to-kernel and kernel-to-network copies. It is only when one broadens one's view even further to see the contortions involved in responding to a Web request that one notices the further redundancies involving the file system. Only when one broadens one's view further still does one see all the manipulations involved in processing a packet and the wasted reads to memory. Finally, it is only when one examines the loading of instructions that one sees the alarming possibility that the protocol code can be several times larger than the packet size.

Thus the use of the first principle of network algorithmics requires a synoptic eye, one that sees the whole system, from HTTP and its headers, to the file system, and down to the instruction caches. While this seems daunting in complexity, Chapter 2 has already argued that simple models of hardware, architecture, operating systems, and protocols can make such a holistic viewpoint possible. For example, I-caches have a number of complex variants, but a simple model of a direct-mapped I-cache with multiple instructions per block is not hard for an operating system designer to keep in mind.

Finally, compared to the beauty and complexity of theoretical techniques such as the ellipsoid algorithm for linear programming and the theory of rapidly mixing Markov chains, techniques in systems such as copy avoidance seem drab and shallow. However, one can argue that the complexity of systems is not in *depth* (i.e., the complexity of each component by itself) but in *breadth* (i.e., the complex relationships between components). Perhaps the breadth of understanding (HTTP, file system, networking code, instruction cache implementation) required to optimize memory bandwidth in a Web server provides some evidence for this thesis.

5.8 EXERCISES

1. **Data caches and copies:** A normal data cache is a mapping from a memory location address to a piece of content. If the content is frequently accessed, then the content can be accessed directly from the fast cache instead of making a memory access. Assuming the cache is a write-back cache, even writes can be written to the cache instead of memory and only written to memory when the cache is overwritten. A modern cache block is fairly large (128 bits), with a mapping from a 32-bit address to 128 bits of data starting at that address.

   We want to address the copying problem where various modules (including the network and file system) copy data via intermediate buffers that are soon overwritten (e.g., socket buffer, application buffer). The chapter did so with software changes. Here we consider whether changing the hardware architecture can help *without software changes* such as IO-Lite, fbufs, and mmap.

   - Even an ordinary data cache may help remove some of the overhead when copying data from location L to location M. Explain why. (Assume that location M is a temporary buffer that is soon overwritten, as in a socket buffer. Assume that if only a single word is written in a large cache block, the remaining words can be marked invalid.) Intuitively, this problem is asking whether there is an equivalent of copy-on-write (used to reduce copying between virtual address spaces) in the world of data caches.

   - Now assume a different data cache design, where a cache is a mapping from *one or more* addresses to the same content. Thus a cache has changed from a one-to-one mapping to a many-to-one mapping. For example, assume a cache where two locations can point to the same content. Thus a cache entry may be (L, M, C), where L and M are addresses and C is the common contents of L and M. A memory access to *either* L or M will return C. What is the advantage over the previous scheme in the previous item?

   - This is all very speculative and wild. Comment on the disadvantages of the idea in the previous item. In particular, many caches use a technique called *set associativity*, where a simple hash function (e.g., low-order bits) is used to select a small set of cache entries that the hardware searches in parallel. Why might the multiple address per cache entry interact poorly with the set associative search?

2. **Application-level optimizations for Web servers:** Operating systems such as the Exokernel [EKO95] take an even more extreme viewpoint and allow the application to customize kernel features for its benefit without compromising safety for other applications. One interesting optimization is to combine the final TCP FIN with the read of the last data segment (an optimization allowed by TCP).

   - Why does this optimization help small Web transfers (which are quite common)?

   - Why is this optimization hard to do in a regular Web server, and why is it easier if the application is integrated with the kernel, as in the Exokernel?

- Explain how this optimization can be migrated to an ordinary Web server by passing information across the interface (**P9**) without compromising safety.

3. **Reverse copyout:** The emulated copy-on-write paper [BS96] describes an interesting degree of freedom (**P13**) for copying page-aligned data between two modules (say, system and application). Imagine that you wish to copy a *partial* page from an application page, X, to a system page, Y. If the page is full, assume that you can swap the two pages efficiently. Assume the partial page has useful data D and some remainder R.

   - If the amount of data D is small compared to R, it is simpler to copy D to the destination page in Y. On the other hand, if D is large (say, almost all of the page) compared to R, devise a simple strategy to minimize copying. Note that if the destination page, Y, has some other data in the remainder of the page, that data must remain after the copy.

   - What is a simple threshold you would use to choose between these two strategies?

CHAPTER 6

Transferring Control

Control thy passions, lest they take vengeance on thee.

— EPICETUS

In a Scott Adams cartoon, Dilbert complains to Dogbert that he is embarassed to work at a company where even paying a simple invoice takes 6 months. The invoice first comes into the mail room for aging, spends some time at the secretary's desk, goes to the desk of the main decision maker, and finally ends up in accounts payable. When processing an invoice in Dilbert's company, the flow of control works its way through layers of command, each of which incurs significant overhead.

A management consultant might suggest that Dilbert's company streamline the processing of an invoice by eliminating mediating layers wherever possible and by making each layer as responsive as possible. However, each layer has some reason for existence. The mailroom aggregates mail delivery service for all departments in the company. The secretary protects the busy boss from interrupts and weeds out inappropriate requests. The boss must eventually decide whether the invoice is worth paying. Finally, the mundane details of disbursing cash are best left to accounts payable.

A modern CPU processing a network message also goes through similar layers of mediation. The device, for example, an Ethernet adaptor, interrupts the CPU, asking somewhat stridently for attention. Control is passed to the kernel. The kernel batches interrupts wherever possible, does the network layer processing for the packet, and finally schedules the application process (say, a Web server) to run. As always, the reception of a single packet provides too limited a picture of the overall processing context. For instance, a Web server will parse the request (such as a GET) in the network packet, look for the file, and institute proceedings to retrieve the file from disk. When the file gets read into memory, a response containing the requested file is sent back, prepended with an HTTP header.

While Chapter 5 concentrated on reducing the overhead of operations that touch the *data* in a packet (e.g., copying, checksumming), this chapter concentrates on reducing the *control* overheads involved in processing a packet. As in Chapter 5, we start by examining the control overheads involved in sending or receiving a packet. We then broaden to our canonical network application, a Web server.

This chapter is organized as follows. Section 6.1 starts by describing the control flow costs involved in a computer: interrupt overheads (involved when a device asks asynchronously for attention), system calls (involved when a user asks the kernel for service, thus moving the flow of control across a protection boundary), and process-context switching (allowing a new

Number	Principle	Used In
P8	Go beyond downcalls used in specifications	Upcalls
P8	Process per message, not per layer	x-Kernel
P13	Link protocol implementation with user code	Mach variants
P13	Process per disk access	Flash
P13	Modularize by task, not clients	Haboob Web server
P4	VM mapping to avoid copies in cache and application	Flash
P15	Bitmap tree	Fast ufalloc()
P12a **P9** **P12**	Incrementally compute interest vector Pass hints from protocol to select () Remember interest across calls	Fast select()
P3c **P2**	Move protection from kernel to adaptor Have kernel authorize adaptor on initialization	ADCs
P13	Batch process interrupts	Most OSs
P2b	Execute protocol in the context of the receive process	LRP (Lazy Receiver Processing)

F I G U R E 6.1 Techniques for reducing control overhead that are discussed in this chapter, together with the corresponding principles.

process to run when the current process is stymied waiting for some resource or has run too long). Thus the rest of this chapter is organized around reducing these control overhead costs, from the largest (context switching) to the smallest (interrupt overhead).

Accordingly, Section 6.2 concentrates on reducing process-context switching by describing how to structure *networking* code (e.g., TCP/IP) to avoid context switching. Section 6.3 then describes how to structure *application code* (e.g, a Web server) to reduce context-switching costs. Sections 6.4 and 6.5 focus on reducing or eliminating system call overhead. Section 6.4 shows how to reduce overhead in the implementation of a crucial system call used by event-driven Web servers to decide which of the connections they are handling are ready to be serviced. Section 6.5 goes further and describes user-level networking that bypasses the kernel in the common case of sending and receiving a packet. Finally, Section 6.6 briefly describes simple ideas to avoid interrupt overhead.

The techniques described in this chapter (and the corresponding principles invoked) are summarized in Figure 6.1.

Quick Reference Guide

The most useful sections for an implementor today are as follows. Section 6.3 describes how to structure *application code* (e.g, a Web server) to reduce context-switching costs, presenting alternatives to event-driven Web servers. Section 6.4 focuses on reducing the overhead of the *select()* system call (or similar calls in other operating systems) used by event-driven servers to decide which client to service next. Section 6.5 shows how to eliminate system call overhead using techniques such as VIA (virtual interface adaptor).

6.1 WHY CONTROL OVERHEAD?

Chapter 5 started with a review of the *copying* overhead involved in a Web server by showing the potential copies (Figure 5.2) involved in responding to a GET request at a server. By contrast, Figure 6.2 shows the potential *control* overhead involved in a large Web server that handles many clients. Note that in comparison with Figure 5.2 for Web copies, Figure 6.2 ignores all aspects of data transfer. Thus Figure 6.2 uses a simplified architectural picture that concentrates on the control interplay between the network adaptor and the CPU (via interrupts), between the application and the kernel (via system calls), and between various application-level processes or threads (via scheduler invocations). The reader unfamiliar with operating systems may wish to consult the review of operating systems in Chapter 2. For simplicity, the picture shows only one CPU in the server (many servers are multiprocessors) and a single disk (some servers use multiple disks and disks with multiple heads). Assume that the server can handle a large number (say, thousands) of concurrent clients.

For the purposes of understanding the possible control overhead involved in serving a GET request, the relevant aspects of the story are slightly different from that in Chapter 5. First, assume the client has sent a TCP SYN request to the server that arrives at the adaptor from which it is placed in memory. The kernel is then informed of this arrival via an *interrupt*. The kernel notifies the Web server via the unblocking of an earlier *system call*; the Web server application will accept this connection if it has sufficient resources.

FIGURE 6.2 Control overhead involved in handling a GET request at a server.

In the second step of processing, some server process parses the Web request. For example, assume the request is GET File 1. In the third step, the server needs to locate where the file is on disk, for example, by navigating directory structures that may also be stored on disk. Once the file is located, in the fourth step, the server process initiates a Read to the file system (another system call). If the file is in the file cache, the read request can be satisfied quickly; failing a cache hit, the file subsystem initiates a disk seek to read the data from disk. Finally, after the file is in an application buffer, the server sends out the HTTP response by writing to the corresponding connection (another system call).

So far the only control overhead appears to be that of system calls and interrupts. However, that is because we have not examined closely the structure of the networking and application code.

First, if the networking code is structured naively, with a single process per layer in the stack, then the process scheduling overhead (on the order of hundreds of microseconds) for processing a packet can easily be much larger than a single packet arrival time. This potential scheduling overhead is shown in Figure 6.2 with a dashed line to the TCP/IP code in the kernel. Fortunately, most networking code is structured more monolithically, with minimal control overhead, although there are some clever techniques that can do even better.

Second, our description of Web processing has focused on a single client. Since we are assuming a large Web server that is working concurrently on behalf of thousands of clients, it is unclear how the Web server should be structured. At one extreme, if each client is a separate process (or thread) running the Web server code, *concurrency* is maximized (because when client 1 is waiting for a disk read, client 2 could be sending out network packets) at the cost of high *process scheduling* overhead.

On the other hand, if all clients are handled by a single event-driven process, then context-switching overhead is minimized, but the single process must internally schedule the clients to maximize concurrency. In particular, it must know when file reads have completed and when network data has arrived.

Many operating systems provide a *system call* for this purpose that we have generically called **FindActive**() in Figure 6.2. For example, in UNIX the specific name for this generic routine is the *select( )* system call. While even an empty system call is expensive because of the kernel-to-application boundary crossing, an inefficient *select( )* implementation can be even more expensive.

Thus there are challenging questions as to how to structure both the networking and server code in order to minimize scheduling overhead and maximize concurrency. For this reason, Figure 6.2 shows the clients partitioned into groups, each of which is implemented in a single process or thread. Note that placing all clients in a single group yields the event-driven approach, while placing each client in a separate group yields the process- (or thread-) per-client approach.

Thus an unoptimized implementation can incur considerable process-switching overhead (hundreds of microseconds) if the application and networking code is poorly structured. Even if process-structuring overhead is removed, system calls can cost tens of microseconds, and interrupts can cost microseconds. To put these numbers in perspective, observe that on a 10-GB Ethernet link, a 40-byte packet can arrive at a PC every 3.2 μsec.

Given that 10-Gbps links are already arriving, it is clear that careful attention has to be paid to control overhead. Note that, as we have seen in Chapter 2, as CPUs get faster, historically the control overheads associated with context switching, system calls, and interrupts have not improved at the same rate. Some progress has been made with more efficient operating systems such as Linux, but the progress will not be sufficient to keep up with increasing link speeds.

We now begin attacking the bottlenecks described in Figure 6.2.

6.2 AVOIDING SCHEDULING OVERHEAD IN NETWORKING CODE

One of the major difficulties with implementing a protocol is to balance modularity (so you implement a big system in pieces and get each piece right, independent of the others) and performance (so you can get the overall system to perform well). As a simple example, consider how one might implement a networking stack. The "obvious modularity" would be to implement the transport protocol (e.g., TCP) as a process, the routing protocol (e.g., IP) as a process, and the applications as a separate process. If that were the case, however, every received packet would take at least two process-context switches, which are expensive. There are, however, a number of creative alternatives that allow modularity as well as efficiency. These were first pointed out by Dave Clark in a series of papers.

Figure 6.3 provides an example that Clark [Cla85] used to illustrate his ideas. It consists of a simple application that reads data from a keyboard and sends it to the network using a reliable transport protocol. When the data is received by some receiver on the network, the data is displayed on the screen. The vertical slices show the various protocol layers, with the topmost slice (routines such as display-get-data and display-receive) being the application protocol, the second slice (routines such as transport-receive and transport-send) being the transport protocol, and the bottom slice (routines such as net-receive and net-dispatch) being the network protocol. The naive way to implement this protocol would be to have a process per slice, which would involve three processes and two full-scale context switches per received or sent packet.

Instead, Clark suggests using only two processes each at the sender and two processes at the receiver (shown as boxed vertical sections) to implement the network protocol stack. In Figure 6.3 the leftmost two sections correspond to receiver processes and the rightmost two sections correspond to sender processes. Thus the sender has a Keyboard Handler process

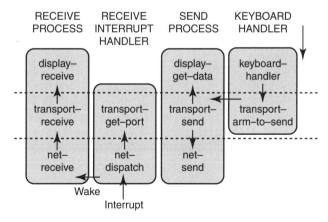

FIGURE 6.3 Implementing a protocol using upcalls.

that gathers data coming in from the keyboard and calls *transport-arm-to-send* when it has got some data. Notice that *transport-arm-to-send* is a transport-layer function that is exported to the Keyboard Handler process and is executed by the Keyboard Handler process. At this point the Keyboard Handler can suspend itself (a context switch). *Transport-arm-to-send* only tells the transport protocol that this connection wished to send data; it does not transfer data.

However, the transport-send process may not send data immediately because of flow control limitations. When the flow control limits are removed (because of acks arriving), the Send Process will execute the transport-*send* routine for this connection. The *send* call will first upcall the application protocol, which exports a routine called *display-get-data* that actually provides the transport protocol with the data for the application. This is advantageous because the application may have received more keyboard data by the time the transport protocol is ready to send, and one might as well send as much data as possible in a packet. Finally, within the context of the same process, transport adds a transport-layer header and makes a call to the network protocol to actually send the packet.

At the receiving end, the packet is received by the receive interrupt handler using a network-layer routine called *net-dispatch* that needs to find which process to dispatch the received packet to. To find out, *net-dispatch* makes an upcall to transport-get-port. This is a routine exported by the transport layer that looks at port numbers in the header to figure out which application (e.g., FTP) must handle the packet. Then a context switch is made and the Receive Handler relinquishes control and wakes up the Receive Process, which executes network-layer functions, transport-layer functions, and finally the application-level code to display the data. Note that a single process is executing all the layers of protocol.

The idea was a bit unusual at the time because the conventional dogma until that point was that layers should only use services of layers below; thus calls between layers had, historically, been "downcalls." However, Clark pointed out that downcalls were perhaps required for protocol *specifications* but were not the only alternative for protocol *implementations*. In our example in particular, upcalls are used to obtain data (e.g., the upcall to *display-get-data*) and for advice from upper layers (upcall to *transport-get-port*).

While upcalls are commonly used in real implementations, there is probably no difference between an upcall and a standard procedure call except for its possible novelty in the context of a networking layered implementation. However, the more important idea, which is perhaps more lasting, is the idea of using only one or two processes to process a message, each process consisting of routines from two or more protocol layers. This idea found its way into systems like the x-kernel [HP91] and into user-level networking, which is described in the next section.

More generally, the idea of considering alternative implementation structures that preserve modularity without sacrificing performance is a classic example of Principle **P8**, which says that implementors should consider alternatives to reference implementations described in specifications. Notice that each protocol layer can still be implemented modularly but the upcalled routines can be registered by upper layers when the system starts up.

6.2.1 Making User-Level Protocol Implementations Real

Most modern machines certainly do not implement each protocol layer in a separate process. Instead, in UNIX all the protocol code (transport, network, and data link) is handled as part of a single kernel "process." When a packet arrives via an interrupt, the interrupt handler notes the arrival of the packet, possibly queues it to memory, and then schedules a kernel process (via what is sometimes called a *software interrupt*) to actually process the packet.

FIGURE 6.4 Demultiplexing a packet to the final destination process using an intermediate demultiplexing process is expensive.

The kernel process does the data link, network, and transport-layer code (using upcalls); by looking at the transport port numbers, the kernel process knows the application. It then wakes up the application. Thus every packet is processed using at least two context switches: one from the interrupt context to the kernel process doing protocol handling, and one from the kernel process to the process running the application code (e.g., the Web, FTP).

The idea behind user-level protocol implementation is to realize the aspect of Clark's idea shown in the receive process of Figure 6.3, where the protocol handlers execute in the same process as the application and can communicate using upcalls. User-level implementations have two possible advantages: We can potentially bypass the kernel and go directly from the interrupt handler to the application, as in the Clark model, saving a context switch. Also, the protocol code can be written and debugged in user space, which is a far friendlier place to implement protocols (debugging tools work in user space and do not work well at all in the kernel).

One extreme way to do this was advocated in Mach, where all protocols were implemented in user space. Also, protocols were allowed to be significantly more general than in Clark's example of Figure 6.3. Thus when a receiving interrupt handler received a packet, it had no way of easily telling to which process it should dispatch the packet (since the network-layer implementations done in the final process contained the demultiplexing code). In particular, one can't just call transport to examine the port number (as in Clark's example) since we can have lots of possible transport protocols and lots of possible network protocols.

A naive method was initially used, as shown in Figure 6.4. This involved a separate demultiplexing process that received all packets and examined them to determine the final destination process, which is then dispatched to. This is quite sad, because our efforts so far have been to reduce context switches, but the new demultiplexing process is actually adding back the missing context switch.

The simple idea used to remedy this situation is to pass extra information (**P9**) across the application–kernel interface so that each application can pass information about what kinds of packets it wants to process. This is shown in Figure 6.5. For example, a mail application may wish for all packets whose Ethernet-type field is IP, whose IP protocol number specifies TCP, and whose TCP destination port number is 25.

Recall that we are talking about the mail application implementing all of IP, TCP, and mail. To do so, the kernel defines an interface, which is typically some form of programming language. For example, the earliest one was the CSPF (CMU Stanford packet filter), which specifies the fields for packets using a stack-based programming language. A more commonly used language is BPF (Berkeley packet filter), which uses a stack-based language; a more efficient language is PathFinder. These demultiplexing algorithms are described in Chapter 8.

FIGURE 6.5   The packet filter approach to demultiplexing.

Note that one has to be careful about passing information from an application to a kernel; any such information should be checked so that malicious or wrong applications cannot destroy the kernel. In particular, one has to prevent applications from providing arbitrary code to kernels, which then causes havoc. Fortunately, there are software technologies that can "sandbox" foreign code so it can do damage only within its own allotted space of memory (its sandbox). For example, a stack-based language can be made to work on a specified size of stack that can be bounds checked at every point. This form of technology has culminated recently in execution of arbitrary Java applets received from the network.

Clearly, if packets are dispatched from the kernel interrupt handler (using the collection of packet filters) to the receiving process, the receiving process should implement the protocol stack. However, replicating the TCP/IP code in every application would cause a lot of code redundancy. Thus TCP/IP is generally (in such systems) implemented as a shared library that is linked in (a single copy is used to which the application has a pointer, but with the code written in a so-called *reentrant* way, to allow reuse).

This is not as easy as it looks because there is some TCP state that is common to all connections, though most are TCP state connection specific. There are other problems because the last write done by an application should be retransmitted by TCP, but the application may exit its process after its last write. However, these problems can be fixed. User-level implementations have been written [TNML93, MB93] to provide excellent performance. Fundamentally, they exploit a degree of freedom (**P13**) in observing that protocols do not have to be implemented in the kernel.

6.3 AVOIDING CONTEXT-SWITCHING OVERHEAD IN APPLICATIONS

The last section concentrated on removing process-scheduling overhead for processing a single packet received by the network by effectively limiting the processing to fielding one interrupt (which, as we discuss in Section 6.6, can also be removed or amortized over several packets) and dispatching the packet to the final process in which the application (that processes the packet) resides. If the destination process is currently running, then there is even no process-scheduling overhead. Thus after all optimizations there can be close to no control overhead for processing a packet.

This is analogous to Chapter 5, in which the first few sections showed how to process a received packet with zero copies. However, in that chapter after broadening one's viewpoint to see the complete application processing, it became apparent that there were further redundant copies caused by interactions with the file system.

In a similar fashion, this section broadens beyond the processing of a single packet to consider how an application processes packets. Once again, as in Chapter 5, we consider a Web server (Figure 6.2) because it is a canonical example of a server that needs to be made more efficient and because of its importance in practice.

In what follows, we will use a Web server as an example of a canonical server that may require the handling of a large number of connections. In another example, Barile [Bar04] describes a TCP-to-UDP proxy server for a telephony server that can handle 100,000 concurrent connections.

How should a Web server be structured? Before tackling this question, it helps to understand the potential concurrency within a single Web server. Readers familiar with operating systems may wish to skim over the next three paragraphs. These are included for readers not as familiar with the secret life of a workstation.[1]

Even with a single CPU and a single disk head, there are opportunities for concurrency. For example, assume that in processing a read for File 1, File 1 is not in cache. Thus the CPU initiates a disk read. Since this may take a few milliseconds to complete, and the CPU can do an instruction almost every nanosecond, it is obvious waste to idle the CPU during this read. Thus a more sensible strategy is to have the CPU switch to processing another client while Client 1's disk read is in progress. This allows processing by the disk on behalf of Client 1 to be overlapped with processing by the CPU for Client 2.

A second example of concurrency between the CPU and a device (that is relevant to a Web server) is overlapping between network I/O (as performed by the adaptor) and the CPU. For example, after a server accepts a connection, it may do a *Read* to an accepted connection for Client 1. If the CPU waits for the *Read* to complete it may wait a long time, potentially also several milliseconds. This is because the remote client has to send a packet that has to make its way through the network and finally be written by the adaptor to the socket corresponding to Client 1 at the server.

By switching to another client, processing by the network on behalf of Client 1 is overlapped with processing by the CPU on behalf of some other client. Similarly, when doing a *Write* to the network, the *Write* may be blocked because of the lack of buffer space in the socket buffer. This buffer space may be released much later when acknowledgments arrive from the destination.

The last three paragraphs show that for a Web server to be efficient, every opportunity for concurrency must be exploited to increase effective throughput. Thus a CPU in a Web server must switch between clients when one client is blocked waiting for I/O. We now consider various ways to structure a server application and their effects on concurrency and scheduling overhead.

6.3.1 Process per Client

In terms of programming, the simplest way to implement a Web server is to structure the processing of each client as a separate process. In other words, every client is in a separate group by itself in Figure 6.2. In Chapter 2, we saw that the operating system scheduler juggles

---

[1]Recall that the intent of network algorithmics and of this book is to allow all constituencies — for example, hardware designers — to understand the relevant issues.

between processes, assigning a new process to a CPU when a current process is blocked. Most modern operating systems also can take into account multiple CPUs and schedule the CPUs such that all CPUs are doing useful work wherever possible.

Thus the Web server application need not do the juggling between clients; the *operating system* does this automatically on the application's behalf. For example, when Client 1 is blocked waiting for the disk controller, the operating system may save all the context for the Client 1 process to memory and allow the Client 2 process to run by restoring its context from memory.

This simplicity, however, comes at a cost. First, as we have seen, process-context switching and restoring is expensive. It requires reads and writes from memory to registers to save and restore context. Recall that the context includes changing the page tables being used (because page tables are per process); thus any virtual memory translations cached within the TLB need to be cached. Similarly, the contents of the data cache and the instruction cache are likely to represent the tastes and preferences of the previously resident process; thus much of it may be useless to the new process. When all caches fail, the initial performance of the switched-in process can be very poor.

Further, spawning a new process when a new client comes in, as was done by some initial Web servers, is also expensive.[2] Fortunately, the overhead to create and destroy processes when clients come and go can be avoided by precomputation and/or lazy process deletion (**P2**, shifting computation in time). When a client finishes its request processing and the connection is terminated, rather than destroy the process, the process can be returned to a pool of idle processes. The process can then be assigned to the next new client that needs a process to shepherd its request through the server.

A second issue is the problem of matchmaking between new arriving clients and processes in the process pool. A naive way to do this is as follows. Each new client is handed to a well-known matchmaking process, which then hands off each new client to some available process in the pool. However, operating system designers have realized the importance of matchmaking. They have invented system calls (for instance, the *Accept* call in UNIX) to do matchmaking at the cost of a system call invocation, as opposed to requiring a process-context switch.

When a process in the pool is done it makes an *Accept* call and waits in line in a kernel data structure. When a new client comes in, its socket is handed off to the idle process that is first in line. Thus the kernel provides matchmaking services directly.

6.3.2 Thread per Client

Even after removing the overheads of creating a process on demand and the overhead of matchmaking, processes are an expensive solution. Since slow wide-area connections to servers are very common and the rate of arrivals to popular Web servers can easily exceed 2000 per second, it is not unusual for a Web server to have 6000 concurrent clients being served at once.

As we have seen, even if the processes are already created, switching between processes incurs TLB and cache misses and requires effort to save and restore context. Further, each process requires memory to store context. This can take away from the memory needed by the file cache.

---

[2]While some of these early schemes may seem primitive in terms of the techniques in this book, they were probably very simple to program and maintain. It is difficult to quantify the trade-off between efficiency and ease of implementation and maintenance.

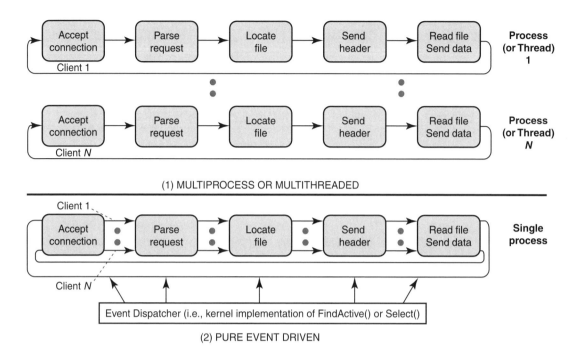

FIGURE 6.6 The two simplest alternatives for structuring a Web server: (1) the use of a single process (or thread) per client; (2) a single process implementation that uses an event manager to tell the process of the status of I/O for each client.

An intermediate stance is to use threads, or lightweight processes. Note that threads generally trust each other, as is appropriate for all the threads processing different clients in a Web server. Thus in Figure 6.6, we can replace the processing of each client with a separate thread per client, all within the protection of a single process. Note that the threads share the same virtual memory. Thus TLB entries do not have to be flushed between threads.

Further, the fact that threads can share memory implies that all threads can use a common cache to share file name translations and even files. Implementing a process per client, on the other hand, implies that file caches can often not be shared efficiently across processes, because each process uses a separate virtual memory space. Thus application caches for Web servers, as described in Chapter 5, will suffer in performance because files common to many clients are replicated.[3] Thus a popular Web server, the Apache Web server, is implemented using a thread per client in Windows.

However, when all is said and done, the overhead for switching between threads, while smaller than that for switching between processes, is still considerable. Fundamentally, the operating system must still save and restore per-thread context such as stacks and registers.

---

[3]However, this replication will not cost much *if* a system such as I/O-Lite, described in Chapter 5, is used. The problem is that many operating systems do not have such mechanisms to allow subsystems to share data.

Also, the memory required to store per-thread or per-process state takes away from the file cache, which then leads to potentially higher miss rates.

6.3.3 Event-Driven Scheduler

If a general-purpose operating system facility is too expensive, the simplest strategy is to avoid it completely. Thus while thread scheduling provides a facility for juggling between clients without further programming, if it is too expensive, the application may benefit from *doing the juggling itself*. Effectively, the application must implement its own internal scheduler that juggles the state of each client.

For example, the application may have to implement a state machine that remembers that Client 1 is in Stage 2 (HTTP processing) while Client 2 is in Stage 3 (waiting for disk I/O) and Client 3 is in Stage 4 (waiting for a socket buffer to clear up to send the next part of the response).

However, the kernel has an advantage over an application program because the kernel sees all I/O completion events. For example, if Client 1 is blocked waiting for I/O, in a per-thread implementation, when the disk controller interrupts the CPU to say that the data is now in memory, the kernel can now attempt to schedule the Client 1 thread.

Thus if the Web server application is to do its own scheduling between clients, the kernel must pass information (**P9**) across the API to allow a single threaded application to view the completion of all I/O that it has initiated. Many operating systems provide such a facility, which we generically called *FindActive()* in Figure 6.2. For example, Windows NT 3.5 has an I/O completion port (IOCP) mechanism, and UNIX provides the *select()* system call.

The main idea is that the application stays in a loop invoking the *FindActive()* call. Assuming there is always some work to do on behalf of some client, the call will return with a list of I/O descriptors (e.g., file 1 data is now in memory, connection 5 has received data) with pending work. When the Web server processes these active descriptors, it loops back to making another *FindActive()* call.

If there is always some client that needs attention (typically true for a busy server), there is no need to sleep and invoke the costs of context switching (e.g., scheduler overhead, TLB misses) when juggling between clients. Of course, such juggling requires that the application keep a state machine that allows it to do its own context switching among the many concurrent requests. Such application-specific internal scheduling is more efficient than invoking the general-purpose, external scheduler. This is because the application knows the minimum set of context that must be saved when moving from client to client.

The Zeus server and the original Harvest/Squid proxy cache server use the single-process event-driven model. Figure 6.6 contrasts the multiprocess (and multithreaded) server architectures with an event-driven architecture. The details of a generic event-driven implementation using a single process can be found in Barile [Bar04], together with pointers to source code. Barile [Bar04] describes generic code that is abstracted to work across platforms (a crucial requirement for today's server environments), including Windows and UNIX.

6.3.4 Event-Driven Server with Helper Processes

In principle, an event-driven server can extract as much concurrency from a stream of client operations as a multiprocess or multithreaded server. Unfortunately, many operating systems, such as UNIX, do not provide suitable support for nonblocking disk operations.

For example, if an event-driven server is not to waste opportunities to do useful work, then when it issues a *read()* to a file that is not in cache, we wish the *read()* to return immediately saying it is unavailable so that the *read()* is nonblocking. This allows the server to move on to other clients. Later, when the disk I/O completes, the application can find out using the next invocation of the *FindActive()* call. On the other hand, if the *read()* call is blocking, then the server main loop would be stuck waiting for the milliseconds required for disk I/O to complete.

The difficulty is that many operating systems, such as Solaris and UNIX, allow nonblocking *read()* and *write()* operations on network connections but may block when used on disk files. These operating systems do allow other asynchronous system calls for disk I/O, but these are not integrated with the *select()* call (i.e., the UNIX equivalent of *FindActive()*). Thus in such operating systems one must choose between the loss of concurrency incurred by blocking on disk I/O and going beyond the single-process model.

The Flash Web server [PDZ99a] goes beyond the single-process model to maximize concurrency. When a file is to be read, the main server process first tests if the file is already in memory using either a standard system call[4] or by locking down the file cache pages so that the server process always knows which files are in the cache.[5] If the file is not in memory, the main server process instructs a helper process to perform the potentially blocking disk read. When the helper is done, it communicates to the main server process via some form of interprocess communication such as a pipe.

Note that unlike the multiprocess model, helpers are needed only for each concurrent disk operation and not for each concurrent client request. In some sense, this model exploits a degree of freedom (**P13**) by observing that there are interesting alternatives between a single process and a process per client.

Besides file reads, helper processes can also be used to do directory lookups to locate the file on disk. While Flash maintains a cache that maps between directory path names and disk files, if there is a cache miss, then there is a need to search through on-disk directory structures. Since such directory lookups can also block, these are also relegated to helper processes. Increasing the pathname cache does increase memory consumption, but the reduced cache miss rate may reduce the number of helper processes required and so decrease memory overall.

Clearly, helper processes should be prespawned to avoid the latency of creating a process each time a helper process is invoked. How many helper processes should be spawned? Too few can cause concurrency loss, and too many results in wasted memory. The solution in Flash [PDZ99a] is to dynamically spawn and destroy helper processes according to load.

6.3.5 Task-Based Structuring

The top of Figure 6.7 depicts the event-driven approach augmented with helper processes. Notice the similarity to the simple event-handler approach shown at the bottom of Figure 6.6, except for the addition of helper processes.

There are some problems with the event-driven architecture with helper processes.

- **Complexity:** The application designer must manage the state machine for juggling client requests without help.

---

[4]The original Flash Web server uses UNIX's *mincore()* command.

[5]If the virtual memory system could swap out cached files under the nose of the server, the server may think a file is in cache when it really is not.

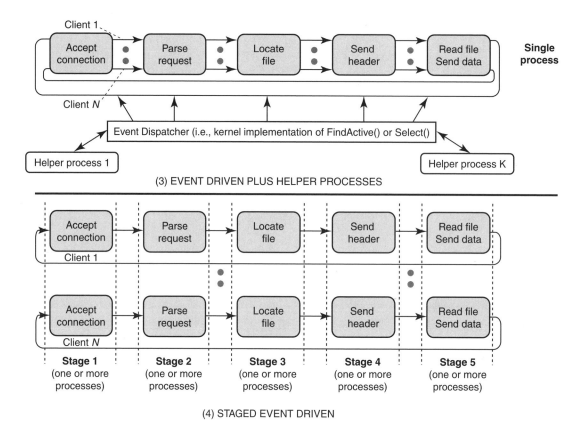

FIGURE 6.7 Two other proposals for Web architectures besides the two shown in Figure 6.6: (3) event-driven plus helper processes; (4) staged event-driven architecture.

- **Modularity:** The code for the server is written as one piece. While Web servers are popular, there are many other Web services that may use some similar pieces of code (e.g., for accepting connections). A more modular approach could allow code reuse.

- **Overload control:** Production Web servers have to deal with wide variations of load from huge client populations. Thus it is crucial to continue to make some progress during overload (without thrashing) and to be as fair as possible across clients.

   The main idea in the staged event-driven architecture [WCB01] is to exploit another degree of freedom (**P13**) in decomposing code. Instead of decomposing into threads *horizontally* by client, as in a multithreaded architecture, the server system is decomposed *vertically* by tasks within each client request cycle, as shown on the bottom of Figure 6.6. Each stage can be handled by one or more threads. Thus the staged model can be considered a refinement of the simple event-driven model. This is because it assigns a main thread and a potential thread to each stage of server processing. Once that is done, the stages communicate via queues, and more refined overload control can be done at each stage.

6.4 FAST SELECT

To motivate the fast-selection problem, Section 6.4.1 presents a mysterious performance problem found in the literature. Section 6.4.2 then describes the usage and implementation of the *select( )* call in UNIX. Section 6.4.3 describes an analysis of the overheads, and applies the implementation principles to suggest ideas for improvement. Based on the analysis, Section 6.4.4 describes an improvement, assuming that the API cannot change. Finally, Section 6.4.5 proposes an even better solution that involves a more dramatic change to the API.

6.4.1 A Server Mystery

The previous section suggested that avoiding process-scheduling overheads was important in a Web server. For example, an event-driven server completely reduces process scheduling overhead by using a single thread for all clients and then using a *FindActive( )* call such as *select( )*. Now, the CERN Web proxy used a process per client, and the Squid (formerly Harvest) Web server [CDea96] used an event-driven implementation. Measurements done in a LAN environment indeed showed [CDea96] that the Squid Web proxy performed an order of magnitude better than the CERN server.

A year later another group repeated these tests in a WAN (i.e., wide area network) environment [MRG97] and found that in the WAN environment there was *no difference* in performance between the CERN and Squid servers. The problem is to elucidate this mystery.

The mystery was finally solved by Banga and Mogul [BM98]. A key observation is that given the same throughput (in terms of connections per second), the higher round-trip delays in a WAN environment lead to a *larger number of concurrent connections* in a WAN setting. For example, in a WAN environment with mean connection times of 2 seconds [BMD99] and a Web server throughput of 3000 connections per second, Little's law (from queuing theory) predicts that the average number of concurrent connections is the product, or 6000.

On the other hand, in a LAN environment with a round-trip delay of 2 msec, the average number of concurrent connections drops to six. Note that if the throughput stays the same, in the wide area setting a large fraction of the connections must be idle (waiting for replies) at any given time.

Given this, the two main causes of overhead were two system calls used by the event-driven server. The standard UNIX implementation of both these calls scales poorly with a large number of connections. The two calls were:

- *select( ):* Event-driven servers running on UNIX use the *select( )* call for the *FindActive( )* call. Experiments by Banga and Mogul [BM98] show that more than half of the CPU is used for kernel and user-level *select( )* functions with 500 connections.

- *ufalloc( ):* The server also needs to allocate the lowest unallocated descriptor for new sockets or files. This seemingly simple call took around a third of the CPU time.

ufalloc( ) performance can easily be explained and fixed. Normally, finding a free descriptor can be efficiently implemented using a free list of descriptors. Unfortunately, UNIX requires choosing the *lowest unused* descriptor. For example, if the currently allocated descriptor list has the elements (in unsorted order) 9, 1, 5, 4, 2, then one cannot determine that the lowest unallocated number is 3 without traversing the entire unsorted list. Fortunately, a simple change to the kernel implementation (**P15**, use efficient data structures) can reduce this overhead to nearly zero.[6]

6.4.2 Existing Use and Implementation of select()

Assuming that *ufalloc()* overhead can easily be minimized by changing the kernel implementation, it is important to improve the remaining bottleneck caused by the *select()* implementation in an event-driven server. Because the causes of the problem are more complex, this section starts by reviewing the use and implementation of *select()* in order to understand the various sources of overhead.

PARAMETERS

Select() is *called* as follows:

- *Input:* An application calls *select()* with three bitmaps of descriptors (one for descriptors it wishes to read from, one for those it wishes to write from, and one for those it wishes to hear exceptions from) as well as a timeout value.
- *Interim:* The application is blocked if there is no descriptor ready.
- *Output:* When something of interest occurs, the call returns with number of ready descriptors (passed by value as an integer) and the specific lists of descriptors of each category (passed by reference, by overwriting input bitmaps).

USAGE IN A WEB SERVER

Having understood the parameters of the *select()* call, it is important to understand how *select()* could be used by an event-driven Web server. A plausible use of *select()* is as follows [BM98]. The server application thread stays in a loop with three major components:

- *Initialize:* The application first zeroes out bitmaps and sets bits for descriptors of interest for read and write. For example, the server application may be interested in reading from file descriptors and writing and reading from network sockets open to clients.
- *Call:* The application then calls *select()* with bitmaps it built in the previous step, and it blocks if no descriptor is ready at the point of call; if a timeout occurs, the application does exception processing.
- *Respond:* After the call returns, the application linearly walks through returned bitmaps and invokes appropriate read and write handlers for descriptors corresponding to set bit positions.

Note that the costs of building the bitmaps in Step 1 and scanning the bitmaps in Step 3 are charged to the user, though they are directly attributable to the costs of preparing for and responding to a *select()* call.

---

[6]While the reader familiar with algorithms will immediately think of a heap, a better solution, which exploits typical computer architectures, is explored in Exercise 3.

IMPLEMENTATION

Having understood the parameters of the *select( )* call, it is important to understand how *select( )* is implemented in the kernel of a typical UNIX variant [WS95]. The kernel does the following (annotated with sources of overhead):

- *Prune:* The kernel starts by using the bitmaps passed as parameters to build a summary of descriptors marked in at least one bitmap (called the *selected* set).

  This requires a linear search through bitmaps of size N regardless of how many descriptors the application is currently interested in.

- *Check:* Next, for each descriptor in the selected set, the kernel checks if the descriptor is ready; if not, the kernel queues the application thread ID on the select queue of the descriptor. The kernel puts the calling application thread to sleep if no descriptors are ready.

  This requires investigation of all selected descriptors, independent of how many are actually ready. This step is more expensive than simply scanning a bitmap.

- *Resume:* When I/O occurs to make a descriptor ready (i.e., a packet arrives to a socket that the server is waiting for data from), the kernel I/O module checks its select queue and wakes up all threads waiting for a descriptor.

  This requires scheduler overhead, which seems fundamentally unavoidable without polling or busy waiting.

- *Rediscover:* Finally, *select( )* rediscovers the list of ready descriptors by making a scan of all selected descriptors to see which have become ready between the time *select( )* was put to sleep and was later awakened. This requires repeating the same expensive checks made in Step 2.

  They are repeated despite the fact that the I/O module knew which descriptors became ready but did not inform the *select( )* implementation.

6.4.3 Analysis of Select()

We start by describing opportunities for optimization in the existing *select( )* implementation and then use our principles to suggest strategies to improve performance.

OBVIOUS WASTE IN *Select()* IMPLEMENTATION

Principle **P1** seeks to remove obvious waste. In order to apply Principle **P1**, it helps to catalog the sources of "obvious waste" in the *select( )* implementations. With each source of waste, we also attach a *scapegoat* that can be blamed for the waste.

1. *Recreating interest on each call:* The same bitmap is used for input and output. This overloading causes the application to rebuild the bitmaps from scratch, though it may be interested in most of the same descriptors across consecutive calls to *select( )*. For

example, if only 10 bits change in a bitmap of size 6000 on each call, the application still has to walk through 6000 bits, to set each if needed.

Blame this on either the interface (API) or on the lack of incremental computing in the application.

2. *Rechecking state after resume:* No information is passed from a protocol module (that wakes up a thread sleeping on a socket) to the *select( )* call that is invoked when the thread resumes. For example, if the TCP module receives data on socket 9, on which thread 1 is sleeping, the TCP module will ensure that thread 1 is woken up. However, no information is passed to thread 1 as to who woke up thread 1; thus thread 1 must again check all selected sockets to determine that socket 9 indeed has data. Clearly, the TCP module knew this when it woke up thread 1.

Blame the kernel implementation.

3. *Kernel rechecks readiness for descriptors known not to be ready:* The Web server application is typically interested in a socket until connection failure or termination. In that case, why repeat tests for readiness if no change in state has been observed? For example, assume that socket 9 is a connection to a remote client with a delay of 1 second to send and receive network packets. Assume that at time t a request is sent to the client on socket 9 and the server is waiting for a response, which arrives at $t + 1$ seconds. Assume that in the interval from t to $t + 1$, the server thread calls *select( )* 15,000 times. Each time *select( )* is called the kernel makes an expensive check of socket 9 to determine that no data has arrived. Instead, the kernel can infer this from the fact that the socket was checked at time t and no network packet has been received for this socket since time t. Thus 15,000 expensive and useless checks can be avoided; when the packet finally arrives at time $t + 1$, the TCP module can pass information to reinstate checking of this socket.

Blame the kernel implementation.

4. *Bitmaps linear with descriptor size:* Both kernel and user have to scan bitmaps proportional to the size of possible descriptors, not to the amount of useful work returned. For example, if there are 6000 possible descriptors a Web server may have to deal with at peak load, the bitmaps are of length 6000. Suppose during some period there are 100 concurrent clients, of which only 10 are ready during each call to *select( )*. Both kernel and application are scanning and copying bitmaps of size 6000, though the application is only interested in 200 bits and only 10 bits are set when each *select( )* returns.

Blame the API.

STRATEGIES AND PRINCIPLES TO FIX SELECT

Given the sources of waste just listed, some simple strategies can be applied using our algorithmic principles.

- *Recreate interest on each call:* Consider changing the API (**P9**) to use separate bitmaps for input and output. Alternatively, preserve the API and use incremental computation. (**P12a**)

- *Recheck state after resume:* Pass information between protocol modules that know when a descriptor is ready and the select module. (**P9**)

- *Have kernel recheck readiness for descriptors known not to be ready.* Kernel keeps state across calls so that it does not recheck readiness for descriptors known not to be ready. (**P12a**, use incremental computation)

- *Use bitmaps linear with ready size, not descriptor size:* Change the API in a fundamental way to avoid the need for state-based queries about all descriptors represented by bitmaps. (**P9**)

6.4.4 Speeding Up Select() without Changing the API

Banga and Mogul [BM98] show how to eliminate the first three (of the four) elements of waste listed earlier.

1. *Avoid rebuilding bitmaps from scratch:* The application code is changed to use *two* bitmaps of descriptors it is interested in. Bitmap *A* is used for long-term memory, and bitmap *B* is used as the actual parameter passed by reference to *select()*. Thus between calls to *select()*, only the (presumably few) descriptors that have changed have to be updated in bitmap *A*. Before calling *select()*, bitmap *A* is copied to bitmap *B*. Because copy can proceed a word at a time, the copy is more efficient than a laborious bit-by-bit inspection of the bitmap. In essence, the new bitmap is being computed incrementally. (**P12a**)

2. *Avoid rechecking all descriptors when select() wakes up:* To avoid this overhead, the kernel implementation is modified such that each thread keeps a hints set *H* that records sockets that have become ready since the last time the thread called *select()*. The protocol or I/O modules are modified such that when new data arrives (network packet, disk I/O completes), the corresponding descriptor index is written to the hints set of all threads that are on the select queue for that descriptor. Finally, after a thread wakes up in *select()*, only the descriptors in *H* are checked. The essence of this optimization is passing hints between layers. (**P9**)

3. *Avoid rechecking descriptors known not to be ready:* The fundamental observation is that a descriptor that is waiting for data need not be checked until asynchronous notification occurs (e.g., the descriptor is placed in hints set *H* described earlier). Clearly, however, any newly arriving descriptors (e.g., newly opened sockets) must be checked. A third, subtle point is that even after network data has arrived for a socket (e.g., 1500 bytes), the application may read only 200 bytes. Thus a descriptor must be checked for readiness even after data first arrives, until there is no more data left (i.e., application reads all data) to signify readiness.

   To implement these ideas, besides the hints set *H* for each thread, the kernel implementation keeps two more sets. The first is an interested set *I* of all descriptors the thread is interested in. The second is a set of descriptors *R* that are known to be ready. The interested set *I* reflects long-term interest; for example, a socket is placed in *I* the first time it is mentioned in a *select()* call and is removed only when the socket is disconnected or reused. Let the set passed to *select( )* be denoted by S. Then I is updated to $I_{new} = I_{old} \cup S$. Note that this incorporates newly selected descriptors without losing previously selected descriptors.[7]

Next, the kernel checks only those descriptors that are in I_{new} but are either (i) in the hints set H or (ii) not in I_{old} or (iii) in the old ready set R_{old}. Note that these three predicates reflect the three categories discussed two paragraphs back. They represent either recent activity, newly declared interest, or unconsumed data resulting from prior activity. The descriptors found by the check to be ready are recorded in R_{new}. Finally, the *select( )* call returns to the user the elements in $R_{new} \cap S$. This is because the user only cares about the readiness of descriptors specified in the selecting set S.

As an example, socket 15 may be checked when it is first mentioned in a *select( )* call and so enters I; socket 15 may be checked next when a network packet of 500 bytes arrives, causing socket 15 to enter H; finally, socket 15 may be checked repeatedly as part of R until the application consumes all 500 bytes, at which point socket 15 leaves R. The basis of this optimization is **P12**, adding state for speed. The optimization maintains state across calls (**P12**) to reduce redundant checks.

6.4.5 *Speeding Up Select( ) by Changing the API*

The technique described in Section 6.4.4 improves performance considerably by eliminating the first three (and chief) sources of overhead in *select( )*. However, it does so by maintaining extra state (**P12**) in the form of three more sets of descriptors (i.e., H, I, and R) that are also maintained as bitmaps. This, taken together with the selection set S passed in each call, requires the scanning and updating of four separate bitmaps.

In a situation where a large number of connections are present but only a few are active at any instant, this fundamentally still requires paying some small overhead, proportional to the total number of connections as opposed to the number of active connections. This is the fourth source of "waste" enumerated earlier, and it appears unavoidable given the present API.

Further, as we saw earlier, even the modified fast *select( )* potentially checks a descriptor multiple times for each event such as a packet arrival (if the application does not consume all the data at once). Such additional checks are unavoidable because *select( )* provides the state of each descriptor.

If one looks closely at the interface, what the application fundamentally requires is to be notified of the stream of events (e.g., file I/O completed, network packet arrived) that causes changes in state. Event-based notifications appear, on the surface, to have some obvious drawbacks that may have prevented them from being used in the past.

- *Asynchronous Notification:* If the application is notified as soon as an event occurs, this can take excessive overhead and be difficult to program. For example, when an application is servicing socket 5, a packet to socket 12 may arrive. Interrupting the application to inform it of the new packet may be a bad idea.

- *Excessive Event Rate:* The application is interested in the events that cause state change and not in the raw event stream. For a large Web transfer, several packets may arrive to a socket and the application may wish to get one notification for a batch, and not one for

---

[7]The reader may wonder whether it suffices to set $I = S$. The exercises explore some of the issues with this alternative implementation.

every packet. The overhead for each notification is in terms of communication costs (CPU) as well as storage for each notification.

Principle **P6** suggests designing efficient specialized routines to overcome bottlenecks. In this spirit, Banga, Mogul, and Druschel [BMD99] describe a new event-based API that avoids both these problems.

- *Synchronous Inquiry:* As in the original *select()* call, the application can inquire for pending events. For example, in the previous example, the application continues to service socket 5 and all other active sockets before asking for (and being told about) events such as packet arrival on socket 5.

- *Coalescing of Events:* If a second event occurs for a descriptor while a first event has been queued for notification, the second notification is omitted. Thus there can be at most one outstanding event notification per descriptor.

The use of this new API is straightforward and roughly follows the style in which applications use the old *select()* API. The application stays in a loop in which it asks synchronously for the next set of events and goes to sleep if there are none. When the call returns, the application goes through each event notification and invokes the appropriate read or write handlers. Implicitly, the setting up of a connection registers interest in the corresponding descriptor, while disconnection removes the descriptor from the interest list.

The implementation is as follows. Associated with each thread is a set of descriptors in which it is interested. Each descriptor (e.g., socket) keeps a reverse mapping list of all threads interested in the descriptor. On I/O activity (e.g., data arrival on a socket), the I/O module uses its reverse mapping list to identify all potentially interested threads. If the descriptor is in the thread's interested set, a notification event is added to a queue of pending events for that thread.

A simple per-thread bitmap, one bit per descriptor, is used to record the fact that an event is pending in the queue and is used to avoid multiple event notifications per descriptor. Finally, when the application asks for the next set of events, these are returned from the pending queue.[8]

6.5 AVOIDING SYSTEM CALLS

For now forget about the intervening discussion of *select()*, and recall the discussion of user-level networking. We seem to have gotten the kernel out of the picture on the receipt or sending of a packet, but sadly that is not quite the case. When an application wants to send data, it must somehow tell the adaptor where the data is.

When the application wants to receive data, it must specify buffers where the received packet data should be written to. Today, in UNIX this is typically done using system calls, where the application tells the kernel about data it wishes to send and buffers it wishes to receive to. Even if we implement the protocol in user space, the kernel must service these system calls (which can be expensive; see Chapter 2) for every packet sent and received.

This appears to be required because there can be several applications sending and receiving data from a common adaptor; since the adaptor is a shared resource, it seems unthinkable for

---

[8]This simple description glosses over some tricky race conditions and overflow conditions.

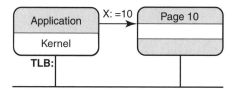

FIGURE 6.8 Reading and writing to memory is not mediated by the kernel.

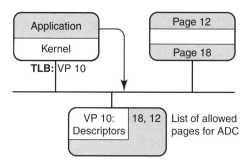

FIGURE 6.9 Application device channels.

an application to write directly to the device registers of a network adaptor without kernel mediation to check for malicious or erroneous use. Or is it?

A simple analogy suggests that alternatives may be possible. In Figure 6.8 we see that when an application wants to set the value of a variable X equal to 10, it does not actually make a call to the kernel. If this were the case, every read and write in a program would be slowed down very badly. Instead, the hardware determines the virtual page of X, translates it to a physical page (say, 10) via the TLB, and then allows direct access as long as the application has Page 10 mapped into its virtual memory.

If Page 10 is not mapped into the application's virtual memory, the hardware generates an exception and causes the kernel to intervene to determine why there is a page access violation. Notice that the kernel was involved in *setting up* the virtual memory for the application (only the kernel should be allowed to do so, for reasons of security) and may be involved if the application violates its page accesses that the kernel set up. However, the kernel is *not involved* in every access. Could we hope for a similar approach for application access to adaptor memory to avoid wasted system calls (**P1**)?

To see if this is possible we need to examine more carefully what information an application sends and receives from an adaptor. Clearly, we must prevent incorrect or malicious applications from damaging other applications or the kernel itself. Figure 6.9 shows an application that wishes to receive data directly from the adaptor. Typically, an application that does so must queue a *descriptor*. A descriptor is a small piece of information that describes the buffer in main memory where the data for the next packet (for this application) should be written to. Thus we should consider carefully and separately both descriptor memory as well as the actual buffer memory.

We can deal with descriptor memory quite easily by recalling that the adaptor memory is memory mapped. Suppose that the adaptor has 10,000 bytes of memory that is considered memory on the bus and that the physical page size of the system is 1000 bytes. This means that the adaptor has 10 physical pages. Suppose we allocate two physical pages to each of five high-performance applications (e.g., Web, FTP) that want to use the adaptor to transfer data. Suppose the Web application gets two physical pages, 9 and 10. Then the kernel maps the physical pages 9 and 10 into the Web application's page table and the physical pages 3 and 4 into the FTP application's page table.

Now the Web application can write directly to physical pages 9 and 10 without any danger; if it tries to write into pages 3 and 4, the virtual memory hardware will generate an exception. Thus we are exploiting existing hardware (**P4c**) in the form of the TLB to protect access to pages. So now let us assume that Page 10 is a sequence of free buffer descriptors written by the Web application; each buffer descriptor describes a page of main memory (assume this can be done using just 32 bits) that will be used to receive the next packet described for the Web application.

For example, Page 10 could contain the sequence 18, 12 (see Figure 6.9). This means that the Web application has currently queued physical pages 18 and 12 for the next incoming packet and its successor. We assume that pages 18 and 12 are in main memory and are physically locked pages that were assigned to the Web application by the kernel when the Web application first started.

When a new packet arrives for the Web application, the adaptor will demultiplex the packet to the descriptor Page 10 using a packet filter, and then it will write the data of the packet (using DMA) to Page 18. When it is done, the adaptor will write the descriptor 18 to a page of written page descriptors (exactly as in fbufs), say, Page 9, that the Web application is authorized to read. It is up to the Web application to finish processing written pages and periodically to queue new free buffer descriptors to the adaptor.

This sounds fine, but there is a serious security flaw. Suppose the Web application, through malice or error, writes the sequence 155, 120 to its descriptor page (which it can do). Suppose further that Page 155 is in main memory and is where the kernel stores its data structures. When the adaptor gets the next packet for the Web application it will write it to Page 155, overwriting the kernel data structures. This causes a serious problem, at least causing the machine to crash.

Why, you may ask, can't virtual memory hardware detect this problem? The reason is that virtual memory hardware (observe the position of the TLB in Figure 6.8) only protects against unauthorized access by processes running on the CPU. This is because the TLB intercepts every READ (or WRITE) access done by the CPU and can do checks. However, devices like adaptors that do DMA bypass the virtual memory system and access memory directly.

This is not a problem in practice because applications cannot program the devices (such as disks, adaptors) to read or write to specific places at the application's command. Instead, access is always mediated by the kernel. If we are getting rid of the kernel, then we have to ensure that everything the application can instruct the adaptor to do is carefully scrutinized.

The solution used in the application device channel (ADC) [DDP94] solution promoted by Druschel, Davy, and Peterson is to have the kernel pass (**P9**, pass hints in interfaces) the adaptor a list of valid physical pages that each application using the adaptor can access directly. This can be done once when the application first starts and before data transfer begins. In other words, the time-consuming computation involved in authorizing pages is shifted in time (**P2**) from the data transfer phase to application initialization. For example, when the Web application first starts, it can ask the kernel for two physical pages, say, 18 and 12, and then ask the kernel to authorize the use of these pages to the adaptor.

The kernel is then bypassed for normal data operation. However, if now the Web application queues the descriptor 155 and a new packet arrives, the adaptor will first check the number 155 against its authorized list for the application (i.e., 18, 12). Since 155 is not in the list, the adaptor will not overwrite the kernel data structures (phew!).

In summary, ADCs are based on shifting protection functions in space (**P3c**) from the kernel to the adaptor, using some precomputed information (list of allowed physical pages, **P2a**) passed from the kernel to the adaptor (**P9**), and augmented with the normal virtual memory hardware (**P4c**).

The architecture community has, in recent years, been promoting the use of *active messages* [vECea92], for similar reasons. An active message is a message that carries the address of the user-level process that will handle the packet.[9]

An active message (such as the ADC approach) avoids kernel intervention and temporary buffering by using preallocated buffers or by using small messages that are responded to directly by the application, thus providing low latency. Low latency, in turn, allows computation and communication to overlap in parallel machines. The active messages implementation [vECea92] allowed only small messages or (large) block transfer. The fast messages implementation [PKC97] goes further to combine user-level scatter–gather interfaces and flow control to enable uniform high performance for a continuum from short to long messages.

WHAT ARE KERNELS GOOD FOR?

It is important to consider this question because the ADC and active message approaches bypass the kernel. Kernels are good for protection (protecting the system and good users from malice or errors) and for scheduling resources among different applications. Thus if we remove the kernel from the run-time data path, it is up to the solution to provide these services in lieu of the kernel. For example, ADCs do protection using the virtual memory hardware (to protect descriptors) and adaptor enforcement (to protect buffer memory).

It also must multiplex the physical communication link (especially on the sending side) among the different application device channels and provide some sort of fairness. To do this in every device would require replicating traditional kernel code in every device; however, it can be argued that some devices, such as the disk and the network adaptor, are special in terms of their performance needs and are worth giving special treatment. There is a movement afoot to make some of these ideas commercial based on the ADC idea and the UUNet solution (similar to ADCs and proposed concurrently) advocated at Cornell [vEBea95]. We now briefly describe this proposal, known as virtual interface architecture (VIA).

6.5.1 The Virtual Interface Architecture (VIA) Proposal

Virtual interface architecture (VIA [CIC97]) is a commercial standard that advocates the ideas in ADCs. The term *virtual interface* makes sense because one can think of an application device channel as providing each application with its own virtual interface that it can manipulate without kernel intervention. The virtual interfaces are, of course, multiplexed on a single physical interface. VIA was proposed by an industry consortium that includes Microsoft, Compaq, and Intel.

---

[9]This is a way of avoiding packet filters completely by passing more information in packets, but it is a bit scary in a networking environment because of the security risks; however, it is typically used only within clusters of machines that trust each other.

VIA uses the following terminology that can easily be understood based on the earlier discussion.

- **Registered Memory:** These are regions of memory that the application uses to send and receive data. These regions are authorized for the application to read and write from; they are also pinned down to avoid paging.

- **Descriptor:** To send or receive a packet, the application uses a user-level library (libvia) to construct a descriptor that is just a data structure with information about the buffer, such as a pointer. VIA allows a descriptor to refer to multiple buffers in registered memory (for scatter–gather) and allows different memory protection tags. Descriptors can be added to a descriptor queue.

- **Doorbells:** These represent an unspecified method to communicate descriptors to the network interface. This can be done via writing part of the interface card's memory or by triggering an interrupt on the card; it varies from implementation to implementation. Doorbells are pointers to descriptors, thus leading to a second level of indirection.

The VIA standard has a few problems that are partly addressed in Dittia et al. [DPJ97] and Buonadonna et al. [BGC02]. These problems (with some sample solutions) are:

- *Small message performance:* To actually send data requires following a doorbell to a descriptor (quite large, around 45 bytes [BGC02]) to the data. For small messages, this can be high overhead. (One way to fix this problem suggested in Buonadonna et al. [BGC02] is to combine the descriptor and the data for small messages.)

- *Doorbell memory:* Just as registered memory is protected, so must doorbells be protected (as in the ADC proposal). Thus the VIA specification requires that each doorbell be mapped to a separate user page, which is a waste of the virtual address space for small descriptors. (One way to avoid this is to combine multiple descriptors into a single page, as suggested in Dittia et al. [DPJ97]. However, this requires some additional machinery.)

The VIA specifications [CIC97] are somewhat vague. For more details the reader may wish to consult more complete system implementations (such as Refs. BGC02 and DPJ97).

6.6 REDUCING INTERRUPTS

We have worked our way down the hierarchy of control overheads from process scheduling to select call implementations to system calls. At the bottom of the list is interrupt overhead. While involving less overhead than process scheduling or system calls, interrupt overhead can be substantial. Each time a packet arrives, fielding the corresponding interrupt from the device disrupts processor pipelines and requires some context switching to service the interrupt. There is no way to avoid interrupts completely. However, one can reduce interrupt overhead using the following tricks.

- **Interrupt only for significant events:** For example, in the ADC solution, the adaptor does not need to interrupt the processor on every packet reception but only for the first packet received in a stream of packets (we can assume the application will check for more packets received) and when the queue of free buffer descriptors becomes empty. This can reduce interrupt overhead to 1 in N packets received, if N packets are received in a burst. This is just an application of batching, or expense sharing (**P2c**).

- **Polling:** The idea here is that the processor (CPU) keeps checking to see if packets have arrived and the adaptor never interrupts. This can be more overhead than interrupt-driven processing if the number of packets received is low, but it can become more efficient for high throughput data streams. Another variation is clocked interrupts [ST]: The CPU periodically polls when a timer fires.

- **Application controlled:** An even more radical idea, once proposed by Dave Clark, is that the sender be able to control when the receiver interrupts by passing a bit in the packet header. For example, a sending FTP could set the interrupt bit only for the last data packet in a file transfer. This is another example of **P10**, passing hints in protocol headers. It is probably too radical for use. However, a more recent paper [DPJ97] proposes implementing a refinement of this idea in an ATM chip that was indeed fabricated.

In general, the use of batching works quite well in practice. However, in some implementations, such as the first bridge implementation (described in Chapter 10), the use of polling is also very effective. Thus more radical ideas, such as clocked or application-controlled interrupts, have become less useful. Note that the RDMA ideas described in Chapter 5 also have the great potential advantage of removing the need for both per-packet system calls and per-packet interrupts for a large data transfer.

6.6.1 Avoiding Receiver Livelock

Besides inefficiencies due to the cost of handling interrupts, interrupts can interact with operating system scheduling to drive end-system throughput to zero, a phenomenon known as *receiver livelock*. Recall that in Example 8 of Chapter 2 we showed that in BSD UNIX the arrival of a packet generates an interrupt. The processor then jumps to the interrupt handler code, bypassing the scheduler, for speed. The interrupt handler copies the packet to a kernel queue of IP packets waiting to be consumed, makes a request for an operating system thread (called a *software interrupt*), and exits.

Recall also that under high network load, the computer can enter what is called *receiver livelock* [MR97], in which the computer spends all its time processing incoming packets, only to discard them later because the applications never run. If there is a series of back-to-back packet arrivals, only the highest-priority interrupt handler will run, possibly leaving no time for the software interrupt and certainly none for the browser process. Thus either the IP or socket queues will fill up, causing packets to be dropped after resources have been invested in their processing.

One basic technique that seems necessary [MR97] is to turn off interrupts when too little application processing is occurring. This can be done by keeping track of how much time is spent in interrupt routines for a device and masking off that device if the fraction spent exceeds a specified percentage of total time. However, merely doing so can drop all packets that arrive during overload, including well-behaved and important packet flows.

A very nice solution to this problem is described by Druschel and Banga [DB96],[10] who suggest combating this problem via two mechanisms. First, they suggest using a separate

---

[10]This solution was also explored in the Exercises for Chapter 2.

queue per destination socket instead of a single shared queue. When a packet arrives, early demultiplexing (Chapter 8) is used to place the packet in the appropriate per-socket queue. Thus if a single socket's queues fill up because its application is not reading packets, other sockets can still make progress.

The second mechanism is to implement the protocol processing at the priority of the receiving process and as part of the context of the received process (and not a separate software interrupt). First, this removes the unfair practice of charging protocol processing for application X to the application, Y, that was running when the packet for X arrives. Second, it means that if an application is running slowly, its per-socket queue fills up and its particular packets will be dropped, allowing others to progress. Third, and most importantly, since protocol processing is done at a lower priority (application processing), it greatly alleviates the livelock problem caused by the partial processing (i.e., protocol processing only) of many packets without the corresponding application processing required to remove these packets from the socket queue.

This mechanism, called *lazy receiver processing* (LRP), essentially uses lazy evaluation (**P2b**), not so much for efficiency but for fairness and to avoid livelock. Solutions that require less drastic changes are described in Mogul and Ramakrishnan [MR97].

6.7 CONCLUSIONS

After the basic restructuring to avoid copying, control overhead is probably the next most important overhead to attack in a networking application. From reducing the overhead of process scheduling to limiting system calls to reducing interrupt overhead, fast server implementations must reduce unnecessary overheads due to these causes. Newer operating systems, such as Linux, are making giant strides in reducing the inherent control overhead costs. However, modern architectures are getting faster in the processing of instructions using cached data without a commensurate speedup in context switching and interrupt processing.

This chapter started by surveying basic techniques for reducing process-scheduling overhead for networking code. These lessons have been taken to heart by the networking community. Hardly any implementor worth his or her salt will do something egregious, such as structuring each layer as a separate process, and not resort freely to upcalls. However, the deeper lesson of Figure 6.3 is not the seemingly arcane structure, but the implicit idea of user-level networking. User-level networking was not developed at the time Clark presented his paper, and it is still not very well known. Note that user-level networking, together with application device channels, makes possible technologies such as VIA, which may become part of real systems in order to avoid system calls when sending and receiving packets.

On the other hand, the art of structuring processing in the application context — for example, a Web server — has received attention only more recently. While event-driven servers (augmented with helper processes) satisfactorily balance the need to maximize concurrency and minimize context-switching overhead, the software engineering aspects of such designs still leave many questions unanswered. Will the event-driven approach suffice in a production environment with rapid changes and facilitate debugging? The staged event-driven approach is a step in this direction, but the engineering of large Web servers will surely require more work.

The event-driven approach also relies on the fast implementation of equivalents of the *select()* call. While the UNIX approaches have fundamental scalability problems, it is reassuring that other popular operating systems, such as Windows [BMD99], have much more efficient APIs.

Allowing applications to communicate directly with network devices using a protected virtual interface is an idea that seems to be gaining ground through the VIA standard. Ideally, adaptors are designed to enable VIA or similar mechanisms. Finally, while interrupts are fundamentally unavoidable, their nuisance value can be greatly mitigated by the use of batching and the use of polling in appropriate environments.

Figure 6.1 shows a list of the techniques used in this chapter, with the corresponding principles. In summary, while Epicetus urged his readers to control their passions, we feel it is equally important for implementors of networking code to be passionate about control.

6.8 EXERCISES

1. **Packet Filters and Upcalls:** In the description on upcalls (Figure 6.3), we showed that the system figured out which application the packet was for by upcalling a transport routine. But if you can do that, who needs packet filters anyway? What hidden assumption is being made here?

2. **Comparing Web Server Structuring Models:** In the text we compared various server structuring mechanisms with respect to simple metrics such as scheduling efficiency and CPU concurrency. Consider the following other metrics for comparison.

   • *Disk Concurrency:* Some systems employ multiple disks and do disk scheduling. Why might the event-driven approach have problems in such an environment, compared to a multithreaded approach? Does the event-driven approach with helper processes have the same problems?

   • *Gathering Statistics:* Web servers need to keep statistics on usage patterns for accounting. Why might gathering statistics be more complex in process-per-client and thread-per-client architectures? Why is it simpler in an event-driven architecture?

3. **Algorithms versus Algorithmics in *ufalloc()* Reimplementation:** In this exercise we will consider how to efficiently reimplement *ufalloc()* to find the lowest unallocated descriptor.

   • First consider using a binary heap. For N identifiers, how many memory accesses are required? How much space is required, in bits?

   • Assume that the machine has a W-bit (e.g., for the Alpha, $W = 64$) word and that there is an efficient instruction (or set of instructions) to find the rightmost zero in a W-bit word. Suppose the allocated descriptors are represented as set bits in a large bitmap (**P14**) of size N. Show how to augment this bitmap with some extra state (**P12**) to efficiently compute the lowest unallocated descriptor.

   • What are the space and time costs of this scheme compared to a simple heap? Can a simple heap be made faster by the (standard) trick of increasing the radix of the heap to have $K > 1$ elements in every heap node?

4. **Modified Implementation of Fast** *select()***:** The text explains how elements are *added* to the sets I, H, and R but does not specify completely how they are *removed*. Explain how elements are removed, especially with respect to the hints set H.

5. **Modified Implementation of Fast** *select()***:** In the fast select implementation of Banga and Mogul [BM98], consider changing the implementation as follows:

   (a) First, I_{new} is set equal to S (and not to $I_{old} \cup S$ as before).

   (b) R_{new} is computed as before.

   (c) What is returned to the user is R_{new} (and not $R_{new} \cap S$) as before.

   Answer the following questions.

   • Explain in words what is different from this implementation and the one proposed by Banga and Mogul.

   • Explain why this implementation may require one to be careful about how it removes elements from the hints set H in order not to miss state changes due to newly arriving packets.

   • Explain how this scheme can be inferior to the existing implementation, assuming no application changes. Find a worst-case scenario.

   • Explain why this implementation can sometimes be *better* than the existing implementation if the application is smart enough not to choose a socket in its selecting set as long as it still has unread data. (In other words, if a socket has unconsumed data, the application is smart enough not to select it until all data has been consumed.)

6. **Comparing the APIC Approach to the ADC Approach**: In the text we described the ADC approach to application-level networking, thereby bypassing the kernel and avoiding system calls. We want to compare this approach to an approach used in the APIC chip. First use a search engine to locate and print out a paper called "The APIC Approach to High-Performance Network Interface Design: Protected DMA and Other Techniques" [DPJ97]. Read the paper carefully, and then answer the following questions about its particular twists to the ADC design for a practical system.

   • There are two types of memory the ADC approach protects: the device registers on the adaptor, and the buffer memory containing the data. The first is protected by overloading the virtual memory scheme; the second is protected by having the kernel hand the adaptor a list of pages that an application can read/write from. Contrast this to the APIC approach to protecting the device registers. Why is an access mask helpful? Why is each connection register mapped both into the application and kernel memory?

   • In the APIC, the buffer memory is protected by having the APIC read (from memory) a kernel descriptor that contains validation information about the buffer. In the ADC approach, the validating information is already in the adaptor. Why add this extra complexity?

   • In the APIC, there is a third kind of memory that needs to be protected: Buffer descriptors contain links to other other descriptors, and this link memory needs to be validated. Why is this not needed in the ADC approach?

- A different way to do link notarization is to have the kernel create an array of pointers to real buffers, one for each application. Only the kernel can read or write this array. The applications queue buffer descriptors as offsets into this array. This is a standard approach in systems called *using one level of indirection.* Compare this approach to the APIC link notarization approach.

- A disadvantage of the APIC approach is that the adaptor has to do a number of READs to main memory to do all its checks. How many such READs are required in the worst case for a received packet? Why might this be insignificant?

- The paper describes splitting a packet into two pieces. Why is this needed? What assumption does this method make about protocols (that an approach based on packet filters does not need)?

CHAPTER 7

Maintaining Timers

That was, is, and shall be: Time's wheel runs back or stops.

— ROBERT BROWNING

A timer module in a system is analogous to a secretary who keeps track of all the appointments of a busy executive. The executive tells the secretary to schedule appointments and sometimes to cancel appointments before they occur. It is the secretary's job to interrupt the executive with a warning just before the scheduled time of an appointment. Many secretaries actually do this using a so-called *tickler file*, which is a moving window over the next *N* days. When the day's appointments are done, the tickler file is rolled to bypass the current day. We will find a strong analogy between a tickler file and a timing wheel, the main data structure of this chapter.

The chapter is organized as follows. Section 7.1 describes why timers are needed. Section 7.2 describes a model of a timer routine and the relevant parameters that are critical for performance. Section 7.3 describes the simplest techniques for maintaining timers, some of which are still appropriate in some cases. Section 7.4 introduces the main data structure, called *timing wheels*. This is followed by two specific instantiations of timing wheels called *hashed wheels* (in Section 7.5) and *hierarchical timing wheels* (in Section 7.6). The chapter ends with a technique called *soft timers* (Section 7.8) that reduces timer overhead by amortizing timer maintenance across other system calls. Figure 7.1 summarizes the principles applied in the various timer schemes.

Quick Reference Guide

The most useful section for an implementor is Section 7.5 on hashed timing wheels, versions of which have appeared in many operating systems, such as FreeBSD and Linux.

7.1 WHY TIMERS?

Why do systems need timers? Systems need timers for failure recovery and also to implement algorithms in which the notion of time or relative time is integral. Several kinds of failures cannot be detected asynchronously. Some can be detected by periodic checking (e.g., disk watchdog timers), and such timers always expire. Other failures can be only be inferred by

Number	Principle	Timer Technique
P14 P2c,4	Use array to store bounded timers Leverage off time-of-day update	Basic timing wheels
P15	Using hashing or hierarchies	Hashed, hierarchical timing wheels
P10	Pass handle to delete timer	Any timer scheme
P4 P3 P11	Leverage off system calls, etc. Relax need for accurate timers Optimize for fast timers	Soft timers

FIGURE 7.1 Principles used by the timer schemes described in this chapter.

the lack of some positive action (e.g., message acknowledgment) within a specified period. If failures are infrequent, these timers rarely expire.

Many systems also implement algorithms that use time or relative time. Examples include algorithms that control the rate of production of some entity (e.g., rate-based flow control in networks) and *scheduling* algorithms. These timers almost always expire.

The performance of algorithms to implement a timer module becomes an issue when any of the following are true. First, performance becomes an issue if the algorithm is implemented by a processor that is interrupted each time a hardware clock ticks and the interrupt overhead is substantial. Second, it becomes an issue if fine-granularity timers are required. Third, it becomes an issue if the average number of active timers is large.

If the hardware clock interrupts the host every tick and the interval between ticks is on the order of microseconds, then the interrupt overhead is substantial. Most host operating systems offer timers of coarse granularity (milliseconds or seconds). Alternatively, in some systems finer-granularity timers reside in special-purpose hardware. In either case, the performance of the timer algorithms will be an issue because they determine the latency incurred in starting or stopping a timer and the number of timers that can be simultaneously outstanding.

As an example, consider communications between members of a distributed system. Since messages can be lost in the underlying network, timers are needed at some level to trigger retransmissions. A host in a distributed system can have several timers outstanding. Consider, for example, a server with 200 connections and three timers per connection. Further, as networks scale to gigabit speeds, both the required resolution and the rate at which timers are started and stopped will increase.

Some network implementations (e.g., the BSD TCP implementation) do not use a timer per packet; instead, only a few timers are used for the entire networking package. The BSD TCP implementation gets away with two timers because the TCP implementation maintains its own timers for all outstanding packets and uses a single kernel timer as a clock to run its own timers. TCP maintains its packet timers in the simplest fashion: Whenever its single kernel timer expires, it ticks away at all its outstanding packet timers. For example, many TCP implementations use two timers: a 200-msec timer and a 500-msec timer.

The naive method works reasonably well if the granularity of timers is low and losses are rare. However, it is desirable to improve the resolution of the retransmission timer to allow speedier recovery. For example, the University of Arizona has a TCP implementation called TCP Vegas [BMP94] that performs better than the commonly used TCP Reno. One of the reasons TCP Reno has bad performance when experiencing losses is the coarse granularity of the timeouts.

Besides faster error recovery, fine-granularity timers also allow network protocols to more accurately measure small intervals of time. For example, accurate estimates of round-trip delay are important for the TCP congestion-control algorithm [Jac88] and the SRM (scalable reliable multicast) framework [FJM+95] that is implemented in the Wb conferencing tool [McC92]. Finally, many multimedia applications routinely use timers, and the number of such applications is increasing. An example can be found in Siemens' CHANNELS run-time system for multimedia [BSV95], where each audio stream uses a timer with granularity that lies between 10 and 20 msec. For multimedia and other real-time applications, it is important to have worst-case bounds on the processing time to start and stop timers.

Besides networking applications, process control and other real-time applications will benefit from large numbers of fine-granularity timers. Also, the number of users on a system may grow large enough to lead to a large number of outstanding timers. This is the reason cited for redesigning the timer facility by the developers of the IBM VM/XA SP1 operating system [Dav89].

In the following sections, we will describe a family of schemes for efficient timer implementations based on a data structure called a *timing wheel*. We will also describe performance results based on a UNIX implementation and survey some of the systems that have implemented timer packages based on the ideas in this chapter.

7.2 MODEL AND PERFORMANCE MEASURES

A timer module [VL87] has four component routines:

STARTTIMER (Interval, *RequestId*, *ExpiryAction*): The client calls this routine to start a timer that will expire after "Interval" units of time. The client supplies a *RequestId* that is used to distinguish this timer from other timers the client has outstanding. Finally, the client can specify what action must be taken on expiry, for instance, calling a client-specified routine or setting an event flag.

STOPTIMER (*RequestId*): This routine uses its knowledge of the client and *RequestId* to locate the timer and stop it.

PERTICKBOOKKEEPING: Let the granularity of the timer be T units. Then every T units this routine checks whether any outstanding timers have expired; if so, it calls STOPTIMER, which in turn calls the next routine.

EXPIRYPROCESSING: This routine does the *ExpiryAction* specified in the STARTTIMER call.

The first two routines are activated on client calls; the last two are invoked on timer ticks. The timer is often an external hardware clock.

Two performance measures can be used to choose between algorithms described in the rest of this chapter. Both are parameterized by n, the average (or worst-case) number of outstanding timers. They are the space (*Space*) required for the timer data structures and the latency (*Latency*), or the time between the invoking of a routine in the timer module and its completion. Assume that the caller of the routine blocks until the routine completes. Both the average and worst-case latency are of interest.

FIGURE 7.2   Timer queue example used to illustrate Scheme 2.

7.3 SIMPLEST TIMER SCHEMES

The two simplest schemes for timer implementation are, in fact, commonly used. In the first scheme, STARTTIMER finds a memory location and sets that location to the specified timer interval. Every T units, PERTICKBOOKKEEPING will decrement each outstanding timer; if any timer becomes zero, EXPIRYPROCESSING is called.

This scheme is extremely fast for all but PERTICKBOOKKEEPING. It also uses one record per outstanding timer, the minimum space possible. It is appropriate if there are only a few outstanding timers, if most timers are stopped within a few ticks of the clock, and if PERTICKBOOKKEEPING is done with suitable performance by special-purpose hardware.

Note that instead of doing a Decrement, we can store the absolute time at which timers expire and do a Compare. This option is valid for all timer schemes we describe; the choice between them will depend on the size of the time-of-day field, the cost of each instruction, and the hardware on the machine implementing these algorithms. In this chapter we will use the Decrement option, except when describing Scheme 2.

In a second simple scheme, used in older versions of UNIX, PERTICKBOOKKEEPING latency is reduced at the expense of STARTTIMER performance. Timers are stored in an ordered list. Unlike Scheme 1, we will store the absolute time at which the timer expires, not the interval before expiry. The timer that is due to expire at the earliest time is stored at the head of the list. Subsequent timers are stored in increasing order, as shown in Figure 7.2. In Figure 7.2 the lowest timer is due to expire at absolute time 10 hours, 23 minutes, and 12 seconds.

Because the list is sorted, PERTICKBOOKKEEPING need only increment the current clock time and compare it with the head of the list. If they are equal or if the time of day is greater, it deletes that list element and calls EXPIRYPROCESSING. It continues to delete elements at the head of the list until the expiry time of the head of the list is strictly less than the time of day. STARTTIMER searches the list to find the position to insert the new timer. In the example, STARTTIMER will insert a new timer, due to expire at 10:24:01, between the second and third elements.

The worst-case latency to start a timer is $O(n)$. The average latency depends on the distribution of timer intervals (from time started to time stopped) and on the distribution of the arrival process according to which calls to STARTTIMER are made.

STOPTIMER need not search the list if the list is doubly linked. When STARTTIMER inserts a timer into the ordered list, it can store a pointer to the element. STOPTIMER can then use this pointer to delete the element in $O(1)$ time from the doubly linked list. This can be used by any timer scheme. This is an application of **P9**, passing hints in layer interfaces. More precisely, the user passes a handle to the timer in the STOPTIMER interface.

If this scheme is implemented by a host processor, the interrupt overhead on every tick can be avoided if there is hardware support to maintain a single timer. The hardware timer is set to expire at the time at which the timer at the head of the list is due to expire.

The hardware intercepts all clock ticks and interrupts the host only when a timer actually expires. Unfortunately, some processor architectures do not offer this capability.

As for Space, Scheme 1 needs the minimum space possible; Scheme 2 needs $O(n)$ extra space for the forward and back pointers between queue elements.

A linked list is one way of implementing a priority queue. For large n, tree-based data structures are better. These include unbalanced binary trees, heaps, post-order and end-order trees, and leftist trees [CLR90, VD75]. They attempt to reduce the latency in Scheme 2 for STARTTIMER from $O(n)$ to $O(\log(n))$. In Myhrhaug [Myh] it is reported that this difference is significant for large n and that unbalanced binary trees are less expensive than balanced binary trees.

Unfortunately, unbalanced binary trees easily degenerate into a linear list; this can happen, for instance, if a set of equal timer intervals is inserted. It would, however, be a good idea to compare the performance of timing wheels against an implementation using simple binary heaps. We will lump these algorithms together as Scheme 3: tree-based algorithms.

Thus the three simple schemes take time that is least logarithmic in the number of timers for either STARTTIMER or PERTICKBOOKKEEPING. This a problem for high-speed implementations. The next section shows how to do better.

7.4 TIMING WHEELS

The design of the first scheme follows a common problem solving paradigm:

First solve a simpler problem, and then use the insight to solve the more complex problem.

The simpler problem we tackle first is as follows. Suppose timers are all set for some small interval, say, MAXINTERVAL, and let the granularity of the timer be 1 unit. This suggests the use of **P4**, bucket-sorting techniques, instead of the sorting techniques suggested by Schemes 2 and 3. However, bucket sorting is really used for static sorting of a set of numbers. Here, new numbers keep being added and deleted, and we still want to maintain order. (In technical algorithmic terms, the timer data structure must implement a priority queue that allows the operations of addition, deletion, and finding the smallest element.) What is the bucket-sorting equivalent of a priority queue?

Given this motivation, it is not hard to have the following picture (shown in Figure 7.3) float into the reader's mind. Imagine that current time is represented by a pointer to an element in a circular array with dimensions [0, MAXINTERVAL -1]. On every timer tick (for per-tick bookkeeping) we simply increment the pointer by 1 mod the size of the array.

To set a timer at j units past current time, we index (Figure 7.3) into Element $i + j$ mod MAXINTERVAL and put the timer at the head of a list of timers that will expire at a time $=$ *CurrentTime* $+ j$ units. Each tick we increment the current timer pointer (mod MAXINTERVAL) and check the array element being pointed to. If the element is 0 (no list of timers waiting to expire), then no more work is done on that timer tick. But if it is nonzero, then we do EXPIRYPROCESSING on all timers that are stored in that list. Thus the latency for STARTTIMER is $O(1)$; PERTICKBOOKKEEPING is $O(1)$ except when timers expire, but this is the best possible. If the timer lists are doubly linked and, as before, we store a pointer to each timer record, then the latency of STOPTIMER is also $O(1)$.

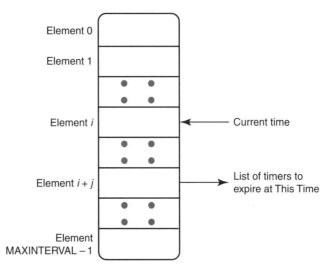

FIGURE 7.3   Array of lists used by Scheme 4 for timer intervals up to MAXINTERVAL.

We can describe this array somewhat more picturesquely as a *timing wheel*, where the wheel turns one array element every timer unit. For a secretary, this is similar to a tickler file. For sorting experts, this is similar to a bucket sort that trades off memory for processing. However, since the timers change value every time instant, intervals are entered as offsets from the current time pointer. It is sufficient if the current time pointer increases every time instant.

A bucket sort sorts N elements in $O(M)$ time using M buckets, since all buckets have to be examined. This is inefficient for large $M > N$. In timer algorithms, however, the crucial observation is that some entity needs to do $O(1)$ work per tick to update the current time; it costs only a few more instructions for the same entity to step through an empty bucket. This is a nice example of using Principle **P4** (leveraging system components) and **P2c** (expense sharing).

The system is already doing some work per tick to increment time. Thus what matters when figuring out the cost of the algorithm is only the *additional expense* caused by the algorithm, not the cost taken in isolation as is typically measured in algorithms classes. Note that this assumption would be false if the system did not do some work on every clock tick and, instead, relied on a piece of hardware to keep the time of day. What matters, unlike the sort, is not the total amount of work to sort N elements, but the average (and worst-case) part of the work that needs to be done per timer tick.

Still, memory is finite: It is difficult to justify 2^{32} words of memory to implement 32-bit timers. So how would you generalize this idea to larger timer values? If you haven't seen it before, try to come up with your own ideas before reading further.

One naive solution is to implement timers within some range using this scheme and the allowed memory. Timers greater than this value are implemented using, say, Scheme 2. Alternatively, this scheme can be extended in two ways to allow larger values of the timer interval with modest amounts of memory. The two techniques are motivated by two algorithmic techniques (**P15**): hashing and radix sort.

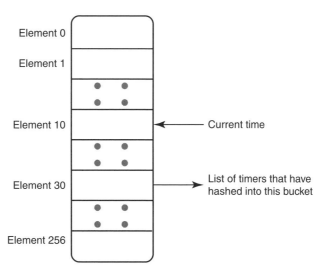

FIGURE 7.4 Array of lists used by Schemes 5 and 6 for arbitrary-size timers: basically a hash table.

7.5 HASHED WHEELS

The design of the first extension follows a second common problem-solving paradigm:

Use analogies to derive techniques for the problem at hand from solutions to a different problem.

Many ideas first occur by analogy, even if the analogy is not always exact. The previous scheme has an obvious analogy to inserting an element in an array using the element value as an index. If there is insufficient memory, can we hash the element value to yield an index? For example, if the table size is a power of 2, an arbitrary-size timer can easily be divided by the table size; the remainder (low-order bits) is added to the current time pointer to yield the index within the array. The result of the division (high-order bits) is stored in a list pointed to by the index.

In Figure 7.4, let the table size be 256 and the timer be a 32-bit timer. The remainder on division is the last 8 bits. Let the value of the last 8 bits be 20. Then the timer index is 10 (current time pointer) + 20 (remainder) = 30. The 24 high-order bits are then inserted into a list that is pointed to by the 30th element.

Other methods of hashing are possible. For example, any function that maps a timer value to an array index could be used. We will defend our choice at the end of Section 7.5. However, we now come to a fork in the road for our design. Whatever hash function we use, there are two ways to maintain each list.

The most straightforward way, which seems best until we look a little closer, is to do Scheme 2 within each bucket. This clearly generalizes Scheme 2 while improving its performance because each of the "little" lists should be smaller than a single list. Now for the details. Unfortunately, its performance depends on the hash function because STARTTIMER can be slow because the 24-bit quantity must be inserted into the correct place in the list. The worst-case latency for STARTTIMER is still $O(n)$.

Assuming that a worst-case STARTTIMER latency of $O(n)$ is unacceptable, we can maintain each time list as an unordered list instead of an ordered list. At first glance this seems like a bad idea. We have certainly made STARTTIMER faster; but if lists are unordered, then it seems that per tick we will have to do a lot more work, seemingly a bad trade-off. Let us look a little closer, however.

Clearly, STARTTIMER now has a worst-case and average latency of $O(1)$. PERTICK-BOOKKEEPING now does take longer. Every timer tick, we increment the pointer (mod *TableSize*); if there is a list there, we must decrement the high-order bits for every element in the array, exactly as in Scheme 1. However, if the hash table has the property described earlier, then the average size of the list will be $O(1)$.

We can make a stronger statement about the average behavior regardless of how the hash distributes. This is perhaps not quite so obvious. Notice that every *TableSize* ticks, we decrement once all timers that are still living. Thus for n timers, we do $n/TableSize$ work on average per tick. If $n < TableSize$, then we do $O(1)$ work on average per tick. If all n timers hash into the same bucket, then every *TableSize* ticks we do $O(n)$ work, but for intermediate ticks we do $O(1)$ work. What this means is that if we want to keep the per-tick work small and bounded, we simply arrange that the number of buckets is some factor larger than the maximum number of concurrent timers we support. We can even reduce this work as much as we want by increasing the number of buckets. This is an example of a result about *amortized complexity*, which is stronger than a result about *average complexity*.

Thus the hash distribution in Scheme 6 controls only the "burstiness" (variance) of the latency of PERTICKBOOKKEEPING, not the average latency. Since the worst-case latency of PERTICKBOOKKEEPING is always $O(n)$ (all timers expire at the same time), we believe that the choice of hash function for Scheme 6 is insignificant. Obtaining the remainder after dividing by a power of 2 is cheap and, consequently, recommended. Further, using an arbitrary hash function to map a timer value into an array index would require PERTICKBOOKKEEPING to compute the hash on each timer tick, which would make it more expensive.

7.6 HIERARCHICAL WHEELS

The second extension of the basic scheme exploits the concept of hierarchy. To represent the number 1000000 we need only 7 digits instead of 1000000 because we represent numbers hierarchically in units of 1's, 10's, 100's, etc. Similarly, to represent all possible timer values within a 32-bit range, we do not need a 2^{32}-element array. Instead we can use a number of arrays, each of different granularity. For instance, we can use four arrays as follows:

- A 100-element array in which each element represents a day

- A 24-element array in which each element represents an hour

- A 60-element array in which each element represents a minute

- A 60-element array in which each element represents a second

Thus instead of $100 * 24 * 60 * 60 = 8.64$ million locations to store timers up to 100 days, we need only $100 + 24 + 60 + 60 = 244$ locations.

As an example, consider Figure 7.5. Let the current time be 11 days, 10 hours, 24 minutes, 30 seconds. Then to set a timer of 50 minutes and 45 seconds, we first calculate the absolute

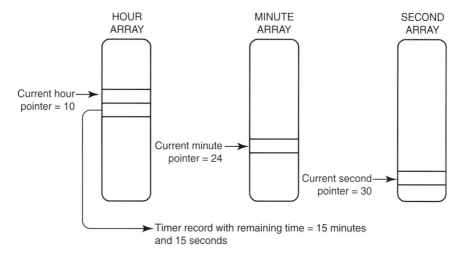

FIGURE 7.5 Hierarchical set of arrays of lists used by Scheme 7 to "map" time more efficiently.

time at which the timer will expire, which is 11 days, 11 hours, 15 minutes, 15 seconds. Then we insert the timer into a list beginning 1 (11 − 10 hours) element ahead of the current hour pointer in the hour array. We also store the remainder (15 minutes and 15 seconds) in this location. We show this in Figure 7.5, ignoring the day array, which does not change during the example.

The seconds array works as usual: Every time the hardware clock ticks we increment the second pointer. If the list pointed to by the element is nonempty, we do EXPIRYPROCESSING for elements in that list. However, the other three arrays work slightly differently.

Even if there are no timers requested by the user of the service, there will always be a 60-second timer that is used to update the minute array, a 60-minute timer to update the hour array, and a 24-hour timer to update the day array. For instance, every time the 60-second timer expires, we will increment the current minute timer, do any required EXPIRYPROCESSING for the minute timers, and reinsert another 60-second timer.

Returning to the example, if the timer is not stopped, eventually the hour timer will reach 11. When the hour timer reaches 11, the list is examined; EXPIRYPROCESSING will insert the remainder of the seconds (15) in the minute array, 15 elements after the current minute pointer(0). Of course, if the minutes remaining were zero, we could go directly to the second array. At this point, the table will look like Figure 7.6.

Eventually, the minute array will reach the 15th element; as part of EXPIRYPROCESSING we will move the timer into the second array 15 seconds after the current value. Fifteen seconds later, the timer will actually expire, at which point the user-specified EXPIRYPROCESSING is performed.

The choice between Scheme 6 and Scheme 7 is tricky. For small values of T and large values of M, Scheme 6 can be better than Scheme 7 for both STARTTIMER and PERTICKBOOKKEEPING. However, for large values of T and small values of M, Scheme 7 will have a better average cost (latency) for PERTICKBOOKKEEPING but a greater cost for STARTTIMER latency.

Observe that if the timer precision is allowed to decrease with increasing levels in the hierarchy, then we need not migrate timers between levels. For instance, in our earlier example

HOUR
ARRAY

MINUTE
ARRAY

SECOND
ARRAY

Current minute →
pointer = 0

Current second →
pointer = 0

Current hour →
pointer = 11

Element 15

Timer record with remaining time = 15 seconds

FIGURE 7.6 The previous example, but after the hour component of the timer expires (using Scheme 7).

we would round off to the nearest hour and only set the timer in hours. When the hour timer goes off, we do the user-specified EXPIRYPROCESSING without migrating to the minute array. Essentially, we now have different timer modes, one for hour timers, one for minute timers, etc. This reduces PERTICKBOOKKEEPING overhead further, at the cost of a loss in precision of up to 50% (e.g., a timer for 1 minute and 30 seconds that is rounded to 1 minute). Alternatively, we can improve the precision by allowing just one migration between adjacent lists.

7.7 BSD IMPLEMENTATION

Adam Costello has implemented [CV98b] a new version of the BSD UNIX callout and timer facilities. Current BSD kernels take time proportional to the number of outstanding timers to set or cancel timers. The new implementation, which is based on Scheme 6, takes constant time to start, stop, and maintain timers; this leads to a highly scalable design that can support thousands of outstanding timers without much overhead.

In the existing BSD implementation, each callout is represented by a CALLOUT structure containing a pointer to the function to be called (C_FUNC), a pointer to the function's argument (C_ARG), and a time (C_TIME) expressed in units of clock ticks. Outstanding callouts are kept in a linked list, sorted by their expiration times. The C_TIME member of each callout structure is differential, not absolute — the first callout in the list stores the number of ticks from now until expiration, and each subsequent callout in the list stores the number of ticks between its own expiration and the expiration of its predecessor.

In BSD UNIX, callouts are set and canceled using TIMEOUT() and UNTIMEOUT(), respectively. TIMEOUT(FUNC, ARG, TIME) registers FUNC(ARG) to be called at the specified time. UNTIMEOUT(FUNC, ARG) cancels the callout with matching function and argument. Because the CALLTODO list must be searched linearly, both operations take time proportional to the number of outstanding callouts. Interrupts are locked out for the duration of the search.

The Costello implementation is based on Scheme 6. Unfortunately, the existing TIME-OUT()/UNTIMEOUT() interface in BSD does not allow the passing of handles, which was used in all our schemes to quickly cancel a timer. The Costello implementation used two solutions to this problem. For calls using the existing interface, a search for a callout given a function pointer and argument is done using a hash table. A second solution was also implemented: A new interface function was defined for removing a callout (UNSETCALLOUT()) that takes a handle as its only argument. This allows existing code to use the old interface and new applications to use the new interface. The performance difference between these two approaches appears to be slight, so the hash table approach appears to be preferable.

In the new implementation, the timer routines are guaranteed to lock out interrupts only for a small, bounded amount of time. The new implementation also extends the SETITIMER() interface to allow a process to have multiple outstanding timers, thereby reducing the need for users to maintain their own timer packages. The changes to the BSD kernel are small (548 lines of code added, 80 removed) and are available on the World Wide Web. The details of this new implementation are described elsewhere [CV98b]; the written report contains several important implementation details that are not given here.

7.8 OBTAINING FINE-GRANULARITY TIMERS

As networks grow faster, one might expect retransmission timers to grow smaller as round-trip delays to destinations decrease. If round-trip delays fall to microseconds, it makes sense to expect the retransmit timers to fall to microseconds as well. Unfortunately, with the BSD approach, one is stuck with a 200-msec timer even when round-trip delays fall to microseconds. The use of a timing wheel by TCP can allow finer-granularity retransmission timers. But the timers can still be no smaller than the granularity of the timer tick, which is typically 1 msec. Thus timer granularity on most systems is rarely finer than 1 msec.

Now many CPUs provide a programmable hardware interrupt chip that can be programmed to interrupt the CPU at a desired frequency. For example, most Pentium CPUs come with an Intel 8253 timer chip. Thus an apparently simple method to improve timer resolution is to increase the frequency of the clock interrupt to, say, 100 kHz. Together with the use of a timing wheel, this would appear to provide timer granularities in the order of 10 μsec.

Unfortunately, there is a flaw in the argument. As we have argued in the model section, modern CPUs tend to keep a lot of state to speed up processing. This includes pipeline state, the use of a large number of registers, and caches and TLBs. An interrupt causes high overhead, because it involves the saving and restoring of CPU state, and can cause changes to locality patterns that result in cache and TLB misses after exiting the interrupt handler. Measurements in Aron and Druschel [AD99] show that the cost of an interrupt on a 300- or 500-Mhz Pentium is around 4.5 μsec. Worse, as processors get faster there is no indication that interrupt processing times will improve.

Thus having a hardware interrupt every 100 kHz will result in roughly 45% overhead merely for responding to interrupts! Since this is clearly infeasible, we must look for a better idea. As the problem is defined, considering the timer module as a black box leaves us no way out. However, systems thinking provides a solution to our dilemma by considering principle **P4** again and leveraging off other system components. Observe that the life of a CPU is chock full of other kinds of transition events that involve state saving and restoring and changes in locality patterns. Such transition events include system calls (e.g., a call to a device handler), exceptions (e.g., a page fault), and hardware interrupts (e.g., an interrupt from the network adaptor).

If we place a check for expired timers as part of the code for such transition events, the overhead for state saving and locality changes is already part of the transition event and is not increased significantly by the timer handler. This is good. Unfortunately, unlike the hardware clock interrupt, the frequency of transition events is unpredictable. This is bad.

Still, it is worthwhile experimenting with a real CPU and measuring the distribution of the times between transition events. Experiments over a wide range of benchmarks in Aron and Druschel [AD99] show that the mean delay between transition events varies from 5 to 30 μsec, depending on what the CPU is running, that delays over 100 μsec occur in only 6% of the cases, and that the maximum delay never exceeded 1 msec.

The data suggests an interesting use of **P3**, relaxing system requirements. Instead of providing a "hard" timer facility that *always* provides microsecond timers, we provide a "soft" timer [AD99] facility that *often* provides 10-μsec timers. We can also bound the error of the soft timer facility by adding a hardware clock interrupt every 1 msec. Thus soft timers are useful for applications that can benefit from an expected case (**P11**) of tens of microseconds and a worst case of 1 msec.

Fortunately, a large fraction of applications that use timers can benefit from such approximate timers. Consider failure recovery, for example, fast retransmission. If most retransmissions are fast except for the occasional retransmission that takes 1 msec, failure performance will improve. Also, consider algorithms where the rate of production of some entity is being controlled. As long as the algorithm correctness can tolerate variability or jitter in the rate, performance should improve in the expected case. For example, Aron and Druschel [AD99] show how a TCP connection can be rate controlled to send packets roughly every 12 μsec. The finer rate control decreases the burstiness of the data, but deviations in the rate do not affect correctness.

It is also tempting to speculate that the right way to handle microsecond, or even nanosecond, timers is to add hardware (**P5**). Such hardware could be in the form of a timer chip that completely handles all timers within the chip using timing wheels or a d-heap. Thus the chip has an internal hardware clock, and the hardware clock interrupt is fielded within the chip; the CPU is interrupted only when a timer expires. However, if timers are frequently cancelled, there can be considerable overhead for the CPU to cancel timers by communicating with the chip.

7.9 CONCLUSIONS

This chapter describes two techniques for efficient timer implementation. The first technique, timing wheels, reduces the overhead of a timer implementation to constant time, regardless of the number of outstanding timers. This allows a timer facility to provide a very large number of timers, a useful feature for today's Internet servers, which sometimes service thousands of concurrent clients. The second technique, soft timers, reduces the operating system overhead incurred by PERTICKBOOKKEEPING. This allows a timer facility to provide fine-grained timers in the expected case, a useful feature as Internet link speeds increase. The principles used within these two schemes are summarized in Figure 7.1.

When timing wheels were first described [VL87], they were generally considered as solving a useless problem. As one system designer put it at the time, "If it ain't broke, why fix it?" — a valid question. It helps, however, to think of schemes for problems that you project will appear in the future. The following information is taken from Justin Gibbs, a key implementor of FreeBSD, though its references to actual product use may be dated.

The scalability of FreeBSD is tested daily on the Internet. Yahoo! serves all of its content through 500 FreeBSD servers distributed throughout the world. Hotmail, the largest provider of Web-based e-mail services, initially used FreeBSD for both e-mail routing and Web services. Thousands of ISPs, including two of the largest ISPs in the nation, Best Internet and USWest, rely on FreeBSD to provide Internet news services, packet routing, Web hosting, and shell services for their users. Not only does FreeBSD perform well for its installed base of over a million desktop users, but it has also proven itself in some of the most demanding applications on the Internet.

FreeBSD has achieved its scalability through continuous attention to system performance. In the latter half of 1997, it became apparent that the timer services used in the FreeBSD kernel would soon became a bottleneck for system throughput. Timer events are employed in several applications that require per-transaction, time-based, notifications. As the number and/or frequency of transactions is scaled higher, the load on the timer interface increases linearly. As an example, the FreeBSD kernel schedules a "watch dog" timer for every disk transaction, which, if fired, initiates error recovery actions. On a typical server machine, over 15% of the CPU was consumed by timer event scheduling under a modest load of 250 concurrent disk transactions. Analysis of the algorithms employed by the old timer interfaces showed that the CPU load would rise linearly with the number of concurrent transactions. System scalability was compromised.

After finding a bug in the Costello implementation that he fixed, Justin Gibbs implemented Hashed Wheels in FreeBSD. Justin's implementation reduced timer overhead in the FreeBSD benchmarks to a fraction of a percent of total CPU usage. The new algorithm also ensures near constant overhead regardless of the transactional load, guaranteeing that the timer facility will scale to many thousands of transactions with ease. Many other operating systems, such as Linux, now use the same idea, as do most real-time operating systems, including ones used in routers. Attention to algorithmics can bear fruit in the long run.

7.10 EXERCISES

1. **Better Hash Functions:** Currently hashed wheels use a very simple and primitive hash function (low-order bits). Find a way to use your favorite hash function to do hashed wheels. (*Hint*: Consider working with absolute time and not relative time.) What particular aspect of performance of a timer module would a better hash function improve? (This idea is due to Travis Newhouse.)

2. **Hierarchical Wheels versus Hashed Wheels and Heaps:** Current implementations of timing wheels use hashed wheels.

   • What is one possible advantage of hierarchical wheels over hashed wheels? Can you quantify the difference precisely?

   • Suppose we do hierarchical wheels by dividing a 32-bit timer into four chunks of 8 bits apiece. What is the difference between such a timing wheel and a 256-way *d*-heap? When might the heap be a better solution?

CHAPTER 8

Demultiplexing

Biologically the species is the accumulation of the experiments of all its successful individuals since the beginning.

— H. G. WELLS

A protocol, like a copy center or an ice cream parlor, should be able to serve multiple clients. The clients of a protocol could be end users (as in the case of the file transfer protocol), software programs (for example, when the tool traceroute uses the Internet protocol), or even other protocols (as in the case of the email protocol SMTP, which uses TCP).

Thus when a message arrives, the receiving protocol must *dispatch* the received message to the appropriate client. This function is called *demultiplexing*. Demultiplexing is an integral part of data link, routing, and transport protocols. It is a fundamental part of the abstract protocol model of Chapter 2.

Traditionally, demultiplexing is done layer by layer using a demultiplexing field contained in each layer header of the received message. Called *layered demultiplexing*, this is shown in Figure 8.1. For example, working from bottom to top in the picture, a packet may arrive on the Ethernet at a workstation. The packet is examined by the Ethernet driver, which looks at a so-called *protocol type field* to decide what routing protocol (e.g., IP, IPX) is being used. Assuming the type field specifies IP, the Ethernet driver may upcall the IP software.

After IP processing, the IP software inspects the protocol ID field in the IP header to determine the transport protocol (e.g., TCP or UDP?). Assuming it is TCP, the packet will be passed to the TCP software. After doing TCP processing, the TCP software will examine the port numbers in the packet to demultiplex the packet to the right client, say, to a process implementing HTTP.

Traditional demultiplexing is fairly straightforward because each layer essentially does an exact match on some field or fields in the layer header. This can be done easily, using, say, hashing, as we describe in Chapter 10. Of course, the lookup costs add up at each layer.

By contrast, this chapter concentrates on *early demultiplexing*, which is a much more challenging task at high speeds. Referring back to Figure 8.1, early demultiplexing determines the entire *path* of protocols taken by the received packet in one operation, when the packet first arrives. In the last example, early demultiplexing would determine in one fell swoop that the path of the Web packet was Ethernet, IP, TCP, Web. A possibly better term is *delayered demultiplexing*. However, this book uses the more accepted name of early demultiplexing.

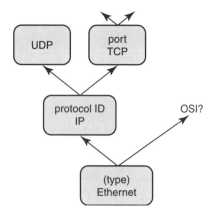

FIGURE 8.1 Traditional layered demultiplexing has each layer demultiplex a packet to the next layer software above using a field in the layer header.

Number	Principle	Used In
P9	Pass header specifications from user to kernel	CSPF
P1 P4c	Use CFG to avoid unnecessary tests Use a register-based specification language	BPF
P15	Factor common checks using a generalized trie	Pathfinder
P2	Specialize code when classifier is modified	DPF

FIGURE 8.2 Principles used in the various demultiplexing techniques discussed in this chapter.

This chapter is organized as follows. Section 8.1 delineates the reasons for early demultiplexing, and Section 8.2 outlines the goals of an efficient demultiplexing solution. The rest of the chapter studies various implementations of early demultiplexing. The chapter starts with the pioneering CMU/Stanford packet filter (Section 8.3), moves on to the commonly used Berkeley packet filter (Section 8.4), and ends with more recent proposals, such as Pathfinder (Section 8.5) and DPF (Section 8.6).

The demultiplexing techniques described in this chapter (and the corresponding principles used) are summarized in Figure 8.2.

Quick Reference Guide

The Berkeley packet filter (BPF) is freely available. However, other demultiplexing algorithms are more efficient. The implementor who wishes to design a demultiplexing routine should consider PathFinder, described in Section 8.5. While dynamic packet filter (DPF, see Section 8.6) is even faster, many implementors may find the need for dynamic code generation in DPF to be an obstacle.

8.1 OPPORTUNITIES AND CHALLENGES OF EARLY DEMULTIPLEXING

Why is early demultiplexing a good idea? The following basic motivations were discussed in Chapter 6.

- *Flexible User-Level Implementations:* The original reason for early demultiplexing was to allow *flexible* user-level implementation of protocols without excessive context switching.

- *Efficient User-Level Implementations:* As time went on, implementors realized that early demultiplexing could also allow *efficient* user-level implementations by minimizing the number of context switches. The main additional trick was to structure the protocol implementation as a shared library that can be linked to application programs.

However, there are other advantages of early demultiplexing.

- *Prioritizing Packets:* Early demultiplexing allows important packets to be prioritized and unnecessary ones to be discarded quickly. For example, Chapter 6 shows that the problem of receiver livelock can be mitigated by early demultiplexing of received packets to place packets directly on a per-socket queue. This allows the system to discard messages for slow processes during overload while allowing better behaved processes to continue receiving messages. More generally, early demultiplexing is crucial in providing quality-of-service guarantees for traffic streams via service differentiation. If all traffic is demultiplexed into a common kernel queue, then important packets can get lost when the shared buffer fills up in periods of overload. Routers today do packet classification for similar reasons (Chapters 12 and 14). Early demultiplexing allows explicit scheduling of the processing of data flows; scheduling and accounting can be combined to prevent anomalies such as priority inversion.

- *Specializing Paths:* Once the path for a packet is known, the code can be specialized to process the packet because the wider context is known. For example, rather than have each layer protocol check for packet lengths, this can be done just once in the spirit of **P1**, avoiding obvious waste. The philosophy of paths is taken to its logical conclusion in Mosberger and Peterson [MP96], who describe an operating system in which paths are first-class objects.

- *Fast Dispatching:* This chapter and Chapter 6 have already described an instance of this idea using packet filters and user-level protocol implementations. Early demultiplexing avoids per-layer multiplexing costs; more importantly, it avoids the control overhead that can sometimes be incurred in delayered multiplexing.

8.2 GOALS

If early demultiplexing is a good idea, is it easy to implement? Early demultiplexing is particularly easy to implement if each packet carries some information in the outermost (e.g., data link or network) header, which identifies the final endpoint. This is an example of **P14**, passing information in layer headers. For example, if the network protocol is a virtual circuit protocol such as ATM, the ATM virtual circuit identifier (VCI) can directly identify the final recipient of the packet.

However, protocols such as IP do not offer such a convenience. MPLS does offer this convenience, but MPLS is generally used only between routers, as described in Chapter 11. Even using a protocol such as ATM, the number of available VCIs may be limited. In lieu of a single demultiplexing field, more complex data structures are needed that we call *packet filters* or *packet classifiers*.

Such data structures take as input a complete packet header and map the input to an endpoint or path. Intuitively, the endpoint of a packet represents the receiving application process, while the path represents the sequence of protocols that need to be invoked in processing the packet prior to consumption by the endpoint. Before describing how packet filters are built, here are the goals of a good early-demultiplexing algorithm.

- *Safety:* Many early-demultiplexing algorithms are implemented in the kernel based on input from user-level programs. Each user program P specifies the packets it wishes to receive. As with Java programs, designers must ensure that incorrect or malicious users cannot affect other users.

- *Speed:* Since demultiplexing is done in real time, the early-demultiplexing code should run quickly, particularly in the case where there is only a single filter specified.

- *Composability:* If N user programs specify packet filters that describe the packets they expect to receive, the implementation should ideally compose these N individual packet filters into a single composite packet filter. The composite filter should have the property that it is faster to search through the composite filter than to search each of the N filters individually, especially for large N.

This chapter takes a mildly biological view, describing a series of packet filter species, with each successive adaptation achieving more of the goals than the previous one. Not surprisingly, the earliest species is nearly extinct, though it is noteworthy for its simplicity and historical interest.

8.3 CMU/STANFORD PACKET FILTER: PIONEERING PACKET FILTERS

The CMU/Stanford packet filter (CSPF) [MRA87] was developed to allow user-level protocol implementations in the Mach operating system. In the CSPF model, application programs provide the kernel with a *program* describing the packets they wish to receive. The program supplied by A operates on a packet header and returns **true** if the packet should be routed to application A. Like the old Texas Instrument calculators, the programming language is a stack-based implementation of an *expression tree* model.

As shown in Figure 8.3, the leaves of the tree represent simple test predicates on packet headers. An example of a test predicate is equality comparison with a fixed value; for example, in Figure 8.3, ETHER.TYPE = ARP represents a check of whether the Ethernet type field in the received packet matches the constant value specified for ARP (address resolution protocol) packets. The other nodes in the tree represent boolean operations such as AND and OR.

Thus the left subtree of the expression tree in Figure 8.3 represents any ARP packet sent from source IP address X, while the right subtree represents any IP packet sent from source IP address X. Since the root represents an OR operation, the overall tree asks for all IP or ARP packets sent by a source X. Such an expression could be provided by a debugging tool to the kernel on behalf of a user who wished to examine IP traffic coming from source X.

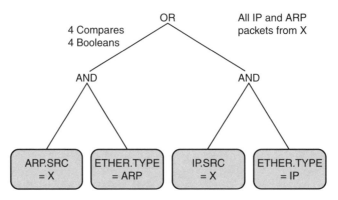

FIGURE 8.3 The CMU/Stanford packet filter (CSPF) allows applications to provide programs that specify an expression tree representing the packets they wish to receive. The tree shown here effectively asks for all IP and ARP packets sent by IP source address *X*.

While the expression tree model provides a *declarative* model of a filter, such filters actually use an *imperative* stack-based language to describe expression trees. To provide safety, CSPF provides stack instructions of limited power; to bound running times there are no jumps or looping constructs. Safety is also achieved by checking program loads and stores in real time to eliminate wild memory references. Thus stack references are monitored to ensure compliance with the stack range, and references to packets are vetted to ensure they stay within the length of the packet being demultiplexed.

8.4 BERKELEY PACKET FILTER: ENABLING HIGH-PERFORMANCE MONITORING

CSPF guarantees security by using instructions of limited power and by doing run-time bounds checking on memory accesses. However, CSPF is not composable and has problems with speed. The next mutation in the design of packet filters occurred with the introduction of the Berkeley packet filter (BPF) [MJ93].

The BPF designers were particularly interested in using BPF as a basis for high-performance network-monitoring tools such as tcpdump, for which speed was crucial. They noted two speed problems with the use of even a single CSPF expression tree of the kind shown in Figure 8.3

- *Architectural Mismatch:* The CSPF stack model was invented for the PDP-11 and hence is a poor match to modern RISC architectures. First, the stack must be simulated at the price of an extra memory reference for each Boolean operation to update the stack pointer. Second, RISC architectures gain efficiency from storing variables in fast registers and doing computation directly from registers. Thus to gain efficiency in a RISC architecture, as many computations as possible should take place using a register value before it is reused. For instance, in Figure 8.3, the CSPF model will result in two separate loads from memory for each reference to the Ethernet type field (to check equality with ARP and IP). On modern machines, it would be better to reduce memory references by storing the type field in a register and finishing all comparisons with the type field in one fell swoop.

- *Inefficient Model:* Even ignoring the extra memory references required by CSPF, the expression tree model often results in more operations than are strictly required. For example, in Figure 8.3, notice that the CSPF expression takes four comparisons to evaluate all the leaves. However, notice that once we know that the Ethernet type is equal to ARP (if we are evaluating from left to right), then the extra check for whether the IP source address is equal to X is redundant (Principle **P1**, seek to avoid waste). The main problem is that in the expression tree model there is no way to "remember" packet parse state as the computation progresses. This can be fixed by a new model that builds a state machine.

CSPF had two other minor problems. It could only parse fields at fixed offsets within packet headers; thus it could not be used to access a TCP header encapsulated within an IP header, because this requires first parsing the IP header-length field. CSPF also processes headers using only 16-bit fields; this doubles the number of operations required for 32-bit fields such as IP addresses.

The Berkeley packet filter (BPF) fixes these problems as follows. First, it replaces the stack-based language with a register-based language, with an indirection operator that can help parse TCP headers. Fields at specified packet offsets are loaded into registers using a command such as "LOAD [12]", which loads the Ethernet type field, which happens to start at an offset of 12 bytes from the start of an Ethernet packet.

BPF can then do comparisons and jumps such as "JUMP_IF_EQUAL ETHERTYPE_IP, TARGET1, TARGET2". This instruction compares the accumulator register to the IP Ethernet type field; if the comparison is true, the program jumps to line number TARGET1; otherwise it jumps to TARGET2. BPF allows working in 8-, 16-, and 32-bit chunks.

More fundamentally, BPF uses a *control flow graph* model of computation, as illustrated in Figure 8.4. This is basically a state machine starting with a root, whose state is updated at each node, following which it transitions to other node states, shown as arcs to other nodes. The state machine starts off by checking whether the Ethernet type field is that of IP; if true, it need only check whether the IP source field is X to return true. If false, it needs to check whether the Ethernet type field is ARP and whether the ARP source is X. Notice that in the left branch of the state machine we do not check whether the IP source address is X. Thus the worst-case number of comparisons is 3 in Figure 8.4, compared to 4 in Figure 8.3.

The Berkeley packet filter is used as a basis for a number of tools, including the well-known tcpdump tool by which users can obtain a readable transcript of TCP packets flowing on a link. BPF is embedded into the BSD kernel as shown in Figure 8.5.

When a packet arrives on a network link, such as an Ethernet, the packet is processed by the appropriate link-level driver and is normally passed to the TCP/IP protocol stack for processing. However, if BPF is active, BPF is first called. BPF checks the packet against each currently specified user filter. For each matching filter, BPF copies as many bytes as are specified by the filter to a per-filter buffer. Notice that multiple BPF applications can cause multiple copies of the same packet to be buffered. The figure also shows another common BPF application besides tcpdump, the reverse ARP demon (rarpd).

There are two small features of BPF that are also important for high performance. First, BPF filters packets before buffering, which avoids unnecessary waste (**P1**) when most of the received packets are not wanted by BPF's applications. The waste is not just memory for buffers but also for the time required to do a copy (Chapter 5).

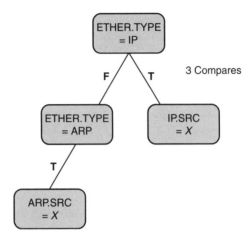

FIGURE 8.4 The Berkeley packet filter uses a state machine or control flow graph as its underlying model, which enables it to avoid redundant comparisons when compared to Figure 8.3.

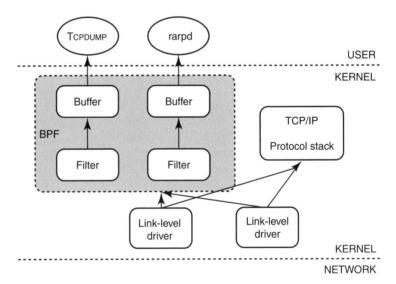

FIGURE 8.5 Packets arriving on a link are sent to both BPF (for potential logging) and the protocol stack (for normal protocol processing). BPF applies all currently specified filters and queues the packet to the appropriate buffer if the filter indicates a match.

Second, since packets can arrive very fast and the read() system call is quite slow, BPF allows batch processing (**P2c**) and allows multiple packets to be returned to the monitoring application in one call. To handle this and yet allow packet boundaries to be distinguished, BPF adds a header to each packet that includes a time stamp and length. Users of tcpdump do not have to use this interface; instead, tcpdump offers a more user-friendly interface: Interface commands are compiled to BPF instructions.

8.5 PATHFINDER: FACTORING OUT COMMON CHECKS

BPF is a more refined adaptation than CSPF because it increases speed for a single filter. However, every packet must still be compared with each filter in turn. Thus the processing time grows with the number of filters. Fortunately, this is not a problem for typical BPF usage. For example, a typical Tcpdump application may provide only a few filters to BPF.

However, this is not true if early demultiplexing is used to discriminate between a large number of packet streams or paths. In particular, each TCP connection may provide a filter, and the number of concurrent TCP connections in a busy server can be large. The need to deal with this change in environment (user-level networking) led to another successful mutation, called *Pathfinder* [BGP+94]. Pathfinder goes beyond BPF by providing *composability*. This allows scaling to a large number of users.

To motivate the Pathfinder solution, imagine there are 500 filters, each of which is exactly the same (Ethernet type field is IP, IP protocol type is TCP) except that each specifies a different TCP port pair. Doing each filter sequentially would require comparing the Ethernet type of the packet 500 times against the (same) IP Ethernet type field and comparing the IP protocol field 500 times against the (same) TCP protocol value. This is wasteful (**P1**).

Next, comparing the TCP port numbers in the packet to each of the 500 port pairs specified in each of the 500 filters is not obvious waste. However, this is exactly analogous to a linear search for exact matching. This suggests that integrating all the individual filters into a single composite filter can considerably reduce unnecessary comparisons when the number of individual filters is large. Specifically, this can be done using hashing (**P15**, using efficient data structures) to perform exact search; this can replace 500 comparisons with just a few comparisons.

A data structure for this purpose is shown in Figure 8.6. The basic idea is to superimpose the CFGs for each filter in BPF so that all comparisons on the same field are placed in a single node. Finally, each node is implemented as a hash table containing all comparison values to replace linear search with hashing.

Figure 8.6 shows an example with at least four filters, two of which specify TCP packets with destination port numbers 2 and 5; for now ignore the dashed line to TCP port 17, which will be used as an example of filter insertion in a moment. Besides the TCP filters, there are one or more filters that specify ARP packets and one or more filters that specify packets that use the OSI protocol.

The root node corresponds to the Ethernet type field; the hash table contains values for each possible Ethernet type field value used in the filters. Each node entry has a value and a pointer. Thus the ARP entry points to nodes that further specify what type of ARP packets must be received; the OSI entry does likewise. Finally, the Ethernet type field corresponding to IP points to a node corresponding to the IP protocol field.

In the IP protocol field node, one of the values corresponding to TCP (which has value 6) will point to the TCP node. In the TCP node, there are three values pointing to the three possible destination port values of 2 and 5 (recall that the 17 has not been inserted yet). When a TCP packet arrives, demultiplexing proceeds as follows.

Search starts at the root, and the Ethernet type field is hashed to find a matching value corresponding to IP. The pointer of this value leads to the IP node, where the IP protocol type field is hashed to find a matching value corresponding to TCP. The value pointer leads to the TCP node, where the destination port value in the packet is hashed to lead to the final matching filter.

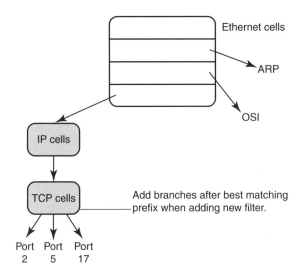

Ethernet cells

ARP

OSI

IP cells

TCP cells

Add branches after best matching prefix when adding new filter.

Port 2   Port 5   Port 17

FIGURE 8.6 The Pathfinder data structure integrates several versions of the BPF control flow graph integrated into a composite structure. In the composite structure all the different field values specified in different filters for a given header field are placed in a single node. Rather than search these values linearly, the header field values are placed in a hash table.

The Pathfinder data structure has a strong family resemblance to a common data structure called a *trie*, which is more fully described in Chapter 11. Briefly, a trie is a tree in which each node contains an array of pointers to subtries; each array contains one pointer for each possible value of a fixed-character alphabet.

To search the trie for a keyword, the keyword is broken into characters, and the ith character is used to index into the ith node on the path, starting with the root. Searching in this way at node i yields a pointer that leads to node $i + 1$, where search continues recursively. One can think of the Pathfinder structure as generalizing a trie by using packet header fields (e.g., Ethernet type field) as the successive characters used for search and by using hash tables to replace the arrays at each node.

It is well known that tries provide fast insertions of new keys. Given this analogy, it is hardly surprising that Pathfinder has a fast algorithm to insert or delete a filter. For instance, consider inserting a new filter corresponding to TCP port 17. As in a trie, the insert algorithm starts with a search for the longest matching prefix (Chapter 11) of this new filter.

This longest match corresponds to the path Ethernet Type = IP and IP Protocol = TCP. Since this path has already been created by the other two TCP filters, it need not be replicated. The insertion algorithm only has to add branches (in this case, a single branch) corresponding to the portion of the new filter beyond the longest match. Thus the hash table in the TCP node need only be updated to add a new pointer to the port 17 filter.

More precisely, the basic atomic unit in Pathfinder is called a *cell*. A cell specifies a field of bits in a packet header (using an offset, length, and a mask), a comparison value, and a pointer. For example, ignoring the pointer, the cell that checks whether the IP protocol field is

TCP is (9, 1, 0xff, 6) — the cell specifies that the ninth byte of the IP header should be masked with all 1's and compared to the value 6, which specifies TCP.

Cells of a given user are strung together to form a *pattern* for that user. Multiple patterns are superimposed to form the Pathfinder trie by not recreating cells that already exist. Finally, multiple cells that specify identical bit fields but different values are coalesced using a hash table.

Besides using hash tables in place of arrays, Pathfinder also goes beyond tries by making each node contain arbitrary code. In effect, Pathfinder recognizes that a trie is a specialized state machine that can be generalized by performing arbitrary operations at each node in the trie. For instance, Pathfinder can handle fragmented packets by allowing *loadable* cells in addition to the *comparison* cells described earlier. This is required because for a fragmented packet only the first fragment specifies the TCP headers; what links the fragments together is a common packet ID described in the first fragment.

Pathfinder handles fragmentation by placing an additional loadable cell (together with the normal IP comparison cell specifying, say, a source address) that is loaded with the packet ID after the first fragment arrives. A cell is specified as loadable by not specifying the comparison value in a cell.

The loadable cell is not initially part of the Pathfinder trie but is instead an attribute of the IP cells. If the first fragment matches, the loaded cell is inserted into the Pathfinder trie and now matches subsequent fragments based on the newly loaded packet ID. After all fragments have been removed, this newly added cell can be removed. Finally, Pathfinder handles the case when the later fragments arrive before the first fragment by postponing their processing until the first fragment arrives.

Although Pathfinder has been described so far as a tree, the data structure can be generalized to a directed acyclic graph (DAG). A DAG allows two different filters to initially follow different paths through the Pathfinder graph and yet come together to share a common path suffix. This can be useful, for instance, when providing a filter for TCP packets for destination port 80 that can be fragmented or unfragmented. While one needs a separate path of cells to specify fragmented and unfragmented IP packets, the two paths can point to a common set of TCP cells.

Finally, Pathfinder also allows the use of OR links that lead from a cell. The idea is that each of the OR links specify a value, and each of the OR links is checked to find a value that matches and then that link is followed.

In order to prioritize packets during periods of congestion, as in Chapter 6, the demultiplexing routine must complete in the minimum time it takes to receive a packet. Software implementations of Pathfinder are fast but are typically unable to keep up with line speeds. Fortunately, the Pathfinder state machine can be implemented in hardware to run at line speeds. This is analogous to the way IP lookups using tries can be made to work at line speeds (Chapter 11).

The hardware prototype described in Bailey et al. [BGP+94] trades functionality for speed. It works in 16-bit chunks and implements only the most basic cell functions; it does, however, implement fragmentation in hardware. The limited functionality implies that the Pathfinder *hardware* can only be used as a cache to speed up Pathfinder *software* that handles the less common cases. A prototype design running at 100 MHz was projected to take 200 nsec to process a 40-byte TCP message, which is sufficient for 1.5 Gbps. The design can be scaled to higher wire speeds using faster clock rates, faster memories, and a pipelined traversal of the state machine.

8.6 DYNAMIC PACKET FILTER: COMPILERS TO THE RESCUE

The Pathfinder story ends with an appeal to hardware to handle demultiplexing at high speeds. Since it is unlikely that most workstations and PCs today can afford dedicated demultiplexing hardware, it appears that implementors must choose between the *flexibility* afforded by early demultiplexing and the limited *performance* of a software classifier. Thus it is hardly surprising that high-performance TCP [CJRS89], active messages [vCGS92], and Remote Procedure Call (RPC) [TNML93] implementations use hand-crafted demultiplexing routines.

Dynamic packet filter [EK96] (*DPF*) attempts to have its cake (gain flexibility) and eat it (obtain performance) at the same time. DPF starts with the Pathfinder trie idea. However, it goes on to eliminate indirections and extra checks inherent in cell processing by *recompiling the classifier into machine code each time a filter is added or deleted.* In effect, DPF produces separate, optimized code for each cell in the trie, as opposed to generic, unoptimized code that can parse any cell in the trie.

DPF is based on *dynamic code generation* technology [Eng96], which allows code to be generated at run time instead of when the kernel is compiled. DPF is an application of Principle **P2**, shifting computation in time. Note that by run time we mean *classifier update* time and not *packet processing* time.

This is fortunate because this implies that DPF must be able to recompile code fast enough so as not to slow down a classifier update. For example, it may take milliseconds to set up a connection, which in turn requires adding a filter to identify the endpoint in the same time. By contrast, it can take a few microseconds to receive a minimum-size packet at gigabit rates. Despite this leeway, submillisecond compile times are still challenging.

To understand why using specialized code per cell is useful, it helps to understand two generic causes of cell-processing inefficiency in Pathfinder:

- *Interpretation Overhead:* Pathfinder code is indeed compiled into machine instructions when kernel code is compiled. However, the code does, in some sense, "interpret" a generic Pathfinder cell. To see this, consider a generic Pathfinder cell C that specifies a 4-tuple: offset, length, mask, value. When a packet P arrives, idealized machine code to check whether the cell matches the packet is as follows:

  LOAD R1, C(Offset); (* load offset specified in cell into register R1 *)
  LOAD R2, C(length); (* load length specified in cell into register R1 *)
  LOAD R3, P(R1, R2); (* load packet field specified by offset into R3 *)
  LOAD R1, C(mask); (* load mask specified in cell into register R1 *)
  AND R3, R1; (* mask packet field as specified in cell *)
  LOAD R2, C(value); (* load value specified in cell into register R5 *)
  BNE R2, R3; (* branch if masked packet field is not equal to value *)

  Notice the extra instructions and extra memory references in Lines 1, 2, 4, and 6 that are used to load parameters from a generic cell in order to be available for later comparison.

- *Safety-Checking Overhead:* Because packet filters written by users cannot be trusted, all implementations must perform checks to guard against errors. For example, every reference to a packet field must be checked at run time to ensure that it stays within the current packet being demultiplexed. Similarly, references need to be checked in real time for memory alignment; on many machines, a memory reference that is not aligned to a multiple of a word size can cause a trap. After these additional checks, the code fragment shown earlier is more complicated and contains even more instructions.

By specializing code for each cell, DPF can eliminate these two sources of overhead by exploiting information known when the cell is added to the Pathfinder graph.

- *Exterminating Interpretation Overhead:* Since DPF knows all the cell parameters when the cell is created, DPF can generate code in which the cell parameters are directly encoded into the machine code as immediate operands. For example, the earlier code fragment to parse a generic Pathfinder cell collapses to the more compact cell-specific code:

LOAD R3, P(offset, length); (* load packet field into R3 *)
AND R3, mask; (* mask packet field using mask in instruction *)
BNE R3, value; (* branch if field not equal to value *)

Notice that the extra instructions and (more importantly) extra memory references to load parameters have disappeared, because the parameters are directly placed as immediate operands within the instructions.

- *Mitigating Safety-Checking Overhead:* Alignment checking can be reduced in the expected case (**P11**) by inferring at compile time that most references are word aligned. This can be done by examining the complete filter. If the initial reference is word aligned and the current reference (offset plus length of all previous headers) is a multiple of the word length, then the reference is word aligned. Real-time alignment checks need only be used when the compile time inference fails, for example, when indirect loads are performed (e.g., a variable-size IP header). Similarly, at compile time the largest offset used in any cell can be determined and a single check can be placed (before packet processing) to ensure that the largest offset is within the length of the current packet.

Once one is onto a good thing, it pays to push it for all it is worth. DPF goes on to exploit compile-time knowledge in DPF to perform further optimizations as follows. A first optimization is to combine small accesses to adjacent fields into a single large access. Other optimizations are explored in the exercises.

DPF has the following potential disadvantages that are made manageable through careful design.

- *Recompilation Time:* Recall that when a filter is added to the Pathfinder trie (Figure 8.6), only cells that were not present in the original trie need to be created. DPF optimizes this expected case (**P11**) by caching the code for existing cells and copying this code directly (without recreating them from scratch) to the new classifier code block. New code must be emitted only for the newly created cells. Similarly, when a new value is added to a hash table (e.g., the new TCP port added in Figure 8.6), unless the hash function changes, the code is reused and only the hash table is updated.

- *Code Bloat:* One of the standard advantages of interpretation is more compact code. Generating specialized code per cell *appears* to create excessive amounts of code, especially for large numbers of filters. A large code footprint can, in turn, result in degraded instruction cache performance. However, a careful examination shows that the number of distinct code blocks generated by DPF is only proportional to the number of *distinct header fields* examined by all filters. This should scale much better than the number of filters. Consider, for example, 10,000 simultaneous TCP connections, for which DPF may emit only three specialized code blocks: one for the Ethernet header, one for the IP header, and one hash table for the TCP header.

The final performance numbers for DPF are impressive. DPF demultiplexes messages 13–26 times faster than Pathfinder on a comparable platform [EK96]. The time to add a filter, however, is only three times slower than Pathfinder. Dynamic code generation accounts for only 40% of this increased insertion overhead.

In any case, the larger insertion costs appear to be a reasonable way to pay for faster demultiplexing. Finally, DPF demultiplexing routines appear to rival or beat hand-crafted demultiplexing routines; for instance, a DPF routine to demultiplex IP packets takes 18 instructions, compared to an earlier value, reported in Clark [Cla85], of 57 instructions. While the two implementations were on different machines, the numbers provide some indication of DPF quality.

The final message of DPF is twofold. First, DPF indicates that one can obtain both performance and flexibility. Just as compiler-generated code is often faster than hand-crafted code, DPF code appears to make hand-crafted demultiplexing no longer necessary. Second, DPF indicates that hardware support for demultiplexing at line rates may not be necessary. In fact, it may be difficult to allow dynamic code generation on filter creation in a hardware implementation. Software demultiplexing allows cheaper workstations; it also allows demultiplexing code to benefit from processor speed improvements.

Technology Changes Can Invalidate Design Assumptions

There are several examples of innovations in architecture and operating systems that were discarded after initial use and then returned to be used again. While this may seem like the whims of fashion ("collars are frilled again in 1995") or reinventing the wheel ("there is nothing new under the sun"), it takes a careful understanding of current technology to know when to dust off an old idea, possibly even in a new guise.

Take, for example, the core of the telephone network used to send voice calls via analog signals. With the advent of fiber optics and the transistor, much of the core telephone network now transmits voice signals in digital formats using the T1 and SONET hierarchies. However, with the advent of wavelength-division multiplexing in optical fiber, there is at least some talk of returning to analog transmission.

Thus the good system designer must constantly monitor available technology to check whether the system design assumptions have been invalidated. The idea of using dynamic compilation was mentioned by the CSPF designers in Mogul et al. [MRA87] but was was not considered further. The CSPF designers assumed that tailoring code to specific sets of filters (by recompiling the classifier code whenever a filter was added) was too "complicated."

Dynamic compilation at the time of the CSPF design was probably slow and also not portable across systems; the gains at that time would have also been marginal because of other bottlenecks. However, by the time DPF was being designed, a number of systems, including VCODE [Eng96], had designed fairly fast and portable dynamic compilation infrastructure. The other classifier implementations in DPF's lineage had also eliminated other bottlenecks, which allowed the benefits of dynamic compilation to stand out more clearly.

8.7 CONCLUSIONS

While it may be trite to say that necessity is the mother of invention, it is also often true. New needs drive new innovations; the lack of a need explains why innovations did not occur earlier. The CSPF filter was implemented when the major need was to avoid a process context switch; having achieved that, improved filter performance was only a second-order effect. BPF was implemented when the major need was to implement a few filters very efficiently to enable monitoring tools like tcpdump to run at close to wire speeds. Having achieved that, scaling to a large number of filters seemed less important.

Pathfinder was implemented to support user-level networking in the x-kernel [HP91], and to allow Scout [MP96] to use paths as a first-class object that could be exploited in many ways. Having found a plausible hardware implementation, perhaps improved software performance seemed less important. DPF was implemented to provide high-performance networking together with complete application-level flexibility in the context of an extensible operating system [EKO95]. Figure 8.2 presents a summary of the techniques used in this chapter, together with the major principles involved.

As in the H. G. Wells quote at the start of the chapter, the DPF species does represent the accumulation of the experiments of all its successful individuals. All filter implementations borrow from CSPF the intellectual leap of separating demultiplexing from packet processing, together with the notion that application demultiplexing specifications can be safely exported to the kernel. DPF and Pathfinder in turn borrow from BPF the basic notion of exploiting the underlying architecture using a register-based, state-machine model. DPF borrows from Pathfinder the notion of using a generalized trie to factor out common checks.

8.8 EXERCISES

1. **Other Uses of Early Demultiplexing:** Besides the uses of early demultiplexing already described, consider the following potential uses.

   - *Quality of Service:* Why might early demultiplexing help offer different qualities of service to different packets in an end system? Give an example.

   - *Integrated Layer Processing:* Integrated layer processing (ILP) was studied in Chapter 5. Discuss why early demultiplexing may be needed for ILP.

   - *Specializing Code:* Once the path of a protocol is known, one can possibly specialize the code for the path, just as DPF specializes the code for each node. Give an example of how path information could be exploited to create more efficient code.

2. **Further DPF Optimizations:** Besides the optimizations already described consider the following other optimizations that DPF exploits.

- *Atom Coalescing:* It often happens that a node in the DPF tree checks for two smaller field values in the same word. For example, the TCP node may check for a source port value and a destination port value. How can DPF do these checks more efficiently? What crucial assumption does this depend on, and how can DPF validate this assumption?

- *Optimizing Hash Tables:* When DPF adds a classifier, it may update the hash table at the node. Unlike Pathfinder, the code can be specialized to the specific set of values in each hash table. Explain why this can be used to provide a more efficient implementation for small tables and for collision handling in some cases.

CHAPTER 9

Protocol Processing

Household tasks are easier and quicker when they are done by somebody else.

— JAMES THORPE

Our mental image of a musician is often associated with giving a recital, and our image of a researcher may involve his mulling over a problem. However, musicians spend more time in less glamorous tasks, such as practicing scales, and researchers spend more time than they wish on mundane chores, such as writing grants. Mastery of a vocation requires paying attention to many small tasks and not just to a few big jobs.

Similarly, tutorials on efficient protocol implementation often emphasize methods of avoiding data-touching overhead and structuring techniques to reduce control overhead. These, of course, were the topics covered in Chapters 5 and 6. This is entirely appropriate because the biggest improvements in endnode implementations often come from attention to such overhead.

However, having created a zero-copy implementation with minimal context switching — and there is strong evidence that modern implementations of network appliances have learned these lessons well – new bottlenecks invite scrutiny. In fact, a measurement study by Kay and Pasquale [KP93] shows that these other bottlenecks can be significant.

There are a host of other protocol implementation tasks that can become new bottlenecks. Chapters 7 and 8 have already dealt with efficient timer and demultiplexing implementations. This chapter deals briefly with some of the common remaining tasks: buffer management, checksums, sequence number bookkeeping, reassembly, and generic protocol processing.

The importance of these protocol-processing "chores" may be increasing, for the following reasons. First, link speeds in the local network are already at gigabit levels and are going higher. Second, market pressures are mounting to implement TCP, and even higher-level application tasks, such as Web services and XML, in hardware. Third, there is a large number of small packets in the Internet for which data manipulation overhead may *not* be the dominant factor.

This chapter is organized as follows. Section 9.1 delves into techniques for managing buffer, that is, techniques for fast buffer allocation and buffer sharing. Section 9.2 presents techniques for implementing CRCs (mostly at the link level) and checksums (mostly at the transport level). Section 9.3 deals with the efficient implementation of generic protocol processing, as exemplified by TCP and UDP. Finally, Section 9.4 covers the efficient implementation of packet reassembly.

The techniques presented in this chapter (and the corresponding principles) are summarized in Figure 9.1.

Number	Principle	Used In
P4b	Use linear buffers, not mbuf chains	Linux sk_buf
P4b	Buddy system without coalescing	BSD 4.2 malloc()
P2b	Sequential chunk allocation, lazy chunk creation	J-machine
P14	Efficient buffer stealing	SFQ
P13	Dynamic buffer thresholds	
P2a	CRC multiple bits at a time using table lookup	Many CRC chips
P2b	Lazy carry evaluation	Fast checksums
P12a	Recompute header checksum	RFC 1624
P4c	Compute data link and application CRC	Infiniband
P11	Predict next TCP header	BSD TCP
P3c	Shift fragmentation from router to source	Path MTU
P11	Fast fragment reassembly	

FIGURE 9.1   Principles used in the various protocol-processing techniques discussed in this chapter.

Quick Reference Guide

The first part of Section 9.1 describes a number of buffering strategies, including UNIX mbufs and Linux sk_bufs, as well as a variety of efficient memory allocators, such as the Kingsley allocator. Implementors interested in fast cyclic redundancy check (CRC) algorithms should read Section 9.2.1; those interested in fast IP checksums should read Section 9.2.2. The first few pages of Section 9.3 describe the classic TCP processing optimization called *header prediction*.

9.1 BUFFER MANAGEMENT

All protocols have to manage buffers. In particular, packets travel up and down the protocol stack in buffers. The operating system must provide services to allocate and deallocate buffers. This requires managing free memory; finding memory of the appropriate size can be challenging, especially because buffer allocation must be done in real time. Section 9.1.1 describes a simple systems solution for doing buffer allocation at high speeds, even for requests of variable sizes.

If the free space must be shared between a number of connections or users, it may also be important to provide some form of fairness so that one user cannot hog all the resources. While static limits work, in some cases it may be preferable to allow dynamic buffer limits, where a process in isolation can get as many buffers as it needs but relinquishes extra buffers when other processes arrive. Section 9.1.2 describes two dynamic buffer-limiting schemes that can be implemented at high speeds.

9.1.1 Buffer Allocation

The classical BSD UNIX implementation, called *mbufs*, allowed a single packet to be stored as a linear list of smaller buffers, where a buffer is a contiguous area of memory.[1] The motivation for this technique is to allow the space allocated to the packet to grow and shrink (for example, as it passes up and down the stack). For instance, it is easy to grow a packet by prepending a new mbuf to the current chain of mbufs. For even more flexibility, BSD mbufs come in three flavors: two small sizes (100 and 108 bytes) and one large size (2048 bytes, called a *cluster*).

Besides allowing dynamic expansion of a packet's allocated memory, mbufs make efficient use of memory, something that was important around 1981, when mbufs were invented. For example, a packet of 190 bytes would be allocated two mbufs (wasting around 20 bytes), while a packet of 450 bytes would be allocated five mbufs (wasting around 50 bytes).

However, dynamic expansion of a packet's size may be less important than it sounds because the header sizes for important packet paths (e.g., Ethernet, IP, TCP) are well known and can be preallocated. Similarly, saving memory may be less important in workstations today than increasing the speed of packet processing. On the other hand, the mbuf implementation makes accessing and copying data much harder because it may require traversing the list.

Thus very early on, Van Jacobson designed a prototype kernel that used what we called *pbufs*. As Jacobson put it in an email note [Jac93]: "There is exactly one, contiguous, packet per pbuf (none of that mbuf chain stupidity)."

While pbufs have sunk into oblivion, the Linux operating system currently uses a very similar idea [Cox96] for network buffers called *sk_buf*. These buffers, like pbufs, are linear buffers with space saved in advance for any packet headers that need to be added later. At times, this will incur wasted space to handle the worst-case headers, but the simpler implementation makes this worthwhile. Both sk_bufs and pbufs relax the specification of a buffer to avoid unnecessary generality (**P7**) and trade memory for time (**P4b**).

Given that the use of linear buffer sizes, as in Linux, is a good idea, how do we allocate memory for packets of various sizes? Dynamic memory allocation is a hard problem in general because users (e.g., TCP connections) deallocate at different times, and these deallocations can fragment memory into a patchwork of holes of different sizes.

The standard textbook algorithms, such as First-Fit and Best-Fit [WJea95], effectively stroll through memory looking for a hole of the appropriate size. Any implementor of a high-speed networking implementation, say, TCP, should be filled with horror at the thought of using such allocators. Instead, the following three allocators should be considered.

SEGREGATED POOL ALLOCATOR

One of the fastest allocators, due to Chris Kingsley, was distributed along with BSD 4.2 UNIX. Kingsley's *malloc()* implementation splits all of memory into a set of segregated pools of memory in powers of 2. Any request is rounded up to its closest power of 2, a table lookup is done to find the corresponding pool list, and a buffer is allocated from the head of that list if available. The pools are said to be segregated because when a request of a certain size fails

---

[1]Craig Partridge attributes the invention of mbufs to Rob Gurwitz [PBW04].

there is no attempt made to carve up available larger buffers or to coalesce contiguous smaller buffers.

Such carving up and coalescing is actually done by a more classical scheme called the *buddy system* (see Wilson et al. [WJea95] for a thorough review of memory allocators). Refraining from doing so clearly wastes memory (**P4b**, trading memory for speed). If all the requests are for exactly one pool size, then the other pools are wasted. However, this restraint is not as bad as it seems because allocators using the buddy system have a far more horrible worst case.

Suppose, for example, that all requests are for size 1 and that every alternate buffer is than deallocated. Then, using the buddy system, memory degenerates into a series of holes of size 1 followed by an allocation of size 1. Half of memory is unused, but no request of size greater than 2 can be satisfied. Notice that this example cannot happen with the Kingsley allocator because the size-1 requests will only deplete the size-1 pool and will not affect the other pools. Thus trafficking between pools may help improve the expected memory utilization but not the worst-case utilization.

LINUX ALLOCATOR

The Linux allocator [Che01], originally written by Doug Lea, is sometimes referred to as *dlmalloc()*. Like the Kingsley allocator, the memory is broken into pools of 128 sizes. The first 64 pools contain memory buffers of exactly one size each, from 16 through 512 bytes in steps of 8. Unlike the case of power-of-2 allocation, this prevents more than 8 bytes of waste for the common case of small buffers. The remaining 64 pools cover the other, higher sizes, spaced exponentially.

The Linux allocator [Che01] does merge adjacent free buffers and promotes the coalesced buffer to the appropriate pool. This is similar to the buddy system and hence is subject to the same fragmentation problem of any scheme in which the pools are not segregated. However, the resulting memory utilization is very good in practice.

A useful trick to tuck away in your bag of tricks concerns how pools are linked together. The naive way would be to create separate free lists for each pool using additional small nodes that point to the corresponding free buffer. But since the buffer is free, this is obvious waste (**P1**). Thus the simple trick, used in Linux and possibly in other allocators, is to store the link pointers for the pool free lists in the corresponding free buffers themselves, thereby saving storage.

The Lea allocator uses memory more efficiently than the Kingsley allocator but is more complex to implement. This may not be the best choice for a wire-speed TCP implementation that desires both speed and the efficient use of memory.

BATCH ALLOCATOR

One alternative idea for memory allocation, which has an even simpler hardware implementation than Kingsley's allocator, leverages batching (**P2c**). The idea, shown in Figure 9.2, is for the allocator to work in large chunks of memory. Each chunk is allocated sequentially. A pointer *Curr* is kept to the point where the last allocation terminated. A new request of size B is allocated after *Curr*, and *Curr* increases to $Curr + B$. This is extremely fast, handles variable sizes, and does not waste any memory — up to the point, that is, when the chunk is used up.

The idea is that when the chunk is used up, another chunk is immediately available. Of course, there is no free lunch — while the second chunk is being used, some spare chunk must be created in the background. The creation of this spare chunk can be done by software,

FIGURE 9.2 Sequentially allocating from a large chunk and using a spare chunk. The magic comes from using the time it takes to completely allocate a chunk to create a new chunk.

while allocates can easily be done in hardware. Similar ideas were presented in the context of the MIT J-machine [DCea87], which relied on an underlying fast messaging service.

Creating a spare chunk can be done in many ways. The problem, of course, is that deallocates may not be done in the same order as allocates, thus creating a set of holes in the chunks that need somehow to be coalesced. Three alternatives for coalescing present themselves. If the application knows that eventually all allocated buffers will be freed, then using some more spare chunks may suffice to ensure that before any chunk runs out some chunk will be completely scavenged. However, this is a dangerous game.

Second, if memory is accessed through a level of indirection, as in virtual memory, and the buffers are allocated in virtual memory, it is possible to use page remapping to gather together many scattered physical memory pages to appear as one contiguous virtual memory chunk. Finally, it may be worth considering compaction. Compaction is clearly unacceptable in a general-purpose allocator like UNIX, where any number of pieces of memory may point to a memory node. However, in network applications using buffers or other treelike structures, compaction may be feasible using simple local compaction schemes [SV00].

9.1.2 Sharing Buffers

If buffer allocation was not hard enough, consider making it harder by asking also for a fairness constraint.[2] Imagine that an implementation wishes to fairly share a group of buffers among a number of users, each of whom may wish to use all the buffers. The buffers should be shared roughly equally among the active users that need these buffers. This is akin to what in economics is called *Pareto optimality* and also to the requirements for fair queuing in routers studied in Chapter 14. Thus it is not surprising that the following buffer-stealing algorithm was invented [McK91] in the context of a stochastic fair queuing (SFQ) algorithm.

BUFFER STEALING

One way to provide roughly Pareto optimality among users is as follows. When all buffers are used up and a new user (whose allocated buffers are smaller than the highest current allocation) wishes one more buffer, *steal* the extra buffer from the highest buffer user. It is easy to see that even if one user initially grabs all the buffers when other users become active, they can get their fair share by stealing.

---

[2]However, to make things easier in return, this section assumes constant-size buffer allocation with all its potential memory wastage.

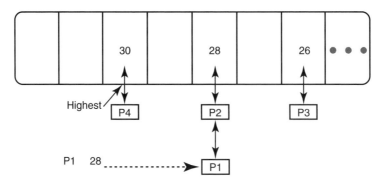

FIGURE 9.3 The Mckenney algorithm for buffer stealing finesses the need for logarithmic heap overhead by relying on the fact that buffer values change by at most 1 on any operation.

The problem is that a general solution to the problem of buffer stealing uses a heap. A heap has $O(\log n)$ cost, where n is the number of users with current allocations. How can this be made faster?

Once again, as is often the case in algorithmics versus algorithms, the problem is caused by reading too much into the specification. If allocations keep changing in *arbitrary* increments and the algorithm wishes always to find the highest allocation, a logarithmic heap implementation is required. However, if we can relax the specification (and this seems reasonable in practice) to assume that a user steals one buffer at a time, then the allocated amounts change not in arbitrary amounts but only by $+1$ or -1. This observation results in a constant-time algorithm (the Mckenney algorithm, Figure 9.3), which also assumes that buffer allocations fall in a bounded set. For each allocation size i, the algorithm maintains a list of processes that have size exactly i. The algorithm maintains a variable called *Highest* that points to the highest amount allocated to any process.

When a process P wishes to steal a buffer, the algorithm finds a process Q with the highest allocation at the head of the list pointed to by *Highest*. While doing so, process P gains a buffer and Q loses a buffer. The books are updated as follows.

When process P gets buffer $i + 1$, P is removed from list i and added to list $i + 1$, updating *Highest* if necessary. When process Q loses buffer $i + 1$, Q is removed from list $i + 1$ and added to list i, updating *Highest* $= i$ if the *Highest* list becomes empty.

Notice this could become arbitrarily inefficient if P and Q could change their allocations by sizes larger than 1. If Q could reduce its allocation by, say, 100 and there are no other users with the same original allocation, then the algorithm would require stepping through 100 lists, looking for the next possible value of highest. Because the maximum amount an allocation can change by is 1, the algorithm moves through only one list. In terms of algorithmics, this is an example of the special opportunities created by the use of finite universes (**P14** suggests the use of bucket sorting and bitmaps for finite universes).

DYNAMIC THRESHOLDS

Limiting access by any one flow to a shared buffer is also important in shared memory switches (Chapter 13). In the context of shared memory switches, Choudhury and Hahne describe an algorithm similar to buffer stealing that they call *Pushout*. However, even using the buffer-stealing algorithm due to McKenney [McK91], Pushout may be hard to implement at high speeds.

Instead, Choudhury and Hahne [CH98] propose a useful alternative mechanism called *dynamic buffer limiting*. They observe that maintaining a single threshold for every flow is either overly limiting (if the threshold is too small) or unduly dangerous (if the threshold is too high). Using a static value of threshold is no different from using a fixed window size for flow control. But TCP uses a *dynamic* window size that adapts to congestion. Similarly, it makes sense to exploit a degree of freedom (**P13**) and use *dynamic thresholds*.

Intuitively, TCP window flow control increases a connection's window size if there appears to be unused bandwidth, as measured by the lack of packet drops. Similarly, the simplest way to adapt to congestion in a shared buffer is to monitor the free space remaining and to increase the threshold proportional to the free space. Thus user i is limited to no more than cF bytes, where c is a constant and F is the current amount of free space. If c is chosen to be a power of 2, this scheme only requires the use of a shifter (to multiply by c) and a comparator (to compare with cF). This is far simpler than even the buffer-stealing algorithm.

Choudhury and Hahne recommend a value of $c = 1$. This implies that a single user is limited to taking no more than half the available bandwidth. This is because when the user takes half, the free space is equal to the user allocation and the threshold check fails. Similarly, if $c = 2$, any user is limited to no more than 2/3 of the available buffer space. Thus unlike buffer stealing, this scheme always holds some free space in reserve for new arrivals, trading slightly suboptimal use of memory for a simpler implementation.

Now suppose there are two users and that $c = 1$. One might naively think that since each user is limited to no more than half, two active users are limited to a quarter. The scheme does better, however. Each user now can take 1/3, leaving 1/3 free. Next, if two new users arrive and the old users do not free their buffers, the two new users can get up to 1/9 of the buffer space.

Thus, unlike buffer stealing, the scheme is not fair in a short-term sense. However, if the same set of users is present for sufficiently long periods, the scheme should be fair in a long-term sense. In the previous example, after the buffers allocated to the first two users are deallocated, a fairer allocation should result.

9.2 CYCLIC REDUNDANCY CHECKS AND CHECKSUMS

Once a TCP packet is buffered, typically a check is performed to see whether the packet has been corrupted in flight or in a router's memory. Such checks are performed by either checksums or cyclic redundancy checks (CRCs). In essence, both CRCs and checksums are hash functions H on the packet contents. They are designed so that if errors convert a packet P to corrupted packet P', then $H(P) \neq H(P')$ with high probability.

In practice, every time a packet is sent along a link, the data link header carries a link level CRC. But in addition, TCP computes a checksum on the TCP data. Thus a typical TCP packet on a wire carries *both* a CRC and a checksum. While this may appear to be obvious waste (**P1**), it is a consequence of layering. The data link CRC covers the data link header, which changes from hop to hop. Since the data link header must be recomputed at each router on the path, the CRC does not catch errors caused *within routers*. While this may seem unlikely, routers do occasionally corrupt packets [SP00] because of implementation bugs and hardware glitches.

Given this, the CRC is often calculated in hardware by the chip (e.g., Ethernet receiver) that receives the packet, while the TCP checksum is calculated in software in BSD UNIX. This division of labor explains why CRC and checksum implementations are so different. CRCs are designed to be powerful error-detection codes, catching link errors such as burst errors. Checksums, on the other hand, are less adept at catching errors; however, they tend to catch common end-to-end errors and are much simpler to implement in software.

The rest of this section describes CRC and then checksum implementation. The section ends with a clever way, used in Infiniband implementations, to finesse the need for software checksums by using *two* CRCs in each packet, both of which can easily be calculated by the same piece of hardware.

9.2.1 Cyclic Redundancy Checks

The CRC "hash" function is calculated by dividing the packet data, treated as a number, with a fixed generator G. G is just a binary string of predefined length. For example, CRC-16 is the string 11000000000000101, of length 17; it is called CRC-16 because the remainder added to the packet turns out to be 16 bits long.

Generators are easier to remember when written in polynomial form. For example, the same CRC-16 in polynomial form becomes $x^{16} + x^{15} + x^2 + 1$. Notice that whenever x^i is present in the generator *polynomial*, position i is equal to 1 in the generator *string*. Whatever CRC polynomial is picked (and CRC-32 is very common), the polynomial is published in the data link implementation specification and is known in advance to both receiver and sender.

A formal description of CRC calculation is as follows. Let r be the number of bits in the generator string G. Let M be the message whose CRC is to be calculated. The CRC is simply the remainder c of $2^{r-1}M$ (i.e., M left-shifted by $r - 1$ bits) when divided by G. The only catch is the division is mod-2 division, which is illustrated next.

Working out the mathematics slightly, $2^{r-1}M = k.G + c$. Thus $2^{r-1}M + c = k.G$ because addition is the same as subtraction in mod-2 arithmetic, a fact strange but true. Thus, even ignoring the preceding math, the bottom line is that *if we append the calculated CRC c to the end of the message, the resulting number divides the generator G.*

Any bit errors that cause the sent packet to change to some other packet will be caught as long as the resulting packet is not divisible by G. CRCs, like good hash functions, are effective because common errors based on flipping a few bits (random errors) or changing any bit in a group of contiguous bits (burst errors) are likely to create a packet that does not divide G. Simple analytical properties of CRCs are derived in Tanenbaum [Tan81].

For the implementor, however, what matters is not *why* CRC works but *how* to implement it. The main thing to learn is how to compute remainders using mod-2 division. The algorithm uses a simple iteration in which the generator G is progressively "subtracted" from the message M until the remainder is "smaller" than the generator G. This is exactly like ordinary division except that "subtraction" is now exclusive-OR, and the definition of whether a number is "smaller" depends on whether its most significant bit (MSB) is 0.

More precisely, a register R is loaded with the first r bits of the message. At each stage of the iteration, the MSB of R is checked. If it is 1, R is "too large" and the CRC string G is "subtracted" from R. Subtraction is done by exclusive-OR (EX-OR) in mod-2 arithmetic. Assuming that the MSB of the generator is always 1, this zeroes out the MSB of R. Finally, if the MSB of R is already 0, R is "small enough" and there is no need to EX-OR.

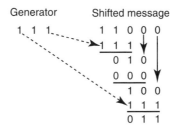

FIGURE 9.4 CRC is calculated by dividing the shifted message with the generator. The intent is to shift in all the message bits and to zero out any most significant bits that are set. Horizontal lines indicate EX-OR operations. Vertical lines denote shifting in the next message bit. Dashed lines show where the generator is brought down. The generator is used for the EX-OR when the MSB of the current result is 1; if not, zero is used.

A single iteration completes by left-shifting R so that the MSB of R is lost, and the next message bit gets shifted in. The iterations continue until all messages are shifted in and the MSB of register R is 0. At this point register R contains the required checksum.

For example, let $M = 110$ and $G = 111$. Then $2^{r-1}M = 11000$. Then the checksum c is calculated as shown in Figure 9.4. In the first step of Figure 9.4, the algorithm places the first 3 bits (110) of the shifted message in R. Since the MSB of 110 is 1, the algorithm hammers away at R by EX-ORing R with the generator $G = 111$ to get 001. The first iteration completes by shifting out the MSB and (Figure 9.4, topmost vertical arrow) shifting in the fourth message bit, to get $R = 010$.

In the second iteration, the MSB of R is 0 and so the algorithm desists. This is represented in Figure 9.4 by computing the EX-OR of R with 000 instead of the generator. As usual, the MSB of the result is shifted in, and the last message bit, also a zero, is shifted in to get $R = 100$. Finally, in the third iteration, because the MSB of R is 1, the algorithm once again EX-ORs R with the generator. The algorithm terminates at this point because the MSB of R is 0. The resulting checksum is R without the MSB, or 11.

NAIVE IMPLEMENTATION

Cyclic redundancy checks have to be implemented at a range of speeds from 1 Gbit/sec to slower rates. Higher-speed implementations are typically done in hardware. The simplest hardware implementation would mimic the foregoing description and use a shift register that shifts in bits one at time. Each iteration requires three basic steps: checking the MSB, computing the EX-OR, and then shifting.

The naive hardware implementation shown in Figure 9.5 would require three clock cycles to shift in a bit; doing a comparison for the MSB in one cycle and the actual EX-OR in another

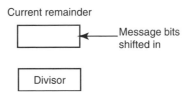

FIGURE 9.5 Naive hardware implementation requires three clock cycles per bit.

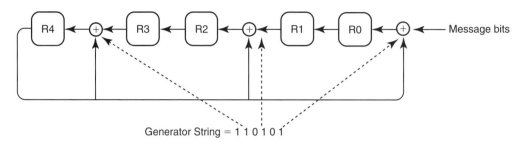

Generator String = 1 1 0 1 0 1

FIGURE 9.6 Linear feedback shift register (LFSR) implementation of a CRC remainder calculation. The EX-ORs are combined with a shift by placing EX-OR gates (the circles) to the right of some registers. Specifically, an EX-OR gate is placed to the right of register i if bit i in the generator string (see dashed lines) is set. The only exception is (what would have been) register $R5$. Such a register need not be stored because it corresponds to the MSB, which is always shifted out.

cycle and the shift in the third cycle. However, a cleverer implementation can be used to shift in one bit every clock cycle by *combining* the test for MSB, the EX-OR, and the shift into a single operation.

IMPLEMENTATION USING LINEAR FEEDBACK SHIFT REGISTERS

In Figure 9.6 the remainder R is stored as five separate 1-bit registers, $R4$ through $R0$, instead of a single 5-bit register, assuming a 6-bit generator string. The idea makes use of the observation that the EX-OR needs to be done only if the MSB is 1; thus in the process of shifting left the MSB, we can feed back the MSB to the appropriate bits of the remainder register. The remaining bits are EX-ORed during their shift to the left.

Notice that in Figure 9.6, an EX-OR gate is placed to the right of register i if bit i in the generator string (see dashed lines) is set. The reason for this rule is as follows. Compared to the simple iterative algorithm, the hardware of Figure 9.6 effectively combines the left shift of iteration J together with the MSB check and EX-OR of iteration $J + 1$. Thus the bit that will be in position i in iteration $J + 1$ is in position $i - 1$ in iteration J.

If this is grasped (and this requires shifting one's mental pictures of iterations), the test for the MSB (i.e., bit 5) in iteration $J + 1$ amounts to checking MSB $- 1$ (i.e., bit 4 in $R4$) in iteration J. If bit 4 is 1, then an EX-OR must be performed with the generator. For example, the generator string has a 1 in bit 2, so $R2$ must be EX-ORed with a 1 in iteration $J + 1$. But bit 2 in iteration $J + 1$ corresponds to bit 1 in iteration J. Thus the EX-OR corresponding to $R2$ in iteration $J + 1$ can be achieved by placing an EX-OR gate to the right of $R2$: The bit that will be placed in $R2$ is EX-ORed during its transit from $R1$.

Notice that the check for MSB has been finessed in Figure 9.6 by using the output of $R4$ as an input to all the EX-OR gates. The effect of this is that if the MSB of iteration $J + 1$ is 1 (recall that this is in $R4$ during iteration J), then all the EX-ORs are performed. If not, and if the MSB is 0, no EX-ORs are done, as desired; this is the same as EX-ORing with zero in Figure 9.4.

The implementation of Figure 9.6 is called a *linear feedback shift register* (LFSR), for obvious reasons. This is a classical hardware building block, which is also useful for the generation of random numbers for, say, QoS (Chapter 14). For example, random numbers using, say, the Tausworth implementation can be generated using three LFSRs and an EX-OR.

FASTER IMPLEMENTATIONS

The bottleneck in the implementation of Figure 9.6 is the shifting, which is done one bit at a time. Even at one bit every clock cycle, this is very slow for fast links. Most logic on packets occurs after the bit stream arriving from the link has been deserialized[3] into wider words of, say, size W. Thus the packet-processing logic is able to operate on W bits in a single clock cycle, which allows the hardware clock to run W times slower than the interarrival time between bits.

Thus to gain speed, CRC implementations have to shift W bits at a time, for $W > 1$. Suppose the current remainder is r and we shift in W more message bits whose value as a number is, say, n. Then in essence the implementation needs to find the remainder of $(2^W \cdot r + n)$ in one clock cycle.

If the number of bits in the current remainder register is small, the remainder of $2^W \cdot r$ can be precomputed (**P2a**) for all r by table lookup. This is the basis of a number of software CRC implementations that shift in, say, 8 bits at a time. In hardware, it is faster and more space efficient to use a matrix of XOR gates to do the same computation. The details of the parallel implementation can be found in Albertengo and Riccardo [AR90], based on the original idea described by Sarwate [Sar88].

9.2.2 Internet Checksums

Since CRC computation is done on every link in the Internet, it is done in hardware by link chips. However, the software algorithm, even shifting 8 bits at a time, is slow. Thus TCP chose to use a more efficient error-detection hash function based on summing the message bits. Just as accountants calculate sums of large sets of numbers by column and by row to check for errors, a *checksum* can catch errors that change the resulting sum.

It is natural to calculate the sum in units of the checksum size (16 bits in TCP), and some reasonable strategy must be followed when the sum of the 16-bit units in the message overflows the checksum size. Simply losing the MSB will, intuitively, lose information about 16-bit chunks computed early in the summing process. Thus TCP follows the strategy of an end-around carry. When the MSB overflows, the carry is added to the least significant bit (LSB). This is called one's *complement addition*.

The computation is straightforward. The specified portion of each TCP packet is summed in 16-bit chunks. Each time the sum overflows, the carry is added to the LSB. Thus the main loop will naively consist of three steps: Add the next chunk; test for carry; if carry, add to LSB. However, there are three problems with the naive implementation.

- *Byte Swapping:* First, in some machines, the 16-bit chunks in the TCP message may be stored byte-swapped. Thus it may appear that the implementation has to reverse each pair of bytes before addition.

- *Masking:* Second, many machines use word sizes of 32 bits or larger. Thus the naive computation may require masking out 16-bit portions.

- *Check for Carry:* Third, the check for carry after every 16-bit word is added can potentially slow down the loop as compared to ordinary summation.

---

[3]This is done by what is often called a *SERDES* chip, for serializer–deserializer chip.

FIGURE 9.7 The 1's complement addition of two 16-bit quantities stays the same (except for byte reversal) when the quantities are represented in byte-reversed form. This is because carries from any bit position flow to the same next-bit position in both original and byte-reversed formats. Consider, for example, how the MSB of *B* flows to the LSB of *A* in both formats.

All three problems can be solved by not being tied to the reference implementation (**P8**) and, instead, by fitting the computation to the underlying hardware (**P4c**). The following ideas and Figure 9.7 are taken from Partridge [Par93].

- *Ignore byte order:* Figure 9.7 shows that swapping every word before addition on a byte-reversed machine is obvious waste (**P1**). The figure shows that whether or not *AB* is stored byte reversed as *BA*, any carry from the MSB of byte *B* still flows to the LSB of byte *A*. Similarly, in both cases, any carry from the MSB of byte *A* flows to the LSB of byte *B*. Thus any 1's-complement addition done on the byte-reversed representation will have the same answer as in the original, except byte reversed. This in turn implies that it suffices to add in byte-reversed form and to do a final byte reversal only at the end.

- *Use natural word length:* If a machine has a 32- or 64-bit word, the most natural thing to do is to maintain the running sum in the natural machine word size. All that happens is that carries accumulate in the higher-order 16 bits of the machine word, which need to be added back to the lower 16 bits in a final operation.

- *Lazy carry evaluation:* Using a larger word size has the nice side effect of allowing lazy evaluation (**P2b**) of carry checking. For example, using a 32-bit word allows an unrolled loop that checks for carries only after every 16 additions [Ste94], because it takes 16 additions in the worst case to have the carry overflow from bit 32.

In addition, as noted in Chapter 5, the overhead of reading in the checksum data into machine registers can be avoided by piggybacking on the same requirement for copying data from the network device into user buffers, and vice versa.

HEADER CHECKSUM

Finally, besides the TCP and UDP checksums on the *data*, IP computes an additional 1's-complement checksum on just the IP *header*. This is crucial for network routers and other hardware devices that need to recompute Internet checksums.

Hardware implementations of header checksum can benefit from *parallel* and *incremental* computation. One strategy for parallelism is to break up the data being checksummed into *W* 16-bit words and to compute *W* different 1's-complement sums in parallel, with a final operation to fold these *W* sums into one 16-bit checksum. A complete hardware implementation of this idea with $W = 2$ is described in Touch and Parham [TP96].

The strategy for incremental computation is defined precisely in RFC 1624 [Rij94]. In essence, if a 16-bit field *m* in the header changes to *m'*, the header checksum can be recalculated by subtracting *m* and adding in *m'* to the older checksum value. There is one subtlety, having to do with the two representations of zero in 1's-complement arithmetic [Rij94], that is considered further in the exercises.

9.2.3 Finessing Checksums

The humble checksum's reason for existence, compared to the more powerful CRC, is the relative ease of checksum implementation in software. However, if there is hardware that already computes a data link CRC on every data link frame, an obvious question is: *Why not use the underlying hardware to compute another checksum on the data?* Doing otherwise results in extra computation by the receiving processor and appears to be obvious waste (**P1**). Once again, it is only obvious waste when looking across layers; at each individual layer (data link, transport) there is no waste.

Clearly, the CRC changes from hop to hop, while the TCP checksum should remain unchanged to check for end-to-end integrity. Thus if a CRC is to be used for both purposes, *two* CRCs have to be computed. The first is the usual CRC, and the second should be on some invariant portion of the packet that includes all the data and does not change from hop to hop.

One of the problems with exploiting the hardware (**P4c**) to compute the equivalent of the TCP checksum is knowing which portion of the packet must be checksummed. For example, TCP and UDP include some fields of the IP header[4] in order to compute the end-to-end checksum. The TCP header fields may also not be at a fixed offset because of potential TCP and IP options. Having a data link hardware device understand details of higher-layer headers seems to violate layering.

On the other hand, all the optimizations that avoid data copying and described in Chapter 5 also violate layering in a similar sense. Arguably, it does not matter what a single endnode does internally as long as the protocol behavior, as viewed externally by a black-box tester, meets conformance tests. Further, there are creative structuring techniques (**P8**, not being tied to reference implementations) of the endnode software that can allow lower layers access to this form of information.

The Infiniband architecture [AS00] does specify that end system hardware compute two CRCs. The usual CRC is called the *variant* CRC; the CRC on the data, together with some of the header, is called the *invariant* CRC. Infiniband transport and network layer headers are simpler than those of TCP, and thus computing the invariant portion is fairly simple.

However, the same idea could be used even for a more complex protocol, such as TCP or IP, while preserving endnode software structure. This can be achieved by having the upper layers pass information about offsets and fields (**P9**) to the lower layers through layer interfaces. A second option to avoid passing too many field descriptions is to precompute the pseudoheader checksum/CRC as part of the connection state [Jac93] and instead to pass the precomputed value to the hardware.

9.3 GENERIC PROTOCOL PROCESSING

Section 9.1 described techniques for buffering a packet, and Section 9.2 described techniques to efficiently compute packet checksums. The stage is now set to actually process such a packet. The reader unfamiliar with TCP may wish first to consult the models in Chapter 2.

---

[4]These portions form what is called the TCP and UDP *pseudoheader* [Ste94].

Since TCP accounts for 90% of traffic [Bra98] in most sites, it is crucial to efficiently process TCP packets at close to wire speeds. Unfortunately, a first glance at TCP code is daunting. While the TCP sender code is relatively simple, Stevens [Ste94] says:

TCP input processing is the largest piece of code that we examine in this text. The function tcp_input *is about 1100 lines of code. The processing of incoming segments is not complicated, just long and detailed.*

Since TCP appears to be complex, Greg Chesson and Larry Green formed Protocol Engines, Inc., in 1987, which proposed an alternative protocol called XTP [Che89]. XTP was carefully designed with packet headers that were easy to parse and streamlined processing paths. With XTP threatening to replace TCP, Van Jacobson riposted with a carefully tuned implementation of TCP in BSD UNIX that is well described in Stevens [Ste94]. This implementation was able to keep up with even 100-Mbps links. As a result, while XTP is still used [Che89], TCP proved to be a runaway success.

Central to Jacobson's optimized implementation is a mechanism called *header prediction* [Jac93]. Much of the complexity of the 1100 lines of TCP receive processing comes when handling rare cases. Header prediction provides a fast path through the thicket of exceptions by optimizing the expected case (**P11**).

TCP HEADER PREDICTION

The first operation on receiving a TCP packet is to find the protocol control block (PCB) that contains the state (e.g., receive and sent sequence numbers) for the connection of which the packet is a part. Assuming the connection is set up and that most workstations have only a few concurrent connections, the few active connection blocks can be cached. The BSD UNIX code [Ste94] maintains a one-behind cache containing the PCB of the last segment received; this works well in practice for workstation implementations.

After locating the PCB, the TCP header must be processed. A good way to motivate header prediction, found in Partridge [Par93], comes from looking at the fields in the TCP header, as shown in Figure 9.8.

After a connection is set up, the destination and source ports are fixed. Since IP networks work hard to send packets in order, the sequence number is likely to be the next in sequence after the last packet received. The control bits, often called flag bits, are typically off, with the exception of the ack bit, which is always set after the initial packet is sent. Finally, most of the time the receiver does not change its window size, and the urgent pointer is irrelevant.

FIGURE 9.8 TCP header fields: The fields most likely to change are the checksum and the ack fields. The other fields carry very little information and can often be predicted from past values.

Thus the only two fields whose information content is high are the ack number and checksum fields.

Motivated by this observation, header prediction identifies the expected case as one of two possibilities: receiving a pure acknowledgment (i.e., the received segment contains no data) or receiving a pure data packet (i.e., the received segment contains an ack field that conveys no new information). In addition, the packet should also reflect business as usual in the following precise sense: No unexpected TCP flags should be set, and the flow control window advertised in the packet should be no different from what the receiver had previously advertised. In pseudocode (simplified from Ref. Jac93):

```
IF (No unexpected flags) AND (Window in packet is as before)
AND (Packet sequence number is the next expected) THEN
    IF (Packet contains only headers and no data)
    Do Ack Processing
/* Release acked bytes, stop timers, awaken process */
ELSE IF (Packet does not ack anything new) /* pure data */
    Copy data to user buffer while checksumming;
    Update next sequence number expected;
    Send Acks if needed and release buffer;
ENDIF
ELSE /* header prediction failed -- take long path */
...
```

Clearly, this code is considerably shorter than the complete TCP receive processing code. However, some of the checks can be made more efficient by leveraging off the fact that most machines can do efficient comparisons in units of a machine word size (**P4a**, exploit locality).

For example, consider the TCP flags contained in the control bits of Figure 9.8. There are six flags, each encoded as a bit: SYN, FIN, RESET, PUSH, URG, ACK. If it is business as usual, all the flags must be clear, with the exception of ACK, which must be set, and PUSH, which is irrelevant. Checking for each of these conditions *individually* would require several instructions to extract and compare each bit.

Instead, observe that the flags field is the fourth word of the TCP header and that the window size is contained in the last 16 bits. In the header prediction code, the sender precomputes (**P2a**) the expected value of this word by filling in all the expected values of the flag and using the last advertised value of the window size.

The expected value of the fourth TCP header word is stored in the PCB entry for the connection. Given this setup, the first two checks in the pseudocode shown earlier can be accomplished in one stroke by comparing the fourth word of the TCP header in the incoming packet with the expected value stored in the PCB. If all goes well, and tests indicate they often do, the expected value of the fourth field is computed only at the start of the connection. It is this test that explains the origin of the name *header prediction*: A portion of the header is being predicted and checked against an incoming segment.

The pseudocode described earlier is abstracted from the implementation by Jacobson in a research kernel [Jac93] that claims to do TCP receiving processing in 30 Sun SPARC instructions! The BSD UNIX code given in Stevens [Ste94] is slightly more complicated, having to deal with mbufs and with the need to eliminate other possibilities, such as the PAWS test [Ste94].

The discussion so far has been limited to TCP receive processing because it is more complex than sending a TCP segment. However, a dual of header prediction exists for the sender side. If only a few fields change between segments, the sender may benefit from keeping a template TCP (and IP) header in the connection block. When sending a segment, the sender need only fill in the few fields that change into the template. This is more efficient if copying the TCP header is more efficient than filling in each field. Caching of sending packet headers is implemented in the Linux kernel.

Before finishing this topic, it is worth recalling Caveat **Q8** and examining how sensitive this optimization is to the system environment. Originally, header prediction was targeted at workstations. The underlying assumption (that the next segment is for the same connection and is one higher in sequence number than the last received segment) works well in this case.

Clearly, the assumption that the next segment is for the same connection works poorly in a server environment. This was noted as early as Jacobson [Jac93], who suggested using a hash of the port numbers to quickly locate the protocol control block. McKenney and Dove confirmed this by showing that using hashing to locate the PCB can speed up receive processing by an order of magnitude in an OLTP (online transaction processing) environment

The FIFO assumption is much harder to work around. While some clever schemes can be used to do sequence number processing for out-of-order packets, there are some more fundamental protocol mechanisms in TCP that build on the FIFO assumption. For example, if packets can be routinely misordered, TCP receivers will send duplicate acknowledgments. In TCP's fast retransmit algorithm [Ste94], TCP senders use three duplicate acknowledgments to infer a loss (see Chapter 14).

Thus lack of FIFO behavior can cause spurious retransmissions, which will lower performance more drastically as compared to the failure of header prediction. However, as TCP receivers evolve to do selective acknowledgment [FMM$^+$99], this could allow fast TCP processing of out-of-order segments in the future.

9.3.1 UDP Processing

Recall that UDP is TCP without error recovery, congestion control, or connection management. As with TCP, UDP allows multiplexing and demultiplexing using port numbers. Thus UDP allows applications to send IP datagrams without the complexity of TCP. Although TCP is by far the dominant protocol, many important applications, such as videoconferencing, use UDP. Thus it is also important to optimize UDP implementations.

Because UDP is stateless, header prediction is not relevant: One cannot store past headers that can be used to predict future headers. However, UDP shares with TCP two potentially time-consuming tasks: demultiplexing to the right protocol control block, and checksumming, both of which can benefit from TCP-style optimizations [PP93].

Caching of PCB entries is more subtle in UDP than in TCP. This is because PCBs may need to be looked up using wildcarded entries for, say, the remote (called *foreign*) IP address and port. Thus there may be PCB 1 that specifies local port L with all the other fields wildcarded, and PCB 2 that specifies local port L and remote IP address X. If PCB 1 is cached and a packet arrives destined for PCB 2, then the cache can result in demultiplexing the packet for the wrong PCB. Thus caching of wildcarded entries is not possible in general; address prefixes cannot be cached for purposes of route lookup (Chapter 11), for similar reasons.

Partridge and Pink [PP93] suggest a simple strategy to get around this issue. A PCB entry, such as PCB 1, that can "hide" or match another PCB entry is never allowed to be cached.

Subject to this restriction, the UDP implementation of Partridge and Pink [PP93] caches both the PCB of the last packet *received* and the PCB of the last packet *sent*. The first cache handles the case of a train of received packets, while the second cache handles the common case of receiving a response to the last packet sent. Despite the cache restrictions, these two caches still have an 87% hit rate in the measurements of Partridge and Pink [PP93].

Finally, Partridge and Pink [PP93] also implemented a copy-and-checksum loop for UDP as in TCP. In the BSD implementation, UDP's *sosend* was treated as a special case of sending over a connected socket. Instead, Partridge and Pink propose an efficient special-purpose routine that first calculates the header checksum and then copies the data bytes to the network buffer while updating the checksum. (Some of these ideas allowed Cray machines to vectorize the checksum loop in the early 1990s.) With similar optimizations used for receive processing, Partridge and Pink report that the checksum cost is essentially zero for CPUs that are limited by memory access time and not processing.

9.4 REASSEMBLY

Both header prediction for TCP and even the UDP optimizations of Partridge and Pink [PP93] assume that the received data stream has no unusual need for computation. For example, TCP segments are assumed not to contain window size changes or to have flags set that need attention. Besides these, an unstated assumption so far is that the IP packets do not need to be *reassembled*.

Briefly, the original IP routing protocol dealt with diverse links with different maximum packet sizes or Maximum Transmission Units (MTUs) by allowing routers to slice up IP packets into fragments. Each fragment is identified by a packet ID, a start byte offset into the original packet, and a fragment length. The last fragment has a bit set to indicate it is the last. Note that an intermediate router can cause a fragment to be itself fragmented into multiple smaller fragments. IP routing can also cause duplicates, loss, and out-of-order receipt of fragments.

At the receiver, Humpty Dumpty (i.e., the original packet) can be put together as follows. The first fragment to arrive at the receiver sets up the state that is indexed by the corresponding packet ID. Subsequent fragments are steered to the same piece of state (e.g., a linked list of fragments based on the packet ID). The receiver can tell when the packet is complete if the last fragment has been received and if the remaining fragments cover all the bytes in the original packets length, as indicated by each fragment's offset. If the packet is not reassembled after a specified time has elapsed, the state is timed out.

While fragmentation allows IP to deal with links of different MTU sizes, it has the following disadvantages [KM87]. First, it is expensive for a router to fragment a packet because it involves adding a new IP header for fragment, which increases the processing and memory bandwidth needs. Second, reassembly at endnodes is considered expensive because determining when a complete packet has been assembled potentially requires sorting the received fragments. Third, the loss of a fragment leads to the loss of a packet; thus when a fragment is lost, transmission of the remaining fragments is a waste of resources.

The current Internet strategy [KM87] is to shift the fragmentation computation in space (**P3c**) from the router and the receiver to the *sender*. The idea behind the so-called *path MTU* scheme is that the onus falls on the sender to compute a packet size that is small enough to pass through all links in the path from sender to receiver. Routers can now refuse to fragment a packet, sending back a control message to the receiver. The sender uses a list of common packet sizes (**P11**, optimizing the expected case) and works its way down this list when it receives a refusal.

The path MTU scheme nicely illustrates algorithmics in action by removing a problem by moving to another part of the system. However, a misconception has arisen that path MTU has completely removed fragmentation in the Internet. This is not so. Almost all core routers support fragmentation in hardware, and a significant amount of fragmented traffic has been observed [SMC01] on Internet backbone links many years after the path MTU protocol was deployed.

Note that the path MTU protocol requires the sender to keep state as to the best current packet size to use. This works well if the sender uses TCP, but not if the sender uses UDP, which is stateless. In the case of UDP, path MTU can be implemented only if the application above UDP keeps the necessary state and implements path MTU. This is harder to deploy because it is harder to change many applications, unlike changing just TCP. Thus at the time of writing, shared file system protocols such as NFS, IP within IP encapsulation protocols, and many media player and game protocols run over UDP and do not support path MTU. Finally, many attackers compromise security by splitting an attack payload across multiple fragments. Thus intrusion detection devices must often reassemble IP fragments to check for suspicious strings within the reassembled data.

Thus it is worth investigating fast reassembly algorithms because common programs such as NFS do not support the path MTU protocol and because real-time intrusion detection systems must reassemble packets at line speeds to detect attacks hidden across fragments. The next section describes fast reassembly implementations at receivers.

9.4.1 Efficient Reassembly

Figure 9.9 shows a simple data structure, akin to the one used in BSD UNIX, for reassembling a data packet. Assume that three fragments for the packet with ID 1080 have arrived. The fragments are sorted in a list by their starting offset number. Notice that there are overlapping bytes because the first fragment contains bytes 1–10, while the second contains 2–21.

Thus if a new fragment with packet ID 1080 arrives containing offsets 25–30, the implementation will typically search through the list, starting from the head, to find the correct position. The correct position is between start offsets 2 and 40 and so is after the second list item.

Each time a fragment is placed in the list, the implementation can check during list traversal if all required bytes have been received up to this fragment. If so, it continues checking to the end of the list to see if all bytes have been received and the last fragment has the last fragment bit set. If these conditions are met, then all required fragments have arrived; the

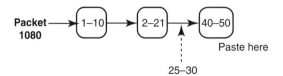

FIGURE 9.9 One data structure for reassembly is a linked list of fragments that is indexed by packet ID and sorted by the start byte offset (first field). The second field is the end offset. Thus the fragment that starts at offset 25 is inserted after the second list element.

implementation then traverses the list again, copying the data of each fragment into another buffer at the specified offset, potentially avoiding copying overlapping portions.

The resulting implementation is quite complex and slow and typically requires an extra copy. Note that to insert a fragment, one has to locate the packet ID's list and then search within the list. This requires two linear searches. Is IP reassembly fundamentally hard?

Oddly enough, there exists a counterexample reassembly protocol that has been implemented in hardware at gigabit speeds: the ATM AAL-5 cell reassembly protocol [Par93], which basically describes how to chop up IP packets into 53-byte ATM cells while allowing reassembly at the cells into packets at the receiver. What makes the AAL-5 reassembly algorithm simple to implement in hardware is not the fixed-length cell (the implementation can be generalized to variable-length cells) but the fact that *cells can only arrive in FIFO order.*

If cells can arrive only in FIFO order, it is easy to paste each successive cell into a buffer just after where the previous cell was placed. When the last cell arrives carrying a last cell bit (just as in IP), the packet's CRC is checked. If the CRC computes, the packet is successfully reassembled. Note that ATM does not require any offset fields because packets arrive in order on ATM virtual circuits.

Unlike ATM cells, IP datagrams can arrive (theoretically) in any order, because IP uses a datagram (post office) model as opposed to a virtual circuit (telephony) model. However, we have just seen that header prediction, and in fact the fast retransmission algorithm, depends crucially on the fact that in the expected case, IP segments arrive in order (**P11**, optimizing the expected case). Combining this observation with that of the AAL-5 implementation suggests that one can obtain an efficient reassembly algorithm, even in hardware, by optimizing for the case of FIFO arrival of fragments, as shown in Figure 9.10.

Figure 9.10 maintains the same sorted list as in Figure 9.9 but also keeps a pointer to the end of the list. Optimizing for the case that fragments arrive in order and are nonoverlapping, when a fragment containing bytes 22–30 arrives, the implementation checks the ending byte number of the last received fragment (stored in a register, equal to 21) against the start offset of the new fragment. Since 22 is 21 + 1, all is well. The new end byte is updated to the end byte of the new fragment (30), and the pointer is updated to point to the newly arrived fragment after linking it at the end of the list. Finally, if the newly arriving fragment is a last fragment, reassembly is done.

Compared to the implementation in Figure 9.9, the check for completion as well as the check to find out where to place a fragment takes constant and not linear time. Similarly, one can cache the expected packet ID (as in the TCP or UDP PCB lookup implementations) to avoid a list traversal when searching for the fragment list. Finally, using data structures such as pbufs instead of mbufs, even the need for an extra copy can be avoided by directly copying a received fragment into the buffer at the appropriate offset.

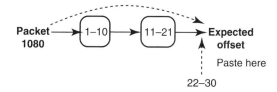

FIGURE 9.10 This implementation is similar to that of Figure 9.9, except it optimizes for the case that the fragments are nonoverlapping and arrive in order.

If the expected case fails, the implementation can revert to the standard BSD processing. For example, Chandranmenon and Varghese [CV98a], which describe this expected-case optimization in which the code keeps two lists and directly reuses the existing BSD code (which is hard to get right!) when the expected case fails. The expected case is reported by Chandranmenon and Varghese [CV98a] as taking 38 SPARC instructions, which is comparable with Jacobson's TCP estimates.

As with header prediction, it is worth applying Caveat **Q8** and examining the sensitivity of this optimization of this implementation to the assumptions. Actually, it turns out to be pretty bad. This is because measurements indicate that many recent implementations, including Linux, have senders send out fragments in reverse order! Thus fragments arrive in reverse order 9% of the time [SMC01].

This seemingly eccentric behavior is justified by the fact that it is only the last fragment that carries the length of the entire packet; by sending it first the sender allows the receiver to know what length buffer to allocate after the first fragment is received, assuming the fragments arrive in FIFO order. Note that the FIFO assumption still holds true. However, Figure 9.10 has a concealed but subtle additional assumption: that fragments will be sent in offset order. Before reading further, think how you might modify the implementation of Figure 9.10 to handle this case.

The solution, of course, is to use the first fragment to decide which of two expected cases to optimize for. If the first fragment is the first fragment (offset 0), then the implementation uses the mode described in Figure 9.10. If the first fragment is the last (last bit set), the implementation jumps to a different state, where it expects fragments in reverse order. This is just the dual of Figure 9.10, where the next fragment should have its last byte number to be 1 less (as opposed to 1 more) than the start offset of the previous fragment. Similarly, the next fragment is expected to be pasted at the start of the list and not the end.

9.5 CONCLUSIONS

This chapter describes techniques for efficient buffer allocation, CRC and checksum calculation, protocol processing such as TCP, and finally reassembly.

For buffer allocation, techniques such as the use of segregated pools and batch allocation promise fast allocation with potential trade-offs: the lack of storage efficiency (for segregated pools) versus the difficulty of coalescing noncontiguous holes (for batch allocation). Buffer sharing is important to use memory efficiently and can be done by efficiently stealing buffers from large users or by using dynamic thresholds.

For CRC calculation, efficient multibit remainder calculation finesses the obvious waste (**P1**) of calculating CRCs one bit at a time, even using LFSR implementations. For checksum calculation, the main trick is to fit the computation to the underlying machine architecture, using large word lengths, lazy checks for carries, and even parallelism. The optimizations for TCP, UDP, and reassembly are all based on optimizing simple expected cases (e.g., FIFO receipt, no errors) that cut through a welter of corner cases that the protocol must check for but rarely occur. Figure 9.1 presents a summary of the techniques used in this chapter together with the major principles involved.

Beyond the specific techniques, there are some general lessons to be gleaned. First, when considering the buffer-stealing algorithm, it is tempting to believe that finding the user with the largest buffer allocation requires a heap, which requires logarithmic time. However, as with timing wheels in Chapter 7, Mckenney's algorithm exploits the special case that buffer sizes only increase and decrease by 1.

The general lesson is that for algorithmics, special cases matter. Theoreticians know this well; for example, the general problem of finding a Hamiltonian cycle [CLR90] is hard for general graphs but is trivial if the graph is a ring. In fact, the practitioner of algorithmics should look for opportunities to change the system to permit special cases that permit efficient algorithms.

Second, the dynamic threshold scheme shows how important it is to optimize one's degrees of freedom (**P13**), especially when considering *dynamic* instead of *static* values for parameters. This is a very common evolutionary path in many protocols: for example, collision-avoidance protocols evolved from using fixed backoff times to using dynamic backoff times in Ethernet; transport protocols evolved from using fixed window sizes to using dynamic window sizes to adjust to congestion; finally, the dynamic threshold scheme of this chapter shows the power of allowing dynamic buffer thresholds.

Third, the discussion of techniques for buffer sharing shows why algorithmics — at least in terms of abstracting common networking tasks and understanding a wide spectrum of solutions for these tasks — can be useful. For example, when writing this chapter it became clear that buffer sharing is also part of many credit-based protocols, such as Ozveren et al. [OSV94] (see the protocol in Chapter 15) — except that in such settings a sender is allocating buffer space at a distant receiver. Isolating the abstract problem is helpful because it shows, for instance, that the dynamic threshold scheme of Choudhury and Hahne can provide finer grain buffer sharing than the technique of Ozveren et al. [OSV94].

Finally, the last lesson from header prediction and fast reassembly is that attempts to design new protocols for faster implementation can often be countered by simpler implementations. In particular, arguing that a protocol is "complex" is often irrelevant if the complexities can be finessed in the expected case.

As a second example, a transport protocol [SN89] was designed to allow efficient sequence number processing for protocols that used large windows and could handle out-of-order delivery. The protocol embedded concepts such as *chunks* of contiguous sequence numbers into the protocol for this purpose. Simple implementation tricks described in the patent [TVHS92] can achieve much the same effect, using large words to effectively represent chunks without redesigning the protocol.

Thus history teaches that attempts to redesign protocols for efficiency (as opposed to more functionality) should be viewed with some scepticism.

9.6 EXERCISES

1. **Dynamic Buffer Thresholds and Credit-Based Flow Control:** Read the credit-based protocol described in Chapter 15. Consider how to modify the buffer-sharing protocol of Chapter 15 to use dynamic thresholds. What are some of the possible benefits? This last question is ideally answered by a simulation, which would make it a longer-term class project.

2. **Incremental Checksum Computation:** RFC 1141 states that when an IP header with checksum H is modified by changing some 16-bit field value (such as the TTL field) m to

a new value m', then the new checksum should become $\overline{H + m + m'}$, where $\overline{X}$ denotes the 1's complement of X. While this works most of the time, the right equation, described in RFC 1624, is to compute $\overline{(H + \overline{m} + m')}$: This is slightly more inefficient but correct. This should show that tinkering with the computation can be tricky and requires proofs.

To see the difference between these two implementations, consider an example given in RFC 1624 with an IP header in which a 16-bit field $m = 0x5555$ changes to $m' = 0x3285$. The 1's-complement sum of all the remaining header bytes is $0xCD7A$. Compute the checksum both ways and show that they produce different results. Given that these two results are really the same in 1's complement notation (different representations of zero), why might it cause trouble at the receiver?

3. **Parallel Checksum Computation:** Figure out how to modify checksum calculation in hardware so as to work on W chunks of the packet in parallel and finally to fold all the results.

4. **Hardware Reassembly:** Suppose the FIFO assumption is not true and fragments arrive out of order. In this problem your assignment is to design an efficient hardware reassembly scheme for IP fragments subject to the restrictions stated in Chapter 2. One idea you could exploit is to have the hardware DMA engine that writes the fragment to a buffer also write a control bit for every word written to memory. This only adds a bit for every 32 bits.

When all the fragments have arrived, all the bits are set. You could determine whether all bits are set by using a summary tree, in which all the bits are leaves and each node has 32 children. A node's bit is set if all its children's bits are set. The summary tree does not require any pointers because all node bit positions can be calculated from child bit positions, as in a heap. Describe the algorithms to update the summary tree when a new fragment arrives. Consider hardware alternatives in which packets are stored in DRAM and bitmaps are stored in SRAM, as well as other creative possibilities.

PART III

Playing with Routers

My work is a game, a very serious game.

— M. C. ESCHER

Part I dealt with models and principles and Part II dealt with applying these models and principles to endnodes. The third part of this book deals with *router algorithmics*. This is the application of network algorithmics to building fast routers. However, many of the techniques apply to bridges, gateways, measurement devices, and firewalls. The techniques are applied mostly in a hardware setting, and much of it has to do with processing packets at wire speeds as links get faster. We study exact lookups, prefix lookups, packet classification, switching, and QoS. We also study some other chores within a router, such as striping and flow control across chip-to-chip links within a router.

CHAPTER 10

Exact-Match Lookups

"Challenge-and-response" is a formula describing the free play of forces that provokes new departures in individual and social life. An effective challenge stimulates men to creative action.

— Arnold Toynbee

In Part III, for simplicity of terminology, we will generically refer to interconnect devices as *routers*. Each chapter in Part III addresses the efficient implementation of a key function for such routers. In the simplest model of a router forwarding path, the destination address of a packet is first looked up to determine a destination port; the packet is then switched to the destination port; finally, the packet is scheduled at the destination port to provide QoS guarantees. In addition, modern high-performance routers also subject packets to internal striping (to gain throughput) and to internal credit-based flow control (to prevent loss on chip-to-chip links). The chapters are arranged to follow the same order, from lookups to switching to QoS.

Thus the first three chapters concentrate on the surprisingly difficult problem of state lookup in routers. The story begins with the simplest exact match lookups in this chapter, progresses to longest-prefix lookups in Chapter 11, and culminates with the most complex classification lookups in Chapter 12.

What is an exact-match lookup? Exact-match lookups represent the simplest form of database query. Assume a database with a set of tuples; each tuple consists of a unique fixed-length key together with some state information. A query specifies a key K. The goal is to return the state information associated with the tuple whose key is K.

Now, exact-match queries are easily implemented using well-studied techniques, such as binary search and hash tables [CLR90]. However, they are still worth studying in this book, for two reasons. First, in the networking context the models and metrics for lookups are different from the usual algorithmic setting. Such differences include the fact that lookups must complete in the time to receive a packet, the use of memory references rather than processing as a measure of speed, and the potential use of hardware speedups. Exact-match lookups offer the simplest opportunity to explore these differences. A second reason to study exact-match lookups is that they are crucial for an important networking function, called *bridging*[1], that is often integrated within a router.

---

[1]A device commonly known as a LAN switch typically implements bridge functionality.

Number	Principle	Used In
P15 P5	Use efficient data structures: binary search table Hardware FPGA for lookup only	First bridge
P15 P2a	Use efficient data structure: perfect hashing Precompute hash function with bounded collisions	Gigaswitch FDDI bridge
P5	Pipeline binary search	

FIGURE 10.1 Principles used in the various exact-match lookup techniques discussed in this chapter.

This chapter is organized around a description of the *history* of bridges. This is done for one chapter in the book, in the hope of introducing the reader to the *process* of algorithmics at work in a real product that changed the face of networking. This chapter also describes some of the stimuli that lead to innovation and introduces some of the people responsible for it.

Arnold Toynbee [TC72] describes history using a challenge–response theory, in which civilizations either grow or fail in response to a series of challenges. Similarly, the history of bridges can be described as a series of three challenges, which are described in the three sections of this chapter: Ethernets Under Fire (Section 10.1), Wire Speed Forwarding (Section 10.2), and Scaling Lookups to Higher Speeds (Section 10.3). The responses to these challenges led to what is now known as 802.1 spanning tree bridges [IEE97].

The techniques described in this chapter (and the corresponding principles) are summarized in Figure 10.1.

Quick Reference Guide

The implementor interested in fast exact-match schemes should consider either parallel hashing techniques inspired by perfect hashing (Section 10.3.1) or pipelined binary search (Section 10.3.2).

10.1 CHALLENGE 1: ETHERNET UNDER FIRE

The first challenge arose in the late 1980s. Ethernet, invented in the 1970s as a low-cost, high-bandwidth interconnect for personal computers, was attacked as behaving poorly at large loads and being incapable of spanning large distances. Recall that if two or more nodes on an Ethernet send data at the same time, a collision occurs on the shared wire. All senders then compute a random retransmission time and retry, where the randomization is chosen to minimize the probability of further collisions.

Theoretical analyses (e.g., Bux and Grillo [BG85]) claimed that as the utilization of an Ethernet grew, the effective throughput of the Ethernet dropped to zero because the entire bandwidth was wasted on retransmissions. A second charge against Ethernet was its small distance limit of 1.5 km, much smaller than the limits imposed by, say, the IBM token ring.

While the limited-bandwidth charge turned out to be false in practice [BMK88], it remained a potent marketing bullet for a long time. The limited-distance charge was, and

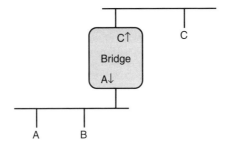

FIGURE 10.2   Toward designing a bridge connecting two Ethernets.

remains, a true limitation of a single Ethernet. In this embattled position, network marketing people at Digital Equipment Corporation (DEC) around 1980 pleaded with their technical experts for a technical riposte to these attacks. Could not their bright engineers find a clever way to "extend" a single Ethernet such that it could become a longer Ethernet with a larger effective bandwidth?

First, it was necessary to discard some unworkable alterntives. Physical layer bit repeaters were unworkable because they did not avoid the distance and bandwidth limits of ordinary Ethernets. Extending an Ethernet using a router did, in theory, solve both problems but introduced two other problems. First, in those days, routers were extremely slow and could hardly keep up with the speed of the Ethernet.

Second, there were at least six different routing protocols in use at that time, including IBM's SNA, Xerox's SNS, DECNET, and Appletalk. Hard as it may be to believe now, the Internet protocols were then only a small player in the marketplace. Thus a router would have to be a complex beast capable of routing multiple protocols (as Cisco would do a few years later), or one would have to incur the extra cost of placing multiple routers, one for each protocol. Thus the router solution was considered a nonstarter.

Routers interconnect links using information in the routing header, while repeaters interconnect links based on physical-layer information, such as bits. However, in classical network layering there is an intermediate layer called the data link layer. For an Ethernet, the data link layer is quite simple and contains a 48-bit unique Ethernet destination address.[2] Why is it not possible, the DEC group argued, to consider a new form of interconnection based only on the data link layer? They christened this new beast a data link layer relay, or a *bridge*.

Let us take an imaginary journey into the mind of Mark Kempf, an engineer in the Advanced Development Group at DEC, who invented bridges in Tewksbury, MA, around 1980. Undoubtedly, he drew something like Figure 10.2, which shows two Ethernets connected by a bridge; the lower Ethernet line contains stations *A* and *B*, while the upper Ethernet contains station *C*.

The bridge should make the two Ethernets look like one big Ethernet so that when *A* sends an Ethernet packet to *C* it magically gets to *C* without *A*'s having to even know there is a bridge in the middle. Perhaps Mark reasoned as follows in his path to a final solution.

Packet Repeater: Suppose *A* sends a packet to *C* (on the lower Ethernet) with destination address *C* and source address *A*. Assume the bridge picks up the entire packet, buffers it, and

---

[2]Note that Ethernet 48-bit addresses have no relation to 32-bit Internet addresses.

waits for a transmission opportunity to send it on the upper Ethernet. This avoids the physical coupling between the collision-resolution processes on the two Ethernets that would be caused by using a bit repeater. Thus the distance span increases to 3 km, but the effective bandwidth is still that of one Ethernet, because every frame is sent on both Ethernets.

Filtering Repeater: The frame repeater idea in Figure 10.2 causes needless waste (**P1**) when *A* sends a packet to *B* by sending the packet unnecessarily on the upper Ethernet. This waste can be avoided if the bridge has a table that maps station addresses to Ethernets. For example, suppose the bridge in Figure 10.2 has a table that maps *A* and *B* to the lower Ethernet and *C* to the upper Ethernet. Then on receipt of a packet from *A* to *B* on the lower Ethernet, the bridge need not forward the frame because the table indicates that destination *B* is on the same Ethernet the packet was received on. If, say, a fraction *p* of traffic on each Ethernet is to destinations on the same Ethernet (locality assumption), then the overall bandwidth of the two Ethernet systems becomes $(1 + p)$ times the bandwidth of a single Ethernet. This follows because the fraction *p* can be simultaneously sent on both Ethernets, increasing overall bandwidth by this fraction. Hence *both* bandwidth and distance increase. The only difficulty is figuring out how the mapping table is built.

Filtering Repeater with Learning: It is infeasible to have a manager build a mapping table for a large bridged network. Can the table be built automatically? One aspect of Principle **P13** (exploit degrees of freedom) is Polya's [Pol57] problem-solving question: "Have you used all the data?" So far, the bridge has looked only at *destination addresses* to forward the data. Why not also look at *source addresses*? When receiving a frame from *A* to *B*, the bridge can look at the source address field to realize that *A* is on the lower Ethernet. Over time, the bridge will learn the ports through which all active stations can be reached.

Perhaps Mark rushed out after his insight, shouting "Eureka!" But he still had to work out a few more issues. First, because the table is initially empty, bridges must forward a packet, perhaps unnecessarily, when the location of the destination has not been learned. Second, to handle station movement, table entries must be timed out if the source address is not seen for some time period *T*. Third, the entire idea generalizes to more than two Ethernets connected together without cycles, to bridges with more than two Ethernet attachments, and to links other than Ethernets that carry destination and source addresses. But there was a far more serious challenge that needed to be resolved.

10.2 CHALLENGE 2: WIRE SPEED FORWARDING

When the idea was first proposed, some doubting Thomas at DEC noticed a potential flaw. Suppose in Figure 10.2 that *A* sends 1000 packets to *B* and that *A* then follows this burst by sending, say, 10 packets to *C*. The bridge receives the thousand packets, buffers them, and begins to work on forwarding (actually discarding) them. Suppose the time that the bridge takes to look up its forwarding table is twice as long as the time it takes to receive a packet. Then after a burst of 1000 back-to-back packets arrive, a queue of 500 packets from *A* to *B* will remain as a backlog of packets that the bridge has not even examined.

Since the bridge has a finite amount of buffer storage for, say, 500 packets, when the burst from *A* to *C* arrives they may be dropped without examination because the bridge has no more buffer storage. This is ironic because the packets from *A* to *B* that are in the buffer will be dropped after examination, but the bridge has dropped packets from *A* to *C* that needed to be forwarded. One can change the numbers used in this example but the bottom line is

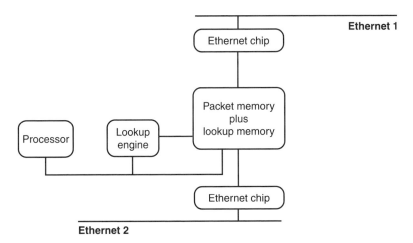

FIGURE 10.3 Implementation of the first Ethernet-to-Ethernet bridge.

unchanged: If the bridge takes more time to forward a packet than the minimum packet arrival time, there are always scenarios in which packets to be forwarded will be dropped, because the buffers are filled with packets that will be discarded.

The critics were quick to point out that routers did not have this problem[3] because routers dealt only with packets addressed to the router. Thus if a router were used, the router–Ethernet interface would not even pick up packets destined for *B*, avoiding this scenario.

To finesse this issue and avoid interminable arguments, Mark proposed an implementation that would do *wire speed forwarding* between two Ethernets. In other words, the bridge would look up the destination address in the table (for forwarding) and the source address (for learning) in the time it took a minimum-size packet to arrive on an Ethernet. Given a 64-byte minimum packet, this left 51.2 μsec to forward a packet. Since a two-port bridge could receive a minimum-size packet on each of its Ethernets every 51.2 μsec, this actually translated into doing two lookups (destination and source) every 25.6 μsec.

It is hard to appreciate today, when wire speed forwarding has become commonplace, how astonishing this goal was in the early 1980s. This is because in those days one would be fortunate to find an interconnect device (e.g., router, gateway) that worked at kilobit rates, let alone at 10 Mbit/sec. Impossible, many thought. To prove them wrong, Mark built a prototype as part of the Advanced Development Group in DEC. A schematic of his prototype, which became the basis for the first bridge, is shown in Figure 10.3.

The design in Figure 10.3 consists of a processor (the first bridge used a Motorola 68000), two Ethernet chips (the first bridge used AMD Lance chips), a lookup chip (which is described in more detail later), and a four-ported shared memory. The memory could be read and written by the processor, the Ethernet chips, and the lookup engine.

The data flow through the bridge was as follows. Imagine a packet *P* sent on Ethernet 1. Both Ethernet chips were set in "promiscuous mode," whereby they received all packets.

---

[3]Oddly enough even routers have the same problem of distinguishing important packets from less important ones in times of congestion, but this was not taken seriously in the 1980s.

Thus the bits of *P* are captured by the upper Ethernet chip and stored in the shared memory in a receive queue. The processor eventually reads the header of *P*, extracts the destination address *D*, and gives it to the lookup engine.

The lookup engine looks up *D* in a database also stored in the shared memory and returns the port (upper or lower Ethernet) in around 1.3 μsec. If the destination is on the upper Ethernet, then the packet buffer pointer is moved to a free queue, effectively discarding the packet; otherwise, the buffer pointer is moved to the transmit queue of the lower Ethernet chip. The processor also provides the source address *S* in packet *P* to the lookup engine for learning.

His design paid careful attention to algorithmics in at least three areas to achieve wire speed forwarding at a surprisingly small manufacturing cost of around $1000.

- **Architectural Design:** To minimize cost, the memory was cheap DRAM with a cycle time of 100 nsec that was used for packet buffers, scratch memory, and the lookup database. The four-port memory (including the separate connection from the lookup engine to the memory) and the buses were carefully designed to maximize parallelism and minimize interference. For example, while the lookup engine worked on doing lookups to memory, the processor continued to do useful work. Note that the processor has to examine the receive queues of both Ethernet chips in dovetailed fashion to check for packets to be forwarded from either the top or bottom Ethernets. Careful attention was paid to memory bandwidth, including the use of page mode (Chapter 2).

- **Data Copying:** The Lance chips used DMA (Chapter 5) to place packets in the memory without processor control. When a packet was to be forwarded between the two Ethernets, the processor only flipped a pointer from the receive queue of one Ethernet chip to the transmit queue of the other processor.

- **Control Overhead:** As with most processors, the interrupt overhead of the 68000 was substantial. To minimize this overhead, the processor used polling, staying in a loop after a packet interrupt and servicing as many packets as arrive, in order to reduce context-switching overhead (Chapter 6). When the receive queues are empty, the processor moves to doing other chores, such as processing control traffic. The first data packet arrival after such an idle period interrupts the processor, but this interrupt overhead is spread over the entire batch of packets that arrive before another idle period begins.

- **Lookups:** Very likely, Mark went through the eight cautionary questions found in Chapter 3. First, to avoid any complaints, he decided to use binary search (**P15**, efficient data structures) for lookup because of its determinism. Second, having a great deal of software experience before he began designing hardware, he wrote some sample 68000 code and determined that software binary search lookup was the bottleneck (**Q2** in Chapter 3) and would exceed his packet processing budget of 25.6 μsec. Eliminating the destination and source lookup would allow him to achieve wire speed forwarding (**Q3**). Recall that each iteration of binary search reads an address from the database in memory, compares it with the address that must be looked up, and uses this comparison to determine the next address to be read. With added hardware (**P5**), the comparison can be implemented using combinatorial logic (Chapter 2), and so a first-order approximation of lookup time is the number of DRAM memory accesses. As the first product aimed for a table size of 8000,[4] this required $\log_2 8000$ memory accesses of 100-nsec each, yielding a lookup time of 1.3 μsec. Given that the processor does useful work during the lookup, two lookups for source and destination easily fit within a 25.6-μsec budget (**Q4**).

To answer **Q5** in Chapter 3 as to whether custom hardware is worthwhile, Mark found that the lookup chip could be cheaply and quickly implemented using a PAL (programmable array logic; see Chapter 2). To answer **Q7**, his initial prototype met wire speed tests constructed using logic analyzers. Finally, **Q8**, which asks about the sensitivity to environment changes, was not relevant to a strictly worst-case design like this.

The 68000 software, written by Bob Shelley, also had to be carefully constructed to maximize parallelism. After the prototype was built, Tony Lauck, then head of DECNET, was worried that bridges would not work correctly if they were placed in cyclic topologies. For example, if two bridges are placed between the same pair of Ethernets, messages sent on one Ethernet will be forwarded at wire speed in the loop between bridges. In response, Radia Perlman, then the DEC routing architect, invented her celebrated *spanning tree* algorithm. The algorithm ensures that bridges compute a loop-free topology by having redundant bridges turn off appropriate bridge ports.

While you can read up on the design of the spanning tree algorithm in Perlman's book [Per92], it is interesting to note that there was initial resistance to implementing her algorithm, which appeared to be "complex" when compared to simple, fast bridge data forwarding. However, the spanning tree algorithm used control messages, called *Hellos*, that are not processed in real time.

A simple back-of-the-envelope calculation by Tony Lauck related the number of instructions used to process a hello (at most 1000), the rate of hello generation (specified at that time to be once every second), and the number of instructions per second of the Motorola 68000 (around 1 million). Lauck's vision and analysis carried the day, and the spanning tree algorithm was implemented in the final product.

Manufactured at a cost of $1000, the first bridge was initially sold at a markup of around eight, ensuring a handsome profit for DEC when sales initially climbed. In 1986 Mark Kempf was awarded U.S. Patent 4,597,07, titled "Bridge circuit for interconnecting networks." DEC made no money from patent licensing, choosing instead to promote the IEEE 802.1 bridge interconnection standards process.

Together with the idea of self-learning bridges, the spanning tree algorithm has passed into history. Ironically, one of the first customers complained that the bridge did not work correctly; field service later determined that the customer had connected two bridge ports to the same Ethernet, and the spanning tree had (rightly) turned the bridge off! While features like autoconfigurability and provable fault tolerance have only recently been added to Internet protocols, they were part of the bridge protocols in the 1980s.

The success of Ethernet bridges led to proposals for several other types of bridges connecting other local area networks and even wide area bridges. The author even remembers working with John Hart (who went on to become CTO of 3Com) and Fred Baker (who went on to become a Cisco Fellow) on building satellite bridges that could link geographically distributed sites. While some of the initital enthusiasm to extend bridges to supplant routers

---

[4]This allows a bridged Ethernet to have only 8000 stations. While this is probably sufficient for most customer sites, later bridge implementations raised this figure to 16K and even 64K.

was somewhat extreme, bridges found their most successful niche in cheaply interconnecting similar local area networks at wire speeds.

However, after the initial success of 10-Mbps Ethernet bridges, enginers at DEC began to worry about bridging higher-speed LANs. In particular, DEC decided, perhaps unwisely, to concentrate their high-speed interconnect strategy around 100-Mbps FDDI token rings [UNH01]. Thus in the early 1990s, engineers at DEC and other companies began to worry about building a bridge to interconnect two 100-Mpbs FDDI rings. Could wire speed forwarding, and especially exact-match lookups, be made 10 times faster?

10.3 CHALLENGE 3: SCALING LOOKUPS TO HIGHER SPEEDS

First, let's understand why binary search forwarding *does not* scale to FDDI speeds. Binary search takes $\log_2 N$ memory accesses to look up a bridge database, where N is the size of the database. As bridges grew popular, marketing feedback indicated that the database size needed to be increased from 8K to 64K. Thus using binary search, each search would take 16 memory accesses. Doing a search for the source and destination addresses using 100-nsec DRAM would then take 3.2 μsec.

Unlike Ethernet, where small packets are padded to ensure a minimum size of 64 bytes, a minimum-size packet consisting of FDDI, routing, and transport protocol headers could be as small as 40 bytes. Given that a 40-byte packet can be received in 3.2 μsec at 100 Mbps, two binary search lookups would use up all of the packet-processing budget for a single link, leaving no time for other chores, such as inserting and removing from link chip queues.

One simple approach to meet the challenge of wire speed forwarding is to retain binary search but to use faster hardware (**P5**). In particular, faster SRAM (Chapter 2) could be used to store the database. Given a factor of 5–10 decrease in memory access time using SRAM in place of DRAM, binary search will easily scale to wire speed FDDI forwarding.

However, this approach is unsatisfactory, for two reasons. First, it is more expensive, because SRAM is more expensive than DRAM. Second, using faster memory gets us lookups at FDDI speeds but will not work for the next speed increment (e.g., Gigabit Ethernet). What is needed is a way to reduce the number of memory accesses associated with a lookup so that bridging can scale with link technology. Of the two following approaches to bridge-lookup scaling, one is based on hashing and the other on hardware parallelism.

10.3.1 *Scaling via Hashing*

In the 1990s, DEC decided to build a fast crossbar switch connecting up to 32 links, called the Gigaswitch [SKO+94]. The switch-arbitration algorithms used in this switch will be described in Chapter 13. This chapter concentrates on the bridge-lookup algorithms used in the Gigaswitch. The vision of the original designers, Bob Simcoe and Bob Thomas, was to have the Gigaswitch be a switch connecting point-to-point FDDI links without implementing bridge forwarding and learning. Bridge lookups were considered to be too complex at 100-Mbps speeds.

Into the development arena strode a young software designer who changed the product direction. Barry Spinney, who had implemented an Ada compiler in his last job, was determined to do hardware design at DEC. Barry suggested that the Gigaswitch be converted to a bridge interconnecting FDDI local area networks. To do so, he proposed designing an

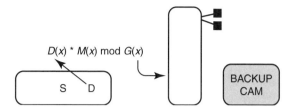

FIGURE 10.4 Gigaswitch hashing uses a hash function with a programmable multiplier, a small, balanced binary tree in every hash bucket, and a backup CAM to hold the rare case of entries that result in more than seven collisions.

FDDI-to-Gigaswitch network controller (FGC) chip on the line cards that would implement a hashing-based algorithm for lookups. The Gigaswitch article [SKO$^+$94] states that each bridge lookup makes at most four reads from memory.

Now, every student of algorithms [CLR90] knows that hashing, on average, is much faster (constant time) than binary search (logarithmic time). However, the same student also knows that hashing is much slower in the worst case, potentially taking linear time because of collisions. How, then, can the Gigaswitch hash lookups claim to take at most four reads to memory in the worst case even for bridge databases of size 64K, whereas binary search would require 16 memory accesses?

The Gigaswitch trick has its roots in an algorithmic technique (**P15**) called *perfect hashing* [DKea88]. The idea is to use a parameterized hash function, where the hash function can be changed by varying some parameters. Then appropriate values of the parameters can be precomputed (**P2a**) to obtain a hash function such that the worst-case number of collisions is small and bounded.

While finding such a good hash function may take (in theory) a large amount of time, this is a good trade-off because this new station's addresses do not get added to local area networks at a very rapid rate. On the other hand, once the hash function has been picked, lookup can be done at wire speeds.

Specifically, the Gigaswitch hash function treats each 48-bit address as a 47-degree polynomial in the Galois field of order 2, GF(2). While this sounds impressive, this is the same arithmetic used for calculating CRCs; it is identical to ordinary polynomial arithmetic, except that all additions are done mod 2. A hashed address is obtained by the equation $A(X) * M(X)$ mod $G(X)$, where $G(X)$ is the irreducible polynomial $X^{48} + X^{36} + X^{25} + X^{10} + 1$, $M(X)$ is a nonzero, 47-degree programmable hash multiplier, and $A(X)$ is the address expressed as a 47-degree polynomial.

The hashed address is 48 bits. The bottom 16 bits of the hashed address is then used as an index into a 64K-entry hash table. Each hash table entry [see Figure 10.4 as applied to the destination address lookup, with $D(x)$ being used in place of $A(x)$] points to the root of a balanced binary tree of height at most 3. The hash function has the property that it suffices to use only the remaining high-order 32 bits of the hashed address to disambiguate collided keys.

Thus the binary tree is sorted by these 32-bit values, instead of the original 48-bit keys. This saves 16 bits to be used for associated lookup information. Thus any search is guaranteed to take no more than four memory accesses, one to lookup the hash table and three more to navigate a height-3 binary tree.

It turns out that picking the multiplier is quite easy in practice. The coefficients of $M(x)$ are picked randomly. Having picked $M(x)$ it sometimes happens that a few buckets have more than seven colliding addresses. In such a case, these entries are stored in a small hardware lookup database called a Content Addressable Memory or CAM (studied in more detail in Chapter 11).

The CAM lookup occurs in parallel with the hash lookup. Finally, in the extremely rare case when several dozen addresses are added to the CAM (say, when new station addresses are learned that cause collisions), the central processor initiates a rehashing operation and distributes the new hash function to the line cards. It is perhaps ironic that rehashing occured so rarely in practice that one might worry whether the rehashing code was adequately tested!

The Gigaswitch became a successful product, allowing up to 22 FDDI networks to be bridged together with other link technologies, such as ATM. Barry Spinney was assigned U.S. patent 5,920,900, "Hash-based translation method and apparatus with multiple-level collision resolution." While techniques based on perfect hashing [DKea88] have been around for a while in the theoretical community, Spinney's contribution was to use a pragmatic version of the perfect hashing idea for high-speed forwarding.

10.3.2 Using Hardware Parallelism

Techniques based on perfect hashing do not completely provide worst-case guarantees. While they do provide worst-case *search* times of three to four memory accesses, they cannot guarantee worst-case *update* times. It is conceivable that an update takes an unpredictably long time while the software searches for a hash function with the specified bound on the number of collisions.

One can argue that exactly the same guarantees are provided every moment by millions of Ethernets around the world and that nondeterministic update times are far preferable to nondeterministic search times. However, proving that long update times are rare in practice requires either considerable experimentation or good analysis. This makes some designers uncomfortable. It leads to a preference for search schemes that have bounded worst-case search and update times.

An alternate approach is to apply hardware parallelism (**P5**) to a deterministic scheme such as binary search. Binary search has deterministic search and update times; its only problem is that search takes a logarithmic number of memory accesses, which is too slow. We can get around this difficulty by *pipelining* binary search to increase lookup throughput (number of lookups per second) without improving lookup latency. This is illustrated in Figure 10.5.

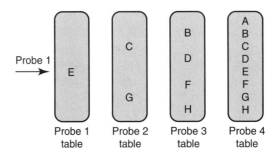

FIGURE 10.5 Pipeling binary search for a database with keys *A* through *H*.

The idea is to have a logarithmic number of processing stages, each with its own memory array. In Figure 10.5 the keys are the characters A through H. The first array has only the root of the trie, the median element E. The second array corresponds to the quartile and third quartile elements C and G, which are the possible keys at the second probe of binary search, and so on. Search keys enter from the left and progress from stage to stage, carrying a pointer that identifies which key in the corresponding stage memory must be compared to the search key. The lookup throughput is nearly one per memory access, because there can be multiple concurrent searches progressing through the stages in order.

Although the figure shows the elements in, say, Stage 2, C and G, as being separated by their spacing in the original table, they can be packed together to save memory in the stages. Thus the overall memory across all stages becomes equal to the memory in a nonpipelined implementation. Indexing into each stage memory becomes slightly more tricky.

Assume Stage i has passed a pointer j to Stage $j + 1$ along with search key S. Stage $j + 1$ compares the search key S to its jth array entry. If the answer is equal, the search is finished but continues flowing through the pipeline with no more changes. If the search key is smaller, the search key is passed to stage $i + 1$ with the pointer $j0$ (i.e., j concatenated with bit 0); if the search key is larger, the pointer passed is $j1$. For example, if the key searched for is F, then the pointer becomes 1 when entering Stage 2 and becomes 10 when entering Stage 3.

The author first heard of this idea from Greg Waters, who later went on to implement IP lookups for the core router company Avici. While the idea looks clever and arcane, there is a much simpler way of understanding the final solution. Computer scientists are well aware of the notion of a binary search tree [CLR90]. Any binary search table can be converted into a fully balanced binary search tree by making the root the median element, and so on, along the lines of Figure 10.5. Any tree is trivially pipelined by height, with nodes of height i being assigned to Stage i.

The only problem with a binary search tree, as opposed to a table, is the extra space required for pointers to children. However, it is well known that for a full binary search tree, such as a heap [CLR90], the pointers can be implicit and can be calculated based on the history of comparisons — as shown earlier. The upshot is that a seemingly abstruse trick can be seen as the combination of three simple and well-known facts from theoretical computer science.

10.4 SUMMARY

This chapter on exact-match lookups is written as a story — the story of bridging. Three morals can be drawn from this story.

First, bridging was a direct response to the challenge of efficiently extending Ethernets without using routers or repeaters; wire speed forwarding was a direct response to the problem of potentially losing important packets in a flood of less important packets. At the risk of sounding like a self-help book, I hold that challenges are best regarded as opportunities and not as annoyances. The mathematician Felix Klein [Bel86] used to say, "You must always have a problem; you may not find what you were looking for but you will find something interesting on the way." For example, it is clear that the main reason bridges were invented — the lack of high-performance multiprotocol routers — is *not* the reason bridges are still useful today.

This brings us to the second moral. Today it is clear that bridges will never displace routers, because of their lack of scalability using flat Ethernet addresses, lack of shortest-cost routing, etc. However, they remain interesting today because bridges are interconnect devices with better cost for performance and higher flexibility than routers for interconnecting a small number of similar local area networks. Thus bridges still abound in the marketplace, often referred to as *switches*. What many network vendors refer to as a *switch* is a crossbar switch, such as the Gigaswitch, that is capable of bridging on every interface. A few new features, notably virtual LANs (VLANs) [Per92], have been added. But the core idea remains the same.

Third, the *techniques* introduced by the first bridge have deeply influenced the next generation of interconnect devices, from core routers to Web switches. Recall that Roger Bannister, who first broke the 4-minute-mile barrier, was followed in a few months by several others. In the same way, the first Ethernet bridge was quickly followed by many other wire speed bridges. Soon the idea began to flow to routers as well. Other important concepts introduced by bridges include the use of memory references as a metric, the notion of trading update time for faster lookups, and the use of minimal hardware speedups. All these ideas carry over into the study of router lookups in the next chapter.

In conclusion, the challenge of building the first bridge stimulated creative actions that went far beyond the first bridge. While wire speed router designs are fairly commonplace today, it is perhaps surprising that there are products still being announced that claim gigabit wire speed processing rates for such abstruse networking tasks as encryption and even XML transformations.

10.5 EXERCISE

1. **ARP Caches:** Another example of an exact-match lookup is furnished by ARP caches in a router or endnode. In an Internet router, when a packet first arrives to a destination, the router must store the packet and send an ARP request to the Ethernet containing the packet. The ARP request is broadcast to all endnodes on the Ethernet and contains the IP address of the destination. When the destination responds with an ARP reply containing the Ethernet address of the destination, the router stores the mapping in an ARP table and sends the stored data packet, with the destination Ethernet address filled in.

   • What lookup algorithms can be used for ARP caches?

   • Why might the task of storing data packets awaiting data translation result in packet reordering?

   • Some router implementations get around the reordering problem by dropping all data packets that arrive to find that the destination address is not in the ARP table (however, the ARP request is sent out). Explain the pros and cons of such a scheme.

CHAPTER 11

Prefix-Match Lookups

You can look it up.

— TRADITIONAL

Consider a flight database in London that lists flights to a thousand U.S. cities. One alternative would be to keep a record specifying the path to each of the thousand cities. Suppose, however, that most flights to America hub though Boston, except flights to California, which hub through Los Angeles. This observation can be exploited to reduce the flight database from a thousand entries to two prefix entries (USA* −− > Boston; USA.CA.* −− > LA).

A problem with this reduction is that a destination city like USA.CA.Fresno will now match both the USA* and USA.CA.* prefixes; the database must return the longest match (USA.CA.*). Thus prefixes have been used to compress a large database, but at the cost of a more complex *longest-matching-prefix* lookup.

As described in Chapter 2, the Internet uses the same idea. In the year 2004, core routers stored only around 150,000 prefixes, instead of potentially billions of entries for each possible Internet address. For example, to a core router all the computers within a university, such as UCSD, will probably be reachable by the same next hop. If all the computers within UCSD are given the same initial set of bits (the network number, or prefix), then the router can store *one* entry for UCSD instead of thousands of entries for each computer in UCSD.

The entire chapter is organized as follows. Section 11.1 provides an introduction to prefix lookups. Section 11.2 describes attempts to finesse the need for IP lookups. Section 11.3 presents nonalgorithmic techniques for lookup based on caching and parallel hardware. Section 11.4 describes the simplest technique based on unibit tries.

The chapter then transitions to describe six new schemes: multibit tries (Section 11.5), level-compressed tries (Section 11.6), Lulea-compressed tries (Section 11.7), tree bitmap (Section 11.8), binary search on prefix ranges (Section 11.9), and binary search on prefix lengths (Section 11.10). The chapter ends with Section 11.11, describing memory allocation issues for lookup schemes.

The techniques described in this chapter (and the corresponding principles) are summarized in Figure 11.1.

Number	Principle	Lookup Technique
P2a, P10	Precompute indices	Tag switching
P2a, P10 P4a	Pass indices computed at run time Exploit ATM switch hardware	IP switching
P11	Cache whole IP addresses	Lookup caches
P5	Hardware parallel lookup	CAMs
P4b	Expand prefixes to gain speed	Controlled expansion
P13	Strides as a degree of freedom	Variable-stride tries
P4b P12, P2a	Compress to gain speed Precomputed count of bits set	Lulea tries
P15 P12 P2a	Use efficient search Add marker state Precompute marker watch	Binary search on prefix lengths
P2a	Precompute range to prefix matching	Binary search on prefixes

FIGURE 11.1 Principles involved in the various prefix-lookup schemes described in this chapter.

Quick Reference Guide

The most important lookup algorithms for an implementor today are as follows. At speeds up to 10 Gbps in hardware or software using DRAM technology, the simplest and most effective scheme is based on multibit tries (Section 11.5). At faster speeds, up to 40 Gbps, especially using more expensive SRAM technology, the most effective algorithm described in this chapter is the tree bitmap (Section 11.8) scheme. A simple reduction of prefix search to binary search is described in Section 11.9; using wide memory words, this scheme is quite effective and, more importantly, is unencumbered by patents. Finally, an important and often not well-appreciated point is the issue of memory allocation for compressed data structures, which is introduced in Section 11.11. While these four sections will probably answer immediate implementation needs, the remaining sections provide insight and alternatives that may help a designer to invent new schemes.

11.1 INTRODUCTION TO PREFIX LOOKUPS

This section introduces prefix notation, explains why prefix lookup is used, and describes the main metrics used to evaluate prefix lookup schemes.

11.1.1 Prefix Notation

Internet prefixes are defined using bits and not alphanumerical characters, of up to 32 bits in length. To confuse matters, however, IP prefixes are often written in dot-decimal notation.

Thus, the 16-bit prefix for UCSD at the time of writing is 132.239. Each of the decimal digits between dots represents a byte. Since in binary 132 is 10000100 and 239 is 11101111, the UCSD prefix in binary can also be written as 1000010011101111*, where the wildcard character * is used to denote that the remaining bits do not matter. All UCSD hosts have 32-bit IP addresses beginning with these 16 bits.

Because prefixes can be variable length, a second common way to denote a prefix is by slash notation of the form *A/L*. In this case *A* denotes a 32-bit IP address in dot-decimal notation and *L* denotes the length of the prefix. Thus the UCSD prefix can also be denoted as 132.239.0.0/16, where the length 16 indicates that only the first 16 bits (i.e., 132.239) are relevant. A third common way to describe prefixes is to use a mask in place of an explicit prefix length. Thus the UCSD prefix can also be described as 128.239.0.0 with a mask of 255.255.0.0. Since 255.255.0.0 has 1's in the first 16 bits, this implicitly indicates a length of 16 bits.[1]

Of these three ways to denote a prefix (binary with a wildcard at the end, slash notation, and mask notation), the last two are more compact for writing down large prefixes. However, for pedagogical reasons, it is much easier to use small prefixes as examples and to write them in binary. Thus in this chapter we will use 01110* to denote a prefix that matches all 32-bit IP addresses that start with 01110. The reader should easily be able to convert this notation to the slash or mask notation used by vendors. Also, note that most prefixes are at least 8 bits in length; however, to keep our examples simple, this chapter uses smaller prefixes.

11.1.2 Why Variable-Length Prefixes?

Before we consider how to deal with the complexity of variable-length-prefix matching, it is worth understanding why Internet prefixes are variable length. Given a telephone number such as 858-549-3816, it is a trivial matter to extract the first three digits (i.e., 858) as the area code. If fixed-length prefixes are easier to implement, what is the advantage of variable-length prefixes?

The *general* answer to this question is that variable-length prefixes make more efficient use of the address space. This is because areas with a large number of endpoints can be assigned shorter prefixes, while areas with a few endpoints can be assigned longer prefixes.

The *specific* answer comes from the history of Internet addressing. The Internet began with a simple hierarchy in which 32-bit addresses were divided into a network address and a host number; routers only stored entries for networks. For flexible address allocation, the network address came in variable sizes: Class A (8 bits), Class B (16 bits), and Class C (24 bits). To cope with exhaustion of Class B addresses, the Classless Internet Domain Routing (CIDR) scheme [RL96] assigns new organizations multiple contiguous Class C addresses that can be aggregated by a common prefix. This reduces core router table size.

Today, the potential depletion of the address space has led Internet registries to be very conservative in the assignment of IP addresses. A small organization may be given only a small portion of a Class C address, perhaps a /30, which allows only four IP addresses within the organization. Many organizations are coping with these sparse assignments by sharing a few

---

[1]The mask notation is actually more general because it allows noncontiguous masks where the 1's are not necessarily consecutive starting from the left. Such definitions of networks actually do exist. However, they are becoming increasingly uncommon and are nonexistent in core router prefix tables. Thus we will ignore this possibility in this chapter.

IP addresses among multiple computers, using schemes such as network address translation, or NAT.

Thus CIDR and NAT have helped the Internet handle exponential growth with a finite 32-bit address space. While there are plans for a new IP (IPv6) with a 128-bit address, the effectiveness of NAT in the short run and the complexity of rolling out a new protocol have made IPv6 deployment currently slow. Despite this, a brave new world containing billions of wireless sensors may lead to an IPv6 resurgence.

The bottom line is that the decision to deploy CIDR helped save the Internet, but it has introduced the complexity of longest-matching-prefix lookup.

11.1.3 Lookup Model

Recall the router model of Chapter 2. A packet arrives on an input link. Each packet carries a 32-bit Internet (IP) address.[2]

The processor consults a forwarding table to determine the output link for the packet. The forwarding table contains a set of *prefixes* with their corresponding output links. The packet is matched to the longest prefix that matches the destination address in the packet, and the packet is forwarded to the corrresponding output link. The task of determining the output link, called *address lookup*, is the subject of this chapter, which surveys lookup algorithms and shows that lookup can be implemented at gigabit and terabit speeds.

Before searching for IP lookup solutions, it is important to be familiar with some basic observations about traffic distributions, memory trends, and database sizes, which are shown in Figure 11.2. These in turn will motivate the requirements for a lookup scheme.

First, a study of backbone traffic [TMW97] as far back as 1997 shows around 250,000 concurrent flows of short duration, using a fairly conservative measurement of flows. Measurement data shows that this number is only increasing. This large number of flows means caching solutions do not work well.

Second, the same study [TMW97] shows that roughly half the packets received by a router are minimum-size TCP acknowledgments. Thus it is possible for a router to receive a stream of minimum-size packets. Hence, being able to prefix lookups in the time to forward a minimum-size packet can finesse the need for an input link queue, which simplifies system design. A second reason is simple marketing: Many vendors claim wire speed forwarding, and these claims can be tested. Assuming wire speed forwarding, forwarding a 40-byte packet should take no more than 320 nsec at 1 Gbps, 32 nsec at 10 Gbps (OC-192 speeds), and 8 nsec at 40 Gbps (OC-768).

Clearly, the most crucial metric for a lookup scheme is lookup speed. The third observation states that because the cost of computation today is dominated by memory accesses, the simplest measure of lookup speed is the worst-case number of memory accesses. The fourth observation shows that backbone databases have all prefix lengths from 8 to 32, and so naive schemes will require 24 memory accesses in the worst case to try all possible prefix lengths.

The fifth observation states that while current databases are around 150,000 prefixes, the possible use of host routes (full 32-bit addresses) and multicast routes means that future backbone routers will have prefix databases of 500,000 to 1 million prefixes.

---

[2]While most users deal with domain names, recall again that these names are translated to an IP address by a directory service called DNS before packets are sent.

Observation	Inference
1. 250,000 concurrent flows in backbone	Caching works poorly in backbone routers
2. 50% are TCP acks	Wire speed lookup needed for 40-byte packets
3. Lookup dominated by memory accesses	Lookup speed measured by number of memory accesses
4. Prefix lengths from 8–32	Naive schemes take 24 memory accesses
5. 150,000 prefixes today and multicast and host routes	With growth, require 500,000–1 million prefixes
6. Unstable BGP, multicast	Updates in milliseconds to seconds
7. Higher speeds need SRAM	Worth minimizing memory
8. IPv6, multicast delays	32-bit lookups more crucial

FIGURE 11.2   Some current data about the lookup problem and the corresponding implications for lookup solutions.

The sixth observation refers to the speed of updates to the lookup data structure, for example, to add or delete a prefix. Unstable routing-protocol implementations can lead to requirements for updates on the order of milliseconds. Note that whether seconds or milliseconds, this is several orders of magnitude below the lookup requirements, allowing implementations the luxury of precomputing (**P2a**) information in data structures to speed up lookup, at the cost of longer update times.

The seventh observation comes from Chapter 2. While standard (DRAM) memory is cheap, DRAM access times are currently around 60 nsec, and so higher-speed memory (e.g., off- or on-chip SRAM, 1–10 nsec) may be needed at higher speeds. While DRAM memory is essentially unlimited, SRAM and on-chip memory are limited by expense or unavailability. Thus a third metric is memory usage, where memory can be expensive fast memory (cache in software, SRAM in hardware) as well as cheaper, slow memory (e.g., DRAM, SDRAM).

Note that a lookup scheme that does not do incremental updates will require two copies of the lookup database so that search can proceed in one copy while lookups proceed on the other copy. Thus it may be worth doing incremental updates simply to reduce high-speed memory by a factor of 2!

The eight observation concerns prefix lengths. IPv6 requires 128-bit prefixes. Multicast lookups require 64-bit lookups because the full group address and a source address can be concatenated to make a 64-bit prefix. However, the full deployment of both IPv6 and multicast is in question. Thus at the time of writing, 32-bit IP lookups remain the most interesting problem. However, this chapter does describe schemes that scale well to longer prefix lengths.

In summary, the interesting metrics, in order of importance, are lookup speed, memory, and update time. As a concrete example, a good on-chip design using 16 Mbits of on-chip memory may support any set of 500,000 prefixes, do a lookup in 8 nsec to provide wire speed forwarding at OC-192 rates, and allow prefix updates in 1 msec.

All the data described in this chapter is based on traces in [TMW97] and the routing databases made available by the IPMA project [Mer]. Thus most academic papers and routing vendors use the same databases to experimentally compare lookup schemes. The largest of these, Mae East, is a reasonable model for a large backbone router.

The following notation is used consistently in reporting the theoretical performance of IP lookup algorithms. N denotes the number of prefixes (e.g., 150,000 for large databases today), and W denotes the length of an address (e.g., 32 for IPv4).

Finally, two additional observations can be exploited to optimize the expected case.

O1: Almost all prefixes are 24 bits or less, with the majority being 24-bit prefixes and the next largest spike being at 16 bits. Some vendors use this to show worst-case lookup times only for 24-bit prefixes; however, the future may lead to databases with a large number of host routes (32-bit addresses) and integration of ARP caches.

O2: It is fairly rare to have prefixes that are prefixes of other prefixes, such as the prefixes 00* and 0001*. In fact, the maximum number of prefixes of a given prefix in current databases is seven.

While the ideal is a scheme that meets worst-case lookup time requirements, it is desirable to have schemes that also utilize these observations to improve average storage performance.

11.2 FINESSING LOOKUPS

The first instinct for a systems person is not to solve complex problems (like longest matching prefix) but to *eliminate* the problem.

Observe that in virtual circuit networks such as ATM, when a source wishes to send data to a destination, a call, analogous to a telephone call, is set up. The call number (VCI) at each router is a moderate-size integer that is easy to look up. However, this comes at the cost of a round-trip delay for call setup before data can be sent.

In terms of our principles, ATM has a previous hop switch pass an index (**P10**, pass hints in protocol headers) into a next hop switch. The index is precomputed (**P2a**) just before data is sent by the previous hop switch (**P3c**, shifting computation in space). The same abstract idea can be used in datagram networks such as the Internet to finesse the need for prefix lookups. We now describe two instantiations of this abstract idea: tag switching (Section 11.2.1) and flow switching (Section 11.2.2).

11.2.1 Threaded Indices and Tag Switching

In threaded indices [CV96], each router passes an index into the next router's forwarding table, thereby avoiding prefix lookups. The indexes are precomputed *by the routing protocol* whenever the topology changes. Thus in Figure 11.3, source S sends a packet to destination D to the first router A as usual; however, the packet header also contains an index i into

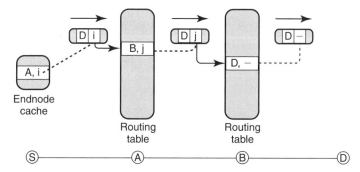

FIGURE 11.3 Replacing the need for a destination lookup in a datagram router by having each router pass an index into the next router's forwarding table.

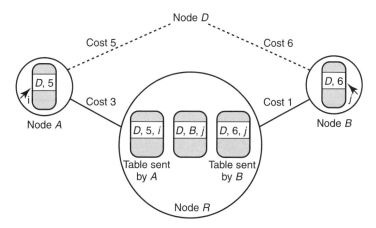

FIGURE 11.4 Setting up the threaded indexes or tags by modifying Bellman–Ford routing.

A's forwarding table. *A*'s entry for *D* says that the next hop is router *B* and that *B* stores its forwarding entry for *D* at index *j*. Thus *A* sends the packet on to *B*, but first it writes *j* (Figure 11.3) as the packet index. This process is repeated, with each router in the path using the index in the packet to look up its forwarding table.

The two main differences between threaded indices and virtual circuit indices (VCIs) are as follows. First, threaded indexes are per *destination* and not per active *source–destination pair* as in virtual circuit networks such as ATM. Second, and most important, threaded indexes are precomputed *by the routing protocol whenever the topology changes*. As a simple example, consider Figure 11.4, which shows a sample router topology where the routers run the Bellman–Ford protocol to find their distances to destinations.

In Bellman–Ford (used, for example, in the intradomain protocol Routing Information Protocol (RIP) [Per92]), a router *R* calculates its shortest path to *D* by taking the minimum of the cost to *D* through each neighbor. The cost through a neighbor such as *A* is *A*'s cost to *D* (i.e., 5) plus the cost from *R* to *A* (i.e., 3). In Figure 11.4, the best-cost path from *R* to *D* is through router *B*, with cost 7. *R* can compute this because each neighbor of *R* (e.g., *A*, *B*) passes its current cost to D to R, as shown in the figure. To compute indices as well, we modify the basic protocol so that *each neighbor reports its index for a destination in addition to its cost to the destination.* Thus, in Figure 11.4, A passes i and B passes j; thus when R chooses B, it also uses B's index j in its routing table entry for D. In summary, each router uses the index of the minimal-cost neighbor for each destination as the threaded index for that destination.

Cisco later introduced tag switching [Rea96], which is similar in concept to threaded indices, except tag switching also allows a router to pass a stack of tags (indices) for multiple routers downstream. Both schemes, however, do not deal well with hierarchies. Consider a packet that arrives from the backbone to the first router in the exit domain. The exit domain is the last autonomously managed network the packet traverses — say, the enterprise network in which the destination of the packet resides.

The only way to avoid a lookup at the first router, R, in the exit domain is to have some earlier router outside the exit domain pass an index (for the destination subnet) to R. But this is impossible because the prior backbone routers should have only one aggregated routing entry for the entire destination domain and can thus pass only one index for all subnets in that domain. The only solution is either to add extra entries to routers outside a domain (infeasible) or to require ordinary IP lookup at domain entry points (the chosen solution). Today tag switching is flourishing in a more general form called *multiprotocol label switching* (MPLS) [Rea96]. However, neither tag switching nor MPLS completely avoids the need for ordinary IP lookups.

11.2.2 Flow Switching

A second proposal to finesse lookups was called *flow switching* [NMH97, PTS95]. Flow switching also relies on a previous hop router to pass an index into the next hop router. Unlike tag switching, however, these indexes are computed on demand when data arrives, and they are then cached.

Flow switching starts with routers that contain an internal ATM switch and (potentially slow) processors capable of doing IP forwarding and routing. Two such routers, R1 and R2, are shown in Figure 11.5. When R2 first sends an IP packet to destination D that arrives on the left input port of R1, the input port sends the packet to its central processor. This is the slow path. The processor does the IP lookup and switches the packet internally to output link L. So far nothing out of the ordinary.

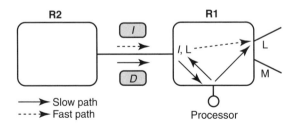

FIGURE 11.5 In IP switching, if R1 wishes to switch packets sent to D that are destined for output link L, R1 picks an idle virtual circuit I, places the mapping I, L in its input port, and then sends I back to R2. If R2 now sends packets to D labeled with VCI I, the packet will get switched directly to the output link without going through the processor.

Life gets more exciting if R1 decides to "switch" packets going to *D*. R1 may decide to do so if, for instance, there is a lot of traffic going to *D*. In that case, R1 first picks an idle virtual circuit identifier *I*, places the mapping $I \rightarrow L$ in its input port hardware, and then sends *I* back to R2. If R2 now sends packets to *D* labeled with VCI *I* to the input port of R1, the input port looks up the mapping from *I* to *L* and switches the packet directly to the output link *L* without going through the processor.

Of course, R2 can repeat this switching process with the preceding router in the path, and so on. Eventually, IP forwarding can be completely dispensed with in the switched portion of a sequence of flow-switching routers.

Despite its elegance, flow switching seems likely to work poorly in the backbone. This is because backbone flows are short lived and exhibit poor locality. A contrarian opinion is presented in Molinero-Fernandez and McKeown [MM02], where the authors argue for the resurrection of flow switching based on TCP connections. They claim that the current use of circuit-switched optical switches to link core routers, the underutilization of backbone links running at 10% of capacity, and increasing optical bandwidths all favor the simplicity of circuit switching at higher speeds.

Both IP and tag switching are techniques to finesse the need for IP lookups by passing information in protocol headers. Like ATM, both schemes rely on passing indices (**P10**). However, tag switching precomputes the index (**P2a**) at an earlier time scale (topology change time) than ATM (just before data transfer). On the other hand, in IP switching the indices are computed on demand (**P2c**, lazy evaluation) after the data begins to flow. However, neither tag nor IP switching completely avoids prefix lookups, and each adds a complex protocol. We now look afresh at the supposed complexity of IP lookups.

11.2.3 *Status of Tag Switching, Flow Switching, and Multiprotocol Label Switching*

While tag switching and IP switching were originally introduced to speed up lookups, IP switching has died away. However, tag switching in the more general form of multi-protocol-label switchings (MPLS) [Cha97]) has reinvented itself as a mechanism for providing flow differention to provide quality of service. Just as a VCI provides a simple label to quickly distinguish a flow, a label allows a router to easily isolate a flow for special service. In effect, MPLS uses labels to finesse the need for packet classification (Chapter 12), a much harder problem than prefix lookups. Thus although prefix matching is still required, MPLS is also de rigeur for a core router today.

Briefly, the required MPLS fast path forwarding is as follows. A packet with an MPLS header is identified, a 20-bit label is extracted, and the label is looked up in a table that maps the label to a forwarding rule. The forwarding rule specifies a next hop and also specifies the operations to be performed on the current set of labels in the MPLS packet. These operations can include removing labels ("popping the label stack") or adding labels ("pushing on to the label stack").

Router MPLS implementations have to impose some limits on this general process to guarantee wire speed forwarding. Possible limits include requiring that the label space be dense, supporting a smaller number of labels than 2^{20} (this allows a smaller amount of lookup memory while avoiding a hash table), and limiting the number of label-stacking operations that can be performed on a single packet.

11.3 NONALGORITHMIC TECHNIQUES FOR PREFIX MATCHING

In this section, we consider two other systems techniques for prefix lookups that do not rely on algorithmic methods: caching and ternary CAMs. Caching relies on locality in address references, while CAMs rely on hardware parallelism.

11.3.1 Caching

Lookups can be sped up by using a cache (**P11a**) that maps 32-bit addresses to next hops. However, cache hit ratios in the backbone are poor [NMH97] because of the lack of locality exhibited by flows in the backbone. The use of a large cache still requires the use of an exact-match algorithm for lookup. Some researchers have advocated a clever modification of a CPU cache lookup algorithm for this purpose [CP99]. In summary, caching can help, but it does not avoid the need for fast prefix lookups.

11.3.2 Ternary Content-Addressable Memories

Ternary content-addressable memories (CAMs) that allow "don't care" bits provide parallel search in one memory access. Today's CAMs can search and update in one memory cycle (e.g., 10 nsec) and handle any combination of 100,000 prefixes. They can even be cascaded to form larger databases. CAMs, however, have the following issues.

- *Density Scaling:* One bit in a TCAM requires 10–12 transistors, while an SRAM requires 4–6 transistors. Thus TCAMs will also be less dense than SRAMs or take more area. Board area is a critical issue for many routers.

- *Power Scaling:* TCAMs take more power because of the parallel compare. CAM vendors are, however, chipping away at this issue by finding ways to turn off parts of the CAM to reduce power. Power is a key issue in large core routers.

- *Time Scaling:* The match logic in a CAM requires all matching rules to arbitrate so that the highest match wins. Older-generation CAMs took around 10 nsec for an operation, but currently announced products appear to take 5 nsec, possibly by pipelining parts of the match delay.

- *Extra Chips:* Given that many routers, such as the Cisco GSR and the Juniper M160, already have a dedicated Application Specific Integrated Circuit (ASIC) (or network processor) doing packet forwarding, it is tempting to integrate the classification algorithm with the lookup without adding CAM interfaces and CAM chips. Note that CAMs typically require a bridge ASIC in addition to the basic CAM chip and sometimes require multiple CAM chips.

In summary, CAM technology is rapidly improving and is supplanting algorithmic methods in smaller routers. However, for larger core routers that may wish to have databases of a million routes in the future it may be better to have solutions (as we describe in this chapter) that scale with standard memory technologies such as SRAM. SRAM is likely always to be cheaper, faster, and denser than CAMs. While it is clearly too early to predict the outcome of this war between algorithmic and TCAM methods, even semiconductor manufacturers have hedged their bets and are providing *both* algorithmic and CAM-based solutions.

P1 = 101*
P2 = 111*
P3 = 11001*
P4 = 1*
P5 = 0*
P6 = 1000*
P7 = 100000*
P8 = 100*
P9 = 110

FIGURE 11.6 Sample prefix database used for the rest of this chapter. Note that the next hops corresponding to each prefix have been omitted for clarity.

11.4 UNIBIT TRIES

It is helpful to start a survey of algorithmic techniques (**P15**) for prefix lookup with the simplest technique: a *unibit trie*. Consider the sample prefix database of Figure 11.6. This database will be used to illustrate many of the algorithmic solutions in this chapter. It contains nine prefixes, called P1 to P9, with the bit strings shown in the figure.

In practice, there is a next hop associated with each prefix omitted from the figure. To avoid clutter, prefix names are used to denote the next hops. Thus in the figure, an address D that starts with 1 followed by a string of 31 zeroes will match P6, P7, and P8. The longest match is P7.

Figure 11.7 shows a unibit trie for the sample database of Figure 11.6. A unibit trie is a tree in which each node is an array containing a 0-pointer and a 1-pointer. At the root all prefixes that start with 0 are stored in the subtrie pointed to by the 0-pointer and all prefixes that start with a 1 are stored in the subtrie pointed to by the 1-pointer.

Each subtrie is then constructed recursively in a similar fashion using the remaining bits of the prefixes allocated to the subtrie. For example, in Figure 11.7 notice that P1 = 101 is stored in a path traced by following a 1-pointer at the root, a 0-pointer at the right child of the root, and a 1-pointer at the next node in the path.

There are two other fine points to note. In some cases, a prefix may be a substring of another prefix. For example, P4 = 1* is a substring of P2 = 111*. In that case, the smaller string, P4, is stored inside a trie node on the path to the longer string. For example, P4 is stored at the right child to the root; note that the path to this right child is the string 1, which is the same as P4.

Finally, in the case of a prefix such as P3 = 11001, after we follow the first three bits, we might naively expect to find a string of nodes corresponding to the last two bits. However, since no other prefixes share more than the first 3 bits with P3, these nodes would only contain one pointer apiece. Such a string of trie nodes with only one pointer each is a called a one-way branch.

Clearly one-way branches can greatly increase wasted storage by using whole nodes (containing at least two pointers) when only a single bit suffices. (The exercises will help you quantify the amount of wasted storage.) A simple technique to remove this obvious waste (**P1**) is to compress the one-way branches.

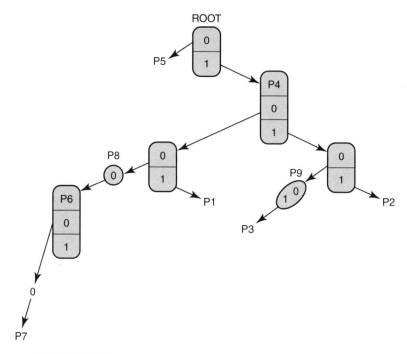

FIGURE 11.7 The one-bit trie for the sample database of Figure 11.6.

In Figure 11.7, this is done by using a text string (i.e. "01") to represent the pointers that would have been followed in the one-way branch. Thus in Figure 11.7, two trie nodes (containing two pointers apiece) in the path to P3 have been replaced by a single text string of 2 bits. Clearly, no information has been lost by this transformation. (As an exercise, determine if there is another path in the trie that can similarly be compressed.)

To search for the longest matching prefix of a destination address D, the bits of D are used to trace a path through the trie. The path starts with the root and continues until search fails by ending at an empty pointer or at a text string that does not completely match. While following the path, the algorithm keeps track of the last prefix encountered at a node in the path. When search fails, this is the longest matching prefix that is returned.

For example, if D begins with 1110, the algorithm starts by following the 1-pointer at the root to arrive at the node containing P4. The algorithm remembers P4 and uses the next bit of D (a 1) to follow the 1-pointer to the next node. At this node, the algorithm follows the 1-pointer to arrive at P2. When the algorithm arrives at P2, it overwrites the previously stored value (P4) by the newer prefix found (P2). At this point, search terminates, because P2 has no outgoing pointers.

On the other hand, consider doing a search for a destination D' whose first 5 bits are 11000. Once again, the first 1 bit is used to reach the node containing P4. P4 is remembered as the last prefix encountered, and the 1 pointer is followed to reach the rightmost node at height 2.

The algorithm now follows the third bit in D' (a 0) to the text string node containing "01." Thus we remember P9 as the last prefix encountered. The fourth bit of D' is a 0, which matches the first bit of "01." However, the fifth bit of D' is a 0 (and not a 1 as in the second bit of "01"). Thus the search terminates with P9 as the longest matching prefix.

The literature on tries [Knu73] does not use *text strings* to compress one-way branches as in Figure 11.7. Instead, the classical scheme, called a *Patricia trie*, uses a *skip count*. This count records the number of bits in the corresponding text string, not the bits themselves. For example, the text string node "01" in our example would be replaced with the skip count "2" in a Patricia trie.

This works fine as long as the Patricia trie is used for *exact* matches, which is what they were used for originally. When search reaches a skip count node, it skips the appropriate number of bits and follows the pointer of the skip count node to continue the search. Since bits that are skipped are not compared for a match, Patricia requires that a complete comparison between the searched key and the entry found by Patricia be done at the end of the search.

Unfortunately, this works very badly with prefix matching, an application that Patricia tries were *not* designed to handle in the first place. For example, in searching for D', whose first 5 bits are 11000 in the Patricia equivalent of Figure 11.7, search would skip the last two bits and get to P3. At this point, the comparison will find that P3 does not match D'.

When this happens, a search in a Patricia trie has to backtrack and go back up the trie searching for a possible shorter match. In this example, it may appear that search could have remembered P4. But if P4 was also encountered on a path that contains skip count nodes, the algorithm cannot even be sure of P4. Thus it must backtrack to check if P4 is correct.

Unfortunately, the BSD implementation of IP forwarding [WS95] decided to use Patricia tries as a basis for best matching prefix. Thus the BSD implementation used skip counts; the implementation also stored prefixes by padding them with zeroes. Prefixes were also stored at the leaves of the trie, instead of within nodes as shown in Figure 11.7. The result is that prefix matching can, in the worst case, result in backtracking up the trie for a worst case of 64 memory accesses (32 down the tree and 32 up).

Given the simple alternative of using text strings to avoid backtracking, doing skip counts is a bad idea. In essence, this is because the skip count transformation does *not* preserve information, while the text string transformation does. However, because of the enormous influence of BSD, a number of vendors and even other algorithms (e.g., Ref. NK98) have used skip counts in their implementations.

11.5 MULTIBIT TRIES

Most large memories use DRAM. DRAM has a large latency (around 60 nsec) when compared to register access times (2–5 nsec). Since a unibit trie may have to make 32 accesses for a 32-bit prefix, the worst-case search time of a unibit trie is at least $32 * 60 = 1.92$ μsec. This clearly motivates *multibit* trie search.

To search a trie in *strides* of 4 bits, the main problem is dealing with prefixes like 10101* (length 5), whose lengths are not a multiple of the chosen stride length, 4. If we search 4 bits at a time, how can we ensure that we do not miss prefixes like 10101*? *Controlled prefix expansion* solves this problem by transforming an existing prefix database into a new database with *fewer prefix lengths* but with potentially *more prefixes*. By eliminating all lengths that are not multiples of the chosen stride length, expansion allows faster multibit trie search, at the cost of increased database size.

FIGURE 11.8   Controlled expansion of the original prefix database shown on the left (which has five prefix lengths, 1, 3, 4, 5, and 6) to an expanded database (which has only 2 prefix lengths, 3 and 6).

For example, removing odd prefix lengths reduces the number of prefix lengths from 32 to 16 and would allow trie search 2 bits at a time. To remove a prefix like 101* of length 3, observe that 101* represents addresses that begin with 101, which in turn represents addresses that begin with 1010* or 1011*. Thus 101* (of length 3) can be replaced by two prefixes of length 4 (1010* and 1011*), both of which inherit the next hop forwarding entries of 101*.

However, the expanded prefixes may collide with an existing prefix at the new length. In that case, the expanded prefix is removed. The existing prefix is given priority because it was originally of longer length.

In essence, expansion trades memory for time (**P4b**). The same idea can be used to remove any chosen set of lengths except length 32. Since trie search speed depends linearly on the number of lengths, expansion reduces search time.

Consider the sample prefix database shown in Figure 11.6, which has nine prefixes, P1 to P9. The same database is repeated on the *left* of Figure 11.8. The database on the *right* of Figure 11.8 is an equivalent database, constructed by expanding the original database to contain prefixes of lengths 3 and 6 only. Notice that of the four expansions of P6 = 1000* to 6 bits, one collides with P7 = 100000* and is thus removed.

11.5.1 Fixed-Stride Tries

Figure 11.9 shows a trie for the same database as Figure 11.8, using expanded tries with a fixed stride length of 3. Thus each trie node uses 3 bits. The replicated entries within trie nodes in Figure 11.9 correspond exactly to the expanded prefixes on the right of Figure 11.8. For example, P6 in Figure 11.8 has three expansions (100001, 100010, 100011).

These three expanded prefixes are pointed to by the 100 pointer in the root node of Figure 11.9 (because all three expanded prefixes start with 100) and are stored in the 001, 010, and 011 entries of the right child of the root node. Notice also that the entry 100 in the root node has a stored prefix P8 (besides the pointer pointing to P6's expansions), because P8 = 100* is itself an expanded prefix.

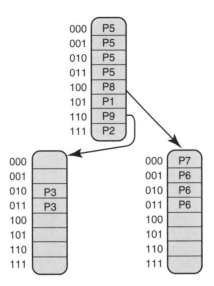

FIGURE 11.9 Expanded trie (which has two strides of 3 bits each) corresponding to the prefix database of Figure 11.8.

Thus each trie node element is a record containing *two* entries: a stored prefix and a pointer. Trie search proceeds 3 bits at a time. Each time a pointer is followed, the algorithm remembers the stored prefix (if any). When search terminates at an empty pointer, the last stored prefix in the path is returned.

For example, if address *D* begins with 1110, search for *D* starts at the 111 entry at the root node, which has no outgoing pointer but a stored prefix (P2). Thus search for *D* terminates with P2. A search for an address that starts with 100000 follows the 100 pointer in the root (and remembers P8). This leads to the node on the lower right, where the 000 entry has no outgoing pointer but a stored prefix (P7). The search terminates with result P7. Both the pointer and stored prefix can be retrieved in one memory access using wide memories (**P5b**).

A special case of fixed-stride tries, described in Gupta et al. [GLM98], uses fixed strides of 24, 4, and 4. The authors observe that DRAMs with more than 2^{24} locations are becoming available, making even 24-bit strides feasible.

11.5.2 Variable-Stride Tries

In Figure 11.9, the leftmost leaf node needs to store the expansions of P3 = 11001*, while the rightmost leaf node needs to store P6 (1000*) and P7 (100000*). Thus, because of P7, the rightmost leaf node needs to examine 3 bits. However, there is no reason for the leftmost leaf node to examine more than 2 bits because P3 contains only 5 bits, and the root stride is 3 bits. There is an extra degree of freedom that can be optimized (**P13**).

In a *variable-stride* trie, the number of bits examined by each trie node can vary, even for nodes at the same level. To do so, the stride of a trie node is encoded with the pointer to the node. Figure 11.9 can be transformed into a variable-stride trie (Figure 11.10) by replacing the leftmost node with a four-element array and encoding length 2 with the pointer to the leftmost

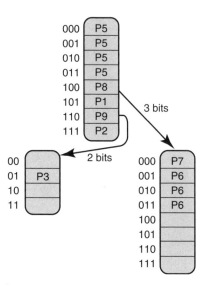

FIGURE 11.10   Transforming the fixed-stride trie of Figure 11.9 into a variable-stride trie by encoding the stride of each trie node along with a pointer to the node. Notice that the leftmost leaf node now only contains four locations (instead of eight), thus reducing the number of locations from 24 to 20.

node. The stride encoding costs 5 bits. However, the variable stride trie of Figure 11.10 has four fewer array entries than the trie of Figure 11.9.

Our example motivates the problem of picking strides to minimize the total amount of trie memory. Since expansion trades memory for time, why not minimize the memory needed by optimizing a degree of freedom (**P13**), the strides used at each node? To pick the variable strides, the designer first specifies the worst-case number of memory accesses. For example, with 40-byte packets at 1-Gbps and 80-nsec DRAM, we have a time budget of 320 nsec, which allows only four memory accesses. This constrains the maximum number of nodes in any search path (four in our example).

Given this fixed height, the strides can be chosen *to minimize storage*. This can be done using dynamic programming [SV99] in a few seconds, even for large databases of 150,000 prefixes. A degree of freedom (the strides) is optimized to minimize the memory used for a given worst-case tree height.

A trie is said to be optimal for height h and a database D if the trie has the smallest storage among all variable-stride tries for database D, whose height is no more than h. It is easy to prove (see exercises) that the trie of Figure 11.10 is optimal for the database on the left of Figure 11.8 and height 2.

The general problem of picking an optimal stride trie can be solved recursively (Figure 11.11). Assume the tree height must be h. The algorithm first picks a root with stride s. The $y = 2^s$ possible pointers in the root can lead to y nonempty subtries $T_1, \ldots T_y$. If the s-bit pointer p_i leads to subtrie T_i, then all prefixes in the original database D that start with p_i must be stored in T_i. Call this set of prefixes D_i.

Suppose we could recursively find the optimal T_i for height $h - 1$ and database D_i. Having used up one memory access at the root node, there are only $h - 1$ memory accesses left to

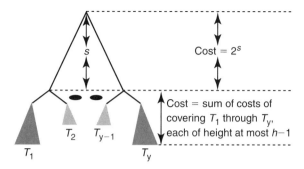

FIGURE 11.11 Picking an optimum variable-stride trie via dynamic programming.

navigate each subtrie T_i. Let C_i denote the storage cost required, counted in array locations, for the optimal T_i. Then for a fixed root stride s, the cost of the resulting optimal trie $C(s)$ is 2^s (cost of root node in array locations) plus $\sum_{i=1}^{y} C_i$. Thus the optimal value of the initial stride is the value of s, where $1 \le s \le 32$, that minimizes $C(s)$.

A naive use of recursion leads to repeated subproblems. To avoid repeated subproblems, the algorithm first constructs an auxiliary 1-bit trie. Notice that any subtrie T_i in Figure 11.11 must be a subtrie N of the 1-bit trie. Then the algorithm uses dynamic programming to construct the optimal cost and trie strides for each subtrie N in the original 1-bit trie for all values of height from 1 to h, building bottom-up from the smallest-height subtries to the largest-height subtries. The final result is the optimal strides for the root (of the 1-bit subtrie) with height h. Details are described in Srinivasan and Varghese [SV99].

The final complexity of the algorithm is easily seen to be $O(N * W^2 * h)$, where N is the number of original prefixes in the original database, W is the width of the destination address, and h is the desired worst-case height. This is because there are $N * W$ subtries in the 1-bit trie, each of which must be solved for heights that range from 1 to h, and each solution requires a minimization across at most W possible choices for the initial stride s. Note that the complexity is linear in N (the largest number, around 150,000 at the time of writing) and h (which should be small, at most 8), but quadratic in the address width (currently 32). In practice, the quadratic dependence on address width is not a major factor.

For example, Srinivasan and Varghese [SV99] show that using a height of 4, the optimized Mae–East database required 423 KB of storage, compared to 2003 KB for the unoptimized version. The unoptimized version uses the "natural" stride lengths 8, 8, 8, 8. The dynamic program took 1.6 seconds to run on a 300-MHz Pentium Pro. The dynamic program is even simpler for fixed-stride tries and takes only 1 msec to run. However, the use of fixed strides requires 737 KB instead of 423 KB.

Clearly, 1.6 seconds is much too long to let the dynamic program be run for every update and still allow millisecond updates [LMJ97]. However, backbone instabilities are caused by pathologies in which the same set of prefixes S are repeatedly inserted and deleted by a router that is temporarily swamped [LMJ97]). Since we had to allocate memory for the full set, including S, anyway, the fact that the trie is suboptimal in its use of memory when S is deleted is irrelevant. On the other hand, the rate at which new prefixes get added or deleted by managers seems more likely to be on the order of days. Thus a dynamic program that takes several seconds to run every day seems reasonable and will not unduly affect worst-case insertion and deletion times while still allowing reasonably optimal tries.

11.5.3 Incremental Update

Simple insertion and deletion algorithms exist for multibit tries. Consider the addition of a prefix P. The algorithm first simulates search on the string of bits in the new prefix P up to and including the last complete stride in prefix P. Search will terminate either by ending with the last (possibly incomplete) stride or by reaching a nil pointer. Thus for adding P10 = 1100* to the database of Figure 11.9, search follows the 110-pointer and terminates at the leftmost leaf trie node X.

For the purposes of insertion and deletion, for each node X in the multibit trie, the algorithm maintains a corresponding 1-bit trie, with the prefixes stored in X. This auxiliary structure need not be in fast memory. Also, for each node array element, the algorithm stores the length of its present best match. After determining that P10 must be added to node X, the algorithm expands P10 to the stride of X. Any array element to which P10 expands (which is currently labeled with a prefix of a length smaller than P10) must be overwritten with P10.

Thus in adding P10 = 1100*, the algorithm must add the expansions of 0* into node X. In particular, the 000 and 001 entries in node X must be updated to be P10.

If the search ends before reaching the last stride in the prefix, the algorithm creates new trie nodes. For example, if the prefix P11 = 1100111* is added, search fails at node X when a nil pointer is found at the 011 entry. The algorithm then creates a new pointer at this location that is made to point to a new trie node that contains P11. P11 is then expanded in this new node.

Deletion is similar to insertion. The complexity of insertion and deletion is the time to perform a search ($O(W)$) plus the time to completely reconstruct a trie node ($O(S)$, where S is the maximum size of a trie node). For example, using 8-bit trie nodes, the latter cost will require scanning roughly $2^8 = 256$ trie node entries. Thus to allow for fast updates, it is crucial to also limit the size of any trie node in the dynamic program described earlier.

11.6 LEVEL-COMPRESSED (LC) TRIES

An LC trie [NK98] is a variable-stride trie in which every trie node contains no empty entries. An LC-trie is built by first finding the largest-root stride that allows no empty entries and then recursively repeating this procedure on the child subtries. An example of this procedure is shown in Figure 11.12, starting with a 1-bit trie on the left and resulting in an LC trie on the left. Notice that P4 and P5 form the largest possible full-root subtrie — if the root stride is 2, then the first two array entries will be empty. The motivation, of course, is to avoid empty array elements, to minimize storage.

However, general variable-stride tries are more tunable, allowing memory to be traded for speed. For example, the LC trie representation using a 1997 snapshot of Mae–East has a trie height of 7 and needs 700 KB of memory. By comparison, an optimal variable-stride trie [SV99] has a trie height of 4 using 400 KB. Recall also that the optimal variable-stride calculates the best trie for a given target height and thus would indeed produce the LC trie *if* the LC trie were optimal for its height.

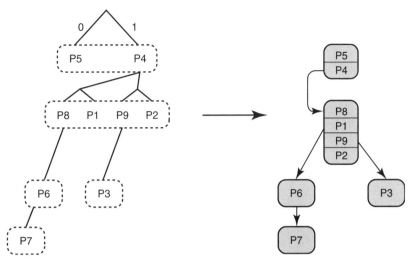

FIGURE 11.12 The level-compressed (LC) trie scheme decomposes the 1-bit trie recursively into full subtries of the largest size possible (left). The children in each full subtrie (shown by the dotted boxes) are then placed in a trie node to form a variable-stride trie that is specific to the database chosen.

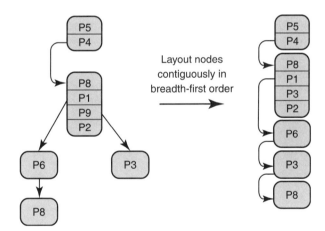

FIGURE 11.13 Array representation of LC tries.

In its final form, the variable-stride LC trie nodes are laid out in breadth-first order (first the root, then all the trie nodes at the second level from left to right, then third-level nodes, etc.), as shown on the right of Figure 11.13. Each pointer becomes an array off-set. The array layout and the requirement for full subtries make updates slow in the worst case. For example, deleting P5 in Figure 11.12 causes a change in the subtrie decomposition. Worse, it causes almost every element in the array representation of Figure 11.13 to be moved upward.

11.7 Lulea-Compressed Tries

Though LC tries and variable-stride tries attempt to compress multibit tries by varying the stride at each node, both schemes have problems. While the use of full arrays allows LC tries not to waste any memory because of empty array locations, it also increases the height of the trie, which cannot then be tuned. On the other hand, variable-stride tries can be tuned to have short height, at the cost of wasted memory because of empty array locations in trie nodes. The Lulea approach [DBCP97], which we now describe, is a multibit-trie scheme that uses fixed-stride trie nodes of large stride but uses *bitmap* compression to reduce storage considerably.

We know that a string with repetitions (e.g., AAAABBAAACCCCC) can be compressed using a bitmap denoting repetition points (i.e., 10001010010000) together with a compressed sequence (i.e., ABAC). Similarly, the root node of Figure 11.9 contains a repeated sequence (P5, P5, P5, P5) caused by expansion.

The Lulea scheme [DBCP97] avoids this obvious waste by compressing repeated information using a bitmap and a compressed sequence without paying a high penalty in search time. For example, this scheme used only 160 KB of memory to store the Mae–East database. This allows the entire database to fit into expensive SRAM or on-chip memory. It does, however, pay a high price in insertion times.

Some expanded trie entries (e.g., the 110 entry at the root of Figure 11.9) have two values, a pointer and a prefix. To make compression easier, the algorithm starts by making each entry have exactly one value by pushing prefix information down to the trie leaves. Since the leaves do not have a pointer, we have only next-hop information at leaves and only pointers at nonleaf nodes. This process is called *leaf pushing*.

For example, to avoid the extra stored prefix in the 110 entry of the root node of Figure 11.9, the P9 stored prefix is pushed to all the entries in the leftmost trie node, with the exception of the 010 and 011 entries (both of which continue to contain P3). Similarly, the P8 stored prefix in the 100 root node entry is pushed down to the 100, 101, 110, and 111 entries of the rightmost trie node. Once this is done, each node entry contains either a stored prefix or a pointer but not both.

The Lulea scheme starts with a conceptual leaf-pushed expanded trie and replaces consecutive identical elements with a single value. A node bitmap (with 0's corresponding to removed positions) is used to allow fast indexing on the compressed nodes.

Consider the root node in Figure 11.9. After leaf pushing, the root has the sequence P5, P5, P5, P5, ptr1, P1, ptr2, P2 (ptr1 is a pointer to the trie node containing P6 and P7, and ptr2 is a pointer to the node containing P3). After replacing consecutive values with the first value, we get P5, -, -, -, ptr1, P1, ptr2, P2, as shown in the middle frame of Figure 11.14. The rightmost frame shows the final result, with a bitmap indicating removed positions (10001111) and a compressed list (P5, ptr1, P1, ptr2, P2).

If there are N original prefixes and pointers within an original (unexpanded) trie node, the number of entries within the compressed node can be shown never to be more than $2N + 1$. Intuitively, this is because N prefixes partition the address space into at most $2N + 1$ disjoint subranges and each subrange requires at most one compressed node entry.

Search uses the number of bits specified by the stride to index into the current trie node, starting with the root and continuing until a null pointer is encountered. However, while following pointers, an uncompressed index must be mapped to an index into the compressed node. This mapping is accomplished by counting bits within the node bitmap.

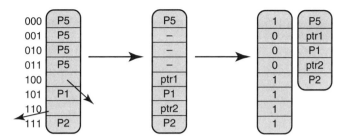

FIGURE 11.14 Compressing the root node of Figure 11.9 (after leaf pushing) using the Lulea bitmap compression scheme.

Consider the data structure on the right of Figure 11.14 and a search for an address that starts with 100111. If we were dealing with just the uncompressed node on the left of Figure 11.14, we could use 100 to index into the fifth array element to get ptr1. However, we must now obtain the same information from the compressed-node representation on the right of Figure 11.14.

Instead, we use the first three bits (100) to index into the root-node bitmap. Since this is the second bit set (the algorithm needs to count the bits set before a given bit), the algorithm indexes into the second element of the compressed node. This produces a pointer ptr1 to the rightmost trie node. Next, imagine the rightmost leaf node of Figure 11.9 (after leaf pushing) also compressed in the same way. The node contains the sequence P7, P6, P6, P6, P8, P8, P8, P8. Thus the corresponding bitmap is 11001000, and the compressed sequence is P7, P6, P8.

Thus in the rightmost leaf node, the algorithm uses the next 3 bits (111) of the destination address to index into bit 8. Since this bit is a 0, the search terminates: There is no pointer to follow in the equivalent uncompressed node. However, to retrieve the best matching prefix (if any) at this node, the algorithm must find any prefix stored before this entry.

This would be trivial with expansion because the value P8 would have been expanded into the 111 entry; but since the expanded sequence of P8 values has been replaced by a single P8 value in the compressed version, the algorithm has to work harder. Thus the Lulea algorithm *counts* the number of bits set before position 8 (which happens to be 3) and then indexes into the third element of the compressed sequence. This gives the correct result, P8.

The Lulea paper [DBCP97] describes a trie that uses fixed strides of 16, 8, and 8. But how can the algorithm efficiently count the bits set in a large bitmap, for example, a 16-bit stride uses 64K bits? Before you read on, try to answer this question using principles **P12** (adding state for speed) and **P2a** (precomputation).

To speed up counting set bits, the algorithm accompanies each bitmap with a summary array that contains a cumulative count (*precomputed*) of the number of set bits associated with fixed-size chunks of the bit map. Using 64-bit chunks, the summary array takes negligible storage. Counting the bits set up to position i now takes two steps. First, access the summary array at position j, where j is the chunk containing bit i. Then access chunk j and count the bits in chunk j up to position i. The sum of the two values gives the count.

While the Lulea paper uses 64-bit chunks, the example in Figure 11.15 uses 8-bit chunks. The large bitmap is shown from left to right, starting with 10001001, as the second array from the top. Each 8-bit chunk has a summary count that is shown as an array above the bitmap.

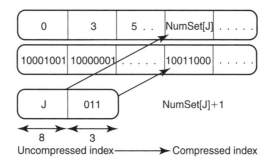

FIGURE 11.15   To allow fast counting of the bits set even in large bitmaps (e.g., 64 Kbits), the bitmap is divided into chunks and a summary count of the bits set before each chunk precomputed.

The summary count for chunk i counts the cumulative bits in the previous chunks of the bitmap (not including chunk i).

Thus the first chunk has count 0, the second has count 3 (because 10001001 has three bits set), and the third has count 5 (because 10001001 has two bits set, which added to the previous chunk's value of 3 gives a cumulative count of 5).

Consider searching for the bits set up to position X in Figure 11.15, where X can be written as J011. Clearly, X belongs to chunk J. The algorithm first looks up the summary count array to retrieve $numSet[J]$. This yields the number of bits set up to but not including chunk J. The algorithm then retrieves chunk J itself (10011000) and counts the number of bits set until the third position of chunk J. Since the first three bits of chunk J are 100, this yields the value 1. Finally, the desired overall bit count is $numSet[J] + 1$.

Notice that the choice of the chunk size is a trade-off between memory size and speed. Making a chunk equal to the size of the bitmap will make counting very slow. On the other hand, making a chunk equal to a bit will require more storage than the original trie node! Choosing a 64-bit chunk size makes the summary array size only 1/64 the size of the original node, but this requires counting the bits set within a 64-bit chunk. Counting can easily be done using special instructions in software and via combinational logic in hardware.

Thus search of a node requires first indexing into the summary table, then indexing into the corresponding bitmap chunk to compute the offset into the compressed node, and finally retrieving the element from the compressed node. This can take three memory references per node, which can be quite slow.

The final Lulea scheme also compresses entries based on their next-hop values (entries with the same next-hop values can be considered the same even though they match different prefixes). Overall the Lulea scheme has very compact storage. Using an early (1997) snapshot of the Mae–East database of around 40,000 entries, the Lulea paper [DBCP97] reports compressing the entire database to around 160 KB, which is roughly 32-bits per prefix.

This is a very small number, given that one expects to use at least one 20-bit pointer per prefix in the database. The compact storage is a great advantage because it allows the prefix database to potentially fit into limited on-chip SRAM, a crucial factor in allowing prefix lookups to scale to OC-768 speeds.

Despite compact storage, the Lulea scheme has two disadvantages. First, counting bits requires at least one extra memory reference per node. Second, leaf pushing makes worst-case insertion times large. A prefix added to a root node can cause information to be pushed to thousands of leaves. The full tree bitmap scheme, which we study next, overcomes these problem by abandoning leaf pushing and using *two* bitmaps per node.

11.8 TREE BITMAP

The tree bitmap [EDV] scheme starts with the goal of achieving the same storage and speed as the Lulea scheme, but it adds the goal of fast insertions. While we have argued that fast insertions are not as important as fast lookups, they clearly are desirable. Also, if the only way to handle an insertion or deletion is to rebuild the Lulea-compressed trie, then a router must keep two copies of its routing database, one that is being built and one that is being used for lookups. This can potentially double the storage cost from 32 bits per prefix to 64 bits per prefix. This in turn can halve the number of prefixes that can be supported by a chip that places the entire database in on-chip SRAM.

To obtain fast insertions and hence avoid the need for two copies of the database, the first problem in Lulea that must be handled is the use of leaf pushing. When a prefix of small length is inserted, leaf pushing can result in pushing down the prefix to a large number of leaves, making insertion slow.

11.8.1 Tree Bitmap Ideas

Thus the first and main idea in the tree bitmap scheme is that there be *two* bitmaps per trie node, one for all the internally stored prefixes and one for the external pointers. Figure 11.16 shows the tree bitmap version of the root node in Figure 11.14.

Recall that in Figure 11.14, the prefixes P8 = 100* and P9 = 110* in the original database are missing from the picture on the left side because they have been pushed down to the leaves to accommodate the two pointers (*ptr*1, which points to nodes containing longer prefixes such as P6 = 1000*, and *ptr*2, which points to nodes containing longer prefixes such as P3 = 11001*). This results in the basic Lulea trie node, in which each element contains either a pointer or a prefix but not both. This allows the use of a *single* bitmap to compress a Lulea node, as shown on the extreme right of Figure 11.14.

By contrast, the same trie node in Figure 11.16 is split into *two* compressed arrays, each with its own bitmap. The first array, shown vertically, is a *pointer array*, which contains a bitmap denoting the (two) positions where nonnull pointers exist and a compressed array containing the nonnull pointers, *ptr*1 and *ptr*2.

The second array, shown horizontally, is the *internal prefix array*, which contains a list of all the prefixes within the first 3 bits. The bitmap used for this array is very different from the Lulea encoding and has one bit set for every possible prefix stored within this node. Possible prefixes are listed lexicographically, starting from *, followed by 0* and 1*, and then on to the length-2 prefixes (00*, 01*, 10*, 11*), and finally the length-3 prefixes. Bits are set when the corresponding prefixes occur within the trie node.

Thus in Figure 11.16, the prefixes P8 and P9, which were leaf pushed in Figure 11.14, have been resurrected and now correspond to bits 12 and 14 in the internal prefix bitmap. In general, for an r-bit trie node, there are $2^{r+1} - 1$ possible prefixes of lengths r or less, which requires the use of a $(2^{r+1} - 1)$ bitmap. The scheme gets its name because the internal prefix

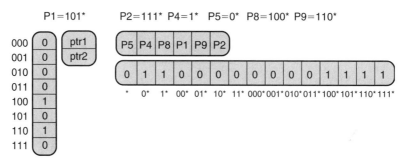

FIGURE 11.16 The tree bitmap scheme allows the compression of Lulea without sacrificing fast insertions by using *two* bitmaps per node. The first bitmap describes internally stored prefixes, and the second describes valid versus null pointers.

bitmap represents a trie in a linearized format: Each row of the trie is captured top-down from left to right.

The second idea in the tree bitmap scheme is to keep the trie nodes as small as possible to reduce the required memory access size for a given stride. Thus a trie node is of fixed size and contains only a pointer bitmap, an internal prefix bitmap, and child pointers. But what about the next-hop information associated with any stored prefixes?

The trick is to store the next hops associated with the internal prefixes stored within each trie node in a separate array associated with this trie node. Putting next-hop pointers in a separate result array potentially requires two memory accesses per trie node (one for the trie node and one to fetch the result node for stored prefixes).

However, a simple lazy evaluation strategy (**P2b**) is *not* to access the result nodes until search terminates. Upon termination, the algorithm makes a final access to the correct result node. This is the result node that corresponds to the last trie node encountered in the path that contained a valid prefix. This adds only a single memory reference at the end, in addition to the one memory reference required per trie node.

The third idea is to use only *one* memory access per node, unlike Lulea, which uses at least two memory accesses. Lulea needs two memory accesses per node because it uses large strides of 8 or 16 bits. This increases the bitmap size so much that the only feasible way to count bits is to use an additional chunk array that must be accessed separately. The tree bitmap scheme gets around this by simply using smaller-stride nodes, say, of 4 bits. This makes the bitmaps small enough that the entire node can be accessed by a single wide access (**P4a**, exploit locality). Combinatorial logic (Chapter 2) can be used to count the bits.

11.8.2 Tree Bitmap Search Algorithm

The search algorithm starts with the root node and uses the first r bits of the destination address (corresponding to the stride of the root node, 3 in our example) to index into the pointer bitmap at the root node at position P. If there is a 1 in this position, there is a valid child pointer. The algorithm counts the number of 1's to the left of this 1 (including this 1) and denotes this count by I. Since the pointer to the start position of the child pointer block (say, y) is known, as is the size of each trie node (say, S), the pointer to the child node can be calculated as $y + (I * S)$.

Before moving on to the child, the algorithm must also check the internal bitmap to see if there are one or more stored prefixes corresponding to the path through the multibit node to position P. For example, suppose P is 101 and a 3-bit stride is used at the root node bitmap, as in Figure 11.16. The algorithm first checks to see whether there is a stored internal prefix 101*. Since 101* corresponds to the 13th bit position in the internal prefix bitmap, the algorithm can check if there is a 1 in that position (there is one in the example). If there was no 1 in this position, the algorithm would back up to check whether there is an internal prefix corresponding to 10*. Finally, if there is a 10* prefix, the algorithm checks for the prefix 1*.

This search algorithm appears to require a number of iterations, proportional to the logarithm of the internal bitmap length. However, for bitmaps of up to 512 bits or so in hardware, this is just a matter of simple combinational logic. Intuitively, such logic performs all iterations in parallel and uses a priority encoder to return the longest matching stored prefix.

Once it knows there is a matching stored prefix within a trie node, the algorithm does not immediately retrieve the corresponding next-hop information from the result node associated with the trie node. Instead, the algorithm moves to the child node while remembering the stored-prefix position and the corresponding parent trie node. The intent is to remember the last trie node T in the search path that contained a stored prefix, and the corresponding prefix position.

Search terminates when it encounters a trie node with a 0 set in the corresponding position of the extending bitmap. At this point, the algorithm makes a final access to the result array corresponding to T to read off the next-hop information. Further tricks to reduce memory access width are described in Eatherton's MS thesis [Eat], which includes a number of other useful ideas.

Intuitively, insertions in a tree bitmap are very similar to insertions in a simple multibit trie wihout leaf pushing. A prefix insertion may cause a trie node to be changed completely; a new copy of the node is created and linked in atomically to the existing trie. Compression results in Eatherton et al. [EDV] show that the tree bitmap has all the features of the Lulea scheme, in terms of compression and speed, along with fast insertions. The tree bitmap also has the ability to be tuned for hardware implementations ranging from the use of RAMBUS-like memories to on-chip SRAM.

11.9 BINARY SEARCH ON RANGES

So far, all our schemes (unibit tries, expanded tries, LC tries, Lulea tries, tree bitmaps) have been trie variants. Are there other algorithmic paradigms (**P15**) to the longest-matching-prefix problem? Now, exact matching is a special case of prefix matching. Both binary search and hashing [CLR90] are well-known techniques for exact matching. Thus we should consider generalizing these standard exact-matching techniques to handle prefix matching. In this section, we examine an adaptation of binary search; in the next section, we look at an adaptation of hashing.

In *binary search on ranges* [LSV98], each prefix is represented as a range, using the start and end of the range. Thus the range endpoints for N prefixes partition the space of addresses into $2N + 1$ disjoint intervals. The algorithm [LSV98] uses binary search to find the interval in which a destination address lies. Since each interval corresponds to a unique prefix match, the

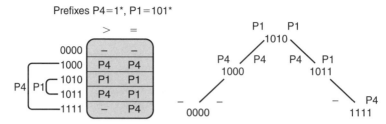

FIGURE 11.17 Binary search on values of a tiny subset of the sample database, consisting of only prefixes P4 = 1* and P1 = 101*.

algorithm *precomputes* this mapping and stores it with range endpoints. Thus prefix matching takes $\log_2(2N)$ memory accesses.

Consider a tiny routing table with only two prefixes, P4 = 1* and P1 = 101*. This is a small subset of the database used in Figure 11.8. Figure 11.17 shows how the binary search data structure is built as a table (left) and as a binary tree (right).

The starting point for this scheme is to consider a prefix as a range of addresses. To keep things simple, imagine that addresses are 4 bits instead of 32 bits. Thus P4 = 1* is the range 1000 to 1111, and P1 = 101* is the range 1010 to 1011. Next, after adding in the range for the entire address space (0000 to 1111), the endpoints of all ranges are sorted into a binary search table, as shown on the left of Figure 11.17.

In Figure 11.17, the range endpoints are drawn vertically on the left. The figure also shows the ranges covered by each of the prefixes. Next, *two* next-hop entries are associated with each endpoint. The leftmost entry, called the > entry, is the next hop corresponding to addresses that are *strictly greater* than the endpoint but strictly less than the next range endpoint in sorted order. The rightmost entry, called the = entry, corresponds to addresses that are *exactly equal* to the endpoint.

For example, it should be clear from the ranges covered by the prefixes that any addresses greater than or equal to 0000 but stricly less than 1000 do not match any prefix. Hence the entries corresponding to 0000 are −, to denote no next hop.[3] Similarly, any address greater than or equal to 1000 but strictly less than 1010 must match prefix P4 = 1*.

The only subtle case, which illustrates the need for two separate entries for > and =, is the entry for 1011. If an address is strictly greater than 1011 but strictly less than the next entry, 1111, then the best match is P4. Thus the > pointer is *P4*. On the other hand, if an address is exactly equal to 1011, its best match is P1. Thus the = pointer is P1.

The entire data structure can be built as a binary search table, where each table entry has three items, consisting of an endpoint, a > next-hop pointer, and a = next-hop pointer. The table has at most $2N$ entries, because each of N prefixes can insert two endpoints. Thus after the next-hop values are precomputed, the table can be searched in $\log_2 2N$ time using binary search on the endpoint values. Alternatively, the table can be drawn as a binary tree, as shown on the right in Figure 11.17. Each tree node contains the endpoint value and the same two next-hop entries.

---

[3] In a core router, no prefix match implies that the message should be dropped; in a router within a domain, no prefix match is often sent to the so-called default route.

The description so far shows that binary search on values can find the longest prefix match after $\log_2 2N$ time. However, the time can be reduced using binary trees of higher radix, such as B-trees. While such trees require wider memory accesses, this is an attractive trade-off for DRAM-based memories, which allow fast access to consecutive memory locations (**P4a**).

Computational geometry [PS85] offers a data structure called a *range tree* for finding the narrowest range. Range trees offer fast insertion times as well as fast $O(\log_2 N)$ search times. However, there seems to be no easy way to increase the radix of range trees to obtain $O(\log_M N)$ search times for $M > 2$.

As described, this data structure can easily be built in linear time using a stack and an additional trie. It is not hard to see that even with a balanced binary tree (see exercises), adding a short prefix can change the > pointers of a large number of prefixes in the table. A trick to allow fast insertions and deletions in logarithmic time is described in Warkhede et al. [WSV01b].

Binary search on prefix values is somewhat slow when compared to multibit tries. It also uses more memory than compressed trie variants. However, unlike the other trie schemes, all of which are subject to patents, binary search is free of such restrictions. Thus at least a few vendors have implemented this scheme into hardware. In hardware, the use of a wide memory access (to reduce the base of the logarithm) and pipelining (to allow one lookup per memory access) can make this scheme sufficiently fast.

11.10 BINARY SEARCH ON PREFIX LENGTHS

In this section, we adapt another classical exact-match scheme, hashing, to longest prefix matching. Binary search on prefix lengths finds the longest match using $\log_2 W$ hashes, where W is the maximum prefix length. This can provide a very scalable solution for 128-bit IPv6 addresses. For 128-bit prefixes, this algorithm takes only seven memory accesses, as opposed to 16 memory accesses using a multibit trie with 8-bit strides. To do so, the algorithm first segregates prefixes by length into separate hash tables. More precisely, it uses an array L of hash tables such that $L[i]$ is a pointer to a hash table containing all prefixes of length i.

Assume the same tiny routing table, with only two prefixes, P4 = 1* and P1 = 101*, of lengths 1 and 3, respectively, that was used in Figure 11.17. Recall that this is a small subset of Figure 11.8. The array of hash tables is shown horizontally in the top frame (A) of Figure 11.18. The length-1 hash table storing P4 is shown vertically on the left and is pointed to by position 1 in the array; the length-3 hash table storing P1 is shown on the right and is pointed to by position 3 in the array; the length-2 hash table is empty because there are no prefixes of length 2.

Naively, a search for address D would start with the greatest-length hash table l (i.e., 3), would extract the first l bits of D into D_l, and then search the length-l hash table for D_l. If search succeeds, the best match has been found; if not, the algorithm considers the next smaller length (i.e., 2). The algorithm moves in decreasing order among the set of possible prefix lengths until it either finds a match or runs out of lengths.

The naive scheme effectively does *linear* search among the distinct prefix lengths. The analogy suggests a better algorithm: binary search (**P15**). However, unlike binary search on prefix *ranges*, this is binary search on prefix *lengths*. The difference is major. With 32 lengths, binary search on lengths takes five hashes in the worst case; with 32,000 prefixes, binary search on prefix ranges takes 16 accesses.

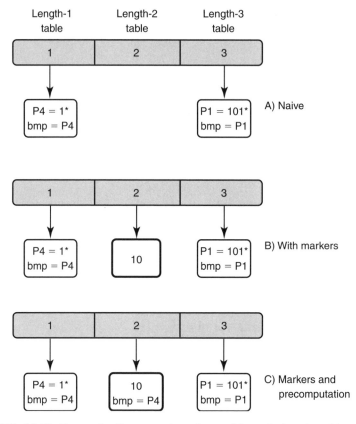

FIGURE 11.18 From naive linear search on the possible prefix lengths to binary search.

Binary search must start at the *median* prefix length, and each hash must divide the possible prefix lengths in half. A hash search gives only two values: *found* and *not found*. If a match is found at length *m*, then lengths strictly greater than *m* must be searched for a longer match. Correspondingly, if no match is found, search must continue among prefixes of lengths strictly less than *m*.

For example, in Figure 11.18, part (A), suppose search begins at the median length-2 hash table for an address that starts with 101. Clearly, the hash search does not find a match. But there is a longer match in the length-3 table. Since only a match makes search move to the right half, an "artificial match," or *marker*, must be introduced to force the search to the right half when there is a potentially longer match.

Thus part (B) introduces a bolded marker entry 10, corresponding to the first two bits of prefix P1 = 101, in the length-2 table. In essence, state has been added for speed (**P12**). The markers allow probe failures in the median to rule out all lengths greater than the median.

Search for an address *D* that starts with 101 works correctly. Search for 10 in the length-2 table (in Part (B) of Figure 11.18) results in a match; search proceeds to the length-3 table, finds a match with *P1*, and terminates. In general, a marker for a prefix *P* must be placed at all lengths that binary search will visit in a search for *P*. This adds only a logarithmic number of markers. For a prefix of length 32, markers are needed only at lengths 16, 24, 28, and 30.

Unfortunately, the algorithm is still incorrect. While markers lead to potentially longer prefixes, they can also cause search to follow false leads. Consider a search for an address *D'* whose first three bits are 100 in part (B) of Figure 11.18. Since the median table contains 10, search in the middle hash table results in a match. This forces the algorithm to search in the third hash table for 100 and to fail. But the correct best matching prefix is at the first hash table — i.e., P4 = 1*. Markers can cause the search to go off on a wild goose chase! On the other hand, a backtracking search of the left half would result in linear time.

To ensure logarithmic time, each marker node *M* contains a variable *M.bmp*, where *M.bmp* is the longest prefix that matches string *M*. This is precomputed when *M* is inserted into its hash table. When the algorithm follows marker *M* and searches for prefixes of lengths greater than *M*, and if the algorithm fails to find such a longer prefix, then the answer is *M.bmp*. In essence, the best matching prefix of every marker is precomputed (**P2a**). This avoids searching all lengths less than the median when a match is obtained with a marker.

The final version of the database containing prefixes P4 and P1 is shown in part (C) of Figure 11.18. A *bmp* field has been added to the 10 marker that points to the best matching prefix of the string 10 (i.e., P4 = 1*). Thus when the algorithm searches for 100 and finds a match in the median length-2 table, it *remembers* the value of the corresponding *bmp* entry P4 before it searches the length-3 table. When the search fails (in the length-3 table), the algorithm returns the *bmp* field of the last marker encountered (i.e., P4).

A trivial algorithm for building the simple binary search data structure from scratch is as follows. First determine the distinct prefix lengths; this determines the sequence of lengths to search. Then add each prefix *P* in turn to the hash table corresponding to *length(P)*. For each prefix, also add a marker to all hash tables corresponding to lengths *L* < *length(P)* that binary search will visit (if one does not already exist). For each such marker *M*, use an auxiliary 1-bit trie to determine the best matching prefix of *M*. Further refinements are described in Waldvogel et al. [WVTP01].

While the search algorithm takes five hash table lookups in the worst case for IPv4, we note that in the expected case most lookups should take two memory accesses. This is because the expected case observation *O1* shows that most prefixes are either 16 or 24 bits (at least today). Thus doing binary search at 16 and then 24 will suffice for most prefixes.

The use of hashing makes binary search on prefix lengths somewhat difficult to implement in hardware. However, its scalability to large prefix lengths, such as IPv6 addresses, has made it sufficiently appealing to some vendors.

11.11 MEMORY ALLOCATION IN COMPRESSED SCHEMES

With the exception of binary search and fixed-stride multibit tries, many of the schemes described in this chapter need to allocate memory in different sizes. Thus if a compressed trie node grows from two to three memory words, the insertion algorithm must deallocate the old node of size 2 and allocate a new node of size 3. Memory allocation in operating systems is a somewhat heuristic affair, using algorithms, such as best-fit and worst-fit, that do not guarantee worst-case properties.

In fact all standard memory allocators can have a worst-case fragmentation ratio that is very bad. It is possible for allocates and deallocates to conspire to break up memory into a patchwork of holes and small allocated blocks. Specifically, if *Max* is the size of the largest memory allocation request, the worst-case scenario occurs when all holes are of size *Max* − 1 and all allocated blocks are of size 1. This can occur by allocating all of memory using requests of size 1, followed by the appropriate deallocations. The net result is that only $\frac{1}{Max}$ of memory is guaranteed to be used, because all future requests may be of size *Max*.

The allocator's use of memory translates directly into the maximum number of prefixes that a lookup chip can support. Suppose that — ignoring the allocator — one can show that 20 MB of on-chip memory can be used to support 640,000 prefixes in the worst case. If one takes the allocator into account and *Max* = 32, the chip can guarantee supporting only 20,000 prefixes!

Matters are not helped by the fact that CAM vendors at the time of writing were advertising a worst-case number of 100,000 prefixes, with 10-nsec search times and microsecond update times. Thus, given that algorithmic solutions to prefix lookup often compress data structures to fit into SRAM, algorithmic solutions *must* also design memory allocators that are fast and that minimally fragment memory.

There is an old result [Rob74] that says that *no allocator* that does not compact memory can have a utilization ratio better than $\frac{1}{\log_2 Max}$. For example, this is 20% for *Max* = 32. Since this is unacceptable, *algorithmic solutions involving compressed data structures must use compaction.* Compaction means moving allocated blocks around to increase the size of holes.

Compaction is hardly ever used in operating systems, for the following reason. If you move a piece of memory *M*, you must correct all pointers that point to *M*. Fortunately, most lookup structures are trees, in which any node is pointed to by at most one other node. By maintaining a *parent* pointer for every tree node, nodes that point to a tree node *M* can be suitably corrected when *M* is relocated. Fortunately, the parent pointer is needed only for updates and not for search. Thus the parent pointers can be stored in an off-chip copy of the database used for updates in the route processor, without consuming precious on-chip SRAM.

Even after this problem is solved, one needs a simple algorithm that decides when to compact a piece of memory. The existing literature on compaction is in the context of garbage collection (e.g., Refs. Wil92, LB96) and tends to use *global* compactors that scan through all of memory in one compaction cycle. To bound insertion times, one needs some form of *local* compactor that compacts only a small amount of memory around the region affected by an update.

11.11.1 Frame-Based Compaction

To show how simple local compaction schemes can be, we first describe an extremely simple scheme that does minimal compaction and yet achieves 50% worst-case memory utilization. We then extend this to improve utilization to closer to 100%.

In *frame merging*, assume that all *M* words of memory are divided into $\frac{M}{Max}$ frames of size *Max*. Frame merging seeks to keep the memory utilization to at least 50%. To do so, all nonempty frames should be at least 50% full. Frame merging maintains the following simple invariant: All *but one* unfilled frame is at least 50% full. If so, and if $\frac{M}{Max}$ is much larger than 1, this will yield a guaranteed utilization of almost 50%.

Allocate and deallocate requests are handled [SV00] with the help of tags added to each word that help identify free memory and allocated blocks. The only additional restriction is that all holes be contained *within* a frame; holes are not allowed to span frames.

Call a frame *flawed* if it is nonempty but is less than 50% utilized. To maintain the invariant, frame merging has one additional pointer to keep track of the current flawed frame, if any. Now, an allocate could cause a previously empty frame to become flawed if the allocation is less than $\frac{Max}{2}$.

Similarly, a deallocate could cause a frame that was filled more than 50% to become less than 50% full. For example, consider a frame that contains two allocated blocks of size 1 and size $Max - 1$ and hence has a utilization of 100%. The utilization could reduce to $\frac{1}{Max}$ if the block of $Max - 1$ is deallocated. This could cause two frames to become flawed, which would violate the invariant.

A simple trick to maintain the invariant is as follows. Assume there is already a flawed frame F and that a new flawed frame, F', appears on the scene. The invariant is maintained by merging the contents of F and F' into F. This is clearly possible because both frames F and F' were less than half full. Note that the only compaction done is *local* and is limited to the two flawed frames, F and F'. Such local compaction leads to fast update times.

The worst-case utilization of frame merging can be improved by increasing the frame size to $kMax$ and by changing the definition of a flawed frame to be one whose utilization is less than $\frac{k}{k+1}$. The scheme described earlier is a special case with $k = 1$. Increasing k improves the utilization, at the cost of increased compaction. More complex allocators with even better performance are described in Sikka and Varghese [SV00].

11.12 LOOKUP-CHIP MODEL

Given speed increases to OC-768 speeds, lookup schemes will probably be implemented on chips rather than on network processors, at least for the very highest speeds. Figure 11.19

FIGURE 11.19 Model of a lookup chip that does a search in hardware using a common SRAM that could be on or off chip.

describes a model of a lookup chip that does search and update. The chip has a Search and an Update process, both of which access a common SRAM memory that is either on or off chip (or both). The Update process allows incremental updates and (potentially) does a memory allocation/deallocation and a small amount of local compaction for every update.

The actual updates can be done either completely on chip, partially in software, or completely in software. If a semiconductor company wishes to sell a lookup chip using a complex update algorithm (e.g., for compressed schemes), it may be wiser also to provide an update algorithm in hardware. If the lookup chip is part of a forwarding engine, however, it may be simpler to relegate the update process completely to a separate CPU on the line card.

Each access to SRAM can be fairly wide if needed, even up to 1000 bits. This is quite feasible today using a wide bus. The search and update logic can easily process 1000 bits in parallel in one memory cycle time. Recall that wide word accesses can help — for example, in the tree bitmap and binary search on values schemes — to reduce search times.

Search and Update use time multiplexing to share access to the common SRAM that stores the lookup database. Thus the Search process is allowed S consecutive accesses to memory, and then the Update process is allowed K accesses to memory. If S is 20 and K is 2, this allows Update to steal a few cycles from Search while slowing down Search throughput by only a small fraction. Note that this increases the latency of Search by K memory accesses in the worst case; however, since the Search process is likely to be pipelined, this can be considered a small additional pipeline delay.

The chip has pins to receive inputs for Search (e.g., keys) and Update (e.g., update type, key, result) and can return search outputs (e.g., result). The model can be instantiated for various types of lookups, including IP lookups (e.g., 32-bit IP addresses as keys and next hops as results), bridge lookups (48-bit MAC addresses as keys and output ports as results), and classification (e.g., packet headers as keys and matching rules as results).

Each addition or deletion of a key can result in a call to deallocate a block and to allocate a different-size block. Each allocate request can be in any range from 1 to *Max* memory words. There is a total of M words that can be allocated. The actual memory can be either off chip, on chip, or both. Clearly, even off-chip solutions will cache the first levels of any lookup tree on chip. On-chip memory is attractive because of its speed and cost. Unfortunately, on-chip memory was limited by current processes to around 32 Mbits at the time of writing. This makes it difficult to support databases of 1 million prefixes.

Internally, the chip will very likely be heavily pipelined. The lookup data structure is partitioned into several pieces, each of which is concurrently worked on by separate stages of logic. Thus the SRAM will likely be broken into several smaller SRAMs that can be accessed independently by each pipeline stage.

There is a problem [SV00] with statically partitioning SRAM between pipeline stages, because memory needs for each stage can vary as prefixes are inserted and deleted. One possible solution is to break the single SRAM into a fairly large number of smaller SRAMs that can be dynamically allocated to the stages via a partial crossbar switch. However, designing such a crossbar at very high speeds is not easy.

All the schemes described in this chapter can be pipelined because they are all fundamentally based on trees. All nodes at the same depth in a tree can be allocated to the same pipeline stage.

11.13 CONCLUSIONS

It is important to gain some perspective after the large number of isolated lookup variants described in this chapter. Thus we conclude with a summary of the state of the art in lookups, and a survey of the common principles used in their design.

State of the Art in Lookups: Lookup schemes are coming under severe pressure in core routers as both table sizes (up to 1 million prefixes) and speed (up to 40 Gbps) ratchet upwards. MPLS, once thought to be a way to finesse lookups, is now mostly used to avoid packet classification for traffic engineering purposes. CAMs are nibbling away at even the core router space, but the large cost, power, and board real estate issues of large CAMs remain issues. Thus many core router vendors are still using and designing algorithmic schemes for lookups.

Oddly enough, even after the algorithmic riches explored in this chapter, simple unibit tries together with SRAM and pipelining work well, even at 40-Gbps speeds. This is because path-compressed unibit tries are relatively compact; their slow search times can be offset by a pipeline together with an initial array lookup. Recall, however, that pipelining is trickier than it looks because of the need to partition memory among stages.

At slower speeds of up to 10 Gbps, simple multibit tries using controlled prefix expansion work well with DRAM. While DRAM is slow, it is plentiful and cheap. The use of RAMBUS-like technologies can allow lookup pipelining even with network processors. The simplicity of this scheme has proved attractive to a number of vendors.

Some vendors even use binary search on values; its speed and memory use are reasonable, especially with B-trees with wide memories to reduce tree height. The binary-search-on-ranges scheme is also unencumbered with patents.

At the highest speeds, the number of pipeline stages can be reduced from 20 to 5 using multibit tries. However, multibit tries must be compressed to fit into limited SRAM, when on or off chip. While Lulea's compression is remarkable, it appears that the algorithm can be used today only via custom solutions sold by a company called Effnet. The Lulea scheme also has slow updates. By contrast, the tree bitmap scheme has fast updates and can be tailored to a wide variety of hardware settings [EDV]. However, there may be patents that restrict the use of tree bitmap as well. It is used today in Cisco's CRS-1 Router.

Finally, binary search on prefix lengths is attractive because of its scaling properties to large address lengths. Unfortunately, its use of hashing makes it hard to guarantee lookup times. Similarly, the slow deployment of IPv6 and multicast, both of which increase the importance of long address lookup, have made this scheme less attractive. It is, however, used by a few vendors in software implementations. It may be a contender in the future.

The bottom line is that algorithmic solutions together with pipelining can scale with link speeds as long as SRAM speeds scale to match packet arrival times. All the schemes studied in this chapter can be pipelined to provide one lookup per memory access time. The choice between CAMs and algorithmic schemes will continue to be hard to quantify and will probably be made on an ad hoc basis for each product.

However, fundamentally, if compressed trie schemes can use less than 32 bits per prefix, compressed tries appear to use fewer transistors and less power than CAMs. This is because in a CAM the lookup logic is distributed in each of N memory cells, whereas in an algorithmic solution the lookup logic, albeit more complicated, is distributed among a small, constant number of stages. A careful VLSI scaling analysis of these two approaches would be very useful.

Underlying Principles: Although this is a chapter about lookups and thinking about lookups requires paying attention to current market trends, it is important not to forget that this is a book about underlying principles. It is plausible that routers in the misty future may use all-optical switches and all-optical processing, even for lookups. In that case, the specific algorithms described in this chapter may be discarded; but perhaps the underlying design principles will remain.

Although the schemes described in this chapter require some algorithmic thinking, they also employ many of the other principles we have stressed. The schemes make heavy use of precomputation, which trades slower insert/delete times for fast search times. The schemes also exploit hardware features such as wide memories, distinguish fast and slow memories, trade memory for time, and optimize the degrees of freedom in a given design. Figure 11.1 summarizes the schemes and the principles used in them.

Finally, this chapter cannot hope to do justice to all the interesting IP lookup schemes that have been published in the academic and patent literature. You can look it up.

11.14 EXERCISES

1. **Caching Prefixes:** Suppose we have the prefixes 10*, 100*, and 1001*. Hugh Hopeful would like to cache prefixes instead of entire 32-bit addresses. Hugh's scheme keeps a set of prefixes in the cache (fast memory), in addition to the complete set of prefixes in slow memory. Hugh's scheme first does a best-matching-prefix search in the cache; if a matching prefix is found, the next hop of the prefix is used. If no matching prefix is found, a best-matching-prefix search is done for the entire database and the resulting prefix cached. Periodically, prefixes that have not been matched for a while are flushed from the cache. Alyssa P. Hacker quickly gives Hugh a counterexample to show him that his scheme is flawed and that caching prefixes is tricky (if not impossible). Can you?

2. **Encoding Prefixes in a Constant Length:** We said in the text that encoding prefixes like 10*, 100*, and 1000* in a fixed length could not be done by padding prefixes with zeroes. It clearly can be done by padding with zeroes and adding an encoding of the prefix length. We want to study a more efficient method.

    - How many possible prefixes on 32 bits can there be?

    - Show how to encode all such prefixes using a fixed length of 33 bits. Make sure that 10*, 100*, and 1000* encode to different values.

    - Can you use this fixed-length encoding of prefixes to have the multiple hash tables used in Section 11.10 be packed into a single hash table? Why might this help to decrease the chances of hash collisions for a given memory size?

3. **Quantifying the Benefits of Compressing One-Way Branches:**

    - For a unibit trie that does not compress one-way branches, show that the maximum number of trie nodes can be $O(N \cdot W)$, where N is the number of prefixes and W is the maximum prefix length. (*Hint*: Generate a trie that uses $\log_2 N$ levels to generate N nodes, and then hang a long string of $N - W$ nodes from each of the N nodes.)

- Show that a unibit trie with text strings to compress one-way branches can have at most $2N$ trie nodes and $2N$ text strings.

- Extend your analysis to multibit trie nodes with a fixed stride. How would you implement text string compression in such tries?

4. **Controlled Prefix Expansion:** Code up an efficient algorithm that expands a set of prefixes to any target set of lengths $L_1, \ldots, L_k$. Check your algorithm using the sample database of Figure 11.8. What is the complexity of your algorithm?

5. **Optimal Variable-Stride Trie:** Prove that the varied-stride trie of Figure 11.10 is optimal for a trie height of 2. Use the recursive formulation shown in the text.

6. **Reducing Memory References in Lulea:** The naive approach to counting bits shown in Figure 11.15 should take three memory references (to access *numSet*, to read the appropriate chunk of the bitmap, and to access the compressed trie node for the actual information.) Show how to use **P4a** to combine the first two accesses into a single access.

7. **Next Node versus Leaf Pushing in Lulea:** Before we applied Lulea compression, we first leaf pushed the expanded trie of Figure 11.9. The motivation was to make every entry either a pointer or a prefix but not both. Suppose we have a special prefix entry at the top of every trie node; if any entry in a trie node has pointer p and prefix P, we push P to the top of the node pointed to by p. Thus we would push the prefix P8 in the 100 entry of the root of Figure 11.9 to the top of the rightmost trie node.

   - We cited leaf pushing as one of the reasons for slow insertion times in the Lulea scheme. Does next-node pushing allow incremental insertion for the Lulea scheme?

   - How would you modify trie search to take into account the fact that prefixes can be stored at the top of (potentially large) trie nodes? How would this increase the search time (in memory accesses) of the Lulea scheme?

8. **CAM Node Compression:** Instead of using the Lulea scheme for compression, we could just store all the prefixes within a trie node without expansion. If we use small trie nodes (3- or 4-bit strides), a chip can potentially read all the entries in a node and internally do a comparison to find the best-matching prefix within the node. Describe the details of such a scheme.

9. **Tree Bitmap Algorithm:** The tree bitmap algorithm described in the text requires rooting through the internal prefix bitmap to decide if there was a matching prefix at a trie node N before moving on. This requires a greater access width (to access the internal prefix bitmaps) and more time. Consider adding state to the next node in the search path (**P12**) and one more final memory access to avoid this overhead.

10. **Multicolumn Binary Search:** In Chapter 4 we saw how to efficiently use binary search when the identifiers were wide. Explain how to combine this idea with that of binary search on prefixes explained in this chapter in order to do IPv6 lookups (up to 128-bit prefixes). How does this scheme compare with the other schemes in terms of lookup performance for IPv6?

11. **Binary Search with Fast Incremental Updates:** (This is difficult.) Find a way to remove all the problems of updates to binary search. The key problem is that if a large

prefix range R contains lots of disjoint prefix ranges $R_1, \ldots R_k$, then the spaces between the ranges R_k must be precomputed to map to R. If we now add a new prefix range, R', that is contained in R but still contains R_1 through R_k, then all the spaces between the ranges R_k must be changed to map to the new range, R'. Since k can be $O(n)$, this could lead to a $O(n)$ update. Try to avoid this problem by storing the binary search database as a tree and storing information about precomputed prefixes that cover the space between ranges as high as possible in the tree, as opposed to storing in the leaves. Details can be found in Warkhede et al. [WSV01b].

12. **Counterexamples for Binary Search on Prefix Lengths:** Even in industry, it is often useful to show by counter example that worst cases can actually exist. This ensures that we are not doing unnecessary work, and it also silences people who say that the worst case will never be too bad. Imagine that Hugh Hopeful is working for the same startup building an IP lookup chip. The company is now considering using binary search on prefix lengths.

   - Suppose we use only markers and no precomputation. This would make insertion a lot faster. Hugh Hopeful suggests that backtracking can only lead to a logarithmic number of extra accesses. Find an example that leads to linear time.

   - Hugh Hopeful finds that in practice real databases add only 25% extra marker storage, much less than the $\log_2 W$ multiplicative factor that we claimed. This is important because he would like to boast of a larger number of prefixes that his chip can handle for the given amount of memory. Give a worst-case example to show that we can add $\log_2 W$ entries per marker.

13. **Rope Search:** Binary search on prefix lengths can be improved by what is called *rope search* in Waldvogel et al. [WVTP01]. If we ever get a match with some entry M at length m, we only search further among the set of lengths corresponding to prefixes that are extensions of M. The basic technique we studied earlier will continue to search among all lengths greater than m in the current set of lengths R. However, many of the lengths $l > m$ may not have a prefix that is an extension of M. Thus this optimization can result in more than halving the set of possible lengths on each match. It may not help the worst case, but it can considerably help the average case. Try to work out details of such a scheme. In particular, a naive approach would keep a list of all potentially matching lengths ($O(W)$ space, where W is the length of an address) with each prefix. Find a way to reduce the state kept with each marker to $O(\log W)$. Details can be found in Waldvogel et al. [WVTP01].

14. **Invariant for Binary Search on Prefix Lengths:** Designing and proving algorithms that correct via invariants is a useful technique even in network algorithmics. The standard invariant for ordinary binary search when searching for key K is: "K is not in the table, or K is in the current range R." Standard binary search starts with R equal to the entire table and constantly halves the range while maintaining the invariant. Find a similar invariant for binary search on prefix ranges.

15. **Semiperfect Hashing:** Hardware chips can fetch up to 1000 bits at a time using wide buses. Exploit this observation to allow up to X collisions in each hash table entry, where the X colliding entries are stored at adjacent locations. Code up a perfect hashing

implementation (of 1000 IP addresses using a set of random hash functions), and compare the amount of memory needed with an implementation based on semiperfect hashing.

16. **Removing Redundancies in Lookup Tables:** Besides the use of compressed structures, another technique to reduce the size of IP lookup tables (especially when the tables are stored in on-chip SRAM) is to remove redundancy. One simple example of redundancy is when a prefix P is longer than a prefix P' and they both have the same next hop. Which prefix can be removed from the table? Can you think of other examples of removing redundancy? How would you implement such compression? Draves et al. [DKVZ99] describe a dynamic programming algorithm for compression, but even simpler alternatives can be effective.

17. **Implementing Tries for Best Matching Prefix:** (Due to V. Srinivasan.) The problem is to use tries to implement a file name completion routine in C or C++, similar to ones found in many shells. Given a unique prefix, the query should return the entire string. For example, with the words *angle*, *epsilon*, and *eagle*: Search(a) should return *angle*, Search(e) should return "No unique completion," Search(ea), Search(eag), etc. should return *eagle*; and Search(b) should return "No matching entries found." Assume all lowercase alphabets. To obtain an index into a trie array use:

index= charVariable - 'a'.

The following definition of a trie node may be helpful.

```
#defineALPHA26
structTRIENODE
{
intcompletionStatus;
charcompletion[MAXLEN];
structTRIENODE*next[ALPHA];
}
```

Can other techniques discussed in the text (e.g., binary search) be applied to this problem? Are insertion costs significant?

CHAPTER 12

Packet Classification

A classification is a definition comprising a system of definitions.

— FRIEDRICH VON SCHLEGEL

Traditionally, the post office forwards messages based on the destination address in each letter. Thus all letters to Timbuctoo were forwarded in exactly the same way at each post office. However, to gain additional revenue, the post office introduced *service differentiation* between ordinary mail, priority mail, and express mail. Thus forwarding at the post office is now a function of the destination address and the traffic class. Further, with the spectre of terrorist threats and criminal activity, forwarding could even be based on the source address, with special screening for suspicious sources.

In exactly the same way, routers have evolved from traditional destination-based forwarding devices to what are called *packet classification routers*. In modern routers, the route and resources allocated to a packet are determined by the destination address as well as other header fields of the packet, such as the source address and TCP/UDP port numbers.

Packet classification unifies the forwarding functions required by firewalls, resource reservations, QoS routing, unicast routing, and multicast routing. In classification, the forwarding database of a router consists of a potentially large number of rules on key header fields. A given packet header can match multiple rules. So each rule is given a cost, and the packet is forwarded using the *least-cost matching rule*.

This chapter is organized as follows. The packet classification problem is motivated in Section 12.1. The classification problem is formulated precisely in Section 12.2, and the metrics used to evaluate rule schemes are described in Section 12.3. Section 12.4 presents simple schemes such as linear search and CAMs. Section 12.5 begins the discussion of more efficient schemes by describing an efficient scheme called *grid of tries* that works only for rules specifying values of only two fields. Section 12.6 transitions to general rule sets by describing a set of insights into the classification problem, including the use of a geometric viewpoint.

Section 12.7 begins the transition to algorithms for the general case with a simple idea to extend 2D schemes. A general approach based on divide-and-conquer is described in Section 12.8. This is followed by three very different examples of algorithms based on divide-and-conquer: simple and aggregated bit vector linear search (Section 12.9), cross-producting (Section 12.10), and RFC, or equivalenced cross-producting (Section 12.11). Section 12.12 presents the most promising of the current algorithmic approaches, an approach based on decision trees.

Num	Principle	Lookup Technique
P12 P2a	Add marker state Precompute filter info	Rectangle and tuple search
P15 P2a	Use Dest and SRC tries Precompute switch pointers	Grid of tries
P15 P12,2a	Divide-and-conquer by first doing field lookups	Bit vector, pruned tuple, cross-producting
P11	Exploit lack of general ranges	Multiple 2D planes
P4a	Exploit bitmap memory locality	Bit vector scheme
P11	Exploit small number of prefixes that match any field	Pruned tuple
P11a,4a	Exploit crossproduct locality	On-demand cross-product
P1	Avoid redundant crossproducts	Equivalent cross-producting

FIGURE 12.1   Summary of the principles used in the classification algorithms described in this chapter.

This chapter will continue to exhibit the set of principles introduced in Chapter 3, as summarized in Figure 12.1. The chapter will also illustrate three general problem-solving strategies: solving simpler problems first before solving a complex problem, collecting different viewpoints, and exploiting the structure of input data sets.

Quick Reference Guide

The most important lookup algorithms for an implementor today are as follows. If memory is not an issue, the fastest scheme is one called recursive flow classification (RFC), described in Section 12.11. If memory is an issue, a simple scheme that works well for classifiers up to around 5000 rules is the Lucent bit vector scheme (Section 12.9). For larger classifiers, the best trade-off between speed and memory is provided by decision tree schemes, such as HiCuts and HyperCuts (Section 12.12). Unfortunately, all these algorithms are based on heuristics and cannot guarantee performance on all databases. If guaranteed performance is required for more than two field classifiers, there is no alternative but to consider hardware schemes such as ternary CAMs.

12.1 WHY PACKET CLASSIFICATION?

Packet forwarding based on a longest-matching-prefix lookup of destination IP addresses is fairly well understood, with both algorithmic and CAM-based solutions in the market. Using basic variants of tries and some pipelining (see Chapter 11), it is fairly easy to perform one packet lookup every memory access time.

Unfortunately, the Internet is becoming more complex because of its use for mission-critical functions executed by organizations. Organizations desire that their critical activities not be subverted either by high traffic sent by other organizations (they require QoS guarantees) or by malicious intruders (they require security guarantees). Both QoS and security guarantees require a finer discrimination of packets, based on fields other than the destination. This is called *packet classification*. To quote John McQuillan [McQ97]:

> *Routing has traditionally been based solely on destination host numbers. In the future it will also be based on source host or even source users, as well as destination URLs (universal resource locators) and specific business policies. . . . Thus, in the future, you may be sent on one path when you casually browse the Web for CNN headlines. And you may be routed an entirely different way when you go to your corporate Web site to enter monthly sales figures, even though the two sites might be hosted by the same facility at the same location. . . . An order entry form may get very low latency, while other sections get normal service. And then there are Web sites comprised of different servers in different locations. Future routers and switches will have to use class of service and QoS to determine the paths to particular Web pages for particular end users. All this requires the use of layers 4, 5, and above.*

This new vision of forwarding is called *packet classification*. It is also sometimes called *layer 4 switching*, because routing decisions can be based on headers available at layer 4 or higher in the OSI architecture. Examples of other fields a router may need to examine include source addresses (to forbid or provide different service to some source networks), port fields (to discriminate between traffic types, such as Napster and E-mail), and even TCP flags (to distinguish between externally and internally initiated connections). Besides security and QoS, other functions that require classification include network address translation (NAT), metering, traffic shaping, policing, and monitoring.

Several variants of packet classification have already established themselves on the Internet. First, many routers implement *firewalls* [CB95] at trust boundaries, such as the entry and exit points of a corporate network. A firewall database consists of a series of packet rules that implement security policies. A typical policy may be to allow remote login from within the corporation but to disallow it from outside the corporation.

Second, the need for predictable and guaranteed service has led to proposals for reservation protocols, such as DiffServ [SWG], that reserve bandwidth between a source and a destination. Third, the cries for routing based on traffic type have become more strident recently — for instance, the need to route Web traffic between Site 1 and Site 2 on, say, Route A and other traffic on, say, Route B. Figure 12.2 illustrates some of these examples.

Classifiers historically evolved from firewalls, which were placed at the edges of networks to filter out unwanted packets. Such databases are generally small, containing 10–500 rules, and can be handled by ad hoc methods. However, with the DiffServ movement, there is potential for classifiers that could support 100,000 rules for DiffServ and policing applications at edge routers.

While large classifiers are anticipated for edge routers to enforce QoS via DiffServ, it is perhaps surprising that even within the core, fairly large (e.g., 2000-rule) classifiers are commonly used for security. While these core router classifiers are nowhere near the anticipated size of edge router classifiers, there seems no reason why they should not continue to grow beyond the sizes reported in this book. For example, many of the rules appear to be denying

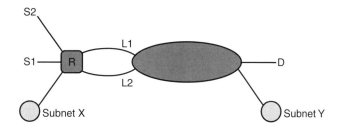

DATABASE AT ROUTER R

To	From	Traffic Type	Forwarding Directive
D	S1	Video	Forward via L1
*	S2	*	Drop all traffic
Y	X	*	Reserve 50 Mbps

FIGURE 12.2 Example of rules that provide traffic-sensitive routing, a firewall rule, and resource reservation. The first rule routes video traffic from S1 to D via L1; not shown is the default routing to D, which is via L2. The second rule blocks traffic from an experimental site, S2, from accidentally leaving the site. The third rule reserves 50 Mbps of traffic from an internal network X to an external network Y, implemented perhaps by forwarding such traffic to a special outbound queue that receives special scheduling guarantees; here X and Y are prefixes.

traffic from a specified subnetwork outside the ISP to a server (or subnetwork) within the ISP. Thus, new offending sources could be discovered and new servers could be added that need protection. In fact, we speculate that one reason why core router classifiers are not even bigger is that most core router implementations slow down (and do not guarantee true wire speed forwarding) as classifier sizes increase.

12.2 PACKET-CLASSIFICATION PROBLEM

Traditionally, the rules for classifying a message are called *rules* and the packet-classification problem is to determine the lowest-cost matching rule for each incoming message at a router.

Assume that the information relevant to a lookup is contained in K distinct *header fields* in each message. These header fields are denoted $H[1], H[2], \ldots, H[K]$, where each field is a string of bits. For instance, the relevant fields for an IPv4 packet could be the destination address (32 bits), the source address (32 bits), the protocol field (8 bits), the destination port (16 bits), the source port (16 bits), and TCP flags (8 bits). The number of relevant TCP flags is limited, and so the protocol and TCP flags are combined into one field — for example, TCP-ACK can be used to mean a TCP packet with the ACK bit set.[1]

---

[1]TCP flags are important for packet classification because the first packet in a connection does not have the ACK bit set, while the others do. This allows a simple rule to block TCP connections initiated from the outside while allowing responses to internally initiated connections.

Other relevant TCP flags can be represented similarly; UDP packets are represented by $H[3] = UDP$.

Thus, the combination $(D, S, \text{TCP-ACK}, 63, 125)$ denotes the header of an IP packet with destination D, source S, protocol TCP, destination port 63, source port 125, and the ACK bit set.

The *classifier*, or *rule database*, router consists of a finite set of rules, $R_1, R_2, \ldots, R_N$. Each rule is a combination of K values, one for each header field. Each field in a rule is allowed three kinds of matches: exact match, prefix match, and range match. In an *exact match*, the header field of the packet should exactly match the rule field — for instance, this is useful for protocol and flag fields. In a *prefix match*, the rule field should be a prefix of the header field — this could be useful for blocking access from a certain subnetwork. In a *range match*, the header values should lie in the range specified by the rule — this can be useful for specifying port number ranges.

Each rule R_i has an associated directive $disp_i$, which specifies how to forward the packet matching this rule. The directive specifies if the packet should be blocked. If the packet is to be forwarded, the directive specifies the outgoing link to which the packet is sent and, perhaps, also a queue within that link if the message belongs to a flow with bandwidth guarantees.

A packet P is said to *match* a rule R if each field of P matches the corresponding field of R — the match type is implicit in the specification of the field. For instance, if the destination field is specified as $1010*$, then it requires a prefix match; if the protocol field is UDP, then it requires an exact match; if the port field is a range, such as 1024–1100, then it requires a range match. For instance, let $R = (1010*, *, TCP, 1024\text{–}1080, *)$ be a rule, with $disp = block$. Then, a packet with header $(10101 \ldots 111, 11110 \ldots 000, TCP, 1050, 3)$ matches R and is therefore blocked. The packet $(10110 \ldots 000, 11110 \ldots 000, TCP, 80, 3)$, on the other hand, doesn't match R.

Since a packet may match multiple rules in the database, each rule R in the database is associated with a nonnegative number, $cost(R)$. Ambiguity is avoided by returning the least-cost rule matching the packet's header. The cost function generalizes the implicit precedence rules that are used in practice to choose between multiple matching rules. In firewall applications or Cisco ACLs, for instance, rules are placed in the database in a specific linear order, where each rule takes precedence over a subsequent rule. Thus, the goal there is to find the *first* matching rule. Of course, the same effect can be achieved by making $cost(R)$ equal to the position of rule R in the database.

As an example of a rule database, consider the topology and firewall database [CB95] shown in Figure 12.3, where a screened subnet configuration interposes between a company subnetwork (shown on top left) and the rest of the Internet (including hackers). There is a so-called bastion host M within the company that mediates all access to and from the external world. M serves as the mail gateway and also provides external name server access. TI, TO are network time protocol (NTP) sources, where TI is internal to the company and TO is external. S is the address of the secondary name server, which is external to the company.

Clearly, the site manager wishes to allow communication from within the network to TO and S and yet wishes to block hackers. The database of rules shown on the bottom of Figure 12.3 implements this intention. Terse explanations of each rule are shown on the right of each rule. Assume that all addresses of machines within the company's network start with the CIDR prefix *Net*. Thus M and TI both match the prefix *Net*. All packets matching any of the first seven rules are allowed; the remaining (last rule) are dropped by the screening router.

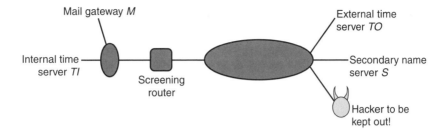

Destination	Source	Destination Port	Source Port	Flags	Comments
M	*	25	*	*	Allow inbound mail
M	*	53	*	UDP	Allow DNS access
M	S	53	*	*	Secondary access
M	*	23	*	*	Incoming telnet
TI	TO	123	123	UDP	NTP time info
*	Net	*	*	*	Outgoing packets
Net	*	*	*	TCP ack	Return ACKs OK
*	*	*	*	*	Block everything!

FIGURE 12.3 The top half of the figure shows the topology of a small company; the bottom half shows a sample firewall database for this company as described in the book by Cheswick and Bellovin [CB95]. The *block* flags are not shown in the figure; the first seven rules have *block = false* (i.e., allow) and the last rule has *block = true* (i.e., block). We assume that all the addresses within the company subnetwork (shown on top left) start with the prefix *Net*, including *M* and *TI*.

A more general firewall could arbitrarily interleave rules that allow packets with rules that drop packets.

As an example, consider a packet sent to M from S with UDP destination port equal to 53. This packet matches Rules 2, 3, and 8 but must be allowed through because the first matching rule is Rule 2.

Note that this description uses N for the number of rules and K for the number of packet fields. K is sometimes called the *number of dimensions*, for reasons that will become clearer in Section 12.6.

12.3 REQUIREMENTS AND METRICS

The requirements for rule matching are similar to those for IP lookups (Chapter 11). We wish to do packet classification at wire speed for minimum-size packets, and thus speed is the dominant metric. To allow the database to fit in high-speed memory it is useful to reduce the amount of memory needed. For most firewall databases, insertion speed is not an issue because rules are rarely changed.

However, this is not true for *dynamic* or *stateful* packet rules. This capability is useful, for example, for handling UDP traffic. Because UDP headers do not contain an ACK bit that can be used to determine whether a packet is the bellwether packet of a connection, the screening router cannot tell the difference between the first packet sent from the outside to an internal server (which it may want to block) and a response sent to a UDP request to an internal client (which it may want to pass). The solution used in some products is to have the outgoing request packet dynamically trigger the insertion of a rule (which has addresses and ports that match the request) that allows the inbound response to be passed. This requires very fast update times, a third metric.

12.4 SIMPLE SOLUTIONS

There are five simple solutions that are often used or considered: linear search, caching, demultiplexing algorithms, MPLS, and content addressable memories (CAMs). While CAMs have difficult hardware design issues, they effectively represent a parallelization of the simplest algorithmic approach: linear search.

12.4.1 *Linear Search*

Several existing firewall implementations do a linear search of the database and keep track of the best-match rule. Linear search is reasonable for small rule sizes but is extremely slow for large rule sets. For example, a core router that does linear search among a rule set of 2000 rules (used at the time of writing by some ISPs) will considerably degrade its forwarding performance below wire speed.

12.4.2 *Caching*

Some implementations even cache the result of the search keyed against the whole header. There are two problems with this scheme. First, the cache hit rate of caching full IP addresses in the backbones is typically at most 80–90% [Par96, NMH97]. Part of the problem is Web accesses and other flows that send only a small number of packets; if a Web session sends just five packets to the same address, then the cache hit rate is 80%. Since caching full headers takes a lot more memory, this should have an even worse hit rate (for the same amount of cache memory).

Second, even with a 90% hit rate cache, a slow linear search of the rule space will result in poor performance.[2] For example, suppose that a search of the cache costs 100 nsec (one memory access) and that a linear search of 10,000 rules costs 1,000,000 nsec = 1 msec (one memory access per rule). Then the average search time with a cache hit rate of 90% is still 0.1 msec, which is rather slow. However, caching could be combined with some of the fast algorithms in this chapter to improve the expected search time even further. An investigation of the use of caching for classification can be found in Xu et al. [XSD00].

---

[2]This is an application of a famous principle in computer architecture called *Amdahl's law*.

12.4.3 Demultiplexing Algorithms

Chapter 8 describes the use of packet rules for demultiplexing and algorithms such as Pathfinder, Berkeley packet filter, and dynamic path finder. Can't these existing solutions simply be reused? It is important to realize that the two problems are similar but subtly different.

The first packet-classification scheme that avoids a linear search through the set of rules is Pathfinder [BGP+94]. However, Pathfinder allows wildcards to occur only at the end of a rule. For instance, $(D, S, *, *, *)$ is allowed, but not $(D, *, Prot, *, SourcePort)$. With this restriction, all rules can be merged into a generalized trie — with hash tables replacing array nodes — and rule lookup can be done in time proportional to the number of packet fields. DPF [EK96] uses the Pathfinder idea of merging rules into a trie but adds the idea of using dynamic code generation for extra performance. However, it is unclear how to handle intermixed wildcards and specified fields, such as $(D, *, Prot, *, SourcePort)$, using these schemes.

Because packet classification allows more general rules, the Pathfinder idea of using a trie does not work well. There does exist a simple trie scheme (set-pruning tries; see Section 12.5.1) to perform a lookup in time $O(M)$, where M is the number of packet fields. Such schemes are described in Decasper et al. [DDPP98] and Malan and Jahanian [MJ98]. Unfortunately, such schemes require $\Theta(N^K)$ storage, where K is the number of packet fields and N is the number of rules. Thus such schemes are not scalable for large databases. By contrast, some of the schemes we will describe require only $O(NM)$ storage.

12.4.4 Passing Labels

Recall from Chapter 11 that one way to finesse lookups is to pass a label from a previous-hop router to a next-hop router. One of the most prominent examples of such a technology is multiprotocol label switching (MPLS) [Cha97]. While IP lookups have been able to keep pace with wire speeds, the difficulties of algorithmic approaches to packet classification have ensured an important niche for MPLS. Refer to Chapter 11 for a description of tag switching and MPLS.

Today MPLS is useful mostly for traffic engineering. For example, if Web traffic between two sites A and B is to be routed along a special path, a label-switched path is set up between the two sites. Before traffic leaves site A, a router does packet classification and maps the Web traffic into an MPLS header. Core routers examine only the label in the header until the traffic reaches B, at which point the MPLS header is removed.

The gain from the MPLS header is that the intermediate routers do not have to repeat the packet-classification effort expended at the edge router; simple table lookup suffices. The DiffServ [SWG] proposal for QoS is actually similar in this sense. Classification is done at the edges to mark packets that deserve special quality of service. The only difference is that the classification information is used to mark the Type of Service [TOS] bits in the IP header, as opposed to an MPLS label. Both are examples of Principle **P10**, passing hints in protocol headers.

Despite MPLS and DiffServ, core routers still do classification at the very highest speeds. This is largely motivated by security concerns, for which it may be infeasible to rely on label switching. For example, Singh et al. [SBV04] describe a number of core router classifiers, the largest of which contains 2000 rules.

12.4.5 *Content-Addressable Memories*

Recall from Chapter 11 that a CAM is a content-addressable memory, where the first cell that matches a data item will be returned using a parallel lookup in hardware. A ternary CAM allows each bit of data to be either a 0, a 1, or a wildcard. Clearly, ternary CAMs can be used for rule matching as well as for prefix matching. However, the CAMs must provide wide lengths — for example, the combination of the IPv4 destination, source, and two port fields is 96 bits.

Because of problems with algorithmic solutions described in the remainder of this chapter, there is a general belief that hardware solutions such as ternary CAMs are needed for core routers, despite the problems [GM01] of ternary CAMs. There are, however, several reasons to consider algorithmic alternatives to ternary CAMs, which were presented in Chapter 11.

Recall that these reasons include the smaller density and larger power of CAMs versus SRAMs and the difficulty of integrating forwarding logic with the CAM. These problems remain valid when considering CAMs for classification. An additional issue that arises is the *rule multiplication* caused by ranges. In CAM solutions, each range has to be replaced by a potentially large number of prefixes, thus causing extra entries. Some algorithmic solutions can handle ranges in rules without converting ranges to rules.

These arguments are strengthened by the fact that, at the time of writing, several CAM vendors were also considering algorithmic solutions, motivated by some of the difficulties with CAMs. While better CAM cell designs that reduce density and power requirements may emerge, it is still important to understand the corresponding advantages and disadvantages of algorithmic solutions. The remainder of the chapter is devoted to this topic.

12.5 TWO-DIMENSIONAL SCHEMES

A useful problem-solving technique is first to solve a simpler version of a complex problem such as packet classification and to use the insight gained to solve the more complex problem. Since packet classification with just *one* field has been solved in Chapter 11, the next simplest problem is *two*-dimensional packet classification.

Two-dimensional rules may be useful in their own right. This is because large backbone routers may have a large number of destination–source rules to handle virtual private networks and multicast forwarding and to keep track of traffic between subnets. Further, as we will see, there is a heuristic observation that reduces the general case to the two-dimensional case.

Since there are only three distinct approaches to one-dimensional prefix matching — using tries, binary search on prefix lengths, and binary search on ranges — it is worth looking for generalizations of each of these distinct approaches. All three generalizations exist. However, this chapter will describe only the most efficient of these (the generalization of tries) in this section.

The appropriate generalization of standard prefix tries to two dimensions is called the *grid of tries*. The main idea will be explained using an example database of seven destination–source rules, shown in Figure 12.4. We arrive at the final solution by first considering two naive variants.

12.5.1 *Fast Searching Using Set-Pruning Tries*

Consider the two-dimensional rule set in Figure 12.4. The simplest idea is first to build a trie on the destination prefixes in the database and then to hang a number of source tries off the leaves

Rule	Destination	Source
R_1	0*	10*
R_2	0*	01*
R_3	0*	1*
R_4	00*	1*
R_5	00*	11*
R_6	10*	1*
R_7	*	00*

FIGURE 12.4   An example with seven destination–source rules.

of the destination trie. Figure 12.5 illustrates the construction for the rules in Figure 12.4. Each valid prefix in the destination trie points to a trie containing some source prefixes. The question is: Which source prefixes should be stored in the source trie corresponding to each destination prefix?

For instance, consider $D = 00*$. Both rules R_4 and R_5 have this destination prefix, and so the trie at D clearly needs to store the corresponding source prefixes $1*$ and $11*$. But storing only these source prefixes is insufficient. This is because the destination prefix $0*$ in rules R_1, R_2, and R_3 also matches any destination that D matches. In fact, the wildcard destination prefix $*$ of R_7 also matches whatever D matches. This suggests that the source trie at $D = 00$ must contain the source prefixes for $\{R_1, R_2, R_3, R_4, R_5, R_7\}$, because these are the set of rules *whose destination is a prefix of D*.

Figure 12.5 shows a schematic representation of this data structure for the database of Figure 12.4. Note that $S1$ denotes the source prefix of rule R_1, $S2$ of rule R_2, and so on. Thus each prefix D in the destination trie *prunes* the set of rules from the entire set of rules down to the set of rules compatible with D. The same idea can be extended to more than two fields, with each field value in the path pruning the set of rules further.

In this trie of tries, the search algorithm first matches the destination of the header in the destination trie. This yields the longest match on the destination prefix. The search algorithm then traverses the associated source trie to find the longest source match. While searching the source trie, the algorithms keep track of the lowest-cost matching rule. Since all rules that have a matching destination prefix are stored in the source trie being searched, the algorithm finds the correct least-cost rule. This is the basic idea behind set-pruning trees [Decasper et al., DDPP98].

Unfortunately, this simple extension of tries from one to two dimensions has a memory-explosion problem. The problem arises because a source prefix can occur in multiple tries. In Figure 12.5, for instance, the source prefixes $S1, S2, S3$ appear in the source trie associated with $D = 00*$ as well as the trie associated with $D = 0*$.

How bad can this replication get? A worst-case example forcing roughly N^2 memory is created using the set of rules shown in Figure 12.6. The problem is that since the destination prefix $*$ matches any destination header, each of the $N/2$ source prefixes are replicated

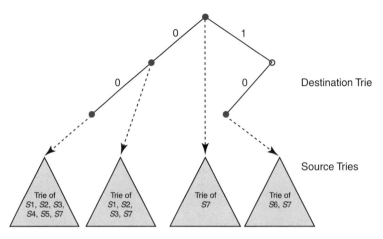

FIGURE 12.5 The set-pruning trie data structure in two dimensions corresponding to the database of Figure 12.4. Destination Trie is a trie for the destination prefixes. The nodes corresponding to a valid destination prefix in the database are shown as filled circles; others are shown as empty circles. Each valid destination prefix D has a pointer to a trie containing the source prefixes that belong to rules whose destination field is a prefix of D.

Rule	Destination	Source
R_1	$D1$	*
R_2	$D2$	*
	⋮	
$R_{N/2}$	$D_{N/2}$	*
$R_{N/2+1}$	*	S_1
$R_{N/2+2}$	*	S_2
	⋮	
R_N	*	S_N

FIGURE 12.6 An example forcing $N^2/2$ memory for two-dimensional set-pruning trees. Similar examples, which apply to a number of other simple schemes, can be used to show $O(N^K)$ storage for K-dimensional rules.

$N/2$ times, one for each destination prefix. The example (see exercises) can be extended to show a $O(N^k)$ bound for general set-pruning tries in K dimensions.

While set-pruning tries do not scale to large classifiers, the natural extension to more than two fields has been used in Decasper et al. [DDPP98] as part of a router toolkit, and in Malan and Jahanian [MJ98] as part of a flexible monitoring system. The performance of set-pruning tries is also studied in Qiu et al. [QVS01]. One interesting optimization introduced in Decasper et al. [DDPP98] and Malan and Jahanian [MJ98] is to avoid obvious waste (**P1**) when two subtries $S1$ and $S2$ have exactly the same contents. In this case, one can replace the pointers to $S1$ and $S2$ by a pointer to a common subtrie, S. This changes the structure from a tree to a directed acyclic graph (DAG). The DAG optimization can greatly reduce storage for set-pruning tries (see Ref. QVS01 for other, related optimizations) and can be used to implement small classifiers, say, up to 100 rules, in software.

12.5.2 Reducing Memory Using Backtracking

The previous scheme pays in memory in order to reduce search time. The dual idea is to pay with time in order to reduce memory. In order to avoid the memory blowup of the simple trie scheme, observe that rules associated with a destination prefix D are copied into the source trie of D' whenever D is a prefix of D'. For instance, in Figure 12.5, the prefix $D = 00*$ has two rules associated with it: R_4 and R_5. The other rules, R_1, R_2, R_3, are copied into D's trie because their destination field $0*$ is a prefix of D.

The copying can be avoided by having each destination prefix D point to a source trie that stores the rules whose destination field is *exactly* D. This requires modifying the search strategy as follows: Instead of just searching the source trie for the best-matching destination prefix D, the search algorithm must now search the source tries associated with all *ancestors* of D.

In order to search for the least-cost rule, the algorithm first traverses the destination trie and finds the longest destination prefix D' matching the header. The algorithm then searches the source trie of D' and updates the least-cost-matching rule. Unlike set-pruning tries, however, the search algorithm is not finished at this point.

Instead, the search algorithm must now work its way back up the destination trie and search the source trie associated with every prefix of D' that points to a nonempty source trie.[3]

Since each rule now is stored exactly once, the memory requirement for the new structure is $O(NW)$, which is a significant improvement over the the previous scheme. Unfortunately, the lookup cost for backtracking is worse than for set-pruning tries: In the worst case, the lookup costs $\Theta(W^2)$, where W is the maximum number of bits specified in the destination or source fields.

The $\Theta(W^2)$ bound on the search cost follows from the observation that, in the worst case, the algorithm may end up searching W source tries, each at the cost of $O(W)$, for a total of $O(W^2)$ time. For $W = 32$ and using 1-bit tries, this is 1024 memory accesses. Even using 4-bit tries, this scheme requires 64 memory accesses.

While backtracking can be very slow in the worst case, it turns out that all classification algorithms exhibit pathological worst-case behavior. For databases encountered in practice, backtracking can work very well. Qiu et al. [QVS01] describe experimental results using backtracking and also describe potential hardware implementations on pipelined processors.

12.5.3 The Best of Both Worlds: Grid of Tries

The two naive variants of two-dimensional tries pay either a large price in memory (set-pruning tries) or a large price in time (backtracking search). However, a careful examination

---

[3]Note that backtracking search can actually search the source tries corresponding to destination prefixes in any order; this particular order was used only to motivate the grid-of-tries scheme. Another search order that minimizes the state required for backtracking is described in Qiu et al. [QVS01].

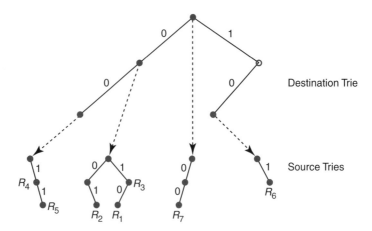

FIGURE 12.7   Avoiding the memory blowup by storing each rule in exactly one trie.

of backtracking search reveals obvious waste (**P1**), which can be avoided using precomputation (**P2a**).

To see the wasted time in backtracking search, consider matching the packet with destination address 001 and source address 001 in Figure 12.7. The search in the destination trie gives $D = 00$ as the best match. So the backtracking algorithm starts its search for the matching source prefix in the associated source trie, which contains rules R_4 and R_5. However, the search immediately fails, since the first bit of the source is 0. Next, backtracking search backs up along the desination trie and *restarts* the search in the source trie of $D = 0*$, the parent of $00*$.

But backing up the trie is a waste because if the search fails after searching destination bits 00 and source bit 0, then any matching rule must be shorter in the destination (e.g., 0) and must contain all the source bits searched so far, *including* the failed bit. Thus backing up to the source trie of $D = 0*$ and then traversing the source bit 0 to the parent of R_2 in Figure 12.7 (as done in backtracking search) is a waste.

The algorithm could predict that this sequence of bits would be traversed when it first failed in the source trie of $D = 00$. This motivates a simple idea: Why not jump directly to the parent of R_2 from the failure point in the source trie of $D = 00*$?

Thus in the new scheme (Figure 12.8), for each failure point in a source trie, the trie-building algorithm *precomputes* what we call a *switch pointer*. Switch pointers allow search to jump directly to the next possible source trie that can contain a matching rule. Thus in Figure 12.8, notice that the source trie containing R_4 and R_5 has a dashed line labeled with 0 that points to a node x in the source trie containing $\{R_1, R_2, R_3\}$. All the dashed lines in Figure 12.8 are switch pointers. Please distinguish the dashed switch pointers from the dotted lines that connect the destination and source tries.

Now consider again the same search for the packet with destination address 001 and source address 001 in Figure 12.8. As before, the search in the destination trie gives $D = 00$ as the best match. Search fails in the corresponding source trie (containing R_4 and R_5) because the source trie contains a path only if the first source bit is a 1. However, in Figure 12.8, instead of failing and backtracking, the algorithm follows the switch pointer labeled 0 directly to node x.

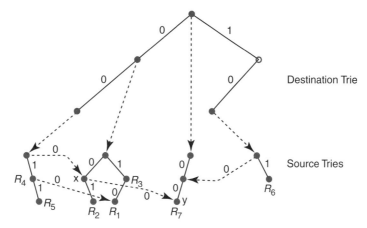

FIGURE 12.8   Improving the search cost with the use of switch pointers.

It then continues matching from node x, without skipping a beat, using the remaining bits of the source.

Since the next bit of the source is a 0, the search in Figure 12.8 fails again. The search algorithm once again follows the switch pointer labeled 0 and jumps to node y of the third source trie (associated with the destination prefix $*$). Effectively, the switch pointers allow skipping over all rules in the next ancestor source trie whose source fields are shorter than the current source match. This in turn improves the search complexity from $O(W^2)$ to $O(W)$.

It may help to define *switch pointers* more precisely. Call a destination string D' an *ancestor* of D if D' is a *prefix* of D. Call D' the *lowest ancestor* of D if D' is the *longest* prefix of D in the destination trie. Let $T(D)$ denote the source trie pointed to by D. Recall that $T(D)$ contains the source fields of exactly those rules whose destination field is D.

Let u be a node in $T(D)$ that *fails* on bit 0; that is, if u corresponds to the source prefix s, then the trie $T(D)$ has no string starting with $s0$. Let D'' be the *lowest* ancestor of D whose source trie contains a source string *starting with prefix $s0$*, say, at node v. Then we place a switch pointer at node u pointing to node v. If no such node v exists, the switch pointer is nil. The switch pointer for failure on bit 1 is defined similarly. For instance, in Figure 12.8, the node labeled x fails on bit 0 and has a switch pointer to the node labeled y.

As a second example, consider the packet header $(00*, 10*)$. Search starts with the first source trie, pointed to by the destination trie node $00*$. After matching the first source bit, 1, search encounters rule R_4. But then search fails on the second bit. Search therefore follows the switch pointer, which leads to the node in the second trie labeled with R_1. The switch pointers at the node containing R_1 are both nil, and so search terminates. Note, however, that search has missed the rule $R_3 = (0*, 1*)$, which also matches the packet header. While in this case R_3 has higher cost than R_1, in general the overlooked rule could have lower cost.

Such problems can be avoided by having each node in a source trie maintain a variable *storedRule*. Specifically, a node v with destination prefix D and source prefix S stores in *storedRule*(v) the least-cost rule whose destination field is a prefix of D and whose source field is a prefix of S. With this precomputation, the node labeled with R_1 in Figure 12.8 would store information about R_3 instead of R_1 if R_3 had lower cost than R_1.

Finally, here is an argument that the search cost in the final scheme is at most $2W$. The time to find the best destination prefix is at most W. The remainder of the time is spent traversing the source tries. However, in each step, the length of the match on the source field increases by 1 — either by traversing further down in the same trie or by following a switch pointer to an ancestral trie. Since the maximum length of the source prefixes is W, the total time spent in searching the source tries is also W. The memory requirement is $O(NW)$, since each of the N rules is stored only once, and each rule requires $O(W)$ space.

Note that k-bit tries (Chapter 11) can be used in place of 1-bit tries by expanding each destination or source prefix to the next multiple of k. For instance, suppose $k = 2$. Then, in the example of Figure 12.8, the destination prefix $0*$ of rules R_1, R_2, R_3 is expanded to 00 and 01. The source prefixes of R_3, R_4, R_6 are expanded to 10 and 11. Using k-bit expansion, a single prefix can expand to 2^{k-1} prefixes. The total memory requirement grows from $2NW$ to $NW2^k/k$, and so the memory increases by the factor $2^{k-1}/k$. On the other hand, the depth of the trie reduces to W/k, and so the total lookup time becomes $O(W/k)$.

The bottom line is that by using multibit tries, the time to search for the best matching rule in an arbitrarily large two-dimensional database is effectively the time for two IP lookups.

Just as the grid of tries represents a generalization of familiar trie search for prefix matching, there is a corresponding generalization of binary search on prefix lengths (Chapter 11) that searches a database of two field rules in $2W$ hashes, where W is the length of the larger of the two fields. This is a big gap from the $\log W$ time required for prefix matching using binary search on prefix lengths. In the special case where the rules do not overlap, the search time reduces even further to $\log^2 W$, as shown in Warkhede et al. [WSV01a]. While these results are interesting theoretically, they seem to have less relevance to real routers, mostly because of the difficulties of implementing hashing in hardware.

12.6 APPROACHES TO GENERAL RULE SETS

So far this chapter has concentrated on the special case of rules on just two header fields. Before moving to algorithms for rules with more than two fields, this section brings together some insights that inform the algorithms in later sections. Section 12.6.1 describes a geometric view of classification that provides visual insight into the problem. Section 12.6.2 utilizes the geometric viewpoint to obtain bounds on the fundamental difficulty of packet classification in the general case. Section 12.6.3 describes several observations about real rule sets that can be exploited to provide efficient algorithms that will be described in subsequent sections.

12.6.1 *Geometric View of Classification*

A second problem-solving technique that is useful is to collect different viewpoints for the same problem. This section describes a *geometric* view of classification that was introduced by Lakshman and Staliadis [LS98] and independently by Adisehsu [Adi98].

Recall from Chapter 11 that we can view a 32-bit prefix like $00*$ as a range of addresses from $000\ldots00$ to $001\ldots11$ on the number line from 0 to 2^{32}. If prefixes correspond to *line segments* geometrically, two-dimensional rules correspond to rectangles (Figure 12.9), three-dimensional rules to cubes, and so on. A given packet header is a point. The problem of packet classification reduces to finding the lowest-cost box that contains the given point.

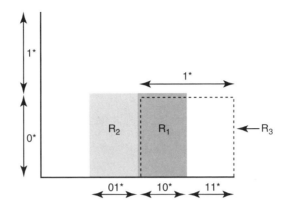

FIGURE 12.9 Geometric view of the first three rules, R_1, R_2, R_3, in the rule database of Figure 12.4. For example, the rule $R_1 = 0*, 10*$ is the box whose projection on the destination axis is the range corresponding to $0*$ and whose projection on the source axis is the range corresponding to $10*$. Note that because $R_3 = 0*, 1*$ has the same destination range as R_1 and a source range that strictly includes the range of R_1, the dashed box, R_3, contains the box R_1.

Figure 12.9 shows the geometric view of the first three two-dimensional rules in Figure 12.4. Destination addresses are represented on the y-axis and source addresses on the x-axis. In the figure, some sample prefix ranges are marked off on each axis. For example, the two halves of the y-axis are the prefix ranges $0*$ and $1*$. Similarly, the x-axis is divided into the four prefix ranges $00*, 01*, 10*$, and $11*$. To draw the box for a rule like $R_1 = 0*, 10*$, draw the $0*$ range on the y-axis and the $10*$ range on the x-axis, and extend the range lines to meet, forming a box. Multiple-rule matches, such as R_1 and R_2, correspond to overlapping boxes.

The first advantage of the geometric view is that it enables the application of algorithms from computational geometry. For example, Lakshman and Staliadis [LS98] adapt a technique from computational geometry known as *fractional cascading* to do binary search for two-field rule matching in $O(\log N)$ time, where N is the number of rules. In other words, two-dimensional rule matching is asymptotically as fast as one-dimensional rule matching using binary search. This is consistent with the results for the grid of tries. The result also generalizes binary search on values for prefix searching as described in Chapter 11.

Unfortunately, the constants for fractional cascading are quite high. Perhaps this suggests that adapting existing geometric algorithms may actually not result in the most efficient algorithms. However, the second and main advantage of the geometric *viewpoint* is that it is suggestive and useful.

For example, the geometric view provides a useful metric, the number of disjoint (i.e., nonintersecting) *classification regions*. Since rules can overlap, this is not the number of rules. In two dimensions, for example, with N rules one can create N^2 classification regions by having $N/2$ rules that correspond geometrically to horizontal strips together with $N/2$ rules that correspond geometrically to vertical strips. The intersection of the $N/2$ horizontal strips with the $N/2$ vertical strips creates $O(N^2)$ disjoint classification regions. For example, the database in Figure 12.6 has this property. Similar constructions can be used to generate $O(N^K)$ regions for K-dimensional rules.

As a second example, the database of Figure 12.9 has four classification regions: the rule R_1, the rule R_2, the points in R_3 not contained in R_1, and all points not contained in R_1, R_2, or R_3. We will use the number of classification regions later to characterize the complexity of a given classifier or rule database.

12.6.2 Beyond Two Dimensions: The Bad News

The success of the grid of tries may make us optimistic about generalizing to larger dimensions. Unfortunately, this optimism is misplaced; either the search time or the storage blows up exponentially with the number of dimensions K for $K > 2$.

Using the geometric viewpoint just described, it is easy to adapt a lower bound from computational geometry. Thus, it is known that general multidimensional range searching over N ranges in k dimensions requires $\Omega((\log N)^{K-1})$ worst-case time if the memory is limited to about linear size [Cha90b, Cha90a] or requires $O(N^K)$ size memory. While $\log N$ could be reasonable (say, 10 memory accesses), $\log^4 N$ will be very large (say, 10,000 memory accesses). Notice that this lower bound is consistent with solutions for the two-dimensional cases that take linear storage but are as fast as $O(\log N)$.

The lower bound implies that for perfectly general rule sets, *algorithmic approaches to classification require either a large amount of memory or a large amount of time.* Unfortunately, classification at high speeds, especially for core routers, requires the use of limited and expensive SRAM. Thus the lower bound seems to imply that content address memories are required for reasonably sized classifiers (say, 10,000 rules) that must be searched at high speeds (e.g., OC-768 speeds).

12.6.3 Beyond Two Dimensions: The Good News

The previous subsection may have left the reader wondering whether there is any hope left for algorithmic approaches to packet classification in the general case. Fortunately, real databases have more *structure*, which can be exploited to efficiently solve multidimensional packet classification using algorithmic techniques.

The *good* news about packet classification can be articulated using four observations. Subsequent sections describe a series of heuristic algorithms, all of which do very badly in the worst case but quite well on databases that satisfy one or more of the assumptions.

The expected case can be characterized using four observations drawn from a set of firewall databases studied in Srinivasan et al. [SVSW98] and Gupta and McKeown [GM99b] (and not from publically available lookup tables as in the previous chapter). The first is identical to an observation made in Chapter 11 and repeated here. The observations are numbered starting from *O2* to be consistent with observation *O1* made in the lookup chapter.

O2: Prefix containment is rare. It is somewhat rare to have prefixes that are prefixes of other prefixes, as, for example, the prefixes 00* and 0001*. In fact, the maximum number of prefixes of a given prefix in lookup tables and classifiers is seven.

O3: Many fields are not general ranges. For the destination and source port fields, most rules contain either specific port numbers (e.g., port 80 for Web traffic), the wildcard range (i.e., ∗), or the port ranges that separate server ports from client ports (1024 or greater and less than 1024). The protocol field is limited to either the wildcard or (more commonly) TCP, UDP. This field also rarely contains protocols such as IGMP and ICMP. While other TCP fields are sometimes referred to, the most common reference is to the ACK bit.

O4: The number of disjoint classification regions is small. This is perhaps the most interesting observation. Harking back to the geometric view, the lower bounds in Chazelle [Cha90a] depend partly on the worst-case possibility of creating N^K classification regions using N rules. Such rules require either N^K space or a large search time. However, Gupta and McKeown [GM99b], after an extensive survey of 8000 rule databases, show that the number of classification regions is much smaller than the worst case. Instead of being exponential in the number of dimensions, the number of classification regions is linear in N, with a small constant.

O5: Source–Destination matching: In Singh et al. [BSV03], several core router classifiers used by real ISPs are analyzed and the following interesting observation is made. Almost all packets match at most five distinct source–destination values found in the classifier. No packet matched more than 20 distinct source–destination pairs. This is a somewhat more refined observation than *O4* because it says that the number of classification regions is small, even when projected only to the source and destination fields. By "small," we mean that the number of regions grows much more slowly than N, the size of the classifier.

12.7 EXTENDING TWO-DIMENSIONAL SCHEMES

The simplest general scheme uses observation *O5* to trivially extend any efficient 2D scheme to multiple dimensions. A number of algorithms simply use linear search to search through all possible rules. This scales well in storage but poorly in time. The source–destination matching observation leads to a very simple idea depicted in Figure 12.10. Use source–destination address matching to reduce linear searching to just the rules corresponding to source–destination prefix pairs in the database that match the given packet header.

By observation *O5*, at most 20 rules match any packet when considering only the source and destination fields. Thus pruning based on source–destination fields will reduce the number of rules to be searched to less than 20, compared to searching the entire database. For example, Singh at al. [SBV04] describe a database with 2800 rules used by a large ISP.

Thus in Figure 12.10, the general idea is to use any efficient two-dimensional matching scheme to find *all* distinct source–destination prefix pairs $(S_1, D_1) \ldots (S_t, D_t)$ that match a header. For each distinct pair (S_i, D_i) there is a linear array or list with all rules that contain (S_i, D_i) in the source and destination fields. Thus in the figure, the algorithm has to traverse the list at (S_1, D_1), searching through all the rules for R_5, R_6, R_2, and R_4. Then the algorithm moves on to consider the lists at (S_2, D_2), and so on.

This structure has two important advantages:

- Each rule is represented only once without replication. However, one may wish to replicate rules to reduce search times even further.

- The port range specifications stay as ranges in the individual lists without the associated blowup associated with range translation in, say, CAMs.

Since the grid-of-tries implementation described earlier is one of the most efficient two-dimensional schemes in the literature, it is natural to instantiate this general schema by using a grid of tries as the two-dimensional algorithm in Figure 12.10.

Unfortunately, it turns out that there is a delicacy about extending the grid of tries. In the the grid of tries, whenever one rule, R, is at least as specific in all fields as a second rule, R',

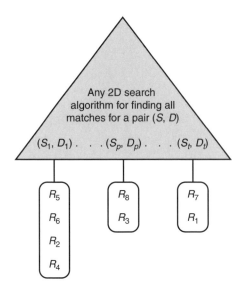

FIGURE 12.10   Extending two-dimensional schemes.

rule R' precomputes its matching directive to be that of R if R is the lower cost of the two rules. This allows the traversal through the grid of tries to safely skip rule R when encountering rule R'. While this works correctly with two-field rules, it requires some further modifications to handle the general case.

One solution, equivalent to precomputing rule costs, is to precompute the list for R' to include all the list elements for R. Unfortunately, this approach can increase storage because each rule is no longer represented exactly once. A more sophisticated solution, called the *extended grid of tries* (EGT) and described in Baboescu et al. [BSV03], is based on extra traversals beyond the standard grid of tries.

The performance of EGT can be described as follows.

Assumption: The extension of two-dimensional schemes depends critically on observation *O5*.

Performance: The scheme takes at least one grid-of-tries traversal plus the time to linearly search c rules, where c is the constant embodied in observation *O5*. Assuming linear storage, the search performance can increase [BSV03] by an additive factor representing the time to search for less specific rules. The addition of a new rule R requires only rebuilding of the individual two-dimensional structure of which R is a part. Thus rule update should be fairly fast.

12.8 USING DIVIDE-AND-CONQUER

The next three schemes (bit vector linear search, on-demand cross-producting, and equivalenced cross-producting) all exploit the simple algorithmic idea (**P15**) of divide-and-conquer. Divide-and-conquer refers to dividing a problem into simpler pieces and then efficiently combining the answers to the pieces. We briefly motivate a skeletal framework of this approach in this section. The next three sections will flesh out specific instantiations of this framework.

FIGURE 12.11 The database of Figure 12.3 "sliced" into columns where each column contains the set of prefixes corresponding to a particular field.

Chapter 11 has already outlined techniques to do lookups on individual fields. Given this background, the common idea in all three divide-and-conquer algorithms is the following. Start by slicing the rule database into columns, with the *i*th column storing all distinct prefixes (or ranges) in field *i*. Then, given a packet *P*, determine the best-matching prefix (or narrowest-enclosing range) for each of its fields separately. Finally, combine the results of the best-matching-prefix lookups on individual fields. The main problem, of course, lies in finding an efficient method for combining the lookup of individual fields into a single compound lookup.

All the divide-and-conquer algorithms conceptually start by slicing the database of Figure 12.3 into individual prefix fields. In the sliced columns, from now on we will sometimes refer to the wildcard character ∗ by the string *default*. Recall that the mail gateway *M* and internal NTP agent *T1* are full IP addresses that lie within the prefix range of *Net*. The sliced database corresponding to Figure 12.3 is shown in Figure 12.11.

Clearly, any divide-and-conquer algorithm starts by doing an individual lookup in each column and then combines the results. The next three sections show that each of the three schemes returns different results with lookup and follows different strategies to combine the individual field results, despite using the same sliced database shown in Figure 12.11.

12.9 BIT VECTOR LINEAR SEARCH

Consider doing a match in one of the individual columns in Figure 12.11, say, the destination address field, and finding a bit string *S* as the longest match. Clearly, this lookup result eliminates any rules that *do not* match *S* in this field. Then the search algorithm can do a linear search in the set of all remaining rules that match *S*. The logical extension is to perform individual matches in each field; each field match will prune away a number of rules, leaving a remaining set. The search algorithm needs to search only the *intersection* of the remaining sets obtained by each field lookup.

This would clearly be a good heuristic for optimizing the average case if the remaining sets are typically small. However, one can guarantee performance even in the worst case

Destination Prefixes	Source Prefixes	DstPort Prefixes	SrcPort Prefixes	Flags Prefixes
M I 11110111	*S* I 11110011	25 I 10000111	123 I 11111111	UDP I 11111101
*T*1 I 00001111	*T*0 I 11011011	53 I 01100111	* I 11110111	TCP I 10110111
Net I 00000111	Net I 11010111	23 I 00010111		*I 10110101
* I 00000101	* I 11010011	123 I 00001111		
		* I 00000111		

FIGURE 12.12   The sliced database of Figure 12.11 together with bit vectors for every possible sliced value. The bit vector has 8 bits, one corresponding to each of the eight possible rules in Figure 12.3. Bit *j* is set for value *M* in field *i* if value *M* matches Rule *j* in field *i*.

(to some extent) by representing the remaining sets as bitmaps and by using wide memories to retrieve a large number of set members in a single memory access (**P4a**, exploit locality).

In more detail, as in Section 12.8, divide-and-conquer is used to slice the database, as in Figure 12.11. However, in addition with each possible value *M* of field *i*, the algorithm stores the set of rules *S(M)* that match *M* in field *i* as a bit vector. This is easy to do when building the sliced table. The algorithm that builds the data structure scans through the rules linearly to obtain the rules that match *M* using the match rule (e.g., exact, prefix, or range) specified for the field.

For example, Figure 12.12 shows the sliced database of Figure 12.11 together with bit vectors for each sliced field value. The bit vector has 8 bits, one corresponding to each of the eight possible rules in Figure 12.3. Bit *j* is set for value *M* in field *i* if value *M* matches Rule *j* in field *i*.

Consider the destination prefix field and the first value *M* in Figure 12.12. If we compare it to Figure 12.3, we see that the first four rules specify *M* in this field. The fifth rule specifies *T*1 (which does not match *M*), and the sixth and eighth rules specify a wildcard (which matches *M*). Finally, the seventh rule specifies the prefix *Net* (which matches *M*, because *Net* is assumed to be the prefix of the company network in which *M* is the mail gateway). Thus the bitmap for *M* is 11110111, where the only bit not set is the fifth bit. This is because the fifth rule has *T*1, which does not match *M*.

When a packet header arrives with fields $H[1] \ldots H[K]$, the search algorithm first performs a longest-matching-prefix lookup in each field *i* to obtain matches M_i and the corresponding set $S(M_i)$ of matching rules. The search algorithm then proceeds to compute the intersection of all the sets $S(M_i)$ and returns the lowest-cost element in the intersection set.

But if rules are arranged in nondecreasing order of cost and all sets are bitmaps, then the intersection set is the AND of all *K* bitmaps. Finally, the lowest-cost element corresponds to the index of the first bit set in the intersection bitmap. But, the reader may object, since there are *N* rules, the intersected bitmaps are *N* bits long. Hence, computing the AND requires $O(N)$ operations. So the algorithm is effectively doing a linear search after slicing and doing individual field matches. Why not do simple linear search instead?

The reason is subtle and requires a good grasp of models and metrics. Basically, the preceding argument above is correct but ignores the large constant-factor improvement that is possible using bitmaps. Thus computing the AND of K bit vectors and searching the intersection bit vector is still an $O(K \cdot N)$ operation; however, the constants are much lower than doing naive linear search because we are dealing with bitmaps. Wide memories (**P4a**) can be used to make these operations quite cheap, even for a large number of rules.

This is because the cost in memory accesses for these bit operations is $N \cdot (K+1)/W$ memory accesses, where W is the width of a memory access. Even with W = 32, this brings down the number of memory accesses by a factor of 32. A specialized hardware classification chip can do much better. Using wide memories and wide buses (the bus width is often the limiting factor), a chip can easily achieve W = 1000 with today's technology. As technology scales, one can expect even larger memory widths.

For example, using W = 1000 and $k = 5$ fields, the number of memory accesses for 5000 rules is $5000 * 6/1000 = 30$. Using 10-nsec SRAM, this allows a rule lookup in 300 nsec, which is sufficient to process minimum-size (40-byte) packets at wire speed on a gigabit link. By using K-fold parallelism, the further factor of $K + 1$ can be removed, allowing 30,000 rules. Of course, even linear search can be parallelized, using N-way parallelism; what matters is the amount of parallelism that can be employed at reasonable cost.

Using our old example, consider a lookup for a packet to M from S with UDP destination port equal to 53 and source port equal to 1029 in the database of Figure 12.3, as represented by Figure 12.12. This packet matches Rules 2, 3, and 8 but must be allowed through because the first matching rule is Rule 2.

Using the bit vector algorithm just described (see Figure 12.12), the longest match in the destination field (i.e., M) yields the bitmap 11110111. The longest match in the source field (i.e., S) yields the bitmap 11110011. The longest match in the destination port field (i.e., 53) yields the bitmap 01100111. The longest match in the source port field (i.e., the wildcard) yields the bitmap 11110111; the longest match in the protocol field (i.e., UDP) yields the bitmap 11111101. The AND of the five bitmaps is 01100001. This bitmap corresponds to matching Rules 2, 3, and 8. The index of the first bit set is 2. This corresponds to the second rule, which is indeed the correct match.

The bit vector algorithm was described in detail in Lakshman and Stidialis [LS98] and also in a few lines in a paper on network monitoring [MJ98]. The first paper [LS98] also describes some trade-offs between search time and memory. A later paper [BV01] shows how to add more state for speed (**P12**) by using summary bits. For every W bits in a bitmap, the summary is the OR of the bits. The main intuition is that if, say, W^2 bits are zero, this can be ascertained by checking W summary bits.

The bit vector scheme is a good one for moderate-size databases. However, since the heart of the algorithm relies on linear search, it cannot scale to both very large databases and very high speeds.

The performance of this scheme can be described as follows.

Assumption: The number of rules will stay reasonably small or will grow only in proportion to increases in bus width and parallelism made possible by technology improvements.

Performance: The number of memory accesses is $N \cdot (K + 1)/W$ plus the number of memory accesses for K longest-matching-prefix or narrowest-range operations. The memory required is that for the K individual field matches (see schemes in Chapter 11) plus

Number	Cross Product					Matching Rule
1	*M, S*, 25, 123, UDP					Rule 1
2	*M, S*, 25, 123, TCP-ACK					Rule 1
3	*M, S*, 25, 123, *default*					Rule 1
4	*M, S*, 25, *default*, UDP					Rule 1
5	*M, S*, 25, *default*, TCP-ACK					Rule 1
6	*M, S*, 25, *default*, *default*					Rule 1
•	•	•	•	•		•
•	•	•	•	•		•
•	•	•	•	•		•
479	*default, default, default, default*, TCP-ACK					Rule 8
480	*default, default, default, default, default*					Rule 8

FIGURE 12.13 A sample of the cross products obtained by cross-producting the individual prefix tables of Figure 12.11.

potentially N^2K bits. Recall that N is the number of rules, K is the number of fields, and W is the width of a memory access. Updating rules is slow and generally requires rebuilding the entire database.

12.10 CROSS-PRODUCTING

This section describes a crude scheme called cross-producting [SVSW98]. In the next section, we describe a crucial refinement we call *equivalenced cross-producting* (but called RFC by the authors [GM99b]) that makes cross-producting more feasible. The top of each column in Figure 12.11 indicates the number of elements in the column. Consider a 5-tuple, formed by taking one value from each column. Call this a *cross product*. Altogether, there are $4 * 4 * 5 * 2 * 3 = 480$ possible cross products. Some sample cross products are shown in Figure 12.13. Considering the destination field to be most significant and the flags field to be least significant, and pretending that values increase down a column, cross products can be ordered from the smallest to the largest, as in any number system.

A key insight into the utility of cross products is as follows.

Given a packet header H, if the longest-matching-prefix operation for each field $H[i]$ is concatenated to form a cross product C, then the least-cost rule matching H is identical to the least-cost rule matching C.

Suppose this were not true. Since each field in C is a prefix of the corresponding field in H, every rule that matches C also matches H. Thus the only case in which H has a different matching rule is if there is some rule R that matches H but not C. This implies that there is some field i such that $R[i]$ is a prefix of $H[i]$ but not of $C[i]$, where $C[i]$ is the contribution of field i to cross product C. But since $C[i]$ is a prefix of $H[i]$, this can happen only if $R[i]$ is longer than $C[i]$. But that contradicts the fact that $C[i]$ is the longest-matching prefix in column/field i.

Thus, the basic cross-producting algorithm [SVSW98] builds a table of all possible cross products and *precomputes* the least-cost rule matching each cross product. This is shown in Figure 12.13. Then, given a packet header, the search algorithm can determine the least-cost matching rule for the packet by performing K longest-matching-prefix operations, together with a single hash lookup of the cross-product table. In hardware, each of the K prefix lookups can be done in parallel.

Using our example, consider matching a packet with header $(M, S, \text{UDP}, 53, 57)$ in the database of Figure 12.3. The cross product obtained by performing best-matching prefixes on individual fields is $(M, S, \text{UDP}, 53, default)$. It is easy to check that the precomputed rule for this cross product is Rule 2 — although Rules 3 and 8 also match the cross product, Rule 2 has the least cost.

The naive cross-producting algorithm suffers from a memory explosion problem: In the worst case, the cross-product table can have N^K entries, where N is the number of rules and K is the number of fields. Thus, even for moderate values, say, $N = 100$ and $K = 5$, the table size can reach 10^{10}, which is prohibitively large.

One idea to reduce memory is to build the cross products on demand (**P2b**, lazy evaluation) [SVSW98]: Instead of building the complete cross-product table at the start, the algorithm incrementally adds entries to the table. The prefix tables for each field are built as before, but the cross-product table is initially empty. When a packet header H arrives, the search algorithm performs a longest-matching prefixes on the individual fields to compute a cross-product term C.

If the cross-product table has an entry for C, then of course the associated rule is returned. However, if there is no entry for C in the cross-product table, the search algorithm finds the best-matching rule for C (possibly using a linear search of the database) and inserts that entry into the cross-product table. Of course, any subsequent packets with cross product C will yield fast lookups.

On-demand cross-producting can improve both the building time of the data structure and its storage cost. In fact, the algorithm can treat the cross-product table as a cache and remove all cross products that have not been used recently. Caching based on cross products can be more effective than full header caching because a single cross product can represent multiple headers (see Exercises). However, a more radical improvement of cross-producting comes from the next idea, which essentially aggregates cross products into a much smaller number of equivalence classes.

12.11 EQUIVALENCED CROSS-PRODUCTING

Gupta and McKeown [GM99b] have invented a scheme called *recursive flow classification* (RFC), which is an improved form of cross-producting that significantly compresses the cross-product table, at a slight extra expense in search time. We prefer to call their scheme *equivalenced cross-producting,* for the following reason. The scheme works by building larger cross products from smaller cross products; the main idea is to place the smaller cross products into equivalence classes before combining them to form larger cross products. This equivalencing of partial cross products considerably reduces memory requirements, because several original cross-product terms map into the same equivalence class.

Recall that in simple cross-producting when a header H arrives, the individual field matches are immediately concatenated to form a cross product that is then looked up in a cross-product table. By contrast, equivalenced cross-producting builds the final cross product in several pairwise combining steps instead of in one fell swoop.

For example, one could form the destination–source cross product and separately form the destination port–source port cross product. Then, a third step can be used to combine these two cross products into a cross product on the first four fields, say, C'. A fourth step is then needed to combine C' with the protocol field to form the final cross product, C. The actual combining sequence is defined by a combining tree, which can be chosen to reduce overall memory.

Just forming the final cross product in several pairwise steps does not reduce memory below N^K. What does reduce memory is the observation that when two partial cross products are combined, many of these pairs are equivalent: Geometrically, they correspond to the same region of space; algebraically, they have the same set of compatible rules.

Thus the main trick is to give each class a class number and to form the larger cross products using the *class numbers* instead of the original matches. Since the algebraic view is easier for computation, we will describe an example of equivalencing using the first two columns of Figure 12.11 under the algebraic view.

Figure 12.14 shows the partial cross products formed by only the destination and source columns in Figure 12.11. For each pair (e.g., M, S) we compute the set of rules that are compatible with such a pair of matches exactly, as in the bit vector linear search scheme. In fact, we can find the bit vector of any pair, such as M, S, by taking the intersection of the rule bitmaps for M and S in Figure 12.12. Thus from Figure 12.12, since the rule bitmap for M is 11110111 and the bitmap for S is 11110011, the intersection bitmap for M, S is 11110011, as shown in Figure 12.14.

Doing this for each possible pair, we soon see that several bitmaps repeat themselves. For example, $M, T0$, and $M, *$ (second and fourth entries in Figure 12.14) have the same bitmap. Two rules that have the same bitmap are assigned to the same equivalence class, and each class is given a class number. Thus in Figure 12.14, the classes are numbered starting with 1; the table-building algorithm increments the class number whenever it encounters a new bitmap. Thus, there are only eight distinct class numbers, compared to 16 possible cross products, because there are only eight distinct bitmaps.

Now assume we combine the two port columns to form six classes from 10 possible cross products. When we combine the port pairs with the destination–source pairs, we combine all possible combinations of the destination–source and port pair class numbers and not the original field matches. Thus after combining all four columns we get $6 * 8 = 48$ cross products. Note that in Figure 12.11, naive cross-producting will form $4 * 4 * 5 * 2 = 160$ cross products from the first four columns. Thus we have saved a factor of nearly 3 in memory.

Of course, we do not stop here. After combining the destination–source and port pair class numbers we equivalence them again using the same technique. When combining class number C with class number C', the bitmap for C, C' is the intersection of the bitmaps for C and C'. Once again pairs with identical bitmaps are equivalenced into groups. After this is done, the

Destination–source prefix pairs	Rule bitmap	Class number
M, S	11110011	C1
M, T0	11010011	C2
M, Net	11010111	C3
M, *	11010011	C2
T1, S	00000011	C4
T1, T0	00001011	C5
T1, Net	00000111	C6
T1, *	00000011	C4
Net, S	00000011	C4
Net, T0	00000011	C4
Net, Net	00000111	C6
Net, *	00000011	C4
*, S	00000001	C7
*, T0	00000001	C7
*, Net	00000100	C8
*, *	00000001	C7

FIGURE 12.14 Forming the partial cross products of the first two columns in Figure 12.11 and then assigning these cross products into the same equivalence class if they have the same rule set (rule bitmap). Notice that 16 partial cross products form only eight classes.

final cross product is formed by combining the classes corresponding to the first four columns with the matches in the fifth column.

Our example combined fields 1 and 2, then fields 3 and 4, and then the first four and finally combined in the fifth (Figure 12.15). Clearly, other pairings are possible, as defined by a binary tree with the fields as nodes and edges representing pairwise combining steps. One could choose the optimal combining tree to reduce memory.

The search process is similar to cross-producting, except the cross products are calculated pairwise (just as they are built) using the same tree. Each pairwise combining uses the two class numbers as input into a table that outputs the class number of the combination. Finally, the class number of the root of the tree is looked up in a table to yield the best-matching rule. Since each class has the same set of matching rules, it is easy to precompute the lowest-cost matching rule for the final classes. Note that the search process does not need to access the rule bitmaps, as is needed for the bit vector linear search scheme. The bitmaps are used only to *build* the structure.

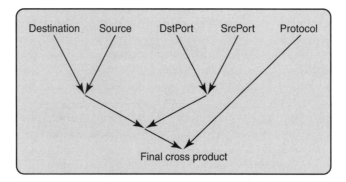

FIGURE 12.15 The combining tree used in the example.

Clearly, each pairwise combining step can take $O(N^2)$ memory because there can be N distinct field values in each field. However, the total memory falls very short of the N^K worst-case memory for real rule databases. To see why this might be the case, we return to the geometric view.

Using a survey of 8000 rule databases, Gupta and McKeown [GM99b] observe that all databases studied have only $O(N)$ classification regions, instead of the N^K worst-case number of classification regions. It is not hard to see that when the number of classification regions is N^K, then the number of cross products in the equivalenced scheme and in the naive scheme is also N^K.

But when the number of classification regions is linear, equivalenced cross-producting can do better. However, it is possible to construct counterexamples where the number of classification regions is linear but equivalenced cross-producting takes exponential memory. Despite such potentially pathological cases, the performance of RFC can be summarized as follows.

Assumption: There is a series of subspaces of the complete rule space (as embodied by nodes in the combining tree) that all have a linear number of classification regions. Note that this is stronger than *O4* and even *O5*. For example, if we combine two fields *i* and *j* first, we require that this intermediate two-dimensional subspace have a linear number of regions.

Performance: The memory required is $O(N^2) * T$, where T is the number of nodes in the combining tree. The sequential performance (in terms of time) is $O(T)$ memory accesses, but the time required in a parallel implementation can be $O(1)$ because the tree can be pipelined. Note that the $O(N^2)$ memory is still very large in practice and would preclude the use of SRAM-based solutions.

12.12 DECISION TREE APPROACHES

This chapter ends with a description of a very simple scheme that performs well in practice, better even than RFC and comparable to or better than the extended grid of tries. This scheme was introduced by Woo [Woo00]. A similar idea, with range tests replacing bit tests, was independently described by Gupta and McKeown [GM99a].

The basic idea is extremely close to the simple set-pruning tries described in Section 12.5.1, with the addition of some important degrees of freedom. Recall that set-pruning tries work one field at a time; thus in Figure 12.8, the algorithm tests *all* the bits for the destination address before testing *all* the bits for the source address. The extension to multiple fields in Decasper et al. [DDPP98] similarly tests all the bits of one field before moving on to another field. The set-pruning trie can be seen as an instance of a general decision tree.

Clearly, an obvious degree of freedom (**P13**) not considered in set-pruning tries is to arbitrarily interleave the bit tests for all fields. Thus the root of the trie could test for (say) bit 15 of the source field; if the bit is 0, this could lead to a node that tests for, say, bit 22 of the port number field. Clearly, there is an exponential number of such decision trees. The schemes in Woo [Woo00] and Gupta and McKeown [GM99a] build the final decision tree using *local optimization* decisions at each node to choose the next bit to test. A simple criterion used in Gupta and McKeown [GM99a] is to balance storage and time.

A second important degree of freedom considered in Woo [Woo00] is to use multiple decision trees. For example, for examples such as Figure 12.6, it may help to place all the rules with wildcards in the source field in one tree and the remainder in a second tree. While this can increase overall search time, it can greatly reduce storage.

A third degree of freedom exploited in both Woo [Woo00] and Gupta and McKeown [GM99a] is to allow a small amount of linear searching after traversing the decision tree. This is similar to the common strategy of using an insert. Consider a decision tree with 10,000 leaves where each leaf is associated with one of four rules. While it may be possible to distinguish these four rules by lengthening the decision tree in height, this lengthened decision tree could add 40,000 extra nodes of storage.

Thus, in balancing storage with time, it may be better to settle for a small amount of linear searching (e.g., among one of four possible rules) at the end of tree search. Intuitively, this can help because the storage of a tree can increase exponentially with its height. Reducing the height by employing some linear search can greatly reduce storage.

The hierarchical cuttings (HiCuts) scheme described in Gupta and McKeown [GM99a] is similar in spirit to that in Woo [Woo00] but uses range checks instead of bit tests at each node of the decision tree. Range checks are slightly more general than bit tests because a range check such as $10 < D < 35$ for a destination address D cannot be emulated by a bit test. A range test (cut) can be viewed geometrically in two dimensions as a line in either dimension that splits the space into half; in general, each range cut is a hyperplane.

In what follows, we describe HiCuts in more detail using an example. The HiCuts local optimization criterion works well when tested on real core router classifiers.

Figure 12.16 shows a fragment of a HiCuts decision tree on the database of Figure 12.3. The nodes contain range comparisons on values of any specified fields, and the edges are labeled **True** or **False**. Thus the root node tests whether the destination port field is less than 50. The fragment follows the case only when this test is false. Notice in Figure 12.3 that this branch eliminates $R1$ (i.e., Rule 1) and $R4$, because these rules contain port numbers 25 and 23, respectively.

The next test checks whether the source address is equal to that of the secondary name server S in Figure 12.3. If this test evaluates to true, then $R5$ is eliminated (because it contains $T0$,), and so is $R6$ (because it contains *Net* and because S does not belong to the internal prefix *Net*). This leads to a second test on the destination port field. If the value is not 53, the only possible rules that can match are $R7$ and $R8$.

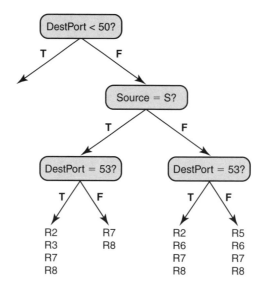

FIGURE 12.16 The HiCuts data structure is essentially a range tree that has pointers corresponding to some ranges of some dimension variable with linear search at the end.

Thus on a packet header in which the destination port is 123 and the source is *S*, the search algorithm takes the right branch at the root, the left branch at the next node, and a right branch at the final node. At this point the packet header is compared to rules *R*7 and *R*8 using linear search. Note that, unlike set pruning trees, the HiCuts decision tree of Figure 12.16 uses ranges, interleaves the range checks between the destination port and source fields, and uses linear searching.

Of course, the real trick is to find a way to build an efficient decision tree that minimizes the worst-case height and yet has reasonable storage. Rather than consider the general optimization problem, which is NP-complete, HiCuts [GM99a] uses a more restricted heuristic based on the repeated application of the following greedy strategy.

- *Pick a field:* The HiCuts paper suggests first picking a field to cut on at each stage based on the number of distinct field values in that field. For example, in Figure 12.16, this heuristic would pick the destination port field.

- *Pick the number of cuts:* For each field, rather than just pick one range check as in Figure 12.16, one can pick *k* ranges or cuts. Of course, these can be implemented as separate range checks, as in Figure 12.16. To choose *k*, the algorithm suggested in Gupta and McKeown [GM99b] is to keep doubling *k* and to stop when the storage caused by the *k* cuts exceeds a prespecified threshold.

Several details are needed to actually implement this somewhat general framework. Assuming the cuts or ranges are equally spaced, the storage cost of *k* cuts on a field is estimated by counting the sum of the rules assigned to each of the *k* cuts. Clearly, cuts that cause rule replication will have a large storage estimate. The threshold that defines acceptable storage is a constant (called *spfac*, for space factor) times the number of rules at the node. The intent is to keep the storage linear in the number of rules up to a tunable constant factor.

Finally, the process stops when all decision tree leaves have no more than *binth* (bin threshold) rules. *binth* controls the amount of linear searching at the end of tree search.

The HiCuts paper [GM99a] mentions the use of the DAG optimization. A more novel optimization, described in Woo [Woo00] and Gupta and McKeown [GM99a], is to eliminate a rule, R, that completely overlaps another rule, R', at a node but has higher cost. There are also several further degrees of freedom (**P13**) left unexplored in Gupta and McKeown [GM99a] and Woo [Woo00]: unequal-size cuts at each node, more sophisticated strategies that pick more than field at a time, and linear searching at nodes other than the leaves.

A more recent paper [BSV03] takes the decision tree approach a step further by allowing the use of several cuts in a single step via multidimensional array indexing. Because each cut is now a general hypercube, the scheme is called *HyperCuts*. HyperCuts appears to work significantly faster than HiCuts on many real databases [BSV03].

In conclusion, the decision tree approach described by Woo [Woo00], Gupta and McKeown [GM99a], and Singh et al. [BSV03] is best viewed as a framework which encompasses a number of potential algorithms. However, experimental evidence [BSV03] shows that this approach works well in practice except on databases that contain a large number of wildcards in one or more fields. The performance of this scheme can be summarized as follows.

Assumption: The scheme assumes there is a sufficient number of distinct fields to make reasonable cuts without much storage replication. This rather general observation needs to be sharpened.

Performance: The memory required can be kept to roughly linear in the number of rules using the HiCuts heuristics. The tree can be of relatively small height if it is reasonably balanced. Search can easily be pipelined to allow $O(1)$ lookup times. Finally, update can be slow if sophisticated heuristics are used to build the decision tree.

12.13 CONCLUSIONS

This chapter describes several algorithms for packet classification at gigabit speeds. The grid of tries provides a two-dimensional classification algorithm that is fast and scalable. All the remaining schemes require exploiting some assumption about real rule databases to avoid the geometric lower bound. While much progress has been made, it is important to reduce the number of such assumptions required for classification and to validate these assumptions extensively.

At the time of writing, decision tree approaches [Woo00, GM99a, SBV04] and the extended grid of tries method [BSV03] appeared to be the most attractive algorithmic schemes. While the latter depends on each packet's matching only a small number of source–destination prefixes, it is still difficult to characterize what assumptions or parameters influence the performance of decision tree approaches.

Of the other general schemes, the bit vector scheme is suitable for hardware implementation for a modest number of rules (say, up to 10,000). Equivalenced cross-producting seems to scale to roughly the same number of rules as the Lucent scheme but perhaps can be improved to lower its memory consumption.

The author and his students have placed code for many of the algorithms described in this chapter on a publicly available Web site [SBV04]. Packet classification has stagnated because of the lack of standard comparisons and freely available code. Readers are encouraged to experiment with and contribute to this code base.

Although the schemes described in this chapter require some algorithmic thinking, they make heavy use of the other principles we have stressed. The two-dimensional scheme makes heavy use of precomputation; the Lucent scheme uses memory locality to turn what is essentially linear search into a fast scheme for moderate rule sizes; all the other schemes rely on some expected-case assumption about the structure of rules, such as the lack of general ranges and the small number of classification regions. Figure 12.1 summarizes the schemes and the principles used in them.

Because best-matching prefix is a special case of lowest-cost matching rule, it is not surprising that rule search schemes are generalizations of prefix search schemes. Thus, the grid of tries and set-pruning tries generalize trie schemes for prefix matching. Multidimensional range-matching schemes generalize prefix-matching schemes based on range matching. Tuple search generalizes binary search on hash tables. While cross-producting is not a generalization of an existing prefix-matching scheme, it can be specialized for prefix lookups as well.

The high-level message of this chapter is as follows. Applications such as QoS routing, firewalls, virtual private networks, and DiffServ will require a more flexible form of forwarding based on multiple header fields. The techniques in this chapter indicate that such forwarding flexibility can go together with high performance using algorithmic solutions without relying on ternary CAMs.

Returning to the quote at the start of this chapter, it should be easy to see how packet classification gets its name if the word *definition* is replaced with *rule*. Notice that classification in the sciences also encompasses overlapping definitions: Men belong to both the mammal and *Homo sapiens* categories. However, it is hard to imagine a biological analog of the concept of a lowest-cost matching rule, or the requirement to classify species several million times a second!

12.14 EXERCISES

1. **Range to Prefix Mappings:** CAMs require the use of prefix ranges, but many rules use general ranges. Describe an algorithm that converts an arbitrary range on, say, 16-bit port number fields to a logarithmic number of prefix ranges. Describe the prefix ranges produced by the arbitrary but common range of greater than 1024. Given a rule R with arbitrary range specifications on port numbers, what is the worst-case number of CAM entries required to represent R? Solutions to this problem are discussed in Refs. SVSW98 and SSV99.

2. **Worst-Case Storage for Set-Pruning Tries:** Generalize the example of Figure 12.6 to K fields to show that storage in set-pruning-trie approaches can be as bad as $O(N^k/k)$.

3. **Improvements to the Grid of Tries:** In the grid of tries, the only role played by the destination trie is in determining the longest-matching destination prefix. Show how to use other lookup techniques to obtain a total search time of $(\log W + W)$ for destination–source rules instead of $2W$.

4. **Aggregate Bit Vector Search:** Use 3-bit summaries in Figure 12.12 and determine the improvement in the worst-case time by adding summaries, and compare it to the

increase in storage for using summaries. Details of the algorithm, if needed, can be found in Baboescu and Varghese [BV01].

5. **Aggregate Bit Vector Storage:** The use of summary bits appears to increase storage. Show, however, a simple modification in which the use of aggregates can reduce storage if the bit vectors contain large strings of zeroes. Describe the modifications to the search process to achieve this compression. Does it slow down search?

6. **On-Demand Cross-Producting:** Consider the database of Figure 12.3, and imagine a series of Web accesses from an internal site to the external network. Suppose the external destinations accessed are $D_1, \ldots, D_M$. How many cache terms will these headers produce in the case of full header caching versus on-demand cross-producting?

7. **Equivalenced Cross-Producting:** Why do the fifth and eighth entries in Figure 12.14 have the same bitmaps? Check your answer two ways, first by intersecting the corresponding bitmaps for the two fields from Figure 12.12 and then by arguing directly that they match the same set of rules.

8. **Combining Trees for RFC:** The equivalenced cross-producting idea in RFC leaves unspecified how to choose a combining tree. One technique is to compute all possible combining trees and then to pick the tree with the smallest storage. Describe an algorithm based on dynamic programming to find the optimal tree. Compare the running times of the two algorithms.

9. **Reducing Rule Databases Using Redundancy:** If a smaller prefix has the same next hop as a longer prefix, the longer prefix can be removed from an IP lookup table. Find similar techniques to spot redundancies in classifiers. Compare your ideas with the techniques described in Gupta and McKeown [GM99b]. Note that as in the case of IP lookups, such techniques to remove redundancy are orthogonal to the classification scheme chosen and can be implemented in a separate preprocessing step.

10. **Generalizing Linear Searching in HiCuts:** In HiCuts, all the linear lists are at the leaves. However, a rule with all wildcarded entries will be replicated at all leaves. This suggests that such rules be placed once in a linear list at the *root* of the HiCuts tree. Generalizing, one could place linear lists at any node to reduce storage. Describe a bottom-up algorithm that starts with the base HiCuts decision tree and then hoists rules to nodes higher up in the tree to reduce storage. Try to do so with minimal impact on the search time.

CHAPTER 13

Switching

I'd rather fight than switch.

— TAREYTON CIGARETTES AD, QUOTED BY *Bartlett's*

In the early years of telephones, the telephone operator helped knit together the social fabric of a community. If John wanted to talk to Martha, John would call the operator and ask for Martha; the operator would then manually plug a wire into a patch panel that connected John's telephone to Martha's. The switchboard, of course, allowed *parallel* connections between disjoint pairs. James could talk to Mary at the same time that John and Martha conversed. However, each new call could be delayed for a small period while the operator finished putting through the previous call.

When transistors were invented at Bell Labs, the fact that each transistor was basically a voltage-controlled switch was immediately exploited to manufacture all-electronic telephone switches using an array of transistors. The telephone operator was then relegated to functions that required human intervention, such as making collect calls. The use of electronics greatly increased the speed and reliability of telephone switches.

A router is basically an automated post office for packets. Recall that we are using the word *router* in a generic sense to refer to a general interconnection device, such as a gateway or a SAN switch. Returning to the familiar model of a router in Figure 13.1, recall that in essence a router is a box that switches packets from input links to output links. The lookup process (**B1** in Figure 13.1), which determines which output link a packet will be switched to, was described in Chapter 11. The packet scheduling done at the outbound link (**B3** in Figure 13.1) is described in Chapter 14. However, the guts of a router remain its internal switching system (**B2** in Figure 13.1), which is discussed in this chapter.

This chapter is organized as follows. Section 13.1 compares router switches to telephone switches. Section 13.2 details the simplicity and limitations of a shared memory switch. Section 13.3 describes router evolution, from shared buses to crossbars. Section 13.4 presents a simple matching algorithm for a crossbar scheduler that was used in DEC's first Gigaswitch product. Section 13.5 describes a fundamental problem with DEC's first Gigaswitch and other input-queued switches, called *head-of-line (HOL) blocking*, which occurs when packets waiting for a busy output delay packets waiting for idle outputs. Section 13.6 covers the knockout switch, which avoids HOL blocking, at the cost of some complexity, by queuing packets at the output.

Section 13.7 presents a randomized matching scheme called PIM, which avoids HOL blocking while retaining the simplicity of input queuing; this scheme was deployed in DEC's

FIGURE 13.1 Router model.

second Gigaswitch product. Section 13.8 describes iSLIP, a scheme that appears to emulate PIM, but without the use of randomization. iSLIP is found in a number of router products, including the Cisco GSR. Since iSLIP works well only for small switches of at most 64 ports, Section 13.9 moves on to cover the use of more scalable switch fabrics. It first describes the Clos fabric, used by Juniper Networks T-series routers to build a 256-port router.

Section 13.9 also introduces the Benes fabric, which can scale to even larger numbers of ports and handles multicast well. A Benes fabric is used in the Washington University WUGS switch. Section 13.10 shows how to scale switches to faster link speeds by using bit-slice parallelism and by using shorter fabric links as implemented in the Avici TSR.

The literature on switching is vast, and this chapter can hardly claim to be representative. I have chosen to focus on switch designs that have been built, analyzed in the literature, and actually used in the networking industry. While these choices clearly reflect the biases and experience of the author, I believe the switches described in this chapter (DEC's Gigaswitch, Cisco's GSR, Juniper's T-series, and Avici's TSR) provide a good first introduction to both the practical and the theoretical issues involved in switch fabrics for high-speed routers. A good review of other, older work in switching can be found in Ahmadi and Denzel [AD89]. A more modern review of architectural choices can be found in Turner and Yamanaka [TY98].

The switching techniques described in this chapter (and the corresponding principles invoked) are summarized in Figure 13.2.

Quick Reference Guide

Most of the switching algorithms described in this chapter have been built. However, for an implementor on a quick first reading, we suggest first reviewing the iSLIP algorithm, which is implemented in the Cisco GSR (Section 13.8). While iSLIP works very well for moderate-size switch fabrics, Section 13.9 describes solutions that scale to large switches, including the Clos fabric used by Juniper Networks and the Benes fabric from Washington University. The Washington University solution is distinguished by its ability to handle multicast well.

Number	Principle	Switch
P5b	Widen memory access for bandwidth	Datapath
P13 P5a	Distribute queue control via tickets Schedule outputs and hunt groups in parallel	Gigaswitch
P11 P15 P3	Optimize for at most $k < N$ output contention Use tree of randomized concentrators for fairness Relax output buffer specification	Knockout
P13 P14 P15	Use per-output input queues N^2 communication feasible for small N Use randomized iterative matching	AN-2
P14 P3	PPEs for round-robin fairness feasible for small N Relax specification of grant-accept dependency	iSLIP
P15 P3b	Use a three-stage Clos network to reduce costs Randomize load distribution to reduce k from $2n$ to n	Juniper T640
P15 P3a P15	Use a (log N)-stage Benes network to reduce costs Use fast randomized routing scheme Use copy-twice multicast and binary tree	Growth fabric
P13	Lay out grid using short wires	Avici TSR

FIGURE 13.2 Principles used in the various switches studied in this chapter.

13.1 ROUTER VERSUS TELEPHONE SWITCHES

Given our initial analogy to telephone switches, it is worthwhile outlining the major similarities and differences between telephone and router switches. Early routers used a simple bus to connect input and output links. A bus (Chapter 2) is a wire that allows only one input to send to one output at a time. Today, however, almost every core router uses an internal crossbar that allows disjoint link pairs to communicate in parallel, to increase effective throughput. Once again, the electronics plays the role of the operator, activating transistor switches that connect input links to output links.

In telephony, a phone connection typically lasts for seconds if not for minutes. However, in Internet switches each connection lasts for the duration of a single packet. This is 8 nsec for a 40-byte packet at 40 Gbps. Recall that caches cannot be relied upon to finesse lookups because of the rarity of large trains of packets to the same destination. Similarly, it is unlikely that two consecutive packets at a switch input port are destined to the same output port. This makes it hard to amortize the switching overhead over multiple packets.

Thus to operate at wire speed, the switching system must decide which input and output links should be matched in a minimum packet arrival time. This makes the control portion of an Internet switch (which sets up connections) much harder to build than a telephone switch. A second important difference between telephone switches and packet switches is the need for packet switches to support *multicast* connections. Multicast complicates the scheduling problem even further because some inputs require sending to multiple outputs.

To simplify the problem, most routers internally segment variable-size packets into fixed-size cells before sending to the switch fabric. Mathematically, the switching component of a router reduces to solving a bipartite matching problem: The router must match as many input links as possible (to as many output links as possible) in a fixed cell arrival time. While optimal algorithms for bipartite matching are well known to run in milliseconds, solving the same problem every 8 nsec at 40 Gbps requires some systems thinking. For example, the solutions described in this chapter will trade accuracy for time (**P3b**), use hardware parallelism (**P5**) and randomization (**P3a**), and exploit the fact that typical switches have 32–64 ports to build fast priority queue operations using bitmaps (**P14**).

13.2 SHARED-MEMORY SWITCHES

Before describing bus- and crossbar-based switches, it is helpful to consider one of the simplest switch implementations, based on shared memory. Packets are read into a memory from the input links and read out of memory to the appropriate output links. Such designs have been used as part of time slot interchange switches in telephony for years. They also work well for networking for small switches.

The main problem is memory bandwidth. If the chip takes in eight input links and has eight output links, the chip must read and write each packet or cell once. Thus the memory has to run at 16 times the speed of each link. Up to a point, this can be solved by using a wide memory access width. The idea is that the bits come in serially on an input link and are accumulated into an input shift register. When a whole cell has been accumulated, the cell can be loaded into the cell-wide memory. Later they can be read out into the output shift register of the corresponding link and be shifted out onto the output link.

The Datapath switch design [Kan99, Kes97] uses a central memory of 4K cells, which clearly does not provide adequate buffering. However, this memory can easily be implemented on-chip and augmented using flow control and off-chip packet buffers. Unfortunately, shared-memory designs such as this do not scale beyond cell-wide memories because minimum-size packets can be at most one cell in size. A switch that gets several minimum-size packets to different destinations can pack several such packets in a single word, but it cannot rely on reading them out at the same time.

Despite this, shared-memory switches can be quite simple for small numbers of ports. A great advantage of shared-memory switches is that they can be memory and power optimal because data is moved in and out of memory only once. Fabric- or crossbar-based switches, which are described in the remainder of this chapter, almost invariably require buffering packets *twice*, potentially doubling memory costs and power costs. It may even be possible to extend the shared-memory idea to larger switches via the randomized DRAM interleaving ideas described in Section 13.10.3.

13.3 ROUTER HISTORY: FROM BUSES TO CROSSBARS

Router switches have evolved from the simplest shared-medium (bus or memory) switches, shown in part A of Figure 13.3, to the more modern crossbar switches, shown in part D of

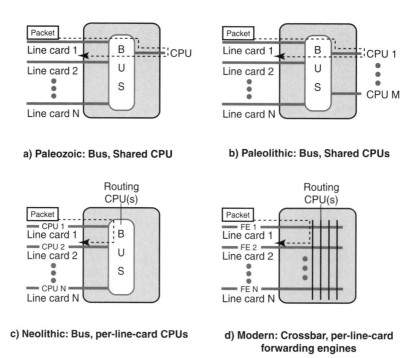

FIGURE 13.3   Evolution of network switches, from shared-bus switches with a shared CPU to crossbar switches with a dedicated forwarding engine per line card. (Adapted from Ref. McK97).

Figure 13.3. A line card in a router or switch contains the interface logic for a data link, such as a fiber-optic line or an Ethernet. The earliest switches connected all the line cards internally via a high-speed bus (analogous to an internal local area network) on which only one pair of line cards can communicate at a time. Thus if Line Card 1 is sending a packet to Line Card 2, no other pair of line cards can communicate.

Worse, in more ancient routers and switches, the forwarding decision was relegated to a shared, general-purpose CPU. General-purpose CPUs allow for simpler and easily changeable forwarding software. However, general-purpose CPUs were often slow because of extra levels of interpretation of general-purpose instructions. They also lacked the ability to control real-time constraints on packet processing because of nondeterminism due to mechanisms such as caches. Note also that each packet traverses the bus twice, once to go to the CPU and once to go from the CPU to the destination. This is because the CPU is on a separate card reachable only via the bus.

Because the CPU was a bottleneck, a natural extension was the addition of a group of shared CPUs for forwarding, any of which can forward a packet. For example, one CPU can forward packets from Line Cards 1 through 3, the second from Line Cards 4 through 6, and so on. This increases the overall throughput or reduces the performance requirement on each individual CPU, potentially leading to a lower-cost design. However, without care it can lead to packet misordering, which is undesirable.

Despite this, the bus remains a bottleneck. A single shared bus has speed limitations because of the number of different sources and destinations that a single shared bus has to handle. These sources and destinations add extra electrical loading that slows down signal rise times and ultimately the speed of sending bits on the bus. Other electrical effects include that of multiple connectors (from each line card) and reflections on the line [McK97].

The classical way to get around this bottleneck is to use a crossbar switch, as shown in Figure 13.3, part d. A crossbar switch essentially has a set of $2N$ parallel buses, one bus per source line card and one bus per destination line card. If one thinks of the source buses as being horizontal and the destination buses as being vertical, the matrix of buses forms what is called a *crossbar*.

Potentially, this provides an N-fold speedup over a single bus, because in the best case all N buses will be used in parallel at the same time to transfer data, instead of a single bus. Of course, to get this speedup requires finding N disjoint source–destination pairs at each time slot. Trying to get close to this bound is the major scheduling problem studied in this chapter.

Although they do not necessarily go together, another design change that accompanied crossbar switches designed between 1995 and 2002 is the use of special-purpose integrated circuits (ASICs) as forwarding engines instead of general-purpose CPUs. These forwarding engines are typically faster (because they are designed specifically to process Internet packets) and cheaper than general-purpose CPUs. Two disadvantages of such forwarding engines include design costs for each such ASIC and the lack of programmability (which makes changes in the field difficult or impossible). These problems have again led to proposals for faster but yet programmable network processors (see Chapter 2).

13.4 THE TAKE-A-TICKET CROSSBAR SCHEDULER

The simplest crossbar is an array of N input buses and N output buses, as shown in Figure 13.4. Thus if line card R wishes to send data to line card S, input bus R must be connected to output bus S. The simplest way to make this connection is via a "pass" transistor, as shown in Figure 13.5. For every pair of input and output buses, such as R and S, there is a transistor that when turned on connects the two buses. Such a connection is known as a *crosspoint*. Notice that a crossbar with N inputs and N outputs has N^2 crosspoints, each of which needs a control line from the scheduler to turn it on or off.

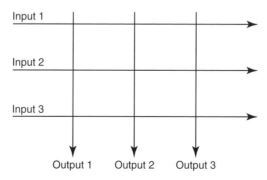

FIGURE 13.4   Basic crossbar switch.

FIGURE 13.5 Connecting input from Line Card R to Line Card S by turning the pass transistor connecting the two buses. Modern crossbars replace this simplistic design by multiplexer trees to reduce capacitance.

While N^2 crosspoints seems large, easy VLSI implementation via transistors makes pin counts, card connector technologies, etc., more limiting factors in building large switches. Thus most routers and switches built before 2002 use simple crossbar-switch backplanes to support 16–32 ports. Notice that multicast is trivially achieved by connecting input bus R to all the output buses that wish to receive from R. However, scheduling multicast is tricky.

In practice, only older crossbar designs use pass transistors. This is because the overall capacitance (Chapter 2) grows very large as the number of ports increases. This in turn increases the delay to send a signal, which becomes an issue at higher speeds. Modern implementations often use large multiplexer trees per output or tristate buffers [All02, Tur02]. Higher-performance systems even pipeline the data flowing through the crossbar using some memory (i.e., a gate) at the crosspoints.

Thus the design of a modern crossbar switch is actually quite tricky and requires careful attention to physical layer considerations. However, crossbar-design issues will be ignored in this chapter in order to concentrate on the algorithmic issues related to switch scheduling. But what should scheduling guarantee?

For correctness, the control logic must ensure that every output bus is connected to at most one input bus (to prevent inputs from mixing). However, for performance, the logic must also maximize the number of line-card pairs that communicate in parallel. While the ideal parallelism is achieved if all N output buses are busy at the same time, in practice parallelism is limited by two factors. First, there may be no data for certain output line cards. Second, two or more input line cards may wish to send data to the same output line card. Since only one input can win at a time, this limits data throughput if the other "losing" input cannot send data.

Thus despite extensive parallelism, the major contention occurs at the output port. How can contention for output ports be resolved while maximizing parallelism? A simple and elegant scheduling scheme for this purpose was first invented and used in DEC's Gigaswitch. An example of the operation of the so-called "take-a-ticket" algorithm [SKO+94] used there is given in Figure 13.6.

The basic idea is that each output line card S essentially maintains a distributed queue for all input line cards R waiting to send to S. The queue for S is actually stored at the input line card itself (instead of being at S) using a simple ticket number mechanism like that at some deli counters. If line card R wants to send a packet to line card S, it first makes a request over a separate control bus to S; S then provides a queue number back to R over the control bus. The queue number is the number of R's position in the output queue for S.

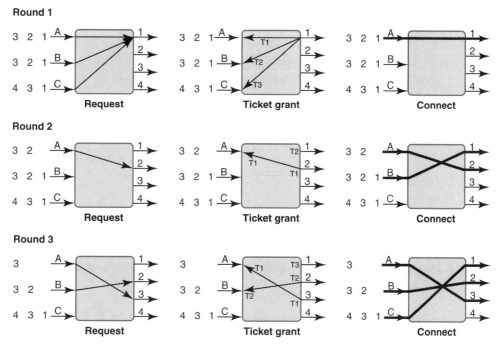

FIGURE 13.6 In the take-a-ticket scheduling mechanism, all input ports have a *single* input queue that is labeled with the output port number to which each packet is destined. Thus in the top frame, inputs *A*, *B*, and *C* send requests to output port 1. Output port 1 (top, middle) gives the first number to *A*, the second to *B*, etc., and these numbers are used to serialize access to output ports.

R then monitors the control bus; whenever *S* finishes accepting a new packet, *S* sends the current queue number it is serving on the control bus. When *R* notices that its number is being "served," *R* places its packet on the input data bus for *R*. At the same time, *S* ensures that the *R–S* crosspoint is turned on.

To see this algorithm in action, consider Figure 13.6, where in the top frame, input line card *A* has three packets destined to outputs 1, 2, and 3, respectively. *B* has three similar packets destined to the same outputs, while *C* has packets destined to outputs 1, 3, and 4. Assume the packets have the same size in this example (though this is not needed for the take-a-ticket algorithm to work).

Each input port works only on the packet at the head of its queue. Thus the algorithm begins with each input sending a request, via a control bus, to the output port to which the packet at the head of its input queue is destined. Thus in the example each input sends a request to output port 1 for permission to send a packet.

In general, a ticket number is a small integer that wraps around and is given out in order of arrival, as in a deli. In this case, assume that *A*'s request arrived first on the serial control bus, followed by *B*, followed by *C*, though the top left picture makes it appear that the requests are sent concurrently. Since output port 1 can service only one packet at a time, it serializes the requests, returning *T*1 to *A*, *T*2 to *B*, and *T*3 to *C*.

Thus in the middle picture of the top row, output port 1 also broadcasts the current ticket number it is serving ($T1$) on another control bus. When A sees it has a matching number for input 1, in the picture on the top right, A then connects its input bus to the output bus of 1 and sends its packet on its input bus. Thus by the end of the topmost row of pictures, A has sent the packet at the head of its input queue to output port 1. Unfortunately, all the other input ports, B and C, are stuck waiting to get a matching ticket number from output port 1.

The second row in Figure 13.6 starts with A sending a request for the packet that is now at the head of its queue to output port 2; A is returned a ticket number, $T1$, for port 2.[1] In the middle picture of the second row, port 1 announces that it is ready for $T2$, and port 2 announces it is ready for ticket $T1$. This results in the rightmost picture of the second row, where A is connected to port 2 and B is connected to port 1 and the corresponding packets are transferred.

The third row of pictures in Figure 13.6 starts similarly with A and B sending a request for ports 3 and 2, respectively. Note that poor C is still stuck waiting for its ticket number, $T3$, which it obtained two iterations ago, to be announced by output port 1. Thus C makes no more requests until the packet at the head of its queue is served. A is returned $T1$ for port 3, and B is returned $T2$ for port 2. Then port 1 broadcasts $T3$ (finally!), port 2 broadcasts $T2$, and port 3 broadcasts $T1$. This results in the final picture of the third row, where the crossbar connects A and 3, B and 2, and C and 1.

The take-a-ticket scheme scales well in control state, requiring only two ($\log_2 N$)-bit counters at each output port to store the current ticket number being served and the highest ticket number dispensed. This allowed the implementation in DEC's Gigaswitch to scale easily to 36 ports [SKO$^+$94], even in the early 1990s, when on-chip memory was limited. The scheme used a distributed scheduler, with each output port's arbitration done by a so-called GPI chip per line card; the GPI chips communicate via a control bus.

The GPI chips have to arbitrate for the (serial) control bus in order to present a request to an output line card and to obtain a queue number. Because the control bus is a broadcast bus, an input port can figure out when its turn comes by observing the service of those who were before it, and it can then instruct the crossbar to make a connection.

Besides small control state, the take-a-ticket scheme has the advantage of being able to handle variable-size packets directly. Output ports can asynchronously broadcast the next ticket number when they finish receiving the current packet; different output ports can broadcast their current ticket numbers at arbitrary times. Thus, unlike all the other schemes described later, there is no header and control overhead to break up packets into "cells" and then do later reassembly. On the other hand, take-a-ticket has limited parallelism because of *head-of-line blocking*, a phenomenon we look at in the next section.

The take-a-ticket scheme also allows a nice feature called *hunt groups*. Any set of line cards (not just physically contiguous line cards) can be aggregated to form an effectively higher-bandwidth link called a *hunt group*. Thus three 100-Mbps links can be aggregated to look like a 300-Mbps link.

The hunt group idea requires only small modifications to the original scheduling algorithm because each of the GPI chips in the group can observe each other's messages on the control bus and thus keep local copies of the (common) ticket number consistent. The next packet

---

[1] Although not shown in the pictures, a ticket should really be considered a pair of numbers, a ticket number and the output port number, so the same ticket number used at different output ports should cause no confusion at input ports.

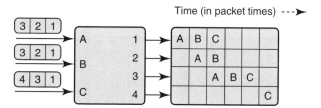

FIGURE 13.7 Example of head-of-line blocking caused by schemes like take-a-ticket. For each output port, a horizontal time scale is drawn labeled with the input port that sent a packet to that output port during the corresponding time period or a blank mark if there is none. Note the large number of blanks, showing potentially wasted opportunities that limit parallelism.

destined to the group is served by the first free output port in the hunt group, much as in a delicatessen with multiple servers. While basic hunt groups can cause reordering of packets sent to different links, a small modification allows packets from one input to be sent to only one output port in a hunt group via a simple deterministic hash. This modification avoids reordering, at the cost of reduced parallelism.

Since the Gigaswitch was a bridge, it had to handle LAN multicast. Because the take-a-ticket scheduling mechanism uses distributed scheduling via separate GPI chips per output, it is hard to coordinate all schedulers to ensure that every output port is free. Further, waiting for all ports to have a free ticket for a multicast packet would result in blocking some ports that were ready to service the packet early, wasting throughput. Hence multicast was handled by a central processor in software and was thus accorded "second-class" status.

13.5 HEAD-OF-LINE BLOCKING

Forgetting about the internal mechanics of Figure 13.6, observe that there were nine potential transmission opportunities in three iterations (three input ports and three iterations); but after the end of the picture in the bottom right, there is one packet in B's queue and two in C's queue. Thus only six of potentially nine packets have been sent, thereby taking limited advantage of parallelism.

This focus on only input–output behavior is sketched in Figure 13.7. The figure shows the packets sent in each packet time at each output port. Each output port has an associated time line labeled with the input port that sent a packet during the corresponding time period, with a blank if there is none. Note also that this picture continues the example started in Figure 13.6 for three more iterations, until all input queues are empty.

It is easy to see visually from the right of Figure 13.7 that only roughly half of the transmission opportunities (more precisely, 9 out of 24) are used. Now, of course, no algorithm can do better for certain scenarios. However, other algorithms, such as iSLIP (see Figure 13.11 in Section 13.8) can extract more parallel opportunities and finish the same nine packets in four iterations instead of six.

In the first iteration of Figure 13.7, all inputs have packets waiting for output 1. Since only one (i.e., A) can send a packet to output 1 at a time, the entire queue at B (and C) is stuck waiting for A to complete. Since the entire queue is held hostage by the progress of the head of the queue, or line, this is called *head-of-line* (HOL) blocking. iSLIP and PIM get around this limitation by allowing packets behind a blocked packet to make progress (for example, the packet destined for output port 2 in the input queue at B can be sent to output port 2 in iteration 1 of Figure 13.7) at the cost of a more complex scheduling algorithm.

The loss of throughput caused by HOL blocking can be analytically captured using a simple uniform-traffic model. Assume that the head of each input queue has a packet destined for each of N outputs with probability $1/N$. Thus if two or more input ports send to the same output port, all but one input are blocked. The entire throughput of the other inputs is "lost" due to head-of-line blocking.

More precisely, assume equal-size packets and one initial trial where a random process draws a destination port at each input port uniformly from 1 to N. Instead of focusing on input ports, let us focus on the probability that an output port O is idle. This is simply the probability that *none* of the N input ports chooses O. Since each input port does not choose O with probability $1 - 1/N$, the probability that all N of them will not choose O is $(1 - 1/N)^N$. This expression rapidly converges to $1/e$. Thus the probability that O is busy is $1 - 1/e$, which is 0.63. Thus the throughput of the switch is not $N * B$, which is what it could be ideally if all N output links are busy operating at B bits per second. Instead, it is 63% of this maximum value, because 37% of the links are idle.

This analysis is simplistic and (incorrectly) assumes that each iteration is independent. In reality, packets picked in one iteration that are not sent must be attempted in the next iteration (without another random coin toss to select the destination). A classic analysis [KHM87] that removes the independent-trials assumption shows that the actual utilization is slightly worse and is closer to 58%.

But are uniform-traffic distributions realistic? Clearly, the analysis is very dependent on the traffic distribution because no switch can do well if all traffic is destined to one server port. Simple analyses show that the effect of head-of-line blocking can be reduced by using hunt groups, by using speedup in the crossbar fabric compared to the links, and by assuming more realistic distributions in which a number of clients send traffic to a few servers.

However, it should be clear that there do exist distributions where head-of-line blocking can cause great damage to throughput. Imagine that every input link has B packets to port 1, followed by B packets to port 2, and so on, and finally B packets to port N. The same distribution of input packets is present in all input ports. Thus clearly, when scheduling the group of initial packets to port 1, essentially head-of-line blocking will limit the switch to sending only one packet per input each time. Thus the switch reduces to $1/N$ of its possible throughput if B is large enough. On the other hand, we will see that switches that use virtual output queues (VOQs) (defined later in this chapter) can, in the same situations, achieve nearly 100% throughput. This is because in such schemes each block of B packets stays in separate queues at each input.

13.6 AVOIDING HEAD-OF-LINE BLOCKING VIA OUTPUT QUEUING

When HOL blocking was discovered, there was a slew of papers that proposed *output* queuing in place of *input* queuing to avoid HOL blocking. Suppose that packets can somehow be sent to an output port without any queuing at the input. Then it is impossible for packet P destined for a busy output port to block another packet behind it. This is because packet P is sent off to the queue at the output port, where it can only block packets sent to the same output port.

The simplest way to do this would be to run the fabric N times faster than the input links. Then even if all N inputs send to the same output in a given cell time, all N cells can be sent through the fabric to be queued at the output. Thus pure output queuing requires an N-fold speedup within the fabric. This can be expensive or infeasible.

A practical implementation of output queuing was provided by the knockout [YHA87] switch design. Suppose that receiving N cells to the same destination in any cell time is rare and that the expected number is k, which is much smaller than N. Then the expected case can be optimized (**P11**) by designing the fabric links to run k times as fast as an input link, instead of N. This is a big savings within the fabric. It can be realized with hardware parallelism (**P5**) by using k parallel buses.

Unlike the take-a-ticket scheme, all the remaining schemes in this chapter, including the knockout scheme, rely on breaking up packets into fixed-size cells. For the rest of the chapter, cells will be used in place of packets, always understanding that there must be an initial stage where packets are broken into cells and then reassembled at the output port.

Besides a faster switch, the knockout scheme needs an output queue that accepts cells k times faster than the speed of the output link. A naive design that uses this simple specification can be built using a fast FIFO but would be expensive. Also, the faster FIFO is overkill, because clearly the buffer cannot sustain a long-term imbalance between its input and output speeds. Thus the buffer specification can be relaxed (**P3**) to allow it to handle only short periods, in which cells arrive k times as fast as they are being taken out. This can be handled by memory interleaving and k parallel memories. A distributor (that does run k times as fast) sprays arriving cells into k memories in round-robin order, and departing cells are read out in the same order.

Finally, the design has to fairly handle the case where the expected case is violated and $N > k$ cells get sent to the same output at the same time. The easiest way to understand the general solution is first to understand three simpler cases.

Two contenders, one winner: In the simplest case of $k = 1$ and $N = 2$, the arbiter must choose one cell fairly from two choices. This can be done by building a primitive 2-by-2 switching element, called a *concentrator*, that randomly picks a winner and a loser. The winner output is the cell that is chosen. The loser output is useful for the general case, in which several primitive 2-by-2 concentrators are combined.

Many contenders, one winner: Now consider when $k = 1$ (only one cell can be accepted) and $N > 2$ (there are more than two cells that the arbiter must choose fairly from). A simple strategy uses divide-and-conquer (**P15**, efficient data structures) to create a *knockout tree* of 2-by-2 concentrators. As in the first round of a tennis tournament, the cells are paired up using $N/2$ copies of the basic 2-by-2 concentrator, each representing a tennis match. This forms the bottom level of the tree. The winners of the first round are sent to a second round of $N/4$ concentrators, and so on. The "tournament" ends with a final, in which the root concentrator chooses a winner. Notice that the loser outputs of each concentrator are still ignored.

Many contenders, more than one winner: Finally, consider the general case where k cells must be chosen from N possible cells, for arbitrary values of k and N. A simple idea is to create k separate knockout trees to calculate the first k winners. However, to be fair, the losers of knockout trees for earlier trees have to be sent to the knockout trees for the subsequent places. This is why the basic 2-by-2 knockout concentrator has two outputs, one for the winner and one for the loser, and not just one for the winner. Loser outputs are routed to the trees for later positions.

Notice that if one had to choose four cells among eight choices, the simplest design would assign the eight choices (in pairs) to four 2-by-2 knockout concentrators. This logic will pick four winners, the desired quantity. While this logic is certainly much simpler than using four separate knockout trees, it can be very unfair. For example, suppose two very heavy traffic sources, $S1$ and $S2$, happen to be paired up, while another heavy source, $S3$, is paired up with a light source. In this case $S1$ and $S2$ would get roughly half the traffic that $S3$ obtains. It is to avoid these devious examples of unfairness that the knockout logic uses k separate trees, one for each position.

The naive way to implement the trees is to *begin* running the logic for the Position j tree strictly after all the logic for the Position $j - 1$ tree has *completed*. This ensures that all eligible losers have been collected. A faster implementation trick is explored in the exercises. Hopefully, this design should convince you that fairness is hard to implement correctly. This is a theme that will be explored again in the discussion of iSLIP.

While the knockout switch is important to understand because of the techniques it introduced, it is complex to implement and makes assumptions about traffic distributions. These assumptions are untrue for real topologies in which more than k clients frequently gang up to concurrently send to a popular server. More importantly, researchers devised relatively simple ways to combat HOL blocking *without* going to output queuing.

13.7 AVOIDING HEAD-OF-LINE BLOCKING BY USING PARALLEL ITERATIVE MATCHING

The main idea behind parallel iterative matching (PIM) [AOST93] is to reconsider input queuing but to retrofit it to avoid head-of-line blocking. It does so by allowing an input port to schedule not just the head of its input queue, but also other cells, which can make progress when the head is blocked. At first glance, this looks very hard. There could be a hundred thousand cells in each queue; attempting to maintain even 1 bit of scheduling state for each cell will take too much memory to store and process.

However, the first significant observation is that cells in each input port queue can be destined for only N possible output ports. Suppose cell $P1$ is before cell $P2$ in input queue X and that both $P1$ and $P2$ are destined for the same output queue Y. Then to preserve FIFO behavior, $P1$ must be scheduled before $P2$ anyway. Thus there is no point in attempting to schedule $P2$ before $P1$ is done. Thus obvious waste can be avoided (**P1**) by not scheduling any cells *other than the first cell sent to every distinct output port*.

Thus the first step is to exploit a degree of freedom (**P13**) and to decompose the single input queue of Figure 13.6 into *a separate input queue per output* at each input port in Figure 13.8. These are called *virtual output queues* (VOQs). Notice that the top left picture of Figure 13.8 contains the same input cells as in Figure 13.7, except now they are placed in separate queues.

The second significant observation is that communicating the scheduling needs of any input port takes a bitmap of only N bits, where N is the size of the switch. In the bitmap, a 1 in position i implies that there is at least one cell destined to output port i. Thus if each of N input ports communicates an N-bit vector describing its scheduling needs, the scheduler needs to process only N^2 bits. For small $N \leq 32$, this is not many bits to communicate via control buses or to store in control memories.

The communicating of requests is indicated in the top left picture of Figure 13.8 by showing a line sent from each input port to each output port for which it has a nonempty VOQ. Notice A

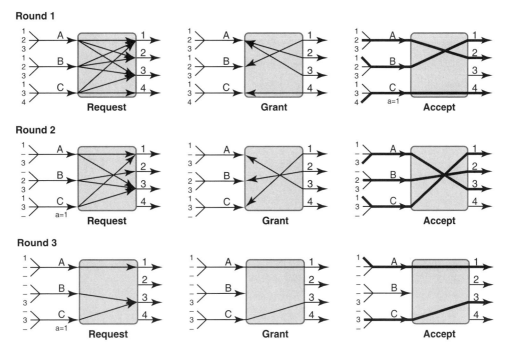

FIGURE 13.8 The parallel iterative matching (PIM) scheme works by having all inputs send requests in *parallel* to all outputs they wish to reach. PIM then uses randomization to do fair matching such that outputs that receive multiple requests pick a random input, and inputs that receive multiple grants randomly pick an output to send to. This three-round process can then be iterated to *improve* the size of the matching.

does not have a line to port 4 because it has no cell for port 4. Notice also that input port C sends a request for the cell destined for output port 4 in input port C, while the same cell is the last cell in input queue C in the single-input-queue scenario of Figure 13.6.

What is still required is a scheduling algorithm that matches resources to needs. Although the scheduling algorithm is clever, in the author's opinion the real breakthrough was observing that, using VOQs, input queue scheduling without HOL blocking is feasible to think about. To keep the example in Figure 13.8 corresponding to Figure 13.6, assume that every packet in the scenario of Figure 13.6 is converted into a single cell in Figure 13.8.

To motivate the scheduling algorithm used in PIM, observe that in the top left of Figure 13.8, output port 1 gets three requests from A, B, and C but can service only one in the next slot. A simple way to choose between requests is to choose randomly (**P3a**). Thus in the *Grant* phase (top middle of Figure 13.8), output port 1 chooses B randomly. Similarly, assume that port 2 randomly chooses A (from A and B), and port 3 randomly chooses A (from A, B, and C). Finally, port 4 chooses its only requester, C.

However, resolving output-port contention is insufficient because there is also input-port contention. Two output ports can randomly grant to the same input port, which must choose exactly one to send a cell to. For example, in the top middle of Figure 13.8, A has an embarrassment of riches by getting grants from outputs 2 and 3. Thus a third, *Accept*, phase is necessary, in which each input port chooses an output port randomly (since randomization was used in the Grant phase, why not use it again?).

Thus in the top right picture of Figure 13.8, *A* randomly chooses port 2. *B* and *C* have no choice and choose ports 1 and 4, respectively. Crossbar connections are made, and the packets from *A* to port 2, *B* to port 1, and *C* to to Port 4 are transferred. While in this case, the corresponding match found was a maximal match (i.e., cannot be improved), in some cases the random choices may result in a match that can be improved further. For example, in the unlikely event that ports 1, 2, and 3 all choose *A*, the match size will only be of size 2.

In such cases, although not shown it in the figure, it may be worthwhile for the algorithm to mask out all matched inputs and outputs and iterate more times (for the same forthcoming time slot). If the match on the current iteration is not maximal, a further iteration will improve the size of the match by at least 1. Note that subsequent iterations cannot worsen the match because existing matches are preserved across iterations. While the worst-case time to reach a maximal match for *N* inputs is *N* iterations, a simple argument shows that the expected number of matches is closer to log *N*. The DEC AN-2 implementation [AOST93] used three iterations for a 30-port switch.

Our example in Figure 13.8, however, uses only one iteration for each match. The middle row shows the second match for the second cell time, in which, for example, *A* and *C* both ask for port 1 (but not *B*, because the *B*-to-1 cell was sent in the last cell time). Port 1 randomly chooses *C*, and the final match is *A*, 3, *B*, 2, and *C*, 1. The third row shows the third match, this time of size 2. At the end of the third match, only the cell destined to port 3 in input queue *B* is not sent. Thus in four cell times (of which the fourth cell time is sparsely used and could have been used to send more traffic) all the traffic is sent. This is clearly more efficient than the take-a-ticket example of Figure 13.6.

13.8 AVOIDING RANDOMIZATION WITH iSLIP

Parallel iterative matching was a seminal scheme because it introduced the idea that HOL could be avoided at reasonable hardware cost. Once that was done, just as was the case when Roger Bannister first ran the mile in under 4 minutes, others could make further improvements. But PIM has two potential problems. First, it uses randomization, and it may be hard to produce a reasonable source of random numbers at very high speeds.[2] Second, it requires a logarithmic number of iterations to attain maximal matches. Given that each of a logarithmic number of iterations takes three phases and that the entire matching decision must be made within a minimum packet arrival time, it would be better to have a matching scheme that comes close to maximal matches in just one or two iterations.

iSLIP is a very popular and influential scheme that essentially "derandomizes" PIM and also achieves very close to maximal matches after just one or two iterations. The basic idea is extremely simple. When an input port or an output port in PIM experiences multiple requests, it chooses a "winning" request uniformly at random, for the sake of fairness. Whereas Ethernet

---

[2]One can argue that schemes like RED require randomness anyway at routers. However, a poor-quality source of random numbers in an RED implementation will be less noticed than poor-quality random numbers within a switch fabric.

provides fairness with randomness, token rings do so using a round-robin pointer implemented by a rotating token.

Similarly, iSLIP provides fairness by choosing the next winner among multiple contenders in round-robin fashion using a rotating pointer. While the round-robin pointers can be initially synchronized and cause something akin to head-of-line blocking, they tend to break free and result in maximal matches over the long run, at least as measured in simulation. Thus the subtlety in iSLIP is not the use of round-robin pointers but the apparent lack of long-term synchronization among N such pointers running concurrently.

More precisely, each output (respectively input) maintains a pointer g initially set to the first input (respectively output) port. When an output has to choose between multiple input requests, it chooses the lowest input number that is equal to or greater than g. Similarly, when an input port has to choose between multiple output-port requests, it chooses the lowest output-port number that is equal to or greater than a, where a is the pointer of the input port. If an output port is matched to an input port X, then the output-port pointer is incremented to the first port number greater than X in circular order (i.e., g becomes $X + 1$, unless X was the last port, in which case g wraps around to the first port number).

This simple device of a "rotating priority" allows each resource (output port, input port) to be shared reasonably fairly across all contenders at the cost of $2N$ extra $\log_2 N$ pointers in addition to the N^2 scheduling state needed on every iteration.

Figures 13.9 and 13.10 show the same scenario as in Figure 13.8 (and Figure 13.6), but using a two-iteration iSLIP. Since each row is an iteration of a match, each match is shown using two rows. Thus the three rows of Figure 13.9 show the first 1.5 matches of the scenario. Similarly, Figure 13.10 shows the remaining 1.5 matches.

The upper left picture of Figure 13.9 is identical to Figure 13.8, in that each input port sends requests to each output port for which it has a cell destined. However, one difference is that each output port has a so-called *grant* pointer g, which is initialized for all outputs to be A. Similarly, each input has a so-called *accept* pointer called a, which is initialized for all inputs to 1.

The determinism of iSLIP causes a divergence right away in the Grant phase. Compare the upper middle of Figure 13.9 with the upper middle of Figure 13.8. For example, when output 1 receives requests from all three input ports, it grants to A because A is the smallest input greater than or equal to $g_1 = A$. By contrast, in Figure 13.8, port 1 randomly chose input port B. At this stage the determinism of iSLIP seems a real disadvantage because A has sent requests to output ports 3 and 4 as well. Because 3 and 4 also have grant pointers $g_3 = g_4 = A$, ports 3 and 4 grant to A as well, ignoring the claims of B and C. As before, since C is the lone requester for port 4, C gets the grant from 4.

When the popular A gets three grants back from ports 1, 2, and 3, A accepts 1. This is because port 1 is the first output equal to greater than A's accept pointer, a_A, which was equal to 1. Similarly C chooses 4. Having done so, A increments a_A to 2 and C increments a_C to 1 (1 greater than 4 in circular order is 1). Only at this stage does output 1 increment its grant pointer, g_1, to B (1 greater than the last successful grant) and port 4 similarly increments to A (1 greater than C in circular order).

Note that although ports 2 and 3 gave grants to A, they do not increment their grant pointers because A spurned their grants. If they did, it would be possible to construct a scenario where output ports keep incrementing their grant pointer beyond some input port I after unsuccessful grants, thereby continually starving input port I. Note also that the match is only of size 2;

Round 1, Iteration 1

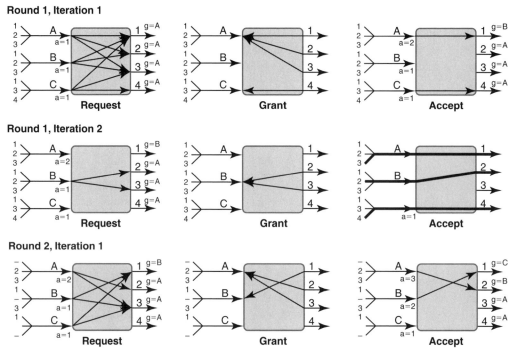

FIGURE 13.9 One and a half rounds of a sample iSLIP scenario.

thus, unlike Figure 13.8, this iSLIP scenario can be improved by a second iteration, shown in the second row of Figure 13.9. Notice that at the end of the first iteration the matched inputs and outputs are not connected by solid lines (denoting data transfer), as shown at the top right of Figure 13.8. This data transfer will await the end of the final (in this case second) iteration.

The second iteration (middle row of Figure 13.9) starts with only inputs unmatched on previous iterations (i.e, *B*) requesting and only to hitherto unmatched outputs. Thus *B* requests to 2 and 3 (and not to 1, though *B* has a cell destined for 1 as well). Both 2 and 3 grant *B*, and *B* chooses 2 (the lowest one that is greater than or equal to its accept pointer of 1). One might think that *B* should increment its accept pointer to 3 (1 plus the last accepted, which was 2). However, to avoid starvation iSLIP *does not* increment pointers on iterations other than the first, for reasons that will be explained.

Thus even after *B* is connected to 2, 2's grant pointer remains at *A* and 2's accept pointer remains at 1. Since this is the final iteration, all matched pairs, including pairs, such as *A*, 1, matched in prior iterations, are all connected and data transfer (solid lines) occurs.

The third row provides some insight into how the initial synchronization of grant and accept pointers gets broken. Because only one output port has granted to *A*, that port (i.e., 1) gets to move on and this time to provide priority to ports beyond *A*. Thus even if *A* had a second packet destined for 1 (which it does not in this example), 1 would still grant to *B*.

The remaining rows in Figure 13.9 and Figure 13.10 should be examined carefully by the reader to check for the updating rules for the grant and accept pointers and to check which

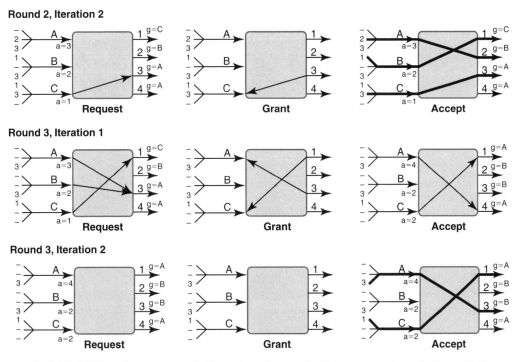

FIGURE 13.10   Last one and a half rounds of the sample iSLIP scenario shown in Figure 13.9.

packets are switched at each round. The bottom line is that by the end of the third row of Figure 13.10 the only cell that remains to be switched is the cell from *B* to 3. This can clearly be done in a fourth cell time.

Figure 13.11 shows a summary of the final scheduling (abstracting away from internal mechanics) of the iSLIP scenario and should be compared in terms of scheduling density with Figure 13.7. While these are just isolated examples, they do suggest that iSLIP (and similarly PIM) tends to waste fewer slots by avoiding head-of-line blocking. Note that both iSLIP and PIM finish the same input backlog in four cell times, as opposed to six.

Note also that when we compare Figure 13.9 with Figure 13.8, iSLIP looks worse than PIM, because it required two iterations per match for iSLIP to achieve the same match sizes

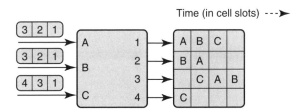

FIGURE 13.11   How iSLIP avoids HOL blocking to increase throughput in the scenario of Figure 13.7.

as PIM does using one iteration per match. However, this is more illustrative of the startup penalty that iSLIP pays rather than a long-term penalty. In practice, as soon as the iSLIP pointers desynchronize, iSLIP does very well with just one iteration, and some commercial implementations use just one iteration: iSLIP is extremely popular.

One might summarize iSLIP as PIM with the randomization replaced by round-robin scheduling of input and output pointers. However, this characterization misses two subtle aspects of iSLIP.

- **Grant pointers are incremented only in the third phase, after a grant is accepted:** Intuitively, if O grants to an input port I, there is no guarantee that I will accept. Thus if O were to increment its grant pointer beyond O, it can cause traffic from I to O to be persistently starved. Even worse, McKeown et al. [Mea97] show that this simplistic round-robin scheme reduces the throughput to just 63% (for Bernoulli arrivals) because the pointers tend to synchronize and move in lockstep.

- **All pointers are incremented only after the first iteration accept is granted:** Once again, this rule prevents starvation, but the scenario is more subtle, which the Exercises will ask you to figure out.

Thus matches on iterations other than the first in iSLIP are considered a "bonus" that boosts throughput without being counted against a port's quota.

13.8.1 Extending iSLIP to Multicast and Priority

iSLIP can be extended to handle priorities and multicast traffic.

PRIORITIES

Priorities are useful to send mission-critical or real-time traffic more quickly through the fabric. For example, the Cisco GSR allows voice-over-IP traffic, to be scheduled at a higher priority than other traffic, because it is rate limited and hence cannot starve other traffic.

The Tiny Tera implementation handles four levels of priorities; thus each input port has 128 VOQs (one for each combination of 32 outputs and four priority levels). Thus each input port supplies to the scheduler 128 bits of control input.

The iSLIP algorithm is modified very simply to handle priorities. First, each output port keeps a separate grant pointer g^k for priority level k, and each input port keeps a separate accept pointer a^k for each priority level k. In essence, the iSLIP algorithm is performed, with each entity (input port, output port) performing the iSLIP algorithm on the highest-priority level among inputs it sees.[3]

More precisely, each output port grants for only the highest-priority requests it receives; similarly, each input port accepts only the highest-priority grant it receives. Notice that an input port I may make a request at priority level 1 for output 5 and a request at priority level 2 for output 6 because these are the highest-priority requests the port had for outputs 5 and 6. If both outputs 5 and 6 grant to I, I does not choose between them based on accept pointers because they are at different priorities; instead I chooses the highest-priority grant. On an accept in the

---

[3]Note that attempting to share the same pointer for all priority levels can cause low-priority traffic from input I to output J to be starved in the face of a combination of high-priority traffic from I to J together with other low-priority traffic to J.

first iteration for priority k between input I and output port O, the priority-k accept pointer at I and the priority-k grant pointer at O are incremented.

MULTICAST

Because of applications such as video conferencing and protocols such as IP multicast, in which routers replicate packets to more than one output port, supporting multicast in switches as a first-class entity is becoming important. Recall that the take-a-ticket scheme described earlier handled multicast as a second-class entity by sending all multicast traffic to a central entity (or entities) that then sent the multicast traffic on a packet-by-packet basis to the corresponding outputs. The take-a-ticket mechanism wastes switch resources (control bandwidth, ports) and provides lower performance (larger latency, less throughput) for multicast.

On the other hand, Figure 13.4 shows that the data path of a simple crossbar switch easily supports multicasting. For example, if Input 1 in Figure 13.4 sends a message on its input bus and the crosspoints are connected so that Input 1's bus is connected to the vertical output buses of Outputs 2 and 3, then Outputs 2 and 3 receive a copy of the packet (cell) at the same time. However, with variable-size packets, the take-a-ticket distributed-control mechanism must choose between waiting for all ports to free up at the same time and sending packets one by one.

The iSLIP extension for multicast, called ESLIP, accords multicast almost the same status as unicast. Ignoring priorities for the moment, there is one additional multicast queue per input. While to avoid HOL blocking one would ideally like a separate queue for each possible subset of output ports, that would require an impractical number of queues (2^{16} for 16 ports). Thus multicast uses only one queue and, as such, is subject to some HOL blocking because a multicast packet cannot begin to be processed unless the multicast packets ahead of it are sent.

Suppose input I has packets for outputs $O1$, $O2$, and $O3$ at the head of I's multicast queue. I is said to have a fanout of 3. Unlike in the unicast case, ESLIP maintains only a shared multicast grant pointer and no multicast accept pointer at all, as opposed to separate grant and accept pointers per port. Note that the use of a shared pointer implies a centralized implementation, unlike the take-a-ticket scheduler. As shown later, the shared pointer allows the entire switch to favor a particular input so that it can complete its fanout completely rather than have several input ports send small portions of their multicast fanout at the same time.

Thus in the example I will send a *multicast* request to $O1$, $O2$, and $O3$. But output ports like $O2$ may also receive unicast requests from other input ports, such as J. How should an output port balance between multicast and unicast packets? ESLIP does so by giving multicast and unicast traffic higher priority in alternate cell slots. For example, in odd slots $O2$ may choose unicast over multicast, and vice versa in even slots.

To continue our example, assume an odd time slot and assume that $O2$ has unicast traffic requests while $O1$ and $O3$ have no unicast requests. Then $O2$ will send a unicast grant, while $O1$ and $O3$ will send multicast grants. $O1$ and $O3$ choose the input to grant to as the first port greater than or equal to the current shared multicast grant pointer, G. Assume that I is chosen, and so $O2$ and $O3$ send multicast grants to I. Unlike unicast, I can accept all its multicast grants.

However, unlike unicast scheduling, the grant pointer for multicast is not incremented to 1 past I until I completes its fanout. Thus on the next cell slot, when the priority is given to multicast, I will be able to transmit to $O2$. At that point, the fanout is completed, the multicast grant pointer increments to $I + 1$, and the scheduler sends back a bit to I saying that the head of its multicast queue has finished transmission so the next multicast packet can be worked on. Notice that a single multicast is not necessarily completed in a single cell slot (which would require all concerned outputs to be free), but by using *fanout splitting* across several slots.

Clearly, iSLIP can incur HOL blocking for multicast. Specifically, if the head of the multicast queue $P1$ is destined for outputs $O1$ and $O2$ and both outputs are busy, but the next packet $P2$ is destined for $O3$ and $O4$ and both are idle, $P2$ must wait for $P1$. It would be much more difficult to implement fanout splitting for packets other than the head of the queue. Once again, this is because one cannot afford to keep a separate VOQ for each possible combination of output-port destinations.

The final ESLIP algorithm, which combines four levels of priority as well as multicasting, is described somewhat tersely in McKeown [McK97]. It is implemented in Cisco's GSR router.

13.8.2 iSLIP Implementation Notes

The heart of the hardware implementation of iSLIP is an arbiter that chooses between N requests (encoded as a bitmap) to find the first one greater than or equal to a fixed pointer. This is what in Chapter 2 is called a *programmable priority encoder*; that chapter also described an efficient implementation that is nearly as fast as a priority encoder. Switch scheduling can be done by one such grant arbiter for every output port (to arbitrate requests) and one accept arbiter for every input port (to arbitrate between grants). Priorities and multicast are retrofitted into the basic structure by adding a filter on the inputs before it reaches the arbiter; for example, a priority filter zeroes out all requests except those at the highest-priority level.

Although in principle the unicast schedulers can be designed using a separate chip per port, the state is sufficiently small to be handled by a single scheduler chip with control wires coming in from and going to each of the ports. Also, the multicast algorithm requires a shared multicast pointer per priority level, which also implies a centralized scheduler. Centralization, however, implies a delay, or latency, to send requests and decisions from the port line cards to and from the central scheduler.

To tolerate this latency, the scheduler [GM99a] works on a pipeline of m cells (8 in Tiny Tera) from each VOQ and n cells (5 in Tiny Tera) from each multicast queue. This in turn implies that each line card in the Tiny Tera must communicate 3 bits per unicast VOQ denoting the size of the VOQ, up to a maximum of 8. With 32 outputs and four priority levels, each input port has to send 384 bits of unicast information. Each line card also communicates the fanout (32 bits per fanout) for each of five multicast packets in each of four priority levels, leading to 640 bits. The $32 * 1024$ total bits of input information is stored in on-chip SRAM. However, for speed the information about the heads of each queue (smaller state, for example, only 1 bit per unicast VOQ) is stored in faster but less dense flip-flops.

Now consider handling multiple iterations. Note that the request phase occurs only on the first iteration and needs to be modified only on each iteration by masking off matched inputs. Thus K iterations appear to take at least $2K$ time steps, because the grant and accept steps of each iteration take one time step. At first glance, the architecture appears to specify that the *grant* phase of iteration $k + 1$ be started after the accept phase of iteration k. This is because one needs to know whether an input port I has been accepted in iteration k so as to avoid doing a grant for such an input in iteration $k + 1$.

What makes partial pipelining possible is a simple observation [GM99a]: If input I receives *any* grant in iteration k, then I must accept exactly one and so be unavailable in iteration $k + 1$. Thus the implementation specification can be relaxed (**P3**) to allow the grant phase of iteration

$k + 1$ to start immediately after the grant phase of iteration k, thus overlapping with the accept phase of iteration k. To do so, we simply use the OR of all the grants to input I (at the end of iteration k) to mask out all of I's requests (in iteration $k + 1$).

This reduces the overall completion time by nearly a factor of 2 time steps for k iterations — from $2k$ to $k + 1$. For example, the Tiny Tera iSLIP implementation [GM99a] does three iterations of iSLIP in 51 nsec (roughly OC-192 speeds) using a clock speed of 175 MHz; given that each clock cycle is roughly 5.7 nsec, iSLIP has nine clock cycles to complete. Since each grant and accept step takes two clock cycles, the pipelining is crucial in being able to handle three iterations in nine cycles; the naive iteration technique would have taken at least 12 clock cycles.

13.9 SCALING TO LARGER SWITCHES

So far this chapter has concentrated on fairly small switches that suffice to build up to a 32-port router. Most Internet routers deployed up to the point of writing have been in this category, sometimes for good reasons. For instance, building wiring codes tend to limit the number of offices that can be served from a wiring closet. Thus switches for local area networks [SP94] located in wiring closets tend to be well served with small port sizes.

However, the telephone network has generally employed a few very large switches that can switch 1000–10,000 lines. Employing larger switches tends to eliminate switch-to-switch links, reducing overall latency and increasing the number of switch ports available for users (as opposed to being used to connect to other switches). Thus, while a number of researchers (e.g., Refs. Tur97 and CFFT97) have argued for such large switches, there was little large-scale industrial support for such large switches until recently.

There are three recent trends that favor the design of large switches.

1. **DWDM:** The use of dense wavelength-division multiplexing (DWDM) to effectively bundle multiple wavelengths on optical links in the core will effectively increase the number of logical links that must be switched by core routers.

2. **Fiber to the home:** There is a good chance that in the near future even homes and offices will be wired directly with fiber that goes to a large central office–type switch.

3. **Modular, multichassis routers:** There is increasing interest in deploying router clusters, which consist of a set of routers interconnected by a high-speed network. For example, many network access points connect up routers via an FDDI link or by a Gigaswitch (see Section 13.4). Router clusters, or *multichassis* routers as they are sometimes called, are becoming increasingly interesting because they allow *incremental growth*, as explained later.

The typical lifetime of a core router is estimated [Sem02] to be 18–24 months, after which traffic increases often cause ISPs to throw away older-generation routers and wheel in new ones. Multichassis routers can extend the lifetime of a core router to 5 years or more, by allowing ISPs to start small and then to add routers to the cluster according to traffic needs.

Thus at the time of writing, Juniper Networks led the pack by announcing its T-series routers, which allow up to 16 single-chassis routers (each of which has up to 16 ports) to be assembled via a fabric into what is effectively a 256-port router. At the heart of the multichassis system is a scalable 256-by-256 switching system. Cisco Networks has recently announced its own version, the CRS-1 Router.

13.9.1 *Measuring Switch Cost*

Before studying switch scaling, it helps to understand the most important cost metrics of a switch. In the early days of telephone switching, crosspoints were electromagnetic switches, and thus the N^2 crosspoints of a crossbar were a major cost. Even today this is a major cost for very large switches of size 1000. But because crosspoints can be thought of as just transistors, they take up very little space on a VLSI die.[4]

The real limits for electronic switches are pin limits on ICs. For example, given current pin limits of around 1000, of which a large number of pins must be devoted to other factors, such as power and ground, even a single bit slice of a 500-by-500 switch is impossible to package in a single chip. Of course one could multiplex several crossbar inputs on a single pin, but that would slow down the speed of each input to half the I/O speed possible on a pin.

Thus while the crossbar does indeed require N^2 crosspoints (and this indeed does matter for large enough N), for values of N up to 200, much of the crosspoint complexity is contained within chips. Thus one places the largest crossbar one can implement within a chip and then one interconnects these chips to form a larger switch. Thus the dominant cost of the composite switch is the cost of the pins and the number of links between chips. Since these last two are related (most of the pins are for input and output links), the total number of pins is a reasonable cost measure. More refined cost measures take into account the type of pins (backplane, chip, board, etc.) because they have different costs.

Other factors that limit the building of large monolithic crossbar switches are the capacitive loading on the buses, scheduler complexity, and issues of rack space and power. First, if one tries to build a 256-by-256 switch using the crossbar approach of 256 input and output buses, the loading will probably result in not meeting the speed requirements for the buses. Second, note that centralized algorithms, such as iSLIP, that require N^2 bits of scheduling state will not scale well to large N.

Third, many routers are limited by availability requirements to placing only a few (often one) ports in a line card. Similarly, for power and other reasons, there are often strict requirements on the number of line cards that can be placed in a rack. Thus a router with a large port count is likely to be limited by packaging requirements to use a multirack, multichassis solution consisting of several smaller fabrics connected together to form a larger, composite router. The following subsections describe strategies for doing just this.

13.9.2 *Clos Networks for Medium-Size Routers*

Despite the lack of current focus on crosspoints in VLSI technology, our survey of scalable fabrics for routers begins by looking at the historically earliest proposal for a scalable switch fabric. Charles Clos first proposed his idea in 1955 to reduce the expense of electromechanical switching in telephone switches. Fortunately, the design also reduces the number of components and links required to connect up a number of smaller switches. It is thus useful in a present-day context. Specifically, a Clos network appears to be used in the Juniper Networks T-series multichassis router product, introduced 47 years later, in 2002.

---

[4]However, in the wheel of time, the number of crosspoints again may begin to matter for optical switches!

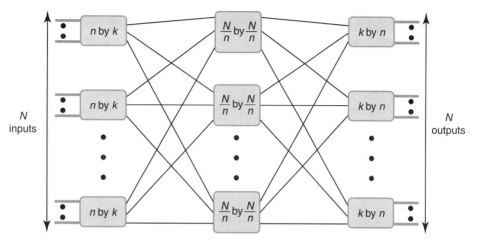

FIGURE 13.12   Three-stage Clos network.

The basic Clos network uses a simple divide-and-conquer (**P15**) approach to reducing crosspoints by switching in three stages, as shown in Figure 13.12. The first stage divides the N total inputs into groups of n inputs each, and each group of n inputs is switched to the second stage by a small (n-by-k) switch. Thus there are N/n "small" switches in the first stage.

The second stage consists of k switches, each of which is an N/n-by-N/n switch. Each of the k outputs of each first-stage switch is connected in order to all the k second-stage switches. More precisely, output j of switch i in the first stage is connected to input i of switch j in the second stage. The third stage is a mirror reversal of the first stage, and the interconnections between the second and third stages are also the mirror reversal of those between the first and second stages. The view from outputs leftward to the middle stage is the same as the view from inputs to the middle stage. More precisely, each of the N/n outputs of the first stage is connected in order to the inputs of the third stage.

A switch is said to be *nonblocking* if whenever the input and output are free, a connection can be made through the switch using free resources. Thus a crossbar is always nonblocking by selecting the crosspoint corresponding to the input–output pair, which is never used for any other pair. On the other hand, in Figure 13.12, every input switch has only k connections to the middle stage, and every middle stage has only one path to any particular switch in the third stage. Thus, for small k it is easily possible to block a new connection because there is no path from an input I to a middle-stage switch that has a free line to an output O.

CLOS NETWORKS IN TELEPHONY

Clos's insight was to see that if $k \geq 2n - 1$, then the resulting Clos network could indeed simulate a crossbar (i.e., is nonblocking) while still reducing the number of crosspoints to be $5.6N\sqrt{N}$ instead of N^2. This can be a big savings for large N. Of course, to achieve this crosspoint reduction, the Clos network has increased latency by two extra stages of switching delay, but that is often acceptable.

The proof of Clos's theorem is easy to see from Figure 13.13. If a hitherto-idle input i wishes to be connected to an idle output o, then consider the first-stage switch S that I is

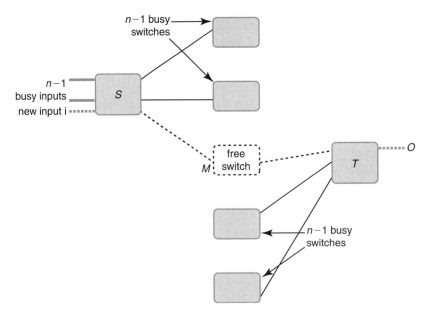

FIGURE 13.13 Proof that a Clos network with $k = 2n - 1$ is nonblocking.

connected to. There can be at most $n - 1$ other inputs in S that are busy (S is an n-by-k switch). These $n - 1$ busy input links of S can be connected to at most $n - 1$ middle-stage switches.

Similarly, focusing on output o, consider the last-stage switch T that o is connected to. Then T can have at most $n - 1$ other outputs that are busy, and each of these outputs can be connected via at most $n - 1$ middle-stage switches. Since both S and T are connected to k middle-stage switches, if $k \geq 2n - 1$, then it is always possible to find a middle-stage switch M that has a free input link to connect to S and a free output link to connect to T. Since S and T are assumed to be crossbars or otherwise nonblocking switches, it is always possible to connect i to the corresponding input link to M and to connect the corresponding output link of M to o.

If $k = 2n - 1$ and n is set to its optimal value of $\sqrt{N/2}$, then the number of crosspoints (summed across all smaller switches in Figure 13.12) becomes $5.6N\sqrt{N}$. For example, for $N = 512$, this reduces the number of crosspoints from 4.2 million for a crossbar to 516,096 for a three-stage Clos switch. Larger telephone switches, such as the No. 1. ESS, which can handle 65,000 inputs, use an eight-stage switch for further reductions in crosspoint size.

CLOS NETWORKS AND MULTICHASSIS ROUTERS

On the other hand, for networking using VLSI switches, what is important is the total number of switches and the number of links interconnecting switches. Recall that the largest possible switches are fabricated in VLSI and that their cost is a constant, regardless of their crosspoint size. Juniper Networks, for example, uses a Clos network to form effectively a 256-by-256 multichassis router by connecting sixteen 16-x-16 T-series routers in the first stage.

Using a standard Clos network for a fully populated multichassis router would require 16 routers in the first stage, 16 in the third stage, and $k = 2 * 16 - 1 = 31$ switches in the middle stage. Clearly, Juniper can (and does) reduce the cost of this configuration by setting $k = n$. Thus the Juniper multichassis router requires only 16 switches in the middle stage.

What happens to a Clos network when k reduces from $2n - 1$ to n? If $k = n$, the Clos network is no longer nonblocking. Instead, the Clos network becomes what is called *rearrangeably nonblocking*. In other words, the new input i can be connected to o as long as it's possible to rearrange some of the existing connections between inputs and outputs to use different middle-stage switches. A proof and possible switching algorithm is described in the Appendix. It can be safely skipped by readers uninterested in the theory.

The bottom line behind all the math in Section A.3.1 in the Appendix is as follows. First, $k = n$ is clearly much more economical than $k = 2n - 1$ because it reduces the number of middle-layer switches by a factor of 2. However, while the Clos network is rearrangably nonblocking, deterministic edge-coloring algorithms for switch scheduling appear at this time to be quite complex. Second, the matching proof for telephone calls assumes that all calls appear at the inputs at the same time; when a new call arrives, existing calls have to be potentially rearranged to fit the new routes. So what does Juniper Networks do when faced with this potential choice between *economy* ($k = n$) and *complexity* (for edge coloring and rearrangement)?

While it's not possible to be sure about what Juniper actually does, because their documentation is (probably intentionally) vague, one can hazard some reasonable guesses. First, it is clear they finesse the whole issue of rearrangement by replacing calls with packets and packets by fixed-size cells within the fabric. Thus in each cell time, cells appear at each input destined to every output; each new cell time requires a fresh application of the matching algorithm, unfettered by the past. Second, their documentation indicates that in place of doing a slow, perfect job using edge coloring, they do a reasonable, but perhaps imperfect, job by distributing the traffic of each input across the middle switches using some form of load balancing.

The Juniper documentation claims that "dividing packets into cells and then distributing them across the Clos fabric achieves the same effect as moving connections in a circuit-switched network because all the paths are used simultaneously." While this is roughly right in a long-term sense, simple deterministic algorithms (in which each input chooses the middle switch to send its next cell in round-robin order; see Exercises) can lead to hot spots in terms of congested middle switches.

Thus it may be that the actual algorithm is deterministic and has possible cases of long-term congestion (which can then be brushed aside by marketing as being pathological). However, it may also be that the actual algorithm is *randomized*. In the simplest version, each input switch picks a random middle switch (**P3a**) for each cell it wishes to transmit.

In a formal probabilistic sense, the expected number of cells each middle switch will receive will be N/n, which is exactly the number of output links each middle switch has. Thus if there is a stream of cells going to distinct outputs,[5] the switch fabric can be expected to achieve 100% throughput in the expected case.

However, randomization is trickier to implement than it may sound. First, just as with hash functions, there is a reasonable probability of "collisions," where too many input switches choose the same output switch. This can reduce throughput and may require buffering within

---

[5]If there are cells going to the same output, there is nothing anyone can do about the loss in throughput anyway.

the switch (or a two-phase process in which inputs make requests to middle switches before sending cells).

The reduced throughput can, of course, be compensated for by using a standard industry trick: *speeding up* internal switch links slightly. Although not given adequate attention in this chapter, speedup is a *very* important technique in real switches to allow simple designs while retaining efficiency.

Second, one has to find a good way to implement the randomization. Fortunately, while there are many poor implementations in existing products, there are, in fact, some excellent hardware random number generators. One good choice [All02] is the Tausworth [L'E96] random number generator. It can be implemented easily using three linear feedback shift registers (LFSRs; see Chapter 9) that are XOR'ed together. Despite its compact implementation, Tausworth passes many sophisticated tests for randomness, such as the diehard test [Mar02].

Third, the algorithms to reassemble cells into packets may be more complex when using randomized load balancing than with deterministic load balancing; in the latter case, the reassembly logic knows where to expect the next packet from.

13.9.3 Benes Networks for Larger Routers

Just as the No. 1. ESS telephone switch switches 65,000 input links, Turner [Tur97, CFFT97] has made an eloquent case that the Internet should (at least eventually) be built of a few large routers instead of several smaller routers. Such topologies can reduce the wasted links for router-to-router connections between smaller routers and thus reduce cost; they can also reduce the worst-case end-to-path length, reducing latency and improving user response times.

Essentially, a Clos network has roughly $N\sqrt{N}$ scaling, in terms of crosspoint complexity using just three stages. This trade-off and general algorithmic experience (**P15**) suggest that one should be able to get $N \log N$ crosspoint complexity while increasing the switch depth to $\log N$. Such switching networks are indeed possible and have been known for years in theory, in telephony, and in the parallel computing industry. Alternatives, such as Butterfly, Delta, Banyan, and Hypercube networks, are well-known contenders.

While the subject is vast, this chapter concentrates only on the Delta and Benes networks. Similar networks are used in many implementations. For example, the Washington University Gigabit switch [CFFT97] uses a Benes network, which can be thought of as two copies of a Delta network. Section A.4 in the Appendix outlines the (often small) differences between Delta networks and others of the same ilk.

The easiest way to understand a Delta network is recursively. Imagine that there are N inputs on the left and that this problem is to be reduced to the problem of building two smaller ($N/2$)-size Delta networks. To help in this reduction, assume a first stage of 2-by-2 switches. A simple scheme (Figure 13.14) is to inspect the output that every input wishes to speak to. If the output is in the upper half (MSB of output is 0), then the input is routed to the upper $N/2$ Delta Network; if the output is in the lower half (i.e., MSB = 1), the input is routed to the lower $N/2$ Delta network.

To economize on the first stage of two-input switches, group the inputs into consecutive pairs, each of which shares a two-input switch, as in Figure 13.14. Thus if the two input cells in a pair are going to different output halves, they can be switched in parallel; otherwise, one will be switched and the other is either dropped or buffered. Of course, the same process can be repeated recursively for both of the smaller ($N/2$)-size Delta networks, breaking them up into a layer of 2-by-2 switches followed by four $N/4$ switches, and so on. The complete

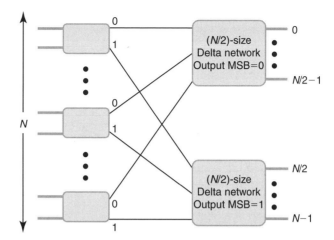

FIGURE 13.14 Constructing a Delta network recursively by reducing the problem of constructing an N-input Delta network to the problem of constructing two $(N/2)$-input Delta networks.

expansion of a Delta network is shown in the first half of Figure 13.15. Notice how the recursive construction in Figure 13.14 can be seen in the connections between the first and second stages in Figure 13.15.

Thus to reduce the problem to 2×2 switches takes $\log N$ stages; since each stage has $N/2$ crosspoints, the binary Delta network has $N \log N$ crosspoint and link complexity. Clearly, we can also construct a Delta network by using d-by-d switches in the first stage and breaking up the initial network into d Delta networks of size N/d each. This reduces the number of stages to $\log_d N$ and link complexity to $n \log_d N$. Given VLSI costs, it is cheaper to construct a switching chip with as large a value of d as possible to reduce link costs.

The Delta network, as do many of its close relatives (see Section A.4) such as the Banyan and the Butterfly, has a nice property called the *self-routing* property. For a binary Delta network, one can find the unique path from a given input to a given output $o = o_1, o_2, \ldots, o_s$ expressed in binary by following the link corresponding to the value of o_i in stage i. This should be clear from Figure 13.14, where we use the MSB at the first stage, the second bit at the second stage, and so on. For $d \geq 2$, write the output address as a radix-d number, and follow successive digits in a similar fashion.

An interesting property that one can intuitively see in Figure 13.14 is that the Delta network is reversible. It is possible to trace a path from an output to an input by following bits of the input in the same way. Thus in Figure 13.14 notice that in going from outputs to inputs, the next-to-last bit of the input selects between two consecutive first-stage switches, and the last bit selects the input. This reversibility property is important because it allows the use of a mirror-reversed version of the Delta (see second half of Figure 13.15) with similar properties as the original Delta.

One problem with the Delta network is congestion. Since there is a unique path from each input to each output, the Delta network is emphatically not a permutation network. For example, if each successive pair of inputs wishes to send a cell to the same output half, only half of the cells can proceed to second stage; if this repeats, only a quarter can proceed to

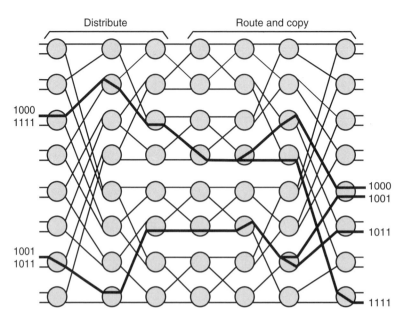

FIGURE 13.15   Doing multicast copy-twice routing using a Benes network, in which the first half distributes load and the second routes and copies. The first half is a Delta network (Figure 13.14), and the second half is a mirror-reversed Delta network.

the third stage; and so on. Thus there are combinations of output requests for which the Delta network throughput can reduce to that of one link, as opposed to N links.

Clearly, one way to make the Delta network less susceptible to congestion for arbitrary permutations of input requests is to add more paths between an input and an output. Generalizing the ideas in a Clos network (Figure 13.12), one can construct a *Benes network* (Figure 13.15), which consists of two ($\log N$)-depth networks: The left half is a standard Delta network, and the right half is a mirror-reversed Delta network. Look at the right half backwards, going left from the outputs: Notice that the connections from the last stage to the next-to-last stage are identical to those between the first and second stages.

One can also visualize a Benes network recursively (**P15**) by extending Figure 13.14 by adding a third stage of 2-by-2 switches and by connecting these third stages to the two ($N/2$)-sized networks in the middle in the same way as the first-stage switches are connected to the two middle ($N/2$)-sized networks (Figure 13.16). Observe that this recursion can be used to directly create Figure 13.15 without creating two separate Delta networks.

Observe the similarity between the recursive version of the Benes network in Figure 13.16 and the Clos network of Figure 13.12. This similarity can be exploited to prove that the *Benes* can route any permutation of output requests in a manner similar to our proof (see earlier box) of the rearrangeably nonblocking property of a Clos network.

In each of two iterations, start by doing a perfect matching between the first and last stages of Figure 13.16, as before, and pick one of the two middle switches. However, rather than stopping here as in the Clos proof, the algorithm must recursively follow the same routing procedure in the ($N/2$)-sized Benes network. Alternatively, the whole process can

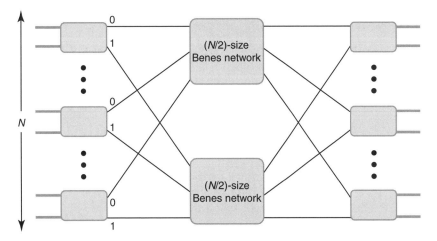

FIGURE 13.16 Recursively constructing a Benes network.

be formulated using edge coloring. The final message is that it is possible to perfectly route arbitrary permutations in a Benes network; however, doing so is fairly complex and is unlikely to be accomplished cheaply in a minimum packet arrival time.

However, recall the earlier argument that a randomized strategy works well, in an expected sense, for Clos networks instead of a more complex and deterministic edge-coloring scheme. Analagous to picking a random middle switch in the Clos network, returning to Figure 13.15 one can pick a random destination for each cell in the first half. One can then route from the random intermediate destination to the actual cell destination (using reverse Delta routing) in the second half. The roots of this idea of using random intermediate destinations go back to Valiant [Val90], who first used it to route in a (single-copy) hypercube.

As in the case of a Clos network using a random choice of middle switches, it can be shown that (in an expected sense) no internal link gets congested as long as no input or output link is congested. Intuitively, the load-splitting half takes all the traffic destined for any output link from any input and spreads it evenly over all the N output links of the first half of Figure 13.15. In the second half, because of the mirror-image structure, all the traffic of the link fans in back to the destined output links.

For example, consider the upper link coming into the first switch in the last stage of Figure 13.15. An important claim is that this upper link will carry half of the traffic to output link 1. This is because this upper link carries all the traffic destined for output link 1 from the top half of the input nodes in the route-and-copy network (mirror-reversed Delta). And by the load-splitting property of the distribute network (the first half of the Delta network), this is half of the traffic destined for output link 1. Similarly, it is possible to argue that the upper link carries half the traffic going to output link 2. Thus if output links 1 and 2 are not saturated, neither will the upper link to switch 1 in the last stage be. One can make a similar argument for any internal link in the second half.

While some of these properties of a Benes network were known before, Turner [Tur97] extended these ideas to include multicast. Notice that our previous example of a scalable switch fabric, the Juniper Clos-based multichassis router, is silent about how multicast is handled. Multicast is handled in a potentially second-class fashion using a server-based approach, as in the take-a-ticket scheme. However, in the Washington University and Growth Network switches [Tur97, CFFT97], Turner showed how to handle multicast traffic in first-class fashion. Thus his vision is for large, scalable, multimedia switches that will need to handle multicast traffic (for, say, video conferencing) as the rule rather than the exception.

To extend the Benes routing ideas to multicast, Turner starts by devising a simpler form of multicast, called *copy-twice* multicast. In this simpler problem, each input may specify two outputs. It is the job of the network to send two copies of the input cell to the two specified output ports. If this can be done and output links can be recycled back to inputs, then the two copies created in the first pass can be extended to four in the second pass and to 2^i copies in i passes through the Benes network.

In Figure 13.15 for example, the fifth input link has a cell destined to 1000 (i.e., output 8) and to 1111 (i.e., to output 15). In the first half, the cell is randomly routed to input 7 of the second half. In the second half, follow the bits of the real outputs, MSB first, until the first point that the two output addresses differ. As usual, a 0 in the current bit is switched upward and a 1 is switched downward. Thus in the first stage of the copy network, the cell is routed to the downlink because both output addresses start with 1.

Life gets more exciting at the second stage because in the second bit from the right, the addresses differ. Thus the second-stage switch in the copy network (more precisely the fourth switch from the top) now replicates the cell in two directions. The two output paths have separated at the first differing bit. From now each of the two cells (the single cell recall is now two cells) follows the address of its corresponding output. Check that following the last two bits of 1000 and 1111 will cause the two cells to reach outputs 8 and 15 in Figure 13.15.

Because of a very similar intuition, it can be shown that doing the copy at the first differing bit does not cause any internal link to be overloaded if the output and input links are not overloaded [Tur97]. In fact, the same result would hold if a copy-3 network (i.e., a network capable of producing three copies in one pass) was used. So why stop at two?

It turns out that when a cell comes into a switch it carries a multicast output-link specifier that has to be translated into two (or more) unicast specifiers for each pass. Similarly, each cell must carry two (or more) addresses during its travels. Thus using a small number like 2 limits the complexity of the port-mapping operation and the header overhead. Using larger numbers would only decrease the number of passes to replicate a multicast cell.

One of the nice features of Turner's multicast design is that larger multicast fanouts can be handled by multiple iterations. This can be logically pictured as a multicast binary tree (**P15**) across several Benes networks connected in series. Of course, in reality the same Benes network is reused, reducing the cost. However, this mental picture indicates why adding a new multicast connection is very efficient. It simply involves adding a new leaf to the tree, with a minimum of disturbance to existing multicast tree nodes or other connections [Tur97].

Thus the Turner switch tends to use resources optimally because of recycling. The design allows resources (crosspoints, mapping tables, etc.) to scale as $N \log N$, can handle any configuration of unicast and multicast traffic, and can add or remove an endpoint from a multicast tree in constant time. Competing switch architectures fail to satisfy all these conditions, sometimes spectacularly. This means that in practice, they can handle only a very limited amount of multicast traffic. Of course, one can argue about the current importance of multicast, which is certainly limited at the time of writing. However, with the rise of videoconferencing over the Internet, one can clearly envision a future where large multimedia switches are key.

Before ending this section, it is worth noting that just as with the Clos switch, the *conceptual simplicity* of a randomized load-balancing strategy for a Benes network comes with some attendant *implementation complexity*. First, since randomized load balancing is not perfect, the Turner switch needs buffers and flow control. Second, it is important to get the randomization done right. The first prototype Washington University switch [CFFT97] used simple load balancing based on a counter. However, when this switch was redesigned as part of a company called Growth Networks [Tur02], the switch used a much more sophisticated randomizer to deal with pathological input patterns. Finally, efficient resequencing of cells takes special effort in this architecture [Tur97].

13.10 SCALING TO FASTER SWITCHES

The preceding section focused on how switches can scale in *size*. This section studies how switches can scale in *speed*. Now, it may be that the speeds of individual fiber channels level off at some point. Many pundits say that fundamental SRAM and optical limits will limit individual fiber channels to OC-768 speeds. The capacity of fiber may then be used for producing more individual channels (e.g., using multiple wavelengths) rather than higher-speed individual channels. The use of more channels then affects switching only in terms of increasing port count and can be handled using the techniques of the previous section.

While this is one viewpoint, the lessons of history should teach us that it is certainly possible for individual applications to increase their speed needs and for technology surprisingly to keep pace by producing faster link speeds that increase from 40 Gbps today to 10 terabits in, say, 5 years. Thus it is worthwhile to look for techniques to scale switches in speed. There are three common techniques: *bit slicing*, the use of *short links*, and the use of *randomized memory sharing*.

13.10.1 *Using Bit Slicing for Higher-Speed Fabrics*

The simplest way to cope with link speed increases is to use a faster clock rate to run the switching electronics. Unfortunately, optical speeds increase exponentially, while ASIC clock rates increase only at around 10% per year. However, by Moore's law, the number of transistors placed on a chip doubles every 18–24 months without a cost increase. Thus the simplest way to cope with link speed increases is to use *parallelism*.

Suppose it were possible to build a crossbar where every link has speed S. Then to handle links of speed kS for some constant k, a design could use k crossbar "slices." For every group of k bits coming from a link, one bit each is sent to each crossbar slice. Thus each slice sees a reduced link speed of $kS/k = S$ and thus can be feasibly implemented. Of course, this implies that the reassembly logic can scale in speed.

If the bits are distributed to slices in deterministic fashion (i.e., bit 1 of the first cell goes to slice 1, bit 2 to slice 2, etc.), the reassembly logic can be simplified because it knows on which slice to expect the next bit. However, care must be taken to avoid synchronization errors. The scheduler can make the same decision for all slices, making the scheduler easy to build.

The Juniper T-series [Sem02] uses four active switch fabric planes (i.e., slices). It also uses a fifth plane as a hot-standby for redundancy. Since each plane uses a request-grant mechanism, if a grant does not return within a timeout, a plane failure can be detected. At this point, only the cells in transit within the failed plane are lost, the failed plane is swapped out for maintenance, and the standby plane is swapped in.

While little discussed so far, redundancy and fault tolerance are crucial for large switch designs because more is at stake. If a small, 8-port router fails, only a few users are affected. But a large, 256-port-by-256-port router must work nearly always, with internal redundancy, masking out faults. This is because external redundancy, in terms of a second such router, is too expensive. Most ISPs require core routers to be NEBS (Network Equipment Building System) [NEB02] compliant. Typically, large routers are expected to have at most 5 minutes of downtime in a year.

13.10.2 *Using Short Links for Higher-Speed Fabrics*

One feature of interconnection networks ignored so far is the physical length of the links used between stages. Links come in various forms, from serial links between chips, to backplane traces, to cable connections between different line cards. Intuitively, the length matters because long wires increase delay and decrease bit rate, unless compensated for using more expensive signaling technology, such as optical signaling.

A look at the Delta and Clos networks shows that these networks use at least a few long wires between stages, whose length scales as $O(N)$. There are, however, interconnect networks that can be packaged with uniformly short wires. These are the so-called low-dimensional mesh networks. Such mesh networks have a checkered history in parallel computing, being used by Cray and Intel supercomputers.

The simplest low-dimensional mesh is the 1D torus, which is basically a line of nodes in which the last node is also connected to the first node to form a logical ring (Figure 13.17). A 2D torus is basically a two-dimensional grid of nodes where the last node in each row or column is also connected to the first node in the same row or column. A 3D torus is the same idea extended to a three-dimensional grid.

Even a 1D torus, which is logically a ring, appears to have one long wire that connects the first and last nodes (Figure 13.17). However, a clever way to amortize this long line length

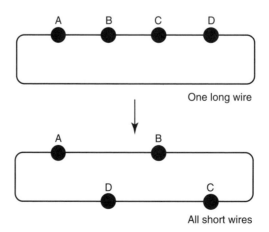

FIGURE 13.17   How a 1D torus can be packaged physically using short wires.

across all nodes is to use a simple degree of freedom (**P13**) and to lay out the first half of the nodes on the forward path of the ring (Figure 13.17) and the second half on the reverse path. While the length of the *A*-to-*B* wire may have doubled, there are no long wires. The same idea can be extended for 2D and 3D toruses by repeating this idea across rows and columns.

Like a Butterfly or Delta network, the problem with a 1D torus, however, is that it suffers from congestion, because there are only two paths between two inputs. It also suffers from high latency because some pairs of nodes have to travel $O(N/2)$ hops. The congestion and latency problems are relieved by using a 3D torus. For example, in a 3D torus that is 8 by 8 by 8, an average message can choose [Dal02] between 90 paths of six hops each.

The Avici TSR Router [Dal02] is an example of a router built using a 3D torus. It can handle up to 560 line cards, and the use of short wires allows it to be packaged very neatly. A 260-line-card configuration can be packaged *without any cables* by connecting only adjacent backplanes using jumpers. The 560-line-card version uses one set of short cables between two rows of racks [Dal02].

Besides the use of short links, the 3D mesh offers a large number of alternate paths for fault tolerance and the ability to be incrementally upgraded with minimal extra cost. By contrast, some interconnection networks tend to require scaling in powers of 2. The Avici TSR router also handles the equivalent of head-of-line blocking by using separate virtual networks. Each virtual network uses separate buffers essentially to create the illusion of several physical switches, one of which can be used when another is blocked.

It appears that HOL blocking is handled by iSLIP, PIM, and the Avici TSR but *not* by the Gigaswitch, the Turner Benes network, or the Clos network. However, switches with buffered switch elements such as the Turner Benes network are not as susceptible to HOL blocking when compared to switches (such as the Gigaswitch) that do not. Given that modern switches can support thousands of cell buffers per crosspoint, HOL blocking may be a red herring for fabrics with internal buffering.

13.10.3 Memory Scaling Using Randomization

In all the switches seen so far, packets have to be stored in buffers during periods of congestion. The standard rule of thumb is for routers to have one RTT (Roundtrip Time) worth of buffering to allow congestion-control algorithms to slow down without causing packet loss. While it may be possible to get around this limit using better higher-level congestion-control algorithms, it appears that the combination of TCP and RED today requires this amount of buffering. Using 200 msec as a conservative estimate for round-trip delay, a 2-terabit router must have 0.4 terabit's worth of packet buffers. Thus as link speeds increase, and assuming no congestion-control innovations, the memory needs will also increase.

Consider an input-buffered switch and packets coming in at OC-768 speeds. Thus a minimum-size packet arrives every 8 nsec and will require at least two accesses to memory: the first to store the packet and the second to read it out for transmission through the fabric. Given that the fastest DRAM available at the time of writing has a cycle time of 50 nsec, it is clear that the only way to meet the memory bandwidth needs using DRAM would be to use a wider memory word.

Unfortunately, one cannot use a wider memory word size than that of a minimum-size packet because it is not possible to guarantee that the next packet will be read out at the same time. One could use SRAMs (at 4-nsec cycle times at the time of writing, this should be just adequate), but then one would have to pay a cost premium of anywhere from a factor of 4 to a factor of 10.[6]

One way out of this dilemma is to use parallel banks of DRAMs. It is possible to keep up with link speeds using 12 DRAM banks working in parallel, each with a 40-byte access width. Intuitively, this seems plausible. For any input stream of packets, send the first packet to DRAM 1, the second to DRAM 2, etc. Unfortunately, because of QoS and scheduling algorithms, it is not clear in which order packets will be read out. Thus it may be that during some period of time all the packets are read out from a few DRAMs only, causing memory bandwidth contention and eventual packet loss.

Such memory contention problems are familiar to computer architects when using interleaved memory. For example, if an array is laid out sequentially across memory banks, it is possible that accesses that are spaced a certain stride apart (e.g., column accesses) may all hit the same bank. One potentially clever way out of the contention problem is to steal a leaf from the designers of the CYDRA-2 stride-insensitive memory [Rau91]. Their idea was to *pseudo-randomly interleave* storage requests to memory such that with high probability any access pattern (other than to the same word) would not cause hot spots.

In the router context, instead of sending packet 1 to DRAM 1 and so on, one would send each packet to a randomly selected DRAM. Of course, as with all randomized interleaving schemes (see the earlier Clos and Benes sections), reassembly gets more complicated, with state having to be kept (in SRAM?) to resequence these packets.

An interesting variation on this theme and that of randomized routing a la Valiant [Val90] is a technique that appears to be used by Juniper Networks in their M40 and M160 routers. From what is possible to glean from their patents [SAFL99], when a packet enters a line card in such a Juniper router it is (without any lookup) sent to a randomly selected other line card, where it is looked up, stored, and finally switched to its correct destination line card.

Why in the world would a leading router company go through one level of randomized indirection and take *two passes* though the fabric for every packet? One explanation may be that this randomization reduces the amount of required DRAM at every input line card from a "worst-case size" to a more "average size." However, it would be nice to have some analysis or simulations to support this thesis.

13.11 CONCLUSIONS

This chapter has surveyed techniques for building switches, from small shared-memory switches to input-queued switches used in the Cisco GSR, to larger, more scalable switch fabrics used in the Juniper T130 and Avici TSR Routers.

Since this is a book about algorithmics, it is important to focus on the techniques and not get lost in the mass of product names. These are summarized in Figure 13.2. Fundamentally, the major idea in PIM and iSLIP is to realize that by using VOQs one can feasibly (with $O(N^2)$ bits) communicate all the desired communication patterns to avoid head-of-line blocking. These schemes go further and show that maximal matching can be done in $N \log N$ time using randomization (PIM) or approximately (iSLIP) using round-robin pointers per port for fairness.

While $N \log N$ is a large number, by showing that this can be done in parallel by each of N ports, the time reduces to $\log N$ (in PIM) and to a small constant (in iSLIP). Given that

---

[6]The cost premium of DRAM versus SRAM is hard to pin down because DRAM prices sometimes fall dramatically.

log N is small, even this delay can be pipelined away to run in a minimum packet time. The fundamental lesson is that even algorithms that appear complex, such as matching, can, with randomization and hardware parallelism, be made to run in a minimum packet time. Further scaling in speed can be done using bit slices.

Larger port counts are handled by algorithmic techniques based on divide-and-conquer. An understanding of the actual costs of switching shows that even a simple three-stage Clos switch works well for port sizes up to 256. However, for larger switch sizes, the Benes network, with its combination of $(2\log N)$ depth Delta networks, is better suited for the job. The main issue in both these scalable fabrics is scheduling. And in both cases, as in PIM, a complex deterministic algorithm is finessed using simple randomization. In both the Clos and Benes networks, the essential similarity of structure allows the use of an initial randomized load-balancing step followed by deterministic path selection from the randomized intermediate destination.

Similar ideas are also used to reduce memory needs by either picking a random intermediate line card or a random choice of DRAM bank to send a given packet (cell) to. The knockout switch uses trees of randomized 2-by-2 concentrators to provide k-out-of-N fairness. Thus randomization is a surprisingly important idea in switch implementations.

It is interesting to note that almost every new switch idea described in this chapter has led to a company. For example, Kanakia worked on shared-memory switches at Bell Labs and then left to found Torrent. Juniper seems to have been started with Sindhu's idea for a new fabric based, perhaps, on the use of staging via a random intermediate line card. McKeown founded Abrizio after the success of iSLIP. Growth Networks was started by Turner, Parulkar, and Cox to commercialize Turner's Benes switch idea, and was later sold to Cisco. Dally took his ideas for deadlock-free routing on low-dimensional meshes and moved them successfully from Cray Computers to Avici's TSR.

Thus if you, dear reader, have an idea for a new folded Banyan or an inverted Clos, you, too, may be the founder of the next great thing in networking. Perhaps some venture capitalist will soon be meeting you in a coffee shop in Silicon Valley to make you an offer you cannot refuse.

In conclusion, for a router designer it's better to switch than to fight — with the difficulties of designing a high-speed bus.

13.12 EXERCISES

1. **Take-a-Ticket State Machine:** Draw a state machine for take-a-ticket. Describe the state machine using pseudocode, with a state machine for each sender and each receiver. Extend the state machine to handle hunt groups.

2. **Knockout Implementation:** There are dependencies between the knockout trees. The simplest implementation passes all the losers from the Position $j-1$ tree to the Position j tree. This would take $k \log N$ gate delays, because each tree takes $\log N$ gate delays. Find a way to pipeline this process such that Tree j begins to work on each batch of losers as they are determined by Tree $j-1$, as opposed to waiting for all losers to be determined. Draw your implementation using 2-by-2 concentrators as your building block and estimate the worst-case delay in concentrator delays.

3. **PIM unfairness:** In the knockout example, using just one tree can lead to unfairness; a collection of locally fair decisions can lead to global unfairness. Surprisingly, PIM can lead to the some form of unfairness as well (but not to persistent starvation). Consider a

2-by-2 switch, where input 1 has unlimited traffic to outputs 1 and 2, and input 2 has unlimited traffic to output 1.

- Show that, on average, input 1 will get two grants from outputs 2 and 1 for half the cell slots and one grant (for output 2 only) for the remaining cell slots. What fraction of output 2's link should input 1 receive?

- Infer, based on the preceding fraction of output 1's bandwidth, what input 1 receives on average versus input 2. Is this fair?

4. **Motivating the iSLIP Pointer Increment Rule:** The following is one unfairness scenario if pointers in iSLIP are incremented incorrectly. For example, suppose in Figure 13.11 that input port *A* always has traffic to output ports 1, 2, and 3, whose grant pointers are initialized to *A*. Suppose also that input ports *B* and *C* also always have traffic to 2. Thus initially *A*, *B*, and *C* all grant to 1, who chooses *A*. In the second iteration, since input port 2 has traffic to *B*, 2 and *B* are matched.

- Suppose *B* increments its grant pointer to 3 based on this second iteration match. Between which port pairs can traffic be continually starved if this scenario persists?

- How does iSLIP prevent this scenario?

5. **ESLIP:** Answer the following questions about ESLIP.

- Describe a scenario where a multicast cell does not finish its fanout in one cycle despite the use of a shared grant pointer and the fact that multicast has priority over unicast in alternate time slots.

- Why is there no need for a shared multicast accept pointer?

6. **Clos Proof Revisited:** The Clos proof is based on a reduction that looks and is simple. However, until you try a few twists that do not work, you may not appreciate its simplicity. In our reduction, each iteration routed *n* pairs, one per input stage, using just one middle switch. Suppose instead that any set of middle switches is used that had free input and output links. Show, by counterexample, why the reduction does not work.

7. **Benes Switch Load-Balancing Proof:** In the Benes switch, the chapter argued that any link one hop from the output cannot be overloaded, assuming perfect load balancing at the first stage. It is helpful to work out with some simple cases to provide intuition before turning, if needed, to the proof provided in Turner [Tur97].

- Repeat the same proof for links one hop away from the network but this time for a two-copy network. Does the proof change for a three-copy network?

- Repeat all the proofs for links two hops away. Do you see a pattern that can now be stated algebraically [Tur97]?

8. **Avici TSR and 3D Grid Layout:** It seems a good bet that layout and packaging will be increasingly important as switches scale up in speeds. Extend the layout drawing in Figure 13.17 for a 1D torus to a 2D and a 3D torus. Then read Dally [Dal02] to learn how the Avici TSR packages its 3D mesh in a box.

CHAPTER 14

Scheduling Packets

A schedule defends from chaos and whim

— ANNIE DILLARD

From arranging vacations to making appointments, we are constantly *scheduling* activities. A busy router is no exception. Routers must schedule the handling of routing updates, management queries, and, of course, data packets. Data packets must be scheduled in real time by the forwarding processors within each line card. This chapter concentrates on the efficient scheduling of data packets while allowing certain classes of data packets to receive different service from other classes.

Returning to our picture of a router (Figure 14.1), recall that packets enter on input links and are looked up using the address lookup component. Address lookup provides an output link number, and the packet is switched to the output link by the switching system. Once the packet arrives at the output port, the packet could be placed in a FIFO (first in, first out) queue. If congestion occurs and the output link buffers fill up, packets arriving at the tail of the queue are dropped. Many routers use such a default output-link scheduling mechanism, often referred to as *FIFO with tail-drop*.

However, there are certainly other options. First, we could place packets in multiple queues based on packet headers and schedule these output queues according to some scheduling policy. There are several policies, such as priority and round-robin, that can schedule packets in a different order from FIFO. Second, even if we had a single queue, we need not always drop from the tail when buffers overflow; we can, surprisingly, even drop a packet when the packet buffer is not full.

Packet scheduling can be used to provide (to a flow of packets) so-called *quality of service* (QoS) guarantees on measures such as delay and bandwidth. We will see that QoS requires packet scheduling together with some form of reservations at routers. We will only briefly sketch some reservation schemes, such as those underlying RSVP [Boy97] and DiffServ [SWG], and we refer the reader to the specifications for more details. This is because the other parts of the QoS picture, such as handling reservations, can be handled out of band at a slower rate by a control processor in the router. Since this book concentrates on implementation bottlenecks, this chapter focuses on packet scheduling.

We will briefly examine the motivation for some popular scheduling choices. More importantly, we will use our principles to look for efficient implementations. Since packet scheduling is done in the real-time path, as is switching and lookup, it is crucial that scheduling decisions can be made in the minimum interpacket times as links scale to OC-768 (40-gigabit) speeds and higher.

FIGURE 14.1   Router model: This chapter concentrates on the third bottleneck, **B3**, scheduling of data packets.

This chapter is organized as follows. Section 14.1 presents the motivation for providing QoS guarantees. Section 14.2 describes random early detect (RED) schemes, which are better suited to TCP congestion control than tail-drop. Section 14.3 offers a simple scheme to limit the bandwidth and burstiness of a flow, and Section 14.4 describes a basic priority scheme. Section 14.5 provides a brief introduction to reservation protocols. Section 14.6 presents simple techniques to apportion the available link bandwidth among competing flows. The section also briefly describes how the accompanying reservations for flow bandwidths can be made. Section 14.7 shows how one can provide good delay guarantees for a flow, at the cost of sorting packet deadlines in real time. Section 14.8 describes several scalable schedulers that are able to schedule a large number of flows with little or no state.

The packet-scheduling techniques described in this chapter (and the corresponding principles involved) are summarized in Figure 14.2.

Quick Reference Guide

The most important scheduling algorithms that an Internet router must implement are RED (Section 14.2), token buckets (Section 14.3), priority queueing (Section 14.4), Deficit round-robin (DRR) (Section 14.6.3), and DiffServ (for DiffServ, consult only the relevant portion of Section 14.8). Other interconnect devices, such as SAN switches and gateways, are not required to implement RED; however, implementing some form of QoS, such as DRR or token buckets, in such devices is also a good idea.

14.1 MOTIVATION FOR QUALITY OF SERVICE

We will be assigning packets flows to queues and sometimes trying to give guarantees to flows. Though we have used the term earlier, we repeat the definition of a *packet flow*. A flow is a stream of packets that traverses the same route from the source to the destination and that requires the same grade of service at each router or gateway in the path. In addition, a flow

Number	Principle	Scheduling Technique
P7	Use power of two parameters	RED
P3	Use policing, not shaping	Token bucket policing
P3 P12 P7	Focus on bandwidth only Maintain list of active queues Use large enough quanta	DRR
P13 P15 P5 P5b	Leap forward, not backward Use a heap to sort tags Use a sorting chip Use a d-heap and wide memory	Leap forward Virtual clock
P3a	Aggregate by hashing flows	SFQ
P3c P10	Shift work to edge routers Pass class in TOS field	DiffServ
P10	Pass drop probability in header	Core stateless

FIGURE 14.2 Summary of packet-scheduling techniques used in this chapter and the corresponding principles.

must be identifiable using fields in a packet header; these fields are typically drawn from the transport, routing, and data link headers only.

The notion of a flow is general and applies to datagram networks (e.g., IP, OSI) and virtual circuit networks (e.g., X.25, ATM). For example, in a virtual circuit network a flow could be identified by a virtual circuit identifier, or VCI. On the other hand, in the Internet a flow could be identified by all packets (a) with a destination address that matches subnet A, (b) with a source address that matches subnet B, and (c) that contain mail traffic, where mail traffic is identified by having either source or destination port numbers equal to 25. We assume that packet classification (Chapter 12) can be used to efficiently identify flows.

Why create complexity in going beyond FIFO with tail-drop? The following needs are arranged roughly in order of importance.

- **Router Support for Congestion:** With link speeds barely catching up with exponentially increasing demand, it is often possible to have congestion in the Internet. Most traffic is based on TCP, which has mechanisms to react to congestion. However, with router support it is possible to improve the reaction of TCP sources to congestion, improving the overall throughput of sources.

- **Fair Sharing of Links among Competing Flows:** With tail-drop routers, customers have noticed that during a period of a backup across the network, important Telnet and e-mail connections freeze. This is because the backup packets grab all the buffers at an output in some router, locking out the other flows at that output link.

- **Providing QoS Guarantees to Flows:** A more precise form of fair sharing is to guarantee bandwidths to a flow. For example, an ISP may wish to guarantee a customer 10 Mbps of

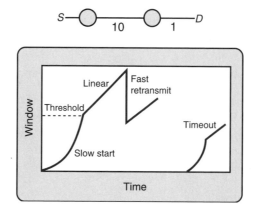

FIGURE 14.3 An illustration of TCP congestion control as a prelude to RED.

bandwidth as part of a virtual private network connecting customer sites. A more difficult task is to guarantee the delay through a router for a flow such as a video flow. Live video will not work well if the network delay is not bounded.

None of these needs should be surprising when one looks at a time-sharing operating system (OS) such as UNIX or Windows NT. Clearly, in times of overload the OS must decide which load to shed; the OS often time-shares among a group of competing jobs for fairness; finally, some operating systems provide delay guarantees on the scheduling of certain real-time jobs, such as playing a movie.

14.2 RANDOM EARLY DETECTION

Random early detection (RED) is a packet-scheduling algorithm implemented in most modern routers, even at the highest speeds, and it has become a de facto standard. In a nutshell, a RED router monitors the average output-queue length; when this goes beyond a threshold, it randomly drops arriving packets with a certain probability, *even though there may be space to buffer the packet*. The dropped packet acts as a signal to the source to slow down early, preventing a large number of dropped packets later.

To understand RED we must review the Internet-congestion-control algorithm. The top of Figure 14.3 shows a network connecting source S and destination D. Imagine the network had links with capacity 1 Mbps and that a file transfer can occur at 1 Mbps. Now suppose the middle link is replaced by a faster, 10-Mbps link. Surely it can't make things worse, can it? Well, in the old days of the Internet it did. Packets arrived at a 10-Mbps rate at the second router, which could only forward packets at 1 Mbps; this caused a flood of dropped packets, which led to slow retransmissions. This resulted in a very low throughput for the file transfer.

Fortunately, the dominant Internet transport protocol, TCP, added a mechanism called *TCP congestion control*, which is depicted in Figure 14.3. The source maintains a window of size W, which is the number of packets the source will send without an acknowledgment. Controlling window size controls the source rate because the source is limited to a rate of W packets in a trip delay to the destination. As shown in Figure 14.3, a TCP source starts W at 1.

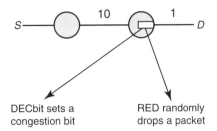

FIGURE 14.4 RED is an early warning system that operates *implicitly* by packet dropping, instead of *explicitly* by sending a bit as in the DECbit scheme.

Assuming no dropped packets, the source increases its window size exponentially, doubling every round-trip delay, until W reaches a threshold. After this, the source increases W linearly.

If there is a single dropped packet (this can be inferred from a number of acknowledgments with the same number), the "gap" is repaired by retransmitting only the dropped packet; this is called *fast retransmit*. In this special case, the source detects some congestion and reduces its window size to half the original size (Figure 14.3) and then starts trying to increase again. If several packets are lost, the only way for the source to recover is by having a slow, 200-msec timer expire. In this case, the source infers more drastic congestion and restarts the window size at 1, as shown in Figure 14.3.

For example, with tail-drop routers, the example network shown at the top of Figure 14.3 will probably have the source ramp up until it drops some packets and then return to a window size of 1 and start again. Despite this oscillation, the average throughput of the source is quite good, because the retransmissions occur rarely as compared to the example without congestion control. However, wouldn't it be nicer if the source could drop to half the maximum at each cycle (instead of 1) and avoid expensive timeouts (200 msec) completely? The use of a RED router makes this more likely.

The main idea in a RED [FJ93] router (Figure 14.4) is to have the router detect congestion *early*, before all its buffers are exhausted, and to warn the source. The simplest scheme, called the *DECbit scheme* [RJ90], would have the router send a "congestion experienced" bit to the source when its average queue size goes beyond a threshold. Since there is no room for such a bit in current IPv4 headers, RED routers simply drop a packet with some small probability. This makes it more likely that a flow causing congestion will drop just a single packet, which can be recovered by the the more efficient fast retransmit instead of a drastic timeout.[1]

The implementation of RED is more complex than it seems. First, we need to calculate the output-queue size using a weighted average with weight w. Assuming that each arriving packet uses the queue size it sees as a sample, the average queue length is calculated by adding $(1 - w)$ times the old average queue size to w times the new sample. In other words, if w is small, even if the sample is large, it only increases the average queue size by a small amount. The average queue size changes slowly as a result and needs a large number of samples to change

---

[1] But what of sources that do not use TCP and use UDP? Since the majority of traffic is TCP, RED is still useful; the RED drops also motivate UDP applications to add TCP-like congestion, a subject of active research. A more potent question is whether RED helps small packet flows, such as Web traffic, which account for a large percentage of Internet traffic.

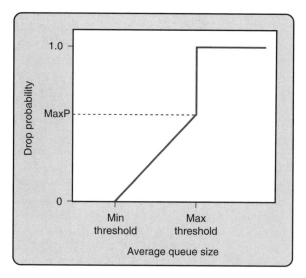

$$AverageQ = (1-W)^*AverageQ + (W^*SampleQsize)$$

FIGURE 14.5   Calculating drop probabilities using RED thresholds.

value appreciably. This is done deliberately to detect congestion on the order of round-trip delays (100 msec) rather than instantaneous congestion that can come and go. However, we can avoid unnecessary generality (**P7**) by allowing the w to be only a reciprocal of a power of 2; a typical value is 1/512. There is a small loss in tunability as compared to allowing arbitrary values of w. However, the implementation is more efficient because the multiplications reduce to easy bit shifting.

However, there's further complexity to contend with. The drop probability is calculated using the function shown in Figure 14.5. When the average queue size is below a minimum threshold, the drop probability is zero; it then increases linearly to a maximum drop probability at the maximum threshold; beyond this all packets are dropped. Once again, we can remove unnecessary generality (**P7**) and use appropriate values, such as MaxThreshold being twice MinThreshold, and MaxP a power of 2. Then the interpolation can be done with two shifts and a subtract.

But wait, there's more. The version of RED so far is likely to drop more than one packet in a burst of closely spaced packets for a source. To make this less likely and fast retransmit more likely to work, the probability calculated earlier is scaled by a function that depends on the number of packets queued (see Peterson and Davy [PD00] for a pithy explanation) since the last drop. This makes the probability increase with the number of nondropped packets, making closely spaced drops less likely.

But wait, there's even more. There is also the possibility of adding different thresholds for different types of traffic; for example, bursty traffic may need a larger Minimum Threshold. Cisco has introduced *weighted RED*, where the thresholds can vary depending on the TOS bits in the IP header. Finally, there is the thorny problem of generating a random number at a router. This can be done by grabbing bits from some seemingly random register on the router; a possible example is the low-order bits of a clock that runs faster than packet arrivals. The net result is that RED, which seems easy, takes some care in practice, especially at gigabit speeds. Nevertheless, RED is quite feasible and is almost a requirement for routers being built today.

14.3 TOKEN BUCKET POLICING

So far with RED we assumed that all packets are placed in a single output queue; the RED drop decision is taken at the input of this queue. Can we add any form of bandwidth guarantees for flows that are placed in a common queue without segregation? For example, many customers require limiting the rate of traffic for a flow. More specifically, an ISP may want to limit NEWS traffic in its network to no more than 1 Mbps. A second example is where UDP traffic is flowing from the router to a slow remote line. Since UDP sources currently do not react to congestion, congestion downstream can be avoided by having a manager limit the UDP traffic to be smaller than the remote line speed. Fortunately, these examples of bandwidth limiting can easily be accomplished by a technique called *token bucket policing*, which uses only a single queue and a counter per flow.

Token bucket policing is a simple derivative of another idea, called *token bucket shaping*. Token bucket shaping [Tur86] is a simple way to limit the burstiness of a flow by limiting its average rate as well as its maximum burst size. For example, a flow could be limited to sending at a long-term average of 100 Kbps but could be allowed to send 4KB as fast as it wants. Since most applications are bursty, it helps to allow *some* burstiness. Downstream nodes are helped by leaky bucket shaping because bursts contribute directly to short-term congestion and packet loss. The implementation is shown conceptually in Figure 14.6.

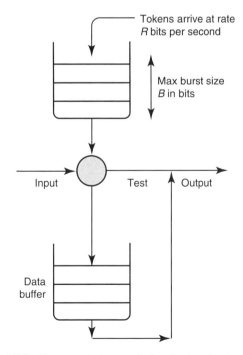

FIGURE 14.6 Conceptual picture of token bucket shaping and policing.

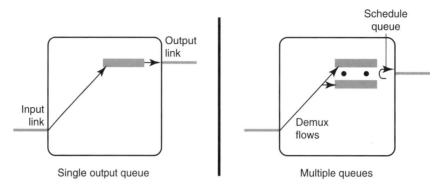

FIGURE 14.7 A single outbound queue (left) versus multiple outbound queues (right). Disciplines based on dropping (such as RED and policing) can be implemented with a single queue, but other possibilities, such as round-robin and priority, are possible with multiple queues.

Imagine that one has a bucket per flow that fills with "tokens" at the specified average rate of R per second. The bucket size, however, is limited to the specified burst size of B tokens. Thus when the bucket is full, all incoming tokens are dropped. When packets arrive for a flow, they are allowed out only if the bucket contains a number of tokens equal to the size of packet in bits. If not, the packet is queued until sufficient tokens arrive. Since there can be at most B tokens, a burst is limited to at most B bits, followed by the more steady rate of R bits per second. This can easily be implemented using a counter and a timer per flow; the timer is used to increment the counter, and the counter is limited never to grow beyond B. When packets are sent out, the counter is decremented.

Unfortunately, token bucket shaping would require different queues for each flow, because some flows may have temporarily run out of tokens and have to wait, while other, later-arriving packets may belong to flows that have accumulated tokens. If one wishes to limit oneself to a single queue, a simpler technique is to limit oneself (**P3**, relax system requirements) to a token bucket policer. The idea would be simply to drop any packet that arrives to find the token bucket empty. In other words, a policer is a shaper without the buffer shown in Figure 14.6. A policer needs only a counter and a timer per flow, which is simple to implement at high speeds using the efficient timer implementations of Chapter 7.

14.4 MULTIPLE OUTBOUND QUEUES AND PRIORITY

So far we have limited ourselves to one single queue for all outbound packets, as shown on the left of Figure 14.7. Random early detection or token bucket policing (or both) can be used to decide whether to drop packets before they are placed on this queue. We now transition to examine scheduling disciplines that are possible with multiple queues. This is shown on the right of Figure 14.7.

First, note that we now need to demultiplex packets based on packet headers to identify which outbound queue to place a packet on. This can be done using the packet-classification techniques described in Chapter 12 or simpler techniques based on inspecting the TOS bits in the IP header. Second, note that we can still implement RED and token bucket policing by dropping packets before they are placed on the appropriate outbound queue.

Third, note that we now have a new problem. If multiple queues have packets to send, we have to decide which queue to service next, and when. If we limit ourselves to *work-conserving* schemes[2] that never idle the link, then the only decision is which queue to service next when the current packet transmission on the output link finishes.

As the simplest example of a multiple queue-scheduling discipline, consider *strict priority*. For example, imagine two outbound queues, one for premium service and one for other packets. Imagine that packets are demultiplexed to these two queues based on a bit in the IP TOS field. In strict priority, we will always service a queue with higher priority before one with lower priority as long as there is a packet in the higher-priority queue. This may be an appropriate way to implement the premium service specification defined in the emerging DiffServ architecture [SWG].

14.5 A QUICK DETOUR INTO RESERVATION PROTOCOLS

This chapter focuses on packet-scheduling mechanisms. However, before we go deeper into scheduling queues, it may help to see the big picture. Thus we briefly discuss reservation protocols that actually set up the parameters that control scheduling. While we do so to make this chapter self-contained, the reader should refer to the original sources (e.g., Ref. Boy97) for a more detailed description.

First, note that reservations are crucial for any form of absolute performance guarantee for flows passing through a router. Consider an ISP router with a 100-Mbs output link. If the ISP wishes to provide some customer flows with a 10-Mbps-bandwidth guarantee, it clearly cannot provide this guarantee to more than 10 flows. It follows that there must be some mechanism to request the router for bandwidth guarantees for a given flow. Clearly, the router must do *admission control* and be prepared to reject further requests if further requests are beyond its capacity.

Thus if we define quality of service (QoS) as the provision of performance guarantees for flows, it can be said that QoS requires reservation mechanisms and admission control (to limit the set of flows we provide QoS to) together with scheduling (to enforce performance guarantees for the selected flows). *Quality of service* is a sufficiently vague term, and the implied performance guarantees can refer to bandwidth, delay, or even variation in delay.

One way to make reservations is for a manager to make reservations for each router in the path of a flow. However, this is tedious and would require the work to be done each time the route of the flow changes and whenever the application that requires reservations is stopped and restarted. One standard that has been proposed is the Resource Reservation Protocol (RSVP) [Boy97], which allows applications to make reservations.

This protocol works in the context of a multicast tree between a sender and a set of receivers (and works for one receiver). The idea is that the sender sends a periodic PATH message along the tree that allows routers and receivers to know in which direction the sender is. Then each receiver that wants a reservation of some resource (say, bandwidth) sends a Resource Reservation Protocol (RSV) message up to the next router in the path. Each router accepts the

---

[2]Token bucket shaping is a commonly used example of a scheduling discipline that is not work conserving.

RSV message if the reservation is feasible, merges the RSV messages of all receivers, and then sends it to its parent router. This continues until all reservations have been set up or failure notifications are sent back. Reservations are timed out periodically, so RSV messages must be sent periodically if a receiver wishes to maintain its reservation.

While RSVP appears simple from this description, it has a number of tricky issues. First, it can allow reservations across multiple senders and can include multiple modes of sharing. For shared reservations, it improves scalability by allowing reservations to be merged; for example, for a set of receivers that want differing bandwidths on the same link for the same conference, we can make a single reservation for the maximum of all requests. Finally, we have to deal with the possibility that the requests of a subset of receivers are too large but that the remaining subset can be accommodated. This is handled by creating *blockade* state in the routers. The resulting specification is quite complex.

By contrast, the DiffServ specification suggests that reservations be done by a so-called *bandwidth broker* per domain instead of by each application. The bandwidth broker architecture was still in a preliminary state at the time of this writing, but it appears potentially simpler than RSVP. However, incompletely specified schemes always appear simpler than completely specified schemes.

14.6 PROVIDING BANDWIDTH GUARANTEES

Given that reservations can be set up at routers for a subset of flows, we now return to the problem of schedulers to enforce these reservations. We will concentrate on bandwidth reservations only in this section, and consider reservations for delay in the next section. We will start with a metaphor in Section 14.6.1 that illustrates the problems; we move on to describe a solution in Section 14.6.2.

14.6.1 The Parochial Parcel Service

To illustrate the issues, let us consider the story of a hypothetical parcel service called the Parochial Parcel Service, depicted in Figure 14.8. Two customers, called Jones and Smith, use the parcel service to send their parcels by truck to the next city.

In the beginning, all parcels were kept in a *single* queue at the loading dock, as seen in Figure 14.9. Unfortunately, it so happened that the loading dock was limited in size. It also happened that during busy periods, Jones would send all his parcels just a little before Smith sent his. The result was that when Smith's parcels arrived during busy periods they were refused; Smith was asked to retry some other time.

To solve this unfairness problem, the Parochial Parcel Service decided to use two queues before the loading dock, one for Jones and one for Smith. When times were busy, some space was left for Smith's queue. The queues were serviced in round-robin order. Unfortunately, even this did not work too well because the evil Jones (see Figure 14.10) cleverly used packages that were consistently larger than those of Smith. Since two large packages of Jones could contain seven of Smith's packages, the net result was that Jones could get 3.5 times the service of Smith during busy periods. Thus Smith was happier, but he was still unhappy.

Another idea that the Parochial Parcel Service briefly toyed with was actually to cut parcels into slices, such as unit cubes, that take a standard time to service. Then the company could service a slice at a time for each customer. They called this *slice-by-slice round-robin*.

FIGURE 14.8 A hypothetical parcel service.

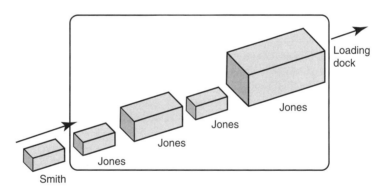

FIGURE 14.9 A FIFO queue for loading parcels that is, unfortunately, hogged by Jones.

When initial field trials produced bitter customer complaints, the Parochial Parcel Service decided they *couldn't* physically cut packages up into slices. However, they realized they *could* calculate the time at which a package will leave in an *imaginary* slice-by-slice system. They could then service packages in the order they would have left in the imaginary system. Such a a system will indeed be fair for any combination of packet (oops, package) sizes.

Unfortunately, simulating the imaginary system is like performing a discrete event simulation in real time. At the very least, this requires keeping the timestamps at which each head package of each queue will depart and picking the earliest such timestamp to service next; thus selection (using priority queues) takes time logarithmic in the number of queues. This must be done whenever a package is sent.

Worse, when a new queue becomes active, potentially all the timestamps have to change. This is shown in Figure 14.11. Jones has a package at the head of his queue that is due to depart

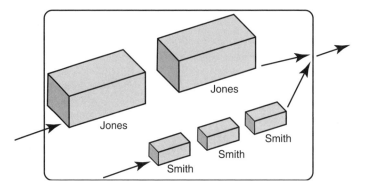

FIGURE 14.10 Two queues and round-robin make Smith happier . . . but not completely happy.

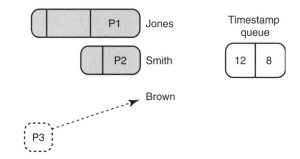

FIGURE 14.11 Brown's entry causes the timestamp of Jones and Smith to change. In general, when a new flow becomes active, the overhead is linear in the number of flows.

at time 12; Smith has a package due to depart at time 8. Now imagine that Brown introduces a packet. Since Brown's package must be scanned once for every three slices scanned in the imaginary slice-by-slice system, the speed of Smith and Jones has gone down from a speed of one in every two slices, to one in every three slices. This potentially means that the arrival of Brown can cause *every* timestamp to be updated, an operation whose complexity is *linear* in the number of flows.

14.6.2 Deficit Round-Robin

What was all this stuff about a parcel service about? Clearly, parcels correspond to packets, the parcel office to a router, and loading docks to outbound links. More importantly, the seemingly facetious slice-by-slice round-robin corresponds to a seminal idea, called *bit-by-bit round-robin*, introduced by Demers, Keshav, and Shenker [DKS89]. Simulated bit-by-bit round-robin provides provably fair bandwidth distribution and some remarkably tight delay bounds; unfortunately, it is hard to implement at gigabit speeds. A considerable improvement to bit-by-bit round-robin is made in the paper by Staliadis and Verma [SV96], which shows how to reduce the linear overhead of the DKS scheme to the purely logarithmic overhead of sorting. Sorting can be done at high speeds with hardware multiway heaps; however, it is still more complex than deficit round-robin for bandwidth guarantees.

Now while bit-by-bit round-robin provides both bandwidth guarantees and delay bounds, our first observation is that many applications can benefit from just bandwidth guarantees. Thus an interesting question is whether there is a simpler algorithm that can provide merely bandwidth guarantees. We are, of course, relaxing system requirements to pave the way for a more efficient implementation, as suggested by **P3**.

If we are only interested in bandwidth guarantees and would like a constant-time algorithm, a natural point of departure is round-robin. So we ask ourselves: Can we retain the efficiency of round-robin and yet add a little state to correct for the unfairness of examples such as Figure 14.10?

A banking analogy motivates the solution. Each flow is given a *quantum*, which is like a periodic salary that gets credited to the flow's bank account on every round-robin cycle. As with most bank accounts, a flow cannot spend (i.e., send packets of the corresponding size) more than is contained in its account; the algorithm does not allow bank accounts to be overdrawn. However, perfectly naturally, the balance remains in the account for possible spending in the next period. Thus any possible unfairness in a round is compensated for in subsequent rounds, leading to long-term fairness.

More precisely, for each flow i, the algorithm keeps a quantum size Q_i and a deficit counter D_i. The larger the quantum size assigned to a flow, the larger the share of the bandwidth it receives. On each round-robin scan, the algorithm will service as many packets as possible for flow i with size less than $Q_i + D_i$. If packets remain in flow i's queue, the algorithm stores the "deficit," or remainder, in D_i for the next opportunity. It is easy to prove that the algorithm is fair in the long term for any combination of packet sizes and that it takes only a few more instructions to implement than round-robin.

Consider the example illustrated in Figures 14.12 and 14.13. We assume that the *quantum* size of all flows is 500 and that there are four flows. In Figure 14.12 the round-robin pointer points to the queue of $F1$; the algorithm adds the quantum size to the deficit counter of $F1$, which is now at 500. Thus $F1$ has sufficient funds to send the packet at the head of its queue (of size 200) but not the second packet, of size 750. Thus the remainder (300) is left in $F1$'s deficit account and the algorithm skips to $F2$, leaving the picture shown in Figure 14.13.

Thus in the second round, the algorithm will send the packet at the head of $F2$'s queue (leaving a deficit of 0), the packet at the head of $F3$'s queue (leaving a deficit of 400), and the packet at the head of $F4$'s queue (leaving a deficit of 320). It then returns to $F1$'s queue. $F1$'s deficit counter now goes up to 800; this reflects a past account balance of 300 plus a fresh deposit of 500. The algorithm then sends the packet of size 750 and the packet of size 20. Assume that no more packets arrive to $F1$'s queue than are shown in Figure 14.13. Thus since the $F1$ queue is empty, the algorithm skips to $F2$.

Curiously, when skipping to $F2$, the algorithm does not leave behind the deficit of $800 - 750 - 20 = 30$ in $F1$'s queue. Instead, it zeroes out $F1$'s deficit counter. Thus the deficit counter is a somewhat curious bank account that is zeroed unless the account holder can prove a "need" in terms of a nonempty queue. Perhaps this is analogous to a welfare account.

14.6.3 Implementation and Extensions of Deficit Round-Robin

As described, DRR has one major implementation problem. The algorithm may visit a number of queues that have no packets to send. This would be very wasteful if the number of possible queues is much larger than the number of active queues. However, there is a simple way to avoid idle skipping of inactive queues by adding redundant state for speed (**P12**).

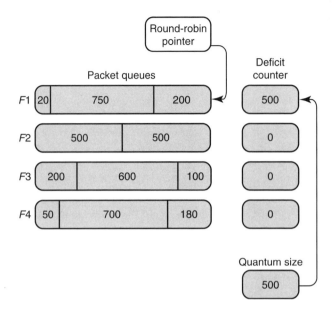

FIGURE 14.12 Deficit round-robin: At the start, all the *deficit* variables are initialized to zero. The round-robin pointer points to the top of the active list. When the first queue is serviced, the *quantum* value of 500 is added to the *deficit* value. The remainder after servicing the queue is left in the *deficit* variable.

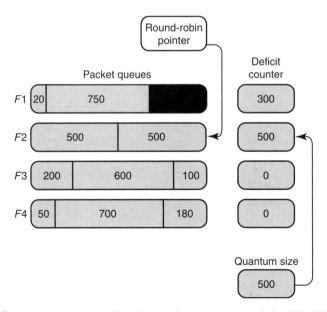

FIGURE 14.13 Deficit round-robin (2): After sending out a packet of size 200, $F1$'s queue had 300 bytes of its quantum left. It could not use it in the current round, since the next packet in the queue is 750 bytes. Therefore, the amount 300 will carry over to the next round, when it can send packets of size totaling 300 (deficit from previous round) + 500 (quantum).

More precisely, the algorithm maintains an auxiliary queue, *ActiveList*, which is a list of indices of queues that contain at least one packet. In the example, $F1$, which was at the head of *ActiveList*, is removed from *ActiveList* after its last packet is serviced. If $F1$'s packet queue were nonempty, the algorithm would place $F1$ at the tail of *ActiveList* and keep track of any unused deficit. Notice that this prevents a flow from getting quantum added to its account while the flow is idle.

Note that DRR shares bandwidth among flows in proportion to quantum sizes. For example, suppose there are three flows, $F1, F2$, and $F3$, with respective quantum sizes 2, 2, *and* 3, who have reservations. Then if all three are active, $F2$ should get a fraction $\frac{2}{2+2+3} = 2/7$ of the output-link bandwidth. If, for example, $F3$ is idle, then $F2$ is guaranteed the fraction $\frac{2}{2+2} = 1/2$ of the output-link bandwidth. In all cases, a flow is guaranteed a *minimum bandwidth*, measured over the period the flow is active, that is proportional to the ratio of its quantum size to the sum of the quantum sizes of all other reservations.

How efficient is the algorithm? The cost to dequeue a packet is a constant number of instructions as long as each flow's quantum is greater than a maximum-size packet. This ensures that a packet is sent every time a queue is visited. For example, if the quantum size of a flow is 1, the algorithm would have to visit a queue 100 times to send a packet of size 100. Thus if the maximum packet size is 1500 and flow $F1$ is to receive twice the bandwidth as flow $F2$, we may arrange for the quantum of $F1$ to be 3000 and the quantum of $F2$ to be 1500. Once again, in terms of our principles, we note that avoiding the generality (**P7**) of arbitrary quantum settings allows a more efficient implementation.

EXTENSIONS OF DEFICIT ROUND-ROBIN

We now consider two extensions of DRR: hierarchical DRR and DRR with a single priority queue.

HIERARCHICAL DEFICIT ROUND-ROBIN

An interesting model for bandwidth sharing is introduced in the so-called *class-based queuing (CBQ)* scheme [FJ95]. The idea is to specify a hierarchy of users that can share an output link. For example, a transatlantic link may be shared by two organizations in proportion to the amount each pays for the link. Consider two organizations, A and B, who pay, respectively, 70% and 30% of the cost of a link and so wish to have assured bandwidth shares in that ratio. However, within organization A there are two main traffic types: Web users and others. Organization A wishes to limit Web traffic to get only 40% of A's share of the traffic when other traffic from A is present. Similarly, B wishes video traffic to take no more than 50% of the total traffic when other traffic from B is present (Figure 14.14).

Suppose at a given instant organization A's traffic is only Web traffic and organization B has both video and other traffic. Then A's Web traffic should get all of A's share of the bandwidth (say, 0.7 Mbps of a 1-Mbps link); B's video traffic should get 50% of the remaining share, which is 0.15 Mbps. If other traffic for A comes on the scene, then the share of A's Web traffic should fall to $0.7 * 0.4 = 0.28$ Mbps. Class-based queuing is easy to implement using a *hierarchical* DRR scheduler for each node in the CBQ tree. For example, we would use a DRR scheduler to divide traffic between A and B. When A's queue gets visited, we run the DRR scheduler for within A, which then visits the Web queue and the other traffic queue and serves them in proportion to their quanta.

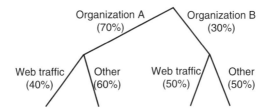

FIGURE 14.14   Example of a class-based queuing specification for bandwidth sharing.

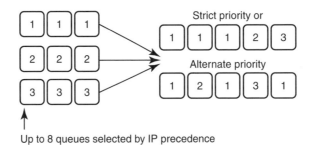

Up to 8 queues selected by IP precedence

FIGURE 14.15   Cisco's modified DRR (MDRR) scheme.

DEFICIT ROUND-ROBIN PLUS PRIORITY

A simple idea implemented by Cisco systems (and called Modified DRR, or MDRR) is to combine DRR with priority to allow minimal delay for voice over IP. The idea, depicted in Figure 14.15, allows up to eight flow queues for a router. A packet is placed in a queue based on bits in the IP TOS fields called the IP *precedence* bits. However, queue 1 is a special queue typically reserved for voice over IP. There are two modes: In the first mode, Queue 1 is given strict priority over the other queues. Thus in the figure, we would serve all three of queue 1's packets before alternating between queue 2 and queue 3. On the other hand, in alternating priority mode, queue 1 visits alternate with visits to a DRR scan of the remaining queues. Thus in this mode, we would first serve queue 1, then queue 2, then queue 1, then queue 3, etc.

14.7 SCHEDULERS THAT PROVIDE DELAY GUARANTEES

So far we have considered only schedulers that provide bandwidth guarantees across multiple queues. Our only exception is MDRR, which is an ad hoc solution. We now consider providing delay bounds. The situation is analogous to a number of chefs sharing an oven, as shown in Figure 14.16. The frozen-food chef (analogous to, say, FTP traffic) cares more about throughput and less about delay; the regular chef (analogous to, say, Telnet traffic) cares about delay, but for the fast-food chef (analogous to video or voice traffic) a small delay is critical for business.

In practice, most routers implement some form of throughput sharing using algorithms such as DRR. However, almost no commercial router implements schedulers that guarantee delay bounds. The result is that video currently works well sometimes, badly at other times. This may be unacceptable for commercial use. One answer to this problem is to have heavily

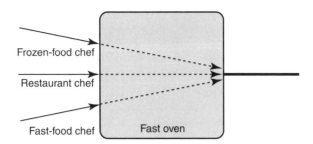

FIGURE 14.16 Three types of chefs sharing an oven, of whom only the fast-food chef needs bounded delay.

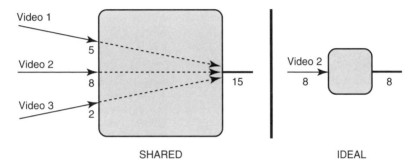

FIGURE 14.17 Defining what an ideal delay bound should be.

underutilized links and to employ ad hoc schemes like MDRR. This may work if bandwidth becomes plentiful. However, traffic does go up to compensate for increased bandwidth; witness the spurt in traffic due to MP3 and Napster traffic.

In theory, the simulated bit-by-bit round-robin algorithm [DKS89] we have already mentioned guarantees isolation and delay bounds. Thus it was used as the basis for the IntServ proposal as a scheduler that could integrate video, voice, and data. However, bit-by-bit round-robin, or weighted fair queuing (WFQ), is currently very expensive to implement. Strict WFQ takes $O(n)$ time per packet, where n is the number of concurrent flows. Recent approximations, which we will describe, take $O(\log(n))$ time. The seminal results in reducing the overhead from $O(n)$ to $O(\log n)$ were due to Staliadis and Verma [SV96] and Bennett and Zhang [BZ96], based on modifications to the bit-by-bit discipline. We will, however, present a version based on another scheme, called *virtual clock*, which we believe is simpler to understand.

Before we study how to implement a delay bound, let us consider what an ideal delay bound should be (Figure 14.17). The left figure shows three video flows that traverse a common output link; the flows have reserved 5, 8, and 2 bandwidth units, respectively, of a 15-unit output link. The right figure shows the ideal "view" of Video 2 if it had its own dedicated router with an output link of 8 units. Thus the ideal delay bound is the delay that a flow would have received in isolation, assuming an output-link bandwidth equal to its own reservation.

Suppose the rate of flow F is r. What is the departure time of a packet p of F arriving at a router dedicated to F that always transmits at r bits per second? Well, if p arrives before the

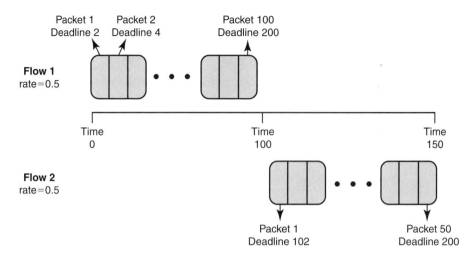

FIGURE 14.18   Accumulated unfairness from the past can impair the fairness of Virtual Clock.

previous packet from flow F (say, *prev*) is transmitted, then p has to wait for *prev* to depart; otherwise p gets transmitted right away. Thus in an ideal system, packet p will depart by: Maximum(Arrival Time(p), Departure Time($prev$)) + Length(p)/r. This recursive equation can easily be solved if we know the arrival times of all packets in flow F up to and including packet p.

Returning to Figure 14.17, if the shared system on the left must emulate the isolated system, it must service every packet before its departure time in the ideal system. In other words, as every packet arrives, we can calculate its deadline in the ideal system as in the preceding paragraph. If the shared system meets all the ideal packet deadlines, then the shared system is as good as or better than the isolated system on the right of Figure 14.17!

We may now consider using a very famous form of real-time scheduler called *earliest deadline first*. The classical idea is that if we wish to meet deadlines, we sort the deadlines of all the packets at the head of each flow queue and send the packet with the *earliest* deadline first. The corresponding packet scheduler, called *virtual clock*, was first introduced by Lixia Zhang [Zha91].

It was first proved [FP95] that virtual clock does a fine job of meeting deadlines. However, it does not quite emulate the system at the right of Figure 14.17 in terms of bandwidth fairness on short time scales. A flow can be locked out for a large amount of time based on past behavior. Consider the example shown in Figure 14.18. Two flows, Flow 1 and Flow 2, are assigned rates of half the link bandwidth each, where the link bandwidth is 1. Assume that Flow 1 has a large supply of packets starting from time 0, while Flow 2's queue is empty until time 100, when it receives a large supply of packets. Thus from time 0 to time 100, since Flow 1 is the only active queue, virtual clock will send 100 packets of size 1 each from Flow 1. The first packet of Flow 1 will have ideal deadline 2, the second 4, and the 100th will have deadline 200. Thus by the time we reach time 100, Flow 1's 101st packet has ideal deadline 202.

If we now bring on 100 packets of Flow 2 at time 100, Flow 2's packets have deadlines 102, 104, 106, ..., and the 50th packet of Flow 2 has deadline 200. Thus during the period from

100 to 150, Flow 2 has taken all the link bandwidth, despite the presence of Flow 1 packets. This hardly looks like the model of Figure 14.17, at least from time 100 to time 150. Notice that packets are all sent within their ideal delays and that even the bandwidth given to both flows is equal across the period from 0 to 150. Unfortunately, we don't want this behavior. We don't want Flow 1 to be penalized, because in the past, when other flows were not present, it took more bandwidth than it needed.

There is a very simple fix for this problem, which was described concurrently in Cobb et al. [CGE96] and Suri et al. [SVC97]. Let us start by calling a flow *oversubscribed* if the flow sends at more than its reserved rates during short periods, as Flow 1 does in Figure 14.18. One can see that an ordinary virtual clock has a throughput unfairness problem because the deadlines of oversubscribed flows can exceed real time by an unbounded amount. For example, Flow 1's deadline can grow without bound if we increase the time when Flow 1 is the only active flow in Figure 14.18.

A careful examination shows that to guarantee delay bounds for other flows, we need only ensure that oversubscribed flow deadlines exceed real time by some threshold δ, where δ is the time taken to send a maximum-size packet at the smallest rate of any flow. For example, in Figure 14.18, this is $1/0.5$, which is 2. Thus to guarantee delay bounds we only need ensure that the virtual clock of an oversubscribed flow is 2 more than real time. To make the difference go up to 100, as in Figure 14.18, is overkill.

To implement this limited "overshoot," we can pull all oversubscribed deadlines back when time advances. Alternately, we can use a famous problem-solving technique and do a mental reversal. This allows us to see another relativistic degree of freedom (**P13**). Instead of pulling back a potentially large set of oversubscribed flows, we can "leap forward" the single counter representing real time. More precisely, we advance the real-time counter to be within δ of the smallest deadline whenever the smallest deadline exceeds the real-time counter by δ. Of course, now the "real-time" counter no longer represents "real-time," but is only the reference "clock" used to stamp deadlines for future packets. The single clock adjustment is more efficient than adjusting multiple deadlines.

For example, using this new mechanism in Figure 14.18, the deadline of the 101st packet of Flow 1 at time 100 would become only 102, and not 202 as in the unmodified scheme. This ensures that Flow 1 and Flow 2 will share the link evenly in the period from time 100 to time 150.

The net result is that the leap-forward version of the virtual clock behaves just as well as ideal bit-by-bit schemes, and it takes $O(\log(n))$ work. The logarithmic overhead is needed only for sorting deadlines using, say, a heap [CLR90]). Leaping forward is also efficient because we can access the element with the smallest tag directly from the top of the heap in constant time. What is the cost of sorting using a heap?

Recall that a d-heap is a tree in which each node of the tree contains d children and each node has a value smaller than the values contained in all its children. If the values in the leaves of the tree are deadlines, then the root contains the earliest deadline. When the earliest deadline flow is scheduled, its leaf deadline value is updated. This can change its parent value, and its parent's parent value, and so on, up to the root. In software, a value of d greater than 2 is not much help, because each of the d children of a node must be compared when any child value changes. However, in hardware, if the d-children are stored in contiguous memory locations, then for values of d up to, say, 32, the hardware can retrieve 32 consecutive memory locations in a single wide memory access of around 1024 bits. Simple combinatorial logic within the chip can then calculate the minimum of these 32 values within the time for a memory access.

Since an update can require changing all parent values in a path from the leaf to the root, and changing each parent value takes one memory access to read and one to write, the worst-case number of memory accesses is equal to twice the maximum height of a 32-way heap, which is $\log_3 2N$, where N is the number of flows. Thus for N less than $32^3 = 32K$, the calculation of the minimum will take only six memory accesses. Thus the $\log N$ term per packet can be made very small in practice by using a large radix for the logarithm.

In terms of our principles, we are using an efficient data structure (**P15**) and are adding hardware (**P5**) in the form of a special-purpose sorting chip. The chip in turn uses wide memories and locality (**P5b**, exploit locality) to reduce memory access times.

A second technique to build heaps does not use wide words but uses pipelining. It is described in the exercises for Chapter 2. Note that these two solutions to making a fast heap represent two of the three memory subsystem design strategies (**P5a, b**, pipelining and wide word parallelism) described in Chapters 3 and 2.

In the case of both DRR and virtual clock, the basic idea works fine if all reserved rates are within small multiples of each other. However, if rates can vary by orders of magnitude (from, say, telemetry applications to video), both schemes introduce a peculiar form of burstiness described in Bennett and Zhang [BZ96]. This burstiness can be fixed using a technique of two queues first introduced in Bennett and Zhang [BZ96] and also used in Suri et al. [SVC97]. However, it adds implementation complexities of its own and may not be needed in practice.

If hardware is not available and the $\log n$ cost is significant, another possible approach [SVC97] is to trade accuracy in deadlines for reduced computation (**P3b**). For example, suppose your deadlines were originally $100.13, 115.27, 61$ and we round up the deadlines (tags) to whole numbers $101, 116, 61$. This reduces the range of numbers to be sorted, which can be exploited by bucket-sorting techniques to reduce sorting overhead. It can also be shown that the reduced deadline accuracy introduces only a small additive penalty to the delay bound.

A second approach to reduce computation, by relaxing specifications (**P3b**), is described in Ramabhadran and Pasquale [RP03]. While there are no worst-case delay guarantees, the scheme appears to provide good delay bounds in most cases, with computation time that is only slightly worse than for DRR.

14.8 SCALABLE FAIR QUEUING

Using multiple queues for each flow, we have seen that: (i) a constant-time algorithm (DRR) can provide bandwidth guarantees for QoS even using software and (ii) a logarithmic time-overhead algorithm can provide bandwidth and delay guarantees; further, the logarithmic overhead can be made negligible using extra hardware to implement a priority queue. Thus it would seem that QoS is easy to implement in routers ranging from small edge routers to the bigger backbone (core) routers.

Unfortunately, studies by Thompson et al. [TMW97] of backbone routers show there to be around 250,000 concurrent flows. With increasing traffic, we expect this number to grow to a million and possibly larger as Internet speed and traffic increase. Keeping state for a million flows can be a difficult task in backbone routers. If the state is kept in SRAM, the amount of memory required can be expensive; if the state is kept in DRAM, state lookup could be slow.

More cogently, advocates of Internet scaling and aggregation point out that Internet routing currently uses only around 150,000 prefixes for over 100 million nodes. Why should QoS require so much state when none of the other components of IP do? In particular, while the QoS state *may* be manageable today, it might represent a serious threat to the scaling of the Internet. Just as prefixes aggregate routes for multiple IP addresses, is there a way to aggregate flow state?

Aggregation implies that backbone routers will treat groups of flows in identical fashion. Aggregation requires that (i) it must be reasonable for the members of the aggregated group to be treated identically and (ii) there must be an efficient mapping from packet headers to aggregation groups. For example, in the case of IP routing, (i) a prefix aggregates a number of addresses that share the same output link, often because they are in the same relative geographic area, and (ii) longest matching prefix provides an efficient mapping from destination addresses in headers to the appropriate prefix.

There are three interesting proposals to provide aggregated QoS, which we describe briefly: random aggregation (stochastic fair queuing), aggregation at the network edge (DiffServ), and aggregation at the network edge together with efficient policing of misbehaving flows (core stateless fair queuing).

14.8.1 Random Aggregation

The idea behind stochastic fair queuing (SFQ) [McK91] is to employ principle **P3a** by trading certainty in fairness for reduced state. In this proposal, backbone routers keep a fixed set of flow queues that is affordable, say, 125,000, on which they do, say, DRR. When packets arrive, some set of packet fields (say, destination, source, and the destination and source ports for TCP and UDP traffic) are hashed to a flow queue. Thus assuming that a flow is defined by the set of fields used for hashing, a given flow will always be hashed to the same flow queue. Thus with 250,000 concurrent flows and 125,000 flow queues, roughly 2 flows will share the same flow queue or hash bucket.

Stochastic fair queuing has two disadvantages. First, different backbone routers can hash flows into different groups because routers need to be able to change their hash function if the hash distributes unevenly. Second, SFQ does not allow some flows to be treated differently (either locally within one router or globally across routers) from other flows, a crucial feature for QoS. Thus, SFQ only provides some sort of scalable and uniform bandwidth fairness.

14.8.2 Edge Aggregation

The three ideas behind the DiffServ proposal [SWG] are: relaxing system requirements (**P3**) by aggregating flows into classes at the cost of a reduced ability to discriminate between flows; shifting the mapping to classes from core routers to edge routers (**P3c**, shifting computation in space); and passing the aggregate class information from the edge to core routers in the IP header (**P10**, passing hints in protocol headers).

Thus, edge routers aggregate flows into classes and mark the packet class by using a standardized value in the IP TOS field. The IP type-of-service (TOS) field was meant for some such use, but it was never standardized; vendors such as Cisco used it within their networks to denote traffic classes such as voice over IP, but there was no standard definition of traffic classes. The DiffServ group generalizes and standardizes such vendor behavior, reserving values for classes that are being standardized. One class being discussed is so-called *expedited*

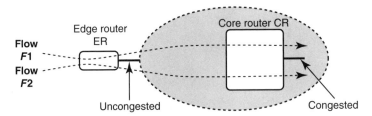

FIGURE 14.19 If flows $F1$ and $F2$ are aggregated by the time they reach the core router CR, how can the core router realize that $F1$ is oversubscribing without keeping state for each (unaggregated) flow?

service, in which a certain bandwidth is reserved for the class. Another is *assured service*, which is given a lower drop probability for RED in output queues.

However, the key point is that backbone routers have a much easier job in DiffServ. First, they map flows to classes based on a small number of field values in a single TOS field. Second, the backbone router has to manage only a small number of queues, mostly one for each class and sometimes one for each subclass within a class; for example, assured service currently specifies three levels of service within the class. Edge routers, though, have to map flows to classes based on ACL-like rules and examination of possibly the entire header. This is, however, a good trade-off because edge routers operate at slower speeds.

14.8.3 Edge Aggregation with Policing

Using edge aggregation, two flows (say, $F1$ and $F2$) that have reserved bandwidth (say, B_1 and B_2, respectively) could be aggregated into a class that has nominally reserved some bandwidth, which is $B \geq B_1 + B_2$ for all flows in the class. Consider Figure 14.19. Suppose $F1$ decides to oversubscribe and to send at a rate greater than B. The edge router ER in Figure 14.19 may currently have sufficient bandwidth to allow all packets of flow $F1$ and $F2$ through. Unfortunately, when this aggregated class reaches the backbone (core) router CR, suppose the core router is limited in bandwidth and must drop packets. Ideally, CR should only drop oversubscribed flows like $F1$ and let all of $F2$'s packets through.

How, though, can CR tell which flows are oversubscribed? It could do so by keeping state for all flows passing through, but that would defeat scaling. A clever idea, called *core-stateless fair queuing* [SSZ], makes the observation that the edge router ER has sufficient information to distinguish the oversubscribed flows. Thus ER can, using principle **P10**, pass information in packet headers to CR.

How, though, should CR handle oversubscribed flows? Dropping all such marked packets may be too severe. If there is enough bandwidth for some oversubscribed flows, it seems reasonable for CR to drop in proportion to the degree a flow is oversubscribed. Thus ER should pass a value in the packet header of a flow that is proportional to the degree a flow is oversubscribed. To implement this idea, CR can drop randomly (**P3a**), with a drop probability that is proportional to the degree of oversubscription. While this has some error probability, it is close enough. Most importantly, random dropping can be implemented without CR keeping any state per flow. In effect, CR is implementing RED, but with the drop probability computed based on a packet header field set by an edge router.

While core-stateless is a nice idea, we note that unlike SFQ (which can be implemented in isolation without cooperation between routers) and DiffServ (which has mustered sufficient support for its standardized use of the TOS field), core-stateless fair queuing is, as of now, only a research proposal [SSZ].

14.9 SUMMARY

In this chapter, we attacked another major implementation bottleneck for a router: scheduling data packets to reduce the effects of congestion, to provide fairness, and to provide quality-of-service guarantees to certain flows. We worked our way upward from schemes, such as RED, that provide congestion feedback to schemes that provide QoS guarantees in terms of bandwidth and delay. We also studied how to scale QoS state to core routers using aggregation techniques such as DiffServ.

A real router will often have to choose various *combinations* of these individual schemes. Many routers today offer RED, token bucket policing, and multiple queues and DRR. However, the major point is that all these schemes, with the exception of the schemes that provide delay bounds, can be implemented efficiently; even schemes that provide delay bounds can be implemented at the cost of fairly simple added hardware. A number of combination schemes can also be implemented efficiently using the principles we have outlined. The exercises explore some of these combinations.

To make this chapter self-contained, we devoted a great deal of the discussion to explanations of topics, such as congestion control and resource reservation, that are really peripheral to the main business of this book. What we really care about is the use of our principles to attack scheduling bottlenecks. Lest that be forgotten, we remind you as always, of the summary, in Figure 14.2 of the techniques used in this chapter and the corresponding principles.

14.10 EXERCISES

1. Consider what happens if there are large variations in the reserved bandwidths of flows, for example, $F1$ with a rate of 1000 and $F2, \ldots, Fn$ with a rate of 1. Assuming that all flows have the same minimum packet size, show that flow $F1$ can be locked out for a long period.

2. Consider the simple idea of sending one packet for each queue with enabled quantum for each round in DRR. In other words, we interleave the packets sent in various queues during a DRR round rather than finishing a quantum's worth for every flow. Describe how to implement this efficiently.

3. Work out the details of implementing a hierarchical DRR scheme.

4. Suppose an implementation wishes to combine DRR with token bucket shaping on the queues as well. How can the implementation ensure that it skips empty queues (a DRR scan should not visit a queue that has no token bucket credits)?

5. Describe how to efficiently combine DRR with multiple levels of priority. In other words, there are several levels of priority; within each level of priority, the algorithm runs DRR.

6. Suppose that the required bandwidths of flows vary by an order of magnitude in DRR. What fairness problems can result? Suggest a simple fix that provides better short-term fairness without requiring sorting.

CHAPTER 15

Routers as Distributed Systems

Come now and let us reason together.

— ISAIAH 1:18, THE BIBLE

Distributed systems are clearly evil things. They are subject to a lack of synchrony, a lack of assurance, and a lack of trust. Thus in a distributed system the time to receive messages can vary widely; messages can be lost and servers can crash; and when a message does arrive it could even contain a virus. In Lamport's well-known words a distributed system is "one in which the failure of a computer you didn't even know existed can render your own computer unusable."

Of course, the main reason to use a distributed system is that people are distributed. It would perhaps be unreasonable to pack every computer on the Internet into an efficiency apartment in upper Manhattan. But a router? Behind the gleaming metallic cage and the flashing lights, surely there lies an orderly world of synchrony, assurance, and trust.

On the contrary, this chapter argues that as routers (recall *routers* includes general interconnect devices such as switches and gateways as well) get faster, the delay between router components increases in importance when compared to message transmission times. The delay across links connecting router components can also vary significantly. Finally, availability requirements make it infeasible to deal with component failures by crashing the entire router. With the exception of trust — trust arguably exists between router components — a router *is* a distributed system. Thus within a router it makes sense to use techniques developed to design reliable distributed systems.

To support this thesis, this chapter considers three sample phenomena that commonly occur within most high-performance interconnect devices — flow control, striping, and asynchronous data structure updates. In each case, the desire for performance leads to intuitively plausible schemes. However, the combination of failure and asynchrony can lead to subtle interactions.

Thus a second thesis of this chapter is that the use of distributed algorithms within routers requires careful analysis to ensure reliable operation. While this is trite advice for protocol designers (who ignore it anyway), it may be slightly more novel in the context of a router's internal microcosm.

The chapter is organized as follows. Section 15.1 motivates the need for flow control on long chip-to-chip links and describes solutions that are simpler than, say, TCP's window flow control. Section 15.2 motivates the need for internal striping across links and fabrics to gain throughput and presents solutions that restore packet ordering after striping. Section 15.3 details

Number	Principle	Used In
P1	Avoid waste caused by partitioned buffers	Internal flow control
P13	Exploit degrees of freedom by decoupling logical from physical reception	Internal striping
P3	Relax binary search requirements to allow duplicate key values	Binary search update

FIGURE 15.1 Principles used in the various distributed systems techniques (for use within a router) discussed in this chapter.

the difficulties of performing asynchronous updates on data structures that run concurrently with search operations.

The techniques described in this chapter (and the corresponding principles invoked) are summarized in Figure 15.1.

In all three examples in this chapter, the focus is not merely on performance, but on the use of design and reasoning techniques from distributed algorithms to produce solutions that gain performance without sacrificing reliability. The techniques used to gain reliability include periodic synchronization of key invariants and centralizing asynchronous computation to avoid race conditions. Counterexamples are also given to show how easily the desire to gain performance can lead, without care, to obscure failure modes that are hard to debug.

The sample of internal distributed algorithms presented in this chapter is necessarily incomplete. An important omission is the use of failure detectors to detect and swap out failed boards, switching fabrics, and power supplies.

Quick Reference Guide

It is important for an implementor to learn how to make link flow control reliable, as described in Section 15.1.2. Implementors are increasingly turning to striping within networking devices and some solutions for link striping are described in Section 15.2.

15.1 INTERNAL FLOW CONTROL

As said in Chapter 13, packaging technology and switch size are forcing switches to expand beyond single racks. These multichassis systems interconnect various components with serial links that span relatively large distances of 5–20 m. At the speed of light, a 20-m link contributes a round-trip link delay of 60 nsec. On the other hand, at OC-768 speeds, a 40-byte minimum-size packet takes 8 nsec to transmit. Thus, eight packets can be simultaneously in transit on such a link.

Worse, link signals propagate slower than the speed of light; also, there are other delays, such as serialization delay, that make the number of cells that can be in flight on a single link even larger. This is quite similar to a stream of packets in flight on a transatlantic link. A single router is now a miniature Internet.

TCP (Transmission Control Protocol) and other transport protocols already solve the problem of *flow control*. If the receiver has finite buffers, sender flow control ensures that any packet sent by the sender has a buffer available when it arrives at the receiver. Chip-to-chip links also require flow control. It is considered bad form to drop packets or cells (we will use cells in what follows) within a router for reasons other than output-link congestion.

It is possible to reuse directly the TCP flow control mechanisms between chips. But TCP is complex to implement. Disentangling mechanisms, TCP is complex because it does error control *and* flow control, both using sequence numbers. However, within a chip-to-chip link, errors on the link are rare enough for recovery to be relegated to the original source computer. Thus, it is possible to apply fairly recent work on flow control [OSV94, KCB94] that is not intertwined with error control.

Figure 15.2 depicts a simple credit flow control mechanism [OSV94] for a chip-to-chip link within a router. The sender keeps a credit register that is initialized to the number of buffers allocated at the receiver. The sender sends cells only when the credit register is positive and decrements the credit register after a cell is sent. At the receiving chip, whenever a cell is removed from the buffer, the receiver sends a credit to the sender. Finally, when a credit message arrives, the sender increments the credit register.

15.1.1 Improving Performance

In Figure 15.2, if the number of buffers allocated is greater than the product of the line speed and the round-trip delay (called the *pipe size*), then transfers can run at the full link speed.

One problem in real routers is that there are often several different traffic classes that share the link. One way to accommodate all classes is to strictly partition destination buffers among classes. This can be wasteful because it requires allocating the pipe size (say, 10 cell buffers) to each class. For a large number of classes, the number of cell buffers will grow alarmingly, potentially pushing the amount of on-chip SRAM required beyond feasible limits. Recall that field programmable gate arrays (FPGAs) especially have smaller on-chip SRAM limits.

FIGURE 15.2 Basic credit-based flow control.

But allocating the full pipe size to all classes at the same time is obvious waste (**P1**) because if every class were to send cells at the same time, each by itself would get only a fraction of the link throughput. Thus it makes sense to *share* buffers. The simplest approach to buffer sharing is to divide the buffer space physically into a common pool together with a private pool for each class.

A naive method to do so would mark data cells and credits as belonging to either the common or the private pools to prevent interference between classes. The naive scheme also requires additional complexity to guarantee that a class does not exceed, say, a pipe size worth of buffers.

An elegant way to achieve the allow buffer sharing without marking cells is described in Ozveren et al. [OSV94]. Conceptually, the entire buffer space at the receiver is partitioned so that each class has a private pool of *Min* buffers; in addition there is a common pool of size $(B - N * Min)$ buffers, where N is the number of classes and B is the total buffer space. Let *Max* denote the pipe size.

The protocol runs in two modes: *congested* and *uncongested*. When congested, each class is restricted to *Min* outstanding cells; when uncongested, each class is allowed the presumably larger amount of *Max* outstanding cells. All cell buffers at the downstream node are anonymous; any buffer can be assigned to the incoming cells of any class. However, by carefully restricting transitions between the two modes, we can allow buffer sharing while preventing deadlock and cell loss.

To enforce the separation between private pools *without* marking cells, the sender keeps track of the total number of outstanding cells S, which is the number of cells sent minus the number of credits received. Each class i also keeps track of a corresponding counter S_i, which is the number of cells outstanding for class i. When $S < N \cdot Min$ (i.e., the private pools are in no danger of depletion), then the protocol is said to be uncongested and every class i can send as long as $S_i \leq Max$.

However, when $S \geq N \cdot Min$, the link is said to be congested and each class is restricted to a smaller limit by ensuring that $S_i \leq Min$. Intuitively, this buffer-sharing protocol performs as follows. During light load, when there are only a few classes active, each active class gets *Max* buffers and goes as fast as it possibly can. Finally, during a continuous period of heavy loading when all classes are active, each class is still guaranteed *Min* buffers.

Hysteresis can be added to prevent oscillation between the two modes. It is also possible to extend the idea of *buffer sharing* for credit-based flow control to *rate sharing* for rate-based flow control using, say, leaky buckets (Chapter 14).

15.1.2 Rescuing Reliability

The protocol sketched in the last subsection uses limited receiver SRAM buffers very efficiently but is not robust to failures. Before understanding how to make the more elaborate flow control protocol robust against failures, it is wiser to start with the simpler credit protocol portrayed in Figure 15.2.

Intuitively, the protocol in Figure 15.2 is like transferring money between two banks: The "banks" are the sender and the receiver, and both credits and cells count as "money." It is easy to see that in the absence of errors the total "money" in the system is conserved. More formally, let *CR* be the credit register, *M* the number of cells in transit from sender to receiver,

C the number of credits in transit in the other direction, and Q the number of cell buffers that are occupied at the receiver.

Then it is easy to see that (assuming proper initialization and that no cells or credits are lost on the link), the protocol maintains the following property at any instant: $CR + M + Q + C = B$, where B is the total buffer space at the receiver. The relation is called an *invariant* because it holds at all times when the protocol works correctly. It is the job of protocol initialization to *establish* the invariant and the job of fault tolerance mechanisms to *maintain* the invariant.

If this invariant is maintained at all times, then the system will never drop cells, because the number of cells in transit plus the number of stored cells is never more than the number of buffers allocated.

There are two potential problems with a simple hop-by-hop flow control scheme. First, if initialization is not done correctly, then the sender can have too many credits, which can lead to cell's being dropped. Second, credits or cells for a class can be lost due to link errors. Even chip-to-chip links are not immune from infrequent bit errors; at high link speeds, such errors can occur several times an hour. This second problem can lead to slowdown or deadlock.

Many implementors can be incorrectly persuaded that these problems can be fixed by simple mechanisms. One immediate response is to argue that these cases won't happen or will happen rarely. Second, one can attempt to fix the second problem by using a timer to detect possible deadlock. Unfortunately, it is difficult to distinguish deadlock from the receiver's removing cells very slowly. Worse, the entire link can slow down to a crawl, causing router performance to fall; the result will be hard to debug.

The problems can probably be cured by a router reset, but this is a Draconian solution. Instead, consider the following resynchronization scheme. For clarity, the scheme is presented using a series of refinements depicted in Figure 15.3.

In the simplest synchronization scheme (Scheme 1, Figure 15.3), assume that the protocol periodically sends a specially marked cell called a *marker*. Until the marker returns, the sender stops sending data cells. At the receiver, the *marker flows through the buffer before being sent back to the upstream node*. It is easy to see that after the marker returns, it has "flushed" the pipe of all cells and credits. Thus at the point the marker returns, the protocol can set the credit register (CR) to the maximum value (B). Scheme 1 is simple but requires the sender to be idled periodically in order to do resynchronization.

So Scheme 2 (Figure 15.3) augments Scheme 1 by allowing the sender to send cells after the marker has been sent; however, the sender keeps track of the cells sent since the marker was launched in a register, say, CSM (for "cells sent since marker"). When the marker returns, the sender adjusts the correction to take into account the cells sent since the marker was launched and so sets $CR = B - CSM$.

The major flaw in Scheme 2 is the inability to bound the delay that it takes the marker to go through the queue at the receiver. This causes two problems. First, it makes it hard to bound how long the scheme takes to correct itself. Second, in order to make the marker scheme itself reliable, the sender must periodically retransmit the marker. Without a bound on the marker round-trip delay, the sender could retransmit too early, making it hard to match a marker response to a marker request without additional complexity in terms of sequence numbers.

To bound the marker round-trip delay, Scheme 3 (Figure 15.3) lets the marker bypass the receiver queue and "reflect back" immediately. However, this requires the marker to return with the number of free cell buffers F in the receiver at the instant the marker was received. Then when the marker returns, the sender sets the credit register $CR = F - CSM$.

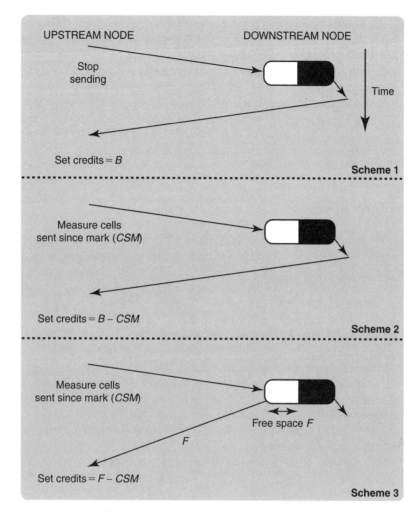

FIGURE 15.3 Three steps to a marker algorithm.

The marker scheme is a special instance of a classical distributed systems technique called a *snapshot*. Informally, a snapshot is a distributed audit that produces a consistent state of a distributed system. Our marker-based snapshot is slightly different from the classical snapshot described in Chandy and Lamport [CL85]. The important point, however, is that snapshots can be used to detect incorrect states of any distributed algorithm and can be efficiently implemented in a two-node subsystem to make any such protocol robust. In particular, the same technique can be used [OSV94] to make the fancier flow control of Section 15.1.1 equally robust.

In particular, the marker protocol makes the credit-update protocol *self-stabilizing*; i.e., it can recover from arbitrary errors, including link errors, and also hardware errors that corrupt registers. This is an extreme form of fault tolerance that can greatly improve the reliability of subsystems without sacrificing performance.

In summary, the general technique for a two-node system is to write down the protocol invariants and then to design a periodic snapshot to verify and, if necessary, correct the invariants. Further techniques for protocols that work on more than two nodes are describe in Awerbuch et al. [APV91]; they are based on decomposing, when possible, multinode protocols into two-node subsystems and repeating the snapshot idea.

An alternative technique for making a two-node credit protocol fault tolerant is the FCVC idea of Kung et al. [KCB94], which is explored in the exercises. The main idea is to use absolute packet numbers instead of incremental updates; with this modification the protocol can be made robust by the technique of periodically resending control state on the two links without the use of a snapshot.

15.2 INTERNAL STRIPING

Flow control within routers is motivated by the twin forces of increasingly large interconnect length and increasing speeds. On the other hand, internal striping or load balancing within a router is motivated by slow interconnect speeds. If serial lines are not fast enough, a designer may resort to striping cells internally across multiple serial links.

Besides serial link striping, designers often resort to striping across slow DRAM banks, to gain memory bandwidth, and across switch fabrics, to scale scheduling algorithms like iSLIP. We saw these trends in Chapter 13. In each case, the designer distributes cells across multiple copies of a slow resource, called a *channel*.

In most applications, the delay across each channel is variable; there is some large skew between the fastest and slowest times to send a packet on each channel. Thus the goals of a good striping algorithm are FIFO delivery in the face of arbitrary skew — routers should not reorder packets because of internal mechanisms — and robustness in the face of link bit errors.

To understand why this combination of goals may be difficult, consider round-robin striping. The sender sends packets in round-robin order on the channels. Round-robin, however, does not provide FIFO delivery without packet modification. The channels may have varying skews, and so the physical arrival of packets at the receiver may differ from their logical ordering. Without sequencing information, packets may be persistently misordered.

Round-robin schemes can be made to guarantee FIFO delivery by adding a packet sequence number that can be used to resequence packets at the receiver. However, many implementations would prefer not to add a sequence number because it adds to cell overhead and reduces the effective throughput of the router.

15.2.1 Improving Performance

To gain ordering without the expense of sequence numbers, the main idea is to exploit a hidden degree of freedom (**P13**) by decoupling *physical reception* from *logical reception*. Physical reception is subject to skew-induced misordering. Logical reception eliminates misordering by using buffering and by having the receiver remove cells using the same algorithm as the sender.

For example, suppose the sender stripes cells in round-robin order using a round-robin pointer that walks through the sending channels. Thus cell A is sent on Channel 1, after which the round-robin pointer at the sender is incremented to 2. The next cell, B, is sent on Channel 2, and so on.

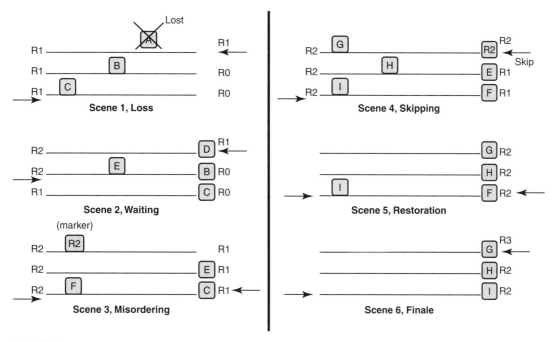

FIGURE 15.4 Misordering and Recovery: A Play in Six Scenes. The final output at the receiver is D, B, C, E, F, G, H, I, and synchronization is achieved after the logical reception of E.

The receiver buffers received cells but does not dequeue a cell when it arrives. Instead, the receiver *also* maintains a round-robin pointer that is initialized to Channel 1. The receiver waits at Channel 1 to receive a cell; when a cell arrives, that cell is dequeued and the receiver moves on to wait for Channel 2. Thus if skew causes cell B (that was sent on Channel 2 after cell A was sent on Channel 1) to arrive before cell 1, the receiver will not dequeue cell B before cell A. Instead, the receiver will wait for cell A to arrive; after dequeuing cell A, the receiver will move on to Channel 2, where it will dequeue the waiting cell, B.

15.2.2 Rescuing Reliability

Synchronization between sender and receiver can be lost due to the loss of a single cell. In the round-robin example shown earlier, if cell A is lost in a large stream of cells sent over three links (Figure 15.4), the receiver will deliver the packet sequence D, B, C, G, E, F, ... and permanently reorder cells.

For switch fabrics and some links, one may be able to assume that cell loss is very rare (say, once a year). Still, such an assumption should make the designer queasy, especially if one loss can cause permanent damage from that point on. To prevent permanent damage after a single cell loss, the sender must periodically resynchronize with the receiver.

To do so, define a *round* as a sequence of visits to consecutive channels before returning to the starting channel. In each round, the sender sends data over all channels. Similarly, in each round, the receiver receives data from all channels. To enable resynchronization, the sender maintains the round number (initialized to *R0*) of all channels, and so does the receiver.

Thus in Figure 15.4, after sending A, B, and C, all the sender channel numbers are at $R1$. However, only channel 1 at the receiver is at $R1$, while the other channels are at $R0$ because the second and third channels have not been visited in the first round-robin scan at the receiver. When the round-robin pointer increments to a channel at the sender or receiver, the corresponding round number is incremented.

Effectively, round numbers can be considered to be implicit per-channel sequence numbers. Thus A can be considered to have sequence number $R1$, the next cell, D, sent on Channel 1 can be considered to have sequence number $R2$, etc.

Thus in Scene 2 of Figure 15.4, the sender has marched on to send D on Channel 1 and E on Channel 2. The receiver is still waiting for a cell on Channel 1, which it finally receives. At this point, the play shifts to Scene 3, where the receiver outputs D and B (in that order) and moves to Channel 3, where it eventually receives cell C.

Basically, the misordering problem in Scene 2 is caused by the receiver's dequeuing a cell sent in Round $R2$ (i.e., D) in Round $R1$ at the receiver. This suggests a simple strategy to synchronize the round numbers in channels: Periodically, the sender should send its current round number on each channel to the receiver. To reduce overhead, such a *marker* cell should be sent after hundreds of data cells are sent, at the cost of having potentially hundreds of cells misordered after a loss.

Because brevity is the soul of wit, the play in Figure 15.4 assumes a marker is sent after D on Channel 1; the sending of markers on other channels is not shown. Thus in Scene 3, notice that a marker is sent on channel 1 with the current round number, $R2$, at the sender.

In Scene 4, the receiver has output D, B, and C, in that order, and is now waiting for Channel 1 again. At this point, the marker containing $R2$ arrives.

A marker is processed at the receiver only when the marker is at the head of the buffer and the round-robin pointer is at the corresponding channel. Processing is done by the following four rules. (1) If the round number in the marker is strictly greater than the current receiver round number, the marker has arrived too early; the round-robin pointer is incremented. (2) If the round numbers are equal, any subsequent cells will have higher round numbers; thus the round-robin pointer is incremented, and the marker is also removed (but not sent to the output).

(3) If the round number in the marker is 1 less than the current channel round number, this is the normal error-free case; the subsequent cell will have the right round number. In this case, the marker is removed but the round-robin pointer at the receiver is *not* incremented. (4) If the round number in the marker is $k > 1$ less than the current channel round number, a serious error (other than cell loss) has occurred and the sender and receiver should reinitialize.

Thus in Scene 4, Rule 2 applies: The marker is destroyed and the round-robin pointer incremented. At this point, it is easy to see that the sender and receiver are now in perfect synchronization, because for each channel at the receiver, the round number when that channel is reached is equal to the round number of the next cell. Thus the play ends with E's being (correctly) dequeued in Scene 4, then F in Scene 5, and finally G in Scene 6. Order is restored, morality is vindicated.

Thus the augmented load-balancing algorithm recovers from errors very quickly (time between sending the marker plus a one-way propagation delay). The general technique underlying the method of Figure 15.4 is to detect state inconsistency on each channel by periodically sending a marker one-way.

One-way sending of periodic state (unlike, say, Figure 15.3) suffices for load balancing as well as for the FCVC protocol (see Exercises) because the invariants of the protocol are one-way. A one-way invariant is an invariant that involves only variables at the two nodes and one link. By contrast, the flow control protocol of Figure 15.2 has an invariant that uses variables on both links.

Periodic sending of state has been advocated as a technique for building reliable Internet protocols, together with timing out state that has not been refreshed for a specified period [Cla88]. While this is a powerful technique, the example of Figure 15.2 shows that perhaps the soft state approach — at least as currently expressed — works only if the protocol invariants are one-way.

For load balancing, besides the one-way invariants on each channel that relate sender and receiver round numbers, there is also a global invariant that ensures that, assuming no packet loss, channel round numbers never differ by more than 1. This node invariant is enforced, after a violation due to loss, by skipping at the receiver.

Even in the case when sequence numbers can be added to cells, logical reception can help simplify the resequencing implementation. Some resequencers use fast parallel hardware sorting circuits to reassemble packets. If logical reception is used, this circuitry is overkill. Logical reception is adequate for the expected case, and a slow scan looking for a matching sequence number is sufficient in the rare error case. Recall that on chip-to-chip links, errors should be very rare. Notice that if sequence numbers are added, FIFO delivery is guaranteed, unlike the protocol of Figure 15.4.

15.3 ASYNCHRONOUS UPDATES

Atomic updates that work concurrently with fast search operations are a necessary part of all the incremental algorithms in Chapters 11 and 10. For example, assume that trie node X points to node Z. Often inserting a prefix requires adding a new node Y so that X points to Y and Y points to Z. Since packets are arriving concurrently at wire speed, the update process must minimally block the search process. The simplest way to do this without locks is to first build Y completely to point to Z and then, in a single atomic write, to swing the pointer at X to point to Y.

In general, however, there are many delicacies in such designs, especially when faced with complications such as pipelining. To illustrate the potential pitfalls and the power of correct reasoning, consider the following example taken from the first bridge implementation.

In the first bridge product studied in Chapter 10, the bridge used binary search. Imagine we had a long list of distinct keys $B, C, D, E, \ldots$ and with all the free space after the last (greatest) key). Consider the problem of adding a new entry, say, A. There are two standard ways to handle this.

The first was is to mimic the atomic update techniques of databases and keep to two copies of the binary search table. When A is inserted, search works on the old copy while A is inserted into a second copy. Then in one atomic operation, update flips a pointer (which the chip uses to identify the table to be searched) to the second copy.

However, this doubles the storage needed, especially if memory is SRAM, and is expensive. Hence many designers prefer a second option: Create a hole for A by moving all elements B and greater one position downward.

15.3.1 *Improving Performance*

To reduce memory needs, update must work on the same binary search table on which search works. To insert element *A* in, say, Figure 15.5, update must move the elements *B*, *C*, and *D* one element down.

If the update and search designers are different, the normal specification for the update designer is always to ensure that the search process sees a consistent binary search table consisting of *distinct* keys. It appears to be very hard to meet this specification without allowing any search to take place until a complete update has terminated. Since an update can take a long time for a bridge database with 32,000 elements, this is unacceptable.

Thus, one could consider relaxing the specification (**P3**) to allow a consistent binary search table that contains *duplicates* of key values. After all, as long as the table is sorted, the presence of two or more keys with the same value cannot affect the correctness of binary search.

Thus the creation of a hole for *A* in Figure 15.5 is accomplished by creating two entries for *D*, then two entries for *C*, and then two entries for *B*, each with a single write to the table. In the last step, *A* is written in place of the first copy of *B*.

To keep the binary search chip simple (see Chapter 10), a route processor was responsible for updates while the chip worked on searches. The table was stored in a separate off-chip memory; all three devices (memory, processor, and chip) can communicate with each other via a common bus. Abstractly, separate search and update processes are concurrently making accesses to memory. Using locks to mediate access to the memory is infeasible because of the consequent slowdown of memory.

Given that the new specification allows duplicates, it is tempting to get away with the simplest atomicity in terms of reads and writes to memory. Search reads the memory and update reads and writes; the memory operations of search and update can arbitrarily interleave. Some implementors may assume that because binary search can work correctly even with duplicates, this is sufficient.

Unfortunately, this does not work, as shown in Figure 15.5.[1] At the start of the scenario (leftmost picture), only *B*, *C*, and *D* are in the first, second, and third table entries. The fourth entry is free. A search for *B* begins with the second entry; a comparison with *C* indicates that binary search should move to the top half, which consists of only entry 1.

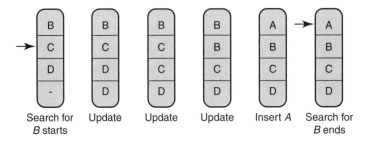

FIGURE 15.5   Concurrent search and update to a binary tree can lead to incorrect search results. A binary search for *B* fails, although *B* is in the table. This is because *B* moves out of the search range during an update that occurs in between search steps.

---

[1] This example is due to Cristi Estan.

Next, search is delayed while update begins to go through the process of inserting *A* by writing duplicates from the bottom up. By the time update is finished, *B* has moved down to the second entry. When search finishes up by examining the first entry, it finds *A* and concludes (wrongly) that *B* is not in the table.

A simple attempt at reasoning correctly exposes this sort of counterexample directly. The standard invariant for binary search is that either the element being searched for (e.g., *B*) is in the current binary search range or *B* is not in the table. The problem is that update can destroy this invariant by moving the element searched for outside the current range.

In the bridge application, the only consequence of this failure is that a packet arriving at a known destination may get flooded to all ports. This will worsen performance only slightly but is unlikely to be noticed by external users!

15.3.2 Rescuing Reliability

A panic reaction to the counterexample of Figure 15.5 might be to jettison single-copy update and retreat to the safety of two copies. However, all the counterexample demonstrates is that a search must complete without intervening update operations. If so, the binary search invariants hold and correctness follows. The counterexample *does not* imply the converse: that an entire update must complete without intervening search operations. The converse property is restrictive and would considerably slow down search.

There are simple ways to ensure that a search completes without intervening updates. The first is to change the architectural model — algorithmics, after all, is the art of changing the problem to fit our limited ingenuity — so that all update writes are centralized through the search chip. When update wishes to perform a write, it posts the write to search and waits for an acknowledgment. After finishing its current search cycle, search does the required write and sends an acknowledgment. Search can then work on the next search task.

A second way, more consonant with the bridge implementation, is to observe that the route processor does packet forwarding. The route processor asks the chip to do search, and it waits for a few microseconds to get the answer. Finally, the route processor does updates only when no packets are being forwarded and hence no searches are in progress. Thus an update can be interrupted by a search, but not vice versa.

The final solution relies on search tolerating duplicates, and it avoids locking by changing the model to centralize updates and searches. Note that centralizing updates is insufficient by itself (without also relaxing the specification to allow duplicates) because this would require performing a complete update without intervening searches.

15.4 CONCLUSIONS

The routing protocol BGP (Border Gateway Protocol) controls the backbone of the Internet. In the last few years, careful scrutiny of BGP has uncovered several subtle flaws. Incompatible policies can lead to routing loops [VGE00], and attempts to make Internal BGP scale using route reflectors also lead to loops [GW02]. Finally, mechanisms to thwart instability by damping flapping routes can lead to penalizing innocent routes for up to an hour [MGVK02].

While credit must go to the BGP designers for designing a protocol that deals with great diversity while making the Internet work most of the time, there is surely some discomfort at these findings. It is often asserted that such bugs rarely manifest themselves in operational networks. But there may be a Three Mile Island incident waiting for us — as in the crash of the old ARPANET [Per92], where a single unlikely corner case capsized the network for a few days.

Even worse, there may be a slow, insidious erosion of reliability that gets masked by transparent recovery mechanisms. Routers restart, TCPs retransmit, and applications retry. Thus failures in protocols and router implementations may only manifest themselves in terms of slow response times, frozen screens, and rebooting computers.

Jeff Raskin says, "Imagine if every Thursday your shoes exploded if you tied them the usual way. This happens to us all of the time with computers, and nobody thinks of complaining." Given our tolerance for pain when dealing with networks and computers, a lack of reliability ultimately translates into a decline of user productivity.

The examples in this chapter fit this thesis. In each case, incorrect distributed algorithm design leads to productivity erosion, not Titanic failures. Flow control deadlocks can be masked by router reboots, and cell loss can be masked by TCP retransmits. Failure to preserve ordering within an internal striping algorithm leads to TCP performance degradation, but not to loss. Finally, incorrect binary search table updates lead only to increased packet flooding. But together, the nickels and dimes of every reboot, performance loss, and unnecessary flood can add up to significant loss.

Thus this chapter is a plea for care in the design of protocols *between* routers and also *within* routers. In the quest for performance that has characterized the rest of the book, this chapter is a lonely plea for rigor. While full proofs may be infeasible, even sketching key invariants and using informal arguments can help find obscure failure modes. Perhaps if we reason together, routers can become as comfortable and free of surprises as an ordinary pair of shoes.

15.5 EXERCISES

1. **FCVC Flow Control Protocol:** The FCVC flow control protocol of Kung et al. [KCB94] provides an important alternative to the credit protocols described in Section 15.1. In the FCVC protocol, shown in Figure 15.6, the sender keeps a count of cells sent H while the receiver keeps a count of cells received R and cells dequeued D. The receiver periodically sends its current value of D, which is stored at the sender as estimate L. The sender is allowed to send if $H - L > Max$. More importantly, if the sender periodically sends H to the receiver, the receiver can deal with errors due to cell loss.

   - Assume cells are lost and that the sender periodically sends H to the receiver. How can the receiver use the values of H and R to detect how many cells have been lost?

   - How can the receiver use this estimate of cell loss to fix D in order to correct the sender?

   - Can this protocol be made self-stabilizing without using the full machinery of a snapshot and reset?

   - Compare the general features of this method of achieving reliability to the method used in the load-balancing algorithm described in the chapter.

2. **Load Balancing with Variable-Size Packets:** Load balancing within a router is typically at the granularity of cells. However, load balancing across routers is often at the

FIGURE 15.6 The FCVC protocol uses a count H of cells sent by sender and an estimate L of the cells dequeued at receiver; flow control is achieved by limiting the difference between H and L. More importantly, the use of absolute packet numbers instead of incremental credits allows the periodic sending of counts to fix errors due to cell loss.

granularity of (variable-sized) packets. Thus simple round-robin striping may not balance load equally because all the large packets may be sent on one link and the small ones on another. Modify the load-balancing algorithm without sequence numbers (using ideas suggested by the deficit round-robin (DRR) algorithm described in Chapter 14) to balance load evenly even while striping variable-size packets. Extend the fault-tolerance machinery to handle this case as well.

3. **Concurrent Compaction and Search:** In many lookup applications, routers must use available on-chip SRAM efficiently and may have to compact memory periodically to avoid filling up memory with unusably small amounts of free space. Imagine a sequence of N trie nodes of size-4 words that are laid out contiguously in SRAM memory after which there is a hole of size-2 words. As a fundamental operation in compaction, the update algorithm needs to move the sequence of N nodes two words to the right to fill the hole. Unfortunately, moving a node two steps to the right can overwrite itself and its neighbor. Find a technique for doing compaction for update with minimal disruption to a concurrent search process. Assume that when a node X is moved, there is at most one other node Y that points to X and that the update process has a fast technique for finding Y given X (see Chapter 11). Use this method to find a way to compact a sequence of trie nodes arbitrarily laid out in memory into a configuration where all the free space is at one end of memory and there are no "holes" between nodes. Of course, the catch is that the algorithm should work without locking out a concurrent search process for more than one write operation every K search operations, as in the bridge binary search example.

PART IV

Endgame

Daring ideas are like chessmen moved forward. They may be beaten, but they may start a winning game.

— GOETHE

We didn't lose the game; we just ran out of time.

— VINCE LOMBARDI

The last part of the book applies network algorithmics to the emerging fields of security and measurement. As the Internet matures, we believe that good abstractions for security and measurement will be key to well-engineered networks. While the problems (e.g., detecting a DoS attack at a high-speed router) seem hard, some remarkable ideas have been proposed. The final chapter reaches closure by distilling the underlying unities behind the many different techniques surveyed in this book and by surveying the future of network algorithmics.

CHAPTER 16

Measuring Network Traffic

Not everything that is counted counts, and not everything that counts can be counted.

— ALBERT EINSTEIN

Every graduate with a business degree knows that the task of optimizing an organization or process begins with *measurement*. Once the bottlenecks in a supply chain are identified and the major cost factors are outlined, improvements can be targeted. The situation is no different in computer networks. For example, in service provider networks, packet counting and logging provide powerful tools for the following.

Capacity Planning: Internet service providers (ISPs) need to determine the traffic matrix, or the traffic between all source and destination subnets they connect. This knowledge can be used on short time scales (say, hours) to perform traffic engineering by reconfiguring optical switches; it can also be used on longer time scales (say, months) to upgrade link capacity.

Accounting: Internet service providers implement complex service level agreements (SLAs) with customers and peers. Simple accounting arrangements based on overall traffic can easily be monitored by a single counter; however, more sophisticated agreements based on traffic type require a counter per traffic type. Packet counters can also be used to decide peering relationships. Suppose ISP A is currently sending packets to ISP C via ISP B and is considering directly connecting (peering) with B; a rational way for A to decide is to count the traffic destined to prefixes corresponding to B.

Traffic Analysis: Many network managers monitor the relative ratio of one packet type to another. For example, a spike in peer-to-peer traffic, such as to Kazaa, may require rate limiting. A spike in ICMP messages may indicate a Smurf attack.

Once causes — such as links that are unstable or have excessive traffic — are identified, network operators can take action by a variety of means. Thus measurement is crucial not just to characterize the network but to better engineer its behavior.

There are several control mechanisms that network operators currently have at their disposal. For example, operators can tweak Open Shortest Path First (OSPF) link weights and BGP policy to spread load, can set up circuit-switched paths to avoid hot spots, and can simply buy new equipment. This chapter focuses only on network changes that address the measurement problem — i.e., changes that make a network more *observable*. However, we recognize that making a network more *controllable*, for instance, by adding more tuning knobs, is an equally important problem we do not address here.

Despite its importance, traffic measurement, at first glance, does not appear to offer any great challenges or have much intellectual appeal. As with mopping a floor or washing dishes, traffic measurement appears to be a necessary but mundane chore.

The goal of this chapter is to argue the contrary: that measurement at high speeds is difficult because of resource limitations and lack of built-in support; that the problems will only grow worse as ISPs abandon their current generation of links for even faster ones; and that algorithmics can provide exciting alternatives to the measurement quandary by focusing on how measurements will ultimately be used. To develop this theme, it is worth understanding right away why the general problem of measurement is hard and why even the specific problem of packet counting can be difficult.

This chapter is organized as follows. Section 16.1 describes the challenges involved in measurement. Section 16.2 shows how to reduce the required width of an SRAM counter using a DRAM backing-store. Section 16.3 details a different technique for reducing counter widths by using randomized counting, which trades accuracy for counter width. Section 16.4 presents a different approach to reducing the number of counters required (as opposed to the width) by keeping track of counters only above a threshold. Section 16.5 shows how to reduce the number of counters even further for some applications by counting only the number of distinct flows.

Techniques in prior sections require computation on every packet. Section 16.6 takes a different tack by describing the sampled NetFlow technique for reducing packet processing; in NetFlow only a random subset of packets is processed to produce either a log or an aggregated set of counters. Section 16.7 shows how to reduce the overhead of shipping NetFlow records to managers. Section 16.8 explains how to replace the independent sampling method of Net-Flow with a consistent sampling technique in all routers that allow packet trajectories to be traced.

The last three sections of the chapter move to a higher-level view of measurement. In Section 16.9 we describe a solution to the accounting problem. This problem is of great interest to ISPs, and the solution method is in the best tradition of the systems approach advocated throughout this book. In Section 16.10 we describe a solution to the traffic matrix problem using the same concerted systems approach. Section 16.11 presents a very different approach to measurement called *passive* measurement, that treats the network as a black box. It includes an example of the use of passive measurement to compute the loss rate to a Web server.

The implementation techniques for the measurement primitives described in this chapter (and the corresponding principles used) are summarized in Figure 16.1.

Quick Reference Guide

Section 16.2 may be of interest to a network device implementor seeking to implement a large number of counters at high speeds. Section 16.5 describes a useful mechanism for quickly counting the list of distinct identifiers in a stream of received packets without keeping large hash tables. Section 16.9 presents a solution proposed by Juniper Networks for accounting. Section 16.10 covers inferring traffic matrices and is useful for implementors building tools for monitoring ISPs.

Number	Principle	Used In
P5c	Low-order counter bits in SRAM, all bits in DRAM	LCF algorithm
P15	Update only counters above threshold	LR algorithm
P3b	Randomized counting	Morris algorithm
P3a	Multiple hashed counters to detect heavy flows	Multistage filters
P3b	Flow counting by hashing flows to bitmaps	Multiresolution bitmap
P3a	Packet sampling to collect representative logs	Sampled NetFlow
P3a	Sampling flows proportional to size	Sampled charging
P3 P4	Aggregating prefixes into buckets Routing protocol helps color prefixes	Juniper's DCU
P4	Using TCP semantics for measurement	Sting

FIGURE 16.1 Principles used in the implementation of the measurement primitives discussed in this chapter.

16.1 WHY MEASUREMENT IS HARD

Unlike the telephone network, where observability and controllability were built into the design, the very simplicity of the successful Internet service model has made it difficult to observe [DG00]. In particular, there appears to be a great semantic distance between what users (e.g., ISPs) want to know and what the network provides. In this tussle [CWSB02] between user needs and the data generated by the network, users respond by distorting [CWSB02] existing network features to obtain desired data.

For example, Traceroute uses the TTL field in an admittedly clever but distorted way, and the Path MTU discovery mechanism is similar. Tools like Sting [Sav99] use TCP in even more baroque fashion to yield end-to-end measures. Even tools that make more conventional use of network features to populate traffic matrices (e.g., Refs. FGea00 and ZRDG03) bridge the semantic gap by correlating vast amounts of spatially separated data and possibly inconsistent configuration information. All this is clever, but it may not be engineering.[1] Perhaps much of this complexity could be removed by providing measurement features directly in the network.

One of the fundamental tools of measurement is *counting*: counting the number of packets or events of a given type. It is instructive to realize that even packet counting is hard as we show next.

16.1.1 Why Counting Is Hard

Legacy routers provide only per-interface counters that can be read by the management protocol SNMP. Such counters count only the aggregate of all counters going on an interface and make

---

[1]Recall the comment by hardened battle veterans on the heroic Charge of the Light Brigade: "It is beautiful, but is it war?"

it difficult to estimate traffic AS-AS matrices that are needed for traffic engineering. They can also be used only for crude forms of accounting, as opposed to more sophisticated forms of accounting that count by traffic type (e.g., real-time traffic may be charged higher) and destination (some destinations may be routed through a more expensive upstream provider).

Thus vendors have introduced filter-based accounting, where customers can count traffic that matches a rule specifying a predicate on packet header values. Similarly, Cisco provides NetFlow-based accounting [Net], where sampled packets can be logged for later analysis, and 5-tuples can be aggregated and counted on the router. Cisco also provides Express Forwarding commands, which allow per-prefix counters [Cis].

Per-interface counters can easily be implemented because there are only a few counters per interface, which can be stored in chip registers. However, doing filter-based or per-prefix counters is more challenging because of the following.

- **Many counters:** Given that even current routers support 500,000 prefixes and that future routers may have a million prefixes, a router potentially needs to support millions of real-time counters.

- **Multiple counters per packet:** A single packet may result in updating more than one counter, such as a flow counter and a per-prefix counter.

- **High speeds:** Line rates have been increasing from OC-192 (10 Gbps) to OC-768 (40 Gbps). Thus each counter matched by a packet must be read and written in the time taken to receive a packet at line speeds.

- **Large widths:** As line speeds get higher, even 32-bit counters overflow quickly. To prevent the overhead of frequent polling, most vendors now provide 64-bit counters.

One million counters of 64 bits each requires a total of 64 Mbits of memory; while two counters of 64 bits each every 8 nec requires 16 Gbps of memory bandwidth. The memory bandwidth needs require the use of SRAM, but the large amount of memory needed makes SRAM of this size too expensive. Thus maintaining counters or packet logs at wire speeds is as challenging as other packet-processing tasks, such as classification and scheduling; it is the focus of much of this chapter.

In summary, this section argues that: (i) packet counters and logs are important for network monitoring and analysis; (ii) naive implementations of packet counting and logs require potentially infeasible amounts of fast memory. The remainder of this chapter describes the use of algorithmics to reduce the amount of fast memory and processing needed to implement counters and logs.

16.2 REDUCING SRAM WIDTH USING DRAM BACKING STORE

The next few sections ignore the general measurement problem and concentrate on the specific problem of packet counting. The simplest way to implement packet counting is shown in Figure 16.2. One SRAM location is used for each of, say, 1 million 64-bit counters. When a packet arrives, the corresponding flow counter (say, based on destination) is incremented.

Given that such large amounts of SRAM are expensive and infeasible, is it required? If a packet arrives, say, every 8 nsec, some SRAM counter must be accessed — as opposed to,

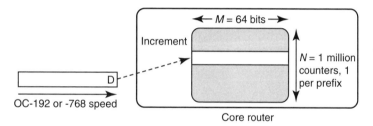

FIGURE 16.2 Basic model for packet counting at high speeds using a large-width counter for each of a large number of flows.

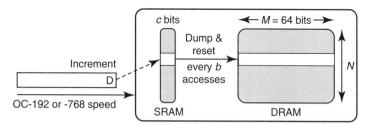

FIGURE 16.3 Using large DRAM counters as a backing store for small SRAM counters, reducing overall cost. For correctness, an SRAM counter must be backed up to DRAM before it overflows.

say, 40-nsec DRAM. However, intuitively keeping a *full* 64-bit SRAM location is obvious waste (**P1**).

Instead, the best hardware features of DRAM and SRAM can be combined (**P5c**). DRAM is at least four times cheaper and often as much as 10 times cheaper, depending on market conditions. On the other hand, DRAM is slow. This is exactly analogous to the memory hierarchy in a computer. The analogy suggests that DRAM and SRAM can be combined to provide a solution that is both cheap and fast.

Observe that if the router keeps a 64-bit DRAM backing location for each counter and a much smaller width (say, 12 bits) for each SRAM counter, then the counter system will be accurate *as long as every SRAM counter is backed up to DRAM before the smaller SRAM counter overflows*. This scheme is depicted in Figure 16.3. What is missing, however, is a good algorithm (**P15**) for deciding when and how to back up SRAM counters.

Assume that the chip maintaining counters is allowed to dump some SRAM counter to DRAM every b SRAM accesses. b is chosen to be large enough that b SRAM access times correspond to 1 DRAM access time. In terms of the smallest SRAM width required, Shah et al. [SIPM02] show that the optimal counter-management algorithm is to dump the *largest* SRAM counter. With this strategy Shah et al. [SIPM02] show that the SRAM counter width c can be significantly smaller than M, the width of a DRAM counter.

More precisely, they show that $2^c \approx \frac{\log b(N-1)}{\log(b/b-1)}$, where N is the total number of counters. Note that this means that the SRAM counter width grows approximately as $\log \log bN$, since $b/b - 1$ can be ignored for large b. For example, with three 64-bit counters every 8 nsec (OC-768) for N equal to a million requires only 8 Mbit of 2.5 μsec SRAM with 51.2 μsec DRAM. Note that in this case the value of b is $51.2/2.5 \approx 21$.

The bottom line is that the naive method would have required 192 Mbit of SRAM compared to 8 Mbit, a factor of 24 savings in expensive SRAM. Overall, this provides roughly a factor of 4 savings in cost, assuming DRAM is four times cheaper than SRAM.

But this begs the question. How does the chip processing counters find the the largest counter? Bhagwan and Lin [BL00] describe an implementation of a pipelined heap structure that can determine the largest value at a fairly high expense in hardware complexity and space. Their heap structure requires pointers of size $\log_2 N$ for each counter just to identify the counter to be evicted. Unfortunately, $\log_2 N$ additional bits per counter can be large (20 for $N = 1$ million) and can defeat the overall goal, which was to reduce the required SRAM bits from 64 to say 10.

The need for a pointer per heap value seems hard to avoid. This is because the counters must be in a fixed place to be updated when packets arrive, but values in a heap must keep moving to maintain the heap property. On the other hand, when the largest value arrives at the top of the heap, one has to correlate it to the counter index in order to reset the appropriate counter and to banish its contents to DRAM. Notice also that all values in the heap, including pointers and values, must be in SRAM for speed.

The following LR algorithm [RV03] simplifies the largest count first (LCF) algorithm of Shah et al. [SIPM02] and is easier to implement. Let j be the index of the counter with the largest value among the counters incremented in the last cycle of b updates to SRAM. Ties may be broken arbitrarily. If $c_j \geq b$, the algorithm updates counter c_j to DRAM. If $c_j < b$, the algorithm updates any counter with value at least b to DRAM. If no such counter exists, $LR(T)$ updates counter C_j to DRAM.

It can be shown that LR [RV03] is also optimal and produces SRAM counter width c, which is equal to that of LCF. The maintaining of all counters above the threshold b can be done using a size-N bitmap in which a 1 implies that the corresponding position has a counter no less than b.

This leaf structure can be augmented with a simple tree that maintains the position of the first 1 (see Exercises). The tree can be easily pipelined for speed, and only roughly 2 bits per counter are required for this additional data structure; thus c is increased from its optimal value, say, x to $x + 2$, a reasonable cost.

Thus the final LR algorithm is a better algorithm (**P15**) and one that is easier to implement, provides a new data structure to efficiently find the first bit set in a bitmap (**P15**), and adds pipelining hardware (**P5**) to gain speed.

The overall approach could be considered superficially similar to the usual use of the memory hierarchy, in which a faster memory acts as a cache for a slower memory. However, unlike a conventional cache this design ensures *worst-case* performance and not *expected* case performance. The goals of the two algorithms are also different: Counter management stores an entry for *all* items but seeks to reduce the width of cache entries, while standard caching stores full widths for only *some* frequent items.

16.3 REDUCING COUNTER WIDTH USING RANDOMIZED COUNTING

The DRAM backing-store approach trades off reduced counter widths for more processing and complexity. A second approach is to trade accuracy and certainty (**P3a, b**) for reduced counter widths. For many applications described earlier, approximate counters may suffice.

FIGURE 16.4 Using threshold compression to reduce the number of counters stored.

The basic idea is as follows. If we increment a b-bit counter only with probability $1/c$, then when the counter saturates, the expected number of counted events is $2^b \cdot c$. Thus a b-bit randomized counter can count c times more events than a deterministic version. But once the notion of approximate counting is accepted, it is possible to do better.

Notice that in the basic idea, the standard deviation (i.e., the expected value of the counter error) is a few c's, which is small at counter values $\gg c$. R. Morris's idea for randomized counting is to notice that for higher counter values, one can tolerate higher absolute values of the error. For example, if the standard deviation is equal to the counter, the real value is likely to be within half to twice the value determined by the counter. Allowing the error to scale with counter values in turn allows a smaller counter width.

To achieve this, Morris's scheme increments a counter with *nonconstant probability that depends on counter value*, so expected error scales with counter size. Specifically, the algorithm increments a counter with probability $1/2^x$, where x is the value of the counter. At the end, a counter value of x represents an expected value of 2^x. Thus the number of bits required for such a counter is $\log \log Max$, where Max is the maximum value required for the counter.

While this is an interesting scheme, its high standard deviation and the need to pick accurate small numbers, especially for high values of the counter, are clear disadvantages. Randomized counting is an example of using **P3b**, trading accuracy for storage (and time).

16.4 REDUCING COUNTERS USING THRESHOLD AGGREGATION

The last two schemes reduce the *width* of the SRAM counter table shown in Figure 16.2. The next two approaches reduce the *height* of the SRAM counter table. They rely on the quote from Einstein (which opened the chapter) that not all the information in the final counter table may be useful to an application, at least for some applications. Effectively, by relaxing the specification (**P3**), the number of counters that need to be maintained can be reduced.

One simple way to compress the counter table is shown in Figure 16.4. The idea is to pick a threshold, say, 0.1% of the traffic, that can possibly be sent in the measurement interval and to keep counters only for such "large" flows. Since, by definition, there can be at most 1000 such flows, the final table reduces to 1000 flow ID, counter pairs, which can be indexed using a CAM. Note that small CAMs are perfectly feasible at high speed.

This form of compression is reasonable for applications that only want counters above a threshold. For example, just as most cell phone plans charge a fixed price up to a threshold and a usage-based fee beyond the threshold, a router may only wish to keep track of the traffic sent by large flows. All other flows are charged a fixed price. Similarly, ISPs wishing to

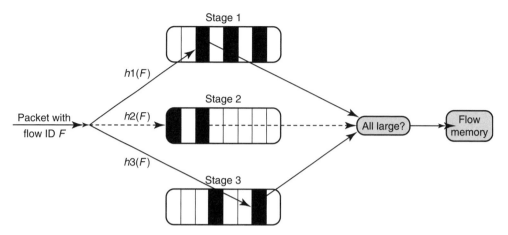

FIGURE 16.5 In a parallel multistage filter, a packet with a flow ID F is hashed using hash function $h1$ into a Stage 1 hash table, $h2$ into a Stage 2 hash table, etc. Each of the hash buckets contains a counter that is incremented by the packet size. If *all* the hash bucket counters are above the threshold (shown bolded), then flow F is passed to the flow memory for more careful observation.

reroute traffic hot spots or detect attacks are only interested in large, "elephant" flows and not the "mice."

However, this idea gives rise to a technical problem. How can a chip detect the elephants above the threshold without keeping track of all flows? The simplest approach would be to keep a counter for all flows, as in Figure 16.2, in order to determine which flows are above the threshold. However, doing so does not save any memory.

A trick [EV02] to directly compute the elephants together with the traffic sent by each elephant is shown in Figure 16.5. The building blocks are hash stages that operate in parallel. First, consider how the filter operates if it had only one stage. A stage is a table of counters indexed by a hash function computed on a packet flow ID; all counters in the table are initialized to 0 at the start of a measurement interval.

When a packet comes in, a hash on its flow ID is computed and the size of the packet is added to the corresponding counter. Since all packets belonging to the same flow hash to the same counter, if a flow F sends more than threshold T, F's counter will exceed the threshold. If we add to the flow memory all packets that hash to counters of T or more, we are guaranteed to identify all the large flows (no false negatives).

Unfortunately, since the number of counters we can afford is significantly smaller than the number of flows, many flows will map to the same counter. This can cause false positives in two ways: first, small flows can map to counters that hold large flows and get added to flow memory; second, several small flows can hash to the same counter and add up to a number larger than the threshold.

To reduce this large number of false positives, the algorithm uses multiple stages. Each stage (Figure 16.5) uses an *independent* hash function. Only the packets that map to counters of T or more at *all* stages get added to the flow memory. For example, in Figure 16.5, if a packet with a flow ID F arrives that hashes to counters 3, 1, and 7, respectively, at the three stages, F will pass the filter (counters that are over the threshold are shown darkened).

On the other hand, a flow G that hashes to counters 7, 5, and 4 will not pass the filter because the second-stage counter is not over the threshold. Effectively, the multiple stages attenuate the probability of false positives exponentially in the number of stages. This is shown by the following simple analysis.

Assume a 100-MB/sec link, with 100,000 flows. We want to identify the flows above 1% of the link during a 1-second measurement interval. Assume each stage has 1000 buckets and a threshold of 1 MB. Let's see what the probability is for a flow sending 100 KB to pass the filter. For this flow to pass one stage, the other flows need to add up to 1 MB − 100 KB = 900 KB.

There are at most 99,900/900 = 111 such buckets out of the 1000 at each stage. Therefore, the probability of passing one stage is at most 11.1%. With four independent stages, the probability that a small flow no larger than 100 KB passes all four stages is the *product* of the individual stage probabilities, which is at most $1.52 * 10^{-4}$.

Note the potential scalability of the scheme. If the number of flows increases to 1 million, we simply add a fifth hash stage to get the same effect. Thus to handle 100,000 flows requires roughly 4000 counters and a flow memory of approximately 100 memory locations; to handle 1 million flows requires roughly 5000 counters and the same size of flow memory. This is logarithmic scaling.

The number of memory accesses at packet arrival time performed by the filter is exactly one read and one write per stage. If the number of stages is small enough, this is affordable, even at high speeds, since the memory accesses can be performed in parallel, especially in a chip implementation. A simple optimization called *conservative update* (see Exercises) can improve the performance of multistage filtering even further. Multistage filters can be seen as an application of Principle **P3a**, trading certainty (allowing some false positives and false negatives) for time and storage.

16.5 REDUCING COUNTERS USING FLOW COUNTING

A second way to reduce the number of counters even further, beyond even threshold compression, is to realize that many applications do not even require identifying flows above a threshold. Some only need a *count* of the number of flows. For example, the Snort (www.snort.org) intrusion-detection tool detects port scans by counting all the distinct destinations sent to by a given source and alarming if this amount is over a threshold.

On the other hand, to detect a denial-of-service attack, one might want to count the number of sources sending to a destination, because many such attacks use multiple forged addresses. In both examples, it suffices to count flows, where a flow identifier is a destination (port scan) or a source (denial of service).

A naive method to count source–destination pairs would be to keep a counter together with a hash table (such as Figure 16.2 except without the counter) that stores all the distinct 64-bit source–destination address pairs seen thus far. When a packet arrives with source and destination addresses S, D, the algorithm searches the hash table for S, D; if there is no match, the counter is incremented and S, D is added to the hash table. Unfortunately, this solution takes too much memory.

An algorithm called *probabilistic counting* [FM85] can considerably reduce the memory needed by the naive solution, at the cost of some accuracy in counting flows. The intuition behind probabilistic counting is to compute a metric of how uncommon a certain pattern within a flow ID is. It then keeps track of the degree of "uncommonness" across all packets seen. If the algorithm sees very uncommon patterns, the algorithm concludes it saw a large number of flows.

More precisely, for each packet seen, the algorithm computes a hash function on the flow ID. It then counts the number of *consecutive zeroes*, starting from the least significant position of the hash result; this is the measure of uncommonness used. The algorithm keeps track of X, the largest number of consecutive zeroes seen (starting from the least significant position) in the hashed flow ID values of all packets seen so far.

At the end of the interval, the algorithm converts X, the largest number of trailing zeroes seen, into an estimate 2^X for the number of flows. Intuitively, if the stream contains two distinct flows, on average one flow will have the least significant bit of its hashed value equal to zero; if the stream contains eight flows, on average one flow will have the last three bits of its hashed value equal to zero — and so on.

Note that hashing is essential for two reasons. First, implementing the algorithm directly on the sequence of flow IDs itself could make the algorithm susceptible to flow ID assignments where the traffic stream contains a flow ID F with many trailing zeroes. If F is in the traffic stream, then even if the stream has only a few flows, the algorithm without hashing will wrongly report a large number of flows. Notice that adding multiple copies of the same flow ID to the stream will not change the algorithm's final result, because all copies hash to the same value.

A second reason for hashing is that accuracy can be boosted using multiple independent hash functions. The basic idea with one hash function can guarantee at most 50% accuracy. By using N independent hash functions in parallel to compute N separate estimates of X, probabilistic counting greatly reduces the error of its final estimate. It does so by keeping the average value of X (as a floating point number, not an integer) and then computing 2^X. Better algorithms for networking purposes are described in Estan et al. [EVF02].

The bottom line is that a chip can count approximately the number of flows with small error but with much less memory than required to track all flows. The computation of each hash function can be done in parallel. Flow counting can be seen as an application of Principle **P3b**, trading accuracy in the estimate for low storage and time.

16.6 REDUCING PROCESSING USING SAMPLED NETFLOW

So far we have restricted ourselves to packet counting. However, several applications might require packet logs. Packet logs are useful for analysts to retrospectively analyze for patterns and attacks.

In networking, there are general-purpose traffic measurement systems, such as Cisco's NetFlow [Net], that report per-flow records for very fine grained flows, where a flow is identified by a TCP or UDP connection. Unfortunately, the large amount of memory needed to store packet logs requires the use of DRAM to store the logs. Clearly, writing to DRAM on every packet arrival is infeasible for high speeds, just as it was for counter management.

Basic NetFlow has two problems.

1. **Processing Overhead:** Updating the DRAM slows down the forwarding rate.

FIGURE 16.6 Using sampling to reduce packet processing while maintaining a packet log for later analysis.

2. **Collection Overhead:** The amount of data generated by NetFlow can overwhelm the collection server or its network connection. Feldman et al. [FGea00] report loss rates of up to 90% using basic NetFlow.

   Thus, for example, Cisco recommends the use of sampling (see Figure 16.6) at speeds above OC-3: Only the sampled packets result in updates to the DRAM flow cache that keeps the per-flow state. For example, sampling 1 in 16 packets or 1 in 1000 packets is common. The advantage is that the DRAM must be written to at most 1 in, say, 16 packets, allowing the DRAM access time to be (say) 16 times slower than a packet arrival time. Sampling introduces considerable inaccuracy in the estimate; this is not a problem for measurements over long periods (errors average out) and if applications do not need exact data.

   The data-collection overhead can be alleviated by having the router aggregate the log information into counters (e.g., by source and destination autonomous systems (AS) numbers) as directed by a manager. However, Fang and Peterson [FP99] show that even the number of aggregated flows is very large. For example, collecting packet headers for Code Red traffic on a class A network [Moo01] produced 0.5 GB per hour of compressed NetFlow data. Aggregation reduced this data only by a factor of 4.

   Sampling is an example of using **P3a**, trading certainty for storage (and time), via a randomized pruning algorithm.

16.7 REDUCING REPORTING USING SAMPLED CHARGING

A technique called *sampled charging* [DLT01] can be used to reduce the collection overhead of NetFlow, at the cost of further errors. The idea is to start with a NetFlow log that is aggregated by TCP or UDP connections and to reduce the overhead of sending this data to a collection station. The goal is to *reduce collection bandwidth* and processing, as opposed to reducing the size of the router log.

The idea, shown in Figure 16.7, is at first glance similar to threshold compression, described in Section 16.4. The router reports only flows above a threshold to the collection station. The only additional twist is that the router also reports a flow with size s that is less than the threshold with probability proportional to s.

Thus the difference between this idea and simple threshold compression is that the final transmitted bandwidth is still small, but some attention is paid to flows below the threshold as well. Why might this be useful? Suppose all TCP individual connections in the aggregated

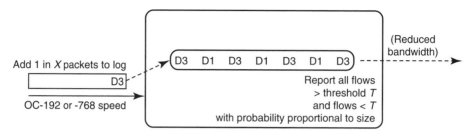

FIGURE 16.7   Using Sampled Charging to only report all large flows over a threshold and report flows below a threshold with probability proportional to their size.

log are small and below threshold but that 50% of the connections are from subnet *A* to subnet *B*.

If the router reported only the connections above threshold, the router would report no flows, because no *individual* TCP flow is large. Thus the collection agency would be unable to determine this unusual pattern in the destination and source addresses of the TCP connections. On the other hand, by reporting flows below threshold with a probability proportional to their size, on average half the flows the router will report will be from *A* to *B*. Thus the collection station can determine this unusual traffic pattern and take steps (e.g., increase bandwidth between these two) accordingly.

Thus the advantage of sampled charging over simple threshold compression is that it allows the manager to infer potentially interesting traffic patterns that are not decided in advance while still reducing the bandwidth sent to the collection node.

For example, sampled charging could also be used to detect an unusual number of packets sent by Napster using the same data sent to the collection station. Its disadvantage is that it still requires a large DRAM log. The large DRAM log scales poorly in size or accuracy as speeds increase.

On the other hand, threshold compression removes the need for the large DRAM log while directly identifying the large traffic flows. However, unless the manager knew in advance that he was interested in traffic between source and destination subnets, one cannot solve the earlier problem. For example, one cannot use a log that is threshold compressed with respect to TCP flows to infer that traffic between a pair of subnets is unusually large. Thus threshold compression has a more compact implementation but is less flexible than sample charging.

More formally, it can be shown that the multistage memory solution in Figure 16.5 requires $\sqrt{M}$ memory, where *M* is the memory required by NetFlow or sampled charging for the same relative error. On the other hand, this solution requires more packet processing. Threshold compression is also less flexible than NetFlow and sampled charging in terms of being able to mine traffic patterns after the fact.

Sampled charging is an example of using **P3b**, trading certainty for bandwidth (and time).

16.8 CORRELATING MEASUREMENTS USING TRAJECTORY SAMPLING

A final technique for *router* measurement is called *trajectory sampling* [DG00]. It is orthogonal to the last two techniques and can be combined with them. Recall that in sampled NetFlow

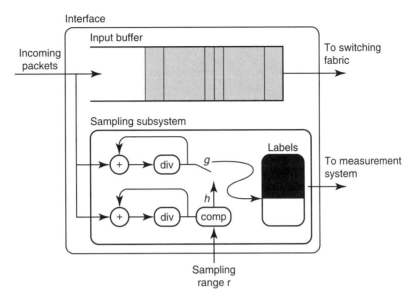

FIGURE 16.8 Trajectory sampling ensures that all routers sample a packet or do not by using the same hash function (as opposed to a random coin) to decide when to sample a packet.

and sampled charging, each router *independently* samples a packet. Thus the set of packets sampled at each router is different even when a set of routers sees the same stream of packets.

The main idea in trajectory sampling is to have routers in a path make *correlated* packet-sampling decisions using a common hash function. Figure 16.8[2] shows packets entering a router line card. The stream is "tapped" before it goes to the switch fabric. For every packet, a hash function h is used to decide whether the packet will be sampled by comparing the hashed value of the packet to a specified range. If the packet is sampled, a second hash function, g, on the packet is used to store a packet label in a log.

Trajectory sampling allows managers to correlate packets on different links. In order to ensure this, two more things are necessary. First, all routers must use the same values of g and h. Second, since packets can change header fields from router to router (e.g., TTL is decremented, data link header fields change), the hash functions are applied only to portions of the network packet that are *invariant*. This is achieved by computing the hash on header fields that do not change from hop to hop together with a few bytes of the packet payload.

A packet that is sampled at *one* router will be sampled at *all* routers in the packet's trajectory or path. Thus a manager can use trajectory sampling to see path effects, such as packet looping, packet drops, and multiple shortest paths, that may not be possible to discern using ordinary sampled NetFlow.

In summary, the two differences between trajectory sampling and sampled NetFlow are: (1) the use of a hash function instead of a random number to decide when to sample a packet; (2) the use of a second hash function on invariant packet content to represent a packet header more compactly.

---

[2]The picture is courtesy of Duffield and Grossglauser [DG00].

16.9 A CONCERTED APPROACH TO ACCOUNTING

In moving from efficient counter schemes to trajectory sampling, we moved from schemes that required only local support at each router to a scheme (i.e., trajectory sampling) that enlists the cooperation of multiple routers to extract more useful information. We now take this theme a step further by showing the power of concerted schemes that can involve all aspects of the network system (e.g., protocols, routers) at various time scales (e.g., route computation, forwarding). We provide two examples: an accounting example based on a scheme proposed by Juniper networks (described in this section) and the problem of traffic matrices (described in the next section).

The specific problem being addressed in this section is that of an ISP wishing to collect traffic statistics on traffic sent by a customer in order to charge the customer differently depending on the type of traffic and the destination of the traffic. Refer to Figure 16.9, which depicts a small ISP, Z, for the discussion that follows.

In the figure, assume that ISP Z wishes to bill Customer A at one rate for all traffic that exits via ISP X and at a different rate for all traffic that exits via ISP Y. One way to do this would be for router R1 to keep a separate counter for each prefix that represents traffic sent to that prefix. In the figure, R1 would have to keep at least 30,000 prefix counters. Not only does this make implementation more complex, but it is also unaligned with the user's need, which will eventually aggregate the 30,000 prefixes into two tariff classes. Further, if routes change rapidly, the prefixes advertised by each ISP may change rapidly, requiring constant update of this mapping by the tool.

Instead, the Juniper DCU solution [Sem02] has two components.

1. **Class Counters:** Each forwarding table entry has a 16-bit class ID. Each bit in the class ID represents one of 16 classes. Thus if a packet matches prefix P with associated class ID C and C has bits set in bits 3, 6, and 9, then the counters corresponding to all three set bits are incremented. Thus there are only 16 classes supported, but a single packet can cause multiple class counters to be incremented. The solution aligns with hardware design realities because 16 counters per link is not much harder than one counter, and

FIGURE 16.9 Example of an ISP with customer and peer links to other ISPs, *X* and *Y*.

incrementing in parallel is easily feasible if the 16 counters are maintained on-chip in a forwarding ASIC. The solution also aligns with real user needs because it cheaply supports the use of up to 16 destination-sensitive[3] counters.

2. **Routing Support:** To attack the problem of changing prefix routes (which would result in the tool's having to constantly map each prefix into a different class), the DCU solution enlists the help of the routing protocol. The idea is that all prefixes advertised by ISP X are given a color (which can be controlled using a simple route policy filter), and prefixes advertised by ISP Y are given a different color. Thus when a router such as $R1$ gets a route advertisement for prefix P with color c, it automatically assigns prefix P to class c. This small change in the routing protocol greatly reduces the work of the tool.

Juniper also has other schemes [Sem02], including counters based on packet classifiers and counters based on MPLS tunnels. These are slightly more flexible than DCU accounting because they can take into account the source address of a packet in determining its class. But these other schemes do not have the administrative scalability of DCU accounting because they lack routing support.

The DCU accounting scheme is an example of **P4**, leveraging off existing system components, and **P3**, relaxing system requirements (e.g., only a small number of aggregate classes).

16.10 COMPUTING TRAFFIC MATRICES

While the DCU solution is useful only for accounting, a generalization of some of the essential ideas can help in solving the *traffic matrix* problem. This is a problem of great interest to many ISPs.

To define the traffic matrix problem, consider a network (e.g, Z in Figure 16.9) such as those used by ISPs Sprint and AT&T. The network can be modeled as a graph with links connecting router nodes. Some of the links from a router in ISP Z go to routers belonging to other ISPs ($E2$, $E3$) or customers ($E1$, $E4$, $E5$). Let us call such links *external* links. Although we have lumped them together in Figure 16.9, external links directed toward the ISP router are called *input* links, and external links directed away from an ISP router are called *output* links.

The traffic matrix of a network enumerates the amount of traffic that was sent (in some arbitrary period, say, a day) between *every* pair of input and output links of the network. For example, the traffic matrix could tell managers of ISP Z in Figure 16.9 that 60 Mbits of traffic entered during the day from Customer A, of which 20 Mbits exited on the peering link $E2$ to ISP X, and 40 Mbps left on link $E5$ to Customer B.

Network operators find traffic matrices (over various time scales ranging from hours to months) indispensable. They can be used to make more optimal routing decisions (working around suboptimal routing by changing OSPF weights or setting up MPLS tunnels), for knowing when to set up circuit-switched paths (avoiding hot spots), for network diagnosis (understanding causes of congestion), and for provisioning (knowing which links to upgrade on a longer time scale of months).

Unfortunately, existing legacy routers provide only a single aggregate counter (the SNMP link byte counter) of all traffic traversing a link, which aggregates traffic sent between all

---

[3]It can also be made sensitive to the type of service by also using the DiffServ byte to determine the class.

pairs of input and output links that traverse the link. Inferring the traffic matrix from such data is problematic because there are $O(V^2)$ possible traffic pairs in the matrix (where V is the number of external links), and many sparse networks may have only, say, $O(V)$ links (and hence $O(V)$ counters). Even after knowing how traffic is routed, one has $O(V)$ equations for $O(V^2)$ variables, which makes deterministic inference (of all traffic pairs) impossible. This dilemma has led to two very different solution approaches. We now describe these two existing solutions and a proposed new approach.

16.10.1 Approach 1: Internet Tomography

This approach (see Refs. MTea02 and ZRDG03 for good reviews of past work) recognizes the impossibility of deterministic inference from SNMP counters cited earlier, and instead attempts statistical inference, with some probability of error. At the heart of the inference technique is some model of the underlying traffic distribution (e.g., Gaussian, gravity model) and some statistical (e.g., maximum likelihood) or optimization technique (e.g., quadratic programming [ZRDG03][4]).

Early approaches based on Gaussian distributions did very poorly [MTea02], but a new approach based on gravity models does much better, at least on the AT&T backbone. The great advantage of tomography is that it works without retrofitting existing routers, and it is also clearly cheap to implement in routers. A possible disadvantage of this method is the potential errors in the method (off by as large as 20% in Zhang et al. [ZRDG03]), its sensitivity to routing errors (a single link failure can throw an estimate off by 50%), and its sensitivity to topology.

16.10.2 Approach 2: Per-Prefix Counters

Designers of modern routers have considered other systems solutions to the traffic matrix problem based on changes to router implementations and (sometimes) changes to routing protocols (see DCU scheme described earlier). For example, one solution being designed into some routers built at Cisco [Cis] and some start-ups is to use per-prefix counters. Recall that prefixes are used to aggregate route entries for many millions of Internet addresses into, say, 100,000–150,000 prefixes at the present time.

A router has a forwarding engine for each input line card that contains a copy of the forwarding prefix table. Suppose each prefix P has an associated counter that is incremented (by the number of bytes) for each packet entering the line card that matches P. Then by pooling the per-prefix counters kept at the routers corresponding to each input link, a tool can reconstruct the traffic matrix. To do so, the tool must associate prefix routes with the corresponding output links using its knowledge of routes computed by a protocol such as OSPF. In Figure 16.9, if $R1$ keeps per-prefix counters on traffic entering from link $E1$, it can sum the 10,000 counters corresponding to prefixes advertised by ISP X to find the traffic between Customer A and ISP X.

One advantage of this scheme is that it provides perfect traffic matrices. A second advantage is that it can be used for differential traffic charging based on destination address, as in the DCU proposal. The two disadvantages are the implementation complexity of maintaining per-prefix counters (and the lack thereof in legacy routers) and the large amount of data that needs to be collected and synthesized from each router to form traffic matrices.

---

[4]Some authors limit the term *tomography* to the use of statistical models; thus Zhang et al. [ZRDG03] refer to their work as *tomogravity*. But this is splitting hairs.

16.10.3 Approach 3: Class Counters

Our idea is that each prefix is mapped to a small class ID of 8–14 bits (256–16,384 classes) using the forwarding table. When an input packet is matched to a prefix P, the forwarding entry for P maps the packet to a class counter that is incremented. For up to 10,000 counters, the class counters can easily be stored in on-chip SRAM on the forwarding ASIC, allowing the increment to occur internally in parallel with other functions.

For accounting, the DCU proposal (Section 16.9) already suggests that routers use policy filters to color routes by tariff classes and to pass the colors using the routing protocol. These colors can then be used to automatically set class IDs at each router. For the traffic matrix, a similar idea can be used to colorize routes based on the matrix equivalence class (e.g., all prefixes arising from same external link or network in one class).

How can class counters be used? For example, many ISPs have points of presence (or PoPs) in major cities, and just calculating the the aggregate PoP-to-PoP traffic matrix is very valuable [BDJT01]. Today this is done by aggregating the complete router-to-router matrix to find this. This can be done directly by classes by setting each PoP into a separate class. For example, in Figure 16.9, $R4$ and $R5$ may be part of the same PoP, and thus $E4$ and $E5$ would be mapped to the same class. Measurement data from 2003 [SMW02] indicates a great reduction in the number of classes, with 150 counters sufficing to handle the largest ISP.

The class counter scheme is an example of Principle **P4**, leveraging off existing system components. It is also an example of Principle **P3**, relaxing system requirements (e.g., using only a small number of aggregate classes).

16.11 STING AS AN EXAMPLE OF PASSIVE MEASUREMENT

So far this chapter has dealt exclusively with *router* measurement problems that involve changes to router implementations and to other subsystems, such as routing protocols. While such changes can be achieved with the cooperation of a few dominant router vendors, they do face the difficulty of incremental deployment. By contrast to the schemes already described, passive measurement focuses on the ability to trick a network into providing useful measurement data without changing network internals. The basic idea is to get around the lack of measurement support provided by the Internet protocol suite.

Imagine you are no longer an ISP but a network manager at the Acme Widget Company. An upstart ISP is claiming to provide better service than your existing ISP. You would like to conduct a test to see whether this true. To do so, you want to determine end-to-end performance measurements from your site to various Web servers across the country using both ISPs in turn.

The standard solution is to use tools, such as Ping and Traceroute, that are based on sending ICMP messages. The difficulty with these tools is that ISPs regularly filter or rate-limit such messages because of their use by hackers.

An idea that gets around this limitation was introduced by the Sting [Sav99] tool, invented by Stefan Savage. The main idea is to send measurement packets in the clothing of TCP packets; ISPs and Web servers cannot drop or rate-limit such packets without penalizing good clients. Then every protocol mechanism of TCP becomes a degree of freedom (**P13**) for the measurement tool.

Consider the problem of determining the loss probability between a source and a distant Web server. This may be useful to know if most of the traffic is sent in only one direction, as in a video broadcast. Even if Ping were not rate-limited, Ping only provides the combined loss probability in both directions.

The Sting idea to find the loss probability from the source to the server is as follows. The algorithm starts by making a normal TCP connection to the server and sending N data packets to the server in sequence. Acknowledgments are ignored; after all, it's measurements we are after, not data transfer.

After the *data-seeding* stage, the algorithm moves into a second stage, called *hole filling*. Hole filling starts with sending a single data packet with sequence number 1 greater than the last packet sent in the first phase. If an acknowledgment is received, all is well; no data packets were lost.

If not, after sufficient retransmission, the receiver will respond with the highest number, X, received in sequence. The sender tool now sends *only* the segment corresponding to $X + 1$. Eventually, an updated acknowledgment arrives with the next highest received in sequence. The receiver fills in this next hole and marches along until all "holes" are filled. At the end of the second phase, the sender knows exactly which data packets were lost in the first phase and can compute the loss rate.

It is more of a challenge to compute the reverse loss rate, because the receiver TCP may batch acknowledgments. However, once it is grasped that the tool is not limited to behaving like a normal TCP connection, all the stops can be loosed. By sending packets out of order in the first phase and a series of bizarre ploys, the receiver is conned into providing the required information.

At this point, the theoretician may shake his head sadly and say, "It's a bunch of tricks. I always knew these network researchers were not quite the thing." Indeed, Sting employs a collection of tricks to compute its particular metrics. But the *idea* of using TCP's venerable protocol mechanisms as a palette for measurement is perhaps an eye-opener. It influenced later measurement tools, such as TBIT [PF01], which used the same general idea to measure the extent to which new TCP features were deployed.

Of course, the idea is not limited to TCP but applies to any protocol. Any protocol, including BGP, can be subverted for the purposes of measurement. Philosophically, this is, however, dangerous ground, because the tools used by the measurement maven (presumably on the side of the angels) are now the same as used by the hacker (presumably on the dark side). For example, denial-of-service attacks exploit the same inability of a server to discriminate between standard usages of a protocol and adaptations thereof.

While Sting is less of an exercise in efficient implementation than it is an exercise in adding features, it can be regarded as an example of **P4**, leveraging off features of existing TCP implementations.

16.12 CONCLUSION

This chapter was written to convince the reader that measurement is an exciting field of endeavor. Many years ago, the advice to an ambitious youngster was, "Go West, young man" because the East was (supposedly) played out.

Similarly, it may be that protocol *design* is played out while protocol *measurement* is not. After all, TCP and IP have been cast in stone these many years; despite some confusion as to its parentage, one can only invent the Internet once. Reinventing the Internet is even harder, if one follows the fate of the next-generation Internet proposal. But there will always be new ways to understand and measure the Internet, especially using techniques that depend on minimal cooperation.

The first part of the chapter focused on the problems of the most basic measurement issue at high speeds: packet counting. This is a real problem faced by every high-speed-router vendor as they deal, on the one hand, with increasing ISP demands for for observability, and, on the other hand, with hardware limitations. Algorithmics can help by clever uses of memories (**P5c**), by changing the specification to focus only on large counters or flow counts (**P3**), by unusual uses of sampling (**P3a**), and finally by determining real user needs to reduce the space of counters required by aggregation for accounting or traffic matrices (**P7**). Figure 16.1 presents a summary of the techniques used in this chapter together with the major principles involved.

The chapter concluded with a small excursion into the field of passive measurement. Unlike all the other schemes described in this chapter, passive measurement schemes do not require implementation or protocol changes and hence are likely to continue to be a useful source of measurement data. Thus it seems fitting to end this chapter with Savage's summary of the main idea behind Sting: "Stop thinking of a protocol as a protocol. Think of it as … an opportunity."

16.13 EXERCISES

1. **Using DRAM-Backed Up Counters:** This chapter only described the implementation of packet counting, not byte counting. Suggest extensions to byte counting.

2. **Finding the First Set Bit:** Using the techniques and assumptions stated in Chapter 2, find a fast parallel implementation of the find-first-bit-set operation for a large (say, of length 1 million) bit vector in the context of the counter-management algorithm described in the text.

3. **Conservative Update of Multistage Hash Counting:** In the multistage filter, there is obvious waste (**P1**) in the way counters are incremented. Supposes a flow F, of size 2, hashes into three buckets whose counters are 15, 16, and 40. The naive method increases the counters to 17, 18, and 42. However, to avoid false negatives it suffices to increase only the smallest counter to 17 and to ensure that all other counters are at least as large. Thus, with this more conservative update strategy [EV02], the counters become 17, 17, and 40. Argue why this optimization does not cause false negatives and can only improve the false-positive rate.

4. **Trajectory Sampling:** Extend trajectory sampling to the case where different routers wish to have the flexibility to store a different number of packet labels because of different storage capabilities. Describe a mechanism that accommodates this and how this affects the potential uses for trajectory sampling.

5. **Passive Measurement and Denial of Service:** In SYN flooding attacks, an attack sends TCP SYN packets to a destination D it wishes to attack using a series of fictitious source addresses. When D replies to the (often) fictitious host, these packets are not replied to. Thus D accumulates a backlog of connections that are "half-open" and eventually refuses

to accept new connections. Assume you are working at a university and you have an unused Class *A* address space. How might you use this address space to infer denial-of-service attacks going on to various destinations on the Internet? Assume that attackers pick fake source addresses randomly from the 32-bit address space. More details for the curious reader can be found in [MVS01].

CHAPTER 17

Network Security

Hacking is an exciting and sometimes scary phenomenon, depending on which side of the battlements you happen to be standing.

— Marcus J. Ranum

From denial-of-service to Smurf attacks, hackers that perpetrate exploits have captured both the imagination of the public and the ire of victims. There is some reason for indignation and ire. A survey by the Computer Security Institute placed the cost of computer intrusions at an average of $970,000 per company in 2000.

Thus there is a growing market for *intrusion detection*, a field that consists of detecting and reacting to attacks. According to IDC, the intrusion-detection market grew from $20 million to $100 million between 1997 and 1999 and is expected to reach $518 million by 2005 [Ger99].

Yet the capabilities of current intrusion detection systems are widely accepted as inadequate, particularly in the context of growing threats and capabilities. Two key problems with current systems are that they are slow and that they have a high false-positive rate. As a result of these deficiencies, intrusion detection serves primarily a monitoring and audit function rather than as a real-time component of a protection architecture on par with firewalls and encryption.

However, many vendors are working to introduce *real-time* intrusion detection systems. If intrusion detection systems can work in real time with only a small fraction of false positives, they can actually be used to *respond* to attacks by either deflecting the attack or tracing the perpetrators.

Intrusion detection systems (IDSs) have been studied in many forms since Denning's classic statistical analysis of host intrusions [Den87]. Today, IDS techniques are usually classified as either *signature detection* or *anomaly detection*. Signature detection is based on matching events to the signatures of known attacks.

In contrast, anomaly detection, based on statistical or learning theory techniques, identifies aberrant events, whether known to be malicious or not. As a result, anomaly detection can potentially detect new types of attacks that signature-based systems will miss. Unfortunately, anomaly detection systems are prone to falsely identifying events as malicious. Thus this chapter does *not* address anomaly-based methods.

Meanwhile signature-based systems are highly popular due to their relatively simple implementation and their ability to detect commonly used attack tools. The lightweight detection system Snort [Roe99] is one of the more popular examples because of its free availability and efficiency.

Given the growing importance of real-time intrusion detection, intrusion detection furnishes a rich source of packet patterns that can benefit from network algorithmics. Thus this chapter samples three important subtasks that arise in the context of intrusion detection. The first is an *analysis* subtask, string matching, which is a key bottleneck in popular signature-based systems such as Snort. The second is a *response* subtask, traceback, which is of growing importance given the ability of intruders to use forged source addresses. The third is an *analysis* subtask to detect the onset of a new worm (e.g., Code Red) without prior knowledge.

These three subtasks only scratch the surface of a vast area that needs to be explored. They were chosen to provide an indication of the richness of the problem space and to outline some potentially powerful tools, such as Bloom filters and Aho–Corasick trees, that may be useful in more general contexts. Worm detection was also chosen to showcase how mechanisms studied earlier in the book can be combined in powerful ways.

This chapter is organized as follows. The first few sections explore solutions to the important problem of searching for suspicious strings in packet payloads. Current implementations of intrusion detection systems such as Snort (www.snort.org) do multiple passes through the packet to search for each string. Section 17.1.1 describes the Aho–Corasick algorithm for searching for multiple strings in one pass using a trie with backpointers. Section 17.1.2 describes a generalization of the classical Boyer–Moore algorithm, which can sometimes act faster by skipping more bits in a packet.

Section 17.2 shows how to approach an even harder problem — searching for *approximate* string matches. The section introduces two powerful ideas: min-wise hashing and random projections. This section suggests that even complex tasks such as approximate string matching can plausibly be implemented at wire speeds.

Section 17.3 marks a transition to the problem of responding to an attack, by introducing the IP traceback problem. It also presents a seminal solution using probabilistic packet marking. Section 17.4 offers a second solution, which uses packet logs and no packet modifications; the logs are implemented efficiently using an important technique called a *Bloom filter*. While these traceback solutions are unlikely to become deployed when compared to more recent standards, they introduce a significant problem and invoke important techniques that could be useful in other contexts.

Section 17.5 explains how algorithmic techniques can be used to extract automatically the strings used by intrusion detection systems such as Snort. In other words, instead of having these strings be installed manually by security analysts, could a system automatically extract the suspicious strings? We ground the discussion in the context of detecting worm attack payloads.

The implementation techniques for security primitives described in this chapter (and the corresponding principles) are summarized in Figure 17.1.

Quick Reference Guide

Sections 17.1.1 and 17.1.2 show how to speed up searching for *multiple* strings in packet payloads, a fundamental operation for a signature-based IDS. The Aho–Corasick algorithm of Section 17.1.1 can easily be implemented in hardware. While the traceback ideas in Section 17.4 are unlikely to be useful in the near future, the section introduces an important data structure, called a Bloom filter, for representing

Number	Principle	Used In
P15	Integrated string matching using Aho–Corasick	Snort
P3a, 5a	Approximate string match using min-wise hashing	Altavista
P3a	Path reconstruction using probabilistic marking	Edge sampling
P3a	Efficient packet logging via Bloom filters	SPIE
P3a	Worm detection by detecting frequent content	EarlyBird

FIGURE 17.1 Principles used in the implementation of the various security primitives discussed in this chapter.

sets and also describes a hardware implementation. Bloom filters have found a variety of uses and should be part of the implementor's bag of tricks. Section 17.5 explains how signatures for attacks can be *automatically* computed, reducing the delay and difficulty required to have humans generate signatures.

17.1 SEARCHING FOR MULTIPLE STRINGS IN PACKET PAYLOADS

The first few sections tackle a problem of detecting an attack by searching for suspicious strings in payloads. A large number of attacks can be detected by their use of such strings. For example, packets that attempt to execute the Perl interpreter have *perl.exe* in their payload. For example, the arachNIDS database [Vis] of vulnerabilities contains the following description.

> *An attempt was made to execute perl.exe. If the Perl interpreter is available to Web clients, it can be used to execute arbitrary commands on the Web server. This can be used to break into the server, obtain sensitive information, and potentially compromise the availability of the Web server and the machine it runs on. Many Web server administrators inadvertently place copies of the Perl interpreter into their Web server script directories. If perl is executable from the cgi directory, then an attacker can execute arbitrary commands on the Web server.*

This observation has led to a commonly used technique to detect attacks in so-called signature-based intrusion detection systems such as Snort. The idea is that a router or monitor has a set of rules, much like the classifiers in Chapter 12. However, the Snort rules go beyond classifiers by allowing a 5-tuple rule specifying the type of packet (e.g., port number equal to Web traffic) *plus* an arbitrary string that can *appear anywhere in the packet payload*.

Thus the Snort rule for the attempt to execute perl.exe will specify the protocol (TCP) and destination port (80 for Web) as well as the string "perl.exe" occurring anywhere in the payload. If a packet matches this rule, an alert is generated. Snort has 300 such augmented rules, with 300 possible strings to search for.

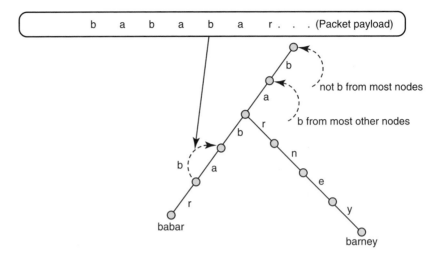

FIGURE 17.2 The Aho–Corasick algorithm builds an alphabetical trie on the set of strings to be searched for. A search for the string "barney" can be found by following the "b" pointer at the root, the "a" pointer at the next node, etc. More interestingly, the trie is augmented with failure pointers that prevent restarting at the top of the trie when failure occurs and a new attempt is made to match, shifted one position to the right.

Early versions of Snort do string search by matching each packet against each Snort rule in turn. For each rule that matches in the classifier part, Snort runs a Boyer–Moore search on the corresponding string, potentially doing several string searches per packet. Since each scan through a packet is expensive, a natural question is: Can one search for all possible strings in one pass through packet?

There are two algorithms that can be used for this purpose: the Aho–Corasick algorithm [AC75] and a modified algorithm due to Commentz-Walter [CW79], which we describe next.

17.1.1 Integrated String Matching Using Aho–Corasick

Chapter 11 used a trie to search for matching prefixes. Clearly, a trie can also be used to search for a string that starts at a known position in a packet. Thus Figure 17.2 contains a trie built on the set of two strings "babar" and "barney"; both are well-known characters in children's literature. Unlike in Chapter 11, the trie is built on characters and not on arbitrary groups of bits. The characters in the text to be searched are used to follow pointers through the trie until a leaf string is found or until failure occurs.

The hard part, however, is looking for strings that can start anywhere in a packet payload. The naivest approach would be to assume the string starts at byte 1 of the payload and then traverse the trie. Then if a failure occurs, one could start again at the top of trie with the character that starts at byte 2.

However, if packet bytes form several "near misses" with target strings, then for each possible starting position, the search can traverse close to the height of the trie. Thus if the payload has L bytes and the trie has maximum height h, the algorithm can take $L \cdot h$ memory references.

For example, when searching for "babar" in the packet payload shown in Figure 17.2, the algorithm jogs merrily down the trie until it reaches the node corresponding to the second "a" in "babar." At that point the next packet byte is a "b" and not the "r" required to make progress in the trie. The naive approach would be to back up to the start of the trie and start the trie search again from the second byte "a" in the packet.

However, it is not hard to see that backing up to the top is obvious waste (**P1**) because the packet bytes examined so far in the search for "babab" have "bab" as a suffix, which is a prefix of "babar." Thus, rather than back up to the top, one can precompute (much as in a grid of tries; see Chapter 12) a failure pointer corresponding to the failing "b" that allows the search to go directly to the node corresponding to path "bab" in the trie, as shown by the leftmost dotted arc in Figure 17.2.

Thus rather than have the fifth byte (a "b") lead to a null pointer, as it would in a normal trie, it contains a failure pointer that points back up the trie. Search now proceeds directly from this node using the sixth byte "a" (as opposed to the second byte) and leads after seven bytes to "babar."

Search is easy to do in hardware after the trie is precomputed. This is not hard to believe because the trie with failure pointers essentially forms a state machine. The Aho–Corasick algorithm has some complexity that ensues when one of the search strings, R, is a suffix of another search string, S. However, in the security context this can be avoided by relaxing the specification (**P3**). One can remove string S from the trie and later check whether the packet matched R or S.

Another concern is the potentially large number of pointers (256) in the Aho–Corasick trie. This can make it difficult to fit a trie for a large set of strings in cache (in software) or in SRAM (in hardware). One alternative is to use, say, Lulea-style encoding (Chapter 11) to compress the trie nodes.

17.1.2 Integrated String Matching Using Boyer–Moore

The exercises at the end of Chapter 3 suggest that the famous Boyer–Moore [BM77] algorithm for *single*-string matching can be derived by realizing that there is an interesting degree of freedom that can be exploited (**P13**) in string matching: One can equally well start comparing the text and the target string from the last character as from the first.

Thus in Figure 17.3 the search starts with the fifth character of the packet, a "b," and matches it to the fifth character of, say, "babar" (shown below the packet), an "r." When this fails, one of the heuristics in the Boyer–Moore algorithm is to shift the search template of "babar" two characters to the right to match the rightmost occurrence of "b" in the template.[1] Boyer–Moore's claim to fame is that in practice it skips over a large number of characters, unlike, say, the Aho–Corasick algorithm.

To generalize Boyer–Moore to multiple strings, imagine that the algorithm concurrently compares the fifth character in the packet to the fifth character, "e," in the other string, "barney" (shown above the packet). If one were only doing Boyer–Moore with "barney," the "barney" search template would be shifted right by four characters to match the only "b" in barney.

---

[1]There is a second heuristic in Boyer–Moore [CLR90], but studies have shown that this simple Horspool variation works best in practice.

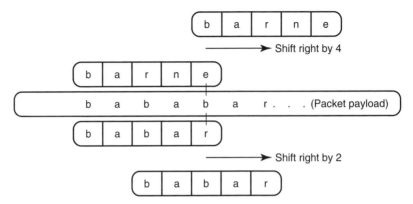

FIGURE 17.3   Integrated Boyer–Moore by shifting a character.

When doing a search for both "barney" and "babar" concurrently, the obvious idea is to shift the search template by the smallest shift proposed by any string being compared for. Thus in this example, we shift the template by two characters and do a comparison next with the seventh character in the packet.

Doing a concurrent comparison with the last character in all the search strings may seem inefficient. This can be taken care of as follows. First, chop off all characters in all search strings beyond L, the shortest search string. Thus in Figure 17.3, L is 5 and "barney" is chopped down to "barne" to align in length with "babar."

Having aligned all search string fragments to the same length, now build a trie starting *backwards* from the last character in the chopped strings. Thus, in the example of Figure 17.3 the root node of the trie would have an "e" pointer pointing toward "barne" and an "r" pointer pointing towards "babar." Thus comparing concurrently requires using only the current packet character to index into the trie node.

On success, the backwards trie keeps being traversed. On failure, the amount to be shifted is precomputed in the failure pointer. Finally, even if a backward search through the trie navigates successfully to a leaf, the fact that the ends may have been chopped off requires an epilogue, in terms of checking that the chopped-off characters also match. For reasonably small sets of strings, this method does better than Aho–Corasick.

The generalized Boyer–Moore was proposed by Commentz-Walter [CW79]. The application to intrusion detection was proposed concurrently by Coit, Staniford, and McAlerney [CSM01] and Fisk and Varghese [FV01]. The Fisk implementation [FV01] has been ported to Snort.

Unfortunately, the performance improvement of using either Aho–Corasick or the integrated Boyer–Moore is minimal, because many real traces [CSM01, FV01] have only a few packets that match a large number of strings, enabling the naive method to do well. In fact, the new algorithms add somewhat more overhead due to slightly increased code complexity, which can exhibit cache effects, as shown in Chapter 3.

While the code as it currently stands needs further improvement, it is clear that at least the Aho–Corasick version does produce a large improvement for *worst-case* traces, which may be crucial for a hardware implementation. The use of Aho–Corasick and integrated Boyer–Moore can be considered straightforward applications of efficient data structures (**P15**).

FIGURE 17.4   Checking for matching with a random projection of the target string "babar" allows the detecting of similar strings with substitution errors in the payload.

17.2 APPROXIMATE STRING MATCHING

This section briefly considers an even harder problem, that of approximately detecting strings in payloads. Thus instead of settling for an exact match or a prefix match, the specification now allows a few errors in the match. For example, with one insertion "p-erl.exe" should match "perl.exe" where the intruder may have added a character.

While the security implications of using the mechanisms described next need much more thought, the mechanisms themselves are powerful and should be part of the arsenal of designers of detection mechanisms.

The first simple idea can handle substitution errors. A *substitution error* is a replacement of one or more characters with others. For example, "parl.exe" can be obtained from "perl.exe" by substituting "a" for "e." One way to handle this is to search not for the complete string but for one or more random projections of the original string.

For example, in Figure 17.4, instead of searching for "babar" one could search for the first, third, and fourth characters in "babar." Thus the misspelled string "babad" will still be found. Of course, this particular projection will not find a misspelled string such as "rabad." To make it hard for an adversary, the scheme in general can use a small set of such random projections. This simple idea is generalized greatly in a set of papers on *locality-preserving hashing* (e.g., Ref. IM97).

Interestingly, the use of random projections may make it hard to efficiently shift one character to the right. One alternative is to replace the random projections by deterministic projections. For example, if one replaces every string by its two halves and places each half in an Aho–Corasick trie, then any one substitution error will be caught without slowing down the Aho–Corasick processing. However, the final efficiency will depend on the number of false alarms.

The simplest random projection idea, described earlier, does not work with insertions or deletions that can displace every character one or more steps to the left or right. One simple and powerful way of detecting whether two or more sets of characters, say, "abcef" and "abfecd," are similar is by computing their *resemblance* [Bro98].

The resemblance of two sets of characters is the ratio of the size of their intersection to the size of their union. Intuitively, the higher the resemblance, the higher the similarity. By this definition, the resemblance of "abcef" and "abfecd" is 5/6 because they have five characters in common.

Unfortunately, resemblance per se does not take into account order, so "abcef" completely resembles "fecab." One way to fix this is to rewrite the sets with order numbers attached so that "abcef" becomes "1a2b3c4e5f" while "fecab" now becomes "1f2e3c4a5b." The resemblance, using pairs of characters as set elements instead of characters, is now nil. Another method that captures order in a more relaxed manner is to use shingles [Bro98] by forming the two sets to be compared using as elements all possible substrings of size *k* of the two sets.

Resemblance is a nice idea, but it also needs a fast implementation. A naive implementation requires sorting both sets, which is expensive and takes large storage. Broder's idea [Bro98] is to quickly compare the two sets by computing a random (**P3a**, trade certainty for time) permutation on two sets. For example, the most practical permutation function on integers of size at most $m - 1$ is to compute $P(X) = ax + b \bmod m$, for random values of a and b and prime values of the modulus m.

For example, consider the two sets of integers $\{1, 3, 5\}$ and $\{1, 7, 3\}$. Using the random permutation $\{3 x + 5 \bmod 11\}$, the two sets become permuted to $\{8, 3, 9\}$ and $\{8, 4, 3\}$. Notice that the minimum values of the two randomly permuted sets (i.e., 3) are the same.

Intuitively, it is easy to see that the higher the resemblance of the two sets, the higher the chance that a random permutation of the two sets will have the same minimum. Formally, this is because the two permuted sets will have the same minimum if and only if they contain the same element that gets mapped to the minimum in the permuted set. Since an ideal random permutation makes it equally likely for any element to be the minimum after permutation, the more elements the two sets have in common, the higher the probability that the two minimums match.

More precisely, the probability that two minimums match is equal to the resemblance. Thus one way to compute the resemblance of two sets is to use some number of random permutations (say, 16) and compute all 16 random permutations of the two sets. The fraction of these 16 permutations in which the two minimums match is a good estimate of the resemblance.

This idea was used by Broder [Bro98] to detect the similarity of Web documents. However, it is also quite feasible to implement at high link speeds. The chip must maintain, say, 16 registers to keep the current minimum using each of the 16 random hash functions. When a new character is read, the logic permutes the new character according to each of the 16 functions in parallel. Each of the 16 hash results is compared in parallel with the corresponding register, and the register value is replaced if the new value is smaller.

At the end, the 16 computed minima are compared in parallel against the 16 minima for the target set to compute a bitmap, where a bit is set for positions in which there is equality. Finally, the number of set bits is counted and divided by the size of the bitmap by shifting left by 4 bits. If the resemblance is over some specified threshold, some further processing is done.

Once again, the moral of this section is not that computing the resemblance is the solution to all problems (or in fact to any specific problem at this moment) but that fairly complex functions can be computed in hardware using multiple hash functions, randomization, and parallelism. Such solutions interplay principle **P5** (use parallel memories) and principle **P3a** (use randomization).

17.3 IP TRACEBACK VIA PROBABILISTIC MARKING

This section transitions from the problem of *detecting* an attack to *responding* to an attack. Response could involve a variety of tasks, from determining the source of the attack to stopping the attack by adding some checks at incoming routers.

The next two sections concentrate on *traceback*, an important aspect of response, given the ability of attackers to use forged IP source addresses. To understand the traceback problem it helps first to understand a canonical denial-of-service (DOS) attack that motivates the problem.

In one version of a DOS attack, called *SYN flooding*, wily Harry Hacker wakes up one morning looking for fun and games and decides to attack CNN. To do so he makes his computer fire off a large number of TCP connection requests to the CNN server, each with a different forged source address. The CNN server sends back a response to each request R and places R in a pending connection queue.

Assuming the source addresses do not exist or are not online, there is no response. This effect can be ensured by using random source addresses and by periodically resending connection requests. Eventually the server's pending-connection queue fills up. This denies service to innocent users like you who wish to read CNN news because the server can no longer accept connection requests.

Assume that each such denial-of-service attack has a traffic signature (e.g., too many TCP connection requests) that can be used to detect the onset of an attack. Given that it is difficult to shut off a public server, one way to respond to this attack is to trace such a denial-of service back to the originating source point despite the use of fake source addresses. This is the IP traceback problem.

The first and simplest systems approach (**P3**, relax system requirements) is to finesse the problem completely using help from routers. Observe that when Harry Hacker sitting in an IP subnetwork with prefix S sends a packet with fake source address H, the first router on the path can detect this fact if H does not match S. This would imply that Harry's packet cannot disguise its subnetworks, and offending packets can be traced at least to the right subnetwork.

There are two difficulties with this approach. First, it requires that edge routers do more processing with the source address. Second, it requires trusting edge routers to do this processing, which may be difficult to ensure if Harry Hacker has already compromised his ISP. There is little incentive for a local ISP to slow down performance with extra checks to prevent DOS attacks to a remote ISP.

A second and cruder systems approach is to have managers that detect an attack call their ISP, say, A. ISP A monitors traffic for a while and realizes these packets are coming from prior-hop ISP B, who is then called. B then traces the packets back to the prior-hop provider and so on until the path is traced. This is the solution used currently.

A better solution than *manual* tracing would be *automatic* tracing of the packet back to the source. Assume one can modify routers for now. Then packet tracing can be trivially achieved by having each router in the path of a packet P write its router IP address in sequence into P's header. However, given common route lengths of 10, this would be a large overhead (40 bytes for 10 router IDs), especially for minimum-size acknowledgments. Besides the overhead, there is the problem of modifying IP headers to add fields for path tracing. It may be easier to steal a small number of unused message bits.

This leads to the following problem. Assuming router modifications are possible, find a way to trace the path of an attack by marking as few bits as possible in a packet's header.

For a single-packet attack, this is very difficult in an information theoretic sense. Clearly, it is impossible to construct a path of 10 32-bit router IDs from, say, a 2-byte mark in a packet. One can't make a silk purse from a sow's ear.

However, in the systems context one can optimize the expected case (**P11**), since most interesting attacks consist of hundreds of packets at least. Assuming they are all coming from

FIGURE 17.5 Reconstructing an attack path by having each router stamp its ID independently, with probability p, into a single node ID field. The receiver reconstructs order by sorting, assuming that closer routers will produce more samples.

the same physical source, the victim can shift the path computation over time (**P2**) by making each mark contribute a piece of the path information.

Let's start by assuming a single 32-bit field in a packet that can hold a single router ID. How are the routers on the path to synchronize access to the field so that each router ID gets a chance, over a stream of packets, to place its ID in the field?

A naive solution is shown in Figure 17.5. The basic idea is that each router independently writes its ID into a *single* node ID field in the packet with probability p, possibly overwriting a previous router's ID. Thus in Figure 17.5, the packet already has $R1$ in it and can be overwritten by $R3$ to $R1$ with probability p.

The hope, however, is that over a large sequence of packets from the attacker to the victim, every router ID in the path will get a chance to place its ID without being overwritten. Finally, the victim can sort the received IDs by the number of samples. Intuitively, the nodes closer to the victim should have more samples, but one has to allow for random variation.

The two problems with this naive approach is that too many samples (i.e., attack packets) are needed to deal with random variation in inferring order. Also, the attacker, knowing this scheme, can place malicious marks in the packet to fool the reconstruction scheme into believing that fictitious nodes are close to the victim because they receive extra marks.

To foil this threat, p must be large, say, 0.51. But in this case, the number of packets required to receive the router IDs far away from the victim becomes very large. For example, with $p = 0.5$ and a path of length $L = 15$, the number of packets required is the reciprocal of the probability that the router furthest from the victim sends a mark that survives. This is $p(1 - p)^{L-1} = 2^{-15}$, because it requires the furthest router to put a mark and the remaining $L - 1$ routers not to. Thus the average number of packets for this to happen is $\frac{1}{2^{-15}} = 32,000$. Attacks have a number of packets, but not necessarily this many.

The straightforward lesson from the naive solution is that randomization is good for synchronization (to allow routers to independently synchronize access to the single node ID field) but not to reconstruct order. The simplest solution to this problem is to use a hop count (the attacker can initialize each packet with a different TTL, making the TTL hard to use) as well as a node ID. But a hop count by itself can be confusing if there are multiple attacks going on. Clearly a mark of node X with hop count 2 may correspond to a different attack path from a mark of node Y with hop count 1.

The solution provided in the seminal paper [SWKA00] avoids the aliasing due to hop counts by conceptually starting with a pair of consecutive node IDs and a hop count to form a triple (R, S, h), as shown in Figure 17.6.

FIGURE 17.6 Edge sampling improves on node sampling by sampling edges and not nodes. This allows trivial order reconstruction based on edge distance and not sample frequency.

When a router R receives a packet with triple (X, Y, h), R generates a random number between 0 and 1. If the number is less than the sampling probability p, router R writes its own ID into the mark triple, rewriting it as $(R, -, 0)$, where the $-$ character indicates that the next router in the path has still to be determined. If the random number is greater than p, then R must maintain the integrity of the previously written mark. If $h = 0$, R writes R to the second field because R is the next router after the writer of the mark. Finally, if the random number is greater than p, R increments h.

It should be clear that by assuming that every edge gets sampled once, the victim can reconstruct the path. Note also that the attacker can only add fictitious nodes to the start of the path. But how many packets are required to find all edges? Given that ordering is explicit, one can use arbitrary values of p.

In particular, if p is approximately $1/L$, where L is the path length to the furthest router, the probability we computed before of the furthest router sending an edge mark that survives becomes $p(1 - p)^{L-1} \approx p/(1 - p)e$, where e is the base of natural logarithms. For example, for $p = 1/25$, this is roughly $1/70$, which is fairly large compared to the earlier attempt.

What is even nicer is that if we choose $p = 1/50$ based on the largest path lengths encountered in practice on the Internet (say, 50), the probability does not grow much smaller even for much smaller path lengths. This makes it easy to reconstruct the path with hundreds of packets as opposed to thousands.

Finally, one can get rid of obvious waste (**P1**) and avoid the need for two node IDs by storing only the Exclusive-OR of the two fields in a single field. Working backwards from the last router ID known to the victim, one can Exclusive-OR with the previous edge mark to get the next router in the path, and so on. Finally, by viewing each node as consisting of a sequence of a number of "pseudonodes," each with a small fragment (say, 8 bits) of the node's ID, one can reduce the mark length to around 16 bits total.

17.4 IP TRACEBACK VIA LOGGING

A problem with the edge-sampling approach of the previous section is that it requires changes to the IP header to update marks and does not work for single-packet attacks like the Teardrop attack. The following approach, traceback via logging [SPea01], avoids both problems by adding more storage at routers to maintain a compressed packet log.

As motivations, neither of the difficulties the logging approach gets around are very compelling. This is because the logging approach still requires modifying router forwarding, even though it requires no header modification. This is due to the difficulty of convincing

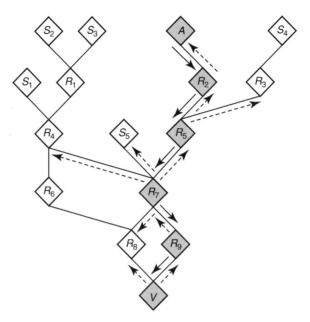

FIGURE 17.7 Using a packet log to trace an attack packet *P* backwards from the victim *V* to the attacker *A* by having the currently traced node ask all its neighbors (the dotted lines) if they have seen *P* (solid line).

vendors (who have already committed forwarding paths to silicon) and ISPs (who wish to preserve equipment for, say, 5 years) to make changes. Similarly, single-packet attacks are not very common and can often be filtered directly by routers.

However, the idea of maintaining compressed searchable packet logs may be useful as a general building block. It could be used, more generally, for, say, a network monitor that wishes to maintain such logs for forensics after attacks. But even more importantly it introduces an important technique called *Bloom filters*.

Given an efficient packet log at each router, the high-level idea for traceback is shown in Figure 17.7. The victim *V* first detects an attack packet *P*; it then queries all its neighboring routers, say, R_8 and R_9, to see whether any of them have *P* in their log of recently sent packets. When R_9 replies in the affirmative, the search moves on to R_9, who asks its sole neighbor, R_7. Then R_7 asks its neighbors R_5 and R_4, and the search moves backward to *A*.

The simplest way to implement a log is to reuse one of the techniques in trajectory sampling (Chapter 16). Instead of logging a packet we log a 32-bit hash of invariant content (i.e., exclude fields that change from hop to hop, such as the TTL) of the packet. However, 32 bits per packet for all the packets sent in the last 10 minutes is still huge at 10 Gbps. Bloom filters, described next, allow a large reduction to around 5 bits per packet.

17.4.1 Bloom Filters

Start by observing that querying either a packet log or a table of allowed users is a *set member-ship query*, which is easily implemented by a hash table. For example, in a different security

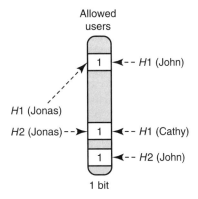

Is Jonas an allowed user?

FIGURE 17.8 A Bloom filter represents a set element by setting k bits in a bitmap using k independent hash functions applied to the element. Thus the element John sets the second (using $H1$) and next-to-last (using $H2$) bits. When searching for Jonas, Jonas is considered a member of the set only if all bit positions hashed to by Jonas have set bits.

context, if John and Cathy are allowed users and we wish to check if Jonas is an allowed user, we can use a hash table that stores John and Cathy's IDs but not Jonas.

Checking for Jonas requires hashing Jonas's ID into the hash table and following any lists at that entry. To handle collisions, each hash table entry must contain a list of IDs of all users that hash into that bucket. This requires at least W bits per allowed user, where W is the length of each user ID. In general, to implement a hash table for a set of identifiers requires at least W bits per identifier, where W is the length of the smallest identifier.

Bloom filters, shown in Figure 17.8, allow one to reduce the amount of memory for set membership to a few bits per set element. The idea is to keep a bitmap of size, say, $5N$, where N is the number of set elements. Before elements are inserted, all bits in the bitmap are cleared.

For each element in the set, its ID is hashed using k independent hash functions (two in Figure 17.8, $H1$ and $H2$) to determine bit positions in the bitmap to set. Thus in the case of a set of valid users in Figure 17.8, ID John hashes into the second and next-to-last bit positions. ID Cathy hashes into one position in the middle and also into one of John's positions. If two IDs hash to the same position, the bit remains set.

Finally, when searching to see if a specified element (say, Jonas) is in the set, Jonas is hashed using all the k hash functions. Jonas is assumed to be in the set if all the bits hashed into by Jonas are set. Of course, there is some chance that Jonas may hash into the position already set by, say, Cathy and one by John (see Figure 17.8). Thus there is a chance of what is called a *false positive*: answering the membership query positively when the member is not in the set.

Notice that the trick that makes Bloom filters possible is relaxing the specification (**P3**). A normal hash table, which requires W bits per ID, does not make errors! Reducing to 5 bits per ID requires allowing errors; however, the percentage of errors is small. In particular, if there is an attack tree and set elements are hashed packet values, as in Figure 17.7, false positives mean only occasionally barking up the wrong tree branch(es).

Line cards   RAM   SPIE card
             MUX   (or box)   Ring buffer DRAM

FIFO

S32 2^K-bit RAM

Sk

Readout
every
R msec

Readout
by
control
processor

Time
= t

Signature taps   Signature aggregation   History memory

FIGURE 17.9 Hardware implementation of packet logging using Bloom filters. Note the use of two-level memory: SRAM for random read-modify-writes and DRAM for large row writes.

More precisely, the false-positive rate for an *m*-size bitmap to store *n* members using *k* hash functions is

$$\left(1 - (1 - 1/m)^{kn}\right)^k \approx (1 - e^{kn/m})^k$$

The equation is not as complicated as it may appear: $(1 - 1/m)^{kn}$ is the probability that any bit is *not* set, given *n* elements that each hashes *k* times to any of *m* bit positions. Finally, to get a false positive, all of the *k* bit positions hashed onto by the ID that causes a false positive must be set.

Using this equation, it is easy to see that for $k = 3$ (three independent hash functions) and 5 bits per member ($m/n = 5$), the false-positive rate is roughly 1%. The false-positive rate can be improved up to a point by using more hash functions and by increasing the bitmap size.

17.4.2 Bloom Filter Implementation of Packet Logging

The Bloom filter implementation of packet logging in the SPIE system is shown in Figure 17.9 (the picture is courtesy of Sanchez et al. [SMea01]). Each line card calculates a 32-bit hash digest of the packet and places it in a FIFO queue. To save costs, several line cards share, via a RAM multiplexor, a fast SRAM containing the Bloom filter bitmap.

As in the case of counters in Chapter 16, one can combine the best features of SRAM and DRAM to reduce expense. One needs to use SRAM for fast front-end *random access* to the bitmap. Unfortunately, the expense of SRAM would allow storing only a small number of packets. To allow a larger amount, the Bloom filter bitmaps in SRAM are periodically read out to a large DRAM ring buffer. Because these are no longer random writes to bits, the write to DRAM can be written in DRAM pages or rows, which provide sufficient memory bandwidth.

17.5 DETECTING WORMS

It would be remiss to end this chapter without paying some attention to the problem of detecting worms. A worm (such as Code Red, Nimda, Slammer) begins with an exploit sent by an attacker to take over a machine. The exploit is typically a buffer overflow attack, which is caused by sending a packet (or packets) containing a field that has more data than can be handled by the buffer allocated by the receiver for the field. If the receiver implementation is careless, the extra data beyond the allocated buffer size can overwrite key machine parameters, such as the return address on the stack.

Thus with some effort, a buffer overflow can allow the attacking machine to run code on the attacked machine. The new code then picks several random IP addresses[2] and sends similar packets to these new victims. Even if only a small fraction of IP addresses respond to these attacks, the worm spreads rapidly.

Current worm detection technology is both *retroactive* (i.e., only after a new worm is first detected and analyzed by a human, a process that can take days, can the containment process be initiated) and *manual* (i.e., requires human intervention to identify the signature of a new worm). Such technology is exemplified by Code Red and Slammer, which took days of human effort to identify, following which containment strategies were applied in the form of turning off ports, applying patches, and doing signature-based filtering in routers and intrusion detection systems.

There are difficulties with these current technologies.

1. *Slow Response:* There is a proverb that talks about locking the stable door after the horse has escaped. Current technologies fit this paradigm because by the time the worm containment strategies are initiated, the worm has already infected much of the network.

2. *Constant Effort:* Every new worm requires a major amount of human work to identify, post advisories, and finally take action to contain the worm. Unfortunately, all evidence seems to indicate that there is no shortage of new exploits. And worse, simple binary rewriting and other modifications of existing attacks can get around simple signature-based blocking (as in Snort).

Thus there is a pressing need for a new worm detection and containment strategy that is real time (and hence can contain the worm before it can infect a significant fraction of the network) and is able to deal with new worms with a minimum of human intervention (some human intervention is probably unavoidable to at least catalog detected worms, do forensics, and fine-tune automatic mechanisms). In particular, the detection system should be *content agnostic*. The detection system should not rely on external, manually supplied input of worm signatures.

---

[2]By contrast, a *virus* requires user intervention, such as opening an attachment, to take over the user machine. Viruses also typically spread by using known addresses, such as those in the mail address book, rather than random probing.

Instead, the system should *automatically* extract worm signatures, even for new worms that may arise in the future.

Can network algorithmics speak to this problem? We believe it can. First, we observe that the only way to detect new worms and old worms with the same mechanism is to abstract the basic properties of worms.

As a first approximation, define a worm to have the following abstract features, which are indeed discernible in all the worms we know, even ones with such varying features as Code Red (massive payload, uses TCP, and attacks on the well-known HTTP port) and MS SQL Slammer (minimal payload, uses UDP, and attacks on the lesser-known MS SQL port).

1. *Large Volume of Identical Traffic:* These worms have the property that at least at an intermediate stage (after an initial priming period but before full infection), the volume of traffic (aggregated across all sources and destinations) carrying the worm is a significant fraction of the network bandwidth.

2. *Rising Infection Levels:* The number of infected sources participating in the attack steadily increases.

3. *Random Probing:* An infected source spreads infection by attempting to communicate to random IP addresses at a fixed port to probe for vulnerable services.

Note that detecting all three of these features may be crucial to avoid false positives. For example, a popular mailing list or a flash crowd could have the first feature but not the third.

An algorithmics approach for worm detection would naturally lead to the following detection strategy, which automatically detects each of these abstract features with low memory and small amounts of processing, works with asymmetric flows, and does not use active probing. The high-level mechanisms[3] are:

1. *Identify Large Flows in Real Time with Small Amounts of Memory:* In Section 16.4 we showed how to describe mechanisms to identify flows with large traffic volumes for any definition of a flow (e.g., sources, destinations). A simple twist on this definition is to realize that the content of a packet (or, more efficiently, a hash of the content) can be a valid flow identifier, which by prior work can identify in real time (and with low memory) a high volume of repeated content. An even more specific idea (which distinguishes worms from valid traffic such as peer-to-peer) is to compute a hash based on the content as well as the destination port (which remains invariant for a worm).

2. *Count the Number of Sources:* In Section 16.5 we described mechanisms using simple bitmaps of small size to estimate the number of sources on a link using small amounts of memory and processing. These mechanisms can easily be used to count sources corresponding to high traffic volumes identified by the previous mechanism.

3. *Determine Random Probing by Counting the Number of Connection Attempts to Unused Portions of the IP Address:* One could keep a simple compact representation of portions of the IP address space known to be unused. One example is the so-called Bogon list, which lists unused 8-bit prefixes (can be stored as a bitmap of size 256). A second

---

[3]Each of these mechanisms needs to be modulated to handle some special cases, but we prefer to present the main idea untarnished with extraneous details.

example is a secret space of IP addresses (can be stored as single prefix) known to an ISP to be unused. A third is a set of unused 32-bit addresses (can be stored as a Bloom filter).

Of course, worm authors could defeat this detection scheme by violating any of these assumptions. For example, a worm author could defeat Assumption 1 by using a very slow infection rate and by mutating content frequently. Assumption 3 could be defeated using addresses known to be used. For each such attack there are possible countermeasures. More importantly, the scheme described seems certain to detect at least all existing worms we know of, though they differ greatly in their semantics. In initial experiments at UCSD as part of what we call the EarlyBird system, we also found very few false positives where the detection mechanisms complained about innocuous traffic.

17.6 CONCLUSION

Returning to Marcus Ranum's quote at the start of this chapter, hacking must be exciting for hackers and scary for network administrators, who are clearly on different sides of the battlements. However, hacking is also an exciting phenomenon for practitioners of network algorithmics — there is just so much to do. Compared to more limited areas, such as accounting and packet lookups, where the basic tasks have been frozen for several years, the creativity and persistence of hackers promise to produce interesting problems for years to come.

In terms of technology currently used, the set string–matching algorithms seem useful and may be ignored by current products. However, other varieties of string matching, such as regular expression matches, are in use. While the approximate matching techniques are somewhat speculative in terms of current applications, past history indicates they may be useful in the future.

Second, the traceback solutions only represent imaginative approaches to the problem. Their requirements for drastic changes to router forwarding make them unlikely to be used for current deployment as compared to techniques that work in the control plane. Despite this pessimistic assessment, the underlying techniques seem much more generally useful.

For example, sampling with a probability inversely proportional to a rough upper bound on the distance is useful for efficiently collecting input from each of a number of participants without explicit coordination. Similarly, Bloom filters are useful to reduce the size of hash tables to 5 bits per entry, at the cost of a small probability of false positives. Given their beauty and potential for high-speed implementation, such techniques should undoubtedly be part of the designer's bag of tricks.

Finally, we described our approach to content-agnostic worm detection using algorithmic techniques. The solution combines existing mechanisms described earlier in this book. While the experimental results on our new method are still preliminary, we hope this example gives the reader some glimpse into the possible applications of algorithmics to the scary and exciting field of network security. Figure 17.1 presents a summary of the techniques used in this chapter, together with the major principles involved.

17.7 EXERCISES

1. **Traceback by Edge Sampling:** Extend the IP traceback edge-sampling idea to reduce the space required. As described in the text, try to do this by chopping the node ID required in

the base scheme into smaller (say, 8-bit) fragments. It may help to consider each of the fragment IDs to be the IDs of four virtual nodes that are housed in a single physical node, thus effectively extending the path and the number of samples needed for reconstruction.

2. **Bloom Filters and Trajectory Sampling:** Can you use Bloom filters to improve the label storage required by trajectory sampling in Chapter 16? Explain.

3. **Sampling and Packet Logging:** Can you use packet sampling to reduce the amount of memory required by the logging traceback solution? What are the disadvantages and advantages?

4. **Traceback by Packet Logging:** Why does the implementation in Figure 17.9 go through the indirection of a hash to 32 bits (as in trajectory sampling) and then to a Bloom filter?

5. **Aho–Corasick as a State Machine:** In many applications, one may wish to ignore certain padding characters that can be inserted by an intruder to make strings hard to detect. How might you extend Aho–Corasick to ignore these padding characters while searching for suspicious strings?

6. **Resemblance and Min-wise Hashing:** Generalize the Broder methods to approximately search for multiple strings and return the string with highest resemblance.

7. **Approximate Matching and Worm Detection:** Could the methods for approximate search generalize to detecting worms that mutate?

CHAPTER 18

Conclusions

The end of a matter is better than its beginning.

— ECCLESIASTES, THE BIBLE

We began the book by setting up the rules of the network algorithmics game. The second part of the book dealt with server implementations and the third part with router implementations. The fourth and last part of the book dealt with current and future issues in measurement and security.

The book covers a large number of specific techniques and a variety of settings — there are techniques for fast server design versus techniques for fast routers, techniques specific to operating systems versus techniques specific to hardware. While all these topics are part of the spectrum of network algorithmics, there is a risk that the material can appear to degenerate into a patchwork of assorted topics that are not linked together in any coherent way.

Thus as we draw to a close, it is appropriate to try and reach closure by answering the following questions in the next four sections.

- *What has the book been about?* What were the main problems, and how did they arise? What are the main techniques? While endnode and router techniques appear to be different when considered superficially, are there some underlying characteristics that unite these two topics? Can these unities be exploited to suggest some cross-fertilization between these areas? (Section 18.1)

- *What is network algorithmics about?* What is the underlying philosophy behind network algorithmics, and how does it differ from algorithms by themselves? (Section 18.2)

- *Is network algorithmics used in real systems?* Are the techniques in this book exercises in speculation, or are there real systems that use some of these techniques? (Section 18.3)

- *What is the future of network algorithmics?* Are all the interesting problems already solved? Are the techniques studied in this book useful only to understand existing work or to guide new implementations of existing tasks? Or are there always likely to be new problems that will require fresh applications of the principles and techniques described in this book? (Section 18.4)

18.1 WHAT THIS BOOK HAS BEEN ABOUT

The main problem considered in this book is bridging the performance gap between good network abstractions and fast network hardware. Abstractions — such as modular server code and prefix-based forwarding — make networks more usable, but they also exact a performance penalty when compared to the capacity of raw transmission links, such as optical fiber. The central question tackled in this book is whether we can have our cake and eat it too: retain the usability of the abstractions and yet achieve wire speed performance for the fastest-transmission links.

To make this general assertion more concrete, we review the main contents of this book in two sub-sections: Section 18.1.1 on endnode algorithmics and Section 18.1.2 on router algorithmics. This initial summary is similar to that found in Chapter 1. However, we go beyond the description in Chapter 1 in Section 18.1.3, where we present the common themes in endnode and router algorithmics and suggest how these unities can potentially be exploited.

18.1.1 Endnode Algorithmics

Chapters 5–9 of this book concentrate on endnode algorithmics, especially for servers. Many of the problems tackled under endnode algorithmics involve getting around complexities due to software and structure — in other words, complexities of our own making as opposed to necessarily fundamental complexities. These complexities arise because of the following characteristics of endnodes.

- *Computation versus Communication:* Endnodes are about general-purpose computing and must handle possible unknown and varied computational demands, from database queries to weather prediction. By contrast, routers are devoted to communication.

- *Vertical versus Horizontal Integration:* Endnodes are typically horizontally integrated, with one institution building boards, another writing kernel software, and another writing applications. In particular, kernels have to be designed to tolerate unknown and potentially buggy applications to run on top of them. Today, routers are typically vertically integrated, where the hardware and all software is assembled by a single company.

- *Complexity of Computation:* Endnode protocol functions are more complex (application, transport) as compared to the corresponding functions in routers (routing, data link).

As a consequence, endnode software has three important artifacts that seem hard to avoid, each of which contributes to inefficiencies that must be worked around or minimized.

1. *Structure:* Because of the complexity and vastness of endnode software, code is structured and modular to ease software development. In particular, unknown applications are allowed using a standard application programming interface (API) between the core operating system and the unknown application.

2. *Protection:* Because of the need to accommodate unknown applications, there is a need to protect applications from each other and to protect the operating system from applications.

3. *Generality:* Core routines such as buffer allocators and the scheduler are written with the most general use (and the widest variety of applications) in mind and thus are unlikely to be as efficient as special-purpose routines.

Bottleneck	Chapter	Cause	Sample Solution
Copying	5	Protection, structure	Passing by reference optimized by caching (IO-Lite)
Context switching	6	Complex scheduling	User-level protocols, event-driven Web servers
System calls	6	Protection, structure	Application device channels
Slow select	6	Scaling with number of clients	Kernel keeps state across calls
Timers	7	Scaling with number of timers	Timing wheels
Demuxing	8	Scaling with number of classifiers	Generalized tries (Pathfinder)
Buffer allocation	9	Generality	Linear buffers
Checksums/ CRCs	9	Generality Scaling with link speeds	Multibit computation
Protocol code	9	Generality	Header prediction

FIGURE 18.1 Endnode bottlenecks covered in this book. Associated with each bottleneck is the chapter in which the material is reviewed, the underlying cause, and one or more sample solutions.

In addition, since most endnodes were initially designed in an environment where the endnode communicated with only a few nodes at a time, there is little surprise that when these nodes were retrofitted as servers, a fourth artifact was discovered.

4. *Scalability:* By scalability, we often mean in terms of the number of concurrent connections. A number of operating systems use simple data structures that work well for a few concurrent connections but become major bottlenecks in a server environment, where there is a large number of connections.

With this list of four endnode artifacts in mind, Figure 18.1 reviews the main endnode bottlenecks covered in this book, together with causes and workarounds. This picture is a more detailed version of the corresponding figure in Chapter 1.

18.1.2 *Router Algorithmics*

In router algorithmics, by contrast, the bottlenecks are caused not by structuring artifacts (as in some problems in endnode algorithmics) but by the scaling problems caused by the need for global Internets, together with the fast technological scaling of optical link speeds. Thus the global Internet puts pressure on router algorithmics because of both *population* scaling and *speed* scaling.

For example, simple caches worked fine for route lookups until address diversity and the need for CIDR (both caused by population scaling) forced the use of fast longest-matching prefix. Also, simple DRAM-based schemes sufficed for prefix lookup (e.g., using expanded tries) until increasing link speeds forced the use of limited SRAM and compressed tries. Unlike endnodes, routers do not have protection issues, because they largely execute one code base. The only variability comes from different packet headers. Hence protection is less of an issue.

Bottleneck	Chapter	Cause	Sample Solution
Prefix lookups	11	CIDR, link speed scaling, Prefix database size scaling	Expanded multibit tries Compressed multibit tries
Packet classification	12	Service differentiation Link speed and size scaling	Decision trees and heuristics Hardware parallelism (CAMs)
Switching	13	Electrical scaling of buses Scaling in bandwidth Head-of-line blocking Scalability in number of ports	Crossbar switches VOQs, fast approximate matches Hierarchical fabrics, randomized resource-contention algorithms
Fair queuing	14	Service differentiation in resource scheduling Link speed scaling Memory scaling	Weighted fair queuing DRR, fast heaps SFQ, DiffServ, Core stateless
Measurement	16	Link speed scaling, number of counters	Low-order bits in SRAM + DRAM Juniper's DCU
Security	17	Scaling in number and intensity of attacks	Traceback with Bloom filters Frequent content-based worm detection

FIGURE 18.2 Router bottlenecks covered in this book. Associated with each bottleneck is the chapter in which the material is reviewed, the underlying cause, and one or more sample solutions.

With the two main drivers of router algorithmics in mind, Figure 18.2 reviews the main router bottlenecks covered in this book together with causes and workarounds. This picture is a more detailed version of the corresponding figure in Chapter 1.

While we have talked about routers as *the* canonical switching device, many of the techniques discussed in this book apply equally well to any switching device, such as a bridge (Chapter 10 is devoted to lookups in bridges) or a gateway. It also applies to intrusion detection systems, firewalls, and network monitors who do not switch packets but must still work efficiently with packet streams at high speeds.

18.1.3 Toward a Synthesis

In his book *The Character of Physical Law*, Richard Feynman argues that we have a need to understand the world in "various hierarchies, or levels." Later, he goes on to say that "all the sciences, and not just the sciences but all the efforts of intellectual kinds, are an endeavor to see the connections of the hierarchies ... and in that way we are gradually understanding this tremendous world of interconnecting hierarchies."

We have divided network algorithmics into two hierarchies: endnode algorithmics and router algorithmics. What are the connections between these two hierarchies? Clearly, we have used the same set of 15 principles to understand and derive techniques in both areas. But are there other unities that can provide insight and suggest new directions?

There are differences between endnode and router algorithmics. Endnodes have large, structured, and general-purpose operating systems that require work arounds to obtain high performance; routers, by contrast, have fairly primitive operating systems (e.g., Cisco IOS) that bear some resemblance to a real-time operating system. Most endnodes' protocol functions are implemented (today) in software, while the critical performance functions in a router are implemented in hardware. Endnodes compute, routers communicate. Thus routers have no file system and no complex process scheduling.

But there are similarities as well between endnode and router algorithmics.

*   *Copying* in endnodes is analogous to the data movement orchestrated by *switching* in routers.

*   *Demultiplexing* in endnodes is analogous to *classification* in routers.

*   *Scheduling* in endnodes is analogous to *fair queuing* in routers.

Other than packet classification, where the analogy is more exact, it may seem that the other correspondences are a little stretched. However, these analogies suggest the following potentially fruitful directions.

1. Switch-based endnode architectures: The analogy between copying and switching, and the clean separation between I/O and computation in a router, suggests that this may also be a good idea for endnodes. More precisely, most routers have a crossbar switch that allows parallel data transfers using dedicated ASICs or processors; packets meant for internal computation are routed to a separate set of processors. While we considered this briefly in Chapter 2, we did not consider very deeply the implications for endnode operating systems.

By dedicating memory bandwidth and processing to I/O streams, the main computational processors can compute without interruptions, system calls, or kernel thread, because I/O is essentially serviced and placed in clean form by a set of I/O processors (using separate memory bandwidth that does not interfere with the main processors) for use by the computational processors when they switch computational tasks. With switch-based bus replacements such as Infiniband, and the increasing use of protocol offload engines such as TCP chips, this vision may be realizable in the near future. However, while the hardware elements are present, there is need for a fundamental restructuring of operating systems to make this possible.

2. Generalized endnode packet classification: Although there seems to be a direct correspondence between packet classification in endnodes (Chapter 8) and packet classification in routers (Chapter 12), the endnode problem is simpler because it works only for a constrained set of classifiers, where all the wildcards are at the end. Router classifiers, on the other hand, allow arbitrary classifiers, requiring more complicated algorithmic machinery or CAMs.

It seems clear that if early demultiplexing is a good idea, then there are several possible definitions of a *path* (*flow* in router terminology), other than a TCP connection. For example, one might want to devote resources to all traffic coming from certain subnets or to certain protocol types. Such flexibility is *not* allowed by current classifiers, such as BPF and DPF (Chapter 8). It may be interesting to study the extra benefits provided by more general classifiers in return for the added computational burden.

3. Fair queuing in endnodes: Fair queuing in routers was originally invented to provide more discriminating treatment to flows in times of overload and (later) to provide quality of service to flows in terms of, say, latency. Both these issues resonate in the endnode environment. For example, the problem of receiver livelock (Chapter 6) requires discriminating between flows during times of overload. The use of early demultiplexing and separate IP queues per flow in lazy receiver processing seems like a first crude step toward fair queuing. Similarly, many endnodes do real-time processing, such as running MPEG players, just as routers have to deal with the real-time constraints of, say, voice-over-IP packets.

Thus, a reasonable question is whether the work on fair schedulers in the networking community can be useful in an operating system environment. When a sending TCP is scheduling between multiple concurrent connections, could it use a scheduling algorithm such as DRR for better fairness? At a higher level, could a Web server use worst-case weighted fair queuing to provide better delay bounds for certain clients? Some work following this agenda has begun to appear in the operating system community, but it is unclear whether the question has been fully explored.

So far, we have suggested that endnodes could learn from router design in overall I/O architecture and operating system design. Routers can potentially learn the following from endnodes.

1. Fundamental Algorithms: Fundamental algorithms for endnodes, such as selection, buffer allocation, CRCs, and timers, are likely to be useful for routers, because the router processor is still an endnode, with very similar issues.

2. More Structured Router Operating Systems: While the internals of router operating systems, such as Cisco's IOS and Juniper's JunOS, are hidden from public scrutiny, there is at least anecdotal evidence that there are major software engineering challenges associated with such systems as time progresses (leading to the need to be compatible with multiple past versions) and as customers ask for special builds. Perhaps routers can benefit from some of the design ideas behind existing operating systems that have stood the test of time.

While protection may be fundamentally unnecessary (no third-party applications running on a router), how should a router operating system be structured for modularity? One approach to building a modular but efficient router operating system can be found in the router plugins system [DDPP98] and the Click operating system [KMea00].

3. Vertically Integrated Routers: The components of an endnode (applications, operating system, boxes, chips) are often built by separate companies, thus encouraging innovation. The interface between these components is standardized (e.g., the API between applications and operating system), allowing multiple companies to supply new solutions. Why should a similar vision not hold for routers some years from now when the industry matures? Currently, this is more of a business than a technical issue because existing vendors do not want to open up the market to competitors. However, this was true in the past for computers and is no longer true; thus there is hope.

We are already seeing router chips being manufactured by semiconductor companies. However, a great aid to progress would be a standardized router operating system that is serious and general enough for production use by several, if not all, router companies.[1] Such a router operating system would have to work across a range of router architectures, just as operating systems span a variety of multiprocessor and disk architectures.

Once this is the case, perhaps there is even a possibility of "applications" that run on routers. This is not as far-fetched as it sounds, because there could be a variety of security and measurement programs that operate on a subset of the packets received by the router. With the appropriate API (and especially if the programs are operating on a logged copy of the

---

[1]Click is somewhat biased toward endnode bus-based routers as opposed to switch-based routers with ASIC support.

router packet stream), such applications could even be farmed out to third-party application developers. It is probably easy to build an environment where a third-party application (working on logged packets) cannot harm the main router functions, such as forwarding and routing.

18.2 WHAT NETWORK ALGORITHMICS IS ABOUT

Chapter 1 introduced network algorithmics with the following definition.

Definition: Network algorithmics is the use of an interdisciplinary systems approach, seasoned with algorithmic thinking, to design fast implementations of network processing tasks.

The definition stresses the fact that network algorithmics is interdisciplinary, requires systems thinking, and can sometimes benefit from algorithmic thinking. We review each of these three aspects (interdisciplinary thinking, systems thinking, algorithmic thinking) in turn.

18.2.1 Interdisciplinary Thinking

Network algorithmics represents the intersection of several disciplines within computer science that are often taught separately. Endnode algorithmics is a combination of networking, operating systems, computer architecture, and algorithms. Router algorithmics is a combination of networking, hardware design, and algorithms. Figure 18.3 provides examples of uses of these disciplines that are studied in the book.

For example, in Figure 18.3 techniques such as header prediction (Chapter 9) require a deep networking knowledge of TCP to optimize the expected case, while internal link striping (Chapter 15) requires knowing how to correctly design a striping protocol. On the other hand, application device channels (Chapter 6) require a careful understanding of the protection issues in operating systems.

Similarly, locality-driven receiver processing requires understanding the architectural function and limitations of the instruction cache. Finally, in router algorithmics it is crucial to understand hardware design. Arbiters like iSLIP and PIM were designed to allow scheduling decisions in a minimum packet arrival time.

Later in this chapter we argue that other disciplines, such as statistics and learning theory, will also be useful for network algorithmics.

Endnode algorithmics

Discipline	Example
Networking	Header prediction (Chapter 6)
Operating systems	Application device channels (Chapter 6)
Computer architecture	Locality-driven receiver processing (Chapter 5)
Algorithms	Timing wheels (Chapter 7)

Router algorithmics

Discipline	Example
Networking	Link striping (Chapter 15)
Hardware design	Switch arbiters (Chapters 2 and 13)
Algorithms	Fast IP lookup (Chapter 11)

FIGURE 18.3 Examples of disciplines used in this book along with sample applications.

18.2.2 Systems Thinking

Systems thinking is embodied by Principles **P1** though **P10**. Principles **P1** through **P5** were described earlier as systems principles. Systems unfold in space and time: in space, through various components (e.g., kernel, application), and in time, through certain key time points (e.g., application initialization time, packet arrival time). Principles **P1** through **P5** ask that a designer expand his or her vision to see the entire system and then to consider moving functions in space and time to gain efficiency.

For example, Principle **P1**, avoiding obvious waste, is a cliché by itself. However, our understanding of systems, in terms of separable and modular hierarchies, often precludes the synoptic eye required to see waste across system hierarchies. For example, the number of wasted copies is apparent only when one broadens one's view to that of a Web server (see I/O-Lite in Chapter 5). Similarly, the opportunities for dynamic code generation in going from Pathfinder to DPF (see Chapter 8) are apparent only when one considers the code required to implement a generic classifier.

Similarly, Principle **P4** asks the designer to be aware of existing system components that can be leveraged. Fbufs (Chapter 5) leverage off the virtual memory subsystem, while timing wheels (Chapter 7) leverage off the existing time-of-day computation to amortize the overhead of stepping through empty buckets. Principle **P4** also asks the designer to be especially aware of the underlying hardware, whether to exploit local access costs (e.g., DRAM pages, cache lines), to trade memory for speed (either by compression, if the underlying memory is SRAM, or by expansion, if memory is DRAM), or to exploit other hardware features (e.g., replacing multiplies by shifts in RED calculations in Chapter 14).

Principle **P5** asks the designer to be even bolder and to consider adding new hardware to the system; this is especially useful in a router context. While this is somewhat vague, Principles **5a** (parallelism via memory interleaving), **P5b** (parallelism via wide words), and **P5c** (combining DRAM and SRAM to improve overall speed and cost) appear to underlie many clever hardware designs to implement router functions. Thus memory interleaving and pipelining can be used to speed up IP lookups (Chapter 11), wide words are used to improve the speed of the Lucent classification scheme (Chapter 12), and DRAM and SRAM can be combined to construct an efficient counter scheme (Chapter 16).

Once the designer sees the system and identifies wasted sequences of operations together with possible components to leverage, the next step is to consider moving functions in time (**P2**) and space (**P3c**). Figure 18.4 shows examples of endnode algorithmic techniques that move functions between components. Figure 18.5 shows similar examples for router algorithmics.

Besides moving functions in space, moving functions in time is a key enabler for efficient algorithms. Besides the more conventional approaches of precomputation (**P2a**), lazy evaluation (**P2b**), and batch processing (**P2c**), there are subtler examples of moving functions to different times at which the system is instantiated. For example, in fbufs (Chapter 5), common VM mappings between the application and kernel are calculated when the application first starts up. Application device channels (Chapter 6) have the kernel authorize buffers (on behalf of an application) to the adaptor when the application starts up. Dynamic packet filter (DPF) (Chapter 8) specializes code when a classifier is updated. Tag switching (Chapter 11) moves the work of computing labels from packet-forwarding time to route-computation time.

Finally, Principles **P6** through **P10** concern the use of alternative system structuring techniques to remove inefficiencies. **P6** suggests considering specialized routines or alternative interfaces; for example, Chapter 6 suggests that event-driven APIs may be more efficient than

FIGURE 18.4 Endnode algorithmics: examples of moving functions in space.

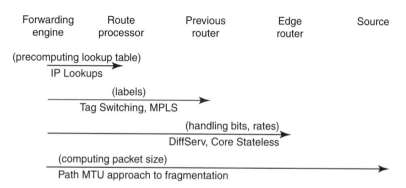

FIGURE 18.5 Router algorithmics: examples of moving functions in space.

the state-based interface of the *select()* call. **P7** suggests designing interfaces to avoid unnecessary generality; for example, in Chapter 5, fbufs map the fbuf pages into the same locations in all processes, avoiding the need for a further mapping when moving between processes. **P8** suggests avoiding being unduly influenced by reference implementations; for example, in Chapter 9, naive reference implementations of checksums have poor performance.

Principles **P9** and **P10** suggest keeping existing interfaces but adding extra information to interfaces (**P9**) or packet headers (**P10**). For example, efficiently reimplementing the *select()* call (Chapter 6) requires passing information between the protocol module and the select module. Passing information in packet headers, on the other hand, has a huge array of examples, including RDMA (Chapter 5), MPLS (Chapter 11), DiffServ, and core stateless fair queuing (Chapter 14).

18.2.3 Algorithmic Thinking

Algorithmic thinking refers to thinking about networking bottlenecks the way algorithm designers approach problems. Overall, algorithmic approaches are less important than other systems approaches, as embodied by Principles **P1** through **P10**. Also, it is dangerous to blindly reuse existing algorithms.

The first problem that must be confronted in using algorithmic thinking is how to frame the problem that must be solved. By changing the problem, one can often find more effective solutions. Consider the following problem, which we avoided in Chapter 11.

◆ *Example*: *Pipelining and Memory Allocation.* A lookup engine is using a trie. The lookup engine must be pipelined for speed. The simplest solution is to pipeline the trie by level. The root is at the first stage, the children of the root are assigned to the second stage, the nodes at height 2 to the third stage, etc. Unfortunately, the memory needs for each stage can vary as prefixes are inserted and deleted. There are the following spectrum of approaches.

- *Centralized memory:* All the processing stages share a single memory. Memory allocation is easy, but the centralized memory becomes a bottleneck.

- *One memory per stage:* Each processing stage has its own memory, minimizing memory contention. However, since the memory is statically allocated at fabrication time, any memory unused by a stage cannot be used by another stage.

- *Dynamically allocate small 1-port memories to stages:* As suggested in Chapter 11, on-chip memory is divided into M SRAMs, which are connected to stage processors via a crossbar. As a processor requires more or less memory, crossbar connections can be changed to allocate more or fewer memories to each stage. This scheme requires large M to avoid wasting memory, but large M can lead to high capacitive loads.

- *Dynamically allocate medium-size 2-port memories to stages:* The setting is identical to the last approach, except that each memory is now a 2-port memory that can be allocated to two processors. Using this it is is possible to show that N memories are sufficient for N processors, with almost no memory wastage.

- *Dynamically change the starting point in the pipeline:* In a conventional linear pipeline, all lookups start at the first stage and leave at the last. Florin Baboescu has suggested an alternative: Using a lookup table indexed on the first few bits, assign each address to a different first processor in the pipeline. Thus different addresses have different start and end processors. However, this gives considerably more flexibility in allocating memory to processors by changing the assignment of addresses to processors.

- *Pipeline by depth:* Instead of pipelining a tree by height, consider pipelining by depth. All leaves are assigned to the last stage, K, all parents of the leaves to stage $K - 1$, etc.

These approaches represent the interplay between principles **P13** (optimizing degrees of freedom) and **P5** (add hardware). However, each approach results in a different algorithmic problem! Thus a far more important skill than solving a hard problem is the skill required to frame the right problems that balance overall system needs.

Principles **P11** and **P13** help choose the right problem to solve. The pipelining example shows that choosing the degrees of freedom (**P13**) can change the algorithmic problem solved.

Similarly, Principle **P11**, optimizing the expected case, can sometimes help decide what the right measure is to optimize. This in turn influences the choice of algorithm. For example, simple TCP header prediction (Chapter 9) optimizes the expected case when the next packet is from the same connection and is the next data packet or ack. If this is indeed the expected case, there is no need for fancy connection lookup structures (a simple one-element cache) or fancy structures to deal with sequence number bookkeeping. However, if there are several concurrent connections, as in a server, a hash table may be better for connection lookup. Similarly, if packets routinely arrive out of order, then more fancy sequence number bookkeeping schemes [TVHS92] may be needed.

Principle **P12**, adding state for speed, is a simple technique used often in standard algorithmic design. However, it is quite common for just this principle by itself (without fancy additional algorithmic machinery) to help remove systems bottlenecks. For example, the major bottleneck in the *select()* call implementation is the need to repeatedly check for data in network connections known not to be ready. By simply keeping state across calls, this key bottleneck can be removed. By contrast, the bottlenecks caused by the bitmap interface can be removed by algorithmic means, but these are less important.

Having framed the appropriate problem using **P11**, **P12**, and **P13**, principles **P14** and **P15** can be used to guide the search for solutions.

Principle **P14** asks whether there are any important special cases, such as the use of finite universes, that can be leveraged to derive a more efficient algorithm. For example, the McKenney buffer-stealing algorithm of Chapter 9 provides a fast heap with $O(1)$ operations for the special case when elements to the heap change by at most 1 on each call.

Finally, principle **P15** asks whether there are algorithmic methods that can be adapted to the system. It is dangerous to blindly adapt existing algorithms because of the following possibilities that can mislead the designer.

- *Wrong Measures:* The measure for most systems implementations is the number of memory accesses and not the number of operations. For example, the fast *ufalloc()* operation uses a selection tree on bitmaps instead of a standard heap, leveraging off the fact that a single read can access W bits, where W is the size of a word. Again, the important measure in many IP lookup algorithms is search speed and not update speed.

- *Asymptotic Complexity:* Asymptotic complexity hides constants that are crucial in systems. When every microsecond counts, surely constant factors are important. Thus the switch matching algorithms in Chapter 13 have much smaller constants than the best bipartite matching algorithms in the literature and hence can be implemented.

- *Incorrect Cost Penalties:* In timing wheels (Chapter 7), a priority heap is implemented using a bucket-sorting data structure. However, the cost of strolling through empty buckets, a severe cost in bucket sort, is unimportant because on every timer tick, the system clock must be incremented anyway. As a second example, the dynamic programming algorithm to compute optimal lookup strides for multibit tries (Chapter 11) is $O(N * W^2)$, where N is the number of prefixes and W is the address width. While this appears to be quadratic, it is linear in the important term N (100,000 or more) and quadratic in the address width (32 bits, and the term is smaller in practice).

In spite of all these warnings, algorithmic methods are useful in networking, ranging from the use of Pathfinder-like tries in Chapter 8 to the use of tries and binary search (suitably modified) in Chapter 11.

18.3 NETWORK ALGORITHMICS AND REAL PRODUCTS

Many of the algorithms used in this book are found in real products. The following is a quick survey.

Endnode Algorithmics: Zero-copy implementations of network stacks are quite common, as are implementations of memory-mapped files; however, more drastic changes, such as IO-Lite, are only used more rarely, such as by the iMimic server software. The RDMA specification is well developed. Event-driven Web servers are quite common, and many operating systems other than UNIX (such as Windows NT) have fast implementations of *select( )* equivalents. The VIA standard avoids system calls using ideas similar to ADCs.

Most commercial systems for early demultiplexing still rely on BPF, but that is because few systems require so many classifiers that they need the scalability of a Pathfinder or a DPF. Some operating systems use timing wheels, notably Linux and FreeBSD. Linux uses fast buffer-manipulation operations on linear buffers. Fast IP checksum algorithms are common, and so are multibit CRC algorithms in hardware.

Router Algorithmics: Binary search lookup algorithms for bridges were common in products, as were hashing schemes (e.g., Gigaswitch). Multibit trie algorithms for IP lookups are very common; recently, compressed versions, such as the tree bitmap algorithm, have become popular in Cisco's latest CRS-1 router. Classification is still generally done by CAMs, and thus much of Chapter 12 is probably more useful for software classification.

In some chapters, such as the chapter on switching (Chapter 13), we provided a real product example for every switching scheme described (see Figure 13.2, for example). In fair queuing, DRR, RED, and token buckets are commonly implemented. General weighted fair queuing, virtual clock, and core stateless fair queuing are hardly ever used. Finally, much of the measurement and security chapters is devoted to ideas that are not part of any product *today*.

It is useful to see many of these ideas come together in a complete system. While it is hard to find details of such systems (because of commercial secrecy), the following two large systems pull together ideas in endnode and router algorithmics.

SYSTEM EXAMPLE 1: FLASH WEB SERVER

The Flash [PDZ99a] Web server was designed at Rice University and undoubtedly served as the inspiration (and initial code base) for a company called iMimic. A version of Flash called Flash-lite uses the following ideas from endnode algorithmics.

- *Fast copies:* Flash-lite uses IO-Lite to avoid redundant copies.
- *Process scheduling:* Flash uses an event-driven server with helper processes to minimize scheduling and maximize concurrency.
- *Fast select:* Flash uses an optimized implementation of the *select( )* call.
- *Other optimizations:* Flash caches response headers and file mappings.

SYSTEM EXAMPLE 2: CISCO 12000 GSR ROUTER

The Cisco GSR [Sys] is a popular gigabit router and uses the following ideas from router algorithmics.

- *Fast IP lookups:* The GSR uses a multibit tree to do IP lookups.
- *Fast switching:* The GSR uses the iSLIP algorithm for fast bipartite matching of VOQs.
- *Fair queuing:* The GSR implements a modified form of DRR called MDRR, where one queue is given priority (e.g., for voice-over-IP). It also implements a sophisticated form of

RED called *weighted RED* and token buckets. All these algorithms are implemented in hardware.

18.4 NETWORK ALGORITHMICS: BACK TO THE FUTURE

The preceding three sections of this chapter talked of the past and the present. But are all the ideas played out? Has network algorithmics already been milked to the point where nothing new is left to do? We believe this is not the case. This is because we believe network algorithmics will be enriched in the near future in three ways: new *abstractions* that require new solutions will become popular; new connecting *disciplines* will provide new approaches to existing problems; and new *requirements* will require rethinking existing solutions. We expand on each of these possibilities in turn.

18.4.1 New Abstractions

This book dealt with the fast implementation of the standard networking abstractions: TCP sockets at endnodes and IP routing at routers. However, new abstractions are constantly being invented to increase user productivity. While these abstractions make life easier for users, unoptimized implementations of these abstractions can exact a severe performance penalty. But this only creates new opportunities for network algorithmics. Here follow some examples of such abstractions.

- *TCP offload engines:* While the book has concentrated on software TCP implementations, movements such as iSCSI have made hardware TCP offload engines more interesting. Doing TCP in hardware and handling worst-case performance at 10 Gbps and even 40 Gbps is very challenging. For example, to do complete offload, the chip must even handle out-of-order packets and packet fragments (see Chapter 9) without appreciable slowdown.

- *HTML and Web server processing:* There have been a number of papers trying to improve Web server performance that can be considered an application of endnode algorithmics. For example, persistent HTTP [Mog95] can be considered an application of **P1** to the problem of connection overhead. A more speculative approach to reduce DNS lookup times in Web accesses by passing hints (**P10**) is described in Chandranmenon and Varghese [CV01].

- *Web services:* The notion of Web services, by which a Web page is used to provide a service, is getting increasingly popular. There are a number of protocols that underly Web services, and standard implementations of these services can be slow.

- *CORBA:* The common object request broker architecture is popular but quite slow. Gokhale and Schmidt [GS98] apply to the problem four of the principles described in this book (eliminating waste, **P1**, optimizing the expected case, **P11**, passing information between layers, **P9**, and exploiting locality for good cache behavior, **P4a**). They show that such techniques from endnode algorithmics can improve the performance of the SunSoft Inter-Orb protocol by a factor of 2–4.5, depending on the data type. Similar optimizations should be possible in hardware.

- *SSL and other encryption standards:* Many Web servers use the secure socket layer (SSL) for secure transactions. Software implementations of SSL are quite slow. There is an increasing interest in hardware implementations of SSL.

- *XML processing:* XML is rapidly becoming the *lingua franca* of the Web. Parsing and converting from XML to HTML can be a bottleneck.

- *Measurement and security abstractions:* Currently, SNMP and NetFlow allow very primitive measurement abstractions. The abstraction level can be raised only by a tool that integrates all the raw measurement data. Perhaps in the future routers will have to implement more sophisticated abstractions to help in measurement and security analysis.

- *Sensor networks:* A sensor network may wish to calculate new abstractions to solve such specific problems as finding high concentrations of pollutants and ascertaining the direction of a forest fire.

If history is any guide, every time an existing bottleneck becomes well studied, a new abstraction appears with a new bottleneck. Thus after lookups became well understood, packet classification emerged. After classification, came TCP offload; and now SSL and XML are clearly important. Many pundits believe that wire speed security solutions (as implemented in a router or an intrusion detection system) will be required by the year 2006. Thus it seems clear that future abstractions will keep presenting new challenges to network algorithmics.

18.4.2 New Connecting Disciplines

Earlier we said that a key aspect of network algorithmics is its interdisciplinary nature. Solutions require a knowledge of operating systems, computer architecture, hardware design, networking, and algorithms. We believe the following disciplines will also impinge on network algorithmics very soon.

- *Optics:* Optics has been abstracted away as a link layer technology in this book. Currently, optics provides a way to add extra channels to existing fiber using dense wavelength-division multiplexing. However, optical research has made amazing strides. There are undoubtedly exciting possibilities to rethink router design using some combination of electronics and optics.[2]

- *Network processor architecture:* While this field is still in its infancy as compared to computer architecture, there are surely more imaginative approaches than current approaches that assign packets to one of several processors. One such approach, described in Sherwood et al. [SVC03], uses a wide word state machine as a fundamental building block.

- *Learning theory:* The fields of security and measurement are crying out for techniques to pick out interesting patterns from massive traffic data sets. Learning theory and data mining have been used for these purposes in other fields. Rather than simply reusing, say, standard clustering algorithms or standard techniques such as hidden Markov models, the real breakthroughs may belong to those who can find variations of these techniques that can be implemented at high speeds with some loss of accuracy. Similarly, online analytical processing (OLAP) tools may be useful for networking, with twists to fit the networking milieu. An example of a tool that has an OLAP flavor in a uniquely network setting can be found in Estan et al. [ESV03].

---

[2]Electronics still appears to be required today because of the lack of optical buffers and the difficulty of optical header processing.

- *Databases:* The field of databases has a great deal to teach networking in terms of systematic techniques for querying for information. Recently, an even more relevant trend has been the subarea of continuous queries. Techniques developed in databases can be of great utility to algorithmics.

- *Statistics:* The field of statistics will be of even more importance in dealing with large data sets. Already, NetFlow and other tools have to resort to sampling. What inferences can safely be made from sampled data? As we have seen in Chapter 16, statistical methods are already used by ISPs to solve the traffic matrix problem from limited SNMP data.

18.4.3 New Requirements

Much of this book has focused on processing time as the main metric to be optimized while minimizing dollar cost. Storage was also an important consideration because of limited on-chip storage and the expense of SRAM. However, even minimizing storage was related to speed, in order to maximize the possibility of storing the entire data structure in high-speed storage.

The future may bring new requirements. Two important such requirements are (mechanical) space and power. Space is particularly important in PoPs and hosting centers, because rack space is limited. Thus routers with small form factors are crucial. It may be that optimizing space is mostly a matter of mechanical design together with the use of higher and higher levels of integration. However, engineering routers (and individual sensors in sensor networks) for power may require attention to algorithmics

Today power per rack is limited to a few kilowatts, and routers that need more power do so by spreading out across multiple racks. Power is a major problem in modern router design. It may be possible to rethink lookup, switching, and fair queuing algorithms in order to minimize power. Such power-conscious designs have already appeared in the computer architecture and operating systems community. It is logical to expect this trend to spread to router design.

18.5 THE INNER LIFE OF A NETWORKING DEVICE

We have tried to summarize in this chapter the major themes of this book in terms of the techniques described and the principles used. We have also tried to argue that network algorithmics is used in real products and is likely to find further application in the future because of new abstractions, new connecting disciplines, and new requirements. While the specific techniques and problems may change, we hope the *principles* involved remain useful.

Besides the fact that network algorithmics is *useful* in building better and faster network devices, we hope this book makes the case that network algorithmics is also *intellectually stimulating*. While it may lack the *depth* of hard problems in theoretical computer science or physics, perhaps what can be most stimulating is the *breadth*, in terms of the disciplines it encompasses.

An endnode, for instance, may appear as a simple processing state machine at the highest level of abstraction. A more detailed inspection would see a Web request packet arriving at a server interface, the interrupt firing, and the protocol code being scheduled via a software interrupt. Even within the protocol code, each line of code has to be fetched, hopefully from the i-cache, and each data item has to go through the VM system (via the TLB hopefully) and the data cache. Finally, the application must get involved via a returned system call and a process-scheduling operation. The request may trigger file system activity and disk activity.

A router similarly has an interesting inner life. Reflecting the macrocosmos of the Internet *outside* the router is a microcosmos *within* the router consisting of major subsystems, such as line cards and the switch fabric, together with striping and flow control across chip-to-chip links.

Network algorithmics seeks to understand these hidden subsystems of the Internet to make the Internet faster. This book is a first attempt to begin understanding — in Feynman's phrase — this "tremendous world of interconnected hierarchies" within routers and endnodes. In furthering this process of understanding and streamlining these hierarchies, there are still home runs to be hit and touchdowns to be scored as the game against networking bottlenecks continues to be played.

APPENDIX

Detailed Models

This appendix contains further models and information that can be useful for some readers of this book. For example, the protocols section may be useful for hardware designers who wish to work in networking but need a quick self-contained overview of protocols such as TCP and IP to orient themselves. On the other hand, the hardware section provides insights that may be useful for software designers without requiring a great deal of reading. The switch section provides some more details about switching theory.

A.1 TCP AND IP

To be self-contained, Section A.1.1 provides a very brief sketch of how TCP operates, and Section A.1.2 briefly describes how IP routing operates.

A.1.1 *Transport Protocols*

When you point your Web browser to www.cs.ucsd.edu, your browser first converts the destination host name (i.e., cs.ucsd.edu) into a 32-bit Internet address, such as 132.239.51.18, by making a request to a local DNS name server [Per92]; this is akin to dialing directory assistance to find a telephone number. A 32-bit IP address is written in dotted decimal form for convenience; each of the four numbers between dots (e.g., 132) represents the decimal value of a byte. Domain names such as cs.ucsd.edu appear only in user interfaces; the Internet transport and routing protocols deal only with 32-bit Internet addresses.

Networks lose and reorder messages. If a network application cares that all its messages are received in sequence, the application can subcontract the job of reliable delivery to a transport protocol such as transmission control protocol (TCP). It is the job of TCP to provide the sending and receiving applications with the illusion of two shared data queues in each direction — despite the fact that the sender and receiver machines are separated by a lossy network. Thus whatever the sender application writes to its local TCP send queue should magically appear in the same order at the local TCP receive queue at the receiver, and vice versa.

Since Web browsers care about reliability, the Web browser at sender S (Figure A.1) first contacts its local TCP with a request to set up a *connection* to the destination application. The destination application is identified by a well-known port number (such as 80 for Web traffic) at the destination IP address. If IP addresses are thought of as telephone numbers, port numbers can be thought of as extension numbers. A connection is the shared state information — such

433

FIGURE A.1 Time–space figure of a possible scenario for a conversation between Web client *S* and Web server *D* as mediated by the reliable transport protocol TCP. Assume that the ack to the SYN-ACK is piggybacked on the 20-byte GET message.

as sequence numbers and timers — at the sender and receiver TCP programs that facilitate reliable delivery.

Figure A.1 is an example of a time–space figure, with time flowing downward and space represented horizontally. A line from *S* to *D* that slopes downward represents the sending of a message from *S* to *D*, which arrives at a later time.

To set up a connection, the sending TCP (Figure A.1) sends out a request to start the connection, called a SYN message, with a number *X* the sender has not used recently. If all goes well, the destination will send back a SYN-ACK to signify acceptance, along with a number *Y* that the destination has not used before. Only after the SYN-ACK is the first data message sent.

The messages sent between TCPs are called TCP *segments*. Thus to be precise, the following models will refer to TCP segments and to IP packets (often called *datagrams* in IP terminology).

In Figure A.1, the sender is a Web client, whose first message is a small (say) 20-byte HTTP GET message for the Web page (e.g., index.html) at the destination. To ensure message delivery, TCP will retransmit all segments until it gets an acknowledgment. To ensure that data is delivered in order and to correlate acks with data, each byte of data in a segment carries a sequence number. In TCP only the sequence number of the first byte in a segment is carried explicitly; the sequence numbers of the other bytes are implicit, based on their offset.

When the 20-byte GET message arrives at the receiver, the receiving TCP delivers it to the receiving Web application. The Web server at D may respond with a Web page of (say) 1900 bytes that it writes to the receiver TCP input queue along with an HTTP header of 100 bytes, making a total of 2000 bytes. TCP can choose to break up the 2000-byte data arbitrarily into segments; the example of Figure A.1 uses two segments of 1500 and 500 bytes.

Assume for variety that the second segment of 500 bytes is lost in the network; this is shown in a time–space picture by a message arrow that does not reach the other end. Since the receiver does not receive an ACK, the receiver retransmits the second segment after a timer expires. Note that ACKs are cumulative: A single ACK acknowledges the byte specified and all previous bytes. Finally, if the sender is done, the sender begins closing the connection with a FIN message that is also acked (if all goes well), and the receiver does the same.

Once the connection is closed with FIN messages, the receiver TCP keeps no sequence number information about the sender application that terminated. But networks can also cause duplicates (because of retransmissions, say) of SYN and DATA segments that appear later and confuse the receiver. This is why the receiver in Figure A.1 does not believe any data that is in a SYN message until it is validated by receiving a third message containing the unused number Y the receiver picked. If Y is echoed back in a third message, then the initial message is not a delayed duplicate, since Y was not used recently. Note that if the SYN is a retransmission of a previously closed connection, the sender will not echo back Y, because the connection is closed.

This preliminary dance featuring a SYN and a SYN-ACK is called TCP's three-way handshake. It allows TCP to forget about past communication, at the cost of increased latency to send new data. In practice, the validation numbers X and Y do double duty as the initial sequence numbers of the data segments in each direction. This works because sequence numbers need not start at 0 or 1 as long as both sender and receiver use the same initial value.

The TCP sequence numbers are carried in a TCP header contained in each segment. The TCP header contains 16 bits for the destination port (recall that a port is like a telephone extension that helps identify the receiving application), 16 bits for the sending port (analogous to a sending application extension), a 32-bit sequence number for any data contained in the segment, and a 32-bit number acknowledging any data that arrived in the reverse direction. There are also flags that identify segments as being SYN, FIN, etc. A segment also carries a routing header[1] and a link header that changes on every link in the path.

If the application is (say) a videoconferencing application that does not want reliability guarantees, it can choose to use a protocol called UDP (user datagram protocol) instead of TCP. Unlike TCP, UDP does not need acks or retransmissions, because it does not guarantee reliability. Thus the only sensible fields in the UDP header corresponding to the TCP header are the destination and source port numbers. Like ordinary mail versus certified mail, UDP is cheaper in bandwidth and processing but offers no reliability guarantees. For more information about TCP and UDP, Stevens [Ste94] is highly recommended.

---

[1] The routing header is often called the Internet protocol, or IP, header.

FIGURE A.2   A sample network topology corresponding to the Internet of Figure A.1.

A.1.2 Routing Protocols

Figure A.2 shows a more detailed view of a plausible network topology between Web client *S* and Web server *D* of Figure A.1. The source is attached to a local area network such as an Ethernet, to which is also connected a router, *R1*. Routers are the automated post offices of the Internet, which consult the destination address in an Internet message (often called a *packet*) to decide on which output link to forward the message.

In the figure, the source *S* belongs to an administrative unit (say, a small company) called a *domain*. In this simple example, the domain of *S* consists only of an Ethernet and a router, *R1*, that connects to an Internet service provider (ISP) through router *R2*. Our Internet service provider is also a small outfit, and it consists only of three routers, *R2*, *R3*, and *R4*, connected by fiber-optic communication links. Finally, *R4* is connected to router *R5* in *D*'s domain, which leads to the destination, *D*.

Internet routing is broken into two conceptual parts, called *forwarding* and *routing*. First consider forwarding, which explains how packets move from *S* to *D* through intermediate routers.

When *S* sends a TCP packet to *D*, it first places the IP address of *D* in the routing header of the packet and sends it to neighboring router, *R1*. Forwarding at endnodes such as *S* and *D* is kept simple and consists of sending the packet to an adjoining router. *R1* realizes it has no information about *D* and so passes it to ISP router *R2*. When it gets to *R2*, *R2* must choose to send the packet to either *R3* or *R4*. *R2* makes its choice based on a forwarding table at *R2* that specifies (say) that packets to *D* should be sent to *R4*. Similarly, *R4* will have a forwarding entry for traffic to *D* that points to *R5*. A description of how forwarding entries are compressed using prefixes can be found in Section 2.3.2. In summary, an Internet packet is forwarded to a destination by following forwarding information about the destination at each router. Each router need not know the complete path to *D*, but only the next hop to get to *D*.

While forwarding must be done at extremely high speeds, the forwarding tables at each router must be built by a routing protocol. For example, if the link from *R2* to *R4* fails, the routing protocol within the ISP domain should change the forwarding table at *R2* to forward packets to *D* to *R3*. Typically, each domain uses its own routing protocol to calculate shortest-path routes within the domain. Two main approaches to routing within a domain are *distance vector* and *link state*.

In the distance vector approach, exemplified by the protocol RIP [Per92], the neighbors of each router periodically exchange distance estimates for each destination network. Thus in Figure A.2, *R2* may get a distance estimate of 2 to *D*'s network from *R3* and a distance estimate of 1 from *R*4. Thus *R*2 picks the shorter-distance neighbor, *R*4, to reach *D*. If the link from *R*2 to *R*4 fails, *R*2 will time-out this link, set its estimate of distance to *D* through *R*4 to infinity, and then choose the route through *R*3. Unfortunately, distance vector takes a long time to converge when destinations become unreachable [Per92].

Link state routing [Per92] avoids the convergence problems of distance vector by having each router construct a *link state packet* listing its neighbors. In Figure A.2, for instance, *R*3's link state packet (LSP) will list its links to *R*2 and *R*4. Each router then broadcasts its LSP to all other routers in the domain using a primitive flooding mechanism; LSP sequence numbers are used to prevent LSPs from circulating forever. When all routers have each other's LSP, every router has a map of the network and can use Dijkstra's algorithm [Per92] to calculate shortest-path routes to all destinations. The most common routing protocol used *within* ISP domains is a link state routing protocol called *open shortest path first* (OSPF) [Per92].

While shortest-path routing works well within domains, the situation is more complex for routing between domains. Imagine that Figure A.2 is modified so that the ISP in the middle, say, ISP *A*, does not have a direct route to *D*'s domain but instead is connected to ISPs *C* and *E*, each of which has a path to *D*'s domain. Should ISP *A* send a packet addressed to *D* to ISP *C* or *E*? Shortest-path routing no longer makes sense because ISPs want to route based on other metrics (e.g., dollar cost) or on policy (e.g., always send data through a major competitor, as in so-called "hot potato" routing).

Thus interdomain routing is a more messy kettle of fish than routing within a domain. The most commonly used interdomain protocol today is called the *border gateway protocol* (BGP) [Ste99], which uses a gossip mechanism akin to distance vector, except that each route is augmented with the path of domains instead of just the distance. The path ostensibly makes convergence faster than distance vector and provides information for policy decisions.

To go beyond this brief sketch of routing protocols, the reader is directed to *Interconnections* by Radia Perlman [Per92] for insight into routing in general and to *BGP-4* by John Stewart [Ste99] as the best published textbook on the arcana of BGP.

A.2 HARDWARE MODELS

For completeness, this section contains some details of hardware models that were skipped in Chapter 2 for the sake of brevity. These detailed models are included in this section to provide somewhat deeper understanding for software designers.

A.2.1 From Transistors to Logic Gates

The fundamental building block of the most complex network processor is a *transistor* (Figure A.3). A transistor is a voltage-controlled switch. More precisely, a transistor is a device with three external attachments (Figure A.3): a gate, a source, and a drain. When an input voltage *I* is applied to the gate, the source–drain path conducts electricity; when the input voltage is turned off, the source–drain path does not conduct. The output *O* voltage occurs at the drain. Transistors are physically synthesized on a chip by having a polysilicon path (gate) cross a diffusion path (source–drain) at points governed by a mask.

The simplest logic gate is an *inverter* (also known as a *NOT* gate). This gate is formed (Figure A.3) by connecting the drain to a power supply and the source to ground (0 volts). The circuit functions as an inverter because when *I* is a high voltage (i.e., *I* = 1), the transistor

FIGURE A.3 A transistor is a voltage-controlled switch allowing the source-to-drain path to conduct current when the gate voltage is high. An inverter is a transistor whose source is connected to ground and whose drain is connected to a power supply.

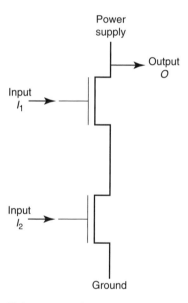

FIGURE A.4 Using two transistors in series to create a NAND gate.

turns on, "pulling down" the output to ground (i.e., $O = 0$). On the other hand, when $I = 0$, the transistor turns off, "pulling up" the output to the power supply (i.e., $O = 1$). Thus an inverter output flips the input bit, implementing the NOT operation. Although omitted in our pictures, real gates also add a resistance in the path to avoid "shorting" the power supply when $I = 1$, by connecting it directly to ground.

The inverter generalizes to a NAND gate (Figure A.4) of two inputs I_1 and I_2 using two transistors whose source–drain paths are connected in series. The output O is pulled down to ground if and only if both transistors are on, which happens if and only if both I_1 and I_2 are 1. Similarly, a NOR gate is formed by placing two transistors in parallel.

A.2.2 Timing Delays

Figure A.3 assumes that the output changed instantaneously when the input changed. In practice, when I is turned from 0 to 1, it takes time for the gate to accumulate enough charge to allow the source–drain path to conduct. This is modeled by thinking of the gate input as charging a gate capacitor (C) in series with a resistor (R). If you don't remember what capacitance and resistance are, think of charge as water, voltage as water pressure, capacitance as the size of a container that must be filled with water, and resistance as a form of friction impeding water flow. The larger the container capacity and the larger the friction, the longer the time to fill the container. Formally, the voltage at time t after the input I is set to V is $V(1 - e^{-t/RC})$. The product RC is the charging time constant; within one time constant the output reaches $1 - 1/e = 66\%$ of its final value.

In Figure A.3, notice also that if I is turned off, output O pulls up to the power supply voltage. But to do so the output must charge one or more gates to which it is connected, each of which is a resistance and a capacitance (the sum of which is called the *output load*). For instance, in a typical 0.18-micron process,[2] the delay through a single inverter driving an output load of four identical inverters is 60 picoseconds.

Charging one input can cause further outputs to charge further inputs, and so on. Thus for a combinatorial function, the delay is the sum of the charging and discharging delays over the worst-case path of transistors. Such path delays must fit within a minimum packet arrival time. Logic designs are simulated to see if they meet timing using approximate analysis as well as accurate circuit models, such as Spice. Good designers have intuition that allows them to create designs that meet timing. A formalization of such intuition is the method of logical effort [SSH99], which allows a designer to make quick timing estimates. Besides the time to charge capacitors, another source of delay is wire delay.

A.2.3 Hardware Design Building Blocks

This section describes some standard terminology for higher-level building blocks used by hardware designers that can be useful to know.

PROGRAMMABLE LOGIC ARRAYS AND PROGRAMMABLE ARRAY LOGICS

A programmable logic array (PLA) has the generality of a software lookup table but is more compact. Any binary function can be written as the OR of a set of product terms, each of which is the AND of a subset of (possibly complemented) inputs. The PLA thus has all the inputs pass through an AND plane, where the desired product terms are produced by making the appropriate connections. The products are then routed to an OR plane. A designer produces specific functions by making connections within the PLA. A more restrictive but simpler form of PLA is a PAL (programmable array logic).

STANDARD CELLS

Just as software designers reuse code, so also do hardware designers reuse a repertoire of commonly occurring functions, such as multiplexors and adders.

The functional approach to design is generally embodied in *standard cell* libraries and *gate array* technologies, in which a designer must map his or her specific problem to a set

---

[2]Semiconductor processes are graded by the smallest gate lengths they can produce. Shrinking process width decreases capacitances and resistances and so increases speed.

FIGURE A.5 To store the output of an inverter indefinitely in the absence of writes, the output is fed back to the input after a second inversion. Two further transistors are used to allow writes and to block the feedback refresh.

of building blocks offered by the technology. At even higher abstraction levels, designers use synthesis tools to write higher-level language code in Verilog or VHDL for the function they wish to implement. The VHDL code is then synthesized into hardware by commercial tools. The trade-off is reduced design time, at some cost in performance. Since a large fraction of the design is not on the critical path, synthesis can greatly reduce time to market. This section ends with a networking example of the use of reduction for a critical path function.

A.2.4 Memories: The Inside Scoop

This section briefly describes implementation models for registers, SRAMs, and DRAMs.

REGISTERS

How can a bit be stored such that in the absence of writes and power failures, the bit stays indefinitely? Storing a bit as the output of the inverter shown in Figure A.3 will not work, because, left to itself, the output will discharge from a high to a low voltage via "parasitic" capacitances. A simple solution is to use *feedback*: In the absence of a write, the inverter output can be fed back to the input and "refresh" the output. Of course, an inverter flips the input bit, and so the output must be inverted a second time in the feedback path to get the polarity right, as shown in Figure A.5. Rather than show the complete inverter (Figure A.3), a standard triangular icon is used to represent an inverter.

Input to the first transistor must be supplied by the write input when a write is enabled and by the feedback output when a write is disabled. This is accomplished by two more "pass" transistors. The pass transistor whose gate is labeled "Refresh Enable" is set to high when a write is disabled, while the pass transistor whose gate is labeled "Write Enable" is set to high when a write is enabled. In practice, refreshes and writes are done only at the periodic pulses of a systemwide signal called a *clock*. Figure A.5 is called a *flip-flop*.

A *register* is an ordered collection of flip-flops. For example, most modern processors (e.g., the Pentium series) have a collection of 32- or 64-bit on-chip registers. A 32-bit register contains 32 flip-flops, each storing a bit. Access from logic to a register on the same chip is extremely fast, say, 0.5–1 nsec. Access to a register off-chip is slightly slower because of the delay to drive larger off-chip loads.

FIGURE A.6 A DRAM cell stores a bit using charge on a capacitor that leaks away slowly and must be refreshed periodically.

STATIC RAM

A static random access memory (SRAM) contains N registers addressed by $\log N$ address bits A. SRAM is so named because the underlying flip-flops refresh themselves and so are "static." Besides flip-flops, an SRAM needs a decoder that decodes A into a unary value used to select the right register. Accessing an SRAM on-chip is only slightly slower than accessing a register because of the added decode delay. At the time of writing, it was possible to obtain on-chip SRAMs with 0.5-nsec access times. Access times of of 1–2 nsec for on-chip SRAM and 5–10 nsec for off-chip SRAM are common. On-chip SRAM is limited to around 64 Mbits today.

DYNAMIC RAM

The SRAM bit cell of Figure A.5 requires at least five transistors. Thus SRAM is always less dense or more expensive than memory technology based on dynamic RAM (DRAM). In Figure A.6, a DRAM cell uses only a single transistor connected to an output capacitance. The transistor is only used to connect the write input to the output when the write enable signal on the gate is high. The output voltage is stored on the output capacitance, which is significantly larger than the gate capacitance; thus the charge leaks, but slowly. Loss due to leakage is fixed by refreshing the DRAM cell externally within a few milliseconds.

To obtain high densities, DRAMs use "pseudo-three-dimensional trench or stacked capacitors" [FPCe97]; together with the factor of 5–6 reduction in the number of transistors, a DRAM cell is roughly 16 times smaller than an SRAM cell [FPCe97].

The compact design of a DRAM cell has another important side effect: A DRAM cell requires higher latency to read or write than the SRAM cell of Figure A.5. Intuitively, if the SRAM cell of Figure A.5 is selected, the power supply quickly drives the output bit line to the appropriate threshold. On the other hand, the capacitor in Figure A.6 has to drive an output line of higher capacitance. The resulting small voltage swing of a DRAM bit line takes longer to sense reliably. In addition, DRAMs need extra delay for two-stage decoding and for refresh. DRAM refreshes are done automatically by the DRAM controller's periodically enabling RAS for each row R, thereby refreshing all the bits in R.

A.2.5 Chip Design

Finally, it may be useful for networking readers to understand how chips for networking functions are designed.

After partitioning functions between chips, the box architect creates a design team for each chip and works with the team to create chip specification. For each block within a chip, logic designers write software register transfer level (RTL) descriptions using a hardware design language such as Verilog or VHDL. Block sizes are estimated and a crude floor plan of the chip is done in preparation for circuit design.

At this stage, there is a fork in the road. In *synthesized* design, the designer applies synthesis tools to the RTL code to generate hardware circuits. Synthesis speeds the design process but generally produces slower circuits than custom-designed circuits. If the synthesized circuit does not meet timing (e.g., 8 nsec for OC-768 routers), the designer redoes the synthesis after adding constraints and tweaking parameters. In *custom* design, on the other hand, the designer can design individual gates or drag-and-drop cells from a standard library. If the chip does not meet timing, the designer must change the design [SSH99]. Finally, the chip "tapes out," and is manufactured, and the first yield is inspected.

Even at the highest level, it helps to understand the chip design process. For example, systemwide problems can be solved by repartitioning functions between chips. This is easy when the chip is being specified, is an irritant after RTL is written, and causes blood feuds after the chip has taped out. A second "spin" of a chip is something that any engineering manager would rather work around.

INTERCONNECTS, POWER, AND PACKAGING

Chips are connected using either point-to-high connections known as *high-speed serial links*, shared links known as *buses*, or parallel arrays of buses known as *crossbar switches*. Instead of using N^2 point-to-point links to connect N chips, it is cheaper to use a shared bus. A bus is similar to any shared media network, such as an Ethernet, and requires an arbitration protocol often implemented (unlike an Ethernet) using a centralized arbiter. Once a sender has been selected in a time slot, other potential senders must not send any signals. Electrically, this is done by having transmitters use a *tristate* output device that can output a 0 or a 1 or be in a high-impedance state. In high-impedance state, there is no path through the device to either the power supply or ground. Thus the selected transmitter sends 0's or 1's, while the nonselected transmitters stay in high-impedance state.

Buses are limited today to around 20 Gb/sec. Thus many routers today use parallel buses in the form of crossbar switches (Chapter 13). A router can be built with a small number of chips, such as a link interface chip, a packet-forwarding chip, memory chips to store lookup state, a crossbar switch, and a queuing chip with associated DRAM memory for packet buffers.

A.3 SWITCHING THEORY

This section provides some more details about matching algorithms for Clos networks and the dazzling variety of interconnection networks.

A.3.1 Matching Algorithms for Clos Networks with k = n

A Clos network can be proved to be rearrangably nonblocking for $k = n$. The proof uses *Hall's theorem* and the notion of *perfect matchings*. A bipartite graph is a special graph with two sets of nodes I and O; edges are only between a node in I and a node in O. A perfect matching is a subset E of edges in this graph such that every node in I is the endpoint of exactly one edge in E, and every node in O is also the endpoint of exactly one edge in E. A perfect match marries every man in I to every woman in O while respecting monogamy. Hall's theorem states that a necessary and sufficient condition for a perfect matching is that every subset X of I of size d has at least d edges going to d distinct nodes in O.

To apply Hall's theorem to prove the Clos network is nonblocking, we show that any arrangement of N inputs that wish to go to N different outputs can be connected via the Clos network. Use the following iterative algorithm. In each iteration, match input switches (set I) to output switches (set O) after ignoring the middle switches. Draw an edge between an input switch i and an output switch o if there is at least one input of i that wishes to send to an output directly reachable through o.

Using this definition of an edge, here is *Claim 1:* Every subset X of d input switches in I has edges to at least d output switches in O. Suppose Claim 1 were false. Then the total number of outputs desired by all inputs in X would be strictly less than nd (because each edge to an output switch can correspond to at most n outputs). But this cannot be so, because d input switches with n inputs each must require exactly nd outputs.

Claim 1 and Hall's theorem can be used to conclude that there is a perfect matching between input switches and output switches. Perform this matching, after placing back *exactly one* middle switch M. This is possible because every middle switch has a link to every input switch and a link to every output switch. This allows routing one input link in every input switch to one output link in every switch. It also makes unavailable all the n links from each input switch to the middle switch M and all output links from M.

Thus the problem has been reduced from having to route n inputs on each input switch using n middle switches to having to route $n - 1$ inputs per input switch using $n - 1$ middle switches. Thus n iterations are sufficient to route all inputs to all outputs without causing resource conflicts that lead to blocking.

Thus a simple version of this algorithm would take n perfect matches; the best existing algorithm for perfect matching [HK73] takes $O(N/n^{1.5})$ time. A faster approach is via edge coloring; each middle switch is assigned a color, and we color the edges of the demand multigraph between input switches and output switches so that no two edges coming out of a node have the same color.[3] However, edge coloring can be done directly (without n iterations as before) in around $O(N \log N)$ time [CH82].

A.4 THE INTERCONNECTION NETWORK ZOO

There is a dazzling variety of $(\log N)$-depth interconnection networks, all based on the same idea of using bits in the output address to steer to the appropriate portion, starting with the most significant bit. For example, one can construct the famous Butterfly network in a very similar way to the recursive construction of the Delta network of Figure 13.14. In the Delta network, all the inputs to the top $(N/2)$-size Delta network come from the 0 outputs of the first stage in order. Thus the 0 output of the first first-stage switch is the first input, the 0 output of the second switch is the second input, etc.

---

[3]Intuitively, each set of edges colored with a single color corresponds to one matching and one middle switch, as in our first algorithm.

By contrast, in a Butterfly, the second input of the upper $N/2$ switch is the 0 output of the middle switch of the first stage (rather than the second switch of the first stage). The 0 output of the second switch is then the third input, while the 0 output of the switch following the middle switch gets the fourth input, etc. Thus the two halves are interleaved in the Butterfly but not in the Delta, forming a classic bowtie or butterfly pattern. However, even with this change it is still easy to see that the same principle is operative: outputs with MSB 0 go to the top half, while outputs with MSB 1 go to to the bottom.

Because the Butterfly can be created from the Delta by renumbering inputs and outputs, the two networks are said to be *isomorphic*. Butterflies were extremely popular in parallel computing [CSG99], gaining fame in the BBN Butterfly, though they seem to have lost ground to low-dimensional meshes (see Section 13.10) in recent machines.

There is also a small variant of the Butterfly, called the *Banyan*, that involves pairing the inputs even in the first stage in a more shuffled fashion (the first input pairs with the middle input, etc.) before following Butterfly connections to the second stage. Banyans enjoyed a brief resurgence in the network community when it was noticed that if the outputs for each input are in sorted order, then the Banyan can route without internal blocking. An important such switch was the Sunshine switch [Gea91]. Since sorting can be achieved using Batcher sorting networks [CLR90], these were called Batcher–Banyan networks. Perhaps because much the same effect can be obtained by randomization in a Benes or Clos network without the complexity of sorting, this approach has not found a niche commercially.

Finally, there is another popular network called the *hypercube*. The networks described so far use d-by-d building block switches, where d is a constant such as 2, *independent* of the size of N. By contrast, hypercubes use switches with $\log N$ links per switch. Each switch is assigned a binary address from 1 to N and is connected to all other switches that differ from it in exactly one bit. Thus, in a very similar fashion to traversing a Delta or a Butterfly, one can travel from input switch to an output switch by successively correcting the bits that are different between output and input addresses, in any order. Unfortunately, the $\log N$ link requirement is onerous for large N and can lead to an "impractical number of links per line card" [Sem02].

BIBLIOGRAPHY

AC75   A. Aho and M. Corasick. Efficient string matching: An aid to bibliographic search. *Communications of the ACM*, 18(6):333–343, 1975.

AD89   H. Ahmadi and W. Denzel. A survey of modern high-performance switching techniques. *IEEE Journal on Selected Areas in Communication*, 7(9):1091–1103, 1989.

AD99   M. Aron and P. Druschel. Soft timers: Efficient microsecond timer support for network processing. In *Proceedings of the 17th Symposium on Operating System Principles (SOSP)*, 1999.

Adi98   H. Adisheshu. *Services for next-generation routers*. Ph.D. dissertation, Washington University Computer Science Department, 1998.

All02   B. Alleyne. Personal communication. 2002.

AMO93   R. Ahuja, T. Magnanti, and J. Orlin. *Network Flows*. Upper Saddle River, NJ: Prentice-Hall, 1993.

AOST93   T. Anderson, S. Owicki, J. Saxe, and C. Thacker. High-speed switch scheduling for local area networks. *ACM Transactions on Computer Systems*, 11(4):319–352, 1993.

APV91   B. Awerbuch, B. Patt-Shamir, and G. Varghese. Self-stabilization by local checking and correction. In *Proceedings of the 32nd IEEE Symposium on Foundations of Computer Science*, Oct. 1991.

AR90   G. Albertengo and S. Riccardo. Parallel CRC generation. *IEEE Micro*, Oct. 1990.

AS00   Infiniband Architecture Specification. *Infiniband Specification*, Oct. 2000.

Assa   Infiniband Trade Assocation. Infiniband architecture. At *http://www.infinibandta.org/home*.

Assb   Web Polygraph Association. Web polygraph. At *http://www.web-polygraph.org/*.

Bar04   I. Barile. I/O multiplexing and scalable socket servers. *Dr. Dobbs Journal*, Feb. 2004.

BDJT01   S. Bhattacharyya, C. Diot, J. Jetcheva, and N. Taft. Pop-level and access-link traffic dynamics in a Tier-1 pop. In *SIGCOMM Internet Measurement Workshop*, 2001.

Be82   A. Birell et al. Grapevine: An exercise in distributed computing. *Comm. of the ACM*, 25(4):202–208, 1982.

Bel86   E. T. Bell. *Men of Mathematics: reissue ed.* New York: Touchstone Books, 1986.

Ben82   J. L. Bentley. *Writing efficient programs*. Upper Saddle River, NY: Prentice Hall, 1982.

Ben95   A. Benner. *Fiber Channel: Gigabit Communications and I/O for Computer Networks*. New York: McGraw-Hill, 1995.

BG85   W. Bux and D. Grillo. Flow control in local-area networks of interconnected token rings. *IEEE Transactions on Communications*, COM-33(10):1058–1066, Oct. 1985.

BGC02   P. Buonadonna, A. Geweke, and D. Culler. An implementation and analysis of the Virtual Interface Architecture. In *SC98: High-Performance Networking and Computing Conference*, San Jose, CA, 2002.

BGP+94   M. Bailey, B. Gopal, M. Pagels, L. Peterson, and P. Sarkar. PATHFINDER: A pattern-based packet classifier. In *Proceedings of the First Symposium on Operating Systems Design and Implementation (OSDI)*, pages 115–123, 1994.

BL00   R. Bhagwan and W. Lin. Fast and scalable priority queue architecture for high-speed network switches. In *IEEE INFOCOM*, pages 538–547, 2000.

Bla96   T. Blackwell. Speeding up protocols for small messages. In *Proceedings of ACM SIGCOMM*, 1996.

BM77   R. S. Boyer and J. S. Moore. A fast string searching algorithm. *Communications of the ACM*, 20(10):762–772, Oct. 1977.

BM98   G. Banga and J. Mogul. Scalable kernel performance for Internet servers under realistic loads. In *USENIX Annual Technical Conference*, New Orleans, 1998.

BMD99   G. Banga, J. Mogul, and P. Druschel. A scalable and explicit event delivery mechanism for UNIX. In *USENIX Annual Technical Conference*, pages 253–265, June 1999.

BMK88   D. R. Boggs, J. C. Mogul, and C. A. Kent. Measured capacity of an Ethernet: Myths and reality. In *Proceedings ACM SIGCOMM*, vol. 18, pages 222–234, 1988.

BMP94   L. Brakmo, S. O. Malley, and L. Peterson. TCP Vegas: New techniques for congestion detection and avoidance. In *Proceedings ACM SIGCOMM*, 1994.

Boy97   J. Boyle. Internet draft: RSVP extensions for CIDR aggregated data flows. In *Internic*, 1997.

BP93   D. Banks and M. Prudence. A high-performance network architecture for a PA-RISC workstation. In *IEEE Journal on Selected Areas in Communications*, February 1993.

Bra98   H. W. Braun. Characterizing traffic workload. At *www.caida.org*, 1998.

Bro98   A. Broder. On the resemblance and containment of documents. In *Sequences '91*, 1998.

Bru99   J. Brustoloni. Interoperation of copy avoidance in network and file I/O. In *Proceedings IEEE Infocom*, New York, March 1999.

BS96   J. Brustoloni and P. Steenkiste. Effects of buffering semantics on I/O performance. In *Proceedings of the 2nd USENIX Symposium on Operating Systems Design and Implementation*, October 1996.

BSV95   S. Boecking, V. Seidel, and P. Vindeby. Channels — a run-time system for multimedia protocols. In *ICCCN*, 1995.

BSV03   F. Baboescu, S. Singh, and G. Varghese. Packet classification for core routers: Is there an alternative to CAMs? In *Proceedings IEEE INFOCOM*, 2003.

BV01   F. Baboescu and G. Varghese. Scalable packet classification. In *Proceedings ACM SIGCOMM*, 2001.

BZ96   J. Bennett and H. Zhang. Hierarchical packet fair queuing algorithms. In *Proceedings SIGCOMM*, 1996.

Car96   A. Carlton. An explanation of the SPEC Web96 Benchmark. Standard Performance Evaluation Corporation white paper, 1996. At *http://www.specbench.org/*, November 1996.

CB95   W. Cheswick and S. Bellovin. *Firewalls and Internet Security*. Reading, MA: Addison-Wesley, 1995.

CC95   M. Crovella and R. Carter. Dynamic server selection in the internet. In *Proceedings of HPCS '95*, August 1995.

CDea96   A. Chankhunthod, P. Danzig, et al. A hierarchical Internet object cache. In *USENIX Annual Technical Conference*, pages 153–164, 1996.

CFFT97   T. Chaney, A. Fingerhut, M. Flucke, and J. Turner. Design of a gigabit ATM switch. In *Proceedings IEEE INFOCOM*, pages 2–11, 1997.

CGE96   J. Cobb, M. Gouda, and A. El Nahas, Time-shift scheduling: Fair scheduling of flows in high-speed networks. In *Proceedings of ICNP*, 1996.

CH82   R. Cole and J. Hopcroft. On edge-coloring bipartite graphs. *SIAM Journal of Computation*, 11:540–546, 1982.

CH98   A. Choudhury and E. Hahne. Dynamic queue length thresholds for shared-memory packet switches. *IEEE/ACM Transactions on Networking*, 6(2):130–140y, 1998.

Cha90a   B. Chazelle. Lower bounds for orthogonal range searching. I: The reporting case. In *Journal of the ACM*, 37, 1990.

Cha90b   B. Chazelle. Lower bounds for orthogonal range searching. II: The arithmetic model. In *Journal of the ACM*, 37, 1990.

Cha97   IETFMPLS Charter. Multiprotocol Label Switching. At *http://www.ietf.org/html-charters/mpls-charter.html*, 1997.

Che89   G. Chesson. XTP/PE design considerations. In *IFIP Workshop on Protocols for High-Speed Networks*, 1989.

Che01   B. Chelf. Dynamic memory management. In *Linux Magazine*. At *http://www.linux-mag.com/2001-06/compile_03.html*, June 2001.

CIC97   Compaq, Intel, and Microsoft Corporations. Virtual Interface Architecture Specification. At *http://www.viaarch.org*, 1997.

Cis   Cisco express forwarding commands. At *http://www.cisco.com*.

CJRS89   D. D. Clark, V. Jacobson, J. Romkey, and H. Salwen. An analysis of TCP processing overhead. *IEEE Communications*, 27(6):23–29, 1989.

CL85   K. M. Chandy and L. Lamport. Distributed snapshots: Determining global states of distributed systems. *ACM Transactions on Computer Systems*, 3(1):63–75, Febuary 1985.

Cla85   D. D. Clark. Structuring of systems using upcalls. In *Proceedings of the 10th ACM Symposium on Operating Systems Principles (SOSP)*, pages 171–180, December 1985.

Cla88   D. D. Clark. The design philosophy of the DARPA Internet protocols. In *Proceedings ACM SIGCOMM*, pages 106–114, August 1988.

CLR90   T. Cormen, C. Leiserson, and R. Rivest. *Introduction to Algorithms*. Cambridge, MA: MIT Press/McGraw-Hill, 1990.

Cona   RDMA Consortium. Architectural specifications for RDMA over TCP/IP. At *http://www.rdmaconsortium.org/home*.

Conb   SPEC Consortium. Specweb99 benchmark. At *http://www.specbench.org/osg/web99/*.

Cox96   A. Cox. Kernel Korner: Network buffers and memory management. In *Linux journal*. At *www.linuxjournal.com*, Oct. 1996.

CP98   T. Chiueh and P. Pradhan. High-performance IP routing table lookup using CPU caching. In *IEEE INFOCOM*, 1998.

CP99   T. Chiueh and P. Pradhan. High-performance IP routing table lookup using CPU caching. In *Proceedings IEEE INFOCOM*, pages 1421–1428, 1999.

CSG99   D. Culler, J. Singh, and A. Gupta. *Parallel Computer Architecture: A Hardware/Software Approach*. San Francisco: Morgan Kaufmann, 1999.

CSM01   C. Coit, S. Staniford, and J. McAlerney. Towards faster pattern matching for intrusion detection or exceeding the speed of snort. In *Proceedings of the 2nd DARPA Information Survivability Conference and Exposition (DISCEX II)*, June 2001.

CT90   D. Clark and D. Tennenhouse. Architectural considerations for a new generation of protocols. In *Proceedings of ACM SIGCOMM*, 1990.

CV96   G. Chandranmenon and G. Varghese. Trading packet headers for packet processing, In *ACM/IEEE Transactions Networking*, 17(1), April 1996.

CV98a   G. Chandranmenon and G. Varghese. Reconsidering fragmentation and reassembly. In *Symposium on Principles of Distributed Computing*, pages 21–29, 1998.

CV98b   A. Costello and G. Varghese: Redesigning the BSD callout and timeout facilities. In *Software Practice and Experience*, July 1998.

CV01   G. Chandranmenon and G. Varghese. Reducing Web latencies using precomputed hints. In *Proceedings IEEE INFOCOM*, 2001.

CW79   B. Commentz-Walter. A string matching algorithm fast on the average. In *Proceedings of the 6th International Colloquium on Automata, Languages and Programming*, vol. 71. New York: Springer, July 1979.

CWSB02   D. Clark, J. Wroclawski, K. Sollins, and R. Braden. Tussle in cyberspace: Defining tomorrow's Internet. In *Proceedings ACM SIGCOMM*, 2002.

Dal02   W. Dally. Scalable switching fabrics for Internet routers. In *Avici Networks White Paper*. At *http://www.avici.com/technology/whitepapers*, 2002.

Dav89   G. Davison. Calendar p's and q's. In *Communications of the ACM*, 32(10):1241–1242, Oct. 1989.

DB96   P. Druschel and G. Banga. Lazy receiver processing: A network subsystem architecture for server systems. In *Proceedings of the UNIX 2nd OSDI Conference*, 1996.

DBCP97   M. Degermark, A. Brodnik, S. Carlsson, and S. Pink. Small forwarding tables for fast routing lookups. In *Proceedings ACM SIGCOMM*, pages 3–14, 1997.

DCea87   W. Dally, L. Chao, et al. Architecture of a message-driven processor. In *Proceedings of the International Symposium on Computer Architecture (ISCA)*, June 1987.

DDP94   P. Druschel, B. Davie, and L. Peterson. Experiences with a high-speed network adapter: A software perspective. In *Proceedings ACM SIGCOMM*, Sept. 1994.

DDPP98   D. Decasper, Z. Dittia, G. Parulkar, and B. Plattner. Router plugins: A software architecture for next-generation routers. In *Proceedings ACM SIGCOMM*, Sept. 1998.

Den87   D. Denning. An intrusion-detection model. *IEEE Transactions on Software Engineering*, 13(2):222–232, Feb. 1987.

DG00   N. Duffield and M. Grossglauser. Trajectory sampling for direct traffic observation. In *Proceedings ACM SIGCOMM*, pages 271–282, Aug. 2000.

DKea88   M. Dietzfelbinger, A. Karlin, et al. Dynamic perfect hashing: Upper and lower bounds. In *29th IEEE Symposium on the Foundations of Computer Science (FOCS)*, 1988.

DKS89   A. Demers, S. Keshav, and S. Shenker. Analysis and simulation of a fair queueing algorithm. *Proceedings of the Sigcomm '89 Symposium on Communications Architectures and Protocols*, 19(4): 1–12, Sept. 1989. Part of ACM Sigcomm Computer Communication Review.

DKVZ99   R. Draves, C. King, S. Venkatachary, and B. Zill. Constructing optimal IP routing tables. In *Proceedings IEEE INFOCOM*, 1999.

DLT01   N. Duffield, C. Lund, and M. Thorup. Charging from sampled network usage. In *SIGCOMM Internet Measurement Workshop*, November 2001.

DP93   P. Druschel and L. Peterson. Fbufs: A high-bandwidth cross-domain transfer facility. In *Proceedings of the Fourteenth ACM Symposium on Operating System Principles*, pages 189–202, December 1993.

DPJ97   Z. D. Dittia, G. M. Parulkar, and J. R. Cox, Jr. The APIC approach to high-performance network interface design: Protected DMA and other techniques. In *Proceedings of IEEE INFOCOM*, 1997.

Eat   W. Eatherton. Hardware-based Internet protocol prefix lookups. University of Washington Electrical Engineering Department, MS thesis, 1995.

EDV   W. Eatherton, Z. Dittia, and G. Varghese. Tree bitmap: Hardware software IP lookups with incremental updates. At *http://www-cse.ucsd.edu/users/varghese/PAPERS/willpaper.pdf*.

EK96   D. Engler and M. F. Kaashoek. DPF: Fast, flexible message demultiplexing using dynamic code generation. In *Proceedings ACM SIGCOMM*, pages 53–59, 1996.

EKO95   D. Engler, F. Kaashoek, and J. O'Toole. Exokernel: An operating system architecture for application-level resource management. In *Symposium on Operating Systems Principles*, pages 251–266, 1995.

Eng96   D. Engler. VCODE: A retargetable, extensible, very fast dynamic code generation system. In *SIGPLAN Conference on Programming Language Design and Implementation*, pages 160–170, 1996.

ESV03   C. Estan, S. Savage, and G. Varghese. Automatically inferring patterns of resource consumption in network traffic. *Proceedings ACM SIGCOMM*, 2003.

EV02   C. Estan, G. Varghese. New directions in traffic measurement and accounting. In *Proceedings of ACM SIGCOMM*, August 2002.

EVF02   C. Estan, G. Varghese and M. Fisk. *Counting the Number of Active Flows on a High-speed Link*. Technical Report 0705, CSE Department, UCSD, May 2002.

FGea00   A. Feldmann, A. Greenberg, et al. Deriving traffic demands for operational IP networks: Methodology and experience. In *Proceedings ACM SIGCOMM*, pages 257–270, Aug. 2000.

FJ93   S. Floyd and V. Jacobson. Random early detection gateways for congestion avoidance. In *ACM/IEEE Transactions Networking*, 1993.

FJ95   S. Floyd and V. Jacobson. Link-sharing and resource management models for packet networks. In *ACM/IEEE Transactions Networking*, 1995.

FJM$^+$95 S. Floyd, V. Jacobson, S. McCanne, C. Liu, and L. Zhang. A reliable multicast framework for light-weight sessions and application-level framing. In *Proceedings ACM SIGCOMM*, 1995.

FM85   P. Flajolet and G. Martin. Probabilistic counting algorithms for database applications. *Journal of Computer and System Sciences*, 31(2):182–209, Oct. 1985.

FMM$^+$99 S. Floyd, J. Mahdavi, M. Mathis, M. Podolsky, and A. Romanow. An extension to the selective acknowledgment (SACK) option for TCP, 1999.

FP93   K. Fall and J. Pasquale. Exploiting in-kernel data paths to improve I/O throughput and CPU availability. In *USENIX Winter*, pages 327–334, 1993.

FP95   N. Figueira and J. Pasquale. Leave-in-time: A new service discipline for real-time communications in a packet-switching network. In *Proceedings ACM SIGCOMM*, Sept. 1995.

FP99   W. Fang and L. Peterson. Inter-AS traffic patterns and their implications. In *Proceedings of IEEE GLOBECOM*, Dec. 1999.

FPCe97   R. Fromm, S. Perissakis, N. Cardwell, et al. The energy efficiency of IRAM architectures. In *International Symposium on Computer Architecture (ISCA '97)*, June 1997.

FV01   M. Fisk and G. Varghese. *Fast Content-Based Packet Handling for Intrusion Detection*. UCSD Technical Report CS2001-0670, April 2001.

Gea91   J. Giacopelli et al. Sunshine: A high-performance self-routing packet switch architecture. *IEEE Journal on Selected Areas in Communication*, 9(8), Oct. 1991.

Ger99   A. Germanow. *Plugging the Holes in Ecommerce: The market for Intrusion Detection and Vulnerability Assessment Software, 1999–2003.*Technical Report B19538, International Data Corporation, 1999.

GLM98   P. Gupta, S. Lin, and N. McKeown. Routing lookups in hardware at memory access speeds. In *IEEE INFOCOM*, April 1998.

GM99a   P. Gupta and N. McKeown. Designing and implementing a fast crossbar scheduler. In *IEEE Micro*, Feb. 1999.

GM99b   P. Gupta and N. McKeown. Packet classification on multiple fields. In *Proceedings ACM SIGCOMM*, pages 147–160, 1999.

GM01   P. Gupta and N. McKeown. Algorithms for packet classification. In *IEEE Network*, 15:2, 2001.

GS98   A. Gokhale and D. Schmidt. Principles for optimizing CORBA Internet inter-ORB protocol performance. In *Hawaiian International Conference on System Sciences*, 1998.

GW02   T. Griffin and G. Wilfong. On the correctness of IBGP configuration. In *Proceedings ACM SIGCOMM*, pages 17–30, 2002.

HK73   J. Hopcroft and R. Karp. An $n^{5/2}$ algorithm for maximum matchings in bipartite graphs. *SIAM Journal on Computation*, 2:225–231, 1973.

HP91   N. C. Hutchinson and L. L. Peterson. The x-kernel: An architecture for implementing network protocols. *IEEE Transactions on Software Engineering*, 17(1):64–76, 1991.

HP96   J. Hennessey and D. Patterson. *Computer Architecture: A Quantitative Approach*, 2nd ed. San Francisco, CA: Morgan Kaufmann, 1996.

HS78   E. Horowitz and S. Sahni. *Fundamentals of Computer Algorithms*. Rockville, MD: Computer Science Press, 1978.

IEE97   IEEE. Media access control (MAC) bridging of Ethernet v2.0 in local area networks. At *http://standards.ieee.org/reading/ieee/std/lanman/802.1H-1997.pdf*, 1997.

IM97   P. Indyk, R. Motwani, et al. Locality-preserving hashing in multidimensional spaces. In *Proceedings of the 29th ACM Symposium on Theory of Computing*, pages 618–625, 1997.

Jac88   V. Jacobson. Congestion avoidance and control. In *Proceedings ACM SIGCOMM*, 1988.

Jac93   V. Jacobson. TCP in 30 instructions. In *Message sent to comp.protocols.tcp newsgroup*, Sept. 1993.

Kan99   H. Kanakia. Datapath switch. *ATT Bell Labs Internal Memorandum*, 1999.

KCB94   H. T. Kung, A. Chapman, and T. Blackwell. The FCVC credit-based flow control protocol. In *Proceedings ACM SIGCOMM*, Sept. 1994.

Kes91   S. Keshav. On the efficient implementation of fair queueing. In *Internetworking: Research and Experience*, vol. 2, pp. 157–173, Sept. 1991.

Kes97   S. Keshav. *Computer Networks: An Engineering Approach*. Reading, MA: Addison-Wesley, 1997.

KHM87   M. Karol, M. Hluchyj, and S. Morgan. Input versus output queuing on a space division switch. *IEEE Transactions on Communications*, pages 1347–1356, Dec. 1987.

KLS86   N. Kronenberg, H. Levy, and W. Strecker. Vaxclusters: A closely coupled distributed system. In *ACM Transactions on Computer Systems*, 4(2), 1986.

KM87   C. A. Kent and J. C. Mogul. Fragmentation considered harmful. *Proceedings ACM SIGCOMM*, Aug. 1987.

KMea00   E. Kohler, R. Morris, et al. The Click modular router. *ACM Transactions on Computer Systems*, Aug. 2000.

Knu73   D. Knuth. *Fundamental Algorithms. Vol 3: Sorting and searching*. Reading, MA: Addison-Wesley, 1973.

KP93   J. Kay and J. Pasquale. The importance of non-data touching processing overheads in TCP/IP. In *Proceedings ACM SIGCOMM*, Sept. 1993.

Kur   R. Kurzweil. What's creativity and who's creative? At *http://www.closertotruth.com/topics/ creativitythinking/103/103transcript.html.*

Lam89   B. Lampson. Hints for computer system design. In *Proceedings of the 9th ACM Symposium on Operating Systems Principles (SOSP) 1989*, 1989.

LB96   K. Lai and M. Baker. A performance comparison of UNIX operating systems on the Pentium. In *Proceedings of the 1996 USENIX Conference*, San Diego, CA, Jan. 1996.

L'E96   P. L'Ecuyer. Maximally equidistributed combined Tausworth generators. *Mathematics of Computation*, 65:203–213, 1996.

LMJ97   C. Labovitz, G. Malan, and F. Jahanian. Internet routing instability. In *Proceedings ACM SIGCOMM*, Oct. 1997.

LS98   T. V. Lakshman and D. Stidialis. High-speed policy-based packet forwarding using efficient multidimensional range matching. In *Proceedings ACM SIGCOMM*, Sept. 1998.

LSV98   B. Lampson, V. Srinivasan, and G. Varghese. IP lookups using multiway and multicolumn search. In *Proceedings of IEEE INFOCOM*, April 1998.

Mar02   G. Marsaglia. Diehard Web page. At *http://stat.fsu.edu/ geo/diehard.html*, 2002.

MB93   C. Maeda and B. Bershad. Protocol service decomposition for high-performance networking. In *Proceedings of the 14th ACM Symposium on Operating Systems Principles (SOSP)*, 1993.

MC80   C. Mead and L. Conway. *Introduction to VLSI Systems*. Reading, MA: Addison-Wesley, 1980.

McC92   S. McCanne. A distributed whiteboard for network conferencing. In *UC Berkeley CS 268 Computer Networks Term Project*, 1992.

McK91   P. McKenney. Stochastic fairness queueing. In *Internetworking: Research and Experience*, vol. 2, pp. 113–131, Jan. 1991.

MD92   P. McKenney and K. Dove. Efficient demultiplexing of incoming TCP packets. In *Proceedings ACM SIGCOMM*, 1992.

McK97   N. McKeown. A fast switched backplane for a gigabit switched router. *Business Communications Review*, 27(12), Dec. 1997.

McQ97   J. McQuillan. Layer 4 switching. In *Data Communications*, Oct. 1997.

Mea97   N. McKeown et al. The tiny tera: A packet switch core. In *IEEE Micro*, Jan. 1997.

Mer   Merit. Routing table snapshot at the Mae-East NAP. At *ftp://ftp.merit.edu/statistics/ipma*.

MGVK02   Z. Mao, R. Govindan, G. Varghese, and R. Katz. Route flap damping can exacerbate BGP convergence. In *Proceedings ACM SIGCOMM*, pages 221–234, 2002.

MJ93   S. McCanne and V. Jacobson. The BSD packet filter: A new architecture for user-level packet capture. In *USENIX Winter Conference*, pages 259–270, 1993.

MJ98   G. Malan and F. Jahanian. An extensible probe architecture for network protocol measurement. In *Proceedings ACM SIGCOMM*, Sept. 1998.

MM02   P. Molinero-Fernandez and N. McKeown. TCP switching: Exposing circuits to IP. *IEEE Micro Magazine*, 22(1):82–89, Jan./Feb. 2002.

Mog95   J. Mogul. The case for persistent-connection http. *Proceedings ACM SIGCOMM*, 1995.

Moo01   D. Moore. Personal conversation. Also see CAIDA Analysis of Code Red, 2001. At *http://www.caida.org/analysis/security/code-red/*.

MP96   D. Mosberger and L. Peterson. Making paths explicit in the Scout operating system. In *Proceedings of the USENIX Symposium on Operating Systems Design and Implementation*, pages 153–167, 1996.

MPBM96   D. Mosberger, L. Peterson, P. Bridges, and S. O'Malley. Analysis of techniques to improve protocol latency. In *Proceedings of ACM SIGCOMM*, 1996.

MR97   J. Mogul and K. K. Ramakrishnan. Eliminating receive livelock in an interrupt-driven kernel. In *ACM Transactions on Computer Systems*, pages 303–313, Aug. 1997.

MRA87   J. Mogul, R. Rashid, and M. Accetta. The packet filter: An efficient mechanism for user-level network code. In *Proceedings of the 11th ACM Symposium on Operating Systems Principles (SOSP)*, vol. 21, pages 39–51, 1987.

MRG97   C. Maltzahn, K. Richardson, and D. Grunwald. Performance issues of enterprise-level Web proxies. In *Measurement and Modeling of Computer Systems*, pages 13–23, 1997.

MTea02   A. Medina, N. Taft, et al. Traffic matrix estimation: Existing techniques and new directions. In *Proceedings ACM SIGCOMM*, 2002.

MVS01   D. Moore, G. Voelker, and S. Savage. Inferring denial-of-service activity. In *Proceedings of the 2001 USENIX Security Symposium*.

Myh   B. Myhrhaug. Sequencing set efficiency. In *Pub. A9, Norwegian Computing Center*.

NEB02   NEBS. Network Equipment Building System (NEBS) requirements. At *http://www.telecordia.com*, 2002.

Net   Cisco netflow. At *http://www.cisco.com/warp/public/732/Tech/netflow*.

NK98   S. Nilsson and G. Karlsson. Fast address lookup for Internet routers. In *Proceedings of IEEE Broadband Communications '98*, April 1998.

NMH97   P. Newman, G. Minshall, and L. Huston. IP switching and gigabit routers. In *IEEE Communications Magazine*, Jan. 1997.

OSV94   C. Ozveren, R. Simcoe, and G. Varghese. Reliable and efficient hop-by-hop flow control. In *Proceedings ACM SIGCOMM*, Sept. 1994.

Par93   C. Partridge. *Gigabit Networking*. Reading, MA: Addison-Wesley, 1993.

Par96   C. Partridge. Locality and route caches. In *NSF Workshop on Internet Statistics Measurement*, San Diego, Feb. 1996.

PBW04   C. Partridge, S. Blumenthal, and D. Walden. Data networking at BBN. In *IEEE Annals of Computing*, to appear.

PD00   L. Peterson and B. Davy. *Computer Networking: A Systems Approach*, 2 ed. San Francisco: Morgan-Kaufmann, 2000.

PDZ99a   V. Pai, P. Druschel, and W. Zwaenepoel. Flash: An efficient and portable Web server. In *USENIX 1999 Annual Technical Conference*, 1999.

PDZ99b   V. Pai, P. Druschel, and W. Zwaenepoel. I/O-Lite: A unified I/O buffering and caching system. In *Proceedings of the 3rd USENIX Symposium on Operating Systems Design and Implementation*, Feb. 1999.

Pe95   H. Patterson et al. Informed prefetching and caching. In *Proceedings of the 15th ACM Symposium of Operating Systems Principles (SOSP)*, Dec. 1995.

Per92   R. Perlman. *Interconnections: Bridges and Routers*. Reading, MA: Addison-Wesley, 1992.

PF01   J. Padhye and S. Floyd. On inferring TCP behavior. In *Proceedings ACM SIGCOMM*, pages 271–282, Aug. 2001.

PKC97   S. Pakin, V. Karamcheti, and A. A. Chien. Fast messages: Efficient, portable communication for workstation clusters and MPPs. In *IEEE Concurrency*, April 1997.

Pol57   G. Polya. *How to Solve it*, 2nd ed. Princeton, NJ: Princeton University Press, 1957.

PP93   C. Partridge and S. Pink. A faster UDP. *IEEE/ACM Transactions on Networking*, 1(4), Aug. 1993.

PS85   F. Preparata and M. Shamos. *Computational Geometry: An Introduction*. New York: Springer-Verlag, 1985.

PTS95   G. Parulkar, J. Turner, and D. Schmidt. IP over ATM: A new strategy for integrating IP and ATM. In *Proceedings ACM SIGCOMM*, Aug. 1995.

QVS01   L. Qiu, G. Varghese, and S. Suri. Fast firewall implementations for software- and hardware-based routers. In *Proceedings of the 9th International Conference on Network Protocols (ICNP)*, Nov. 2001.

Rau91   B. Rau. Pseudo-randomly interleaved memory. In *Proceedings of the International Symposium on Computer Architecture (ISCA)*, 1991.

Rea96   Y. Rekhter et al. Tag switching architecture overview Internet draft. At *http://www-kr.cisco.com/warp/public/732/tag/switarc_draft.html*, 1996.

Ric01   F. Riccardi. Posted note. In *Linux Kernel Archive*, April 2001.

Rij94   A. Rijsinghani. Computation of the Internet checksum via incremental update. In *RFC 1624, www.ietf.org/rfc/rfc1624.txt*, May 1994.

RJ90   K. K. Ramakrishnan and R. Jain. A binary feedback scheme for congestion avoidance in computer networks. In *ACM Transactions on Computer Systems*, 1990.

RL96   Y. Rekhter and T. Li. An architecture for IP address allocation with CIDR. In *RFC 1518*, 1996.

Rob74   J. M. Robson. Bounds for some functions concerning dynamic storage allocation. In *Journal of the Association for Computing Machinery*, July 1974.

Roe99   M. Roesch. Snort — Lightweight intrusion detection for networks. In *Proceedings of the 13th Systems Administration Conference*. USENIX, 1999.

RP03   S. Ramabhadran and J. Pasquale. A low-complexity packet scheduler with bandwidth fairness and delay bounds. In *Proceedings ACM SIGCOMM*, Aug. 2003.

RV03   S. Ramabhadran and G. Varghese. Efficient implementation of a statistics counter architecture. In *Proceedings ACM SIGMETRICS*, 2003.

SAFL99   P. Sindhu, R. Anand, D. Ferguson, and B. Liencres. *High-Speed Switching Device*, U.S. Patent 5905725, 1999.

Sar88   D. Sarwate. Computation of cyclic redundancy checks by table lookup. *Communications of the ACM*, 31(8), 1988.

Sav99   S. Savage. Sting: A TCP-based network measurment tool. In *USENIX Symposium on Intenet Technologies and Systems*, 1999.

SBV04   S. Singh, F. Baboescu, and G. Varghese. Packet classification using multidimensional cutting. In *Proceedings ACM SIGCCOMM*, 2004.

Sem02   C. Semeria. T-series routing platforms: System and forwarding architecture. In *Juniper Networks White Paper, Part Number 200027-001*, 2002.

SG01   D. Shah and P. Gupta. Fast updates on ternary CAMs for packet lookups and classification. In *IEEE Micro*, 21(1), Jan. 2001.

SIPM02   D. Shah, S. Iyer, B. Prabhakar, and N. McKeown. Maintaining statistics counters in router line cards. In *IEEE Micro*, Jan. 2002.

SKO⁺94   R. Souza, P. Krishnakumar, C. Ozveren, R. Simcoe, B. Spinney, R. Thomas, and R. Walsh. GIGAswitch: A high-performance packet switching platform. In *Digital Technical Journal*, 6(1):9–22, Winter 1994.

SKP00   T. Spalink, S. Karlin, and L. Peterson. *Evaluating Network Processors in IP Forwarding.* Computer Science Technical Report TR-626-00, Princeton University, Nov. 2000.

SMC01   C. Shannon, D. Moore, and K. Claffy. Characteristics of fragmented IP traffic on Internet links. In *ACM SIGCOMM Internet Measurement Workshop*, Nov. 2001.

SMea01   L. Sanchez, W. Milliken, et al. Hardware support for hash-based IP traceback. In *Proceedings of the 2nd DARPA Information Survivability Conference and Exposition.* DISCEX, 2001.

SMW02   N. Spring, R. Mahajan, and D. Wetherall. Measuring ISP topologies using RocketFuel. In *Proceedings ACM SIGCOMM*, 2002.

SN89   K. Sabnani and A. Netravali. A high-speed transport protocol for datagram/virtual circuit networks. In *Proceedings ACM SIGCOMM*, Sept. 1989.

Sno   Snort. The Open Source Network Intrusion Detection System. At *http://www.snort.org/*.

SP94   R. Simcoe and T. Pei. Perspectives on ATM switch architecture and the influence of traffic pattern assumptions on switch design. In *ACM Computer Communication Review*, 1994.

SP00   J. Stone and C. Partridge. When the CRC and TCP checksum disagree. In *Proceedings ACM SIGCOMM*, pages 309–319, 2000.

SPea01   A. Snoeren, C. Partridge, et al. Hash-based IP traceback. In *Proceedings ACM SIGCOMM*, pages 295–306, 2001.

SSH99   I. Sutherland, R. Sproull, and D. Harris. *Logical Effort, Designing Fast CMOS Circuits.* San Diego: Morgan Kaufmann, 1999.

SSMe01   J. Satran, D. Smith, K. Meth, et al. iSCSI. At *Internet Draft draft-ietf-ips-iSCSI-07.txt*, July 2001.

SSV99   V. Srinivasan, S. Suri, and G. Varghese. Packet classification using tuple space search. In *Proceedings ACM SIGCOMM*, pages 135–146, 1999.

SSZ   I. Stoica, S. Shenker, and H. Zhang. Core-stateless fair queuing: Achieving approximately fair bandwidth allocations in high-speed networks. In *Proceedings ACM SIGCOMM*, 1998.

ST   J. Smith and B. Traw. Operating systems support for end-to-end Gbps networking. Technical report, Distributed Systems Laboratory, University of Pennsylvania.

Ste94   W. R. Stevens. *TCP/IP Illustrated*, Vol. 1. Reading, MA: Addison-Wesley, 1994.

Ste98   W. R. Stevens. *UNIX Network Programming.* Upper Saddle River, NJ: Prentice Hall, 1998.

Ste99   J. W. Stewart. *BGP-4: Interdomain Routing in the Internet.* Reading, MA: Addison-Wesley, 1999.

SV96   D. Staliadis and A. Varma. Frame-based fair queueing: A new traffic scheduling algorithm for packet-switched networks. In *Proceedings ACM SIGMETRICS*, 1996.

SV99   V. Srinivasan and G. Varghese. Faster IP lookups using controlled prefix expansion. In *ACM Transactions on Computer Systems*, Feb. 1999.

SV00   S. Sikka and G. Varghese. Memory-efficient state lookups. In *Proceedings ACM SIGCOMM*, Aug. 2000.

SVC97   S. Suri, G. Varghese, and G. Chandranmenon. Leap forward virtual clock: A new fair queuing scheme with guaranteed delays and throughput fairness. In *Proceedings of Infocom '97*, 1997.

SVC03   T. Sherwood, G. Varghese, and B. Calder. A pipelined memory architecture for high-throughput network processors. *International Symposium on Computer Architecture*, 2003.

SVSW98   V. Srinivasan, G. Varghese, S. Suri, and M. Waldvogel. Fast scalable level-four switching. In *Proceedings of SIGCOMM '98*, Sept. 1998.

SWG   Differentiated Services Working Group. Differentiated Services (diffserv) Charter. At *http://www.ietf.org/html.charters/diffserv-charter.html*.

SWKA00 S. Savage, D. Wetherall, A. Karlin, and T. Anderson. Practical network support for IP traceback. In *Proceedings ACM SIGCOMM*, pages 295–306, 2000.

Sys Cisco Systems. Cisco 12000 Series Internet Routers. At *http://www.cisco.com/warp/public/cc/pd/rt/12000/tech/index.shtml*.

Tan81 A. S. Tanenbaum. *Computer Networks*. Englewood Cliffs, NJ: Prentice Hall, 1981.

Tan92 A. Tanenbaum. *Modern Operating Systems*. Upper Saddle River, NJ: Prentice Hall, 1992.

TC72 A. Toynbee and J. Caplan. *A Study of History*, abridged version. New York: Oxford University Press, 1972.

TK95 M. N. Thadani and Y. A. Khalidi. *An Efficient Zero-Copy I/O Framework for UNIX*. Technical Report SMLI TR-95-39, Sun Microsystems Laboratories, May 1995.

TMW97 K. Thompson, G. Miller, and R. Wilder. Wide-area traffic patterns and characterizations. In *IEEE Network*, Dec. 1997.

TNML93 C. Thekkath, T. Nguyen, E. Moy, and E. Lazowska. Implementing network protocols at user level. In *Proceedings ACM SIGCOMM*, 1993.

TP96 J. Touch and B. Parham. Implementing the Internet checksum in hardware. In *RFC 1936, www.ietf.org/rfc/rfc1936.txt*, April 1996.

Tsu P. Tsuchiya. A search algorithm for table entries with noncontiguous wildcarding. In *Unpublished report, Bellcore*.

Tur86 J. S. Turner. New directions in communications (or Which way to the information age?). In *IEEE Communications*, 1986.

Tur97 J. Turner. Design of a gigabit ATM switch. In *Proceedings IEEE INFOCOM*, Oct. 1997.

Tur02 J. Turner. Personal communication. 2002.

TVHS92 R. Thomas, G. Varghese, G. Harvey, and R. Souza. Method for keeping track of sequence numbers in a large space. U.S. Patent 5,086,428, Sept. 1992.

TY98 J. Turner and N. Yamanaka. Architectural choices in large scale ATM switches. In *IEICE Transactions*, 1998.

UNH01 UNH Interoperability Lab. FDDI tutorials. At *http://www.iol.unh.edu/training/fddi.html*, 2001.

Val90 L. Valiant. A bridging model for parallel computation. *Communications of the ACM*, 33(8), 1990.

vCGS92 T. von Eicken, D. Culler, S. Goldstein, and K. Schauser. Active messages: A mechanism for integrated communication and computation. In *Proceedings of the 19th International Symposium on Computer Architecture (ISCA)*, pages 256–266, 1992.

VD75 J. G. Vaucher and P. Duval. A comparison of simulation event list algorithms. In *CACM 18*, 1975.

vEBea95 T. von Eicken, A. Basu, et al. U-Net: A user-level network interface for parallel and distributed computing. In *Proceedings of the 15th ACM Symposium on Operating Systems Principles (SOSP)*, 1995.

vECea92 T. von Eicken, D. Culler, et al. Active messages: A mechanism for integrated communication and computation. In *19th International Symposium on Computer Architecture*, pages 256–266, 1992.

VGE00 K. Varadhan, R. Govindan, and D. Estrin. Persistent route oscillations in interdomain routing. *Computer Networks*, 32(1):1–16, 2000.

Vis Max Vision. Advanced reference archive of current heuristics for network intrusion detection systems (arachNIDS). At *http://www.whitehats.com/ids/*.

VL87   G. Varghese and A. Lauck. Hashed and hierarchical timing wheels: Data structures for the efficient implementation of a timer facility. In *Proceedings of the 11th ACM Symposium on Operating Systems Principles (SOSP)*, 1987.

WCB01   M. Welsh, D. E. Culler, and E. A. Brewer. SEDA: An architecture for well-conditioned, scalable Internet services. In *Proceedings of the 22nd Symposium on Operating Systems Principles (SOSP)*, pages 230–243, 2001.

WH00   J. Wang and C. Huang. A high-speed single-phase-clocked CMOS priority encoder. In *IEEE International Symposium on Circuits and Systems*, May 2000.

Wil92   P. Wilson. Uniprocessor garbage collection techniques. In *Springer-Verlag Lecture Notes in Computer Science*, number 637, Sept. 1992.

WJea95   P. Wilson, M. Johnstone, et al. Dynamic storage allocation: A survey and critical review. In *Proceedings of the International Workshop on Memory Management*, Kinross, Scotland, 1995.

Woo00   T. Woo. A modular approach to packet classification: Algorithms and results. In *Proceedings IEEE INFOCOM*, 2000.

WS95   G .R. Wright and W. R. Stevens. *TCP/IP Illustrated*, vol. 2. Reading, MA: Addison-Wesley, 1995.

WSV01a   P. Warkhede, S. Suri, and G. Varghese. Fast packet classification for two-dimensional conflict-free filters. In *Proceedings IEEE INFOCOM*, pages 1434–1443, 2001.

WSV01b   P. Warkhede, S. Suri, and G. Varghese. Multiway range trees: Scalable IP lookups with fast updates. In *IEEE Globecom 2001 Internet Symposium*, Nov. 2001.

WVTP01   M. Waldvogel, G. Varghese, J. Turner, and B. Plattner. Scalable high-speed IP routing lookups. In *ACM Transactions on Computer Systems*, Nov. 2001.

XSD00   J. Xu, M. Singhal, and J. Degroat. A novel cache architecture to support layer-four packet classification at memory access speeds. In *Proceedings IEEE INFOCOM*, pages 1445–1454, 2000.

YHA87   Y. Yeh, M. Hluchyj, and A. Acampora. The Knockout Switch: A simple modular architecture for high-performance packet switching. *IEEE Journal on Selected Areas in Communication*, pages 1426–1435, Oct. 1987.

Zha91   L. Zhang. Virtual clock: A new traffic control algorithm for packet-switched networks. In *ACM Transactions on Computer Systems*, 1991.

ZRDG03   Y. Zhang, M. Roughan, N. Duffield, and A. Greenberg. Fast, accurate computation of large-scale IP matrices from link loads. In *Proceedings ACM SIGMETRICS*, 2003.

INDEX